Operations Research
in Production Planning,
Scheduling,
and Inventory Control

Operations Research in Production Planning, Scheduling, and Inventory Control

Lynwood A. Johnson
Douglas C. Montgomery
Georgia Institute of Technology

JOHN WILEY & SONS, INC; New York · London · Sydney · Toronto

Library of Congress Cataloging in Publication Data:

Johnson, Lynwood A.
  Operation research in production planning, scheduling, and inventory control.

  Includes bibliographies.
  1. Production management—Mathematical models. 2. Inventory control—Mathematical models. 3. Operations research. I. Montgomery, Douglas C., joint author. II. Title.

TS155.J56   658.5′03   73-17331
ISBN 0-471-44618-1

Printed in the United States of America

10–9 8 7 6 5 4 3

Preface

This is a quantitatively oriented textbook dealing with production and inventory management. Specifically, we concentrate on operations research methodology applied to problems of production planning, scheduling, forecasting, and inventory control. The book evolved from class notes for a senior-level course in the design of production-inventory systems at the Georgia Institute of Technology and from several graduate courses in forecasting, scheduling, and production planning. Although most of our presentation is in the context of industrial systems, the concepts and methods are generally applicable to nonindustrial problems. The text is suitable for seniors or first-year graduate students in industrial and systems engineering, operations research, management science, or business administration, provided that their background includes introductory courses in operations research and probability and statistics.

Our purpose is to teach modeling concepts that are useful in solving production management problems. In accomplishing this objective, we have provided a thorough coverage of basic models that have found extensive practical application. Also we discuss many intermediate-level topics, including several results not previously available in textbook form and a few not previously published. Our secondary objective is to present a logical organization to the various quantitative results that are useful in the field of production planning and control. Therefore, the book should be valuable to practitioners who design production-inventory systems.

There are five substantive chapters. Chapter 2 deals with inventory theory, including simple deterministic models, constraints, single-period stochastic models, general periodic review and continuous review stochastic models, base stock systems, and dynamic lot-size models. Chapter 3 treats production planning models that assume demand is static, including linear programming models for product mix, process selection, and other applications, single-facility lot-size problems, and various multistage planning techniques. Chapter 4 extends the material of Chapter 3 to incorporate dynamic demand, including linear and dynamic programming approaches, aggregate planning models, lot-size programming, and multistage dynamic models. Chapter 5 discusses scheduling problems, including combinatorial algorithms and local dispatching rules for job shops, project scheduling and control techniques, and both exact and heuristic procedures for assembly line balancing. Chapter 6 deals with forecasting, including regression and moving average methods, various forms of exponential smoothing, adaptive forecasting methods, Bayesian methods, and Box-Jenkins models. Finally, Chapter 7 discusses several important aspects of developing management control systems that utilize these techniques.

We deliberately included more material than is necessary for a first course, so that the instructor will have flexibility to discuss certain topics in greater depth or to vary his course content from one offering to another. A senior-level introductory course might consist of Chapter 1, certain sections of Chapters 2 to 4, Chapter 5, several early sections of Chapter 6, and Chapter 7. A course sequence for first-year graduate students could cover essentially the entire book, perhaps concentrating on the more advanced material, depending on the students' preparation.

We recognize our obligations to people who have pioneered and developed the application of quantitative methodology in production and inventory management. A partial list includes J. F. Magee, R. G. Brown, H. M. Wagner, T. M. Whitin, G. Hadley, A. F. Veinott, Jr., W. I. Zangwill, F. Hanssmann, A. Charnes, and W. W. Cooper. In many instances, we adopted the terminology and notation of these authors in order to promote standardization and to facilitate the student's transition into the more specialized literature.

Many individuals contributed toward the completion of the book. We particularly thank W. L. Berry for his review of the manuscript, S. J. Deutsch for the data in Example 6–14 and a review of Chapter 6, L. E. Contreras for his assistance in preparing several examples in Chapters 3 and 6, and R. N. Lehrer for providing resources to develop and prepare the manuscript. Finally, we thank Mrs. Vicki DeLoach for her careful typing.

Atlanta, Georgia, 1973   *Lynwood A. Johnson*
                                                                        Douglas C. Montgomery

CONTENTS

Operations Research
in Production Planning,
Scheduling,
and Inventory Control

chapter 1
Analysis of Production-Inventory Systems

This book deals with the use of operations research methodology in the development of management systems for controlling the acquisition and processing of materials, or analogous commodities, by an organization. The emphasis is on the use of mathematical models to aid decision-making in the areas of procurement, production, distribution, and capacity planning. In this chapter, we describe the general nature of these problem areas and discuss the role of operations research in providing solutions.

1-1   The Problem Environment

1-1.1 The Material Flow System

Figure 1-1 gives a general model for the physical system to be managed. The firm acquires raw materials and component parts from outside suppliers and

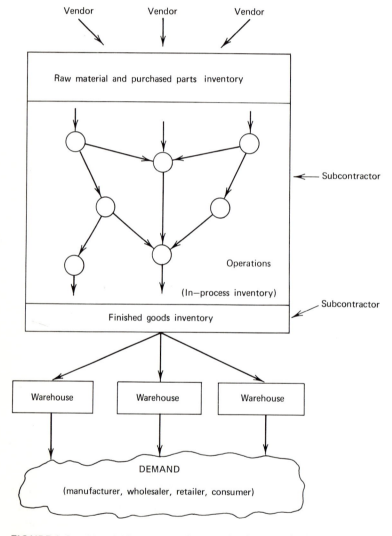

FIGURE 1-1.   Material flow system for a production organization.

stores them until needed in production. The function of managing purchasing and the associated purchased material inventories is called *procurement*. Procurement provides the input to the *production* system, consisting of production centers that process the raw materials and component parts into finished products. The capacity of a production center is determined by the *manpower* and *facilities* comprising that center. A *routing* is a sequence of production centers through which the material flows to produce the product. Each finished product has one or more *routings* by which it can be produced. At a production center, *operations* are performed that utilize a certain amount of the capacity of the center for each unit of product processed. Materials being processed or waiting to be processed comprise the in-process *inventory*. Subcontractors may supply semifinished or finished products to augment the internal capacity of the firm.

Finished products may be inventoried in regional warehouses as well as at the plant where production takes place. The management of the quantity and location of finished goods inventory is a part of the function of *distribution*. Products leave the system to satisfy customer demand. The customer may be a consumer, a retailer, a wholesaler, or another manufacturer.

Three attributes of the material flow are of primary interest to production management: *quantity/time*, *quality*, and *cost*. Quantity/time means the quantity of material processed in each time period at each processing center. Quality refers to the degree of conformance of the product to established specifications. Cost is the value of all resources expended in producing the product. To regulate these attributes, formal procedures for planning and controlling their levels are established. Thus, a progressive company will have organizational units and information systems for production planning and control, inventory control, quality control, and cost control. This book focuses on planning and control of the quantity/time attribute. Because the type of system required for this purpose depends heavily on the nature of the production process being controlled, the next section will briefly describe the major classes of production processes.

1-1.2 Types of Systems

There are four basic types of material flow systems: the continuous production system, the intermittant production system, the project system, and the pure inventory system. The *continuous production system* typically involves producing a few families of closely related products in large volume in plants where facilities are arranged according to the (common) routing of the products. *Intermittent production systems* occur when a large number of products must be made, so that processing centers must frequently change from one product to another. If most of the products have the same routing, the production facilities can be arranged accordingly, and this special case is called a *flow shop* process. On the other hand, when product routings vary widely, the facilities are arranged on a functional basis, and we call the process a *job shop*.

Problems of planning and scheduling production are more complex for intermittant production systems than for continuous production systems. Within the intermittent production system classification, the job shop presents more management problems than the flow shop does. Complexity is a function of many factors, such as the number of products, including component parts and subassemblies; the number of products and parts in production at any given time; whether the products are produced to customer order or to inventory; the number of alternative routings for products; the volume of production; the degree of standardization of component parts; the number of stages in production; whether production orders in a job shop are internally generated to satisfy demand for parts in assembly or whether they come from outside the firm; whether capacity is primarily a function of facilities or of work force; the flexibility of facilities and labor; whether or not production is machine paced; and opportunities for changing the sequence of production during processing. In general, the more alternatives available to production management in their control of material flow and production resources, the more difficult it is to execute this management function well.

The *project system* applies to a production effort that will be done infrequently, often only once. Construction projects, fabrication of large custom-designed machines, and research and development activities are examples where the control of men, materials, and facilities presents a unique management problem. Typically, the goal is to complete the project by a certain date at the lowest cost possible, considering the restrictions resulting from the precedence relations among the activities comprising the project and the availability of resources. This can be quite complicated if a lack of experience or future chance events create uncertainty about the activities to be performed and the time and resources required for any given activity.

The *pure inventory system* is a special case where there is procurement, but no production, prior to distribution. A retail store that buys products for immediate resale is a pure inventory system, as is the stocking of spare parts for maintenance purposes. A basic characteristic of the pure inventory process is the absence of resource availability and other constraints (for instance, labor, machine time, raw materials, and routing restrictions) that are common in production systems.

In studying the production operations of a manufacturing firm, we may observe several types of systems. For example, the purchased material inventory and the finished goods inventory appear to be pure inventory processes. The final stages of production may be a high-volume assembly line, while the initial stages may produce the component parts and be organized and run as a job shop. In developing a management system for this firm, one should consider the interactions between the subsystems and not design their control procedures independently. This is a challenge in practice, because, as you will see in the following chapters, most methodology has been developed for a particular type of material flow system, and not for combinations of different systems.

1-1.3 Decision Problems

Table 1-1 indicates the nature of decisions necessary to control procurement, production, and distribution. Some of these decisions are made on a routine basis to regulate the flow of material through the system; others are made less frequently and result in establishment of policies and capacities that serve as constraints in the routine decision-making process.

For a pure inventory process, the basic decisions are what items to carry in stock, when to reorder, how much to reorder, and who is to be the supplier. To make these decisions rationally, an inventory management system should involve a forecasting procedure and a reordering policy. When a large number of items are carried in inventory, both forecasting and decision analysis usually are formally developed subsystems. The decision analysis is conducted through use of explicitly stated reordering rules that routinely match current inventory positions with predicted requirements, and considering various economic factors, decide when and how much to order.

When production is involved, the decision processes becomes more complicated. Figure 1-2 illustrates the management functions and resulting decisions necessary to plan and control production and classifies them by the length of the planning horizon needed to consider adequately factors relevant to the decision. *Long-range* decisions involve definition of the product lines, establishment of customer service policies, selection of distribution channels, determination of production and warehouse capacity, and perhaps allocation of

TABLE 1-1 Production Management Problems

PROBLEM AREA	REQUIRED DECISIONS
Procurement	What, when, how much, from whom
Production	What, how, when, how much
Inventories	What, where, when, how large
Distribution	What, where to, when, how much
Work force	What skills, where, how large, when
Facilities	What kind, where, what capacity, when

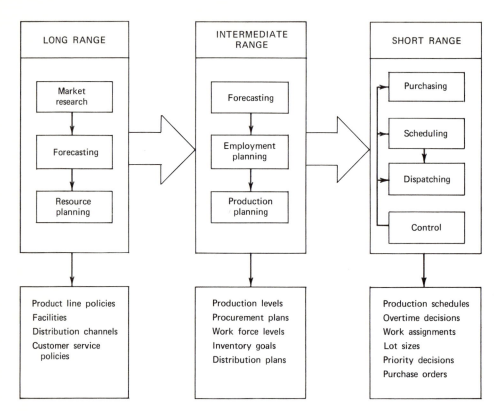

FIGURE 1-2. Stages in the planning and scheduling of production.

that capacity to the different product lines. These decisions are made and reviewed quarterly or annually and require planning horizons of one to five years. Market research, long-range forecasting, and resource planning are necessary activities.

Intermediate-range planning is done within the framework of policy and resource constraints resulting from the long-range planning process. Planning horizons of three months to a year are often sufficient. More detail is required in that production and procurement plans are broken down by product item (or small families of similar products). Necessary management functions include forecasting, work force planning, and production planning. Typically these activities are carried out on a monthly cycle, although it is not unusual to see a shorter review period used.

Short-range activities involve scheduling, dispatching, and control of production. Decisions involve adjustment of production rates to adapt to forecast errors, material shortages, machine breakdowns, and other uncertainties; assignment of workers to work stations; determination of priorities and the sequence of production; assignment of work to work stations; use of overtime; and adjustment of in-process inventory levels. Formally these activities may be carried out weekly or daily, but often they are a continuous function of the production control department and line supervision. Decisions can be made at any time. The planning horizon is short, usually one or two weeks, but could be longer if the manufacturing cycle time is long.

In this text, we shall be concerned mostly with procedures for making intermediate- and short-range decisions. The planning horizon usually will be a year or less. Also, we shall concentrate on models of repetitive decision processes instead of one-time decision problems.

1-1.4 Criteria for Decisions

Decisions about material flow are made with reference to certain general objectives:

1. Maximize revenue from sales.
2. Minimize procurement, production, and distribution costs.
3. Provide a good level of customer service (delivery performance).
4. Stabilize employment levels.
5. Reduce investment in inventories.
6. Hold down investment in facilities.

If we adopt a system-wide perspective, we observe that these objectives are interdependent. A policy that performs well with regard to some objectives may do poorly in attaining others. Management must consider the tradeoffs involved when making decisions. This is difficult to do for two reasons. First, the interactions are complex, especially when many products and facilities are involved. Second, organizations rarely have individuals with the breadth of background and the vision necessary to comprehend the impact of decisions on the several functional units of the firm. Marketing managers, production managers, customer service managers, and controllers do not all see things the same way, perhaps because of what they do and how their performance is measured. The marketing manager is evaluated on the level of sales, while the production manager is measured by cost performance, efficiencies, or how well he meets a given schedule. Naturally, this affects the relative weights they allocate to objectives such as those listed above. Thus the background of people given responsibility for planning production may bias their decisions. Plans and schedules then often are determined through a procedure of negotiation with any line managers who are sufficiently dissatisfied to complain. The chances are remote that an optimal program will be achieved in this manner.

What we seek is an objective means of making decisions that explicitly considers the various management goals. Our approach will be to develop mathematical models, wherein we attempt to quantitatively measure how the attainment of each objective is related to the levels of the decision variables. Typically, we shall try to measure performance in some standard unit, such as dollars. The following economic factors may be relevant:

1. Revenue from sales.
2. Variable costs of production, procurement, and distribution.
3. Losses associated with shortages.
4. Costs of holding inventory.
5. Costs of changing production rates.
6. Costs of changing work force level.
7. Costs of changing facilities (capacity).

The nature of these revenues and costs will be discussed in detail at appropriate points in the text.

Typically, the objective of our analysis will be to choose values for our decision variables that maximize the difference between total variable revenue and total variable cost over the planning horizon. If the planning horizon is sufficiently long, say longer than a year, discounting should be used to account for the time value of money.

Objectives that for one reason or another are not measured in economic terms may be treated as constraints in the decision process. For example, in an inventory problem, when the consequences of shortages are difficult to quantify objectively, the solution may be constrained to those policies that result in no more than a two-day backlog, or to those having at most a 0.10 probability of a stockout.

A third but perhaps less desirable means of treating objectives is to incorporate them subjectively in a review by management of recommended decisions resulting from prior formal analysis. While the opportunity for this process should be provided when the management goals are complex, the decision analysis should be made as explicit as possible by measuring the attainment of each objective in quantitative terms and incorporating this into the decision model, either as part of the objective function or as a constraint.

1-2 An Overview of the Book

This book is an introduction to operations research methodology in the solution of production management problems. We may define operations research as the scientific approach to management decision making. The essence of operations research is use of a mathematical model to describe a decision problem, and by analysis or solution of that model to determine an optimum decision or policy.

Mathematical modeling allows the complexities and uncertainties associated with the decision problem to be put into a logical framework amenable to analytic manipulation and solution. This can permit the manager to solve his operational problems in an effective and efficient manner. The use of mathematical models frequently sharpens management thinking and helps provide consistancy in the decision-making process. Models may also allow management to ask "what if" questions and obtain answers that would be costly or impossible to obtain through direct experimentation with the company.

Model formulation is largely an art, and requires considerable knowledge of the system under study. The model must be formulated so that it contains the essential decison variables and sufficient detail so that a good solution to the decision problem will be obtained. On the other hand, too much detail in the model can result in extreme difficulties in manipulation and solution, and even destroy the usefulness of the model. It is necessary to find a proper balance between reality and analytic tractability.

It is also important to note that the optimal solution to the model is not necessarily the optimal solution to the real problem. This is because simplifications and generalizations have been made in the model formulation. The model solution must be used as a starting point for further analysis incorporating management judgment, experience, and intuition to ultimately arrive at the correct decision.

Many organizations now have formal operations research groups; others have elected to place technical people with operations research competency at various locations in the company structure. Although operations research activity has been extended to almost all levels and functions of business and industry, most of the successful applications of operations research have been in the field of production and inventory management. This is because the decision variables, cost structures, and information availability make these problems amenable to an analytic approach. Furthermore, the large potential payoff from improved management of production and inventories has made this an attractive area for operations research practitioners.

The objectives of this book are twofold: to provide a better understanding of production management problems through the study of models of various systems, and to teach modeling concepts. To accomplish these objectives we have given a thorough treatment of many of the most common and useful models. We also have attempted to incorporate some of the more important and recent literature in this field, hopefully summarizing and classifying the results in a useful fashion. We have not tried to cover all aspects of production management, omitting the more descriptive, traditional material and any discussion of information-processing systems concepts. This material is important, but is well treated in existing texts (1, 2). Also, we have not included survey or review material on mathematical programming, network theory, probability, or other useful bodies of knowledge.

Most of our presentation is in the context of planning and scheduling production for an industrial system, or controlling inventories of a product in a retailing or warehousing operation. However, we hope the reader will be imaginative enough to visualize how these approaches, models, and solution methods can be applied in controlling operations of other types of systems—hospitals, banks, transportation, professional firms, construction, government agencies, and educational institutions.

Chapter 2 is concerned with models of pure inventory systems, primarily for single-item, static, lot-size problems, under both deterministric and stochastic demand. A few examples of multiple-item, constrained models are presented however. The chapter closes with an introduction to simple dynamic inventory systems.

Chapter 3 extends the pure inventory system to incorporate production capability and the various types of constraints associated with production processes. Static demand is assumed throughout the chapter. Linear programming models for product mix, blending, and process selection are presented. Single-facility lot-size and multistage planning techniques, including multiproduct scheduling and multistage inventory models, are discussed.

Chapter 4 extends the material of Chapter 3 to the multiperiod case with dynamic demand. Linear programming models, dynamic programming and network models, aggregate planning techniques, lot-size programming, and various multistage techniques are discussed. An introduction to dynamic models with stochastic elements is also given.

Basic scheduling techniques for job shop systems, large-scale projects, and continuous production systems, or assembly lines, are given in Chapter 5.

Chapter 6 describes statistical techniques for generation and control of forecasts needed as input to production planning and inventory control models. Regression and moving average models, various forms of exponential smoothing, adaptive control procedures, Bayesian methods, and the Box-Jenkins approach are discussed. Special attention is given to the analysis of forecast errors, forecasting over lead times, and forecasting the probability distribution of demand.

Chapter 7 contains a discussion of the use of operations research methodology in the design of management systems for control of production and inventories. It touches on problem definition, system design, economic justification, implementation, and system maintenance.

1-3 References

1. **Buffa, E. S., and W. H. Taubert,** *Production-Inventory Systems: Planning and Control,* Revised Edition, Richard D. Irwin, Inc., Homewood, Ill., 1972.

2. **Magee, J. F., and D. M. Boodman,** *Production Planning and Inventory Control,* Second Edition, McGraw-Hill, New York, 1967.

chapter 2
Inventory Systems

2-1   Introduction

2-1.1 Inventory Problems

In this chapter we consider methods for the analysis of inventory problems. For our purposes, an inventory may be considered an accumulation of a commodity that will be used to satisfy some future demand for that commodity. Our orientation is principally toward inventories of materials—raw material, purchased parts, semifinished products and finished products in manufacturing, spare parts in maintenance operations, purchased products in retailing, and purchased supplies in service operations. It should be pointed out, however, that the same principles and methods used to develop control procedures for material inventories can be used for inventories of other types of resources, such as cash or working capital in financial management, reservoir levels in hydroelectric operations, and space on transportation media.

To formalize our description of an inventory process, we can consider the system pictured in Figure 2-1 to be the inventory level of an item, which is affected by an input process and an output process. Let $P(t)$ be the rate at which material is added to inventory at time t and $W(t)$ be the rate at which material is withdrawn from inventory. Usually, we shall assume that the output is in response to a demand, at rate $D(t)$, which is from some external source and is not under our control. Actually, we may be able to influence demand by pricing or advertising policies, or the demand may be generated by a production process that we operate. The latter case will be considered later, but initially we shall assume that $D(t)$ is not a controllable variable. The output rate will equal the demand rate unless the inventory is exhausted, when it is said to be in an "out-of-stock," "stockout," or "outage" condition.

The input process is partially under our control in that we shall decide when and how much to order from our source of supply. Because of variable time delays in the supplier filling our orders, and possibly because of other reasons to be described later, the actual input rate, $P(t)$, may deviate somewhat from our desires.

The state of the inventory system may be described by variables such as the following:

$I(t)$ = the on-hand inventory level at time t

$B(t)$ = the backorder level at time t

$O(t)$ = the on-order position at time t

$Y(t)$ = the net inventory at time t

$X(t)$ = the inventory position at time t

The on-hand inventory is the quantity of material actually in stock at a given time. When the inventory is out of stock, that is, $I(t) = 0$, any demand that takes place is considered a shortage. Some of this demand may be "backlogged" ("backordered"), if it is accumulated and is to be satisfied as soon as

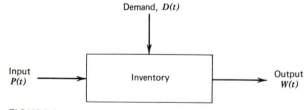

FIGURE 2-1. An inventory system.

sufficient material is received from the supplier. Other shortages may be lost to the system, as when a customer at a retail store goes elsewhere to satisfy his needs, or when a substitute part is used because the originally desired part is out of stock. If backlogging is permitted, the number of units backordered at any time will be of interest.

The net inventory is defined as the on-hand inventory level minus the backorder level. Thus

$$Y(t) = I(t) - B(t) \qquad (2\text{-}1)$$

Note that either $I(t)$ or $B(t)$ or both will be zero at any time.

Because of delays in the supplier filling orders, there may be some material ordered but not yet delivered. This should be considered in evaluating the state of the system, and to do so, we define the inventory position of the system to be the net inventory plus the on-order quantity, $O(t)$, or

$$X(t) = Y(t) + O(t) = I(t) - B(t) + O(t) \qquad (2\text{-}2)$$

We can express these state variables in terms of the input, output, and demand rates, if we make some assumption about the disposition of shortages. Assuming shortages are all backordered, we have

$$Y(t) = Y(0) + \int_0^t [P(u) - D(u)] \, du \qquad (2\text{-}3)$$

where $Y(0)$ is the net inventory level at time zero. Also

$$I(t) = \max [0, Y(t)] \qquad (2\text{-}4)$$

$$B(t) = \max [0, -Y(t)] \qquad (2\text{-}5)$$

and

$$W(t) = \begin{cases} D(t), & \text{if } Y(t) > 0 \\ 0, & \text{if } Y(t) = 0 \\ P(t), & \text{if } Y(t) < 0 \end{cases} \qquad (2\text{-}6)$$

If we assume all shortages are lost to the system,

$$B(t) = 0 \qquad (2\text{-}7)$$

$$Y(t) = I(t) = I(0) + \int_0^t [P(u) - W(u)] \, du, \qquad (2\text{-}8)$$

where $W(t)$ is $D(t)$ if $Y(t) > 0$, and 0 if $Y(t) = 0$.

The inventory problem is to determine an ordering policy, telling when to order and how much to order, that is in some sense economical to operate. This ordering policy will influence the input function, $P(t)$, which in turn affects the inventory and shortage variables defined above. It will be seen that many important economic factors in the operation of an inventory system are a function of these state variables.

To define and solve inventory problems, we must consider the following questions.

1. What decision variables define our ordering policy? These are the controllable variables in our problem. For example, our policy might be to order Q units when the inventory position drops to r units. The decision variables are Q and r, and the purpose of analysis is to find good numerical values for them.

2. What is the appropriate measure of effectiveness for our choice of an inventory policy? We must identify the relevant revenues, costs, and other factors that express our preference for one policy over another.

3. How does the effectiveness measure vary with our choice of an inventory policy? Typically, we shall attempt to construct a mathematical model that formally expresses this relationship.

4. How do we determine the particular policy to use once we have developed a model? In some situations we may be able to use mathematical methods to obtain a solution that is optimal with regard to the model; in other, more complex cases, the model may be used to help select one of several alternative policies by predicting the effect of operating the system under each policy. In the latter case, the goodness of the ultimate solution will depend on the procedure used to select the candidate policies.

In the next several sections, we shall discuss these questions in general. Following that, the remainder of the chapter will contain analyses of a number of common inventory processes.

2-1.2 Functions of Inventories

Inventorying of a commodity should be justified by benefits accruing from one or more functions served by inventories. Among the more important reasons for inventories are those related to economies of scale in production and procurement, to fluctuating requirements over time, to a desire for flexibility in scheduling sequential facilities, to speculation on price or cost, and to uncertainty about requirements and replenishment lead times.

Typically the total cost of producing or purchasing a lot (batch) of material is a concave function of the size of the lot. That is, the average procurement cost per unit will decrease (or at least will not increase) as the lot size increases. These economies of scale may result from fixed costs associated with procurement, effects of learning on production costs, quantity price discounts in purchasing, and so forth. This condition of nonincreasing marginal cost makes it attractive to specify large lot sizes, ordered infrequently to satisfy a given demand, as opposed to a policy of ordering smaller lots more frequently.

However, the average inventory level is a function of the lot size—large lots resulting in a larger average inventory than small lots. Also, to produce a product in batches may require the accumulation of inventories of materials and components prior to production. The amount required will depend on the size of the lot to be produced. Thus, we see that to obtain the economic benefits of batch production, we must carry inventories.

When faced with a demand that fluctuates over time, as for a seasonal product, we may want to build inventory during periods of low demand in anticipation of peak demand in other periods. This buildup inventory might permit us to operate at a fairly constant production rate over the entire season, thereby avoiding the costs of changing production rates. This inventory also will help avoid overtime, subcontracting, lost sales, and backorder penalties during periods of peak demand.

When we manage a series of production facilities, inventories of material in process between facilities will permit more independence in the scheduling of these facilities. If there were no inventory permitted between stages, the production rates of these stages would have to be carefully balanced to avoid material shortages at the following operation and shutdown of the prior operation because of the temporary inability of the following operation to keep up. Such close control may be economically undesirable and can be avoided if a buffer inventory between stages is permitted.

Inventories are sometimes carried because of anticipated changes in the cost of commodities. For example, a manufacturer who believes that his suppliers of an important raw material will soon raise their price may stock unusually large quantities to take advantage of the lower price.

Inventories may be carried because of uncertainties that exist. Future requirements for an item usually are not known with certainty, but instead must be forecast, and these forecasts are, of course, subject to error. To protect against losses resulting from shortages when the actual demand exceeds the forecast, it is often economic to carry inventory above that that would result from planning based strictly on the forecast. This extra inventory is called "safety stock," and the amount required is a function of the uncertainty in the forecast. Uncertainty that makes carrying inventory attractive also may result from sources related to the resupply process. Random variation in lead times means that it will be impossible to predict exactly the usage between ordering from the supplier and receiving the order quantity from him. Safety stock to avoid shortages when the lead time is unusually long may be justified.

An important but difficult to analyze function of inventories is to improve service to customers. By holding inventories of finished goods in several regional distribution warehouses, a manufacturer will be able to deliver a customer's order quicker than if the order had to be filled from a central factory warehouse, or if the order had to be manufactured from semifinished materials and then shipped. If we measure customer service in terms of the average delay in filling an order, we see that it can be improved by carrying more inventory; however, a major problem in the analysis of a given situation to determine the optimal locations and quantities of stock is the difficulty of objectively evaluating benefits to accrue from a given improvement in customer service.

From this brief description of some of the primary functions of inventories, one can begin to appreciate that the study of inventory systems involves analysis of the tradeoffs of the benefits from carrying inventory versus the costs of carrying inventory. In the next section, we discuss the relevant economic factors in more detail.

2-1.3 Measures of Effectiveness

Certain revenues and costs are affected by the choice of an inventory policy. Analysis to determine a good policy will involve identification of these relevant economic factors and construction of a model to show how they are related to the controllable variables in the inventory policy. The revenue and cost parameters then must be estimated from accounting or other data. In this section we describe some of the more important economic considerations in inventory studies; however, we do not discuss methods for their estimation.

Revenues from sources external to the organization may be affected by the inventory policy. These would include income from the normal sales of finished goods and income resulting from disposal of surplus inventory, as, for example, in the case of a highly seasonal item at the conclusion of its season. For a given product the revenue in a period of time will be a function of the inventory provided and the demand realized. Often it is reasonable to assume that the revenue in a period is a linear function of the amount sold at a "regular" price and the amount of stock disposed of at a reduced, or "markdown" price.

The major classes of costs are procurement, inventory holding, shortage, and system operating costs. Procurement costs, both in purchasing and production situations, can consist of a component that is independent of the procurement lot size and a component that varies with the lot size. The former is the fixed cost per lot, sometimes called the "ordering cost" in purchasing or the "setup cost" in production. To purchase a lot requires processing of purchase orders, receiving reports, accounting records, and so on, as well as certain fixed expenses in physically receiving and storing the lot. If the lot is to be produced instead of purchased by the firm, there are the paperwork processing costs and in addition, costs associated with preparing machines, equipment, and workers to produce this particular product and with taking down the setup after the lot has been produced. These costs will be incurred whether only a few units are produced or a large number are made. The variable costs per lot depend on the price schedule of a supplier or on the variable production costs in manufacturing. If we purchase the lot, the supplier will charge us a total price that depends on the lot size for the lot. He may offer quantity discounts, so that the total variable cost per lot is not a linear function of the lot size. If we produce the lot, the total variable cost will, of course, be a function of the lot size, but because of factors such as worker learning and quality problems following a new setup, the relationship between lot size and total variable cost may not be linear. In modeling procurement costs, we often assume the cost of a lot is $A + V(Q)$, where A is the fixed cost per lot and $V(Q)$ is the total variable cost. In case it is appropriate to assume $V(Q)$ is a linear function of Q, we may write $V(Q) = CQ$, where C is the constant unit variable cost.

Inventory holding costs result from out-of-pocket losses such as inventory taxes, insurance, pilferage, damage, deterioration, handling, and storage space requirements. In addition, there are opportunity losses associated with the funds tied up in inventory. Working capital is required to finance inventories, so in a sense inventories are equivalent to sums of money that are unavailable for investment in other opportunities open to the firm. To insure that each dollar of inventory investment justifies itself, it is customary to charge it with the amount it could earn if invested elsewhere. This is an opportunity loss rather than an out-of-pocket cost.

A common method of modeling inventory holding costs is to assume they are proportional to average inventory. If $I(t)$ is the inventory at time t, the average inventory over a period $(0, T)$ is defined as

$$\bar{I} = \frac{1}{T} \int_0^T I(t)\, dt \qquad (2\text{-}9)$$

With reference to Figure 2-2, $\bar{I}$ is the area under the inventory curve divided by T. If h is the cost to carry a unit in inventory for one unit of time, the average inventory holding cost per unit time over the interval $(0, T)$ is given by $h\bar{I}$. (Note that the total inventory carrying cost over $(0, T)$ is $Th\bar{I}$.) Often we assume

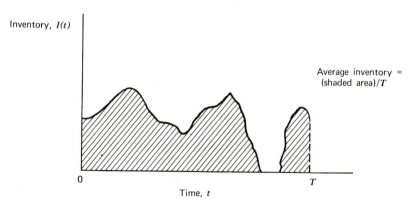

FIGURE 2-2.   Inventory variation over time and average inventory.

that h is comprised of a cost proportional to the dollar value of a unit of inventory plus a cost that is independent of the dollar value, such as a storage cost. Then we write $h = iC + w$, where i is the cost of carrying \$1 of inventory for one unit of time, C is the dollar value of a unit, and w is the storage cost per unit of average inventory per unit time. The factor i is called the inventory carrying cost rate and is typically in the range 0.15–0.25, annually. In many inventory models w is omitted, and the average inventory holding cost per unit time becomes $iC\bar{I}$.

If a demand for a temporarily out-of-stock item occurs, the economic loss depends on whether the shortage is backordered, is satisfied by substitution of a similar item, or is cancelled by the customer. In all cases there may be added information-processing costs and loss of goodwill because of customer dissatisfaction. In the backorder case, there may be costs of expediting and special handling and shipping of the backordered item. If the item is to be used in a manufacturing operation by the firm maintaining the inventory, the operation might have to shut down with loss of production while the inventory is in a backorder condition. If a substitute is sent to the customer, there will at least be a goodwill loss if the substituted item is inferior to that ordered. If the substituted item is more expensive to procure but the customer pays the price of the originally ordered item, there is an opportunity loss equal to the difference in costs of the two items. When a customer cancels an order, there will be a loss of revenue since the sale is not consummated. However, since we do not have to procure an item to meet that demand, the actual opportunity cost is the difference between the revenue from the sale and the cost of the item; that is, it is the lost contribution to profit and overhead. There may also be secondary effects from a lost sale if the customer's dissatisfaction from the shortage causes him to alter his future ordering of this item and possibly other items he buys from the company.

Probably the simplest model for shortage costs is to assume a constant loss, π, associated with each unit demanded when the inventory is out of stock. This would be appropriate for the lost sales and substitution cases. However, if the item is backordered it would seem more realistic to assume that the loss was proportional to the time required to fill the backorder. Thus, we might wish to define a cost, $\hat{\pi}$, of carrying a backorder of one unit for one unit of time. Note that $\hat{\pi}$ is to backorders what h is to inventory. Over a period $(0, T)$ we might model the *total* shortage loss as

$$\pi b + \hat{\pi} T \bar{B} \tag{2-10}$$

where b is the total number of shortages and $\bar{B}$ is the average backorder position during $(0, T)$. The latter is given by

$$\bar{B} = \frac{1}{T} \int_0^T B(t)\, dt \tag{2-11}$$

with $B(t)$ the backorder position at time t. The *average* shortage loss per unit time during the interval $(0, T)$ would then be

$$\frac{\pi b}{T} + \hat{\pi}\bar{B} \qquad (2\text{-}12)$$

To this point, we have discussed briefly the major classes of losses that are affected by our choice of an inventory policy to tell us when and how much to order. For each of these classes, procurement, inventory holding, and shortage, we described the most elementary models for calculating their magnitude over a period of time. We should mention, however, that a fourth category of costs may be important. If the inventory policies under consideration have different requirements for data processing and for management time, the cost of operating the inventory control system under each alternative policy must be considered in a decision to select the best policy. A policy that requires review of inventory levels once a week will cost more to operate than a system that has a review period of a month.

In the remainder of this chapter, we shall present a number of analyses where we define the effectiveness measure for a policy to be the average cost per unit time for procurement, inventory holding, shortages, and system operation. We then seek to determine the policy that minimizes this objective function of average cost per unit time. In a few cases we shall not explicitly include shortage costs in our objective function, but instead shall treat shortages by adding a constraint such as, "No shortages permitted," in the deterministic demand case, or, "The proportion of time the system is out of stock is not to exceed 0.05," or, "90 % of the orders are to be filled on time," in the case where demand cannot be predicted with certainty. Such constraints represent goals of management, and are used when it is difficult to estimate objectively the losses created by shortages. When constraints are present, the role of analysis is to find the policy satisfying the constraints, which minimizes the objective function.

Here we should mention the role of discounting in the economic analysis of inventory policies. It is a fact that a dollar a year from now is not equivalent to a dollar today. Money has value with time and any economic analysis should consider both the magnitude and timing of the cash flows resulting from a decision. Readers familiar with these concepts will be able to appreciate the following arguments; others probably will want to scan this paragraph for conclusions only. If K_t is the economic loss in period t resulting from a given inventory policy, and j is the interest rate per period, reflecting the time value of money, the discounted cost of the policy over a planning horizon of T periods is

$$\sum_{t=1}^{T} K_t(1 + j)^{-t} \qquad (2\text{-}13)$$

To put this on a cost per unit time basis, we compute the equivalent uniform cost per period by multiplying the discounted value by the annuity, or capital recovery, factor

$$\left[\sum_{t=1}^{T} K_t(1+j)^{-t}\right]\left[\frac{j(1+j)^T}{(1+j)^T-1}\right] \equiv \hat{K} \qquad (2\text{-}14)$$

Equation 2-14 is the measure of effectiveness to be minimized. Note that if $K_t = K$, for $t = 1, 2, \ldots, T$,

$$\hat{K} = K\left[\frac{j(1+j)^T}{(1+j)^T-1}\right]\sum_{t=1}^{T}(1+j)^{-t} = K \qquad (2\text{-}15)$$

Thus, if the cost is the same in each period, minimization of the average cost per period, K, is the same as minimization of the equivalent uniform cost per period, $\hat{K}$. The conclusion is that if the decision results in about the same cost in each period, say a year, average annual cost is an appropriate effectiveness measure. (Naturally, this argument assumes that the length of the compounding period is short enough so that the timing of the cash flow within a period is of little significance.)

2-1.4 Uncertainty in Inventory Processes

There are many sources of uncertainty in inventory processes. Perhaps the most common is the demand process. Typically, we are not sure when a demand for the inventoried commodity will occur, and when one does happen, the number of units requested may be uncertain. Thus, the total number of units demanded over a fixed period of time will be a random variable, having a probability distribution that depends on the length of the period. If this probability distribution is the same for each period of length t, we say that we have a *static* demand process; otherwise, we have a *dynamic* demand process.

Another type of uncertainty related to the demand process is whether or not a customer whose demand occurs when the inventory is out of stock will wait for delivery. Some customers may backorder; some will not.

In the replenishment process, the lead time to obtain a replenishment order from the source of supply may be a random variable, so that the usage during the lead time cannot be predicted exactly. Also, the quantity and quality of the delivered order may differ from that requested, as when you order 1000 units and the vendor delivers only 700 (possibly because he was low on inventory), or when you start 1000 units into production to replenish your finished goods inventory, but because of quality problems only 900 acceptable units are completed.

There also may be uncertainty introduced through the information-processing system. For example, one of the important factors entering into a decision to purchase or produce is the current inventory level of the item. This information is provided by an inventory accounting system, which is a data-processing routine involving recording of inventory input and output transactions to keep a running inventory balance. It is not unusual for the balance reported to differ from the amount actually in inventory, because of errors in reporting transactions.

There will be uncertainty about the revenue and cost factors used in the analysis. If production standards are involved in the problem, these must be estimated and thus are subject to error.

In the remainder of this chapter, we shall present several examples of inventory analysis where uncertainty is explicitly considered through use of probability models, as well as other examples where uncertainty is ignored, with all factors in the problem assumed to be known with certainty.

2-1.5 Inventory Policies

In this section, we describe the structure of several policies for inventory management. These rules often are found in practice and have good performance characteristics under static demand processes. The best particular policy structure and the best values of the parameters of the policy for a given situation will, of course, depend on the nature of the economic losses affected by the policy.

Consider an inventory control policy where we observe the inventory level at discrete time points, spaced T time units apart. We call T the *review period* length. At each review point we have the opportunity to order a resupply lot of an arbitrary size. Suppose we decide to adopt the rule of ordering only if our observed inventory level, I, is less than or equal to r units, called the *reorder point*, and if we have to order we order the difference between a *target inventory*, R, and the observed inventory. More formally, at the jth review point, the order size, Q_j, is given by

$$Q_j = \begin{cases} 0, & I_j > r \\ R - I_j, & I_j \leq r \end{cases} \tag{2-16}$$

Our policy consists of three parameters, R, r, and T, and we shall denote it by (R, r, T). In the literature, this is referred to as a *periodic-review R-r policy*. Note that it is a decision rule that tells us when to order and how much to order.

Figure 2-3 illustrates the operation of the R-r policy. At review point 1 we find the inventory is above the reorder point, so we do not order. At review point 2, we order $Q_2 = R - I_2$ units, because the inventory, I_2, is below the reorder point. Note that the order is not received immediately, so that the inventory level continues to drop until the end of the lead time when the order

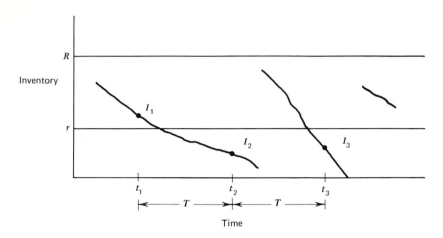

FIGURE 2-3.   Periodic review (R, r) policy.

is added to inventory. In the illustration, the order placed at review point 3 is not received until after the inventory is exhausted, and shortage losses likely were incurred.

A special case of the (R, r, T) policy is obtained by letting $r = R$, so that an order for $R - I_j$ is placed at *every* review point j. This (R, T) policy is called an *order up to R policy* by some writers. It would be appropriate to use this policy only if there were no fixed cost associated with a procurement.

Now suppose that we are able to monitor the inventory level continuously, and were willing to order at any time it seemed desirable. We can conceive of a *continuous-review (R, r) policy* where if at any time, t, the inventory $I(t)$ drops to the reorder point r, or below, we order $Q(t) = R - I(t)$ units. Thus the (R, r) policy is the limiting form of the (R, r, T) policy as $T \to 0$. If units are demanded one at a time, orders will be placed at times when $I(t) = r$, and the order size will always be $Q = R - r$. In this situation, we usually denote the policy by (Q, r) instead of $(Q + r = R, r)$. The (Q, r) policy is called the *fixed reorder quantity policy*, with Q being the constant lot size and r the reorder point. If $r = R$, replenishment orders will be placed after every withdrawal, with the order size equal to the amount of the withdrawal. This means that the on-hand plus on-order inventory level is always R. This policy is called a *base stock system*, and R is the base stock level.

Figure 2-4 is an illustration of a (Q, r) system. Orders are placed each time the inventory reaches the reorder point, but they are not received until after a delivery lead time. Note that if the usage during the lead time exceeds the reorder point, shortages will occur. Observe also that the time between orders is variable, but the order quantity is constant.

To be more precise, the inventory level, I, in the policies described above,

Inventory Systems   **24**

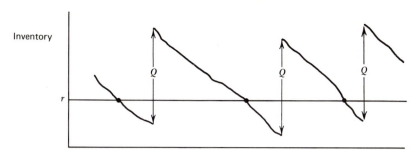

Inventory

r

Time

FIGURE 2-4. Continuous review (Q, r) policy.

should be the inventory position, that is, net inventory plus the already on-order quantity. This avoids operational difficulties when the lead time is longer than the review period and when the order size is not sufficient to bring the on-hand inventory above the reorder point when the order is received.

In the case of a dynamic demand process, the policy may have the same structure as those discussed above; however, the parameters of the policy will change with time.

The policies described in this section illustrate the nature of decision rules for inventory management. In the next section, we shall discuss the approach to selection of a good policy.

2-1.6 Analysis of Inventory Systems

Analysis of inventory problems initially involves a study of the system to determine its basic structure and boundaries, the objectives thought important in system operation, and the variables that affect the degree of attainment of these objectives. Some of the variables are under our control; others are not. In prior sections, we have discussed the basic nature of inventory systems, including the functions and economics of inventories, several common management policies, and uncontrollable variables, such as demand and lead time.

Once the problem is understood, the next step usually is to construct a mathematical model to predict the overall effectiveness of a given choice for the controllable variables, such as lot size and reorder point, and a given realization of the uncontrollable variables. As stated earlier, our effectiveness measure typically will be average loss per unit time. If the uncertainty in the uncontrollable variables is to be explicitly described by a probability distribution, we shall use the expected value of losses in a unit of time as our criterion function.

Having a mathematical statement of system losses in terms of our decision variables, we seek the values of these variables that minimize this criterion function. However, we may have to consider some constraints on our solution. For example, in a multiitem inventory problem we may have a limit on the amount of warehouse space available, or a management-imposed constraint limiting the amount of capital we can invest in inventories. We also may establish a constraint because we cannot, or do not choose to, estimate the payoff with regard to a certain objective. For example, we may feel that we cannot rationally determine the losses resulting from a shortage. So we do not include shortage losses in our objective function, but instead add a constraint such as "Permit no shortages," in the deterministic case, or "The probability of a shortage during any cycle is to be at most 0.05," in the probabilistic case. Such constraints establish a minimum level of performance that is to be achieved by the system.

To complete the model, all constraints must be expressed as mathematical functions of the decision variables. Together with the objective function, they form a mathematical optimization problem that may be solved by methods of calculus, dynamic programming, linear programming, or other special algorithms. Once a solution is obtained, we usually want to examine the sensitivity of the solution to the parameters of the model. This allows us to judge the importance of estimation errors.

In the following sections, we shall present a number of model types and solution procedures. The purpose is not to be all inclusive, but to provide examples of analyses of a variety of inventory problems, with the objective of developing an understanding of the modeling process. To help structure results in inventory theory, the reader will find it helpful to classify problems as *static* or *dynamic*, *deterministic* or *probabilistic*, *single item* or *multiitem*, and *single stage* or *multistage*. Multistage systems, often called *multiechelon* systems, will be treated in Chapters 3 and 4.

2-2 Deterministic Single-Item Models with Static Demand

In this section we present a collection of single-item inventory models for which the rate of demand for the commodity is assumed known with certainty and constant. We also assume that the lead time and other system parameters, such as costs, are known with certainty, constant and independent of the quantity ordered. Models for such an inventory system are said to be deterministic, single-item inventory models. Finally, we assume that all shortages are backlogged, to be satisfied when replenishment orders are received. While the above assumptions may seem quite unrealistic, these models often serve as useful approximations to many real-world inventory systems, and will provide a relatively simple introduction to modeling and controlling inventory processes.

The fundamental problem for these inventory systems is to determine when to place an order for additional stock and how much stock should be ordered. Because the demand rate is constant, we shall adopt a policy of ordering in lots of a fixed size whenever the inventory level drops to the reorder point. The problem is then what values to use for lot size and reorder point. To answer these questions, we shall formulate a mathematical model that expresses the average annual cost as a function of these two decision variables, and then determine the order quantity and reorder point that minimize this cost.

Based on these assumptions, four deterministic models are considered. The inventory behavior for each model is shown in Figure 2-5, and the distinguishing characteristics of the models are given in Table 2-1. It will be seen that Models II, III, and IV are special cases of Model I. Therefore, our approach will be to obtain an expression for the average annual cost for Model I and reduce it to

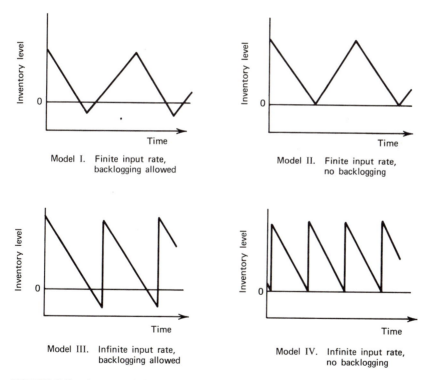

Model I. Finite input rate, backlogging allowed

Model II. Finite input rate, no backlogging

Model III. Infinite input rate, backlogging allowed

Model IV. Infinite input rate, no backlogging

FIGURE 2-5.   Inventory behavior for the static, deterministic models.

Deterministic Single-Item Models with Static Demand   27

TABLE 2-1 Production Rate and Stockout Assumptions for the Deterministic Models

MODEL	PRODUCTION RATE	SHORTAGE COST
I	Finite	Finite
II	Finite	Infinite
III	Infinite	Finite
IV	Infinite	Infinite

the other models under the appropriate assumptions regarding the shortage cost and production rate.

In order to develop an expression for the average annual cost for Model I, some definitions and notation will be required. Let

D = demand rate in units per year

P = production rate in units per year

A = fixed cost of a replenishment order

C = unit variable cost of production (or purchase)

h = inventory carrying cost per unit per year, usually expressed as $h = iC$, where i is the annual inventory carrying cost rate

π = shortage cost per unit short, independent of the duration of the shortage

$\hat{\pi}$ = shortage cost per unit short per year

τ = replenishment lead time, the time between the placement and receipt of an order

Q = order quantity

r = reorder point

$I_{\max}$ = maximum on-hand inventory level

b = maximum backorder level permitted

T = cycle length, the length of time between placement (or receipt) of replenishment orders

K = average annual cost which is a function of the inventory policy.

The behavior of the inventory system which conforms to our Model I assumptions is shown in Figure 2-6. Because we use a fixed lot size and the demand rate is constant, orders will be placed (and received) at equally spaced intervals of length $T = Q/D$. The cycle time, T, is just the time required to use up Q units at the rate D. Thus specification of Q is equivalent to specification of T. The reorder point is chosen so that the backorder position is b when the

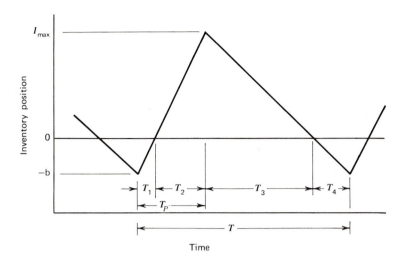

FIGURE 2-6. A cycle for the model I system.

order is received. It will be shown that choice of b is equivalent to choice of the reorder point, since demand during the lead time is constant. It is convenient to develop the cost model in terms of the decision variables Q and b, and then calculate the reorder point implied by b.

Model I assumes that the input rate, P, is finite, as when we are producing the lot and units are added to inventory one at a time. Note from Figure 2-6 that when the backorder position (indicated graphically as a negative inventory level) reaches b, production is started at a rate P. Since P exceeds D, the inventory position will increase at a rate $P - D$, satisfying the backorders and finally building inventory, until Q units have been produced. At that point in the cycle, the inventory level will be a maximum. The time to produce a lot is $T_P = Q/P$, so that

$$I_{max} = \frac{Q}{P}(P - D) - b$$

$$= Q\left(1 - \frac{D}{P}\right) - b$$

During a portion of the cycle, $T_2 + T_3$, there is inventory and inventory carrying costs are incurred. During the remainder of the cycle, $T_1 + T_4$, the system is in a backorder condition and shortages losses are realized. Note that $T_1 = b/(P - D)$, the time to eliminate the backorder position once production is started; $T_2 = I_{max}/(P - D)$, the time to build an inventory of I_{max} from a zero position; $T_3 = I_{max}/D$, the time to consume the maximum inventory; and $T_4 = b/D$, the time to build a backorder position of b.

Deterministic Single-Item Models with Static Demand   29

The average inventory over the cycle is the area under the inventory triangle, divided by T (see Equation 2-9). Denoting this by $\bar{I}$, we have

$$\bar{I} = \frac{1}{T}\left\{\frac{[Q(1 - D/P) - b]^2}{2D(1 - D/P)}\right\} = \frac{[Q(1 - D/P) - b]^2}{2Q(1 - D/P)}$$

The average backorder position over the cycle is the area under the backorder triangle, divided by T (see Equation 2-11). Calling this $\bar{B}$, we have

$$\bar{B} = \frac{1}{T}\left[\frac{b^2}{2D(1 - D/P)}\right] = \frac{b^2}{2Q(1 - D/P)}$$

The average cost per cycle is the sum of the procurement, inventory, and shortage costs during the cycle (all cycles are identical). This cost per cycle is

$$A + CQ + hT\bar{I} + \hat{\pi}T\bar{B} + \pi b$$

In the above, hT is the cost of carrying a unit in inventory for T time units and $\hat{\pi}T$ is the cost to carry a backorder for a time T. To obtain the average annual cost, K, we multiply the cost per cycle by the number of cycles per year, D/Q. Doing this and writing $h = iC$, we obtain

$$K(Q, b) = \frac{AD}{Q} + CD + iC\bar{I} + \hat{\pi}\bar{B} + \frac{\pi b D}{Q} \tag{2-17}$$

Substituting for $\bar{I}$ and $\bar{B}$,

$$K(Q, b) = \frac{AD}{Q} + CD + \frac{iC[Q(1 - D/P) - b]^2}{2Q(1 - D/P)} + \frac{\hat{\pi}b^2}{2Q(1 - D/P)} + \frac{\pi b D}{Q} \tag{2-17a}$$

The decision variables in Equation 2-17a are the order quantity, Q, and the maximum backorder level b. (Note that b uniquely determines the reorder point.) The optimum values of these decision variables may be found by solving the two simultaneous equations given by

$$\frac{\partial K}{\partial Q} = \frac{\partial K}{\partial b} = 0$$

The solution to these equations yields, for $\hat{\pi} \neq 0$,

$$Q^* = \sqrt{\frac{2AD}{iC(1 - D/P)} - \frac{(\pi D)^2}{iC(iC + \hat{\pi})}}\sqrt{\frac{iC + \hat{\pi}}{\hat{\pi}}} \tag{2-18}$$

and

$$b^* = \frac{(iCQ^* - \pi D)(1 - D/P)}{(iC + \hat{\pi})} \tag{2-19}$$

When $\pi = 0$, finite positive values will be obtained for Q^* and b^*, and the minimum average annual cost will be

$$K^* \equiv K(Q^*, b^*) = CD + \sqrt{\frac{2ADiC(1 - D/P)\hat{\pi}}{(iC + \hat{\pi})}}. \tag{2-20}$$

However, when $\hat{\pi} > 0$ and $\pi > 0$, one may obtain a negative value under the radical in (2-18), if π is sufficiently large. In such a case, the optimal policy is to permit no shortages ($b^* = 0$) and use Model II, which results in a lot size given by Equation 2-23.

When $\hat{\pi} = 0$ and $\pi > 0$, it can be shown that the optimal policy is either to allow no shortages or to not stock the item at all. In the latter case, all demand will be backlogged before being satisfied. This corresponds to a "production to order" policy in manufacturing, or a retail policy where an item will not be ordered from the producer until a sufficient backlog has accumulated.

The reorder point in terms of the *inventory position* is $D\tau - b$, the lead time usage. For any b and Q the reorder point in terms of the *net inventory* may also be computed. Let τ be the time required between placing an order and the start of production, and let $m = [\tau/T]$, the greatest integer less than or equal to τ/T. We note that m is the number of orders outstanding at the time an order is placed, so that mQ is the on-order inventory immediately prior to ordering. For any Q and b, the reorder point in terms of the *net inventory* is given by

$$r = \begin{cases} \tau D - mQ - b, & \text{if } \tau - mT \leq T_3 + T_4 \\ [(m + 1)(Q/D) - \tau](P - D) - b, & \text{if } \tau - mT > T_3 + T_4 \end{cases} \tag{2-21}$$

Note from Figure 2-6 that if $\tau - mT \leq T_3 + T_4$, the reorder point will be crossed from above during the part of the cycle when there is no production, while if $\tau - mT > T_3 + T_4$, the reorder point is crossed from below during the production part of the cycle. The reader is asked to verify these results in Exercise 2-31.

The remaining models may be treated as special cases of Model I. In Model II, we suppose the cost of a shortage is infinite. Obviously, we would not plan for backorders in this case, so we add a constraint that $b = 0$. The cost equation becomes

$$K(Q) = \frac{AD}{Q} + CD + iC\frac{Q}{2}\left(1 - \frac{D}{P}\right) \tag{2-22}$$

which is minimized by

$$Q^* = \sqrt{\frac{2AD}{iC(1 - D/P)}} \tag{2-23}$$

We observe that Equation 2-22 is obtained from Equation 2-17a by setting $b = 0$. For Model II, the reorder point is given by Equation 2-21 with $b = 0$.

Next suppose that the rate of addition of a lot to inventory, P, is infinite. Assuming π and $\hat{\pi}$ both finite, this gives rise to Model III. We obtain the appropriate cost equation and solution by taking the limit of Equations 2-17a, 2-18, and 2-19 as $P \to \infty$. This yields

$$K(Q, b) = \frac{AD}{Q} + CD + \frac{iC(Q - b)^2}{2Q} + \frac{(2\pi Db + \hat{\pi}b^2)}{2Q} \qquad (2\text{-}24)$$

$$Q^* = \sqrt{\frac{2AD}{iC} - \frac{(\pi D)^2}{iC(iC + \hat{\pi})}} \sqrt{\frac{iC + \hat{\pi}}{\hat{\pi}}} \qquad (2\text{-}25)$$

$$b^* = \frac{(iCQ^* - \pi D)}{(iC + \hat{\pi})} \qquad (2\text{-}26)$$

for $\hat{\pi} \neq 0$. The reorder point in terms of *net inventory* for this model would be

$$r = \tau D - mQ - b \qquad (2\text{-}27)$$

Finally, suppose that the input rate is infinite and that the cost of a shortage is infinite (so that $b = 0$ is required). We call this Model IV. The appropriate equations are obtained from Equations 2-22 and 2-23 by letting P approach infinity. The cost model is

$$K(Q) = \frac{AD}{Q} + CD + iC\frac{Q}{2} \qquad (2\text{-}28)$$

and the optimal solution is

$$Q^* = \sqrt{\frac{2AD}{iC}} \qquad (2\text{-}29)$$

The reorder point in terms of *net inventory* is

$$r = \tau D - mQ \qquad (2\text{-}30)$$

Model IV is the simplest inventory model and is sometimes referred to as the "classical economic lot-size model."

Instead of applying the constraint $b = 0$ or taking the limit as $P \to \infty$ in the results for Model I, Models II, III, and IV could also have been developed by starting with the inventory geometry, such as in Figure 2-6, and obtaining an expression for K. The optimum value of the system parameters could have been determined easily by solving the equations resulting from the appropriate first partial derivatives of K. The reader is asked to do this.

We have obtained the optimum Q^* and b^* by equating the first partial derivatives of K to zero and solving the resulting equations. However, this satisfies only the necessary conditions for an extreme point. It can be shown that the sufficient conditions for a minimum are satisfied by the solutions so obtained. Once again, the reader is asked to do this as an exercise.

□**EXAMPLE 2-1**   A company purchases valves that are used at the rate of 200 per year. The cost of each valve is $50 and the cost of placing each order is

$5. The inventory carrying-cost rate is assumed to be 0.10. Shortage losses are a fixed cost of 20 cents per unit and a variable cost of $10 per unit per year. The lead time is six months. The optimal order quantity and reorder point may be found by using Model III with $D = 200$, $i = 0.10$, $\pi = 0.20$, $\hat{\pi} = 10$, $C = 50$, $A = 5$, and $\tau = 0.5$. Using Equations 2-25 and 2-26, we obtain $Q^* = 23.8 \cong 24$ and $b^* = 8.74 \cong 9$. The cycle length is $T = 24/200 = 0.12$ year. Thus the reorder point is

$$r^* = \tau D - mQ^* - b^* = (0.5)(200) - \left[\frac{0.5}{0.12}\right](24) - 9$$

$$= 100 - 4(24) - 9 = -5$$

Note that the reorder point is negative, indicating that an order for 24 units should be placed when the backorder level reaches five valves. $\square$

$\square$**EXAMPLE 2-2** Frequently the manager of an inventory system must make the decision whether to purchase or manufacture an item. The models developed in this section often may be used in making this decision. Suppose that an item may be purchased for $25 per unit and manufactured at the rate of 10,000 units per year for $22 each. However, if purchased the ordering cost is only $5 compared to a setup cost of $50 if it is manufactured. The yearly demand for this item is 2500 units and the inventory holding cost rate is 10 percent. Obviously either Model II or Model IV is appropriate, depending on whether the decision is to manufacture or to purchase. Suppose we decide to purchase. The minimum average annual cost is, from (2-20) (letting $P \to \infty$ and $\hat{\pi} \to \infty$),

$$K^* = CD + \sqrt{2ADiC} = (25)(2500) + \sqrt{2(5)(2500)(0.10)(25)} = \$62,750$$

If we manufacture the item, then from (2-20)

$$K^* = CD + \sqrt{1 - D/P} \sqrt{2ADiC} = (22)(2500) + \sqrt{1 - 2500/10,000}$$
$$\sqrt{2(50)(2500)(0.10)(22)} = \$61,422$$

and we see that the item should be produced. The lot size and reorder point may be determined as usual using Model IV. $\square$

2-3 Multiple Items and Constraints

The models described in the preceding section are for inventory systems consisting of a single item. However, most inventory systems stock many different items. We may treat each item individually, using the earlier results of this chapter, so long as there are no interactions among the items. For example, warehouse capacity may be limited, forcing items to compete for floor space; there may be an upper limit on the number of orders that may be placed per year; or there may be an upper limit on the maximum dollar investment allowed in inventory. In this section we shall consider the treatment of constraints such as those described above in multiple-item inventory systems.

We may write the average annual cost of a multiple-item inventory system as just the sum of the average annual costs for the individual items. For example, if there are n items, and the system may be described by, say, Model IV, then

$$K = \sum_{j=1}^{n} K_j = \sum_{j=1}^{n} \left[C_j D_j + \frac{A_j D_j}{Q_j} + i_j C_j \frac{Q_j}{2} \right] \qquad (2\text{-}31)$$

where $j = 1, 2, \ldots, n$ denotes the item.

In general, we can always write the average annual cost of an n-item inventory system as a function of the $2n$ decision variables, the $\{Q_j\}$ and the $\{r_j\}$. The interaction between the n items, or the constraint, may also be written as a function of the $2n$ decision variables. For example, suppose there is an upper limit F to the square feet of warehouse floor space and that one unit of item j occupies f_j square feet of floor space. If Model IV is applicable, and the floor space constraint is not to be violated at any time, then

$$\sum_{j=1}^{n} f_j Q_j = F \qquad (2\text{-}32)$$

We shall not treat the case where orders may be phased so that the maximum inventory levels of all items are never simultaneously attained.

Therefore, we may always express the average annual cost as some function, say K, of the $2n$ decision variables and the constraint may be expressed as a function g of the same decision variables. Thus, the problem is to choose $\{Q_j\}$ and $\{r_j\}$ so as to minimize

$$K = K(Q_1, Q_2, \ldots, Q_n; r_1, r_2, \ldots, r_n) \qquad (2\text{-}33)$$

subject to the constraint

$$g(Q_1, Q_2, \ldots, Q_n; r_1, r_2, \ldots, r_n) = d \qquad (2\text{-}34)$$

where d is some appropriate quantity depending on the nature of the constraint. This type of optimization problem may be treated by the method of Lagrange multipliers. The procedure is as follows. First solve the problem ignoring the constraint (2-34), that is, choose minimum cost Q_j and r_j for each item separately. If these $\{Q_j\}$ and $\{r_j\}$ satisfy the constraint, then they are the optimal parameters for the multiitem system. On the other hand, if they do not satisfy the constraint, then we form the function

$$L = K(Q_1, Q_2, \ldots, Q_n; r_1, r_2, \ldots, r_n)$$
$$+ \lambda[g(Q_1, Q_2, \ldots, Q_n; r_1, r_2, \ldots, r_n) - d] \qquad (2\text{-}35)$$

where λ is a Lagrange multiplier. The optimal $\{Q_j\}$ and $\{r_j\}$ can be determined by solving the $2n + 1$ equations in $2n + 1$ unknowns given by

$$\frac{\partial L}{\partial \lambda} = 0; \quad \frac{\partial L}{\partial Q_j} = 0; \quad \frac{\partial L}{\partial r_j} = 0, \quad j = 1, 2, \ldots, n \qquad (2\text{-}36)$$

It is well known that the set of $\{Q_j\}$ and $\{r_j\}$, which are the solutions to (2-36), yield the absolute minimum of K subject to the constraint (2-35).

□**EXAMPLE 2-3** A small electronics company purchases three types of subcomponents. The management desires never to have an investment in these items in excess of \$15,000. No backorders are allowed and the inventory carrying-cost rate for each item is 20 percent. The pertinent data for each item is shown in Table 2-2. Determine the optimal lot size for each item. The optimal lot sizes, ignoring the constraint, are found by using Model IV as

$$Q_1 = \sqrt{\frac{2(50)(1000)}{(0.2)(50)}} = 100, \quad Q_2 = \sqrt{\frac{2(50)(1000)}{(0.2)(20)}} = 158,$$

$$Q_3 = \sqrt{\frac{2(50)(2000)}{(0.2)(80)}} = 112$$

If these lot sizes are used, the maximum investment in inventory would be

$$(50)(100) + (20)(158) + (80)(112) = \$17,120$$

Since this is greater than the maximum allowable investment in inventory, the constraint is active and the Lagrange multiplier method must be used. The problem becomes

$$\text{minimize } K = \sum_{j=1}^{3} \left[C_j D_j + \frac{A_j D_j}{Q_j} + iC_j \frac{Q_j}{2} \right]$$

subject to

$$\sum_{j=1}^{3} C_j Q_j = d$$

where d is the maximum inventory investment allowed. Now we construct the

TABLE 2-2   Data for Example 2-3

	ITEM 1	ITEM 2	ITEM 3
Demand rate, D_j	1000	1000	2000
Item cost, C_j	50	20	80
Setup cost, A_j	50	50	50

Lagrangian function,

$$L = \sum_{j=1}^{3} \left[C_j D_j + \frac{A_j D_j}{Q_j} + iC_j \frac{Q_j}{2} \right] + \lambda \left[\sum_{j=1}^{3} C_j Q_j - d \right]$$

and

$$\frac{\partial L}{\partial Q_j} = -\frac{A_j D_j}{Q_j^{\,2}} + \frac{iC_j}{2} + \lambda C_j = 0; \qquad j = 1, 2, 3$$

$$\frac{\partial L}{\partial \lambda} = \sum_{j=1}^{3} C_j Q_j - d = 0$$

These have the unique, optimal solution

$$Q_j^* = \sqrt{\frac{2 A_j D_j}{C_j(i + 2\lambda^*)}}; \qquad j = 1, 2, 3$$

where λ^* is the solution of the equation

$$\sum_{j=1}^{3} C_j \sqrt{\frac{2 A_j D_j}{C_j(i + 2\lambda^*)}} = d$$

or

$$\sum_{j=1}^{3} \sqrt{\frac{2 A_j D_j C_j}{i + 2\lambda^*}} = d$$

Substituting into this last equation we obtain

$$\sqrt{\frac{(2)(50)(1000)(50)}{0.20 + 2\lambda^*}} + \sqrt{\frac{(2)(50)(1000)(20)}{0.20 + 2\lambda^*}} + \sqrt{\frac{(2)(50)(2000)(80)}{0.20 + 2\lambda^*}} = 15,000$$

whose solution is

$$\lambda^* = 0.05$$

Therefore, the optimal $\{Q_j^*\}$ are

$$Q_1^* = \sqrt{\frac{(2)(50)(1000)}{(50)(0.30)}} = 82, \qquad Q_2^* = \sqrt{\frac{(2)(50)(1000)}{(20)(0.30)}} = 118,$$

$$Q_3^* = \sqrt{\frac{(2)(50)(2000)}{(80)(0.30)}} = 91$$

Substitution of these $\{Q_j^*\}$ values into the constraint will show that it does hold as a strict equality.□

The Lagrange multiplier technique may also be applied to inventory systems in which two or more constraints are imposed simultaneously. Suppose, for example, that a floor space constraint is imposed simultaneously with a constraint on maximum inventory investment. This problem is more difficult computationally, since either or both of the constraints may be inactive.[1] The procedure may be described as follows. First, determine the minimum cost $\{Q_j\}$, ignoring both constraints. If these $\{Q_j\}$ satisfy the constraints, then they are optimal. When this is not the case, include one of the constraints, say floor space, in the analysis and determine the appropriate $\{Q_j\}$. If these $\{Q_j\}$ satisfy the investment constraint, they are optimal. If they do not, solve the problem including only the investment constraint. If these $\{Q_j\}$ satisfy the floor space constraint, they are optimal. When they do not, then we are sure both constraints are active, and two Lagrange multipliers are introduced to obtain a function of the form

$$L = K(Q_1, Q_2, \ldots, Q_n; r_1, r_2, \ldots, r_n)$$

$$+ \lambda_1[g_1(Q_1, Q_2, \ldots, Q_n; r_1, r_2, \ldots, r_n) - d_1]$$
$$+ \lambda_2[g_2(Q_1, Q_2, \ldots, Q_n; r_1, r_2, \ldots, r_n) - d_2] \quad (2\text{-}37)$$

The optimal $\{Q_j\}$ would now be the solution to

$$\frac{\partial L}{\partial Q_j} = 0, \qquad \frac{\partial L}{\partial r_j} = 0; \qquad j = 1, 2, \ldots, n$$

$$\frac{\partial L}{\partial \lambda_1} = 0, \qquad \frac{\partial L}{\partial \lambda_2} = 0$$

It is important to examine the case where one or both constraints may be inactive in order to obtain the correct solution to this type of problem.

2-4 Quantity Discounts

To this point, we have assumed that the cost of procuring a lot of Q units is of the form $A + CQ$, where the unit variable cost, C, is independent of the quantity ordered. In many cases, this model may not be appropriate. In a purchasing situation, vendors often offer price discounts if the purchased quantity is large. In production, the marginal production cost may decrease, because of a learning process affecting workers' performance, elimination of process quality problems, and so on. In this section, two models will be treated to illustrate analysis of lot-size problems when the unit variable procurement cost is a function of the lot size.

2-4.1 All Units Discounts[2]

Suppose that the procurement cost for a lot of size Q is $A + C_j Q$, if $N_{j-1} \leq Q < N_j, j = 1, 2, \ldots, J$, where $C_j < C_{j-1}$. N_0 is the minimum quantity that

---

[1] It is conceivable that the two constraints are inconsistent and there would be no solution. We assume that they are consistent.

[2] This terminology apparently due to Hadley and Whitin (3).

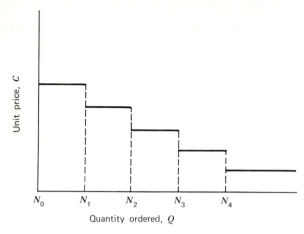

FIGURE 2-7. Unit price as a function of order size—all-units discount.

can be ordered and N_J is the maximum order size, usually unlimited. We shall assume that no shortages are to be permitted and the input rate is infinite, as in the case of a purchased item. Thus, we have the situation of Model IV, but with a discontinuous procurement cost function. Figures 2-7 and 2-8 illustrate this form of discount.

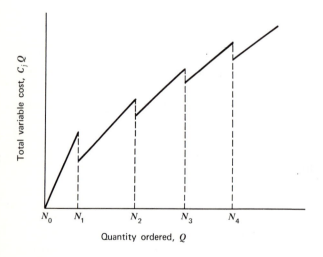

FIGURE 2-8. Total variable cost of a lot, $C_j Q$—all-units discount.

Let

$$K_j(Q) = \frac{AD}{Q} + C_jD + iC_j\frac{Q}{2} \qquad (2\text{-}38)$$

K_j is a mathematical function of Q, which over the range $N_{j-1} \le Q < N_j$ gives the average annual cost of an order of size Q. The average annual cost function then is written as

$$K(Q) = K_j(Q), \quad \text{if } N_{j-1} \le Q < N_j, \qquad (j = 1, 2, \ldots, J) \qquad (2\text{-}39)$$

Figure 2-9 illustrates a typical average annual cost function for $J = 3$. The solid line segments represent the function $K(Q)$; the dashed curves show the behavior of the functions $K_j(Q)$ outside the range of Q where the price C_j applies. For this illustration, the minimum point on the applicable portion of the K_3 curve is at N_2, the minimum point on the K_2 segment is at Q_2^*, and the minimum point on the K_1 segment is at N_1. The overall minimum is at N_2. Note that for any Q, $K_j(Q) < K_{j-1}(Q)$, so that the minimum value of the K_j curve must be less than that of the K_{j-1} segment.

To find the optimal value of Q, we find the minimum cost point on each segment of K and compare the costs at these points to determine the global minimum. This procedure can be stated more precisely as follows: Let Q_j^* be the value of Q that minimizes $K_j(Q)$ in the range $N_{j-1} \le Q_j < N_j$, and define Q^* as the overall optimal lot size. Then $K(Q^*) = \min_j K_j(Q_j^*)$.

To find the minimum cost value, $K_j(Q_j^*)$, in each segment, first find Q_j^*. Let $Q_j{}^0$ be the minimum point of the mathematical function $K_j(Q)$,

$$Q_j{}^0 = \sqrt{\frac{2AD}{iC_j}} \qquad (2\text{-}40)$$

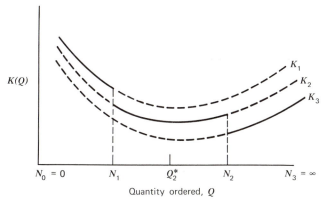

FIGURE 2-9. A typical average annual cost curve—all-units discount.

Then if Q_j^0 is in the range $[N_{j-1}, N_j)$, $Q_j^* = Q_j^0$. If $Q_j^0 < N_{j-1}$, $Q_j^* = N_{j-1}$; and if $Q_j^0 \geq N_j$, $Q_j^* = N_j^-$. These three cases were illustrated by the K_2, K_3, and K_1 segments, respectively, in Figure 2-9. In the latter case of $Q_j^0 \geq N_j$, the overall optimal lot size cannot lie in the region $Q < N_j$. This follows from the facts that $Q_j^0 < Q_{j+1}^0$ and $K_j(Q_j^*) > K_{j+1}(Q_j^*)$. Thus we should begin with the K_J segment and proceed to find Q_J^*, Q_{J-1}^*, $\ldots$, until we first reach an interval, say k, where $Q_k^* = Q_k^0$. The optimal solution must be one of the values Q_k^0, Q_{k+1}^*, $\ldots$, Q_J^*.

This algorithm is better learned through study of the following example.

☐**EXAMPLE 2-4**   A manufacturer uses large quantities of a purchased part in his assembly operations. He wants to use a constant purchase lot size, and he specifies that no shortages be planned. The following data are relevant to the problem of determining the optimal lot size:

   a.   Annual requirements—300,000 units, uniformly required over the year.

   b.   Manufacturer's fixed cost of placing an order—$80.

   c.   Annual cost of interest, insurance, and taxes on average inventory investment—20 percent of the value of average inventory.

   d.   Cost of storage—10 cents per month, based on average quantity stored.

   e.   Vendor's price schedule—a fixed charge of $20 per order, plus a charge per unit determined according to the following schedule:

ORDER SIZE		UNIT VARIABLE COST
	$0 < Q < 10{,}000$	$1.00
10,000	$\leq Q < 30{,}000$	0.98
30,000	$\leq Q < 50{,}000$	0.96
50,000	$\leq Q$	0.94

To solve this problem, we first write the total annual cost function, noting that the fixed cost per order is $100, the sum of the manufacturer's internal cost and the vendor's fixed charge, and that there is a storage cost charge of $1.20 per year per unit of average inventory. For $N_{j-1} \leq Q < N_j$, the price is C_j and the average annual cost is

$$K_j(Q) = \frac{(80 + 20)(300{,}000)}{Q} + (300{,}000)C_j + [(0.20)C_j + 1.20]\frac{Q}{2};$$

$$j = 1, 2, 3, 4$$

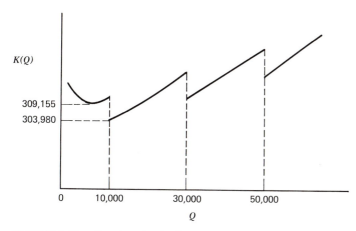

$K(Q)$

309,155

303,980

0   10,000   30,000   50,000

Q

FIGURE 2-10. Cost function for Example 2-4.

The values of C_j, N_{j-1}, and N_j are given in the price schedule. The minimum point on the entire K_j curve is at

$$Q_j^0 = 1000 \sqrt{\frac{60}{1.20 + 0.2C_j}}$$

For $j = 4$, $C_4 = \$0.94$ and $Q_4^0 = 6580 < N_3 = 50,000$, so the minimum cost point on the K_4 segment occurs at $Q_4^* = 50,000$.

For $j = 3$, $C_3 = \$0.96$ and $Q_3^0 = 6570 < N_2 = 30,000$, so $Q_3^* = 30,000$. (Obvious, actually, since $Q_3^0 < Q_4^0$.)

For $j = 2$, $C_2 = \$0.98$ and $Q_2^0 = 6560 < N_1 = 10,000$, so $Q_2^* = 10,000$. (Again obvious from knowledge that Q_2^0 will be less than Q_4^0.)

For $j = 1$, $C_1 = \$1$ and $Q_1^0 = 6550$. This value is in the range for which C_1 applies; therefore $Q_1^* = 6550$.

The costs must be calculated for Q_1^*, Q_2^*, Q_3^*, and Q_4^*:

$K(6550) = \$309,155$

$K(10,000) = \$303,980$—minimum

$K(30,000) = \$309,880$

$K(50,000) = \$317,500$

The optimal lot size is $Q^* = 10,000$ units. The average time between orders is 0.033 year. The total cost curve is shown in Figure 2-10.□

2-4.2 Incremental Discounts

The discount model of the previous section could be called an "all units" discount, because the price associated with an interval was applied to all Q

units purchased. To illustrate analysis of another form of discount schedule, suppose that the price associated with an interval applies only to the units within that interval. Assuming $N_0 = 0$, the first N_1 units would cost C_1 each; the next $(N_2 - N_1)$ units, C_2 each; the next $(N_3 - N_2)$ units, C_3 each, and so on. Hadley and Whitin (3) refer to this form as an "incremental discount" schedule.

The procurement cost for Q units would be $A + V(Q)$, where $V(Q)$ is the total variable cost of the lot and is given by

$$V(Q) = \sum_{k=1}^{j-1} C_k(N_k - N_{k-1}) + C_j(Q - N_{j-1}), \qquad N_{j-1} \leq Q < N_j$$

$$= V(N_{j-1}) + C_j(Q - N_{j-1}), \qquad N_{j-1} \leq Q < N_j \qquad (2\text{-}41)$$

$V(Q)$ is illustrated in Figure 2-11.

The average annual cost is

$$K(Q) = K_j(Q), \quad \text{if } N_{j-1} \leq Q < N_j$$

where

$$K_j(Q) = [A + V(Q)]\frac{D}{Q} + i\left[\frac{V(Q)}{Q}\right]\frac{Q}{2}$$

$$= [A + V(N_{j-1}) + C_j(Q - N_{j-1})]\frac{D}{Q} + \frac{i}{2}[V(N_{j-1}) + C_j(Q - N_{j-1})]$$

$$(2\text{-}42)$$

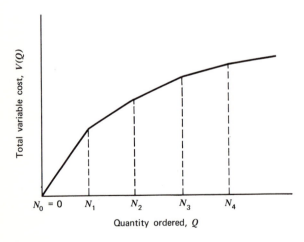

FIGURE 2-11. Total variable cost of a lot, $V(Q)$ — incremental discount schedule.

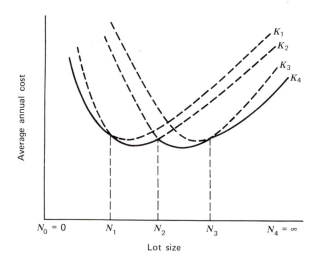

FIGURE 2-12. A typical average annual cost curve— incremental discount.

The term $V(Q)/Q$ in Equation 2-42 represents the average price per unit and is used to find the dollar value of average inventory. The formulation of Equation 2-42 assumes no shortages will be allowed and an infinite input rate (Model IV). Figure 2-12 illustrates the average annual cost curve. It can be shown that the optimal lot size will never equal the quantity defining a price break.

To find the optimal lot size, compute for $j = 1, 2, \ldots, J$,

$$Q_j^0 = \sqrt{\frac{2D[A + V(N_{j-1}) - C_j N_{j-1}]}{iC_j}} \tag{2-43}$$

If $N_{j-1} \le Q_j^0 < N_j$, compute $K_j(Q_j^0)$. Choose lot size Q^* as the value of Q_j^0 yielding the minimum $K_j(Q_j^0)$.

☐ EXAMPLE 2-5   Suppose the price schedule of Example 2-4 had been of the incremental discount type. Then the total annual cost would be $K_j(Q)$, when $N_{j-1} \le Q < N_j$, where[3]

$$K_j(Q) = [100 + V(N_{j-1}) + C_j(Q - N_{j-1})] \frac{300,000}{Q}$$

$$+ \frac{(0.20)}{2} [V(N_{j-1}) + C_j(Q - N_{j-1})] + (1.20)\frac{Q}{2}$$

---

[3] The last term in K_j is the annual storage cost, based on average inventory. See problem statement in Example 2-4.

with

j	C_j	N_j	$V(N_j)$	$V(Q) = V(N_{j-1}) + C_j(Q - N_{j-1})$
1	$1.00	10,000	$10,000	Q
2	0.98	30,000	29,600	$200 + 0.98Q$
3	0.96	50,000	48,800	$800 + 0.96Q$
4	0.94	—	—	$1800 + 0.94Q$

Using the values given,

$$K(Q) = \begin{cases} K_1(Q) = \dfrac{30 \cdot 10^6}{Q} + 300,000 + 0.70Q, \ 0 < Q < 10,000 \\[3ex] K_2(Q) = \dfrac{90 \cdot 10^6}{Q} + 294,020 + 0.698Q, \ 10,000 \leq Q < 30,000 \\[3ex] K_3(Q) = \dfrac{270 \cdot 10^6}{Q} + 288,080 + 0.696Q, \ 30,000 \leq Q < 50,000 \\[3ex] K_4(Q) = \dfrac{570 \cdot 10^6}{Q} + 282,180 + 0.694Q, \ 50,000 \leq Q \end{cases}$$

The minimum points on curves K_1, K_2, K_3, and K_4 are obtained using Equation 2-43, with the denominator including the storage cost component, 1.20.

$$Q_1^0 = 6550$$
$$Q_2^0 = 11,360$$
$$Q_3^0 = 19,660$$
$$Q_4^0 = 28,700$$

The values Q_3^0 and Q_4^0 are not in the range where K_3 and K_4 apply, respectively; therefore they are not considered further. The optimal lot size is either Q_1^0 or Q_2^0. To determine which, we must calculate average annual costs. It turns out that $K(6550) = \$309,360$ and $K(11,360) = \$309,860$, so the optimal lot size is 6550 units. The optimal time between orders is 0.022 year. This example is illustrated in Figure 2-13.

Comparing the solution to this example with that of Example 2-4, where the price schedule was interpreted as an all units discount, we note that the optimal lot size is 6550 here versus 10,000 there. This reduction in lot size was expected because with the incremental discount where the price discount does not apply to all units, there is less incentive to order in large lots.☐

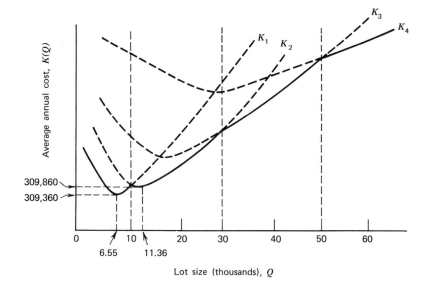

FIGURE 2-13. Cost function for Example 2-5.

2-5 Stochastic Single-Period Models

This section begins the treatment of inventory systems in which the demand and perhaps the lead time are considered to be random variables, with known probability distributions. Eventually we shall consider both single-period and multiperiod models. For the present, however, we shall discuss only single-period models.

The following situation is to be considered. Items are produced (or purchased) for a single period of demand at a cost of C dollars per item. At this point, we assume there is no fixed procurement cost. Each unit brings a price of V dollars when it is sold. Units left at the end of the period are charged a holding cost[4] H. Denote by I the number of units on hand before the ordering decision at the start of the period, and let D be a random variable that represents the demand during the period. We assume that D is continuous, with density function $f(D)$. Discrete demand can also be treated, and the interested reader is referred to Exercise 2-44 at the end of the chapter. The problem is to determine the

[4] The quantity H can be interpreted more generally as the inventory holding cost, plus the cost of removing the item from inventory at the end of the period, less any revenue received if the item is sold on disposal. Thus H could be negative.

optimum inventory level, say R^*, that should be on hand at the start of the period so that the expected cost is minimized. Once the optimal stock level is known, the amount to be procured at the start of the season can be computed as $\max(0, R^* - I)$.

This model describes the inventory process of an item whose demand occurs during a relatively short interval, after which it becomes obsolete (for example, newspapers and certain apparel), spoils (such as produce and Christmas trees), or else is not in demand for a long period, say until next season (such as Christmas cards and antifreeze). It can also describe that of an item that can be obtained only once, such as a spare part that must be bought at the time of initial production. The distinguishing characteristic of this model is that there is only one opportunity for procuring the item and that is at the start of the period.

The amount sold during the period if R units are on hand at the beginning of the period is

$$\left. \begin{array}{ll} D, & \text{if } D < R \\ R, & \text{if } D \geq R \end{array} \right\} = \min(D, R) \tag{2-44}$$

The amount of excess inventory at the end of the period is

$$\xi(R, D) = \begin{cases} R - D, & \text{if } D < R \\ 0, & \text{if } D \geq R \end{cases} \tag{2-45}$$

and the shortage condition at the end of the period is

$$\psi(R, D) = \begin{cases} 0, & \text{if } D \leq R \\ D - R, & \text{if } D > R \end{cases} \tag{2-46}$$

The expected costs for the period consist of the sum of the expected costs of ordering, holding inventory, and shortage. Denoting the expected costs by $E\{K(R)\}$, and assuming the initial on-hand inventory, I, to be zero, we may write

$$E\{K(R)\} = CR + H \int_0^\infty \xi(R, D) f(D)\, dD + V \int_0^\infty \psi(R, D) f(D)\, dD$$

$$= CR + H \int_0^R (R - D) f(D)\, dD + V \int_R^\infty (D - R) f(D)\, dD \tag{2-47}$$

Notice that we have assumed the cost of a shortage to be the lost revenue, V. If an additional cost of shortage, say π dollars per unit, exists, it can be added directly to V and the last integral on the right-hand side of Equation 2-47 would become

$$(V + \pi) \int_R^\infty (D - R) f(D)\, dD$$

Denote the expected costs of holding inventory and shortage by $G(R)$. Therefore

$$G(R) = H \int_0^R (R - D)f(D)\,dD + V \int_R^\infty (D - R)f(D)\,dD \qquad (2\text{-}48)$$

and the expected inventory costs will be minimized by choosing R so as to minimize $C(R - I) + G(R)$, for $R \geq I$. The constraint $R \geq I$ must be added since we assume that items on hand at the start of the period cannot be returned, or thrown away. The optimum R, say R^*, is the solution to

$$\frac{dE\{K(R)\}}{dR} = 0 \qquad (2\text{-}49)$$

or

$$C + H \int_0^R f(D)\,dD - V \int_R^\infty f(D)\,dD = 0 \qquad (2\text{-}50)$$

Equation 2-50 can be written as

$$C + HF(R) - V[1 - F(R)] = 0$$

where F is the cumulative distribution function of demand. This implies that

$$F(R^*) = \frac{V - C}{V + H} \qquad (2\text{-}51)$$

We see that R^* is defined only if $V \geq C$. If $V < C$ we would not operate the inventory system. Furthermore, since

$$\frac{d^2 E\{K(R)\}}{dR^2} = (H + V)f(R) > 0$$

the solution for R^* from Equation 2-51 yields a global minimum. This is equivalent to saying that $G(R)$ is a *convex* function.

Therefore, our optimum policy is to

$$\begin{cases} \text{Order } (R^* - I), & \text{if } R^* > I \\ \text{Do not order}, & \text{if } R^* \leq I \end{cases} \qquad (2\text{-}52)$$

where R^* satisfies Equation 2-51.

□**EXAMPLE 2-6** Suppose the demand in gallons for a soft drink syrup during a week is exponentially distributed with a mean of 100, that is

$$f(D) = 0.01e^{-0.01t}, \qquad t > 0$$

The syrup is produced in batches, one each week. If not used within a week following production, it spoils. The production cost is $1 a gallon. Any unused syrup must be disposed of at the end of the week at a cost of 10 cents per gallon for handling and waste treatment. A shortage of syrup results in lost sales. A gallon of syrup normally yields $2 in sales revenue, net of remaining manufacturing and distribution costs. Letting $R*$ denote the optimal batch size, we have from (2-51):

$$F(R*) = \int_0^{R*} 0.01e^{-0.01t}\, dt = \frac{2.00 - 1.00}{2.00 + 0.10}$$

$$1 - e^{-0.01R*} = 0.476$$

$$R* = 64.6 \text{ gallons} \qquad \square$$

The results given in Equations 2-51 and 2-52 are for the special case of *linear* shortage and holding costs, that is, $G(R)$ as defined in Equation 2-48. However, for any $G(R)$ that is strictly convex, the optimum policy is

$$\begin{cases} \text{Order } (R* - I), & \text{if } R* > I \\ \text{Do not order}, & \text{if } R* \leq I \end{cases}$$

where $R*$ is the value of R that satisfies Equation 2-49, that is

$$\frac{dG(R)}{dR} + C = 0$$

A Model with a Fixed Ordering Cost. Suppose a fixed cost, say A, is charged for placing an order, and that the shortage and holding penalty costs are linear. In this situation the expected cost for stocking an amount $R \geq I$ is

$$\begin{cases} A + C(R - I) + G(R), & \text{if } R > I \\ G(I), & \text{if } R = I \end{cases} \qquad (2\text{-}53)$$

Consider the costs shown in Figure 2-14. Define $R*$ as the value of the inventory level R that minimizes $CR + G(R)$, and define $r*$ as the smallest value of R

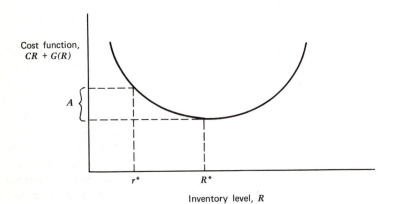

FIGURE 2-14. The function $CR + G(R)$ versus R.

for which $Cr^* + G(r^*) = A + CR^* + G(R^*)$. From examining Figure 2-14, it is clear that if $I > R^*$, then $A + CR + G(R) > CI + G(I)$ for all $R > I$. Therefore, $A + C(R - I) + G(R) > G(I)$, where the left-hand side of this last inequality is the cost of ordering up to R and the right-hand side is the cost of not ordering. Therefore, if $I > R^*$, the optimum policy is not to order. Now consider the case where $r^* \leq I \leq R^*$. From Figure 2-14 it is evident that $A + CR + G(R) \geq CI + G(I)$ for all $r^* \leq I < R \leq R^*$. Thus

$$A + C(R - I) + G(R) \geq G(I),$$

and once again the optimum policy is not to order. Finally, consider $I < r^*$. From Figure 2-14 it follows that $A + CR^* + G(R^*) < CI + G(I)$, or

$$A + C(R^* - I) + G(R^*) < G(I),$$

so that the cost is minimized if we order $(R^* - I)$.

The optimum ordering policy is to

$$\begin{cases} \text{Order } (R^* - I), & \text{if } I < r^* \\ \text{Do not order,} & \text{if } I \geq r^* \end{cases} \tag{2-54}$$

where R^* is as before, that is

$$F(R^*) = \frac{V - C}{V + H} \tag{2-55}$$

and r^* is the smallest value that satisfies

$$Cr^* + G(r^*) = A + CR^* + G(R^*) \tag{2-56}$$

From the discussion in Section 2-1.5, we recognize this ordering policy as an (R, r) policy. The (R, r) policy is the optimal operating doctrine for many types of inventory systems. We shall study further examples of this policy in Section 2-6.2.

As before, these results can be extended easily to the case where $G(R)$ is strictly convex. In such a case, the optimum ordering policy is

$$\begin{cases} \text{Order } (R^* - I), & \text{if } I < r^* \\ \text{Do not order,} & \text{if } I \geq r^* \end{cases}$$

where R^* is the value of R that satisfies

$$\frac{dG(R)}{dR} + C = 0$$

and r^* is the smallest value that satisfies

$$Cr^* + G(r^*) = A + CR^* + G(R^*)$$

2-6 Periodic Review
Models

A logical extension of the analysis of the preceding section is to a planning horizon of more than one period. In this section, we shall discuss multiperiod models in which a review of the inventory level and an ordering decision is made only at fixed intervals of time. These *periodic review* models are important for several reasons. First, many real-world inventory systems are operated according to a policy of this type. Second, they are more amenable to mathematical analysis than are continuous review models. Finally, the theoretical analysis often leads to decision rules that can be implemented relatively easily.

2-6.1 Multiperiod Models with No Fixed Ordering Cost

Consider a situation in which the planning horizon consists of N periods. Assume that a review is made at the start of each period, the delivery lead time is zero, shortages are backlogged (except at the end of period N, when they are lost), and that demands in each of the N periods are independent and *identically* distributed continuous random variables[5] with probability density $f(D)$. The purchase cost, C, is independent of the number of units ordered, the holding cost per unit is H, and the shortage cost per unit short is π. Finally, define a cost discounting factor α, $0 < \alpha \leq 1$, such that $\alpha = (1 + k)^{-1}$, where k is the interest rate per period.

Assume that an *order up to R* policy is to be followed. That is, if I_j is the net inventory at the *start* of period j, then the policy implies

$$\begin{cases} \text{Order } R_j - I_j, & \text{if } R_j > I_j \\ \text{Do not order,} & \text{if } R_j \leq I_j \end{cases}$$

It can be shown that in the absence of a fixed ordering cost, the order up to R policy is an optimal policy. The cost in period j is

$$\begin{cases} C(R_j - I_j) + G(R_j), & \text{if } R_j > I_j \\ G(I_j), & \text{if } R_j \leq I_j \end{cases}$$

where G is the single-period expected sum of holding and shortage costs,

$$G(R_j) = H \int_0^{R_j} (R_j - D)f(D)\, dD + \pi \int_{R_j}^{\infty} (D - R_j)f(D)\, dD$$

---

[5] For discrete demand, replace integrals in the development that follows by summations.

The optimization problem involves finding an order quantity R_j^* for each period $j = 1, 2, \ldots, N$ such that the expected discounted cost[6]

$$K = E\left\{ \sum_{j=1}^{N} \alpha^{j-1}[C(R_j - I_j) + G(R_j)] \right\} \qquad (2\text{-}57)$$

is minimized.

Dynamic programming may be used to minimize Equation 2-57. The appropriate recursive relationship is

$$K_j(I_j) = \min_{R_j \geq I_j} \{C(R_j - I_j) + G(R_j) + \alpha E[K_{j+1}(R_j - D)]\}, \quad j = 1, 2, \ldots, N$$
$$(2\text{-}58)$$

where $K_{N+1}(I_{N+1}) = 0$, and

$$E[K_{j+1}(R_j - D)] = \int_0^\infty K_{j+1}(R_j - D)f(D)\, dD$$

In (2-58), $K_j(I_j)$ is the minimum expected discounted cost over the periods $j, j + 1, \ldots, N$, when the net inventory at the start of period j is I_j. Note that $C(R_j - I_j) + G(R_j)$ is the expected cost in period j and $K_{j+1}(R_j - D)$ is the minimum attainable cost over the last $N - j$ periods as a function of the decision in period j and the demand that occurs in period j. Averaging over D and discounting to the start of period j yields the last term in Equation 2-58. Readers who are not comfortable with dynamic programming formulations may wish to skip to Section 2-6.3.

A backwards solution procedure for (2-58) is used. That is, for period N compute $K_N(I_N)$ given $K_{N+1}(I_{N+1})$, then compute $K_{N-1}(I_{N-1})$ given $K_N(I_N)$, etc., until $K_1(I_1)$ is determined.

□ **EXAMPLE 2-7** The demand for an item in each of two periods is uniformly distributed from 0–10, i.e., $f(D) = 0.10, 0 \leq D \leq 10$. The cost of purchasing is \$2 per item. If excess inventory remains at the end of a period, it is charged at \$6 per item. The shortage cost is \$10 per item. We wish to find the optimum two-period policy for $\alpha = 1$. Consider period 2. Equation 2-58 becomes

$$K_2(I_2) = \min_{R_2 \geq I_2} \{2(R_2 - I_2) + G(R_2) + 0\}$$

and since the shortage and holding costs are linear, the R_2^* that minimizes the quantity in braces is

$$F(R_2^*) = \frac{\pi - C}{\pi + H} = \frac{10 - 2}{10 + 6} = 0.5$$

Thus the optimal $R_2^* = 5$. Now in general,

$$G(R) = 6\int_0^R (R - D)(0.1)\, dD + 10\int_R^{10} (D - R)(0.1)\, dD$$

$$= 0.8R^2 - 10R + 50$$

---

[6] In this section, we depart from using the symbol K to represent the average cost per period.

Therefore

$$E[K_2(R_1 - D)] = \int_0^{10} K_2(R_1 - D)(0.1)\, dD$$

$$= \int_0^{R_1 - R_2^*} G(R_1 - D)(0.1)\, dD$$

$$+ \int_{R_1 - R_2^*}^{10} [C(R_2^* - R_1 + D) + G(R_2^*)](0.1)\, dD$$

$$= \int_0^{R_1 - 5} \{0.8(R_1 - D)^2 - 10(R_1 - D) + 50\}(0.1)\, dD$$

$$+ \int_{R_1 - 5}^{10} \{2(5 - R_1 + D) + 50 - 10(5) + 0.8(5)^2\}(0.1)\, dD$$

$$= \tfrac{8}{300}R_1{}^3 - \tfrac{4}{10}R_1{}^2 - \tfrac{1100}{30}$$

Now consider period 1. The recursion (2-58) becomes

$$K_1(I_1) = \min_{R_1 \geq I_1} \{2(R_1 - I_1) + 0.8R_1{}^2 - 10R_1 + 50 + \tfrac{8}{300}R_1{}^3 - \tfrac{4}{10}R_1{}^2 - \tfrac{1100}{30}\}$$

$$= \min_{R_1 \geq I_1} \{-2I_1 + \tfrac{40}{3} - 10R_1 + \tfrac{4}{10}R_1{}^2 + \tfrac{8}{300}R_1{}^3\}$$

Differentiating $K_1(I_1)$ with respect to R_1 and equating to zero yields

$$-10 + \tfrac{8}{10}R_1 + \tfrac{24}{300}R_1{}^2 = 0$$

whose positive solution is $R_1 = 7.25$. Therefore, the optimal policy is to order up to 7.25 units if the initial stock on hand does not exceed 7.25 units. At the start of period 2, if the amount on hand does not exceed five units, order up to five units.$\square$

For even small values of N, the dynamic programming formulation is computationally difficult. However, an approximate solution may be obtained relatively easily by considering the *unbounded horizon* version of the model. As $N \to \infty$, a reasonable unbounded horizon analog of (2-58) is the *functional equation*

$$K(I) = \min_{R \geq I} \{C(R - I) + G(R) + \alpha E[K(R - D)]\} \qquad (2\text{-}59)$$

where $0 < \alpha < 1$ (we must require that $\alpha < 1$ to insure that $\alpha E[K(R - D)]$ is finite). The optimal value of R is determined from

$$\frac{dK(I)}{dR} = C + H\int_0^R f(D)\, dD - \pi \int_R^\infty f(D)\, dD + \alpha \int_0^\infty \frac{dK(R - D)}{dR} f(D)\, dD$$

$$= 0$$

But $[dK(R - D)]/dR = -C$, since for every additional unit on hand at the start of the period the cost for the period will decrease by C, as those units do not have to be ordered. Therefore, the optimal R^* is the solution to

$$C + H \int_0^R f(D) \, dD - \pi \int_R^\infty f(D) \, dD - \alpha C \int_0^\infty f(D) \, dD = 0$$

or

$$F(R^*) = \frac{\pi - C(1 - \alpha)}{\pi + H} \tag{2-60}$$

If the number of periods in the planning horizon is greater than three or four, then this approximate solution, obtained by assuming the number of periods to be infinite, will usually be satisfactory. Furthermore, the following relationship between the optimal $\{R_j^*\}$ for the finite horizon model and R^* for the unbounded horizon model always holds:

$$R_N^* \leq R_{N-1}^* \leq \cdots \leq R_1^* \leq R^*$$

That is, in the finite-horizon model one orders less as the end of the planning horizon approaches, and none of the critical values $\{R_j^*\}$ can exceed R^* for the unbounded horizon case.

□**EXAMPLE 2-8** Suppose the demand for an item in each of five periods is uniformly distributed between 0 and 10, that is, $f(D) = 0.10$, $0 \leq D \leq 10$. The shortage cost is \$20 per unit, the holding cost is \$10 per item, and the purchase cost is \$10. The discount factor is $\alpha = 0.8$, and we assume that the planning horizon is long enough to employ the unbounded horizon approximation. From Equation 2-60 we compute

$$F(R^*) = \frac{20 - 10(1 - 0.8)}{20 + 10} = \frac{18}{30}$$

and since

$$F(R^*) = \frac{R^*}{10}$$

we see that $R^* = 6$.□

We observe that our development has been for the case of linear shortage and holding costs. More general results may be obtained. If the function G is strictly convex, then the finite-horizon formulation (2-58) leads to a set of $\{R_j^*\}$ that yield an absolute minimum. In the unbounded horizon case, if G is strictly convex, the optimal R^* is the solution to

$$\frac{dG(R)}{dR} + C(1 - \alpha) = 0 \tag{2-61}$$

A Model with Lost Sales. This model is similar to the backlog case, but when demand in any period exceeds the inventory level, the unfilled demand is lost. Thus the next period begins with zero initial inventory. The finite horizon dynamic programming recursion for the lost sales case is

$$K_j(I_j) = \min_{R_j \geq I_j} \left\{ C(R_j - I_j) + G(R_j) + \alpha \left[\int_0^{R_j} K_{j+1}(R_j - D)f(D)\, dD \right. \right.$$

$$\left. \left. + \int_{R_j}^{\infty} K_{j+1}(0)f(D)\, dD \right] \right\}, \qquad j = 1, 2, \ldots, N \quad (2\text{-}62)$$

where $K_{N+1}(I_{N+1}) = 0$. The shortage cost coefficient in $G(R_j)$ is $V + \pi$, which is the cost of a lost sale, including the lost revenue V and any additional penalty π. Let $\pi' = V + \pi$.

It is difficult to solve (2-62) for even moderate values of N. However, the corresponding unbounded horizon model has a simple solution. A logical infinite-stage analog for (2-62) is the functional equation

$$K(I) = \min_{R \geq I} \left\{ C(R - I) + G(R) + \alpha \left[\int_0^R K(R - D)f(D)\, dD + \int_R^{\infty} K(0)f(D)\, dD \right] \right\}$$

$$(2\text{-}63)$$

Assuming the shortage and holding costs to be linear, that is,

$$G(R) = H \int_0^R (R - D)f(D)\, dD + \pi' \int_R^{\infty} (D - R)f(D)\, dD$$

we may find the optimal R^* as the solution to

$$\frac{dK(I)}{dR} = C + H \int_0^R f(D)\, dD - \pi' \int_R^{\infty} f(D)\, dD - \alpha C \int_0^R f(D)\, dD = 0$$

which implies that

$$F(R^*) = \frac{\pi' - C}{\pi' + H - \alpha C} \qquad (2\text{-}64)$$

Once again the relationship

$$R_N^* \leq R_{N-1}^* \leq \cdots \leq R_1^* \leq R^*$$

is still valid.

A Model with Positive Delivery Lead Time. We shall now present a model with a positive delivery lead time, that is, units ordered in period j do not arrive until period $j + \tau$, where $\tau > 0$. If backlogging is allowed, then it can be shown that in the finite horizon case the optimal $\{R_j^*\}$ are the solution to

$$K_j(X_j) = \min_{R_j \geq X_j} \left\{ C(R_j - X_j) + \alpha^\tau \int_0^{\infty} G(R_j - W)f^{(\tau+1)}(W)\, dW \right.$$

$$\left. + \alpha \int_0^{\infty} K_{j+1}(R_j - D)f(D)\, dD \right\}, \qquad j = 1, 2, \ldots, N \quad (2\text{-}65)$$

where X_j is the amount on hand plus on order at the beginning of period j, $K_{N+1}(X_{N+1}) = 0$, and $f^{(\tau+1)}(W)$ is the density function of the sum of $\tau + 1$ demands, each of which are independently and identically distributed random variables with probability density function f. That is, the random variable $W = D_j + D_{j+1} + \cdots + D_{j+\tau}$, and the density function of W, $f^{(\tau+1)}(W)$, is the $(\tau + 1)$-fold *convolution* of f. Clearly this model is similar to the zero lead time model in Equation 2-58, but with a different expected shortage and holding cost, say $J(R)$, where

$$J(R) = \int_0^\infty G(R - W)f^{(\tau+1)}(W) \, dW$$

As the solution to the finite horizon case is usually difficult, the unbounded horizon model

$$K(X) = \min_{R \geq X} \left\{ C(R - X) + \alpha^\tau J(R) + \alpha \int_0^\infty K(R - D)f(D) \, dD \right\} \quad (2\text{-}66)$$

is often employed. For the case of $J(R)$ strictly convex, the optimal R^* for the unbounded horizon model is determined from

$$\alpha^\tau \frac{dJ(R)}{dR} + C(1 - \alpha) = 0 \quad (2\text{-}67)$$

If unfilled demand is lost, then the case of positive delivery lead times is very difficult to analyze, because of a resulting dimensionality problem that increases with τ.

2-6.2 Multiperiod Models with a Fixed Ordering Cost

Suppose that a fixed cost A is incurred every time an order is placed. That is, in period j the ordering cost is

$$u(R_j - I_j) = \begin{cases} 0, & \text{if } R_j = I_j \\ A + C(R_j - I_j), & \text{if } R_j > I_j \end{cases} \quad (2\text{-}68)$$

This situation can also be formulated as a dynamic programming model. The appropriate recursion is

$$K_j(I_j) = \min_{R_j \geq I_j} \{u(R_j - I_j) + G(R_j) + \alpha E[K_{j+1}(R_j - D)]\}, \quad j = 1, 2, \ldots, N$$

$$(2\text{-}69)$$

where $K_{N+1}(I_{N+1}) = 0$.

Theoretically, at least, it is possible to obtain the optimal solution to (2-68) by dynamic programming methods. However, as a general rule, it is extremely difficult computationally. Moreover, there are no simple solutions in the unbounded horizon case as there are when $A = 0$.

Although the computational aspects of the model are formidable, the *structure* of an optimal policy may be determined. Scarf (5), among others, has shown that the form of an optimal policy is an (R, r) policy if the function G is convex. Thus, even though we cannot easily determine the exact optimal values of $\{r_j\}$ and $\{R_j\}$, we should consider using a policy from this class instead of some other ordering policy.

2-6.3 A Heuristic Treatment of the Periodic Review Case with Backorders

The order up to R policy is often used in situations where it is of interest to determine the optimal review period length, T, as well as the optimal target inventory. The formulation given in Section 2-6.1 does not easily allow this to be done. In this section we shall present an approximate treatment of a periodic review inventory system for which there is both a fixed cost of ordering, A, and a fixed cost of making a review, J. Both of these costs are independent of the parameters R and T. We shall also assume that backorders occur only in very small quantities, that is, the cost of a backorder, π, is high relative to the cost of carrying inventory. In practice, it may also be necessary to treat procurement lead time as a random variable. We assume that, if procurement lead time is a random variable, orders are received in the same sequence in which they are placed, and that the lead times for different orders are independent random variables.

Let $\xi(x; t)$ be the probability density of demand x in the time interval of length t, and let D be the average demand rate (the expected demand in a unit of time). The annual ordering and review cost is just $(A + J)/T$. The time between the arrival of two successive orders is approximately the review period length, T.

Suppose that the lead time is a random variable, say τ, such that $\tau_a \leq \tau \leq \tau_b$, with probability density function $g(\tau)$. Thus

$$\int_{\tau_a}^{\tau_b} g(\tau)\, d\tau = 1$$

Then if τ_1 and τ_2 are the lead times for the orders placed at times t and $t + T$, respectively, then the expected number of demands backordered at the end of each period must be

$$\int_{\tau_a}^{\tau_b} \int_{\tau_a}^{\tau_b} \int_{R}^{\infty} (x - R)\xi(x; \tau_2 + T)g(\tau_2)g(\tau_1)\, dx\, d\tau_2\, d\tau_1 \qquad (2\text{-}70)$$

or

$$\int_R^\infty (x - R)f(x; T)\, dx \qquad (2\text{-}71)$$

where

$$f(x; T) = \int_{\tau_a}^{\tau_b} \xi(x; \tau_2 + T)g(\tau_2)\, d\tau_2 \qquad (2\text{-}72)$$

This follows, since τ_1 may be integrated out of Equation 2-70.

Define $f(x; T)$ to be $\xi(x; \tau + T)$ when the procurement lead time is constant and Equation 2-72 when the procurement lead time is a random variable. Then in either case, the expected number of backorders per period is given by Equation 2-71, and the average number of backorders incurred per year is

$$\frac{1}{T}\int_R^\infty (x - R)f(x; T)\, dx \equiv \frac{1}{T}\bar{b}(R, T) \qquad (2\text{-}73)$$

Thus the average annual cost of backorders is simply $\pi\bar{b}(R, T)/T$.

Let μ be the expected value of lead-time demand. Because the mean rate of demand is constant at D over time, the expected net inventory decreases linearly from $R - \mu$ immediately following the arrival of an order to $R - \mu - DT$ just prior to the arrival of the next order. Because we have assumed that backorders are incurred in only very small quantities, the integral over time of the net inventory is approximately equal to the time integral of the on-hand inventory. Therefore, the average annual cost of carrying inventory must be approximately

$$iC\left[\frac{(R - \mu) + (R - \mu - DT)}{2}\right] = iC\left[R - \mu - \frac{DT}{2}\right] \qquad (2\text{-}74)$$

The average annual variable cost is

$$K(R, T) = \frac{A + J}{T} + iC\left[R - \mu - \frac{DT}{2}\right] + \frac{\pi\bar{b}(R, T)}{T} \qquad (2\text{-}75)$$

For a given T, the value of R, say R^*, that minimizes Equation 2-75 is the solution to

$$\frac{\partial K(R, T)}{\partial R} = 0$$

This implies that R^* must satisfy

$$F'(R^*; T) = \frac{iCT}{\pi} \qquad (2\text{-}76)$$

where $F'(R; T) = \int_R^\infty f(x; T)\, dx$ is the complementary cumulative of $f(x; T)$.

Equation 2-75 may also be optimized with respect to T by solving $\partial K(R, T)/\partial T = 0$ simultaneously with (2-76). However, this would require the use of some numerical technique. It is usually sufficient to tabulate the cost K as a function of T, using the R^* for the given T to compute K, and in this manner determine T^*.

☐**EXAMPLE 2-9** A large supplier of electronic components has decided to control the inventory of a certain item by a periodic review, order up to R policy. The mean demand rate for this item is 500 units per year. The lead time τ is nearly constant at three months. The demand in the time $\tau + T$ can be represented by a normal distribution with mean $500(\tau + T)$ and variance $800(\tau + T)$. The cost of each unit is \$10, the inventory carrying charge is computed using $i = 0.10$, the cost of making a review and placing an order is \$15, and the cost of a backorder is estimated to be \$30. It is desired to find the optimal R and T. If T is specified, we may find R^* easily. For example, suppose we wish to review the inventory level every three months. Then $\tau + T = 0.5$, and the expected demand in $\tau + T$ is $500(0.5) = 250$, and the variance of demand in this time is $800(0.5) = 400$. Thus R^* is the solution to

$$\Phi'\left(\frac{R - 250}{20}\right) = \frac{(0.1)(10)(0.25)}{30} = 0.0803$$

where

$$\Phi'(u) = \int_u^\infty (2\pi)^{-1/2} e^{-z^2/2} \, dz$$

is the complementary cumulative distribution of the standard normal random variable. From the normal tables, Table A-2 in the Appendix,

$$\frac{R - 250}{20} = 1.40$$

Thus

$$R^* = 250 + 20(1.40) = 278$$

If T is not specified, then the average annual cost becomes

$$K(R, T) = \frac{15}{T} + (0.1)(10)[R - 125 - 250T] + \frac{15}{T}\int_R^\infty (x - R) f(x; T) \, dx$$

where the density $f(x; T)$ is normal with mean $500(0.25 + T)$ and variance $800(0.25 + T)$. It can be shown that for a normal random variable x, having mean μ and variance σ^2,

$$\int_a^\infty (x - a)n(x; \mu, \sigma^2) \, dx = \sigma\phi\left(\frac{a - \mu}{\sigma}\right) + (\mu - a)\Phi'\left(\frac{a - \mu}{\sigma}\right)$$

where

$$\phi(z) = (2\pi)^{-1/2} e^{-z^2/2}$$

and

$$n(x;\, \mu,\, \sigma^2) = \frac{1}{\sigma}\, \phi\!\left(\frac{x - \mu}{\sigma}\right)$$

(The reader is asked to verify this in Exercise 2-60.)[7] Using this result, we may write the cost $K(R,\, T)$ as

$$K(R,\, T) = \frac{15}{T} + (0.1)(10)[R - 125 - 250T]$$
$$+ \frac{15}{T}\left\{\sqrt{800(0.25 + T)}\,\phi\!\left(\frac{R - 500(0.25 + T)}{\sqrt{800(0.25 + T)}}\right)\right.$$
$$\left. + [500(0.25 + T) - R]\Phi'\!\left(\frac{R - 500(0.25 + T)}{\sqrt{800(0.25 + T)}}\right)\right\}$$

Using this expression, we may now tabulate $K(R^*,\, T)$ as a function of T, where the optimum R^* depends on the particular T chosen. Such a tabulation is shown below. We would choose $T^* = 0.30$ as the optimum review period and

T(YEARS)	R*(UNITS)	K(R*, T) (DOLLARS)
0.25	278	195
0.30	323	176
0.35	350	184

$R^* = 323$ as the optimum target inventory, as these parameters result in a minimum cost. In computing the optimal T, an increment of 0.05 years was used, and hence the optimum T^* is only accurate to within 0.025 years. Smaller increments could be used if it is felt that more accurate results are required.☐

2-7 Continuous Review Models

2-7.1 A Heuristic Treatment of the Fixed Reorder Quantity Policy with Backorders

Suppose that the inventory position of an item is monitored after every transaction and that the policy is to order a lot of size Q when the inventory level drops

---

[7] See Example 2-10 for an alternate way to evaluate the integral.

to a reorder point, r. This policy was described in Section 2-1.5 and illustrated by Figure 2-4.

Assume that the demand in any given interval of time is a random variable whose probability distribution is stationary. The expected value of demand in a unit of time, say a year, is D. We suppose units are demanded one at a time or in small quantities, so that there will be no appreciable overshoot of the reorder point at the time it is reached. The replenishment lead time is τ. Initially we assume τ is constant and sufficiently small to insure that at most one replenishment order will be outstanding. We let x denote the demand during a lead time and $f(x)$ denote its probability distribution.

The fixed cost of a procurement is A and the unit variable procurement cost is C. The cost of carrying a unit of inventory for one unit of time is h. All shortages are backordered at a cost of π per unit short, regardless of the duration of the shortage.

Our approach will be to compute the costs associated with a given cycle and multiply by the number of cycles per year to obtain an expression for average annual cost. Because of the probabilistic nature of demand, the number of cycles per year is a random variable that averages D/Q.

The procurement cost per cycle is $A + CQ$.

The shortage cost per cycle is $\pi \bar{b}(r)$, where $\bar{b}(r)$ is the expected number of shortages per cycle and is a function of the reorder point r. A shortage can occur only if the demand during a lead time exceeds the reorder point quantity. The amount of the shortage at the end of a cycle, when the replenishment order is received, is $b(x, r) = \max [0, x - r]$, which has expected value

$$\bar{b}(r) = \int_r^\infty (x - r) f(x) \, dx \qquad (2\text{-}77)$$

The inventory carrying cost per cycle is $(hQ/D)\bar{I}(Q, r)$, where Q/D is the average length of a cycle, hQ/D is the cost to carry a unit of inventory for a cycle, and $\bar{I}(Q, r)$ is the average on-hand inventory during the cycle. The latter depends on Q and r. Obtaining an exact expression for $\bar{I}$ is difficult and an approximate result will be used here, which is good if the time the system is in a backorder condition during a cycle is small compared to the cycle length. In this case, the average net inventory, $\bar{Y}$, is approximately equal to the average on-hand inventory, $\bar{I}$. (Remember that over any period of time the average on-hand inventory minus the average backorder position equals the average net inventory). The net inventory is at its minimum immediately before receipt of an order and at its maximum immediately after receipt of the order. The expected net inventory levels at these two points are $r - \mu$ and $Q + r - \mu$, respectively, where μ is the expected demand during a lead time. Assuming a linear decrease over the cycle, we average the high and low values to obtain

$$\bar{I} \cong \bar{Y} = \frac{Q}{2} + r - \mu \qquad (2\text{-}78)$$

The quantity $Q/2$ often is called the *cycle stock* and $r - \mu$ is referred to as the *safety stock*. Thus safety stock for this system is the amount by which the reorder point exceeds the average usage during a lead time.

Our cost per cycle is then approximately

$$A + CQ + h\frac{Q}{D}\left[\frac{Q}{2} + r - \mu\right] + \pi \bar{b}(r)$$

Multiplying by the average number of cycles per year, we obtain the average annual cost

$$K(Q, r) = \frac{AD}{Q} + CD + h\left[\frac{Q}{2} + r - \mu\right] + \frac{\pi D\bar{b}(r)}{Q} \tag{2-79}$$

To minimize K, we solve

$$\frac{\partial K}{\partial Q} = -\frac{AD}{Q^2} + \frac{h}{2} - \frac{\pi D\bar{b}(r)}{Q^2} = 0$$

$$\frac{\partial K}{\partial r} = h + \frac{\pi D}{Q}\frac{\partial}{\partial r}\bar{b}(r) = 0$$

The first equation yields the optimal Q for a given reorder point r:

$$Q = \sqrt{\frac{2D[A + \pi\bar{b}(r)]}{h}} \tag{2-80}$$

In the second equation

$$\frac{\partial \bar{b}}{\partial r} = \frac{\partial}{\partial r}\int_r^\infty (x - r)f(x)\,dx = -\int_r^\infty f(x)\,dx = -F'(r)$$

where $F'(r)$ is the complementary cumulative distribution of x evaluated at r. Therefore, solving the second equation for r in terms of Q gives

$$F'(r) = \frac{hQ}{\pi D} \tag{2-81}$$

Note that Equation 2-81 says that for a given lot size, Q, the reorder point r should be chosen so that the probability of a shortage during a lead time is $hQ/\pi D$.

To find the optimal pair (Q^*, r^*) that minimize K, we use the following iterative procedure:

1. Assume $\bar{b}(r) = 0$ and compute Q with Equation 2-80. Call this value Q_1.

2. Use Equation 2-81 with $Q = Q_1$ to find the reorder point. Call this value r_1.

3. Use Equation 2-80 with $r = r_1$ to find a new lot size Q_2, having first found $\bar{b}(r_1)$ from Equation 2-77.

4. Repeat step 2 with $Q = Q_2$, etc. Convergence occurs when at iteration i, $Q_i = Q_{i-1}$ or $r_i = r_{i-1}$. Usually this is rapid.

If at any point in the algorithm, while using Equation 2-81, $hQ/\pi D > 1$ is obtained, we interpret this as indicating that the cost of a shortage is so small that it is desirable to incur a large number of backorders. Hence our approximation of the on-hand inventory by the net inventory was not appropriate and a more exact model is required.

When the lead time is on the order of Q/D, or greater, there may be more than one order outstanding. In this case, the reorder point, r, is expressed in terms of the inventory position; that is, an order is placed every time the inventory position drops to r.

When the lead time is a random variable, say with density function $g(t)$, we consider $f(x)$ to be the marginal distribution of lead time demand derived from the conditional distribution $\xi(x; \tau)$ by the following operation:

$$f(x) = \int_0^\infty \xi(x; \tau)g(\tau)\, d\tau \qquad (2\text{-}82)$$

Our analysis then procedes as in the case of constant lead time. Actually, this approach is not theoretically correct if more than one order is outstanding, but in many situations, especially when the time interval between placing orders is not very short, the method is satisfactory. A more thorough discussion of the effects of variability in lead times is given by Hadley and Whitin (3).

☐**EXAMPLE 2-10** A manufacturer of textile products uses a certain chemical in its finishing process at an expected annual rate of 10,000 gallons. This expected rate is constant over time; however, the actual demand in a period may vary randomly. The chemical is purchased and the demand during the procurement lead time is estimated to be normally distributed with a mean of 300 gallons and a standard deviation of 40 gallons. The fixed procurement cost is $70 per order and the variable procurement cost is $3 a gallon. The company uses an annual inventory carrying cost rate of 20 percent. Shortages result in rescheduling production, with the resulting cost assumed proportional to the size of the shortage. This loss is estimated at $1.50 per gallon short. A fixed reorder quantity system is to be used.

This is a backorders case, since all demand for the chemical is eventually satisfied, so we use the cost model given by (2-79), with $D = 10,000$, $A = 70$, $h = iC = (0.2)(3) = 0.6$, $\mu = 300$, $\pi = 1.5$, and

$$\bar{b}(r) = \int_r^\infty (x - r)n(x; 300, 1600)\, dx$$

where $n(x; \mu, \sigma^2)$ is the normal density with mean μ and variance σ^2. Equations

2-80 and 2-81 are

$$Q = \sqrt{\frac{(2)(10,000)[70 + 1.5\bar{b}(r)]}{0.6}} = (182.5)\sqrt{70 + 1.5\bar{b}(r)}$$

and

$$F'(r) = \Phi'\left(\frac{r - 300}{40}\right) = \frac{(0.6)Q}{(1.5)(10,000)} = 0.00004Q$$

To evaluate $\bar{b}(r)$, we can use the result given in Example 2-9,

$$\int_r^\infty (x - r)n(x; \mu, \sigma^2)\, dx = \sigma\phi\left(\frac{r - \mu}{\sigma}\right) - (r - \mu)\Phi'\left(\frac{r - \mu}{\sigma}\right)$$

for computation or we can use Appendix Table A-3, which gives values of the unit-normal linear-loss integral

$$L'(u) = \int_u^\infty (z - u)\phi(z)\, dz$$

It can be shown (Exercise 2-61) that if x is $n(x; \mu, \sigma^2)$, $\bar{b}(r) = \sigma L'[(r - \mu)/\sigma]$.

Initially we assume $\bar{b}(r) = 0$ and compute $Q_1 = 1530$. Using a lot size of 1530, the optimal reorder point, r_1, satisfies

$$\Phi'\left(\frac{r_1 - 300}{40}\right) = (0.00004)(1530) = 0.0612$$

so that $r_1 = 300 + (1.54)(40) \cong 362$.

With a reorder point of 362,

$$\bar{b}(362) = 40L'\left(\frac{362 - 300}{40}\right) = 40L'(1.54)$$

$$= (40)(0.02674) = 1.07$$

and

$$Q_2 = (182.5)\sqrt{70 + (1.5)(1.07)} = 1547$$

Repeating the determination of a reorder point:

$$\Phi'\left(\frac{r_2 - 300}{40}\right) = (0.00004)(1547) = 0.0619$$

$$r_2 = 300 + (1.54)(40) = 362$$

We have converged on the solution $Q^* = 1547$ and $r^* = 362$. For this policy, the probability of a shortage during a lead time is 0.0619 and the expected number of backorders per cycle is 1.07. The minimum average annual cost of $30,964 is obtained by substituting Q^* and r^* into Equation 2-79.□

2-7.2 A Heuristic Treatment of the Fixed Reorder Quantity System with Lost Sales

Now consider the fixed reorder quantity policy when all shortages are lost. We make the same assumptions as in the backorders case, except that the shortage cost π now includes the lost profit on an item.

If we again consider a cycle to be the time between receipt of lots, we can conceive of an average cycle length $\bar{T}$, consisting of an average time $\bar{T}_1$ when the on-hand inventory is positive plus an average time $\bar{T}_2$ when the on-hand inventory is zero. Because no backorders are permitted, $\bar{T}_1 = Q/D$ and the average number of cycles per year is $(\bar{T})^{-1} = (\bar{T}_1 + \bar{T}_2)^{-1} = D/(Q + D\bar{T}_2)$. If the cost of a shortage is not small, $\bar{T}_2$ will be much less than Q/D, so that the expected number of cycles per year can be approximated by D/Q.

The procurement cost per cycle is $A + CQ$, and the shortage cost per cycle is $\pi\bar{b}(r)$, where $\bar{b}(r)$ is the expected number of lost sales per cycle and is given by Equation 2-77. In the lost sales case, the net inventory and the on-hand inventory are the same. The on-hand inventory at the end of a cycle, immediately prior to receipt of a lot, is $a(x, r) = \max(0, r - x)$, where x is the lead time demand. The expected on-hand inventory at the end of a cycle is

$$
\begin{aligned}
\bar{a}(r) &= \int_0^r (r - x) f(x)\, dx \\
&= \int_0^\infty (r - x) f(x)\, dx + \int_r^\infty (x - r) f(x)\, dx \\
&= r - \mu + \bar{b}(r)
\end{aligned}
\tag{2-83}
$$

The average on-hand inventory over the cycle is approximately the average of $\bar{a}(r) + Q$ and $\bar{a}(r)$, the expected maximum and minimum values, respectively, of the on-hand inventory during the cycle. Therefore

$$
\bar{I} = \frac{Q}{2} + r - \mu + \bar{b}(r)
\tag{2-84}
$$

The average cost per cycle is

$$
A + CQ + h\frac{Q}{D}\left[\frac{Q}{2} + r - \mu + \bar{b}(r)\right] + \pi\bar{b}(r)
\tag{2-85}
$$

Multiplying by the expected number of cycles per year,

$$
K(Q, r) = \frac{AD}{Q} + CD + h\left[\frac{Q}{2} + r - \mu\right] + \left(h + \frac{\pi D}{Q}\right)\bar{b}(r)
\tag{2-86}
$$

The conditions $\partial K / \partial Q = 0$ and $\partial K / \partial r = 0$ lead to

$$Q = \sqrt{\frac{2D[A + \pi \bar{b}(r)]}{h}} \qquad (2\text{-}87)$$

$$F'(r) = \frac{hQ}{hQ + \pi D} \qquad (2\text{-}88)$$

The optimal lot size and reorder point are determined from Equations 2-87 and 2-88, using the iterative procedure described for the backorders case.

□**EXAMPLE 2-11** A beer distributor uses a fixed reorder quantity system to control his inventory of a locally popular brand of beer. His weekly demand is approximately normally distributed with a mean of 800 cases and a standard deviation of 40 cases. He pays $2.50 for a case and makes a net profit of $1.10 on each case he sells. His fixed cost of procurement from the brewer is $50 per lot, and the lead time is two weeks. He uses an inventory carrying-cost rate of 20 percent per year. He feels that the majority of shortages are lost sales.

To determine his order quantity and reorder point, we first note that the lead time demand is normally distributed with a mean of 1600 cases and a standard deviation of $\sqrt{(40)^2 + (40)^2} = 56.6$ cases. The expected annual demand is $D = (52)(800) = 41,600$ cases. The cost of a shortage is $\pi = \$1.10$, without including any penalty for "loss of goodwill," etc., which actually might be appropriate in a situation such as this. The annual inventory carrying cost per case is $h = iC = (0.20)(2.50) = \$0.50$. Therefore the expected annual cost is

$$K(Q, r) = \frac{(50)(41,600)}{Q} + (2.5)(41,600)$$

$$+ (0.50)\left[\frac{Q}{2} + r - 1600\right] + \left[0.50 + \frac{(1.1)(41,600)}{Q}\right]\bar{b}(r)$$

where

$$\bar{b}(r) = \int_r^\infty (x - r)n(x; 1600, 3200) \, dx$$

$$= (56.6)\phi\left(\frac{r - 1600}{56.6}\right) + [1600 - r]\Phi'\left(\frac{r - 1600}{56.6}\right)$$

$$= (56.6)L'\left(\frac{r - 1600}{56.6}\right)$$

In the expression for $\bar{b}(r)$, we used the result given in Example 2-9 for a normally distributed random variable.

To solve, we use Equations 2-87 and 2-88:

$$Q = \sqrt{\frac{(2)(41,600)[50 + (1.1)\bar{b}(r)]}{0.50}} = (406)\sqrt{50 + 1.1\bar{b}(r)}$$

$$F'(r) = \Phi'\left(\frac{r - 1600}{56.6}\right) = \frac{(0.5)Q}{(0.5)Q + (1.1)(41,600)} = \frac{Q}{Q + 91,250}$$

Assuming $\bar{b}(r) = 0$, we obtain $Q_1 = 2878$. The first reorder point value is found from

$$\Phi'\left(\frac{r_1 - 1600}{56.6}\right) = \frac{2878}{2878 + 91,250} = 0.0305$$

$$r_1 = 1600 + (1.87)(56.6) \cong 1706$$

Then

$$\bar{b}(1714) = (56.6)L'(1.87) = (56.6)(0.01195) = 0.675$$

$$Q_2 = (406)\sqrt{50 + (1.1)(0.675)} = 2890$$

$$\Phi'\left(\frac{r_2 - 1600}{56.6}\right) = \frac{2890}{2890 + 91,250} = 0.0307$$

$$r_2 = 1600 + (1.87)(56.6) \cong 1706$$

The solution is $Q^* = 2890$ and $r^* = 1706$. □

2-7.3 Base Stock Systems with Constant Lead Times

A base stock system is a special case of the fixed reorder quantity policy where $Q = 1$. Let $R = r + Q = r + 1$, where r is the reorder point in terms of the inventory position. The base stock system is characterized by the single parameter, R, called the *base stock level*, if it is understood that an order is placed every time a unit is demanded. This means that at all times the sum of the on-hand inventory and the on-order amount is to equal R. The problem is to determine R.

Assume that shortages are backordered and that the replenishment lead time, τ, is constant. As before, x is the lead time demand and is assumed to have stationary probability density function $f(x)$. At any point in time, the amount on order will equal the demand, x, during the just-ended time period of length τ. The net inventory is $R - x$, so that the expected on-hand inventory and expected backorder positions at any point in time are given by

$$\bar{I} = \int_0^R (R - x)f(x)\,dx \qquad (2\text{-}89)$$

and

$$\bar{B} = \int_R^\infty (x - R)f(x)\, dx \tag{2-90}$$

The cost model is the sum of the inventory and backorder costs per unit time:

$$K(R) = h\bar{I} + \hat{\pi}\bar{B}$$

$$= h\int_0^R (R - x)f(x)\, dx + \hat{\pi}\int_R^\infty (x - R)f(x)\, dx \tag{2-91}$$

where h has its usual meaning and $\hat{\pi}$ is the cost to carry a unit backorder for one unit of time. It is not necessary to include the fixed ordering cost, A, since the policy requires that an order be placed after each demand. Also the variable procurement cost, C, may be omitted. The optimal R is determined from the following condition:

$$\frac{dK}{dR} = h\int_0^R f(x)\, dx - \hat{\pi}\int_R^\infty f(x)\, dx = 0$$

which leads to

$$F(R^*) = \frac{\hat{\pi}}{h + \hat{\pi}} \tag{2-92}$$

or

$$F'(R^*) = \frac{h}{h + \hat{\pi}} \tag{2-93}$$

Equation 2-93 says that the optimal base stock level will result in the system being in a backorder state a fraction $h/(h + \hat{\pi})$ of the time. As $\hat{\pi}$ increases, this fraction decreases, as it logically should. We note also that when the demand process is stationary, as is assumed here, $F(R)$ is the fraction of customer demand filled from stock (that is, "on time") and is a measure of system performance that often interests managers. Sometimes it is called the *service level* of the system.

The model can be enriched somewhat by assuming that there is also a fixed loss π associated with each backorder. During any interval of length τ, this will result in an expected loss of $\pi\mu F'(R)$, since $F'(R)$ is the fraction of demand backordered (also the probability the system is out of stock) and $\mu = E(x)$ is the expected demand during the interval. The contribution to the expected loss per unit time is obtained by dividing by τ: $\pi(\mu/\tau)F'(R)$. Letting $D = \mu/\tau$, the expanded objective function is

$$K(R) = h\int_0^R (R - x)f(x)\, dx + \hat{\pi}\int_R^\infty (x - R)f(x)\, dx + \pi D F'(R) \tag{2-94}$$

The optimal base stock level is R^*, satisfying

$$(h + \hat{\pi})F(R^*) - \pi D f(R^*) = \hat{\pi} \tag{2-95}$$

Continuous Review Models   67

For the lost sales case, $\hat{\pi} = 0$ and π includes the lost unit profit. The optimal base stock level would be determined from

$$F(R^*) - \frac{\pi D}{h} f(R^*) = 0 \qquad (2\text{-}96)$$

In case lead-time demand is to be treated as an integer-valued random variable with probability mass function $p(x)$, we have R an integer and

$$K(R) = h \sum_{x=0}^{R} (R - x)p(x) + \hat{\pi} \sum_{x=R+1}^{\infty} (x - R)p(x) + \pi D \sum_{x=R}^{\infty} p(x) \qquad (2\text{-}97)$$

The optimal value R^* is the smallest integer R satisfying

$$\Delta K(R) \equiv K(R + 1) - K(R) \geq 0$$

or

$$\Delta K(R) = h \sum_{x=0}^{R} p(x) - \hat{\pi} \sum_{x=R+1}^{\infty} p(x) - \pi D p(R) \geq 0$$

or

$$(h + \hat{\pi})P(R) - \pi D p(R) - \hat{\pi} \geq 0 \qquad (2\text{-}98)$$

where $P(x)$ is the cumulative distribution of x.

2-7.4 Base Stock Systems with Variable Lead Times

When the lead time is a random variable, the analysis becomes more complex. We give one example, which also illustrates the application of queueing theory methods to the study of inventory problems. Consider τ to be an exponentially distributed random variable having density $g(\tau) = v e^{-v\tau}$. The demand process is assumed Poisson with parameter λ, so that the demand in any time interval of length t has probability mass function

$$p(x; \lambda t) = \frac{e^{-\lambda t}(\lambda t)^x}{x!}$$

Our approach will be to find the probability distribution of the net inventory at any time, which in turn will be used in computing expected losses per unit time. Assuming that demand is discrete, let α_j be the probability that the net inventory level, Y, is j. In the lost sales case, $j = 0, 1, 2, \ldots, R$. For the back-orders case $j = \ldots, -2, -1, 0, +1, \ldots, R$. In modeling this process, it is convenient to think of the state of the system as being the number of units on order, $R - Y$. Let β_i be the probability that the on-order amount at any time equals i. Note that $\beta_i = \alpha_{R-i}$, that $i = 0, 1, \ldots, R$ in the lost sales case, and that $i = 0, 1, 2, \ldots$ in the backorders case.

A queueing system analogy has customers as demands, service times as lead times, number of service channels as R in the lost sales case and unlimited in the backorders case, and number of units in the system as number of units on order. No waiting line is permitted. The arrival process is Poisson and the service times are exponential. The steady-state equations for the backorders case are

$$\left. \begin{aligned} v\beta_1 - \lambda\beta_0 &= 0 \\ (i+1)v\beta_{i+1} + \lambda\beta_{i-1} - (\lambda + iv)\beta_i &= 0; \qquad (i = 1, 2, \ldots) \end{aligned} \right\} \quad (2\text{-}99)$$

For the lost sales case, the steady-state equations are

$$\left. \begin{aligned} v\beta_1 - \lambda\beta_0 &= 0 \\ (i+1)v\beta_{i+1} + \lambda\beta_{i-1} - (\lambda + iv)\beta_i &= 0; \qquad (i = 1, 2, \ldots, R-1) \\ \lambda\beta_{R-1} - Rv\beta_R &= 0 \end{aligned} \right\} \quad (2\text{-}100)$$

Of course, we also require

$$\Sigma\beta_i = 1; \qquad 0 \le \beta_i \le 1 \tag{2-101}$$

The solution to Equations 2-99 and 2-101 gives for the backorders case

$$\beta_i = \frac{1}{i!}\left(\frac{\lambda}{v}\right)^i e^{-\lambda/v}; \qquad (i = 0, 1, 2, \ldots) \tag{2-102}$$

Solution to Equations 2-100 and 2-101 yields for the lost sales case

$$\beta_i = \frac{1}{i!}\left(\frac{\lambda}{v}\right)^i \left[\sum_{k=0}^{R}\frac{1}{k!}\left(\frac{\lambda}{v}\right)^k\right]^{-1}; \qquad (i = 0, 1, \ldots, R) \tag{2-103}$$

Using these state probabilities, we can develop a cost model to determine the optimal base stock level, R. We describe the procedure for the backorders case.

If backorders are allowed, we obtain the net inventory level probabilities by letting $i = R - j$ in Equation 2-102, which gives[8]

$$\alpha_j = \frac{1}{(R-j)!}\left(\frac{\lambda}{v}\right)^{R-j} e^{-\lambda/v}; \qquad (j = \ldots, -1, 0, +1, \ldots, R) \quad (2\text{-}104)$$

It may be shown that the expected on-order position is $\lambda/v = \lambda\bar{\tau}$, where $\bar{\tau}$ is the average lead time length and λ is the demand rate, and that the expected net inventory level is $R - \lambda\bar{\tau}$. It will be convenient to define $\rho = \lambda/v = \lambda\bar{\tau}$. The average on-hand inventory is

$$\begin{aligned} \bar{I} &= \sum_{j=0}^{\infty} j\alpha_j = \sum_{j=0}^{R} j\frac{1}{(R-j)!}\rho^{R-j}e^{-\rho} \\ &= RP(R-1;\rho) - \rho P(R-2;\rho) \end{aligned} \tag{2-105}$$

[8] Hadley and Whitin (3, pp. 207–209) show that these results hold for any lead time distribution having mean $\bar{\tau}$, if lead times are independent random variables.

where $P(j; \rho) = \sum\limits_{x=0}^{j} \dfrac{1}{x!} \rho^x e^{-\rho}$, the cumulative Poisson distribution. The average backorder level is

$$\bar{B} = -\sum_{j=-\infty}^{0} j\alpha_j = -\sum_{j=-\infty}^{0} j \frac{1}{(R-j)!} \rho^{R-j} e^{-\rho}$$

$$= RP(R-1; \rho) - \rho P(R-2; \rho) - (R-\rho)$$

$$= \bar{I} - (R-\rho) \tag{2-106}$$

The expected number of backorders in a unit of time is the demand rate λ times the fraction of time (probability) the system is out of stock, which is

$$\gamma = \sum_{j=-\infty}^{0} \alpha_j = \sum_{j=-\infty}^{0} \frac{1}{(R-j)!} \rho^{R-j} e^{-\rho}$$

$$= \sum_{k=R}^{\infty} \frac{1}{k!} \rho^k e^{-\rho}$$

$$= 1 - P(R-1; \rho) \tag{2-107}$$

The average cost per unit time is

$$K(R) = h\bar{I} + \hat{\pi}\bar{B} + \pi\lambda\gamma$$

$$= (h + \hat{\pi})[RP(R-1; \rho) - \rho P(R-2; \rho)] - \hat{\pi}(R-\rho)$$

$$+ \pi\lambda[1 - P(R-1; \rho)] \tag{2-108}$$

The first difference of K is

$$\Delta K(R) = K(R+1) - K(R) = (h + \hat{\pi})P(R; \rho) - \pi\lambda p(R; \rho) - \hat{\pi} \tag{2-109}$$

The optimal base stock level is the smallest integer value of R for which $\Delta K(R) \geq 0$.

The lost sales case is considered in Exercise 2-92.

□EXAMPLE 2-12   An automobile distributor wishes to control his inventory of a popular model car with a base stock system. That is, whenever he sells a car, he will order a similar one from the manufacturer. When he is out of stock, his customers will wait for delivery. Assume that demand is Poisson with a mean of five cars per week and that lead times are exponentially distributed with a mean of four weeks. This model automobile costs the dealer about $4000 and he sells it for an average of $4800, considering the cash value of any trade-in (which he immediately sells wholesale to a used-car dealer.) He uses an inventory carrying-cost rate of 20 percent annually.

To find the appropriate base stock level, we use the model of Equation 2-108 with $\lambda = 5$, $v = 0.25$, $\rho = \lambda/v = 20$, and $h = (0.20)(4000) = 800$. To arrive at values for $\hat{\pi}$ and π, we assume that the only effect of a backorder is to postpone the receipt of the $800 profit on the sale. If we assume that the dealer can earn a 15 percent annual return on his capital, the cost of a backorder for a year would be $\hat{\pi} = (0.15)(800) = 120$. We assume there is no fixed backorder cost; that is, $\pi = 0$. Therefore

$$K(R) = (800 + 120)[RP(R - 1; 20) - 20P(R - 2; 20)] - 120(R - 20)$$

and R^* is the smallest integer for which

$$(800 + 120)P(R; 20) - 120 > 0$$

or

$$P(R; 20) > 0.130$$

From Table A-1, we find $P(14; 20) = 0.1049$ and $P(15; 20) = 0.1565$; therefore, $R^* = 15$.

With a base stock level of 15 automobiles, the dealer will have an average inventory of 0.25 car, will have an average backorder position of 5.25 cars, and will be out of stock about 90 percent of the time. These results were obtained from Equations 2-105, 2-106, and 2-107, respectively. □

2-8 Lot-Size Problems with Dynamic Demand

When the demand process changes over time, the associated inventory planning problem is said to be *dynamic*. In the previous sections of this chapter, we have treated only the static case, assuming either that demand was deterministic at a constant rate, or that demand was stochastic with a stationary probability distribution. In this section, we consider two cases of policy determination under dynamic, deterministic demand. In Chapter 4, we will expand on the treatment of dynamic models, when we discuss multiperiod production planning problems.

2-8.1 Continuous Review Lot-Size Problem

As an initial illustration of dynamic analysis, let us consider a case where we have a finite planning horizon of length T and where lots may be added to inventory at arbitrary times during this period. No shortages are to be permitted. The demand rate at time t is $\delta(t)$. When $\delta(t)$ is not constant over time, it is no longer optimal to have all lots of the same size. Let

n = number of lots to be procured during $(0, T)$

Q_j = size of the lot added to inventory at time t_j

A = fixed cost associated with procurement of a lot

C = unit variable procurement cost

h = inventory carrying cost per unit per unit time

$D(t)$ = cumulative demand in the interval $(0, t)$

$I(t)$ = inventory level at time t

The problem is to choose n lots of sizes $Q_1, Q_2, \ldots, Q_n$, to be added to inventory at times $t_1, t_2, \ldots, t_n$, respectively, to minimize

$$K_n = nA + CD(T) + H_n \tag{2-110}$$

where nA is the total fixed procurement cost, $CD(T)$ is the total variable procurement cost, and H_n is the total inventory carrying cost during the planning horizon. Note that n is a decision variable as well as the $\{t_j\}$ and $\{Q_j\}$. Since $CD(T)$ is a constant, we omit it in the following solution.

The inventory level at time t is given by

$$I(t) = I(0) + \sum_{i=1}^{j} Q_i - D(t), \qquad t_j \leq t \leq t_{j+1} \tag{2-111}$$

for $j = 0, 1, \ldots, n$, where we define $t_0 \equiv 0$ and $t_{n+1} \equiv T$. We note that an optimal policy will have zero inventory at times $t_1, t_2, \ldots, t_n$ (and T). To see this, consider a time point t_j, before a lot is added to inventory. If $I(t_j) > 0$, the inventory cost H_n could be reduced by $h(t_j - t_{j-1})I(t_j)$ by decreasing the lot size at time t_{j-1} by $I(t_j)$ units. No other costs would be affected. Thus, we have $I(t_j) = 0, j = 1, 2, \ldots, n$, under the optimal policy.

Using this result along with the constraint $I(t) \geq 0$, we have

$$Q_j = \int_{t_j}^{t_{j+1}} \delta(t)\, dt = D(t_{j+1}) - D(t_j); \qquad j = 1, 2, \ldots, n \tag{2-112}$$

and

$$D(t_1) = I(0) \tag{2-113}$$

so that $t_1 = D^{-1}[I(0)]$. The inventory level at t is

$$I(t) = \begin{cases} I(0) - \int_0^t \delta(u)\, du, & \text{for } 0 \leq t \leq t_1 \\ \\ Q_j - \int_{t_j}^t \delta(u)\, du, & \text{for } t_j \leq t \leq t_{j+1} \quad (j = 1, 2, \ldots, n) \end{cases}$$

or in terms of the cumulative demand function

$$I(t) = \begin{cases} I(0) - D(t), & \text{for } 0 \leq t \leq t_1 \\ D(t_{j+1}) - D(t), & \text{for } t_j \leq t \leq t_{j+1} \quad (j = 1, 2, \ldots, n) \end{cases} \tag{2-114}$$

The total inventory carrying costs are given by

$$H_n = h \sum_{j=0}^{n} \int_{t_j}^{t_{j+1}} I(t) \, dt \qquad (2\text{-}115)$$

Substituting for $I(t)$,

$$H_n = h \int_{0}^{t_1} [I(0) - D(t)] \, dt + h \sum_{j=1}^{n} \int_{t_j}^{t_{j+1}} [D(t_{j+1}) - D(t)] \, dt$$

$$= h \left[t_1 I(0) - \int_{0}^{t_1} D(t) \, dt \right] + h \sum_{j=1}^{n} \left[D(t_{j+1})(t_{j+1} - t_j) - \int_{t_j}^{t_{j+1}} D(t) \, dt \right]$$

$$= h \left[t_1 I(0) + \sum_{j=1}^{n} (t_{j+1} - t_j) D(t_{j+1}) \right] - h \sum_{j=0}^{n} \int_{t_j}^{t_{j+1}} D(t) \, dt$$

Using $D(t_1) = I(0)$,

$$H_n = h \sum_{j=0}^{n} (t_{j+1} - t_j) D(t_{j+1}) - h \int_{0}^{T} D(t) \, dt \qquad (2\text{-}116)$$

For a given n, H_n is minimized by selecting $t_1, t_2, \ldots, t_n$ such that

$$D(t_1) = I(0) \qquad (2\text{-}117)$$

$$\frac{\partial H_n}{\partial t_j} = (t_j - t_{j-1}) \frac{\partial D(t_j)}{\partial t_j} + D(t_j) - D(t_{j+1}) = 0, \qquad (j = 2, 3, \ldots n) \quad (2\text{-}118)$$

$$D(t_{n+1}) = D(T) \qquad (2\text{-}119)$$

Equation 2-118 can be further simplified using $\partial D(t_j)/\partial t_j = \delta(t_j)$,

$$\frac{\partial H_n}{\partial t_j} = (t_j - t_{j-1})\delta(t_j) + D(t_j) - D(t_{j+1}) = 0$$

or

$$D(t_{j+1}) = D(t_j) + (t_j - t_{j-1})\delta(t_j), \qquad (j = 2, 3, \ldots, n) \qquad (2\text{-}120)$$

The following is a method of completing the solution: (1) For a given n, solve for $\{t_j^*\}$, the values of $\{t_j\}$ satisfying Equations 2-117, 2-118, and 2-119. If $D(t)$ is a simple mathematical function of t and n is small, this can be done directly. Otherwise, use (2-117) to find t_1^*; then choose a value for t_2 and solve for t_3, $t_4, \ldots, t_n$, satisfying the first $n - 2$ relations of (2-118). The last relation probably will yield a $D(t_{n+1}) \neq D(T)$, so try different values for t_2 until $D(t_{n+1}) = D(T)$. Evaluate K_n for this set of $\{t_j^*\}$ and n to obtain K_n^*. (2) Vary n and repeat step 1. Choose the policy that minimizes K_n^*. (3) Determine the optimal lot sizes from Equation 2-112 using the $\{t_j^*\}$.

☐ **EXAMPLE 2-13** During the next year, the demand rate for a product is expected to vary according to $\delta(t) = 1000 - 400t$, $0 \leq t \leq 1$, where t is in years. The item is purchased for $20 per unit, and the fixed procurement cost is $200 per order. The inventory carrying cost rate is 20 percent annually. No shortages are permitted. The initial inventory is 192 units. No final inventory is required. The problem is to determine when and in what quantities to order during the next year.

Suppose only one order is to be placed. This should be done when the initial inventory is exhausted. Since $D(t) = 1000t - 200t^2$, the cumulative requirements will equal 192 at $t_1 = 0.20$. Thus, order $Q_1 = D(T) - I(0) = 800 - 192 = 608$ units at that time. By Equation 2-116, $H_1 = \$980$, with $h \equiv iC = 4$, and thus $K_1^* = A + H_1 = \$1180$.

If exactly two orders are to be placed, the first should be placed at $t_1 = 0.20$ and the second at a time t_2, satisfying Equation 2-120 for $j = 2$:

$$D(t_3) = D(t_2) + (t_2 - t_1)\delta(t_2)$$

Using Equation 2-119, $D(t_3) = D(T) = 800$, and we have

$$800 = 1000t_2 - 200t_2^2 + (t_2 - 0.20)(1000 - 400t_2)$$

Solving, we obtain $t_2 = 0.626$, so that

$$Q_1 = D(0.626) - D(0.200) = 548 - 192 = 356$$

$$Q_2 = D(1) - D(0.626) = 800 - 548 = 252$$

Using these results, we find $H_2 = \$551$ and $K_2^* = 2A + H_2 = \$951$. The optimal two-lot policy is better than the optimal one-lot policy, since $K_2^* < K_1^*$.

Now consider $n = 3$. Again $t_1 = 0.20$. The values for t_2 and t_3 must satisfy

$$D(t_3) = D(t_2) + (t_2 - 0.2)(1000 - 400t_2)$$
$$D(t_4) = D(t_3) + (t_3 - t_2)(1000 - 400t_3) \equiv D(T) = 800$$

The solution is $t_2^* = 0.383$ and $t_3^* = 0.577$, for which

$$Q_1 = D(0.383) - D(0.200) = 354 - 192 = 162$$

$$Q_2 = D(0.577) - D(0.383) = 511 - 354 = 157$$

$$Q_3 = D(1) - D(0.577) \quad\;\; = 800 - 511 = 289$$

This policy gives $H_3 = \$428$ and $K_3^* = \$1028$. Since $K_3^* > K_2^*$, we decide to terminate our analysis and use a two-lot policy.

The solution is to order 356 units for delivery at time 0.20 and 252 units for delivery at time 0.626. □

2-8.2 Periodic Review Lot-Size Problem [Wagner-Whitin Algorithm (6)]

Now we consider the planning horizon to be divided into N periods, having known demands $D_1, D_2, \ldots, D_N$. A single lot may be procured in each period.

Let Q_t denote the size of the lot procured in period t. There is a fixed cost of A_t if a lot is ordered in period t and the unit variable cost is C_t, which can vary from period to period. No shortages are to be planned. There is an inventory cost of h_t to carry a unit in stock from period t to period $t + 1$. The initial inventory is assumed to be zero. The problem is to determine the lot sizes, Q_1, $Q_2, \ldots, Q_N$, which minimize the sum of procurement costs and inventory carrying costs over the N periods.

For the particular cost structure assumed, it can be shown that an optimal policy has the property that $I_{t-1}Q_t = 0$, for $t = 1, 2, \ldots, N$. That is, the requirements in a period are satisfied either *entirely* from procurement in the period or *entirely* from procurement in a prior period. This will be proved in Chapter 4, when we give a more complete treatment of dynamic models.

The property of an optimal solution stated above implies that we need consider only procurement programs where $Q_t = D_t + D_{t+1} + \cdots + D_{t+k}$, for some $k = t, t + 1, \ldots, N$. To efficiently investigate such programs, we can use the following algorithm.

Let F_k be the minimum cost program for periods $1, 2, \ldots, k$, when $I_k = 0$ is required. Let j be the last period prior to k having an ending inventory of zero. Thus $I_j = 0$, $I_k = 0$, and $I_t > 0$, for $t = j + 1, j + 2, \ldots, k - 1$. Therefore, $Q_{j+1} = D_{j+1} + D_{j+2} + \cdots + D_k$. Define M_{jk} to be the cost incurred in periods $j + 1$ through k. It is

$$M_{jk} = A_{j+1} + C_{j+1}Q_{j+1} + \sum_{t=j+1}^{k-1} h_t I_t \tag{2-121}$$

Since

$$I_t = Q_{j+1} - \sum_{r=j+1}^{t} D_r = \sum_{r=t+1}^{k} D_r, \quad \text{for } j < t < k$$

$$M_{jk} = A_{j+1} + C_{j+1}Q_{j+1} + \sum_{t=j+1}^{k-1} h_t \sum_{r=t+1}^{k} D_r \tag{2-122}$$

With this definition[9] of M_{jk}, we can write the following recursive equation for F_k.

$$F_k = \min_{0 \le j < k} [F_j + M_{jk}], \quad (k = 1, 2, \ldots, N) \tag{2-123}$$

where $F_0 \equiv 0$. The logic motivating Equation 2-123 is that for a k-period horizon with zero initial and final inventories and no shortages allowed, there will be some period where the last procurement is made. Call this period $j + 1$, and by the property of an optimal solution, $I_j = 0$. Assume that we have found the optimal policy, and hence minimum cost F_t, for every $t < k$, where we assumed $I_t = 0$. Thus we know F_j and can compute M_{jk}. The minimum cost for a k-period horizon results from selecting the optimal period for the last

[9] To be complete, we must add that $M_{jk} = 0$, if $D_{j+1} + D_{j+2} + \cdots + D_k = 0$. This is because Q_{j+1} would be zero in such a case, and no fixed cost would be incurred.

TABLE 2-3 Data for Example 2-14

MONTH (t)	1	2	3	4	5	6
Expected demand (D_t)	60	100	140	200	120	80
Fixed cost (A_t)	150	140	160	160	170	190
Variable unit cost (C_t)	7	7	8	7	6	10
Unit inventory cost (h_t)	1	1	2	2	2	2

procurement. By trying all $j < k$, we can find the value of j, say j_k^*, which minimizes $F_j + M_{jk}$. Last procurement is in period $j_k^* + 1$.

The procedure is to determine in sequence the values $F_1, F_2, \ldots, F_N$. When F_N is found, we have the minimum cost value for the N-period horizon and can use j_N^* to work backward to extract the optimal lot sizes. The method is best learned through study of an example.

$\Box$**EXAMPLE 2-14** A seasonal product has a six month selling season. The item is purchased, with a procurement possible at the start of each month. Table 2-3 contains relevant data. There is no initial inventory. No shortages are to be planned. The quantities to be procured in each period must be determined.

First consider a one-period horizon. Obviously, $Q_1 = D_1 = 60$, and $F_1 = F_0 + M_{01} = F_0 + A_1 + C_1 Q_1 = 0 + 150 + (7)(60) = 570$.

Now consider the first two periods. Last production could take place either in period 1 or in period 2. We must evaluate both cases:

$$F_2 = \min \begin{cases} F_0 + M_{02} = F_0 + A_1 + C_1(D_1 + D_2) + h_1 D_2 \\ \qquad = 0 + 150 + (7)(60 + 100) + (1)(100) = 1370 \\ F_1 + M_{12} = F_1 + A_2 + C_2 D_2 = 570 + 140 + (7)(100) = 1410 \end{cases}$$
$$= 1370$$

We see that for a two-period horizon, the optimal period of last procurement is period 1 and the optimal last point of zero inventory is at the end of period 0 (that is, $j_2^* = 0$).

For a three-period horizon,

$$F_3 = \min \begin{cases} F_0 + M_{03} = F_0 + A_1 + C_1(D_1 + D_2 + D_3) \\ \qquad\qquad\qquad + h_1(D_2 + D_3) + h_2 D_3 = 2630 \\ F_1 + M_{13} = F_1 + A_2 + C_2(D_2 + D_3) + h_2 D_3 = 2530 \\ F_2 + M_{23} = F_2 + A_3 + C_3 D_3 = 2650 \end{cases}$$
$$= 2530$$

The optimal period of last procurement is 2 and $j_3^* = 1$.

Inventory Systems **76**

TABLE 2-4   Values of $F_j + M_{jk}$ for Example 2-14

PERIOD OF LAST PROCUREMENT ($j + 1$)	LAST PERIOD WITH ZERO INVENTORY (j)	PLANNING HORIZON (k)					
		1	2	3	4	5	6
1	0	570	1370	2630	4830	6390	7590
2	1		1410	2530	4530	5970	7090
3	2			2650	4650	6090	7210
4	3				4090	5170	6050
5	4					4980	5620
6	5						5970
F_k		570	1370	2530	4090	4980	5620
j_k^*		0	0	1	3	4	4

For a four-period horizon,

$$
F_4 = \min
\begin{cases}
F_0 + M_{04} = F_0 + A_1 + C_1\left(\sum_{t=1}^{4} D_t\right) + h_1\left(\sum_{t=2}^{4} D_t\right) \\
\qquad\qquad + h_2(D_3 + D_4) + h_3 D_4 = 4830 \\
F_1 + M_{14} = F_1 + A_2 + C_2\left(\sum_{t=2}^{4} D_t\right) \\
\qquad\qquad + h_2(D_3 + D_4) + h_3 D_4 = 4530 \\
F_2 + M_{24} = F_2 + A_3 + C_3(D_3 + D_4) + h_3 D_4 = 4650 \\
F_3 + M_{34} = F_3 + A_4 + C_4 D_4 = 4090
\end{cases}
$$

$$= 4090, \text{ for which } j_4^* = 3$$

The same procedure is followed in computing F_5 and F_6. The results are summarized in Table 2-4. The reader should verify several of the computations.

From Table 2-4, we see that the minimum cost over the six-period planning horizon is $F_6 = 5620$. Because $j_6^* = 4$, we order in period 5 an amount $Q_5^* = D_5 + D_6 = 200$, and we set $Q_6^* = 0$. We know $I_4^* = 0$, hence we next consider a four-period horizon. For a four-period horizon, $j_4^* = 3$ and therefore $I_3^* = 0$ and $Q_4^* = D_4 = 200$. Considering a three-period horizon, we obtain $j_3^* = 1$; hence, $I_1^* = 0$, $Q_2^* = D_2 + D_3 = 240$, and $Q_3^* = 0$. For a one-period horizon, $j_1^* = 0$ and $Q_1^* = D_1 = 60$. The optimal plan is to order lots of 60, 240, 0, 200, 200, and 0 over the six-period horizon.□

When there is an initial inventory of $I_0 > 0$, the algorithm will work provided we redefine the demand schedule to be the requirements remaining after we

TABLE 2-5   Values of $F_j + M_{jk}$ for Example 2-15

PERIOD OF LAST PROCUREMENT $(j + 1)$	LAST PERIOD WITH ZERO INVENTORY (j)	PLANNING HORIZON (k)				
		1	2	3	4	5
1	0	0	340.8	596.8	942.4	1352.0
2	1		200.0	328.0	558.4	865.6
3	2			400.0	515.2	720.0
4	3				528.0	630.4
5	4					715.2
F_k		0	200.0	328.0	515.2	630.4
j_k^*		0	1	1	2	3

have used our initial inventory. This technique is illustrated in the following example.

□**EXAMPLE 2-15**   Consider treating the situation of Example 2-13 as a periodic review system with five periods, each of length 0.2, during the planning horizon. The demand schedule would be $D_1 = 192$, $D_2 = 176$, $D_3 = 160$, $D_4 = 144$, and $D_5 = 128$, adding to a total of 800 units. The initial inventory is 192 units, so only 608 units will have to be procured during the planning horizon. Starting with the first period and allocating the initial inventory against demand until it is exhausted, the revised schedule $D_1 = 0$, $D_2 = 176$, $D_3 = 160$, $D_4 = 144$, and $D_5 = 128$ is obtained.

The relevant cost parameters are $A_t = 200$, $C_t = 20$, and $h_t = 0.8$, for all $t = 1, 2, \ldots, 5$. The unit inventory cost for a unit of time is 4, or 0.8 for a period of length 0.2. Since the unit variable cost, C_t, is the same in each period, the term $C_{j+1} Q_{j+1}$ can be omitted in Equation 2-121. Application of the algorithm results in Table 2-5.

The solution extracted from Table 2-5 is $Q_1^* = 0$, $Q_2^* = 336$, $Q_3^* = 0$, $Q_4^* = 272$, and $Q_5^* = 0$. (Compare with the solution to Example 2-13.)□

This section was intended to be only an introduction to dynamic models. The subject is covered more completely in Chapter 4.

2-9   References

1.   **Arrow, K. J., S. Karlin, and H. Scarf,** *Studies in the Mathematical Theory of Inventory and Production,* Stanford University Press, Stanford, Calif., 1958.

2. **Hanssmann, F.,** *Operations Research in Production and Inventory Control,* John Wiley & Sons, New York, 1962.

3. **Hadley, G., and T. M. Whitin,** *Analysis of Inventory Systems,* Prentice-Hall, Englewood Cliffs, N.J., 1963.

4. **Morse, P. M.,** *Queues, Inventories, and Maintenance,* John Wiley & Sons, New York, 1958.

5. **Scarf, H.,** "A Survey of Analytic Techniques in Inventory Theory," Chapter 7 in H. Scarf, D. Gilford, and M. Shelly (eds.), *Multistage Inventory Models and Techniques,* Stanford University Press, Stanford, Calif., 1963.

6. **Wagner, H., and T. M. Whitin,** "Dynamic Version of the Economic Lot Size Model," *Management Science,* **5**, (1), 1958, 89–96.

2-10   Exercises

2-1   A manufactured product has a constant demand rate of 10,000 units per year. The machine used to manufacture this item has a production rate of 140,000 units per year, therefore the product will be produced in batches rather than continuously. Because the units are produced sequentially, the rate of addition to inventory is finite. The machine setup cost is $400 and the unit variable production cost is $25. No shortages are to be allowed.

(a)   If the annual inventory carrying-cost rate is 0.20, what is the economic production lot size?

(b)   If the manufacturer uses a lot size of 4000, what inventory carrying-cost rate is he implicitly assuming? That is, for what inventory carrying-cost rate would 4000 be optimal?

2-2   A product is produced in lots of 20,000 units. The machine on which the product is made produces the item at a rate of 400,000 units per year, with product being added to inventory continuously while the machine is producing. Demand for the product is uniform over the year at a rate of 160,000 units per year. Production is not started until a backorder position of 4000 units has been reached. The setup cost is $400, the unit variable production cost is $20, the inventory carrying cost rate is 20 percent annually, and the backorder cost is $5 per unit short per year. Give values for each of the following:

(a)   Maximum inventory.

(b)   Average inventory investment over the entire year.

(c)   Annual inventory carrying costs.

(d)   Annual backorder costs.

(e)   Annual setup costs.

(f)   Fraction of time the system is in a backorder position.

2-3   An item is purchased in lots of 2000 units. Its annual demand is uniform over the year at the rate of 18,000 units annually. The replenishment lead time is constant at 0.27 year. What is the reorder point in terms of the on-hand inventory?

2-4   The following data is for an item purchased for resale by a retail store:

Annual demand rate, constant	100,000 units
Fixed cost of placing an order	$40
Unit variable cost	$10
Annual inventory carrying-cost rate	0.20
Annual backorder cost rate	$2 per unit
All shortages are backordered	
The entire lot is delivered in one shipment	

(a)   Calculate the economic lot size.

(b)   If the lead time is one month, what is the reorder point?

(c)   What will be the average inventory level? The maximum inventory level? The maximum backorder level? The average backorder level?

(d)   What fraction of total demand will be delivered late?

2-5   The XYZ Company manufactures metal window frames. The demand for a certain model is constant and known to be 20,000 units per year. The XYZ Company can produce up to 25,000 units in its own plants and may purchase up to 10,000 units from a subcontractor. For a manufactured lot, the setup cost is $150 and the unit variable cost is $1.75. For a purchased lot, the fixed cost is $25 and the unit variable cost is $2.00. A 20 percent annual inventory carrying-cost rate is used. Shortages are backordered at a fixed cost of $1 per unit short. Determine the optimal inventory policy for this model window frame.

2-6   The demand for a commodity is known and constant at the rate of 1000 units per day. The item is purchased and the procurement lead time is virtually constant. Under the policy being used, orders are placed so that a lot is received every 30 days. The order size is constant. Shortages are backordered. The fixed cost per order is $80, the unit variable cost is $5, the inventory carrying cost rate is 0.20 per year, and the cost of a shortage is $2 per unit backlogged per month. What is the appropriate order size? The optimal amount on hand at the start of a 30-day cycle? The maximum shortage?

2-7   Formulate a model for total annual cost as a function of the order size Q and the maximum backorder level b, given the following facts:

(a)   Demand is constant at a known rate per year.

(b)   There is a fixed cost associated with the placing of an order.

(c)   The inventory carrying costs are made up of two parts: an investment charge proportional to the average dollar investment in inventory, and a storage cost proportional to the maximum inventory.

(d)   Shortages are backordered, at a fixed charge for every unit backordered.

(e)   The item is purchased and the entire lot is delivered in one shipment.

2-8   A purchased item has a demand rate of 4000 units per year. The fixed cost per order is $60, the cost per unit is $4, and the annual inventory carrying cost rate is 0.15. Shortages are allowed and backordered. The cost per year for a unit backordered is $1.

(a)   What is the economic lot size and what is the optimal number of backorders to tolerate per cycle?

(b)   If management wants a policy resulting in no more than 50 units backordered at any time, what lot size should be used?

2-9   *A Model With Lost Sales.* Examine the deterministic situation where shortages are allowed, but none can be backlogged. All shortages thus are "lost sales." Assume that a loss of π dollars per unit short is experienced. Show that it is never optimal to inventory the item and permit lost sales.

2-10   *A Model With A Mixture of Backorders and Lost Sales.* Examine the deterministic situation in which shortages are allowed, but only a fraction q of them are backordered and the remaining fraction $1 - q$ are lost forever. Thus, a mixture of backorders and lost sales exists. Show that the reorder point and order quantity to maximize profit will also minimize inventory costs, if the cost of a lost sale also includes the opportunity cost of lost profit. Assuming an infinite production rate, find the optimal order quantity and reorder point for this model.

2-11   Consider a deterministic inventory model in which no shortages are allowed and the production rate is infinite. The fixed ordering cost is thought to be A dollars per order, but in reality it is A' dollars per order. Find an expression for the ratio of the actual average annual cost to the true minimum average annual cost. Plot this ratio as a function of A/A'. In what region are we insensitive to errors in estimating A? Is it better to underestimate A or overestimate?

2-12   *Discrete Demand.* We usually treat demand in a deterministic inventory model as a continuous quantity. This often is only an approximation, of course, since in most cases demand must always be for a discrete number of units. However, if the total demand is reasonably large, the continuous approximation is usually valid. For small values of D, we must account for the integrality of demand. Instead of equating the first derivative (with respect to Q) of average annual cost to zero, we work instead with the first difference of K with respect to Q, $\Delta K(Q)$. Here $\Delta K(Q) = K(Q + 1) - K(Q)$, and the optimal Q, say Q^*, can be found by noting that $\Delta K(Q^*) \geq 0$ and $\Delta K(Q^* - 1) \leq 0$. Show that if the production rate is infinite and no shortages are allowed, this implies that Q^* is the largest Q that satisfies

$$Q(Q - 1) < \frac{2AD}{iC}$$

2-13   When treating simple, deterministic inventory models, we implicitly assumed a continuous review process. Now consider a deterministic inventory system in which an order is placed every T units of time. The demand rate is D, each unit costs C dollars, A is the fixed cost of placing an order, and no stockouts are allowed. Find the length of the optimal review period, that is, the review period such that the average annual variable cost is minimized. Show that this periodic review formulation is equivalent to the usual continuous review formulation.

2-14   A manufacturer produces a product that is perishable in that it deteriorates in storage. He feels that the maximum time he can hold a unit in inventory is two weeks. He produces in batches and the process is such that the entire batch is completed and added to inventory at one time. The annual demand rate is 5200 units. The setup cost is $400, the inventory carrying-cost rate is 0.20, the unit variable cost is $100, and no shortages are allowed. Find the economic lot size, subject to the shelf life constraint.

2-15   Consider the following four items:

	ITEM			
	1	2	3	4
Demand/year	1000	5000	10,000	8000
Ordering cost	$6	$10	$10	$8
Cost/unit	$10	$3	$5	$2
Floor space required	5.0 ft²	1.0 ft²	1.0 ft²	1.5 ft²

Assume that the annual inventory carrying cost rate is 0.10, and that 15,000 square feet of floor space are available. What is the optimal inventory policy for these items? Determine the cost to management of having only 15,000 square feet of floor space.

2-16   A company inventories three items. The pertinent data is shown below.

	ITEM		
	1	2	3
Demand/year	1000	5000	4000
Item cost	$1.50	$2.50	$4
Carrying-cost rate	0.20	0.20	0.20
Setup cost	$15	$25	$20
Shortage cost/unit	$1	$1	$1

(a)   Determine the optimal inventory policy if no more than $2000 can be invested in inventory at any point in time.

(b)   What is the cost per year to management of this constraint on inventory investment?

2-17   An electrical repair firm inventories three kinds of small motors. The pertinent data is shown below. The inventory carrying cost is computed using $i = 0.15$. Management has decreed that no more than $8000 can be invested in inventory at any one point in time. Additionally, the warehouse has only 7500 square feet that can be allocated to these motors. Find the optimal inventory policy for these motors.

	MOTOR		
	1	2	3
Demand/year	1500	2000	3000
Cost/item	$10	$5	$7.50
Ordering cost	$50	$50	$50
Floor space/item	0.5 ft²	1.0 ft²	2.5 ft²

2-18   A number (n) of products are purchased from the same vendor. To save on ordering costs, it is decided that all products are to be ordered at the same time, yielding the same cycle length (T) for all items. Find an expression for the optimal cycle length, using the notation defined below:

D_j = annual demand rate for product j, $(j = 1, 2, \ldots, n)$

C_j = unit variable cost of product j

A = fixed cost of placing an order (for all n items)

i = annual inventory carrying cost rate

2-19   Consider a situation in which n items are to be inventoried, and there is no fixed cost of placing an order. The demand is constant at D_j units per year for item j, the cost of the jth item is C_j, and the annual unit inventory carrying cost is i times the item cost. Suppose there is an upper limit, say N, to the number of orders that can be placed per year. Show that closed-form solutions exist for the Lagrange multiplier as well as for the optimal lot sizes. How would you interpret the Lagrange multiplier in this problem? Does a closed-form solution exist if each item incurs a cost of A_j dollars every time an order is placed? Develop the necessary equations to verify your answer.

2-20   A manufacturer produces an item for inventory in lots. The annual demand rate is constant at 120,000 units, the production rate is 600,000 units per year, the setup cost is $800, the unit variable production cost is $6, the annual inventory carrying cost rate is 0.10, and no shortages are to be permitted.

(a)   Write the expression for average annual cost as a function of the production lot size.

(b)   Determine the optimal lot size and the optimal time between production runs.

(c)   If the lead time between the decision to put a lot into production and the start of production is two months, determine the reorder point.

(d)   If the maximum storage capacity for this item is 12,000 units, determine the optimum production lot size and reorder point.

(e)   Suppose the unit variable cost depends on the lot size according to the following function:

LOT SIZE	UNIT COST (ALL UNITS)
$0 < Q < 10{,}000$	$6.00
$10{,}000 \leq Q < 30{,}000$	5.80
$30{,}000 \leq Q$	5.70

What is the optimal lot size without the storage space constraint? With the storage space constraint?

2-21 Determine the optimal order quantity for a purchased part having the following characteristics:

Estimated annual usage, constant rate	10,000 units
Cost of processing each purchase order	$32
Annual storage cost per unit of maximum inventory	$0.50
Annual interest, taxes, and insurance as a fraction of the value of average inventory investment	0.20

Unit price schedule

For an order of 1 to 999 units	$3.00 each
For an order of 100 to 1999 units	$2.95 each
For an order of 2000 or more	$2.90 each

No shortages are to be allowed

The entire lot is delivered in one shipment

2-22 A product is purchased for resale. Shortages are backordered at a cost of $4 per unit per year. The cost of carrying inventory is $1 per unit per year, based on average inventory. The annual demand is 10,000 units per year. The fixed cost per lot is $50, and the unit variable cost is $2, if $0 < Q < 2000$, and $1.97, if $2000 \leq Q$. This is an all-units discount. Write an expression for average annual cost as a function of the lot size and the maximum backorder level. Solve for the optimal lot size. Sketch the average annual cost curve.

2-23 A raw material is consumed at the rate of 180,000 pounds per year. The fixed cost for placing an order for this item is $60 per order. The annual inventory holding costs are estimated at 20 percent of the investment in average inventory. No shortages are to be allowed. The price paid for the material is a function of the amount ordered according to the following schedule (an incremental discount schedule):

ORDER QUANTITY IN POUNDS	PRICE PER POUND
$0 < Q < 6000$	$1.70
$6000 \leq Q < 10,000$	1.60
$10,000 \leq Q$	1.50

What is the minimum cost order quantity? Sketch the graph of total annual cost versus the quantity ordered.

2-24 Badley Motors, Inc. sells new automobiles at the almost constant rate of eight per day. The cost of carrying one automobile in inventory for one day is $1, and the fixed cost of ordering a new shipment of cars is estimated to be $50 per order. The lot adjacent to Badley will hold a maximum of 12 cars and the display room provides space for three additional cars. Should the stock on hand exceed the storage capacity, the extra stock will have to be driven to the Badley Used Cars lot and stored there until room becomes available at Badley Motors. The extra handling cost involved when this action is required is estimated at $2 per car so handled.

(a) How many automobiles should be ordered at a time and how often should orders be placed if a fixed order size policy is to be used, lead time is known and constant, demand variance is very small, and there are to be at least three cars on hand at all times?

(b) Solve the problem above using an order cost of $27 (instead of $50).

(c) Solve the above problem using an order cost of $30 and an inventory holding cost of $4 per car per day.

2-25 A product is purchased and received in lots of size Q. The annual demand rate is constant at 10,000 units, the fixed cost per order is $64, the variable cost per unit is $4, the inventory carrying-cost rate is 25 percent annually, and no shortages are to be allowed. The inventory carrying-cost rate does not include rental cost for inventory storage, which is based on maximum inventory, and computed as follows: storage space for up to 500 units, $1 per unit per year; storage space for each unit in excess of 500, $1.50 per unit per year. Compute the economic lot size.

2-26 The Ace Publishing Company is printing a textbook for a course in production control. They estimate the demand to be 5000 books per year. The production cost of each book is $8.75, inventory carrying costs are computed using $i = 0.18$, each order requires a fixed setup cost of $500, and up to 15,000 books may be printed and bound per year. No shortages are allowed, for if the publisher is out of stock, a professor will adopt another text. Suppose, however, that the publisher is in error, and the actual demand for the book is 7500 copies per year. How much has this lack of perfect information affected the optimal inventory policy? How much would the publisher be willing to pay to have a "perfect" estimate of demand?

2-27 Derive the expressions for $\bar{I}$ and $\bar{B}$, which were substituted into Equation 2-17.

2-28 Derive Equations 2-18, 2-19, and 2-20.

2-29 Is it possible for the quantity under the radical in Equation 2-18 to be negative? If so, what is the solution?

2-30 In the static deterministic case with backlogging, what is the solution if $\pi > 0$ and $\hat{\pi} = 0$? (Also, see Exercise 2-9.)

2-31 Develop Equation 2-21.

2-32 Equation 2-21 gives the reorder point in terms of the net inventory. What would be the corresponding reorder point in terms of the inventory position; that is, in terms of the net inventory plus on-order quantity?

2-33 A manufacturer uses a particular part at an almost constant rate of 10,000 pieces per year. He can produce this part at a rate of 100,000 units per year, with a variable cost of $40 per piece. He has the capacity to do this, but because of the nature of his machinery and his labor costs, a fixed setup cost of $5000 is associated with every lot he produces. He can purchase the part from either or both of two vendors. Vendor A quotes a price of $44 per piece, requires a minimum lot size of 1000 pieces, and can supply up to 6000 pieces per year. Vendor B charges a fixed cost of $200 per lot, a price of $43.50, and can supply up to 4000 pieces per year. The manufacturer uses an annual inventory carrying cost of 20 percent. He wants no shortages of this part. What is his optimal procurement policy?

2-34 Consider an item that is to be produced only once. Demand during the single selling period is assumed to be normally distributed with mean 200 and variance 400. The item costs $4.50 per unit and sells for $8.50 per unit. How many units should be produced in order to maximize expected profit? If the production quantity was chosen to equal the expected demand, what would be the expected profit?

2-35 The single-period stochastic problem can be formulated in the context of opportunity losses associated with shortages and overages. Let c_1 be the opportunity loss for each unit of on-hand inventory at the end of the period and c_2 be the opportunity loss associated with each unit short during the period. Then the expected opportunity loss during the period is

$$K(R) = c_1 \int_0^R (R - D)f(D)\, dD + c_2 \int_R^\infty (D - R)f(D)\, dD$$

Show that R^* minimizes $K(R)$, where R^* satisfies

$$F(R^*) = \frac{c_2}{c_1 + c_2}$$

Verify that for the profit model of Section 2-5, $c_1 = C + H$ and $c_2 = V - C$ lead to Equation 2-51. Interpret these opportunity losses.

2-36 The demand for an item has a density function $f(D)$, where D is the demand during a week. The item is replenished by a supplier at the start of each week. If a shortage occurs during the week, the loss is π_1 dollars for each unit short up to M units and π_2 dollars for each unit short in excess of M units. Assume that if an item is left in stock at the end of the week, it is carried over to the next week at a cost of H dollars per unit. The problem is to determine the optimal stock level (R) at the start of each week. Formulate the objective function symbolically, and solve.

2-37 A producer of antifreeze is faced with the problem of how much antifreeze to produce for the coming winter season. He has on hand 50,000 gallons that were not sold last year. His demand in millions of gallons is a random variable having the following probability density function:

$$f(D) = \begin{cases} 1, & \text{for } 1 \le D \le 2 \\ 0, & \text{for any other value of } D \end{cases}$$

For every gallon stocked in excess of demand, it costs 50 cents for carrying this quantity in inventory until the next year. The production cost is $1.50 per gallon and the sale price in wholesale lots is $2.50 per gallon. The cost of a shortage may be taken as the lost profit per gallon. We may assume that the demand for antifreeze is almost instantaneous.
Find the optimum amount of antifreeze to be produced this season.

2-38 The demand for a seasonal retail product is estimated to be uniformly distributed between 100 and 300 units. The procurement cost is $10 per unit and the sales revenue is $60 per unit. Units unsold at the end of the season have no value and are to be charged an inventory holding cost of $10 per unit. If a shortage occurs, there is a shortage penalty of $20 per unit, in addition to the lost profit. What should be the stock level at the start of the season?

2-39 Suppose in the situation of Exercise 2-38, there is also a fixed procurement cost of $100. If the retailer has I units already on hand prior to making his stocking decision at the start of the period, what is his optimal procurement policy?

2-40 Suppose in the situation of Exercise 2-39, there is an opportunity to return units to the supplier for a credit of $10 per unit, as well as to purchase additional units, in adjusting the start of the period inventory. For either a purchase or a return there is a fixed cost of $100. What is the optimal policy?

2-41 A department store must purchase an item in advance of a special sale. The unit selling price is V, the unit cost is C, and the terminal value of an item not sold during the sale is $L(L < C)$. The demand for the item is assumed to have density function $f(D)$. Show that the optimal initial stock level is R^*, defined by

$$F(R^*) = \frac{V - C}{V - L}$$

2-42 Solve Exercise 2-41 for the case where the store's storage space is limited and any initial inventory in excess of M units must be stored elsewhere and later retrieved as the main inventory is depleted. The extra handling for units procured in excess of M is estimated to cost h dollars per unit.

2-43 An apparel manufacturer has the opportunity to make a special purchase of an imported woolen fabric that he can make into men's suits for the coming season. However, he may place only one order and will not be able to reorder at a later date. His problem is to determine how much to order on the one opportunity that he has.

The cost of a yard of fabric is $6 and the selling price of a yard (when converted into a suit) is $14. The cost of manufacture is $4.50 a yard. Material purchased but not used must be disposed of at the end of the season for an estimated $3 a yard. Demand is estimated to be normally distributed with a mean of 10,000 yards and a standard deviation of 1000 yards.

How much fabric should be purchased?

2-44 Consider the discrete version of the single-period, stochastic problem described in Section 2-5. We suppose that the demand, D, is a discrete random variable having probability mass function, $p(D)$, and that the stock level, R, must also be discrete. Show that the optimal initial stock level when there is no fixed procurement cost is R^*, where R^* satisfies the inequality

$$P(R^* - 1) \le \frac{V - C}{V + H} \le P(R^*)$$

If there are I units already on hand at the start of the period immediately prior to ordering, what is the optimal ordering policy?

2-45 What is the solution to Exercise 2-44 if there is also a fixed procurement cost of A?

2-46 A seasonal article that must be ordered in advance and stocked by a department store sells for $100 and costs the store $50 to purchase. Any units not sold during the season must be sold at a sacrifice to a special dealer for $35 per unit. The following probability distribution of demand during the season is assumed:

DEMAND	PROBABILITY
5	0.10
6	0.15
7	0.20
8	0.25
9	0.20
10	0.10

If the store has only one opportunity to stock the article, how many units should it purchase? What would be the expected on-hand inventory at the end of the season if eight units were stocked initially?
(See Exercises 2-44 and 2-45 for the approach to discrete analysis.)

2-47 A service station finds that its weekly sales of regular gasoline may be considered to be a normally distributed random variable with a mean of 2000 gallons and a standard deviation of 200 gallons. It is able to replenish its stock only once each week, and there is no fixed cost for this. The shortage loss is estimated at $0.04 per gallon and the storage cost for gas unsold at the end of the week is $0.005 per gallon. Determine the optimal stock level.

2-48 The owners of a new service station plan to give a set of drinking glasses to each opening-week customer who buys more than seven gallons of gasoline. A set costs 40 cents and, if not used, can be returned to the supplier who will refund 30 cents.
The owners estimate that between 500 and 1000 sets will be required according to the following probability distribution:

$$f(D) = \begin{cases} (0.001)(8 - 0.008D), & \text{for } 500 \leq D \leq 1000 \\ 0, & \text{otherwise} \end{cases}$$

(Although "sets" are actually discrete, the large demand permits approximation by a continuous model.)
If the owners decide to order 750 sets and no opportunity exists for replenishment during the week, what value are they implicitly assigning to the cost of a shortage of a set?

2-49 Consider the single-period inventory model with a fixed procurement cost, A, as discussed in Section 2-5. If demand is exponential with parameter λ, that is,

$$f(D) = \frac{1}{\lambda} e^{-D/\lambda}$$

find an approximate general solution for the optimal parameters R and r. Under what conditions is this approximation valid?

2-50 Consider the single-period, stochastic problem of Section 2-5. Suppose now that the unit variable procurement cost is a function of the quantity ordered. Develop the optimal ordering policy for the case of an all-units price discount schedule.

2-51 Repeat Exercise 2-50 for the case of an incremental discount schedule.

2-52 A retailer has a special sale for which he stocks some or all of n specialty items. The jth item has a unit cost of C_j, a unit selling price of V_j, and a probabilistic demand described by the probability distribution $f_j(D_j)$. Units remaining at the end of the sale can be disposed of for a value of $L_j < C_j$. The retailer has only M dollars with which to stock initially his inventory for the sale. There is no opportunity to reorder. How should he determine how much of each product to stock?

2-53 Use the procedure developed in Exercise 2-52 to solve the following problem, where all demands are assumed to be normally distributed.

ITEM	UNIT COST	UNIT PRICE	TERMINAL VALUE	EXPECTED DEMAND	DEMAND VARIANCE
1	$20	$28	$15	100	25
2	10	15	3	200	1600
3	10	15	3	200	100
4	20	25	10	200	1600

The retailer has a limit of $10,000 on his initial stock level. How many units of each item should he stock?

2-54 At the time of installation of a set of machines in a manufacturing plant, the maintenance department has the opportunity to order spare parts from the manufacturer of the machinery. A certain spare part costs $600, if purchased then. It cannot be bought at a later date. The demand for this part over the life of the machinery is thought to be a Poisson variable with a mean of 5. The machines are expected to be used for 10 years, and any spare parts remaining at the end of that time will be of no value. If a shortage occurs, the part will have to be specially produced in the company's own machine shop at a cost estimated at $3000, including lost production. Without considering inventory carrying costs, how many of this part should be stocked? (See also Exercise 2-55.)

2-55   Solve Exercise 2-54 considering an inventory carrying cost at the rate of 20 percent annually. (One approach would be to assume that the inventory cost is charged only on spare parts remaining at the end of 10 years. A second method would be to assume that the actual demand takes place at equally spaced time points within the 10-year period and develop an expression for the on-hand inventory at any point in time. From this the inventory carrying cost can be computed. Since the time period is long, future inventory costs and future shortage penalties should be discounted before being considered with present time procurement costs. Use a 10 percent annual rate of interest. Work this exercise using both approaches and compare the results).

2-56   Consider a single-period problem where demand has probability density function $f(D)$, the item costs C dollars, sells for a price of V dollars, and has a disposal value at the end of the period of L dollars. However, there is a fixed cost of M dollars to sell the group of items, if any, remaining at the end of the season. If sale of the terminal inventory is not elected, these units are scrapped at no cost and for no value. How many units should be stocked initially?

2-57   Consider a single-period problem where demand has probability density function $f(D)$. The item costs C dollars. If a shortage occurs during the period, there is a fixed shortage penalty of ψ dollars, independent of the amount of the shortage. How many units should be stocked initially?

2-58   A vendor who sells souvenirs at baseball games is planning for the World Series games to be held in his city. He is certain there will be at least two games played, but feels there is only a 0.60 probability of a third game and only a 0.20 probability of a fourth game in his locale. For a certain item, which he must stock prior to the first game and cannot reorder, he estimates that sales for the four possible games can be approximately described as normally distributed random variables with means 4000, 2000, 1000, and 1000 and standard deviations 200, 160, 100, and 100, respectively. If the item costs him $1, sells for $3, and has no value if unsold during the Series, how many should he stock?

2-59   Consider a single-period inventory problem with only one opportunity for procurement and that occurring at the start of the period. The demand in the period is assumed normally distributed with mean μ and variance σ^2. The procurement process is such that if R units are ordered from the supplier, the quantity actually delivered will be a normally distributed random variable with mean R and variance v. Let c_1 be the loss for every unit actually procured, but not sold during the period, and let c_2 be the loss for every unit of shortage during the period. Show that the optimal order quantity is determined from

$$F(-R^*) = \frac{c_1}{c_1 + c_2}$$

where F is the cumulative distribution of a normally distributed random variable having mean $-\mu$ and variance $\sigma^2 + v$.

2-60 Suppose x is a normally distributed random variable having mean μ and variance σ^2. The normal density function will be denoted by $n(x; \mu, \sigma^2)$. Let $\phi(z)$ be the standard normal density and $\Phi(z)$ and $\Phi'(z)$ be the associated cumulative and complementary cumulative distributions, respectively. Show that for any number a

$$\int_a^\infty (x - a)n(x; \mu, \sigma^2)\, dx = \sigma\phi\!\left(\frac{a - \mu}{\sigma}\right) + (\mu - a)\Phi'\!\left(\frac{a - \mu}{\sigma}\right)$$

and

$$\int_{-\infty}^a (a - x)n(x; \mu, \sigma^2)\, dx = \sigma\phi\!\left(\frac{a - \mu}{\sigma}\right) + (a - \mu)\Phi\!\left(\frac{a - \mu}{\sigma}\right)$$

2-61 (A continuation of Exercise 2-60.) Define

$$L'(u) \equiv \int_u^\infty (z - u)\phi(z)\, dz$$

and

$$L(u) \equiv \int_{-\infty}^u (u - z)\phi(z)\, dz$$

L' and L are called the right and left unit-normal linear-loss integrals, respectively. Values of these integrals can be obtained from Table A-3. Verify the following properties.

$$L'(-u) = u + L'(u)$$
$$L(-u) = L(u) - u$$
$$L'(u) = L(-u)$$

$$\int_a^\infty (x - a)n(x; \mu, \sigma^2)\, dx = \sigma L'\!\left(\frac{a - \mu}{\sigma}\right)$$

$$\int_{-\infty}^a (a - x)n(x; \mu, \sigma^2)\, dx = \sigma L\!\left(\frac{a - \mu}{\sigma}\right)$$

$$= (a - \mu) + \sigma L'\!\left(\frac{a - \mu}{\sigma}\right)$$

2-62 Suppose x is a discrete random variable described by a Poisson distribution $p(x; \mu)$, where μ is the expected value of x. Show that for some number a

$$\sum_{x=a}^{\infty} (x - a)p(x; \mu) = \mu - a + aP(a - 1; \mu) - \mu P(a - 2; \mu)$$

and

$$\sum_{x=0}^{a} (a - x)p(x; \mu) = aP(a; \mu) - \mu P(a - 1; \mu)$$

where $P(x; \mu)$ is the cumulative Poisson distribution.

2-63 Find the optimal inventory policy for an item that will be demanded during a two-period planning horizon. The demand in each period has density function

$$f(D) = \tfrac{1}{20}e^{-D/20}, \qquad D > 0$$

The inventory holding cost is $1 per unit per period. Shortages are backlogged at a cost of $2 per unit short. The item costs $2 per unit. There is no fixed ordering cost, and the item may be procured at the start of each period.

2-64 A certain item in a military supply system will be demanded over the next two years. The demand in either year can be assumed to be uniformly distributed over the interval 0 to 300. The cost of each item is $50, the holding cost per unit per year is $25, and the backorder cost is $30 per unit short. This item may be procured at the beginning of each year.

(a) What is the optimal inventory policy?

(b) Rework part (a) assuming a discount factor of $\alpha = 0.75$.

(c) Assume that the infinite period model is an adequate approximation and find the optimal inventory policy. What is the difference between the cost incurred in part (a) and part (c)? On the basis of this cost, do you think the infinite period model assumption was justified?

2-65 A retailer reviews the stock of cartons of a particular shirt every week. The number of cartons of shirts demanded in any time period is assumed to be Poisson distributed with mean 20 per week. Each carton of shirts costs the retailer $27.50 and sells for $50. An inventory carrying-cost rate of 0.20 is used. Demands occurring when the retailer is out of stock are backordered at a cost of $5. The procurement lead time can be assumed to be constant at four days. Determine the optimal inventory policy.

2-66 A manufacturer uses a purchased part whose demand over any time period of length t can be assumed to be normally distributed with mean

$200t$ and variance $400t$. The parts cost \$15 each. The lead time is two weeks. The annual inventory carrying cost rate is 15 percent. Shortages are backordered at a cost of \$10 each. If the inventory is reviewed every six weeks under a fixed reorder period system, find the optimal target inventory level. Suppose the length of the review period is also a decision variable. Find the optimal fixed reorder period policy, when the cost of an inventory review is \$100.

2-67 *A Periodic Review Model with Lost Sales.* Consider the approximate treatment of the periodic review case treated in Section 2-6.3. Suppose demands occurring when the system is out of stock are lost forever. Develop an appropriate inventory model, and an expression for the optimal target inventory.

2-68 Rework Exercise 2-65 for the case where shortages are lost sales and there is a goodwill loss of \$3 per carton in addition to the lost profit. (See Exercise 2-67, also.)

2-69 Develop a model for the fixed period system of Section 2-6.3 when expected demand is small and must be treated as a discrete random variable. Obtain the solution.

2-70 *A Periodic Review Model with a Mixture of Backorders and Lost Sales.* Consider a periodic review, stochastic demand inventory model in which only a fraction q of the shortages can be backordered and the remaining fraction $(1 - q)$ is lost forever. Let $f(x; T) \, dx$ be the probability that x units are demanded in a review period plus a lead time (Equation 2-72), and denote the expected value of lead time demand by μ. Define π_0 to be the additional cost of a lost sale over a backorder, including lost profit. Show that the average annual variable cost is

$$K(R, T) = \frac{A + J}{T} + iC\left[R - \mu - \frac{DT}{2} \right]$$

$$+ \left[iC(1 - q) + \frac{\pi + \pi_0(1 - q)}{T} \right] \bar{b}(R)$$

where $\bar{b}(R) = \int_R^\infty (x - R)f(x; T) \, dx$, and that for a given T the optimal R must satisfy

$$F'(R, T) = \frac{iCT}{iCT(1 - q) + \pi + \pi_0(1 - q)}$$

How would you obtain the optimal R *and* T?

2-71 A slow-moving retail item is controlled by a periodic review system of the (R, r) type, with a four-week review period. Specifically, if the inventory level is less than or equal to three, an order is placed for an amount equal to the difference between seven and the actual inventory. Thus, the target inventory is $R = 7$ and the reorder point is $r = 3$. Procurement lead time is negligible. The item costs $100 and sells for $210. There is a fixed procurement cost of $150 per order. Shortages are lost sales, with a goodwill loss of $10 per unit short. The annual inventory carrying cost rate is 20 percent. Demand in a four-week period is a random variable having the following probability distribution:

SALES	PROBABILITY	SALES	PROBABILITY
0	0.04	5	0.15
1	0.10	6	0.10
2	0.16	7	0.03
3	0.20	8	0.02
4	0.20	≥ 9	0

Calculate the average on-hand inventory, the average number of shortages per unit time, the average number of orders per unit time, and the average number of units ordered per unit time. Then compute the average cost per unit time for this (R, r) policy. (You may want to use Markov chain analysis in solving the problem.)

2-72 Repeat Exercise 2-71 assuming all shortages are backordered at a cost of $10 per unit.

2-73 The inventory of a purchased item is to be controlled with a continuous review (Q, r) policy. The fixed cost of an order is $100, the cost per unit is $5, the annual inventory carrying cost rate is 20 percent, and the expected annual demand is 10,000 units. Lead time demand is normally distributed with a mean of 400 and a standard deviation of 30.

(a) Find the reorder point if the probability of a shortage during any lead time is to be 0.05.

(b) All shortages are backordered at a cost of $4 per unit. What should be the reorder point in order to minimize average annual costs, if a lot size of 1000 is to be used?

(c) If a reorder point of 400 is used, what would be the expected annual cost of backorders? Assume each backorder costs $4.

(d) For a reorder point of 400 and a backorder cost of $4 per unit, find the lot size that will minimize average annual costs.

(e) What are optimal values for lot size and reorder point when shortages are backordered at a cost of $4 per unit?

2-74 A drapery manufacturer controls his finished goods inventory with a fixed reorder quantity system. A particular style has a demand that is normally distributed with a mean of 500 pair per week and a standard deviation of 50 pair. Procurement lead time is two weeks. The fixed procurement cost is $300, the unit variable cost is $40 per pair, the selling price is $50 per pair, and the annual inventory carrying-cost rate is 20 percent. Shortages are backordered at a cost of $2 per pair short. Determine the optimal lot size and reorder point.

2-75 Repeat Exercise 2-74 assuming all shortages are lost. In addition to lost profit, there is a $2 per pair shortage charge.

2-76 In Exercise 2-74, suppose that the procurement lead time was a random variable, being two weeks with probability 0.6 and three weeks with probability 0.4. Find the optimal lot size and reorder point.

2-77 In Exercise 2-74, suppose that the lead time could be reduced to one week through expediting at a cost of $100 per lot. What is the optimal inventory policy?

2-78 For the fixed reorder quantity system with lost sales, derive the results of Equations 2-87 and 2-88.

2-79 Consider the fixed reorder quantity system used to control the inventory of a slow-moving item, where demand must be treated as a discrete random variable and Q and r are to be integer valued. Let $p(x)$ be the probability distribution of lead-time demand. For the backorders case, develop a procedure to find the optimal order size and reorder point.

2-80 Repeat Exercise 2-79 for the lost sales case.

2-81 Consider the fixed reorder quantity system used to control the inventory of an item whose procurement cost is subject to price breaks. Treating demand as continuous, develop a solution procedure for the case of an all-units discount schedule.

2-82 Repeat Exercise 2-81 for the case of an incremental discount schedule.

2-83 Consider the fixed reorder quantity system applied to an item that is produced to inventory. When a lot is produced, units are added to inventory at the constant rate of P units per unit time. The time between observing the inventory at the reorder point and starting production is τ. Assuming demand is a continuous random variable, develop a model and solve for both the lost sales and the backorders cases.

2-84 Consider the fixed reorder quantity system where demand is a continuous random variable and shortages are backordered. Suppose the only shortage penalty is a fixed loss of ψ dollars if a shortage occurs during a cycle. Develop a model and solve.

2-85 *A Continuous Review Model with A Mixture of Backorders and Lost Sales.* Consider a continuous review, stochastic demand inventory model in which only a fraction q of demand that occurs when the system is out of stock can be backordered and the remaining fraction $(1 - q)$ of such demand is lost forever. Let π_0 be the additional cost of a lost sale, including lost profit, and $f(x)$ be the density function of lead-time demand such that $E(x) = \mu$. Show that the average annual variable cost is

$$K(Q, r) = \frac{AD}{Q} + iC[Q + r - \mu]$$

$$+ \left[iC(1 - q) + \frac{\pi D}{Q} + \frac{\pi_0 D(1 - q)}{Q} \right] \bar{b}(r)$$

and that the optimal Q and r must satisfy

$$Q = \sqrt{\frac{2D[A + \pi \bar{b}(r) + \pi_0(1 - q)\bar{b}(r)]}{iC}}$$

$$F'(r) = \frac{iCQ}{iCQ(1 - q) + \pi D + \pi_0 D(1 - q)}$$

2-86 A manufacturing plant maintains an inventory of spare parts and supplies for use in maintenance operations. The usage of a certain part is Poisson with an expected rate of five parts per week. The inventory of this part is controlled by a base stock system. The lead time for procurement is two weeks and is constant. The part costs $300. An inventory carrying-cost rate of 20 percent annually is used. Shortages are backordered at a loss of $700 a week per unit short, resulting from machine downtime. What base stock level should be used?

2-87 Rework Exercise 2-86 assuming that shortages are not backordered, but that an emergency procurement is made when a shortage occurs, and that the added cost of the special procurement is $200. No other shortage losses are experienced.

2-88 A retail product is controlled by a base stock system, having a constant procurement lead time of three weeks. Demand in a three-week period is normally distributed with a mean of 400 and a standard deviation of 50. The unit cost is $100 and the unit selling price is $180. The annual inventory carrying cost rate is 20 percent. Shortages are backordered at a fixed cost of $5 per backorder plus a time-dependent cost of $2 per unit short per week. What base stock level should be used?

2-89 Suppose the management of the retail store in Exercise 2-88 arbitrarily decided to use a base stock level of 400 units, because of difficulties in estimating the time-dependent backorder loss. Assuming the other costs and revenues are known, what value are they imputing to backorder cost ($\hat{\pi}$)? Repeat for a base stock level of 500.

2-90   A base stock system is used to control a slow-moving item in a retail store. Customer orders are for a single unit and occur at the rate of 0.30 orders per week. The number of orders in a week is assumed to be Poisson distributed. The replenishment lead time is exponentially distributed with a mean of one week. Shortages result in lost sales. The item costs $60 and is sold for $100. The cost of ordering and receiving an item is $10. The inventory carrying cost rate is 0.20 annually. What base stock level should be used?

2-91   Consider the base stock system with constant lead time, where a fraction q of the shortages may be backordered and the remaining $1 - q$ are lost sales. Develop a model similar to Equation 2-94 and solve.

2-92   *Base Stock System with Lost Sales.* Consider the base stock system with variable lead time as described in Section 2-7.4. Suppose that no backorders are allowed; all shortages are lost sales. The steady-state equations are given in Equation 2-100. Show that their solution is

$$\beta_i = \frac{1}{i!}\left(\frac{\lambda}{v}\right)^i \beta_0, \qquad (i = 0, 1, 2, \ldots, R)$$

where

$$\beta_0 = e^{-\rho}/P(R; \rho) \quad \text{and} \quad \rho = \lambda/v$$

Then

$$\alpha_j = \frac{1}{(R - j)!} \rho^{R-j} e^{-\rho}/P(R; \rho), \qquad (j = 0, 1, \ldots, R)$$

Show also that the average inventory is

$$\bar{I} = R - \frac{\rho P(R - 1; \rho)}{P(R; \rho)}$$

and that the fraction of time the system is out of stock is

$$\gamma = \frac{\rho^R e^{-\rho}}{R! P(R; \rho)}$$

Using these results formulate a cost model similar to Equation 2-108 and solve.

[*Comment.* These results hold for any lead time distribution having a mean $\bar{\tau} = 1/v$. See Morse (4).]

2-93   A department store sells towels throughout the year; however, the demand rate varies widely over time because of white sales, customer buying habits, etc. For a certain towel, the estimated sales in dozens by month for the next 12 months are 60, 12, 10, 15, 15, 50, 30, 60, 20, 15, 20, and 30. The company can order a lot from the manufacturer at the start of each month. Delivery is immediate. The fixed cost per lot is $100 and the towels cost $40 per dozen. The store uses an annual inventory carrying cost rate of 20 percent. If no shortages are to be permitted and actual demand equals the estimates, what order sizes should be used during the year?

2-94 Solve Exercise 2-93 assuming an initial inventory of 70 dozen towels.

2-95 Procurement of a seasonal product is to be planned over a six-month horizon. One lot can be ordered each month. The initial inventory is 20 units. Demand estimates and costs are given in the table below. Find the optimal procurement program, if no shortages are allowed.

MONTH	DEMAND	UNIT COST	FIXED COST/LOT	INVENTORY COST/UNIT
May	40	5	100	2
June	60	5	100	1
July	100	8	150	1
August	40	8	150	1
September	100	8	200	2
October	200	10	200	2

2-96 The demand rate for a product over the next year is expected to be $200 + 1600t$, $0 \leq t \leq 1$. The product is purchased in lots, which can be ordered at any time. The fixed procurement cost is $200 per lot, the item costs $10 per unit, and the annual inventory carrying cost rate is 20%. The initial inventory is 100 units. What is the optimal procurement policy during the next year, if no shortages are permitted?

2-97 *Service Level Concepts.* Consider a continuous review (Q, r) system with static probabilistic demand. Some measures of how well the system is satisfying demand are (1) the probability of a shortage during a cycle, α; (2) the probability of one or more cycles having shortages during a unit of time, say a year, β; (3) the expected number of shortages per cycle, $\bar{b}(r)$; (4) the expected number of shortages per year; (5) the fraction of time the system is out of stock, γ; and (6) the fraction of demand satisfied immediately from inventory, sometimes called the *service level*. Note that γ is the fraction of demand delivered late in the backlogging case and is the fraction of demand lost in the lost sales case. If $f(x)$ is the probability distribution of lead time demand, we can write

(a) $\alpha = F'(r)$

(b) $\beta = 1 - (1 - \alpha)^n$, where $n = D/Q$

(c) $\bar{b}(r) = \int_r^\infty (x - r)f(x)\, dx$

(d) Shortages per unit time $= n\bar{b}(r)$

(e) $\gamma = \begin{cases} \bar{b}(r)/Q, & \text{in the backorders case} \\ \bar{b}(r)/[Q + \bar{b}(r)], & \text{in the lost sales case} \end{cases}$

(f) Service level $= 1 - \gamma$

Write expressions for each of these measures when $f(x)$ is normal with mean μ and variance σ^2.

2-98 Repeat Exercise 2-97 for $f(x)$ Poisson with parameter μ.

2-99 Suppose you want to determine the reorder point for a fixed reorder quantity system, so that a service level of $1 - \gamma$ is obtained. (See Exercise 2-97.) Assume lead time demand is normally distributed with mean μ and variance σ^2. Show that the reorder point is of the form $r = \mu + k\sigma$, where the safety stock multiplier is determined from

$$\theta(k) = \begin{cases} \gamma Q/\sigma, & \text{for the backorders case} \\ Q\gamma/(1 - \gamma)\sigma, & \text{for the lost sales case} \end{cases}$$

and

$$\theta(k) = \phi(k) - k\Phi'(k)$$

2-100 *Turnover Rate.* An inventory-control performance measure commonly used by managers is the "turnover rate," defined as the ratio of average annual sales to average on-hand inventory. Find the optimal turnover rate for the static, deterministic demand case, when no shortages are allowed. Find an expression for the turnover rate as a function of Q, r, and D for the fixed reorder quantity system. How could this be used to design the system, if management specified a target turnover rate? Analyze the relationships between the objectives of a high turnover rate and a high service level for the fixed reorder quantity system. (See Exercise 2-99.)

chapter 3
Production Planning—Static Models

3-1 Introduction

Production planning is the activity of establishing production goals over some future time period, called the *planning horizon*. The objective of production planning is to plan the optimal use of resources to meet stated production requirements or to take advantage of potential sales opportunities.

As input, production planning will use the following kinds of information:

1. Current inventory levels.
2. Current backlog position.

3. Forecasts of future demand.
4. Current work in process.
5. Current work force levels.
6. Capacity of each production center.
7. Material availability.
8. Production standards.
9. Cost standards and selling prices.
10. Management policies.

This information is gathered and analyzed periodically to develop production plans. The output from this activity may take a variety of forms, specifying the following type of things for each period of the planning horizon:

1. Quantities of each product to be produced.
2. Quantities of a given product to be produced by each of several alternative processes.
3. Quantities of each product to be produced by a given process (such as plant, department, line, machine, etc.).
4. Target inventory levels by product.
5. Work force level.
6. Overtime, additional shifts, unused capacity, etc.
7. Quantities of material and semifinished product to be transported between stages in a multistage (for example, multiplant) production system.
8. Subcontracting plans.
9. Purchased material requirements.

The decisions made in production planning affect several classes of costs and revenues:

1. Production costs.
2. Production rate change costs.
3. Capacity change costs.
4. Inventory holding costs.
5. Customer service and shortage losses.
6. Procurement costs.

Production costs are usually divided into categories of fixed and variable costs. The fixed cost is, of course, independent of the quantity to be produced. Typically, it results from getting the process ready to produce the product (*setup cost*) and from cleaning up the process at the termination of production (*takedown cost*). When changing machines from one product to another, the cost of preparing the process for the new product may be a function of the sequence of products; that is, it may depend on the product being removed from production as well as the new product. In such a case, we say that setup costs are *sequence dependent*.

Variable production costs are actual costs for labor, material, power, supplies, etc., which depend on the level of production. The usual assumption is that the unit variable cost is constant over the range of production being considered, so that total variable cost can be obtained by multiplying the quantity produced by the unit variable cost. However, when production is in lots, or batches, the average unit variable cost may depend on the size of the lot. As the lot is produced, quality problems may be solved and worker learning takes place, so that the marginal cost of a unit will decrease as production continues. This is the "learning curve" effect, and results in a concave-shaped total variable cost curve.

The opposite effect on total variable cost will occur if increased production means that less efficient or more costly production processes must be used. For example, when *overtime* is necessary to meet a production schedule, the direct cost of a unit of product increases because of labor cost premiums paid for overtime hours. Also, production efficiency on overtime may be less than on straight (regular) time. These same comments apply to added shifts. Other examples of situations leading to convex-shaped total variable cost curves are when less efficient labor or machinery must be employed, and when more expensive processes, such as subcontracting, must be used to obtain higher production rates.

When making decisions about changing the production rate of a product from one period to the next, it is necessary to consider the costs associated with the change. Naturally, if the desired production rate exceeds the regular time capacity, overtime or subcontracting will be necessary and undoubtedly will result in a higher unit cost. However, here we are talking about the costs associated with making the changes in production levels. Costs of changing machines and equipment, transferring workers, added production planning and control efforts, relocation of material, etc., are costs that could be avoided if the plant produced the same products at the same rates from period to period.

If changes in work force level decisions are necessary because of changes in production levels, there will be losses associated with hiring or laying off workers. Employment and training costs, cost of employee transfer and re-training, intangible effects on public and employee relations, and separation pay fall into this category.

In the longer run, production planning decisions will interact with plans to change capacity by the acquisition or disposal of plant and equipment. If these alternatives are available, the appropriate economic factors must be identified and estimated. Since we shall assume physical capacity is fixed in our treatment of production planning, these costs will not be described here.

Production planning decisions affect inventory levels. Plans may call for building up inventories in slack periods for use in later peak periods. They may call for production in large batches, which requires large inventories. They may create large in-process inventories because of scheduled batch sequence changes between operations. They may specify different production rates for successive operations, resulting in an inventory between them. A description of the costs associated with such inventories is given in Section 2-1.3 and will not be repeated here. Just as in the pure inventory process, inventories serve many useful functions in the production system, thereby reducing costs from other sources. (See Section 2-1.2 for a general discussion of the functions of inventories.) The problem is one of trading off the cost of inventories against the value of inventories; we seek optimal inventory levels in production planning.

Failure to meet customer demand on time may result in tangible loss of profit or expediting costs and intangible loss of good will. Also, the inability of salesmen to make competitive delivery promises may result in no customer order at all. There are two ways that production planning and control actions result in these losses. The first is the failure to coordinate production with demand, which results in shortages and late deliveries. The second is the generation of excessive idle time, which results in the actual output being less than the rated output. If the lost production could be sold, the company has a shortage loss because of poor efficiency.

Finally, production planning may determine the ability to economically acquire materials used in production, and it affects how much finished or semifinished product must be procured from outside sources ("subcontractors").

In this chapter we begin to describe the modeling of decision problems in production planning. While it is true that some of the models of Chapter 2 are appropriate for simple production-inventory systems, in general, more complex models are needed to represent adequately problems involving multiple products, multiple sources of product, resource limitations, and other characteristics common to production planning. The following are some of the features to be introduced:

1. *Multiple products* competing for limited resources, such as machine time, labor, working capital, etc. The problem is to allocate effectively available resources to the production of the various products.

2. *Multiple sources*, or processes, by which a product can be produced. Some examples would be different routings within a plant, different plants, make versus buy (subcontract) alternatives, overtime versus regular time, alternative materials, and different methods of cutting or stamping parts from

material. The problem is to determine how much of the product to make by each process.

3. *Multiple facilities* arranged in a multistage structure so that the output from one stage becomes the input to a following stage. The problem is to schedule production at each facility, thereby controlling the inventories between stages and insuring that external demand on the final stage is met.

The models in Chapter 3 are *static* in that the rate of demand for a product is assumed to be constant over time. If demand is stochastic, we further assume that the probability distribution of demand in periods of a given length does not change from period to period. Chapter 4 extends the analysis to the dynamic situation, where characteristics of the demand process vary over time.

We have chosen to illustrate the modeling of many of the problem situations in Chapters 3 and 4 using linear programming models. We did this because the linear programming model has a simple form that can be easily understood and, more importantly, is often a realistic description of the real-world production planning problem. If the latter is not a reasonable assumption in a given application, then nonlinear models should be considered; however, at this time it is difficult, often impossible, to solve nonlinear programming models of the size required to describe many production planning problems.

3-2   Product Mix Decisions

For many firms, the most important decisions relating to production are those that determine the product mix for a given period of time. There may be a number of products that the company could produce and sell in the period and the problem is to decide how much of each product to schedule. The objective is to utilize limited resources to maximize the net value of the output from the production facilities. Production and sale of a given quantity of a product results in a certain contribution to overhead and profit (that is, the difference between variable sales revenue and variable production cost) and uses up certain resources, such as materials, labor, machine time at various production centers, etc. The problem is to find the production program that maximizes the total contribution to profit and overhead during the period, subject to constraints imposed by resource limitations and considering customer orders already in hand and potential sales (forecasts).

The following features characterize a product mix problem:

1. Maximization of contribution to profit and overhead.
2. Constraints resulting from resource limitations.
3. Bound constraints on planned production.

3-2.1 Linear Programming Formulations

The product mix problem is most naturally modeled as a mathematical programming problem. We shall illustrate this by giving a linear programming model. Let

X_i = quantity of product i, $i = 1, 2, \ldots, n$, produced in the period

b_k = amount of resource k, $k = 1, 2, \ldots, K$, available during the period

a_{ik} = number of units of resource k required to produce one unit of product i .

U_i = maximum sales potential of product i in the period

L_i = required minimum production level of product i in the period

r_i = revenue, net of variable selling expense, from selling one unit of product i

c_i = unit variable cost of producing a unit of product i

We assume that $(r_i - c_i)X_i$ is the contribution to overhead and profit resulting from the production and sale of X_i units of product i, where we suppose that all production of product i up to U_i units can be sold in the period. Furthermore, we assume that production of X_i units of product i will use up $a_{ik}X_i$ units of resource k. Our objective is to maximize the total contribution to overhead and profit, Z, from all products.

Mathematically, we wish to choose $X_1, X_2, \ldots, X_n$ to maximize

$$Z = \sum_{i=1}^{n} (r_i - c_i)X_i \tag{3-1a}$$

subject to

$$\sum_{i=1}^{n} a_{ik}X_i \le b_k, \qquad (k = 1, 2, \ldots, K) \tag{3-1b}$$

$$X_i \le U_i, \qquad (i = 1, 2, \ldots, n) \tag{3-1c}$$

$$X_i \ge L_i, \qquad (L_i \ge 0, i = 1, 2, \ldots, n) \tag{3-1d}$$

The left-hand side of (3-1b) is the total amount of resource k required by the production program. The lower bound constraints, (3-1d), occur when there is a prior commitment to deliver a given amount, L_i, of a product i in the period, or when management decides to produce at least that much of the product, regardless of the economic consequences.

□**EXAMPLE 3-1** A manufacturer produces a line of household products fabricated from sheet metal. To illustrate his production planning problem, suppose that he makes only four products and that his production system

TABLE 3-1   Production Data for Example 3-1

DEPARTMENT	PRODUCTION RATES IN HOURS PER UNIT				PRODUCTION HOURS AVAILABLE
	PRODUCT 1	PRODUCT 2	PRODUCT 3	PRODUCT 4	
Stamping	0.03	0.15	0.05	0.10	400
Drilling	0.06	0.12	—	0.10	400
Assembly	0.05	0.10	0.05	0.12	500
Finishing	0.04	0.20	0.03	0.12	450
Packaging	0.02	0.06	0.02	0.05	400

consists of five production centers: stamping, drilling, assembly, finishing (painting and printing), and packaging. For a given month, he must decide how much of each product to manufacture, and to aid in this decision, he has assembled the data shown in Tables 3-1 and 3-2. Furthermore, he knows that only 2000 square feet of the type of sheet metal used for products 2 and 4 will be available during the month. Product 2 requires 2.0 square feet per unit and product 4 uses 1.2 square feet per unit.

Formulating this as a linear programming model, we let X_i be the number of units of product i produced in the month and Z be the total contribution to profit and overhead. The problem is to choose nonnegative X_1, X_2, X_3, and X_4 to maximize

$$Z = 4X_1 + 10X_2 + 5X_3 + 6X_4$$

subject to

(1) constraints on production time (e.g., machine-hours):

$$0.03X_1 + 0.15X_2 + 0.05X_3 + 0.10X_4 \leq 400 \quad \text{(Stamping)}$$
$$0.06X_1 + 0.12X_2 \qquad\qquad + 0.10X_4 \leq 400 \quad \text{(Drilling)}$$
$$0.05X_1 + 0.10X_2 + 0.05X_3 + 0.12X_4 \leq 500 \quad \text{(Assembly)}$$
$$0.04X_1 + 0.20X_2 + 0.03X_3 + 0.12X_4 \leq 450 \quad \text{(Finishing)}$$
$$0.02X_1 + 0.06X_2 + 0.02X_3 + 0.05X_4 \leq 400 \quad \text{(Packaging)}$$

(2) constraint on sheet metal availability:

$$2.0X_2 + 1.2X_4 \leq 2000$$

(3) constraints on minimum production and maximum sales:

$$1000 \leq X_1 \leq 6000$$
$$0 \leq X_2 \leq 500$$
$$500 \leq X_3 \leq 3000$$
$$100 \leq X_4 \leq 1000$$

TABLE 3-2 Product Data for Example 3-1

PRODUCT	NET SELLING PRICE/UNIT	VARIABLE COST/UNIT	SALES POTENTIAL MINIMUM	SALES POTENTIAL MAXIMUM
1	$10	$6	1000	6000
2	25	15	—	500
3	16	11	500	3000
4	20	14	100	1000

(The problem was solved by the simplex algorithm to obtain the information described in the following paragraphs. The reader may wish to verify the results.)

The optimal production program is $X_1^* = 5500$, $X_2^* = 500$, $X_3^* = 3000$, and $X_4^* = 100$. We are to make as much of products 2 and 3 as we can sell in the period. Product 4 is produced only because of the lower bound constraint $X_4 \geq 100$. This program uses all of the capacity in stamping and drilling. The unused capacity in the remaining production centers is 13 hours in assembly, 28 hours in finishing, and 195 hours in packaging. Only 1120 square feet of sheet metal are used, leaving 880 square feet unused. The maximum profit is $42,600.

By examining values of the dual variables, we learn that it would not be desirable to produce more of product 4 (at the expense of reducing production of some other product) unless its unit profit were at least $1.78 higher, or $7.78. The marginal value of an additional hour of stamping capacity is $22.22 and of drilling capacity, $55.56. If we could sell one more unit of product 3, we could increase our profit by $3.89 (accounting for the fact that some other product would have to be cut back). The ability to sell one more unit of product 2 would yield no more profit.□

3-2.2 Stochastic Product Mix Problems

Explicit consideration of uncertainty about the demand for a product is difficult in constrained problems, such as product mix determination. In the previous section, a maximum sales potential was given for each product, and scheduled production was not allowed to exceed this value. It was not made clear how this maximum would be determined in practice. A simple approach would be to forecast the expected sales for the month and then, using knowledge of the probability distribution of forecast error (see Chapter 6), to establish the limit above or below the expected sales, depending upon the profitability of the item.

This would be done by subjectively trading off profit potential versus risk of overproduction. Once limits have been established for all products, the problem is modeled as a (deterministic) linear programming problem. Then if one wished to go further in investigating the effects of uncertainty on the solution, sensitivity analysis of the upper bound constraints could be carried out.

In this section, we give two illustrations of more direct treatment of uncertainty about demand. The first involves making probability statements about desired relationships between production and demand and then translating these probability statements into linear inequality constraints, which are added to the linear programming model (3-1). This approach is called *chance-constrained programming*. In the second illustration, we use the probability distributions of demand in formulating a model for expected total contribution to profit and overhead during the period, and then optimize subject to a single resource constraint.

□**EXAMPLE 3-2** *A Chance-Constrained Model.*   Naturally in a product mix situation management is concerned about producing more of a product than they will be able to sell. In model (3-1), we treated this concern by adding constraints of the form $X_i \leq U_i$. Now suppose we use an alternative approach and require that the probability of production, X_i, exceeding the demand, D_i, for product i be less than or equal to α_i, where α_i is set by management policy. Assume D_i is a random variable with known probability distribution $f_i(D_i)$. Then our constraint is

$$P\{D_i \leq X_i\} \leq \alpha_i$$

or

$$\int_{-\infty}^{X_i} f_i(D_i) \, dD_i \equiv F_i(X_i) \leq \alpha_i \qquad (3\text{-}2)$$

where $F_i(D_i)$ is the cumulative probability distribution of demand.

If the demand forecast is μ_i and forecast errors are normally distributed about zero with a variance σ_i^2, then we take $f_i(D_i) = n(D_i; \mu_i, \sigma_i^2)$. Using $\Phi(z)$ to denote the cumulative standard normal distribution, the constraint (3-2) is now

$$\Phi\left(\frac{X_i - \mu_i}{\sigma_i}\right) \leq \alpha_i \qquad (3\text{-}3)$$

Let z_α be a value of the standard normal variable such that $\Phi(z_\alpha) = \alpha$. Because $\Phi(z)$ is monotone increasing in z, we can write (3-3) as

$$\frac{X_i - \mu_i}{\sigma_i} \leq z_{\alpha_i}$$

or

$$X_i \leq \mu_i + z_{\alpha_i}\sigma_i \qquad (3\text{-}4)$$

Note that the constraint (3-4) is a linear inequality and could therefore be used in a linear programming formulation. Notice also that it is of the form $X_i \leq U_i$, and thus, in effect, we have described a method for determining U_i.

For a numerical illustration, reconsider Example 3-1 and suppose that the demand forecast for product 4 is 1000 and it is known that the forecasting procedure yields unbiased forecasts with normally distributed errors having a standard deviation of 100. For various reasons (such as style obsolescence, perishability, and storage cost), management is willing to run only a small risk of using their limited resources to produce more of product 4 than can be sold in the period. Suppose they select $\alpha = 0.10$. They are requiring

$$\Phi\left(\frac{X_4 - 1000}{100}\right) \leq 0.10$$
$$X_4 \leq 1000 + z_{0 \cdot 10}(100)$$

From Table A-2 in the Appendix, we find $z_{0 \cdot 10} = -1.282$, and the upper bound constraint for product 4 is

$$X_4 \leq 872$$

When we add constraints of the form (3-2) to the model (3-1), they replace the upper bound constraints (3-1c). The objective function is not modified, even though the actual contribution to profit and overhead during the period will be a random variable. In using the original objective function, we do not explicitly consider the "losses" associated with overproduction; instead, we treat them by setting maximum probabilities of overproduction. Naturally, the question arises about how well management can select values for the $\{\alpha_i\}$. Since this is done subjectively, there is no assurance that their choices will result in a decision that will maximize the expected contribution to profit and overhead.

A more direct approach would be to try to maximize the expected value of Z, which, assuming overproduction can be disposed of for a unit value $r' < r$, is

$$E(Z) = \sum_{i=1}^{n} \left[(r_i - c_i)X_i - (r_i - r_i') \int_0^{X_i} (X_i - D_i) f_i(D_i) \, dD_i \right]$$

subject to the resource constraints

$$\sum_{i=1}^{n} a_{ik}X_i \leq b_k, \qquad (k = 1, 2, \ldots, K)$$

Note that $E(Z)$ is the original objective function (3-1a), less the expected "loss" from disposing of excess production at a lower price. This model will be developed more carefully in the next example; for now, we only want to point out that $E(Z)$ is nonlinear in the $\{X_i\}$ and thus the problem must be solved by nonlinear programming methods. We treat the case when there is only one resource constraint in Example 3-3.

If the problem is not too large, one may be able to use one of the approaches

Production Planning—Static Models   **112**

to stochastic programming to explicitly treat uncertainty about demand. The interested reader should see Chapter 16 in Reference 15 or Chapter 5 in Reference 4.□

□EXAMPLE 3-3 *A Probabilistic Model with a Single Resource Constraint.* Consider the problem of a merchandise manager for a department store who must purchase items for a special sale. He is considering n different items for stock, but is not certain of the sales potential (demand) for any item. In establishing his inventory levels prior to the start of the sale, he cannot exceed his budget of B dollars. The sale is of short duration, so there is no opportunity to reorder. We might model his problem by letting

X_i = initial stock level of item i

c_i = unit procurement cost of item i

r_i = unit selling price of item i, if sold during the sale

r_i' = unit disposal value of item i, if not sold during the sale

D_i = the demand for item i during the sale, a random variable having probability distribution $f_i(D_i)$

Z = the contribution to profit and overhead from the sale

For a given decision about the $\{X_i\}$ and a given realization of the $\{D_i\}$ during the sale, the quantity of item i sold would be

$$\phi(X_i, D_i) = \min(X_i, D_i),$$

the quantity remaining at the end of the period would be

$$\xi(X_i, D_i) = \max(X_i - D_i, 0),$$

and the payoff from the sale would be

$$Z = \sum_{i=1}^{n} [r_i \phi(X_i, D_i) + r_i' \xi(X_i, D_i) - c_i X_i]$$

If we assume the product demands are mutually independent random variables, the expected contribution to profit and overhead would be

$$
\begin{aligned}
E(Z) &= \sum_{i=1}^{n} \left\{ \int_0^{\infty} [r_i \phi(X_i, D_i) + r' \xi(X_i, D_i)] f_i(D_i)\, dD_i - c_i X_i \right\} \\
&= \sum_{i=1}^{n} \left\{ r_i \left[\int_0^{X_i} D_i f_i(D_i)\, dD_i + X_i \int_{X_i}^{\infty} f_i(D_i)\, dD_i \right] \right. \\
&\qquad \left. + r_i' \int_0^{X_i} (X_i - D_i) f_i(D_i)\, dD_i - c_i X_i \right\} \\
&= \sum_{i=1}^{n} \left\{ (r_i - c_i) X_i + (r_i - r_i') \left[\int_0^{X_i} D_i f_i(D_i)\, dD_i - X_i F_i(X_i) \right] \right\} \quad \text{(3-5)}
\end{aligned}
$$

If there were no budget constraint, we could solve the equations, $\partial E(Z)/\partial X_i = 0$, $i = 1, 2, \ldots n$, for the optimal order quantities, $\{X_i^*\}$. Doing this, we would obtain the condition

$$F_i(X_i^*) \equiv \int_0^{X_i^*} f_i(D_i)\, dD_i = \frac{r_i - c_i}{r_i - r_i'}; \qquad i = 1, 2, \ldots, n \qquad (3\text{-}6)$$

We would be treating each product independently, just as in Section 2-5. However, the problem here is to maximize (3-5) subject to the constraint

$$\sum_{i=1}^{n} c_i X_i \leq B \qquad (3\text{-}7)$$

The approach is to use (3-6) to obtain a solution, ignoring the constraint (3-7), and then determine if this solution satisfies the constraint. If so, that solution is optimal; otherwise, the constraint must be explicitly considered using the Lagrange multiplier method described in Section 2-3.

In the latter case where the constraint is active, we form the Lagrangian,

$$L(X_1, \ldots, X_n, \lambda) = E(Z) - \lambda \left[\sum_{i=1}^{n} c_i X_i - B \right]$$

and solve the $n + 1$ equations,

$$\frac{\partial L}{\partial X_i} = r_i - c_i - (r_i - r_i')F_i(X_i) - \lambda c_i = 0; \qquad i = 1, 2, \ldots, n$$

$$\frac{\partial L}{\partial \lambda} = -\left[\sum_{i=1}^{n} c_i X_i - B \right] = 0$$

resulting in

$$F(X_i^*) = \frac{r_i - (1 + \lambda^*)c_i}{r_i - r_i'}; \qquad i = 1, 2, \ldots, n \qquad (3\text{-}8\text{a})$$

$$\sum_{i=1}^{n} c_i X_i^* = B \qquad (3\text{-}8\text{b})$$

Probably the best way to obtain the solution from this point is to try values for λ^* in (3-8a) until a set $\{X_i^*\}$ is obtained that satisfies (3-8b). The optimal value for the Lagrange multiplier can be interpreted as the increase in $E(Z)$ to result from a unit increase in B. Compare (3-8a) with (3-6) to see how assigning a positive value to λ forces the solution to conform to the budget constraint.

In the case of discrete demand, one may use marginal analysis [see Hanssmann (6)] or dynamic programming methods (see literature under the "multiproduct newsboy problem," the "knapsack problem," and the "flyaway kit problem").

When there are multiple resource constraints, the problem is more difficult and will not be considered here. Discussion of the current state of stochastic programming is beyond the intended scope of our text.□

3-3 Process Selection Problems

In this common type of problem, there are fixed production requirements for each of a number of products during a period. Each product may have several alternative ways (sources, routings, and processes) by which it can be produced. The unit costs and resources utilized will depend on the process selected. Each production resource has a given limited availability in the period, and the various products will compete for this capacity according to the particular production processes selected for each product. The problem is to determine how much of each product to make by each process to minimize production costs, subject to constraints imposed by resource limitations and the requirement that given total amounts of each product be produced. Note that, because production requirements are given, revenue is not a consideration, and hence cost minimization is an appropriate objective.

To formulate an algebraic model, let

X_{ij} = quantity of product i, $i = 1, 2, \ldots, n$, produced by process j, $j = 1, 2, \ldots, J_i$, in the period

D_i = required production of product i in the period

b_k = amount of resource k, $k = 1, 2, \ldots, K$, available in the period

a_{ijk} = number of units of resource k used to produce one unit of product i by process j

c_{ij} = unit variable cost of producing one unit of product i by process j

Z = total production cost in the period

We wish to choose the $\{X_{ij}\}$ to minimize

$$Z = \sum_{i=1}^{n} \sum_{j=1}^{J_i} c_{ij} X_{ij} \tag{3-9a}$$

subject to

$$\sum_{j=1}^{J_i} X_{ij} = D_i \tag{3-9b}$$

$$\sum_{i=1}^{n} \sum_{j=1}^{J_i} a_{ijk} X_{ij} \leq b_k \tag{3-9c}$$

$$X_{ij} \geq 0 \tag{3-9d}$$

for all i, j, and k.

We now give two examples. Example 3-4 illustrates model (3-9) exactly, while Example 3-5 demonstrates how the process selection feature can be incorporated into a product mix model. This latter type of problem is perhaps the most common application of mathematical programming in industry.

$\square$**EXAMPLE 3-4** In the situation of Example 3-1, suppose that the production requirements for the four products were fixed at 3000, 500, 1000, and 2000 units, respectively. Exactly this amount of each product is to be fabricated in the month. The available regular time production hours are as shown in Table 3-1. Additionally, the stamping and drilling of parts for any product can be subcontracted, but this will add 20 percent to the product cost. Both the stamping and drilling operations are done by the subcontractor, who then ships the semifinished parts to the manufacturer for assembly, finishing, and packaging. If necessary, the manufacturer will operate his finishing department on overtime, up to a maximum of 100 machine hours during the month. However, this results in increasing the costs of products 1 and 3 by 20 cents per unit, product 2 by 40 cents per unit, and product 4 by 30 cents per unit. The sheet metal limitation of 2000 square feet for products 2 and 4 applies only to internally stamped and drilled production.

The objective is to meet the production goals at minimum cost. The decision variables are the quantities of each product to be produced by each process, or routing. There are four processes: (1) internal stamping, regular time finishing; (2) internal stamping, overtime finishing; (3) subcontracting, regular time finishing; and (4) subcontracting, overtime finishing. We must identify these different processes because unit costs and resources consumed differ between them. For example, the unit costs of product 1 by the four processes are $6.00, $6.20, $7.20, and $7.40, respectively. Let X_{ij} be the number of units of product i produced by process j. The problem is to minimize

$$Z = 6.0X_{11} + 6.2X_{12} + 7.2X_{13} + 7.4X_{14} + 15.0X_{21} + 15.4X_{22}$$
$$+ 18.0X_{23} + 18.4X_{24} + 11.0X_{31} + 11.2X_{32} + 13.2X_{33} + 13.4X_{34}$$
$$+ 14.0X_{41} + 14.3X_{42} + 16.8X_{43} + 17.1X_{44}$$

subject to

(1) constraints on regular time capacity:

$$\sum_{j=1}^{2}(0.03X_{1j} + 0.15X_{2j} + 0.05X_{3j} + 0.10X_{4j}) \leq 400$$

$$\sum_{j=1}^{2}(0.06X_{1j} + 0.12X_{2j} + 0.10X_{4j}) \leq 400$$

$$\sum_{j=1}^{4}(0.05X_{1j} + 0.10X_{2j} + 0.05X_{3j} + 0.12X_{4j}) \leq 500$$

$$0.04(X_{11} + X_{13}) + 0.20(X_{21} + X_{23})$$
$$+ 0.03(X_{31} + X_{33}) + 0.12(X_{41} + X_{43}) \leq 450$$

$$\sum_{j=1}^{4}(0.02X_{1j} + 0.06X_{2j} + 0.02X_{3j} + 0.05X_{4j}) \leq 400$$

TABLE 3-3 Optimal Production Plan for Example 3-4

PRODUCTION CENTER	PRODUCT 1	PRODUCT 2	PRODUCT 3	PRODUCT 4
1. Stamping, internal	3000	0	1000	1667
2. Drilling, internal	3000	0	1000	1667
3. Stamping and drilling, subcontracted	0	500	0	333
4. Assembly	3000	500	1000	2000
5. Finishing: regular time	3000	300	1000	2000
overtime	0	200	0	0
6. Packaging	3000	500	1000	2000

(2) constraint on overtime finishing capacity:

$$0.04(X_{12} + X_{14}) + 0.20(X_{22} + X_{24})$$
$$+ 0.03(X_{32} + X_{34}) + 0.12(X_{42} + X_{44}) \leq 100$$

(3) constraint on sheet metal availability:

$$2.0(X_{21} + X_{22}) + 1.2(X_{41} + X_{42}) \leq 2000$$

(4) constraints on quantities required:

$$X_{11} + X_{12} + X_{13} + X_{14} = 3000$$
$$X_{21} + X_{22} + X_{23} + X_{24} = 500$$
$$X_{31} + X_{32} + X_{33} + X_{34} = 1000$$
$$X_{41} + X_{42} + X_{43} + X_{44} = 2000$$

(We point out that there are other ways to define the decision variables in this problem that would result in a slightly different formulation. They involve treating the system as a multistage process, and we wait until Section 3-8 to discuss this further.)

The solution is $X_{11}^* = 3000$, $X_{23}^* = 300$, $X_{24}^* = 200$, $X_{31}^* = 1000$, $X_{41}^* = 1667$, and $X_{43}^* = 333$. All other variables are zero. Table 3-3 organizes these results into a more easily comprehended form. The cost of this program is $67,013.

The utilization of production capacity is shown in Table 3-4.

All 2000 square feet of sheet metal are used in producing product 4. This causes all of product 2 and some of product 4 to be procured from the subcontractor.

The values of the dual variables corresponding to the regular time finishing capacity constraint and the sheet metal constraint are 2.00 and 2.33, respectively. This means that an extra hour of regular time finishing capacity would permit

TABLE 3-4 Optimal Utilization of Capacity in Example 3-4

	REGULAR TIME HOURS			OVERTIME HOURS		
DEPARTMENT	AVAIL-ABLE	SCHEDULED	UNUSED	AVAIL-ABLE	SCHEDULED	UNUSED
Stamping	400	306.7	93.3	0	0	0
Drilling	400	346.7	53.3	0	0	0
Assembly	500	490.0	10.0	0	0	0
Finishing	450	450.0	0	100	40.0	60.0
Packaging	400	210.0	190.0	0	0	0

a $2 reduction in total cost and that an extra square foot of sheet metal would result in a $2.33 reduction in total cost.□

□**EXAMPLE 3-5** *Product Mix Decisions with Alternative Production Sources.* Now we combine the decisions of Examples 3-1 and 3-4 into one problem. We suppose that fixed production requirements are not given, but instead that the sales opportunities and minimum production levels of Table 3-2 are the constraints. The goal is maximization of contribution to profit and overhead, as in Example 3-1, but we must consider the production alternatives described in Example 3-4. The decision variables are the same as in Example 3-4; however, the objective function, to be *maximized*, is now

$$Z = 4.0X_{11} + 3.8X_{12} + 2.8X_{13} + 2.6X_{14} + 10.0X_{21} + 9.6X_{22}$$
$$+ 7.0X_{23} + 6.6X_{24} + 5.0X_{31} + 4.8X_{32} + 2.8X_{33} + 2.6X_{34}$$
$$+ 6.0X_{41} + 5.7X_{42} + 3.2X_{43} + 2.9X_{44}$$

With the exception of the last four constraints on production requirements, the constraints for this problem include all those of Example 3-4. In place of the fixed production requirements constraints, we add the following (from Example 3-1):

$$1000 \le \sum_{j=1}^{4} X_{1j} \le 6000$$

$$0 \le \sum_{j=1}^{4} X_{2j} \le 500$$

$$500 \le \sum_{j=1}^{4} X_{3j} \le 3000$$

$$100 \le \sum_{j=1}^{4} X_{4j} \le 1000$$

TABLE 3-5 Optimal Production Plan for Example 3-5

PRODUCTION CENTER	PRODUCT 1	PRODUCT 2	PRODUCT 3	PRODUCT 4
1. Stamping, internal	5500	500	3000	100
2. Drilling, internal	5500	500	3000	100
3. Stamping and drilling, subcontracted	260	0	0	0
4. Assembly	5760	500	3000	100
5. Finishing: regular time	5760	500	3000	100
overtime	0	0	0	0
6. Packaging	5760	500	3000	100
Total planned production	5760	500	3000	100

TABLE 3-6 Optimal Utilization of Capacity in Example 3-5

DEPARTMENT	REGULAR TIME HOURS AVAILABLE	SCHEDULED	UNUSED	OVERTIME HOURS AVAILABLE	SCHEDULED	UNUSED	DUAL VARIABLE
Stamping	400	400.0	0	0	0	0	6.67
Drilling	400	400.0	0	0	0	0	16.67
Assembly	500	500.0	0	0	0	0	56.00
Finishing	450	432.4	17.6	100	0	100	0
Packaging	400	210.2	189.8	0	0	0	0

The solution to this product mix problem is $X_{11}^* = 5500$, $X_{13}^* = 260$, $X_{21}^* = 500$, $X_{31}^* = 3000$, $X_{41}^* = 100$, and $Z_{max} = \$43,328$. Tables 3-5 and 3-6 display the solution more clearly. Only 1120 square feet of sheet metal are used by this program.□

3-4 Blending Problems

This type of problem occurs when a production process involves blending (mixing) several raw materials to make a product conforming to given specifications, and there are a number of alternative combinations (blends) of these materials that will produce an acceptable product. Since the materials have different properties, resulting in their making differing contributions toward meeting the specifications, and have different unit costs, the problem is to determine the least-cost blend of materials that will result in a satisfactory product. The available quantities of the raw materials, as well as the product specifications, create constraints in obtaining the optimal blend. The solution to the problem gives the quantity of each material to be mixed to produce one unit of product.

Some examples are blending of crude oils in the petroleum industry, mineral-bearing ores in the production of metals and alloys, cotton or wool fibers in the textile industry, ingredients in the food-processing industry, and minerals in the production of fertilizers.

To formulate a mathematical model of a blending problem, suppose there are n different materials and m specifications on the properties of the finished product. To arrive at a linear programming model, we must assume that the level of attainment of each property is a linear function of the quantity of each material used. Also, the cost per unit of product must be a linear function of the quantity of each material in the blend. Let

X_j = quantity of material j used per unit of product

c_j = unit cost of material j

a_{ij} = contribution of a unit of material j to the value of property i of the product

b_i = specification on property i of the product

Z = total material cost per unit of product

The problem is to choose nonnegative $X_1, X_2, \ldots, X_n$ to minimize

$$Z = \sum_{j=1}^{n} c_j X_j \qquad (3\text{-}10\text{a})$$

subject to

$$\sum_{j=1}^{n} a_{ij} X_j \begin{Bmatrix} \leq \\ = \\ \geq \end{Bmatrix} b_i, \qquad (i = 1, 2, \ldots, m) \qquad (3\text{-}10\text{b})$$

$$\sum_{j=1}^{n} X_j = 1 \qquad (3\text{-}10\text{c})$$

If the process is such that some of material j is removed and discarded during production, we let d_j be the fraction of a unit of input of material j contained in a unit of finished product and modify (3-10c) to read

$$\sum_{j=1}^{n} d_j X_j = 1 \qquad (3\text{-}10\text{d})$$

Blending problems are characterized by a constraint of the form (3-10c) or (3-10d).

TABLE 3-7 Data for Example 3-6

ORE	METAL A	METAL B	METAL C	METAL D	IMPURITIES	COST/TON
1	25%	10%	10%	25%	30%	$23
2	40	0	0	30	30	20
3	20	10	0	30	40	18
4	0	15	5	20	60	10
5	20	20	0	40	20	27
6	8	5	10	17	60	12

☐**EXAMPLE 3-6** A producer of metal alloys has a special order from a customer to produce an alloy containing four metals, according to the following specifications: metal A, at least 23 percent; metal B, no more than 15 percent; metal C, no more than 4 percent; and metal D, between 35 and 65 percent. No other components are allowed. The producer has access to several grades of ore from which the metals may be refined. Table 3-7 contains information about the composition of each ore and its selling price. The impurities in the ores will be removed in processing.

Let X_j be the number of tons of ore $j, j = 1, 2, \ldots, 6$, used per ton of alloy. We wish to minimize the total cost per ton of alloy,

$$Z = 23X_1 + 20X_2 + 18X_3 + 10X_4 + 27X_5 + 12X_6$$

subject to

(1) specifications on the metal content:

$$0.25X_1 + 0.40X_2 + 0.20X_3 + 0.20X_5 + 0.08X_6 \geq 0.23$$
$$0.10X_1 + 0.10X_3 + 0.15X_4 + 0.20X_5 + 0.05X_6 \leq 0.15$$
$$0.10X_1 + 0.05X_4 + 0.10X_6 \leq 0.04$$
$$0.25X_1 + 0.30X_2 + 0.30X_3 + 0.20X_4 + 0.40X_5 + 0.17X_6 \geq 0.35$$
$$0.25X_1 + 0.30X_2 + 0.30X_3 + 0.20X_4 + 0.40X_5 + 0.17X_6 \leq 0.65$$

(2) material balance constraint:

$$0.70X_1 + 0.70X_2 + 0.60X_3 + 0.40X_4 + 0.80X_5 + 0.40X_6 = 1.00$$

The solution is $X_2^* = 0.9714, X_4^* = 0.8000$, and $X_1^* = X_3^* = X_5^* = X_6^* = 0$. We should use 0.9714 ton of ore 2 and 0.80 ton of ore 4 in making one ton of the alloy. The cost per ton is $Z^* = \$27.43$. The constraint on the maximum amount (4 percent) of metal C in the alloy is active. The value of the dual variable for this constraint is 28.57.☐

Blending Problems   121

3-5 Simultaneous Production of Multiple Products by a Single Activity

A special type of process selection problem involves choosing the manner in which a number of products will be produced from a common material simultaneously by one or more operations. Processing crude oil into petroleum products, crushing stone with a mix of sizes resulting, cutting of apparel parts from the same spread of cloth, and stamping or cutting multiple parts from sheet metal are examples. In this section, we give a general algebraic statement of the problem and an application to cutting rolls of paper in the paper industry.

Let X_j be the quantity of material processed by method j, $j = 1, 2, \ldots, n$, and D_i be the required quantity of product i, $i = 1, 2, \ldots, m$. One unit of material processed by method j will yield a_{ij} units of product i and will cost c_j. The problem is to meet the requirements at minimum cost. Formally, we wish to choose nonnegative $X_1, X_2, \ldots, X_n$ to minimize

$$Z = \sum_{j=1}^{n} c_j X_j \qquad (3\text{-}11\text{a})$$

subject to

$$\sum_{j=1}^{n} a_{ij} X_j \geq D_i, \qquad (i = 1, 2, \ldots, m) \qquad (3\text{-}11\text{b})$$

If relevant, constraints on the amount of material that can be processed by the various methods could be added. Also, there is a "product mix" version of this problem, where the objective is to maximize the value from processing a given amount of material. (See Exercise 3-20.)

☐**EXAMPLE 3-7 Cutting Rolls of Paper.** (This problem is commonly described in operations research texts under the heading "stock slitting.") A paper company has machines that produce large rolls of paper of a given diameter and width, say 200 inches. To fill customer orders, these large rolls must be cut (slit) into narrower widths. The particular widths required will vary from period to period, depending on the nature of customer orders. Suppose that at a given point in time, there is a need for 500 45-inch wide rolls, 300 24-inch wide rolls, and 200 60-inch wide rolls. A plan must be developed for cutting the standard (wide) rolls to meet this demand for the narrower widths. A listing of logical alternative patterns for cutting a standard 200-inch roll is given in Table 3-8. For example, pattern 2 involves cutting three 24-inch widths and two 60-inch widths, leaving 8 inches of waste from the original standard roll.

Let X_j denote the number of standard rolls cut by pattern j. If we assume that

TABLE 3-8 Cutting Patterns for Example 3-7

	CUTTING PATTERN											
	1	2	3	4	5	6	7	8	9	10	11	12
45-inch widths	0	0	1	0	1	2	3	0	1	2	3	4
24-inch widths	0	3	1	5	3	2	0	8	6	4	2	0
60-inch widths	3	2	2	1	1	1	1	0	0	0	0	0
End waste (inches)	20	8	11	20	23	2	5	8	11	14	17	20

any extra 45-, 24-, or 60-inch widths must be thrown away, along with the end waste, our objective is to minimize the number of standard rolls cut in filling the order,

$$Z = \sum_{j=1}^{12} X_j$$

subject to

$$X_3 + X_5 + 2X_6 + 3X_7 + X_9 + 2X_{10} + 3X_{11} + 4X_{12} \geq 500$$
$$3X_2 + X_3 + 5X_4 + 3X_5 + 2X_6 + 8X_8 + 6X_9 + 4X_{10} + 2X_{11} \geq 300$$
$$3X_1 + 2X_2 + 2X_3 + X_4 + X_5 + X_6 + X_7 \geq 200$$
$$X_j \geq 0, \quad (j = 1, 2, \ldots, 12)$$

Actually, X_j must be an integer, but since a large number of rolls will be cut, we assume that solving the linear programming problem and rounding the solution to the next highest integer will be a satisfactory approach. The solution to this linear programming model is $X_6^* = 150$, $X_7^* = 50$, and $X_{12}^* = 12.5$. Probably by rounding the number of rolls to be cut by pattern 12 upward to 13, we would have an optimal or near-optimal integer solution.

Sometimes you see this problem formulated with the objective of minimizing the sum of the total inches of end waste and the total inches of width of extra rolls produced in excess of requirements. For our example, let w_j be the inches of end waste from pattern j and s_i be the overproduction in pieces of width i (s_i is the surplus variable for constraint i). We minimize

$$Z' = \sum_{j=1}^{12} w_j X_j + 45s_1 + 24s_2 + 60s_3$$

Obviously minimization of Z' is equivalent to minimization of Z, above, since $200Z$ exceeds Z' by a constant equal to the total inches of width ordered:

$$(500)(45) + (300)(24) + (200)(60) = 41,700 \qquad \square$$

Simultaneous Production of Multiple Products by a Single Activity   123

3-6 Single-Facility Lot-Size Models

The models and examples given in previous sections of this chapter have contained only linear production cost functions having no fixed component. That is, the cost, $C(X)$, of producing X units of a product was assumed to have the form

$$C(X) = cX \qquad (3\text{-}12)$$

rather than the "fixed charge" structure

$$C(X) = \begin{cases} 0, & \text{if } X = 0 \\ A + cX, & \text{if } X > 0 \end{cases} \qquad (3\text{-}13)$$

When there are significant setup costs and (3-13) is appropriate, the production planning problem is more difficult to model and analyze. In this section we study a simple multiproduct production problem having a single resource constraint and requiring consideration of setup costs. Additional treatment of setup costs is contained in Section 3-8.5 (multistage lot-size models), Exercise 3-10 (mixed-integer programming models), and Chapter 4 (dynamic programming and network models). Example 4-16 gives an interesting linear programming application where the consumption of a resource, labor hours, is related to the production level, X, by a form similar to (3-13).

For now, consider the case of a single production facility that produces n products. Product j is demanded at the constant rate of D_j units per unit time and can be produced at the rate of P_j units per unit time. We assume $P_j > D_j$, so that production of product j will be intermittant (in lots). Also we assume that $\sum_{j=1}^{n} D_j/P_j \leq 1$, which means that the facility has the capacity to meet the demand for all n products (why?). The unit variable cost is c_j, the setup cost is A_j, and the inventory carrying-cost rate is i per dollar of inventory per unit time. No shortages are to be permitted. The problem is to determine when and how much of each product to produce.

Suppose, because of our background in studying Chapter 2, particularly Section 2-2, we decide to adopt the policy of a constant lot size, X_j, for each product j. Then, following Equation 2-22, our total cost per unit time would be

$$K(X_1, X_2, \ldots, X_n) = \sum_{j=1}^{n} \left[\frac{A_j D_j}{X_j} + c_j D_j + i c_j \frac{X_j}{2} \left(1 - \frac{D_j}{P_j} \right) \right] \qquad (3\text{-}14)$$

Solving $\partial K/\partial X_j = 0$, we would obtain

$$X_j^* = \sqrt{\frac{2 A_j D_j}{i c_j (1 - D_j/P_j)}}, \qquad j = 1, 2, \ldots, n \qquad (3\text{-}15)$$

which is Equation 2-23. However, if we used this formula to determine the lot sizes, we undoubtedly would find that they could not be scheduled on the single facility without incurring shortages. Certainly, this is to be expected, since our analysis to this point has ignored the resource constraint of a single facility. The above approach is not correct unless the products are produced on separate facilities and do not compete for capacity.

However, by using a *rotation cycle* policy, we can conveniently arrive at lot sizes that are easily scheduled to avoid shortages. In a rotation cycle, all products have the same cycle time, T, and during an interval of length T, a lot of each product is produced on the facility. The products are run in a fixed sequence ("rotation"), which is repeated from cycle to cycle. Since no shortages are permitted, the lot size for product j must equal the demand during the cycle; that is,

$$X_j = TD_j \tag{3-16}$$

Substituting the constraint (3-16) into the objective function (3-14), we obtain the following expression for the average cost per unit time:

$$K(T) = \sum_{j=1}^{n} \left[\frac{A_j}{T} + c_j D_j + ic_j \frac{TD_j}{2} \left(1 - \frac{D_j}{P_j} \right) \right] \tag{3-17}$$

It is easy to show that $K(T)$ is minimized by

$$T^* = \sqrt{ \frac{ 2 \sum_{j=1}^{n} A_j }{ i \sum_{j=1}^{n} c_j D_j (1 - D_j/P_j) } } \tag{3-18}$$

However, before we can adopt T^* as our cycle length, we must consider the time required for setups during the cycle. Suppose the setup time for product j is s_j. Since the total setup time per cycle plus the total production time per cycle must be no more than the cycle length, we have the following constraint on T:

$$\sum_{j=1}^{n} \left(s_j + \frac{X_j}{P_j} \right) \le T$$

or, using $X_j = TD_j$,

$$T \ge \frac{ \sum_{j=1}^{n} s_j }{ 1 - \sum_{j=1}^{n} (D_j/P_j) } \equiv T_{\min} \tag{3-19}$$

Notice that the denominator of (3-19) is the fraction of time the facility will not be producing. Since $K(T)$ is convex in T, we should use a cycle time equal to the maximum of T^* and $T_{\min}$. To see this, observe from Figure 3-1, that if $T_{\min}$

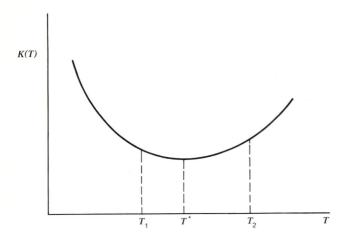

$K(T)$

T_1 T^* T_2 T

FIGURE 3-1. Optimal rotation cycle determination.

is at a point $T_1 < T^*$, T^* is feasible and hence the solution; however, if $T_{\min}$ is at $T_2 > T^*$, T^* is not feasible and $T_{\min}$ gives the lowest cost of all feasible T.

If the setup costs and times are sequence-dependent, the problem of determining the optimal rotation cycle length is somewhat more difficult. Substitution of (3-18) into (3-17) reveals that we can choose the sequence of products (within the cycle) that minimizes the sum of the setup costs during the cycle, and the resulting T^* will minimize $K(T)$.[1] As long as $T^* > T_{\min}$, where $T_{\min}$ depends on the sequence chosen through the sum of the setup times, this is the correct approach. However, if $T^* < T_{\min}$, and another sequence having a larger total setup cost yields a smaller total setup time per cycle, further investigation must be carried out by trading off increases in $\sum A_j$ with decreases in $\sum s_j$ (and hence $T_{\min}$). Fortunately, setup costs often are proportional to setup times and no problem is encountered.

Once we have determined the cycle length, we use (3-16) to find the lot sizes. Example 3-8 illustrates the method and demonstrates that it is possible to schedule the facility so that no shortages occur.

The requirement that a rotation cycle be used changed the original problem to a form that was easy to solve. In general, however, we are not constrained to a rotation cycle. The principal reasons for deviating from it are large differences among the demand rates of the various products and among their setup times or setup costs. There is no universal solution procedure for this more general problem. [For an early theoretical discussion, see Maxwell (11). Practical approaches are given in Magee and Boodman (9).]

[1] The problem of choosing the optimal sequence when setup costs are sequence dependent is a "traveling salesman" problem, whose solution methodology is given in Section 5-2.6.

TABLE 3-9 Data for Example 3-8

PRODUCT	ANNUAL DEMAND	PRODUCTION RATE (UNITS/YEAR)	SETUP COST	SETUP TIME (YEARS)	VARIABLE COST/UNIT
A	3000	10,000	$50	0.001	$10
B	2000	5,000	70	0.002	15
C	5000	50,000	120	0.005	5
D	1000	10,000	80	0.003	20

It may not be important to search for solutions different from that found requiring a rotation cycle. If we were to go one step beyond dropping the rotation cycle constraint and also drop the constraint on facility capacity, we would be assuming in effect that each product is made on a different facility and could determine the lot sizes by (3-15), which was derived assuming complete independence of the products. Substituting (3-15) into (3-14) gives the cost of the "independent" solution. The cost of the best rotation cycle solution is found by evaluating (3-17) for the optimal cycle length. The cost of the best solution to the true problem (having only the single facility capacity constraint) lies somewhere between that of the rotation cycle and that of the independent solution. If this range is small, we cannot improve much by deviating from the rotation cycle.

☐ **EXAMPLE 3-8** Four products are manufactured on the same facility. Relevant data are given in Table 3-9. The inventory carrying-cost rate is 20 percent annually. No shortages are to be permitted.

Before finding the optimal rotation cycle, we verify that it is possible to meet the demand by computing $\sum (D_j/P_j) = 0.90$. This means that the facility must run 90 percent of the time, with the remaining 10 percent available for setups, maintenance, etc. Since the sum of the setup times is $\sum s_j = 0.011$, the minimum cycle length is $T_{min} = 0.011/0.10 = 0.11$ year.

Using Equation 3-18, we obtain

$$T^* = \sqrt{\frac{(2)(320)}{15,900}} = 0.20$$

Because $T^* > T_{min}$, we choose our cycle length to be 0.20 year. The associated lot sizes are, from (3-16), $X_1^* = 600$, $X_2^* = 400$, $X_3^* = 1000$, and $X_4^* = 200$. Using (3-17), we find that the average annual cost using the optimal rotation cycle is $K(0.20) = \$108,190$.

The reader can verify that if we assumed independence of the products and used Equation 3-15, we would obtain lot sizes of 453, 394, 1155, and 211, respectively. The total average annual cost would be $108,158, from (3-14).

Single-Facility Lot-Size Models   127

However, it is not possible to use these lot sizes on a single facility without incurring shortages. Imposing the constraint of a single facility would cause the cost to increase above $108,158, but not more than the $108,190 cost of the rotation cycle. Since the range is only $42, there is no incentive to attempt finding a better feasible solution than the rotation cycle.

The ease of scheduling a rotation cycle can be observed by studying Figure 3-2, where we have plotted the inventory behavior of the four products during

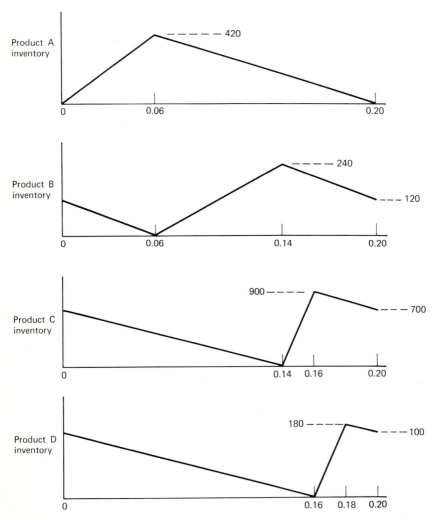

FIGURE 3-2. Behavior of inventory levels of the four products in Example 3-8. (Setup times are not shown.)

a cycle, assuming that they are produced in the order A–B–C–D. From the start of the cycle (time zero) to 0.06, the facility is producing A; from 0.06 to 0.14, B; from 0.14 to 0.16, C; from 0.16 to 0.18, D; and from 0.18 to 0.20, the facility is idle. (For convenience, we did not show the setup times in Figure 3-2 or include them in the immediately preceding description of the utilization of the facility. The reader should note that the effect of setup times on Figure 3-2 is to shift the start of production to the right for each product.)□

3-7 Multiperiod Production Planning Under Static Probabilistic Demand

In Section 2-6, we considered the problem of planning the procurement of a single item when there is one opportunity to reorder in each of a sequence of identical-length periods and the demand in any period is a random variable generated by a stationary stochastic process. Initially we formulated a dynamic programming model of the finite planning horizon problem and then extended it to the infinite horizon case. We pointed out that, for certain commonly assumed cost structures, an (R, r, T) inventory policy is optimal. The (R, r, T) policy requires that the inventory be reviewed every T units of time and action taken only if the inventory position is r or less, in which case an order should be placed equal to the difference between R and the current inventory position. It was also pointed out that an (R, T) policy, which is an (R, r, T) policy with $r = R$, is optimal if there is no fixed cost of ordering and if variable procurement costs are convex. We presented an approximate solution procedure for the (R, r) policy for the infinite horizon case.

In this section, we extend that treatment of periodic review policies by showing how linear programming can be used to determine optimal values of the policy variables when demand and lot sizes are discrete, and by describing how one can explicitly model the effect of a delay in filling customer orders on the probability distribution of demand.[2]

3-7.1 Markov Models and Optimal Periodic Review Policies

We are to develop a policy for producing (to inventory) an item whose demand is expected to continue indefinitely. The policy calls for reviewing the

[2] This material might well have been placed in Chapter 2; however, because of the length of that chapter and the methodology used, we decided to put it here. The reader should be able to follow the presentation without having studied Chapter 2.

inventory position every T units of time, where the period length, T, is given. At any review point, say the start of period t, a production order may be placed, and we assume that the lot is completed in time to be used to satisfy that period's demand, if necessary. We also suppose that there is no backlogging, that is, all shortages are lost; that demand in a period is a discrete random variable, D, having probability distribution $p(D)$; that the maximum inventory level permitted or needed is L; and that consequently only a finite set of values will be considered for the production lot size, X, in any period.

The state variable of the system is the on-hand inventory, I. The production decision at the start of a period will depend on the inventory level at that time. Thus, we might seek a policy, $X(I)$, which gives the appropriate production quantity for every possible value of I. For example, the policy might state, "If $I = 10$, produce $X = 40$ units." Such a decision rule is deterministic because, for a given I, it specifies a given X with certainty.

However, instead of a deterministic decision rule, we shall consider a *randomized decision rule*, $\delta(I)$, which assigns probabilities to the possible production levels. (For simplicity of notation, suppose X can be $0, 1, \ldots, L$.) Under a randomized policy, when the initial inventory is I, we produce X units in the period with probability $\delta(X \mid I)$, $X = 0, 1, \ldots, L$. The function $\delta(I)$ is an $(L + 1)$-component probability vector, having components $0 \le \delta(X \mid I) \le 1$, such that

$$\sum_{X=0}^{L} \delta(X \mid I) = 1$$

Use of a randomized decision rule requires that we employ a chance mechanism (for example, a random number table) in making our decision. The rule gives only the probabilities of choosing each action; however, these probabilities depend on the state variable, I.

To someone encountering the concept of a randomized rule for the first time, it may seem a ridiculuous way to make a decision. However, in certain situations in statistical decision theory and in game theory (where it is called a "mixed strategy"), a randomized rule may be quite logical and superior to any deterministic rule (called a "pure strategy" in game theory).[3] In spite of this, our intuition tells us that in this production planning situation, we should use a deterministic rule. This is, in fact, the case (and thankfully so, since trying to sell management on using a randomized rule for planning production would undoubtedly overtax the persuasive powers of the typical OR analyst). We introduce randomized rules only to aid in the development of a linear programming model, whose solution allows computation of the optimal decision function. It turns out that here this optimal decision rule will always be deterministic.

---

[3] Note that a deterministic rule is a special case of a randomized rule, where $\delta(X \mid I) = 1$, for some X, for every I.

To begin the model formulation, we note that the inventory behavior can be described by a discrete time, discrete state space Markov process. Let a_{ij} be the conditional probability that the inventory at the end of a period is j, given that the inventory at the start of the period (prior to ordering) is i, $(i, j = 0, 1, \ldots, L)$. The element a_{ij} is the probability of a transition from state i to state j during the period and is a function of the decision rule used for ordering and the probability distribution of demand during the period. The process is described by the *transition matrix* $\mathbf{A} = (a_{ij})$, which is an $(L + 1)$ by $(L + 1)$ stochastic matrix. We note that $0 \leq a_{ij} \leq 1$ and $\sum_{j=0}^{L} a_{ij} = 1$, for all i.

We can compute the transition probabilities from $p(D)$ and $\delta(I)$ by noting that to start with i units, produce X units, and end with $j > 0$ units, the demand must have been $D = i + X - j$ units. To end with $j = 0$ units, the demand must have been greater than or equal to $i + X$. Thus,

$$a_{ij} = \sum_{X=0}^{L} \delta(X \mid i)p(i + X - j), \qquad (i = 0, 1, \ldots, L; j = 1, 2, \ldots, L) \quad \text{(3-20a)}$$

$$a_{i0} = \sum_{X=0}^{L} \sum_{D=i+X}^{\infty} \delta(X \mid i)p(D), \qquad (i = 0, 1, \ldots, L) \quad \text{(3-20b)}$$

where in (3-20a), $p(D) = 0$, for $D < 0$.

We are interested in the steady-state probability distribution of the on-hand inventory. Let y_I be the probability that the inventory at the start (or end) of any period is I, and let $\mathbf{Y} = (y_0, y_1, \ldots, y_L)$. If we knew $\mathbf{A}$, we could compute the state probabilities from the equilibrium condition

$$\mathbf{YA} = \mathbf{Y} \tag{3-21}$$

or, writing out the steady-state equations:

$$y_0 a_{0j} + y_1 a_{1j} + \cdots + y_L a_{Lj} = y_j, \qquad (j = 0, 1, \ldots, L) \quad \text{(3-22a)}$$

These equations, of which only L are linearly independent, together with

$$y_0 + y_1 + \cdots + y_L = 1 \tag{3-22b}$$

can be solved for $\mathbf{Y}$.

Now we want to show how our randomized decision rules,

$$\boldsymbol{\Delta} = [\delta(0), \delta(1), \ldots, \delta(L)]$$

enter into the determination of $\mathbf{Y}$. Substituting (3-20) into (3-22a), we obtain

$$\sum_{I=0}^{L} y_I \sum_{X=0}^{L} \sum_{D=I+X}^{\infty} \delta(X \mid I)p(D) = y_0$$

$$\sum_{I=0}^{L} y_I \sum_{X=0}^{L} \delta(X \mid I)p(I + X - j) = y_j, \qquad (j = 1, 2, \ldots, L)$$

Let w_{IX} be the joint probability of starting with I units and deciding to produce X units. Then $w_{IX} = y_I \, \delta(X \mid I)$. Note that

$$\sum_{X=0}^{L} w_{IX} = y_I \sum_{X=0}^{L} \delta(X \mid I) = y_I$$

so that if the $\{w_{IX}\}$ are known,

$$\delta(X \mid I) = \frac{w_{IX}}{y_I} = \frac{w_{IX}}{\displaystyle\sum_{X=0}^{L} w_{IX}} \tag{3-23}$$

Substituting in the steady-state equations,

$$\sum_{I=0}^{L} \sum_{X=0}^{L} \sum_{D=I+X}^{\infty} w_{IX} p(D) = \sum_{X=0}^{L} w_{0X}$$

$$\sum_{I=0}^{L} \sum_{X=0}^{L} w_{IX} p(I + X - j) = \sum_{X=0}^{L} w_{jX}, \qquad (j = 1, 2, \ldots, L) \tag{3-24a}$$

Substituting in (3-22b),

$$\sum_{I=0}^{L} \sum_{X=0}^{L} w_{IX} = 1 \tag{3-24b}$$

Equations 3-24 constitute the linear relationships among the $\{w_{IX}\}$ in steady state. There are $L + 1$ independent constraints and L^2 variables. If we can express the objective function for our production planning problem as a linear equation in the $\{w_{IX}\}$, we can use linear programming methods to solve for their optimal values, subject to the constraints (3-24). Then we can employ (3-23) to obtain the optimal decision function for any I, $\delta^*(I)$, and hence Δ^*, the complete set of decision rules for all possible I. It can be shown that $\delta^*(I)$ will be a nonrandomized decision rule; that is, $\delta^*(X \mid I) = 1$, for some X, (4).

To formulate the objective function, suppose that production costs in a period are a function, $C(X)$, of the production level, X; inventory costs in a period are a function, $H(I)$, of the initial inventory, I; and shortage costs in a period are a function, $S(K)$, of the shortages during the period,

$$K = \max (0, D - I - X)$$

Note that these functions are not required to be of any particular form; however, they remain the same from period to period. The average value per period of these costs can be computed by

$$\bar{C} = \sum_{I=0}^{L} \sum_{X=0}^{L} w_{IX} C(X)$$

$$\bar{H} = \sum_{I=0}^{L} y_I H(I) = \sum_{I=0}^{L} \sum_{X=0}^{L} w_{IX} H(I)$$

$$\bar{S} = \sum_{I=0}^{L} \sum_{X=0}^{L} w_{IX} \sum_{D=I+X}^{\infty} p(D) S(D - I - X)$$

TABLE 3-10   Cost Information for Example 3-9

PRODUCTION COSTS		INVENTORY COSTS		SHORTAGE COSTS	
X	$C(X)$	I	$H(I)$	K	$S(K)$
0	$ 0	0	$ 0	0	$ 0
1	600	1	40	1	1000
2	800	2	80	2	2000
3	1000	3	140	3	3500
4	1150	4	200	4	5000
5	1300	5	260	5	7000
6	1400	6	340	6	9000

Define γ_{IX} to be the cost coefficient associated with the unknown w_{IX}. Then

$$\gamma_{IX} = C(X) + H(I) + \sum_{D=I+X}^{\infty} p(D)S(D - I - X) \qquad (3\text{-}25)$$

The objective function is the average cost per period,

$$Z = \sum_{I=0}^{L} \sum_{X=0}^{L} \gamma_{IX} w_{IX} \qquad (3\text{-}26)$$

which is to be minimized subject to (3-24). This is a linear programming model with $L + 1$ rows and L^2 variables (actually, one may be able to reduce the number of variables by setting $w_{IX} = 0$ for some I and X, say when $I + X - D_{\min} > L$).

Manne (10) originally formulated the problem in this manner. A detailed discussion of this approach versus dynamic programming solution methods is found in Hadley (4, Chapter 11).

☐**EXAMPLE 3-9**   The inventory level of a product is reviewed weekly, at which time a production order can be placed. Production is completed in time for sale in the next week. Shortages are lost. The probability distribution of demand is $p(0) = 0.1, p(1) = 0.2, p(2) = 0.4, p(3) = 0.3$, and $p(D) = 0$, for any other value of D. Table 3-10 contains information about production, inventory, and shortages costs, assuming a maximum inventory level $L = 6$.

Let w_{IX} be the joint probability of having I units on hand at the start of a week and placing a production order for X units at that time. The cost coefficients, $\{\gamma_{IX}\}$, are computed from (3-25). Their values are shown in Table 3-11 for I and X such that $I + X \leq 6$.

TABLE 3-11 Values of γ_{IX} for Example 3-9

I \ X	0	1	2	3	4	5	6
0	$2050	$1600	$1100	$1000	$1150	$1300	$1400
1	1040	940	840	1040	1190	1340	
2	380	680	880	1080	1230		
3	140	740	940	1140			
4	200	800	1000				
5	260	860					
6	340						

The steady-state equations (3-24a) are

State $I = 0$: $w_{00} + 0.9(w_{10} + w_{01}) + 0.7(w_{20} + w_{11} + w_{02})$
$$+ 0.3(w_{30} + w_{21} + w_{12} + w_{03}) = \sum_{X=0}^{6} w_{0X}$$

State $I = 1$: $0.1(w_{10} + w_{01}) + 0.2(w_{20} + w_{11} + w_{02})$
$$+ 0.4(w_{30} + w_{21} + w_{12} + w_{03})$$
$$+ 0.3(w_{40} + w_{31} + w_{22} + w_{13} + w_{04}) = \sum_{X=0}^{5} w_{1X}$$

State $I = 2$: $0.1(w_{20} + w_{11} + w_{02}) + 0.2(w_{30} + w_{21} + w_{12} + w_{03})$
$$+ 0.4(w_{40} + w_{31} + w_{22} + w_{13} + w_{04})$$
$$+ 0.3(w_{50} + w_{41} + w_{32} + w_{23} + w_{14} + w_{05}) = \sum_{X=0}^{4} w_{2X}$$

State $I = 3$: $0.1(w_{30} + w_{21} + w_{12} + w_{03})$
$$+ 0.2(w_{40} + w_{31} + w_{22} + w_{13} + w_{04})$$
$$+ 0.4(w_{50} + w_{41} + w_{32} + w_{23} + w_{14} + w_{05})$$
$$+ 0.3(w_{60} + w_{51} + w_{42} + w_{33} + w_{24} + w_{15} + w_{06}) = \sum_{X=0}^{3} w_{3X}$$

State $I = 4$: $0.1(w_{40} + w_{31} + w_{22} + w_{13} + w_{04})$
$$+ 0.2(w_{50} + w_{41} + w_{32} + w_{23} + w_{14} + w_{05})$$
$$+ 0.4(w_{60} + w_{51} + w_{42} + w_{33} + w_{24} + w_{15} + w_{06}) = \sum_{X=0}^{2} w_{4X}$$

State $I = 5$: $0.1(w_{50} + w_{41} + w_{32} + w_{23} + w_{14} + w_{05})$
$$+ 0.2(w_{60} + w_{51} + w_{42} + w_{33} + w_{24} + w_{15} + w_{06}) = \sum_{X=0}^{1} w_{5X}$$

State $I = 6$: $0.1(w_{60} + w_{51} + w_{42} + w_{33} + w_{24} + w_{15} + w_{06}) = w_{60}$

		VARIABLE IDENTIFIER—SUBSCRIPT ON w																											RIGHT-HAND SIDE
ROW	00	01	02	03	04	05	06	10	11	12	13	14	15	20	21	22	23	24	30	31	32	33	40	41	42	50	51	60	
1		-.1	-.3	-.7	-1.0	-1.0	-1.0	.9	.7	.3	-.7	-1.0	-1.0	.7	.3	.3			.3										0
2		.1	.2	.4	.3			-.9	-.8	-.6	-.7	-1.0	-1.0	.2	.4	.3	-.6	-.7	.4	.3	.3		.3	.3		.3	.3	.3	0
3			.1	.2	.4	.3			.1	.2	.4	.3	.4	-.9	-.8	-.6	-.7	-1.0	.2	.4	.3		.4	.4	.3	.3	.4	.4	0
4				.1	.2	.4	.3			.1	.2	.4	.3	.1	.1	.2	.4	.3	-.9	-.8	-.6	-.7	.2	.2	-.6	.2	.4	.4	0
5					.1	.2	.4				.1	.2	.4			.1	.2	.4		.1	.2	.4	-.9	-.8	.2	-.9	-.8	.2	0
6						.1	.2					.1	.2				.1	.2			.1	.2	.1	.1	.2	.1			0
7	1.0	1.0	1.0	1.0	1.0	1.0	1.0	1.0	1.0	1.0	1.0	1.0	1.0	1.0	1.0	1.0	1.0	1.0	1.0	1.0	1.0	1.0	1.0	1.0	1.0	1.0	1.0	1.0	1.0
x_j	2050	1600	1100	1000	1150	1300	1400	1040	940	840	1040	1190	1340	380	680	880	1080	1230	140	740	940	1140	200	800	1000	260	860	340	

FIGURE 3-3. Tabular display of linear programming model of Example 3-9.

For constraints in our linear programming formulation, we use any five of the above equations, plus

$$\sum_{I=0}^{6} \sum_{X=0}^{6} w_{IX} = 1$$

Figure 3-3 more compactly describes the linear programming model to be solved. We have omitted the state equation for $I = 6$ in forming the model. Under each variable identifier, the coefficients of that variable in the seven equations and the objective function are shown.

This problem was solved to obtain $w_{06}^{*} = 0.1606$, $w_{15}^{*} = 0.1533$, $w_{20}^{*} = 0.1387$, $w_{30}^{*} = 0.2118$, $w_{40}^{*} = 0.1361$, $w_{50}^{*} = 0.0934$, and $w_{60}^{*} = 0.1063$. The associated minimum value of the objective function is 600.16. Using (3-23), we compute the following optimal values of $\delta(X \mid I)$:

I \ X	0	1	2	3	4	5	6
0	0	0	0	0	0	0	1
1	0	0	0	0	0	1	0
2	1	0	0	0	0	0	0
3	1	0	0	0	0	0	0
4	1	0	0	0	0	0	0
5	1	0	0	0	0	0	0
6	1	0	0	0	0	0	0

The optimal decision functions are nonrandomized. If the inventory is one or less, order up to six units, but do not produce if the inventory exceeds one unit. This is an (R, r, T) policy, with $R = 6$ and $r = 1.$ □

3-7.2 A Model with Demand Dependent on Service Time

We suppose that the inventory of an item is being controlled with an (R, T) inventory policy. Demand is stochastic and backlogging is allowed. The fixed cost of producing a lot is negligible, a fact that leads to the choice of an (R, T) policy when the demand process and costs are stationary. We shall use the following notation:

X_t = size of the production lot scheduled to become available for inventory at the start of period t

τ = constant production lead time in multiples of the review period, so that X_t is ordered at the start of period $t - \tau$

D_t = demand in period t, a random variable having mean μ and variance σ^2

I_t = *net inventory* level at the *end* of period t, also a random variable (negative values indicate a backorder position)

R = target inventory position, a parameter of the inventory policy that determines X_t each period.

Consider the decision at the start of period t. A production order, $X_{t+\tau}$, must be placed for delivery to inventory at the start of period $t + \tau$. We know the present net inventory, I_{t-1}, and the quantities $X_t, X_{t+1}, \ldots, X_{t+\tau-1}$, already in production and scheduled to be delivered before the start of period $t + \tau$. Our policy is to order up to R; that is, we choose $X_{t+\tau}$ so that the sum of the net inventory and the on order quantity equals R. The decision rule is

$$X_{t+\tau} = R - I_{t-1} - \sum_{j=t}^{t+\tau-1} X_j \qquad (3\text{-}27)$$

An equivalent way to state the policy is to specify a target expected net inventory, $\hat{I}$, at the end of period $t + \tau$, and to choose $X_{t+\tau}$ so that $E(I_{t+\tau}) = \hat{I}$. More formally, since

$$I_{t+\tau} = I_{t-1} + \sum_{j=t}^{t+\tau}(X_j - D_j) \qquad (3\text{-}28)$$

we have

$$E(I_{t+\tau}) = I_{t-1} + \sum_{j=t}^{t+\tau} X_j - (\tau + 1)\mu \qquad (3\text{-}29)$$

Then, the ordering rule is

$$X_{t+\tau} = (\tau + 1)\mu - \sum_{j=t}^{t+\tau-1} X_j + (\hat{I} - I_{t-1}) \qquad (3\text{-}30)$$

In words, the policy is order the expected demand during the lead time plus one review period, less the amount already on order, plus the discrepancy between the target net inventory and the current actual net inventory.

The reader may wish to verify that rules (3-27) and (3-30) are equivalent when $\hat{I} = R - (\tau + 1)\mu$. This means that we have our choice of building a model to find the optimal R or a model to find the optimal $\hat{I}$. We choose the latter approach here.

Suppose that the $\{D_t\}$ are independent normally distributed random variables, and we use the rule (3-30). Then from (3-28) and (3-30), we note that the net inventory at the end of any period will be normally distributed with mean $\hat{I}$ and variance $\hat{\sigma}^2 = (\tau + 1)\sigma^2$. Let I^+ be the on-hand inventory at the end of a period and I^- be the backlog position at the end of a period. Then

$I = I^+ - I^-$, and

$$E(I^+) = \int_0^\infty In(I; \hat{I}, \hat{\sigma}^2) \, dI \tag{3-31}$$

$$E(I^-) = -\int_{-\infty}^0 In(I; \hat{I}, \hat{\sigma}^2) \, dI \tag{3-32}$$

If our objective is to minimize the sum of expected inventory and back-order costs per period, we form a model such as

$$K(\hat{I}) = hE(I^+) + \pi E(I^-) \tag{3-33}$$

and solve $\partial K/\partial \hat{I} = 0$. The reader is asked to verify the following solution in Exercise 3-36: Choose $\hat{I} = \hat{I}^*$, where

$$\Phi\left(\frac{-\hat{I}^*}{\hat{\sigma}}\right) = \frac{h}{\pi + h} \tag{3-34}$$

In the above, $\Phi(z)$ is the cumulative standard normal distribution. If we define $\gamma \equiv h/(\pi + h)$,

$$\hat{I}^* = -z_\gamma \hat{\sigma} = -z_\gamma \sigma \sqrt{\tau + 1} \tag{3-35}$$

where z_γ is the 100γ percentile of the standard normal distribution. Note that $\gamma = P\{I < 0\}$, the probability of a shortage during a period.

Now consider the same situation when the demand process is affected by the average delay in filling a customer's order. We call this interval the service time of the system and denote it by S. We might model this dependency by assuming the demand in a period, D, has mean $\mu(S) = v(S)\mu$ and standard deviation $\sigma(S) = v(S)\sigma$, where $v(S)$ is a monotone decreasing function of S, such that $v(0) = 1$ and $v(\infty) = 0$. The net inventory, I, has mean $\hat{I}$ and standard deviation $\hat{\sigma}(S) = \sqrt{\tau + 1} \, \sigma(S)$.

The service level is related to the backorder level, which in turn depends on $\hat{I}$ and $\hat{\sigma}(S)$. Hanssmann (5) proposed representing the relationship between S and $E(I^-)$ as follows:

$$S = \frac{E(I^-)}{\mu(S)} \tag{3-36}$$

The logic is that $E(I^-)$ is the expected backorder position at the end of a period, which when divided by the expected usage in a period, gives the average time to fill the backlogged demand.

Hanssmann observed that when this model is used, S can be treated as the decision variable, since when S is specified, $E(I^-)$ can be determined from (3-36), and $E(I^+)$ then can be found from knowledge of $E(I^-)$. One first finds $\hat{I}$ corresponding to $E(I^-)$, using (3-32), and then $E(I^+)$ associated with that $\hat{I}$

from (3-31), being careful to use $\hat{\sigma}(S)$. Hanssmann, in Reference 6, gives tables to facilitate these operations. (See Exercise 3-54.)

Since we have a mixture of backorders and lost sales when $v(S) < 1$, our objective function must include the lost profit when demand is not backlogged. We might adopt the following profit model, where r is the revenue per unit sold, c is the unit variable production cost, h is the inventory carrying cost per unit per period, π is the cost of a backorder, π_0 is the out-of-pocket cost of a lost sale, and Λ is the average net profit per period:

$$\Lambda(S) = (r - c)\mu v(S) - hE(I^+) - \pi E(I^-) - \pi_0[1 - v(S)]\mu \qquad (3\text{-}37)$$

Remember that all terms are functions of the chosen service time S. We find S^* by examining the behavior of Λ as S is varied. Usually it will be sufficient to construct a graph of Λ from a few calculated points and observe the approximate location of the maximum. Having found S^*, we compute $\hat{I}^*$ and, if desired, $R^* = \hat{I}^* + (\tau + 1)\mu(S^*)$.

An alternative to (3-37) is a model for expected cost per period:

$$K(S) = hE(I^+) + \pi E(I^-) + (r - c + \pi_0)[1 - v(S)]\mu \qquad (3\text{-}38)$$

The reader can easily verify that the S^* that maximizes Λ also minimizes K.

3-8 Multistage Planning Problems

3-8.1 Linear Programming Models

To this point we have considered production systems as if they consisted of a single stage. In many situations, however, it may be desirable to model the multifacility features of a system explicitly. This is especially true when the facilities can be operated on different schedules, with coordination required only because some facilities obtain parts or semifinished products from one or more other facilities. By allowing flexibility in scheduling, reduced production costs may be realized; however, this usually is at the expense of additional inventory holding costs resulting from increased inventories between stages. The between-stage inventories act as a buffer to absorb the effect of imbalances between the production rates of successive stages. The larger the inventory, the more independence between the stages.

Mathematical programming models, particularly linear programming models, are commonly used to analyze multistage systems. For problems involving a single product, a network analogy leads to the well-known transportation and transhipment models and to dynamic programming models. All of these models contain one common feature that characterizes multistage models, namely, material balance equations for each inventory point. These equations have the general form

$$I_j = I_j^0 + X_j - \sum_{k \neq j} W_k^j(X_k) \tag{3-39}$$

where I_j^0 is the starting inventory at stage j, X_j is the production (input) at stage j, $W_k^j(X_k)$ is the amount withdrawn to support the production of X_k units at stage k, and I_j is the ending inventory at stage j. If it is possible to have several production facilities supplying stage j, we replace X_j in (3-39) with $\sum_i P_i^j(X_i)$, where $P_i^j(X_i)$ is the number of units of product j resulting from producing X_i units at stage i.

The keys to modeling a multistage system are the decisions about what groupings of production operations constitute the stages in the system, whether or not each stage is to have multiple facilities operating in parallel, and how many inventory points between stages are to be defined. To be more specific, consider the systems pictured in Figure 3-4. Each diagram represents a two-stage production system. In Figure 3-4*a*, the system is viewed as two facilities in series (a *serial* system). The term *facility* is used here to mean a subsystem that is to be scheduled as a whole, so that in particular, it can be modeled without specifically accounting for inventory accumulations between production centers within the facility. A facility could be a single machine, a department, a production line, an entire plant, or a grouping of plants, depending on the nature of the planning decisions. Note that with this definition of a facility, we can see that the methodology studied so far in this chapter is applicable to a single-stage system comprised of a single facility.

When a stage consists of parallel sequences of production centers, where each sequence produces the product of that stage, it may be desirable to model the stage as parallel facilities and define separate decision variables for each facility. This would nearly always be true in cases where a stage involves multiple plants. Both Figures 3-4*b* and 3-4*c* represent a system where the first stage consists of two parallel facilities, each producing the same type of product; the second stage, which uses the product of the first stage, consists of three parallel facilities. In Figure 3-4*b*, the inventory between stages is not identified by facility, while in Figure 3-4*c*, it is. The former model would be used when the inventory is, in fact, stored at a common location, or when it is not important to distinguish between locations. The latter model may be necessary when transportation costs depend heavily on plant locations, when there are storage limitations at the separate inventory locations, or when it is desired to obtain the optimal shipping pattern between stages, as well as the production program at each stage, as direct output from solving the model.

This discussion to this point has been somewhat abstract and we believe that its significance will become apparent only after studying a number of examples. In the remainder of this section, we give several linear programming models

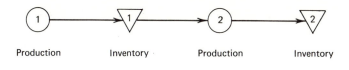

Production   Inventory   Production   Inventory

(a)

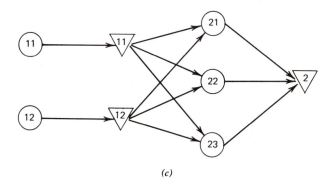

(b)

(c)

FIGURE 3-4. Different configurations for a two-stage system producing a single product. (a) Facilities in series. (b) Facilities in parallel, common inventories. (c) Facilities in parallel, separate inventories between stages.

of multistage planning problems. Later in Section 4-7, the treatment is extended to multiple time period models, where the demand process is dynamic.

□**EXAMPLE 3-10**   Consider the problem of Example 3-4, where we wanted to schedule production of four products in a plant consisting of five production centers: stamping, drilling, assembly, finishing, and packaging. Subcontracting of stamping and drilling was possible, as was overtime production in finishing. We conceived of the system as a single stage having a single facility. Our variables completely defined the routing of the product through the facility.

Now suppose we use a different formulation of the system, where we employ two stages. The first stage consists of the production centers performing stamping and drilling, while the second consists of the production centers performing assembly, finishing, and packaging. The first stage is divided into two parallel facilities: internal stamping and drilling and subcontracted stamping and drilling. The second stage is treated as a single facility. This structure is illustrated in Figure 3-5.

For notation, let W_i be the amount of product i stamped and drilled in the plant, X_i be the amount of product i stamped and drilled by the subcontractor, and Y_{ij} be the amount of product i produced by process j in assembly, finishing, and packaging. Process 1 ($j = 1$) involves only regular time production, while process 2 ($j = 2$) requires that finishing be done on overtime. Also, let a_i be the cost of stamping and drilling a unit of product i internally, including material cost, b_i be the cost of obtaining a stamped and drilled unit of product i from the subcontractor, and c_{ij} be the unit cost of processing a unit of product i through stage 2 using process j.

The objective is to minimize the total cost of production for the period,

$$Z = \sum_{i=1}^{4} (a_i W_i + b_i X_i + c_{i1} Y_{i1} + c_{i2} Y_{i2})$$

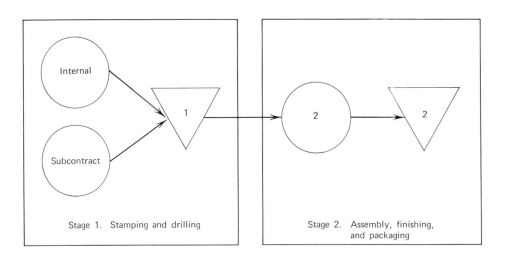

FIGURE 3-5.   Two-stage model of the problem of Example 3-4.

subject to the following constraints:

(1) Stage 1 capacity:

Stamping:	$0.03W_1 + 0.15W_2 + 0.05W_3 + 0.10W_4 \leq 400$
Drilling:	$0.06W_1 + 0.12W_2 + 0.10W_4 \leq 400$
Metal:	$2.0W_2 + 1.2W_4 \leq 2000$

(2) Stage 2 capacity:

Assembly: $\sum_{j=1}^{2} (0.05Y_{1j} + 0.10Y_{2j} + 0.05Y_{3j} + 0.12Y_{4j}) \leq 500$

Finishing: $0.04Y_{11} + 0.20Y_{21} + 0.03Y_{31} + 0.12Y_{41} \leq 450$

$0.04Y_{12} + 0.20Y_{22} + 0.03Y_{32} + 0.12Y_{42} \leq 100$

Packaging: $\sum_{j=1}^{2} (0.02Y_{1j} + 0.06Y_{2j} + 0.02Y_{3j} + 0.05Y_{4j}) \leq 400$

(3) Inventory balance equations:

Stage 1: $\quad W_i + X_i = Y_{i1} + Y_{i2}, \quad (i = 1, 2, 3, 4)$

Stage 2: $\quad Y_{11} + Y_{12} = 3000$

$\quad\quad\quad\quad Y_{21} + Y_{22} = 500$

$\quad\quad\quad\quad Y_{31} + Y_{32} = 1000$

$\quad\quad\quad\quad Y_{41} + Y_{42} = 2000$

The solution is $W_1^* = 3000$, $W_3^* = 1000$, $W_4^* = 1667$, $X_2^* = 500$, $X_4^* = 333$, $Y_{11}^* = 3000$, $Y_{21}^* = 300$, $Y_{22}^* = 200$, $Y_{31}^* = 1000$, and $Y_{41}^* = 2000$. All other variables are zero. Note that this is the production plan shown in Table 3-3. □

Comparing the model of Example 3-10 with that of Example 3-4, we note that here we have 15 contraints and 16 variables, whereas there we had 11 constraints and 16 variables. The extra constraints are the inventory balance equations linking the two stages. Although we generally prefer models with as few constraints as possible, the multistage model has some advantages that may offset its somewhat larger size. First, one does not have to identify all possible combinations of facilities and routings within facilities (we had to do this in Example 3-4 in order to define the variables). Second, and more important, the multistage model is easier to maintain when costs, production rates, or processes change. Only a part of the model will be affected. These are significant advantages in large multiproduct, multiple time period models.

□EXAMPLE 3-11 *An M-Stage Serial System, with Multiple Production Processes at Each Stage.* A production system is assumed to consist of M stages in series, with each stage containing a single production facility and an inventory. A single finished product is manufactured, and we assume that the unit of production at each stage is the quantity needed for a unit of finished product. At any stage j, there may be several sources of production (alternative production processes), such as regular time, overtime, subcontracting, different routings on machines, and so on. Let

X_{jk} = the number of units of product at stage j produced by process k, $(k = 1, 2, \ldots, K_j)$

c_{jk} = unit variable production cost at stage j, if process k is used

b_{jl} = amount of resource type l available at stage j, $(l = 1, 2, \ldots, L_j)$

a_{jkl} = amount of resource l used to produce one unit at stage j by process k

D = number of units of finished product that must be produced in the period

Z = total production cost for the period

Formally, we want to choose the $\{X_{jk}\}$ to minimize

$$Z = \sum_{j=1}^{M} \sum_{k=1}^{K_j} c_{jk} X_{jk} \tag{3-40a}$$

subject to the following constraints:

(1) Resource limitations at each stage:

$$\sum_{k=1}^{K_j} a_{jkl} X_{jk} \leq b_{jl}, \qquad (j = 1, 2, \ldots, M; l = 1, 2, \ldots, L_j) \tag{3-40b}$$

(2) Inventory balance between stages:

$$\sum_{k=1}^{K_j} X_{jk} = \sum_{k=1}^{K_{j+1}} X_{j+1,k}, \qquad (j = 1, 2, \ldots, M-1) \tag{3-40c}$$

(3) Finished product requirement:

$$\sum_{k=1}^{K_M} X_{Mk} = D \tag{3-40d}$$

$\square$

□**EXAMPLE 3-12** *An M-Stage Serial System, with Multiple Products and Production Processes at Each Stage.* We now generalize the model (3-40) of Example 3-12 to include the case of multiple products. We suppose that there are n different finished products produced by the system. Each stage processes n products, such that the ith product of the jth stage is required *only* for producing the ith product of the $(j + 1)$th stage. (In Example 3-13, we illustrate the case where a product of one stage may be used in production of more than one product at following stages. Later, a more general formulation is given in Example 4-21.)

Let X_{ijk} be the number of units of product i produced at stage j by process k, $k = 1, 2, \ldots, K_{ij}$, in the period, and let D_i be the number of finished units of product i required. We wish to minimize

$$Z = \sum_{i=1}^{n} \sum_{j=1}^{M} \sum_{k=1}^{K_{ij}} c_{ijk} X_{ijk} \qquad \text{(3-41a)}$$

subject to

$$\sum_{i=1}^{n} \sum_{k=1}^{K_{ij}} a_{ijkl} X_{ijk} \le b_{jl}, \qquad (j = 1, 2, \ldots, M; l = 1, 2, \ldots, L_j) \quad \text{(3-41b)}$$

$$\sum_{k=1}^{K_{ij}} X_{ijk} = \sum_{k=1}^{K_{i,j+1}} X_{i,j+1,k}, \qquad (i = 1, 2, \ldots, n; j = 1, 2, \ldots, M-1) \quad \text{(3-41c)}$$

$$\sum_{k=1}^{K_{iM}} X_{iMk} = D_i, \qquad (i = 1, 2, \ldots, n) \quad \text{(3-41d)}$$

Equation 3-41c is the material balance equation between stages j and $j + 1$.□

□**EXAMPLE 3-13** Consider the three-stage system shown in Figure 3-6. There is one product produced by each stage. The product of stage 1 is used in the production of products at stages 2 and 3. The product of stage 2 is used in the production of the product at stage 3 and also can be sold directly to customers. The product of stage 3 is sold.

Let

$X_j =$ units of production at stage j

$P_j =$ capacity of stage j in units of product

$a_{ij} =$ number of units of product at stage i required to produce one unit at stage j

$c_j =$ unit variable production cost incurred at stage j

$r_j =$ revenue from the sale of product $j, j = 2, 3$

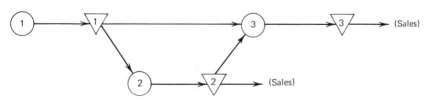

FIGURE 3-6. Production system for Example 3-13.

$$L_j = \text{minimum sales requirements for product } j, j = 2, 3$$

$$U_j = \text{maximum sales possible for product } j, j = 2, 3$$

$$Z = \text{contribution to profit and overhead for the period}$$

This is a product mix model, where we assume that all production of products 2 and 3 up to U_2 and U_3, respectively, can be sold. The problem is to maximize

$$Z = r_3 X_3 + r_2(X_2 - a_{23}X_3) - c_1 X_1 - c_2 X_2 - c_3 X_3$$
$$= (r_3 - a_{23}r_2 - c_3)X_3 + (r_2 - c_2)X_2 - c_1 X_1$$

subject to

$$X_j \le P_j, \quad (j = 1, 2, 3)$$
$$X_1 = a_{12}X_2 + a_{13}X_3$$
$$X_2 \ge a_{23}X_3$$
$$L_2 \le X_2 - a_{23}X_3 \le U_2$$
$$L_3 \le X_3 \le U_3$$

An alternative to this model results from defining additional variables S_2 and S_3, representing the sales of products 2 and 3. Then we maximize

$$Z = r_2 S_2 + r_3 S_3 - c_1 X_1 - c_2 X_2 - c_3 X_3$$

subject to

$$X_j \le P_j, \quad (j = 1, 2, 3)$$
$$X_1 = a_{12}X_2 + a_{13}X_3$$
$$X_2 = a_{23}X_3 + S_2$$
$$X_3 = S_3$$
$$L_2 \le S_2 \le U_2$$
$$L_3 \le S_3 \le U_3$$

This formulation completes the material balance equation at the second stage and adds an inventory balance equation for the third stage. There is no advantage to this approach in the single time period case. However, it can be the only way to model certain product mix problems in the multiple period situation. (For an illustration, see Example 4-22.)□

3-8.2 A Single-Period Stochastic Model

As an introduction to the analysis of multistage systems under uncertainty, we examine a production system consisting of a single facility that converts a purchased material into a finished product. Assume the product is a specialty (or style, or fashion, or seasonal) item whose demand takes place over a short period of time. Demand is a random variable with density function $f(D)$. Because of the short length of the selling period, there is no opportunity for the manufacturer to reorder material from his supplier. At the start of the period, then, he will have an amount, say X_1, in his material inventory and possibly an amount X_2 in his finished product inventory, ready for sale. If he runs out of finished stock during the period, a fraction α of subsequent customers will wait for him to produce a finished item from his available stock of material; the remainder will cancel their order. Product or material remaining at the end of the period must be disposed of. The problem is to determine values for X_1 and X_2.

Let r be the selling price of a unit of product, c_1 be the cost of a unit of material, c_2 be the cost of processing a unit of material into a unit of finished product, L_1 be the disposal value of a unit of material, and L_2 be the disposal value of a unit of finished product. For the problem to be interesting, we should have $L_1 < c_1$ and $L_2 < c_1 + c_2 < r$. The profit for the period, V, depends on X_1, X_2, and D. If $0 \le D \le X_2$, no material will be used, only finished goods. If $X_2 \le D \le X_2 + X_1/\alpha$, all of the initial finished goods inventory will be issued and some material will be processed for customers who will wait. Finally, if $D > X_2 + X_1/\alpha$, all material will be used up. We can express the profit as

$$V(X_1, X_2, D) = \begin{cases} rD - c_1X_1 - (c_1 + c_2)X_2 + L_1X_1 + L_2(X_2 - D), \\ \qquad\qquad\qquad\qquad\qquad \text{if } 0 \le D \le X_2 \\ r[X_2 + \alpha(D - X_2)] - c_1X_1 - c_2\alpha(D - X_2) \\ \qquad - (c_1 + c_2)X_2 + L_1[X_1 - \alpha(D - X_2)], \\ \qquad\qquad\qquad\qquad\qquad \text{if } X_2 < D \le X_2 + X_1/\alpha \\ r(X_1 + X_2) - (c_1 + c_2)(X_1 + X_2), \quad \text{if } X_2 + X_1/\alpha < D \end{cases}$$

$$\equiv \begin{cases} V_1(X_1, X_2, D), & \text{if } 0 \le D \le X_2 \\ V_2(X_1, X_2, D), & \text{if } X_2 < D \le X_2 + X_1/\alpha \\ V_3(X_1, X_2, D), & \text{if } X_2 + X_1/\alpha < D \end{cases}$$

The expected profit is

$$\bar{V}(X_1, X_2) = \int_0^{X_2} V_1(X_1, X_2, D)f(D)\, dD + \int_{X_2}^{X_2 + X_1/\alpha} V_2(X_1, X_2, D)f(D)\, dD$$

$$+ \int_{X_2 + X_1/\alpha}^{\infty} V_3(X_1, X_2, D)f(D)\, dD$$

Taking partial derivatives with respect to X_1 and X_2, we obtain

$$\frac{\partial \overline{V}}{\partial X_1} = (r - c_1 - c_2) - (r - c_2 - L_1)F\left(X_2 + \frac{X_1}{\alpha}\right)$$

$$\frac{\partial \overline{V}}{\partial X_2} = (r - c_1 - c_2) - [(1 - \alpha)r + \alpha c_2 + \alpha L_1 - L_2]F(X_2)$$

$$- \alpha(r - c_2 - L_1)F\left(X_2 + \frac{X_1}{\alpha}\right)$$

Equating these derivatives to zero, we can solve the resulting equations to get the following:

$$F(X_2^*) = \frac{(1 - \alpha)(r - c_1 - c_2)}{[(1 - \alpha)r + \alpha c_2 + \alpha L_1 - L_2]} \tag{3-42}$$

$$F(X_2^* + X_1^*/\alpha) = \frac{r - c_1 - c_2}{r - c_2 - L_1} \tag{3-43}$$

for $\alpha \neq 0$. If $\alpha = 0$, obviously no material inventory would be maintained, and the resulting single-stage problem could be solved by the method of Section 2-5.

□**EXAMPLE 3-14** Suppose $r = \$100$, $c_1 = \$30$, $c_2 = \$40$, $L_1 = \$20$, $L_2 = \$10$, $\alpha = 0.40$, and $f(D)$ is normal with mean 1000 and standard deviation of 200. Equations 3-42 and 3-43 become $F(X_2^*) = 0.243$, and $F(X_2^* + 2.5X_1^*) = 0.750$. Using tables of the standard normal variable, we obtain

$$X_2^* = 1000 - (0.69)(200) = 862$$

$$X_2^* + 2.5X_1^* = 1000 + (0.67)(200) = 1134$$

or

$$X_1^* = 109$$

Thus we should stock 862 units in finished product form and 109 units in raw material form. Note that the combined stock level is less than the expected demand of 1000.□

Hanssmann (6) gives a general formulation of the M-stage version of this problem, where the stages are in series. He also discusses the solution procedure.

3-8.3 Multistage Base Stock Systems

In Section 2-7.3, we considered base stock policies for a single-stage inventory system. Under a base stock policy, a unit is ordered from the supplier every time a unit is demanded and either filled from stock or backlogged. This means that the net inventory plus the quantity on order always equals a constant, called the base stock level. Now we describe an analysis, developed by Simpson (12), for a multistage system consisting of M stages in series, where the inventory at each stage is controlled by a base stock policy, and the demand is stochastic. Shortages are backlogged at every stage. Thus, an external demand of one unit on stage M will trigger an order for one unit on every other stage.

When stage i orders a unit from stage $i - 1$, there is a time lag between the ordering of the unit and its addition to inventory at stage i. This time lag is the sum of the production lead time at stage i, τ_i, and any delay in obtaining a unit of material from the inventory at stage $i - 1$. The latter is greater than zero only if the inventory at stage $i - 1$ is in a backorder position.

Simpson defines the *service time*, S_i, for stage i to be the maximum time to fill an order at that stage. He supposes that the raw material inventory (stage 0) is never empty, so that $S_0 = 0$, and that customer demand at stage M is to be filled without delay, meaning $S_M = 0$ is required. The other $\{S_i\}$ are policy variables that must be established to minimize inventory costs. Observe that $0 \le S_i \le S_{i-1} + \tau_i$ must hold for all i. Note that $S_i = 0$ means that stage i is almost never out of stock, a condition whose assurance requires a large inventory, while $S_i = S_{i-1} + \tau_i$ means that no inventory is carried at stage i.

Let R_i be the base stock level at stage i and let L_i be the maximum time lag in filling an order placed to replenish the stage i inventory. Then, $L_i = S_{i-1} + \tau_i$. Suppose $f(D; t)$ is the probability distribution of demand in any time period of length t. Let α_i be the probability that the service time at stage i exceeds S_i. Assume the $\{\alpha_i\}$ are established by management policy. Then R_i should be determined so that the probability of demand during a period of length $L_i - S_i$ exceeding R_i is only α_i. To see this, suppose $S_i = 0$. Then a shortage will occur at stage i if the demand during L_i exceeds R_i. By policy, this must happen with small probability α_i; therefore,

$$\int_{R_i}^{\infty} f(D; L_i)\, dD = \alpha_i$$

If $S_i > 0$ is permitted, we need less protection, so

$$\int_{R_i}^{\infty} f(D; L_i - S_i)\, dD = \alpha_i \tag{3-44}$$

Now suppose $f(D; t)$ is normal with mean μt and variance $\sigma^2 t$. Then

$$\int_{R_i}^{\infty} n(D; \mu t, \sigma^2 t)\, dD = \alpha_i$$

with $t = L_i - S_i$, implies

$$R_i = \mu(L_i - S_i) + z_{1-\alpha_i}\sigma\sqrt{L_i - S_i} \tag{3-45}$$

In (3-45), $z_{1-\alpha_i}$ is the $100(1 - \alpha_i)$ percentile of the standard normal density.

The stage i net inventory level, I_i, is a random variable that at a given point in time equals the base stock level, R_i, minus the demand during the preceding $L_i - S_i$ units of time. Thus, the expected net inventory level is

$$E(I_i) = R_i - \mu(L_i - S_i)$$

$$= z_{1-\alpha_i}\sigma\sqrt{L_i - S_i} \qquad (3\text{-}46)$$

If h_i is the cost to carry one unit in inventory for one unit of time at stage i, the average inventory holding costs per unit time for the system are approximately

$$\sum_{i=1}^{M} h_i z_{1-\alpha_i}\sigma\sqrt{L_i - S_i} = \sum_{i=1}^{M} h_i z_{1-\alpha_i}\sigma\sqrt{S_{i-1} + \tau_i - S_i} \qquad (3\text{-}47)$$

Here we have approximated the average on-hand inventory by the average net inventory.

We desire to minimize (3-47) subject to the constraints:

$$S_0 = 0$$

$$0 \le S_i \le S_{i-1} + \tau_i, \qquad (i = 1, 2, \ldots, M - 1) \qquad (3\text{-}48)$$

$$S_M = 0$$

Simpson shows that (3-47) is concave, so that the optimal solution occurs at an extreme point of the convex set bounded by (3-48). Therefore the optimal solution has the property that either $S_i = 0$, or $S_i = S_{i-1} + \tau_i$. There are 2^M candidates for the optimal policy and they must all be examined. This is not difficult for small M. [Question: Why did we omit consideration of procurement costs and shortage costs in formulating the objective function (3-47)?]

Simpson also shows how his approach can be extended to multiechelon systems.

□**EXAMPLE 3-15** Consider a system having three production stages in series. There is a raw material inventory prior to the first production stage and a finished goods inventory following the third production stage. Assume $\tau_1 = 2$, $\tau_2 = 4$, and $\tau_3 = 3$ weeks. A base stock system is to be used at each inventory point. Management has established the following probabilities of exceeding the base stock level at the stages: $\alpha_0 = 0.01$, $\alpha_1 = 0.05$, $\alpha_2 = 0.05$, and $\alpha_3 = 0.01$. Also it is specified that $S_0 = S_3 = 0$. Inventory costs are $h_0 = 0$, $h_1 = 2$, $h_2 = 3$, and $h_3 = 5$, in dollars per unit per unit time. Demand in any interval of length t is normally distributed with a mean of $150t$ and variance $100t$. The choice of S_1 and S_2 will affect inventory costs at all stages except the raw material inventory; hence, our objective function is

$$K(S_1, S_2) = (2)(1.645)(10)\sqrt{0 + 2 - S_1} + (3)(1.645)(10)\sqrt{S_1 + 4 - S_2}$$

$$+ (5)(2.326)(10)\sqrt{S_2 + 3 - 0}$$

Our constraints are

$$0 \le S_1 \le 2$$
$$0 \le S_2 \le S_1 + 4$$

There are four extreme point solutions:

S_1	S_2	$K(S_1, S_2)$	
0	0	347	
0	4	355	
2	0	324	(minimum)
2	6	350	

The optimal solution is $S_1^* = 2$, $S_2^* = 0$, and using (3-45) with $S_0 = S_3 = 0$,

$$R_1^* = (100)(0 + 2 - 2) + (1.645)(10)\sqrt{0 + 2 - 2} = 0$$
$$R_2^* = (100)(2 + 4 - 0) + (1.645)(10)\sqrt{2 + 4 - 0} = 640$$
$$R_3^* = (100)(0 + 3 - 0) + (2.326)(10)\sqrt{0 + 3 - 0} = 341$$

There should be no inventory at stage 1, and base stock levels of 640 and 341 should be used at stages 2 and 3, respectively.□

3-8.4 A Multistage Periodic Review Model with Stochastic Demand

In this section, we extend the discussion of Section 3-7.2 to treat multistage systems controlled by periodic review production and inventory policies. We shall use a two-stage example to illustrate the modeling of a serial production system. The approach used was developed by Hanssmann (5).

Suppose a single product is produced by processing a raw material into semifinished material in one production operation and then into a finished product in a second production operation. There are two production facilities and three inventories: raw material, semifinished product, and finished product. (See Figure 3-7.) Assume that the raw material inventory is never out of stock and that the problem is to develop policies for controlling the semifinished and finished product inventories and for determining production lot sizes. Each review period, a replenishment order is placed for each inventory, using an (R, T) policy, and a lot is started into production at each facility.

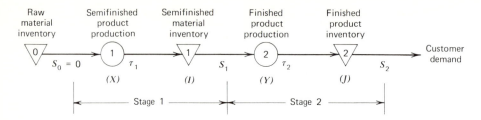

FIGURE 3-7. The two-stage system for Section 3-8.4.

Because the semifinished inventory can be in a backorder condition, the production lot size at the second stage may not equal that of the replenishment order for finished goods in that period. At the first stage, however, the production lot size will always be the same as the replenishment order for semifinished product, since the raw material inventory is never empty.

We shall need the following notation:

τ_i = production lead time at stage i, $i = 1, 2$, in multiples of the review period

I_t = net inventory of semifinished product at stage 1 at the end of period t

X_t = size of the production lot completed at stage 1 and added to semi-finished inventory at the start of period t

J_t = net inventory of finished product at the end of period t

Y_t = size of the production lot completed at stage 2 and added to finished goods inventory at the start of period t

Q = size of the replenishment order for finished goods issued to the second stage production facility at the start of period t

S_2 = average delay in filling a customer's order at the finished goods inventory, measured in multiples of the review period

S_1 = average delay in getting a finished goods replenishment order into production at stage 2, because of shortages of semifinished product at the stage 1 inventory

The quantities S_1 and S_2 are the service times of the two inventory points. Finally, as in Section 3-7.2, we assume customer demand, D, in any period is a normally distributed random variable with mean $\mu(S_2) = v(S_2)\mu$ and standard deviation $\sigma(S_2) = v(S_2)\sigma$, where $v(S_2)$ is a positive fraction that decreases monotonically with S_2.

Now consider the situation at the very start of a period t. At stage 1, there are τ_1 lots in progress, having sizes $X_t, X_{t+1}, \ldots, X_{t+\tau_1-1}$. The τ_2 lots in progress at stage 2 have sizes $Y_t, Y_{t+1}, \ldots, Y_{t+\tau_2-1}$. Net inventories are I_{t-1} and J_{t-1}. Suppose, based on this information, a production order for Q units of finished product is placed at stage 2. Then the production lot size, $Y_{t+\tau_2}$, to be started into production at stage 2 in period t can be computed in the following manner. First, determine the net semifinished inventory at the end of period t,

$$
\begin{aligned}
I_t &= I_{t-1} + X_t - Q \\
&= I_{t-1}^+ - I_{t-1}^- + X_t - Q
\end{aligned}
\tag{3-49}
$$

where I^+ and I^- are on-hand inventory and backorder level, respectively. Next, we calculate

$$
Y_{t+\tau_2} = \begin{cases} Q + I_{t-1}^-, & \text{if } I_t \geq 0 \\ X_t + I_{t-1}^+, & \text{if } I_t \leq 0 \end{cases}
\tag{3-50}
$$

Observe from (3-50) that the production lot size is the minimum of the quantity required and the amount of semifinished material available.

The ordering decision at the start of period t will first affect the finished goods inventory in period $t + \tau_2 + S_1$. The net inventory at the end of that period will be

$$
J_{t+\tau_2+S_1} = J_{t-1} + \sum_{i=t}^{t+\tau_2-1} Y_i + \sum_{i=t}^{t+S_1-1} X_i + Q - \sum_{i=t}^{t+\tau_2+S_1} D_i
\tag{3-51}
$$

The quantity $X_t + X_{t+1} + \cdots + X_{t+S_1-1}$ is the amount of semifinished product that will pass through the semifinished inventory into production at stage 2 before semifinished product becomes available for the order Q. If our policy is to choose Q such that the expected net finished inventory at the end of any period is $\hat{J}$, we have the reordering rule

$$
Q = (\tau_2 + S_1 + 1)\mu(S_2) - \sum_{i=t}^{t+\tau_2-1} Y_i - \sum_{i=t}^{t+S_1-1} X_i + \hat{J} - J_{t-1}
\tag{3-52}
$$

Once Q is determined, I_t and $Y_{t+\tau_2}$ can be obtained from (3-49) and (3-50).

The ordering decision at the first stage will affect the semifinished inventory in period $t + \tau_1$. At the end of that period,

$$
I_{t+\tau_1} = I_t + \sum_{i=t+1}^{t+\tau_1} (X_i - Y_i)
\tag{3-53}
$$

Assuming we want the expected net semifinished inventory at the end of any period to be $\hat{I}$, we can use the reordering rule

$$
X_{t+\tau_1} = \tau_1\mu(S_2) - \sum_{i=t+1}^{t+\tau_1-1} X_i + \hat{I} - I_t
\tag{3-54}
$$

where I_t is obtained from (3-49). In developing (3-54), it was assumed that the expected production lot size at stage 2 is the average demand per period, $\mu(S_2)$.

Having structured the reordering rules, our next step is to determine a procedure for getting good values for the target net inventories, $\hat{I}$ and $\hat{J}$. From the preceding development, we observe that J will be normally distributed with mean $\hat{J}$ and standard deviation $\sqrt{\tau_2 + S_1 + 1}\,\sigma(S_2) \equiv \hat{\sigma}_2$, and I will be normally distributed with mean $\hat{I}$ and approximate standard deviation

$\sqrt{\tau_1 + 1} \, \sigma(S_2) \equiv \hat{\sigma}_1$. Expected on-hand inventory and backlog levels are given by

$$E(I^+) = \int_0^\infty In(I; \hat{I}, \hat{\sigma}_1{}^2) \, dI \tag{3-55}$$

$$E(I^-) = -\int_{-\infty}^0 In(I; \hat{I}, \hat{\sigma}_1{}^2) \, dI \tag{3-56}$$

$$E(J^+) = \int_0^\infty Jn(J; \hat{J}, \hat{\sigma}_2{}^2) \, dJ \tag{3-57}$$

$$E(J^-) = -\int_{-\infty}^0 Jn(J; \hat{J}, \hat{\sigma}_2{}^2) \, dJ \tag{3-58}$$

(See Exercise 3-54 for advice on computing the above.) Our objective function could be expected net profit per period

$$\Lambda = (r - c)v(S_2)\mu - h_1 E(I^+) - h_2 E(J^+) - \pi E(J^-) - \pi_0[1 - v(S_2)]\mu \tag{3-59}$$

where r is the unit sales revenue, c is the unit production cost, h_1 and h_2 are inventory holding costs, π is the unit backorder cost, and π_0 is the cost of a lost sale, in addition to lost profit. An equivalent objective function, to be minimized, is the expected cost per period

$$K = h_1 E(I^+) + h_2 E(J^+) + \pi E(J^-) + (r - c + \pi_0)[1 - v(S_2)]\mu \tag{3-60}$$

It is important to note that Λ and K can be considered functions of the decision variables S_1 and S_2, if we assume, as in Section 3-7.2, that the expected backorder positions are related to the average service times by

$$E(I^-) = S_1\mu(S_2) \tag{3-61}$$

$$E(J^-) = S_2\mu(S_2) \tag{3-62}$$

We choose S_1 and S_2 to maximize Λ, subject to the constraints $0 \le S_1 \le \tau_1$ and $0 \le S_2 \le S_1 + \tau_2$. If S_1 or S_2 equals zero, it means that the expected backorder level is negligible at that inventory point; if $S_1 = \tau_1$, no semifinished inventory is maintained; if $S_2 = S_1 + \tau_2$, no finished inventory is kept; and if $S_1 = \tau_1$ and $S_2 = \tau_1 + \tau_2$, there is only the raw material inventory and all production is to customer order. Once the optimal service levels have been determined, they can be converted into associated values of $\hat{I}$ and $\hat{J}$. (See Exercise 3-55.)

3-8.5 Multistage Economic Lot-Size Problems

When there are significant setup costs associated with production in a multistage system, the analysis becomes much more complex, even in the simplest case of a single product having a known and constant demand rate. Only recently have results begun to appear in the literature. Some have treated the problem as one of determining economic lot sizes at each stage, using the continuous review concept and a modeling approach similar to that used in developing economic lot-size equations for a single-stage system (see Section 2-2). Others have used a periodic review concept, where it is assumed that exactly one production lot can be produced at each stage in each period. We have used that approach for the case of proportional production costs in Sections 3-8.1 and 3-8.3, and we shall take up the concave production cost case (including the setup cost model), assuming periodic review, in Section 4-7. In this section, however, we briefly discuss continuous review economic lot-size models, under static deterministic demand.

Description of the System. We suppose that there are M production facilities in series and that the system produces a single finished product. At each stage production is in lots, with the lot sizes possibly varying from one operation to the next. Therefore, an inventory may exist between any two successive facilities. It is assumed that the demand on the system is at a known and constant rate and that no shortages are to be permitted at any stage, except the final stage (finished goods inventory), where they are backordered. The problem is to determine the optimal lot sizes at each stage, considering setup costs, inventory holding costs, and, at the final stage, backorder costs.

Assume the stages are numbered $1, 2, \ldots, M$, in order of production, so that stage M is the final stage and inventory M is the only point where backorders are permitted. Let

D = continuous demand rate on the final stage inventory

P_i = production rate at stage i, where we assume $P_i > D$, so that the ith facility will operate intermittently

τ_i = time to process a unit through facility i, when production is unit by unit (that is, production does not involve processing the entire lot simultaneously as a batch)

$\bar{I}_i$ = average on-hand inventory at stage i, which includes work in process in facility i, product that has been processed by facility i, but is not yet available for use by stage $i + 1$, and product that is available for use by facility $i + 1$

$\bar{B}_M$ = average backorder position at the finished goods inventory

X_i = lot size at stage i

$T_i = X_i/D$, the time between starting production runs at stage i, also called the cycle time at stage i

In addition to requiring constant lot sizes at each stage, we also make the important assumption that the lot size at any stage i is a positive integer multiple of the lot size at stage $i + 1$; that is,

$$X_i = n_i X_{i+1}, \qquad (n_i = 1, 2, \ldots) \tag{3-63}$$

A discussion of the desirability of this policy will be given later.

Average Inventory Levels. The principal difficulty in developing continuous review models of multistage systems lies in expressing the average inventory level at each stage as a mathematical function of the lot sizes. Knowledge of how average inventory levels vary with lot-size decisions is essential to the determination of an optimal production policy. Therefore, we now obtain expressions for the $\{\bar{I}_i\}$ as a function of the $\{X_i\}$, before constructing a cost model and discussing optimization.

At any inventory point, fluctuations in level, and hence in the average and maximum inventory, will depend on characteristics of the input and withdrawal processes. The input may be discontinuous in time at a finite rate or at an infinite rate (as when the entire replenishment lot arrives at one time). If at any stage input is continuous, it means there is no lot-size production at the prior production operation. Withdrawals also may be discontinuous at a finite or infinite rate, and continuous withdrawal means no lot-size production at the next operation.

An important consideration in determining inventory behavior is whether or not production (input) and consumption (withdrawal) can take place simultaneously, and, if not, whether or not there has to be a nonzero time lag between the termination of production of a lot and its availability for consumption. For each of these situations, there are many possibilities for the manner in which material flows through stage i. We shall consider two general cases, which can be interpreted to encompass many common variations. In Case I, we suppose processing at facility i is unit by unit and that the output from facility i is immediately available for use at stage $i + 1$. Thus, a lot can be used as it is being produced. In Case II, we again assume production at facility i is unit by unit; however, we suppose that the output from facility i must be accumulated until the entire lot is completed. From that time, there is a delay of l_i before the lot is available for use by stage $i + 1$. This delay may be for handling, transportation, or acceptance inspection, or may be required by the manufacturing technology (for example, aging, drying, and curing). We also shall show how this case can be interpreted to represent the situation where facility i processes X_i units as a batch.

Case I. Simultaneous Production and Consumption of a Lot. To analyze Case I, consider what happens when facility 1 begins production (see also Figure 3-8):

    1.   Material is withdrawn from the inventory at stage $i - 1$ at a rate P_i, for a length of time $t_i = X_i/P_i$.

    2.   If the lead time, τ_i, is less than or equal to the time to put the lot into

production, t_i, work in process at facility i builds to a level of $\tau_i P_i$ at time τ_i, and remains at that level until time t_i, when the entire lot has been started into production. If $\tau_i > t_i$, the work in process peaks at X_i units at time t_i and remains at that level until time τ_i. From max (τ_i, t_i), the amount of material in process at facility i decreases as the pipeline empties, until time $\tau_i + t_i$, when production stops.

3. At time τ_i, facility i begins to discharge product, which is immediately added to the inventory available for use by stage $i + 1$. Except possibly over intervals where material is withdrawn by stage $i + 1$, this inventory grows steadily until time $\tau_i + t_i$. After this point in time, the input ceases and the inventory drops as usage occurs.

Figure 3-8 shows the work-in-progress inventory at facility i and the available-for-use inventory at stage i generated by one lot started into production at time zero. In constructing the graph of available inventory, it was assumed that $X_i = 2X_{i+1}$ and that the withdrawal rate, P_{i+1}, is infinite (meaning that X_{i+1} units are withdrawn instantaneously). Note that lots of $X_2 = 250$ are withdrawn at times 5.5 and 15.5 of the cycle. The reader should construct similar plots for the case where $\tau_i = 8$.

To find the average values of these inventories over time, we note that the area under an inventory-time curve represents the number of unit-years of inventory generated by one lot. Since exactly one lot is produced at stage i every $T_i = X_i/D$ years, we can divide the area under the curve by T_i to obtain the average inventory in units. Let $\overline{W}_i$ be the average work-in-process inventory at facility i and $\overline{V}_i$ be the average available-for-use inventory at stage i. It is easy to show that

$$\overline{W}_i = \frac{\tau_i X_i}{T_i} = \tau_i D \qquad (3\text{-}64)$$

regardless of which is larger, τ_i or t_i. The quantity $\overline{W}_i$ is often called the *pipeline inventory* for facility i. It can be reduced only by shortening the production lead time, τ_i. (We comment that this may be an important avenue of investigation in the practical analysis of inventory problems.)

Finding a general expression for $\overline{V}_i$ is much more tedious; however, results have been obtained and reported in Reference 8. We give them without details of their derivation, pointing out only that the timing of the production at stage i is assumed to be such that $\overline{V}_i$ is minimized for given X_i and X_{i+1}, and that (3-63) is assumed to be the policy structure. We have

$$\overline{V}_i = \begin{cases} \dfrac{X_{i+1}}{2}\left[n_i\left(1 - \dfrac{D}{P_i}\right) - \left(1 - \dfrac{D}{P_{i+1}}\right)\right], & \text{if } P_{i+1} \le P_i \quad (3\text{-}65a) \\[4mm] \dfrac{X_{i+1}}{2}\left[n_i\left(1 - \dfrac{D}{P_i}\right) - \left(1 - \dfrac{2D}{P_i}\right) - \dfrac{D}{P_{i+1}}\right], & \text{if } P_{i+1} > P_i \quad (3\text{-}65b) \end{cases}$$

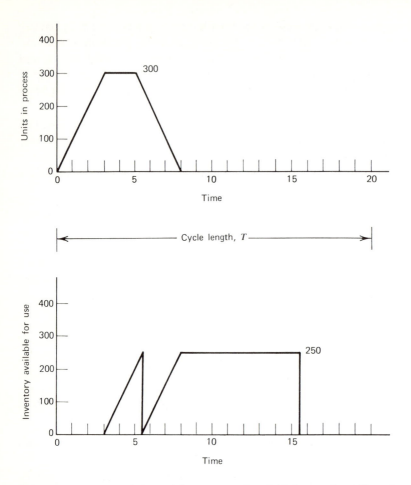

FIGURE 3-8. Graph of the work in process and available inventories at Stage i, when $P_i = 100$, $X_i = 500$, $\tau_i = 3$, $X_{i+1} = 250$, $P_{i+1} = \infty$, and $D = 25$, so that $t_i = 5$ and $T_i = 20$ (Case I).

Letting $X_i = k_i X_M$, where $k_i = n_i n_{i+1} \cdots n_{M-1}$, we can express $\overline{V}_i$ in terms of the final stage lot size, X_M,

$$
\overline{V}_i = \begin{cases} \dfrac{k_{i+1} X_M}{2}\left[n_i\left(1 - \dfrac{D}{P_i}\right) - \left(1 - \dfrac{D}{P_{i+1}}\right)\right], & \text{if } P_{i+1} \leq P_i \quad (3\text{-}66a) \\[3ex] \dfrac{k_{i+1} X_M}{2}\left[n_i\left(1 - \dfrac{D}{P_i}\right) - \left(1 - \dfrac{2D}{P_i}\right) - \dfrac{D}{P_{i+1}}\right], & \text{if } P_{i+1} > P_i \quad (3\text{-}66b) \end{cases}
$$

To appreciate the need for separate formulas depending on the relationship between P_i and P_{i+1}, the reader should plot the available inventory for the example of Figure 3-8 when $P_{i+1} = 125$ and when $P_{i+1} = 50$.

The preceding results hold for stages $1, 2, \ldots, M - 1$. For the final stage,

$$\overline{W}_M = \tau_M D \tag{3-67}$$

and, if no shortages are allowed

$$\overline{V}_M = \frac{X_M}{2}\left(1 - \frac{D}{P_M}\right) \tag{3-68}$$

If backorders are permitted at the final stage, the average on-hand inventory is

$$\overline{V}_M = \frac{[X_M(1 - D/P_M) - b]^2}{2X_M(1 - D/P_M)} \tag{3-69}$$

where b is the maximum backorder position, and the average backorder position is

$$\overline{B}_M = \frac{b^2}{2X_M(1 - D/P_M)} \tag{3-70}$$

Graphs of the final stage inventories are shown in Figure 3-9.

If s_i is the setup, cleaning, and maintenance time for facility i each cycle, and if only one lot can be in production at any time, we must have

$$\tau_i + t_i + s_i \le T_i$$

or, since $t_i = X_i/P_i$ and $T_i = X_i/D$,

$$X_i \ge \frac{(s_i + \tau_i)D}{1 - D/P_i} \tag{3-71}$$

Case II. Delay Following Production of a Lot. Now suppose that there is a delay of l_i following completion of the entire lot, before any of the lot can be used by stage $i + 1$. Because this delay may be for handling or inspection, l_i may depend on the size of the lot. To recognize this possibility, we shall adopt the simple model

$$l_i = \alpha_i + \beta_i X_i \tag{3-72}$$

Now, in addition to the work-in-progress inventory, W, at facility i and the available-for-use inventory, V, at stage i, we must include the inventory of product that has completed processing at facility i, but is unavailable for use at the following stage. The average value of this unavailable inventory will be denoted by $\overline{U}_i$. Variation of the three types of inventory during a cycle is shown in Figure 3-10. Note that the delay does not begin until all production is completed.

To obtain average inventory levels, the areas under the inventory curves are divided by the cycle length, T_i. Again, we give only the general results, derived

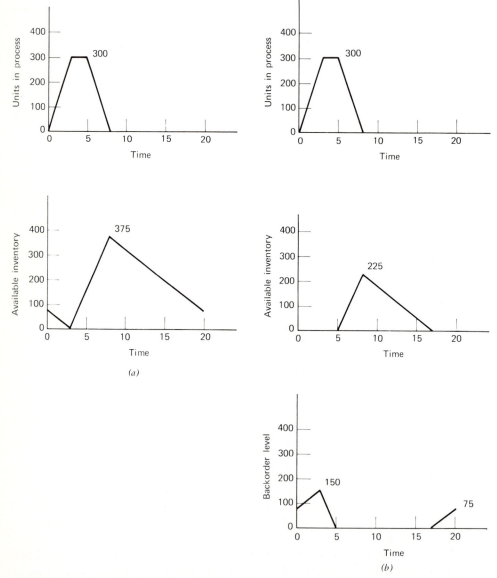

FIGURE 3-9. Stage M inventories and backlog position, when $P_M = 100$, $\tau_M = 3$, $X_M = 500$, $D = 25$, $b = 150$, so that $t_M = 5$ and $T_M = 20$. (Case I.) (a) No shortages allowed. (b) Backorders permitted.

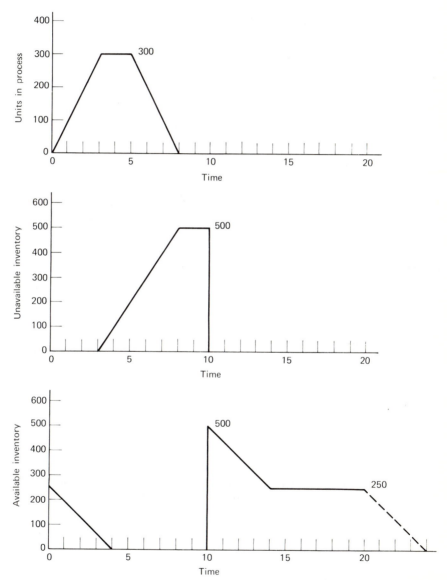

FIGURE 3-10. Graph of the work in process, unavailable, and available inventories at stage i, when $P_i = 100$, $X_i = 500$, $\tau_i = 3$, $l_i = 2$, $X_{i+1} = 250$, $P_{i+1} = 62.5$, and $D = 25$, so that $t_i = 5$ and $T_i = 20$ (Case II).

under the same assumptions as in Case I, and omit the tedious algebraic details of their development. The average inventories are

$$\overline{W}_i = \tau_i D \tag{3-73}$$

$$\overline{U}_i = \left[\frac{X_i}{2P_i} + l_i\right]D$$

$$= \frac{X_i}{2}\left[\frac{D}{P_i} + 2\beta_i D\right] + \alpha_i D \tag{3-74}$$

$$\overline{V}_i = \frac{X_{i+1}}{2}\left[n_i - 1 + \frac{D}{P_{i+1}}\right] \tag{3-75}$$

If we wish to obtain these results in terms of k_{i+1}, n_i, and X_M, we can substitute $X_i = n_i X_{i+1}$ and $X_{i+1} = k_{i+1} X_M$. The average on-hand inventory at any stage $i = 1, 2, \ldots, M - 1$ is then

$$\overline{I}_i = \overline{W}_i + \overline{U}_i + \overline{V}_i$$

$$= \frac{k_{i+1} X_M}{2}\left[n_i\left(1 + \frac{D}{P_i} + 2\beta_i D\right) - \left(1 - \frac{D}{P_{i+1}}\right)\right] + (\tau_i + \alpha_i)D \tag{3-76}$$

For the final stage, $\overline{W}_M$ and $\overline{U}_M$ are given by (3-73) and (3-74), respectively, and the average available inventory on hand when no shortages are allowed is

$$\overline{V}_M = \frac{X_M}{2} \tag{3-77}$$

When backorders are allowed,

$$\overline{V}_M = \frac{(X_M - b)^2}{2X_M} \tag{3-78}$$

where b is the maximum backorder position, and the average backorder level is

$$\overline{B}_M = \frac{b^2}{2X_M} \tag{3-79}$$

The behavior of the finished goods inventory is shown in Figure 3-11. Note that when a lot becomes available for use, backorders are satisfied and the remainder is added to inventory.

If we assume that at most one lot can be in production at facility i at any time, we must constrain the lot size at stage i, as shown in (3-71). Additionally, if we assume that the maximum size of the unavailable inventory is R_i, the lot size is further constrained by

$$\overline{U}_i \leq R_i$$

or

$$X_i \leq \frac{2P_i(R_i - \alpha_i D)}{D(1 + 2\beta_i P_i)} \tag{3-80}$$

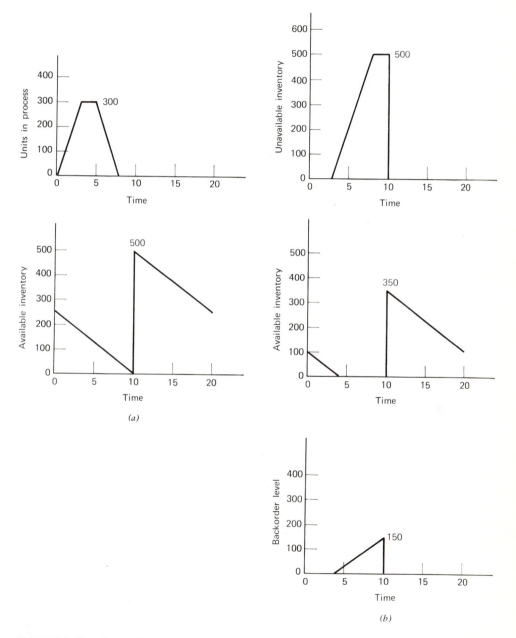

FIGURE 3-11. Stage M inventories and backlog position, when $P_M = 100$, $\tau_M = 3$, $X_M = 500$, $I_M = 2$, $D = 25$, and $b = 150$, so that $t_M = 5$ and $T_M = 20$. (Case II.) (a) No shortages allowed. (b) Backorders permitted.

Batch Production at Facility i. If production at facility i is not unit by unit, but instead the entire lot of X_i units is processed simultaneously as a batch, we can obtain the average inventory levels by adapting the results for Case II. We suppose that facility i withdraws X_i units instaneously from the inventory at stage $i - 1$ and processes them as a batch so that all units complete production at the same time; therefore, we have $P_i = \infty$. The time to process the batch is τ_i, and since it may depend on the batch size, we let

$$\tau_i = \gamma_i + \delta_i X_i \tag{3-81}$$

where for feasibility we must have $\delta_i D \leq 1$ (or else we could not meet the demand). Now the average work-in-progress inventory is

$$\overline{W}_i = (\gamma_i + \delta_i X_i)D \tag{3-82}$$

The average unavailable inventory is given by (3-74), with $P_i = \infty$:

$$\overline{U}_i = (\alpha_i + \beta_i X_i)D$$

The expressions for $\overline{V}_i$, $\overline{V}_M$, and $\overline{B}_M$ are unchanged.

We must modify the constraint (3-71) to reflect the dependence of τ_i on the lot size. The condition,

$$\tau_i + t_i + s_i \leq T_i$$

with τ_i given by (3-81) and $P_i = \infty$, implies

$$X_i \geq \frac{\gamma_i + s_i}{\delta_i} \tag{3-83}$$

Cost Model and Optimization. Now that we have the ability to express the inventory levels as functions of the lot sizes, we can formulate a cost model of the decision problem. We use a simple, but common, form for the objective function. Let

A_i = setup cost at stage i

c_i = unit variable production cost at stage i

h_i = inventory carrying cost per unit per unit time at stage i

$\hat{\pi}$ = backorder cost per unit per unit time at stage M

K = average total relevant cost per unit time

For the entire system of M stages,

$$K(X_1, X_2, \ldots, X_M, b) = \sum_{i=1}^{M} \left[\frac{A_i D}{X_i} + c_i D + h_i \bar{I}_i \right] + \hat{\pi} \overline{B}_M \tag{3-84}$$

where $\bar{I}_i = \overline{W}_i + \overline{U}_i + \overline{V}_i$ and $\overline{B}_M$ are functions of the decision variables $X_1, X_2, \ldots, X_M$, and b, whose form depends on the nature of the production operations. The problem is to minimize K, subject to the constraints

$\{X_i = n_i X_{i+1}\}$, where n_i is a positive integer, and possibly other restrictions such as (3-71) or (3-80). Because of the required relationship between the lot sizes, we have $K = K(n_1, n_2, \ldots, n_{M-1}, X_M, b)$, where generally X_M and b can be treated as continuous variables.

If the number of stages is small, solution for the optimal lot sizes is not difficult. General solutions for the two- and three-stage problems are given in Reference 8. For more than three stages, one can solve the equations, $\partial K/\partial X_M = 0$ and $\partial K/\partial b = 0$, for X_M^* and b^* in terms of $n_1, n_2, \ldots, n_{M-1}$. Substitution of these expressions into (3-84) yields $K(n_1, n_2, \ldots, n_{M-1}, X_M^*, b^*)$, a function of $M - 1$ positive integer-valued variables. Typically in practice, M will be small, probably less than six, and the costs will be such that the $\{n_i^*\}$ will also be reasonably small. This means that in many cases complete enumeration or a simple direct search procedure will quickly yield a solution. The optimization can also be approached through dynamic programming. A dynamic programming model and solution procedure are given in Reference 7 for the Case I situation.

The question now arises as to the optimality of the policy structure itself. We have considered only solutions that (1) have a constant lot size at each stage and (2) have the lot size at any stage i an integer multiple of the lot size at stage $i + 1$, and hence of the lot size at stage M. We adopted the first condition because it is well known that if the demand process is deterministic and constant and if the relevant cost factors do not change with time, an optimal policy for a single-stage system is to keep the lot size constant. Also, this policy has some appeal in practice because of its convenience in planning and execution. Therefore, we used it in our analysis; however, we can offer no proof of its optimality in the multistage case.

The second condition was used because, as will be shown in Chapter 4, when production and inventory costs are concave functions at every stage, it is not economic to set up and begin production such that product is added to inventory when there already is inventory on hand from a previous production run. Thus, in the concave cost case, we should plan our production so that product begins to be added to an inventory at a point in time when the previous inventory has been exhausted. This means that the lot size at a stage must be an integer multiple of the lot size at the following stage. However, the basis for this policy is not true for nonconcave cost functions, nor for systems having production capacity constraints. (The latter certainly would be the case when multiple products are produced by the same system.) While it is true that our objective function has proportional inventory costs and concave production costs, and so meets that criterion, it is not clear that having $X_i = n_i X_{i+1}$, for every i is optimal in a multistage system having constraints imposed by fixed production rates and lead times. Other treatments of this problem where this assumption also has been made are given in References 2 and 14. The analysis of Reference 7 does not require this policy structure.

3-9   References

1. **Charnes, A., W. W. Cooper, and G. H. Symonds,** "Cost Horizons and Certainty Equivalents: An Approach to Stochastic Programming of Heating Oil," *Management Science,* **4** (3), 1958, 235–263.

2. **Crowston, W. B., M. Wagner, and J. F. Williams,** "Economic Lot Size Determination in Multi-Stage Assembly Systems," *Management Science,* **19** (5), 1973, 517–527.

3. **Driebeek, N. J.,** *Applied Linear Programming,* Addison-Wesley, Reading, Mass., 1969.

4. **Hadley, G.,** *Nonlinear and Dynamic Programming,* Addison-Wesley, Reading, Mass., 1964.

5. **Hanssmann, F.,** "Optimal Inventory Location and Control in Production and Distribution Networks," *Operations Research,* **7** (4), 1959, pp. 483–498.

6. **Hanssmann, F.,** *Operations Research in Production and Inventory Control,* John Wiley & Sons, New York, 1962.

7. **Jensen, P. A., and H. A. Kahn,** "Scheduling in a Multistage Production System with Setup and Inventory Costs," *AIIE Transactions,* **IV** (2), 1972, 126–133.

8. **Johnson, L. A.,** "Multistage Economic Lot Size Problems with Static, Deterministic Demand," *Technical Papers,* Twenty-Third Annual Conference of the American Institute of Industrial Engineers, 1972, pp. 387–392.

9. **Magee, J. F., and D. M. Boodman,** *Production Planning and Inventory Control,* Second Edition, McGraw-Hill, New York, 1967.

10. **Manne, A. S.,** "Linear Programming and Sequential Descisions," *Management Science,* **6** (3), 1960, 259–267.

11. **Maxwell, W. L.,** "The Scheduling of Economic Lot Sizes," *Naval Research Logistics Quarterly,* **11** (2), 1964, 89–124.

12. **Simpson, K. S.,** "In-Process Inventories," *Operations Research,* **6** (6), 1958, 863–873.

13. **Smythe, W. R., and L. A. Johnson,** *Introduction to Linear Programming, with Applications,* Prentice-Hall, Englewood Cliffs, N.J., 1966.

14. **Taha, H. A., and R. W. Skeith,** "The Economic Lot Sizes in Multistage Production Systems," *AIIE Transactions,* **II** (2), 1970, 157–162.

15. **Wagner, H. M.,** *Principles of Operations Research,* Prentice-Hall, Englewood Cliffs, N.J., 1969.

3-10 Exercises

3-1   Three products are produced in a plant. For a given period, there is the problem of deciding how much of each product to produce. The table below contains information on the production process, profitability, and sales potential of each item. Note that the production of a unit of product A requires processing in all five departments.

| PRODUCT | PROCESSING TIME IN HOURS PER UNIT | | | | | UNIT PROFIT | SALES | |
	DEPT. I	DEPT. II	DEPT. III	INSPEC- TION	SHIPPING		MIN.	MAX.
A	0.14	0.6	0.2	0.04	0.10	$42	150	250
B	0.10	0.4	0.2	0.04	0.10	40	200	400
C		0.2	0.1	0.04	0.12	36	360	500
Hours of capacity	160	320	160	80	80			

(a)   Formulate a linear programming model.

(b)   If you have access to a computer and a linear programming software package, solve for the optimal production program. What departments have surplus capacity? Which products are at their upper bound and which at their lower bound? For what range of the unit profits is this solution optimal? Investigate the effects of varying the capacities of the different departments.

3-2   A department produces two parts, A and B, made according to the following routings:

	OPERATION	ON MACHINE	UNIT PROCESSING TIME IN HOURS	FRACTION SCRAP
Product A	1	M1	0.03	0.01
	2	M2	0.07	0.05
	3	M3	0.05	0.02
Product B	1	M1	0.12	0.03
	2	M3	0.08	0.10
	3	M4	0.17	0.02
	4	M1	0.04	0.07

Machine operating cost data are as follows:

MACHINE	COST PER HOUR	HOURS OF PRODUCTION TIME AVAILABLE
1	$20	400
2	30	340
3	40	410
4	50	160

Product data are as follows:

PRODUCT	UNIT SELLING PRICE	UNIT RAW MATERIAL COST	SALES LEVEL CONSTRAINTS MINIMUM	MAXIMUM
A	$ 60	$20	100 units	None
B	100	25	150 units	250 units

The problem is to schedule production for the department in the next period. Put this problem in linear programming form. Assume that all defective parts are immediately detected and removed. (*Hint:* Let X_1 and X_2 be the amount of each product *started* in the next period.)

3-3   Formulate the following problem as a linear programming problem. Be certain to define the variables and show the objective function and the constraints.

A plant can manufacture three products, A, B, and C. The plant has four departments, I, II, III, and IV. Product A must be processed in departments I and II; product B in departments I, II, III, and IV; and product C in departments I, III, and IV.

The problem is to determine the most profitable product mix for the plant during the next month. Relevant data are the following:

PRODUCT	OUTPUT RATE IN PIECES PER HOUR DEPT. I	DEPT. II	DEPT. III	DEPT. IV	PROFIT PER PIECE
A	20	40			$3.10
B	30	25	10	22	2.05
C	60		20	5	6.17
Available Hours	150	160	130	100	

Departments I and II must each be scheduled for at least 100 hours. At least 1000 pieces of product A must be manufactured. A purchased part used in the assembly of products A and C is scarce—only 3500 parts are available for the month. Two parts are used in each piece of product A and three parts are used in each piece of product C.

3-4 For the situation of Exercise 3-1, suppose that the demand for each product is assumed to be normally distributed with $\mu_A = 200$, $\sigma_A = 10$, $\mu_B = 300$, $\sigma_B = 15$, $\mu_C = 500$, and $\sigma_C = 20$. Instead of the upper and lower bounds on product availability for sale, suppose management wishes to impose the following constraints on the production program: "The chance that we produce more of product C than we can sell should be no more than 0.10, the chance that we do not produce enough of product A should be less than or equal to 0.20, and the chance that we do not produce enough of product B should be 50–50." How would you incorporate these constraints into the linear programming model?

3-5 A manufacturer is to produce three items for a special sale. All production must take place prior to the start of the selling period. Items left over at the end of the period must be disposed of at a reduced price. He assumes the demand for item i is uniformly distributed over the interval $[a_i, b_i]$; that is

$$f_i(D_i) = \begin{cases} \dfrac{1}{b_i - a_i}, & a_i \le D_i \le b_i \\ 0, & \text{otherwise} \end{cases}$$

He only has $10,000 to finance his presale inventory. Using the data in the table below, find the optimal stock level for each product. If the constraint is active, interpret the value of the Lagrange multiplier.

PRODUCT	UNIT COST	SELLING PRICE	DISPOSAL VALUE	a_i	b_i
1	$10	$20	$ 5	150	250
2	20	35	10	0	400
3	30	50	20	100	300

3-6 Solve the problem of Exercise 3-5 assuming that the probability distribution of demand is normally distributed for each product. Assume that these normal distributions have the same mean and variance as the uniform distributions of Exercise 3-5. Compare answers. (*Note:* The mean of the uniform distribution is $(b + a)/2$ and the variance is $(b - a)^2/12$.)

3-7 *Multiproduct Constrained Stochastic Problem—Incremental Analysis.* Consider the discrete version of Example 3-3. Assume that the probability distribution of demand for product i is $p_i(D_i)$, $D_i = 0, 1, 2, \ldots$, and that all other notation is unchanged.

(a) Write the expression for the expected contribution to profit and overhead.

(b) Develop an expression for the incremental value of changing the stock level of product i from $X_i - 1$ to X_i. That is, compute the following partial difference of $E(Z)$ with respect to X_i:

$$E[Z(X_1, X_2, \ldots, X_i, \ldots, X_n)]$$
$$- E[Z(X_1, X_2, \ldots, X_i - 1, \ldots, X_n)]$$

(c) How could you use information about incremental values to optimally allocate the quantity B?

3-8 *Multiproduct Constrained Stochastic Problem—Dynamic Programming.* Consider the discrete version of Example 3-3. Assume that the probability distribution of demand for product i is $p_i(D_i)$, $D_i = 0, 1, 2, \ldots$, and that all other notation is unchanged. Develop a dynamic programming approach to the solution.

3-9 *Multiproduct Single-Period Stochastic Problem—Fixed Charge Model.* How would you modify the analysis in Example 3-3 if there were a fixed charge, A_i, if product i is produced. That is, the procurement cost function is

$$C_i(X_i) = \begin{cases} 0, & \text{if } X_i = 0 \\ A_i + c_i X_i, & \text{if } X_i > 0 \end{cases}$$

Include the possibility that there are I_i units of product i already in inventory prior to the stocking decision.

3-10 *Setup Costs in the Product Mix Model.* Suppose in the product mix model (3-1) of Section 3-2, the production cost for product i is

$$C_i(X_i) = \begin{cases} 0, & \text{if } X_i = 0 \\ A_i + c_i X_i, & \text{if } X_i > 0 \end{cases}$$

Reformulate the model as a mixed-integer programming model, containing n integer variables such that the ith variable, δ_i, is 0, if $X_i = 0$, and 1, if $X_i > 0$. How would you obtain a solution?

3-11   In the situation of Exercise 3-2, suppose that the production requirements for products A and B in a period were fixed at 3000 and 2000 units, respectively. The product routing data and production rates are as shown in Exercise 3-2; however, suppose that both regular time and overtime options are available in the period. Capacity and cost data are shown in the following table:

MACHINE	MACHINE-HOURS AVAILABLE		MACHINE COST PER HOUR	
	REGULAR TIME	OVERTIME	REGULAR TIME	OVERTIME
1	400	80	$20	$30
2	340	68	30	40
3	160	0	40	50
4	300	60	50	70

Assume the same unit selling prices and unit raw material costs as given in Exercise 3-2. Formulate this production planning problem as a linear programming model.

3-12   Assuming that you solved Exercise 3-11 by defining the decision variables to be the number of *units* of a product produced by a given production alternative, use a somewhat different approach and reformulate the problem when the decision variables are the number of regular time and the number of overtime *machine-hours* scheduled for each product. Compare the two models. Does one approach offer advantages over the other?

3-13   In Exercise 3-12, suppose that the fourth operation for product B can be subcontracted for $1 a unit. Then it may be desirable to have some or all of product B sent to the subcontractor for this last operation. Reformulate the linear programming model. If there were also a fixed cost of $500 when subcontracting is used, how would you proceed with the analysis?

3-14   A plant manufactures three products, A, B, and C. Four production departments are involved. A product may be made through alternative routings. For example, product A can be manufactured through processing in departments I, II, and III, *or* in departments I, II, IV. Profit depends on the routing. The following data are relevant:

	ROUTING ALTERNATIVE	DEPT. I	DEPT. II	DEPT. III	DEPT. IV	PROFIT PER UNIT
		HOURS PER UNIT				
PRODUCT						
A	1	0.21	1.15	3.20	—	$ 6.00
	2	0.21	1.15	—	2.75	5.90
B	1	1.30	2.19	—	—	10.00
	2	1.30	—	1.60	—	11.50
	3	1.30	—	—	2.40	9.70
C	1	—	4.00	2.60	1.00	8.50
Available hours		160	140	150	120	

The hours available for scheduling in the period to be planned are shown on the last row.

At least 10 units of product B must be manufactured in the period. No more than 40 units of product C may be manufactured because of material limitations.

Develop a linear programming formulation of the problem of determining how many units of each product to manufacture in the period.

3-15 Write a general linear programming model for the combined product mix, process selection problem illustrated by Example 3-5.

3-16 In Example 3-6, suppose that the customer order is for 4000 tons of the alloy and that the producer has only the following amounts of the six ores available (in tons): 2500, 2200, 800, 3000, 1000, and 1600.

(a) Formulate the appropriate model.
(b) Write a general linear programming formulation for the resource-constrained blending problem, where the raw materials are in limited supply.

3-17 To produce lawn fertilizer, a manufacturer mixes nitrates, phosphates, and potash with inert ingredients and packages the mix for sale. The four products are 14–5–10, 10–6–4, 8–8–6, and 6–8–6, where the numbers are the percentages by weight of nitrates, phosphates, and potash, respectively.

The manufacturer wishes to plan production for a period given the following data on material availability, material costs, product selling price, and product sales forecasts:

INGREDIENT	QUANTITY AVAILABLE	COST PER TON
Nitrates	2000 tons	$220
Phosphates	1000	80
Potash	1500	130
Inert	No limit	20

PRODUCT	PRICE PER TON	MINIMUM SALES	MAXIMUM SALES
14–5–10	$150	2000 tons	4000 tons
10–6–4	120	3000	8000
8–8–6	90	0	5000
6–8–6	70	1000	9000

Other production and selling costs are estimated at $30 per ton, regardless of the product.

Formulate a linear programming model for the purpose of determining how much of each product to produce in the period, assuming that the manufacturer's policy is to produce at least the minimum sales level predicted for each product.

3-18 A coffee manufacturer produces several brands of coffee from a number of different types of coffee bean. A given brand is made by mixing several types of beans in a given proportion, then roasting, grinding, and packaging the blend. It turns out that the flavor of a brand can be obtained using a number of different blends. These alternative blends have different costs because of differences among bean costs. For any given time period there will be stated production requirements for each brand and given availabilities of each bean type. The problem is to use the available supply of beans to meet the production goals at minimum cost. Formulate a linear programming model, given the following data:

TYPE OF BEAN	COST PER POUND	POUNDS AVAILABLE	SPECIFICATIONS ON COFFEE BRANDS		
			BRAND A	BRAND B	BRAND C
1	$0.23	4000	None	$\geq 20\%, \leq 40\%$	$\geq 40\%$
2	0.20	6000	$\geq 10\%$	$\geq 30\%, \leq 70\%$	$\leq 60\%$
3	0.15	2500	$\geq 40\%, \leq 70\%$		$\leq 10\%$
4	0.10	8000	$\leq 80\%$	$\leq 10\%$	None

Production requirements are 5000 pounds of Brand A, 10,000 pounds of B, and 3000 pounds of C.

3-19 Exercises 3-17 and 3-18 differ somewhat from the "pure" blending problem described in Section 3-4. In Exercise 3-17, there is a product mix feature with limited materials, while in Exercise 3-18 there are several products with limited materials. For each of these situations, write a general linear programming model. These models are extentions of model (3-10).

3-20 Modify model (3-11) in Section (3-5) to fit the situation where there is a limited supply, B, of the material in the period. There are no fixed production requirements for product i; however, from consideration of sales potential, production of product i must lie between L_i and U_i. The unit revenue from the sale of product i is r_i. The objective is to use the available material in an optimal manner.

3-21 A paper company produces large rolls of paper of a given diameter in two standard widths: 240 inches and 150 inches. To fill customer orders, these rolls must be cut into narrower widths. In the current period, there is a need for 300 70-inch wide rolls, 400 90-inch wide rolls, and 600 35-inch rolls. Formulate a mathematical programming model to plan the cutting of standard rolls to fill this order. Assume an unlimited supply of each type of standard roll.

3-22 Modify the formulation of Exercise 3-21 to account for a limitation on the number of standard rolls of each type. Specifically, suppose there are 200 of the 240-inch rolls and 300 of the 150-inch rolls available for cutting.

3-23 A quarry has a stone-crushing operation. A machine crushes large pieces of stone and the output is screened to separate it by degree of fineness, or size. By changing the setup of the machine, output having different size percentages can be obtained. Suppose there are n settings for the machine and let f_{ij} be the fraction of output that is in size category $j, j = 1, 2, \ldots, m$, when the setting is i. In a given period there is a need for D_j tons of size j rock. If c_i is the cost to crush a ton of stone using setting i, write a model to solve the problem of how to meet this demand.

3-24 In the situation of Exercise 3-23, suppose there is a limited supply, B, of large stone for crushing, and the problem is to determine the best way to process it. Let r_j be the selling price of a ton of crushed stone of size j and U_j be the maximum amount of size j that can be sold. Formulate a linear programming model.

3-25 Five products are produced to inventory in lots on the same machine. To make scheduling easier, it has been decided to produce a lot of each product, in sequence, prior to repeating production of a product. A "cycle" consists then of producing five lots and possibly idle time before beginning the next cycle. Demand rates for the five products are assumed to remain constant over time, so all cycles are to be of the same length T. Determine the most economic value for T and the associated lot sizes for each product, given the following data:

PRODUCT	ANNUAL REQUIREMENTS IN UNITS	MACHINE HOURS PER UNIT	MACHINE SETUP COST	UNIT VARIABLE PRODUCTION COST
A	4,000	0.20	$100	$ 5
B	15,000	0.01	120	10
C	2,000	0.10	250	20
D	8,000	0.05	280	10
E	1,000	0.20	120	5

The annual inventory carrying cost rate is 20 percent. Assume the machine is available 2000 hours per year. Also assume setup times are very small.

3-26 Three products are manufactured on a single machine. The demand rate for each item is known and constant. It has been decided that all products are to have a common production cycle time. During this interval the machine will produce a lot of each product. No shortages are permitted. The following data are available:

PRODUCT	ANNUAL DEMAND RATE	ANNUAL PRODUCTION RATE	SETUP COST	SETUP TIME	MANUFACTURING COST PER UNIT
1	15,000	60,000	$150	2 days	$10
2	20,000	40,000	100	1	5
3	6,000	50,000	150	3	30

The annual inventory carrying cost rate is 0.20. Find the optimal cycle time, the associated lot sizes for each product, the fraction of time the machine will be idle, and the average annual cost of this policy. Also compute the average annual cost that would be incurred if the products were produced on separate machines at the same rates and costs as above. What are your conclusions about the desirability of deviating from a rotation cycle?

3-27 *Single-Facility Lot-Size Problem with Backorders.* Modify the analysis of Section 3-6 for the case where backorders are allowed at a cost of $\hat{\pi}_j$ per unit of product j backordered for one unit of time. (See Section 2-2 for the single-product analysis.)

3-28 Three products are produced on the same facility. Their demand rates are known and constant. Shortages can be backordered (see Exercise 3-27). What production policy would you recommend, given the following data:

PRODUCT	ANNUAL DEMAND	PRODUC- TION RATE	SETUP COST	UNIT COST	INVENTORY COST PER UNIT	BACKORDER COST PER UNIT
1	20,000	80,000	$150	$2	$0.50	$ 3.00
2	10,000	50,000	200	4	1.00	10.00
3	30,000	90,000	400	6	1.50	6.00

The inventory and backorder costs are expressed as cost per unit per year. Setup times are negligible.

3-29 *Secondary Production Source with Setup Cost.* Consider the problem of determining the optimal production lot size under the following conditions:

D = annual demand rate (constant)

i = inventory carrying-cost rate (annually)

A_1 = setup cost of primary production facility

c_1 = variable cost per unit produced on primary facility

P_1 = production rate of primary facility in units per year

A_2 = setup cost of secondary production facility

c_2 = variable cost per unit produced on secondary facility

P_2 = production rate of secondary facility in units per year

The policy is that if a lot of more than N units is ordered, both production facilities are used to produce the lot; otherwise only the primary facility is used.

Let X denote the lot size. Assume no shortages are permitted. Develop a procedure for finding the optimal value of X.

3-30 *Reject Allowance Problem.* A customer places an order for D pieces of a part that your company can manufacture on a single machine. This is a custom part and you doubt that the order will be repeated. The customer will pay you r dollars per piece produced within stated quality specifications, subject to the following conditions: (1) he will not pay for more than $D + d$ pieces, $(d > 0)$; (2) he will reject the entire shipment, if it contains less than $D - e$ pieces, $(e \geq 0)$, and will make no payment and will cancel his order.

The cost of manufacturing and delivering the order is estimated to be c dollars per piece. The manufacturing process is such that the probability of any piece being out of specifications is p. Because of a lack of instrumentation, you cannot inspect the output; this will be done by the customer after your shipment is delivered.

The problem is to determine how many pieces to manufacture to satisfy this order.

(a) Develop a model and solution procedure.

(b) Solve for $D = 200, e = 10, d = 5, p = 0.10, c = \$30$, and $r = \$50$.

3-31 *Allowance for Production Losses in Batch Size Determination.* A simple chemical process may be represented as follows:

where X = input in gallons and p = fraction of input lost because of evaporation, etc. Assume p is a random variable having probability density function $f(p)$.

The plant is a special order shop. Assume that an order for D gallons has been received. The problem is to determine the number of gallons of raw material to start (X). The following costs are pertinent:

C_m = cost per gallon of raw material

C_p = cost per gallon of processing (based on input amount)

R = selling price per gallon (up to D gallons)

L = penalty cost (lump sum) if delivered quantity is less than D

The company's policy is to run a batch of X gallons of raw material. If the output exceeds the order size, the excess is thrown away and only D gallons are sent to the customer. On the other hand, if the output is less than D, it is all sent to the customer and a penalty charge of L dollars must be paid. The company will not make an additional run.

How would you find the optimal value of X?

3-32 *Reject Allowance Problem.* A part is produced on a single machine, which has a constant probability p of producing a defective part. A production order calls for D good items. Because inspection takes place after production of the entire lot (of $X \geq D$ units), there is a possibility that the number of good items in the lot will be less than the required D. In that event, the machine would be set up again and additional parts produced until the deficit in good parts is satisfied. In this second production run, the operator inspects each part after production to classify it "good" or "defective." This means a higher unit production cost than on the first run.

Construct an economic model to determine the optimal lot size. Define notation. Be sure to include setup costs. Develop a method of solving the model.

3-33 A chemical product can be produced once every four weeks. The production process is such that the lot size must be an integer multiple of the capacity of a certain piece of equipment. Using this capacity as the unit of measurement, the demand for this product during a four-week period is a random variable having the following probability distribution:

DEMAND, D	$p(D)$
2	0.15
3	0.20
4	0.30
5	0.25
6	0.10

The cost of producing a lot of size X is

$$C(X) = \begin{cases} 0, & \text{if } X = 0 \\ 1000 + 200X, & \text{if } X = 1, 2, 3 \\ 1600 + 150(X - 3), & \text{if } X = 4, 5, \ldots \end{cases}$$

and the cost of having I units of inventory on hand at the start of a month is $H(I) = 50I$. Shortages cannot be backlogged, and the cost of being short K units during a month is given by

$$S(K) = \begin{cases} 0, & \text{if } K = 0 \\ 100 + 500K, & \text{if } K = 1, 2, 3 \\ 1600 + 700(K - 3)^2, & \text{if } K = 4, 5, \ldots \end{cases}$$

Because of storage limitations, the inventory level at the end of any period cannot exceed seven units. The problem is to develop a policy for determining how much to produce each month.

(a) Use the method of Section 3-7.1 to formulate this problem as a linear programming model. Summarize by giving a tableau of the form shown in Figure 3-3.

(b) Assuming you have access to a digital computer and a linear programming software package, solve the model and compute the optimal production policy.

3-34 For a single-item periodic review system with backorders allowed, use the Markov chain/linear programming approach described in Section 3-7.1 to develop a method for determining the optimal production policy.

3-35 Consider the multiproduct version of the situation of Section 3-7.1. Each of n products has known stationary demand distribution and cost functions. Assume that there is a single resource constraint of the form

$$\sum_{j=1}^{n} e_j X_j \le b$$

in each period. Can the Markov chain/linear programming approach be used to develop a production policy for the n products? Explain your answer.

3-36 Show that the optimal solution to the model (3-33) is defined by (3-34). You may need the following properties of the standard normal variable:

$$\int_k^\infty z\phi(z)\, dz = \phi(k)$$

$$\int_k^\infty z^2\phi(z)\, dz = z\phi(k) + 1 - \Phi(k)$$

3-37 Repeat the development and solution of model (3-33) in Section 3-7.2 assuming that the demand in a period is Poisson with mean μ. Then continue the analysis, assuming that the mean is a monotone decreasing function of the service time, S, of the system.

3-38 The production program for a product is reviewed weekly and a production lot is ordered at that time. The policy is to order the difference between the inventory position at that time and a constant target inventory position, R. Thus an (R, T) policy is used, with T equal to one week. The production lead time is four weeks. Demand for the product in any week is normally distributed with a mean of 400 and a standard deviation of 30. The annual inventory carrying cost rate is 0.20 and the unit variable production cost is $26. Shortages are backlogged at a cost of $1 per unit. Production setup costs are negligible. Find the optimal net inventory position at the end of any period. Find the optimal value for R.

3-39 Solve Exercise 3-38 assuming that demand in any week is a normally distributed random variable with mean $400v(S)$ and standard deviation $30v(S)$, where S is the average service time of the system and $v(S)$ is the following function of S:

S, weeks:	0	0.25	0.50	0.75	1.00	1.25	1.50	1.75	2.00	2.25	2.50
$v(S)$:		1.0	0.95	0.90	0.85	0.80	0.75	0.70	0.60	0.50	0.40	0.30

The unit selling price is $30.

3-40 Model the problem of Example 3-4 as a four-stage process, where the stages are (1) stamping and drilling, (2) assembly, (3) finishing, and (4) packaging. (See also Example 3-10.)

3-41 Model the problem of Exercise 3-1 as a three-stage process, where the stages are (1) Departments I and II, (2) Department III, and (3) Inspection and Shipping. Define notation for any cost or revenue coefficients you need, but do not have numerical values for.

3-42 Model the problem of Exercise 3-14 as a four-stage process, where each department is treated as a separate stage. Define notation for any cost or revenue coefficients you need, but do not have numerical values for.

3-43 A company has four plants, each of which manufactures the same product. Production costs differ from one plant to another, as do the costs of raw materials. There are five regional warehouses, and customers pay different prices at each. Given the data in the table at the top of page 181, what is the best production and distribution schedule?

3-44 In the problem of Exercise 3-43, suppose that units can be transhipped from Plant 4 through Plant 1 to any warehouse at an additional cost of $3 per unit (for the interplant shipment) and that units can be shipped

	PLANT					
	1	2	3	4	SELLING	MAXIMUM SALES
Material cost	$ 15	$ 18	$ 14	$ 13	SELLING	SALES
Other production costs	10	9	12	8	PRICE	IN UNITS
Transportation costs:						
Warehouse 1	$ 3	$ 9	$ 5	$ 4	$34	80
Warehouse 2	1	7	4	5	32	110
Warehouse 3	5	8	3	10	31	150
Warehouse 4	7	3	8	12	35	100
Warehouse 5	4	5	6	7	30	150
Plant capacity, units	150	200	175	100		

from Warehouse 2 to Warehouse 3 and Warehouse 4 at a unit cost of $4 and $5, respectively.

(a) Formulate a linear programming model.

(b) Set up in a tableau for solution as a transportation problem.

(c) Solve for the optimal production-distribution program.

3-45 Two products are manufactured by a two-plant production system. Plant A has four production centers and produces three semifinished products, which are used by Plant B to make the two finished products. Plant B has two production centers. Within each plant there are alternative ways to produce the products. The following data are for Plant A:

SEMIFINISHED PRODUCT	PRODUCTION ALTERNATIVE	PRODUCTION RATE IN UNITS PER HOUR IN PLANT A PRODUCTION CENTER			
		1	2	3	4
1	1	20	10		10
	2	20	10	25	
2	1	5		20	5
	2	5	40		10
	3		10	20	20
3	1	1	2	4	10
Production hours available		320	240	320	400
Cost per hour		$100	$200	$300	$250

Note, for example, that production alternative 1 for semifinished product 1 involves processing each unit of that product in centers 1, 2, and 4. Material costs are $100, $150, and $200, respectively, for the three semifinished products.

To produce a unit of finished product 1, two units of semifinished product 1 and one unit of semifinished product 2 are required. To produce a unit of finished product 2, one unit of each of the three semifinished units is required. Additional data for Plant B are given in the following table:

FINISHED PRODUCT	PRODUCTION ALTERNATIVE	PRODUCTION RATE IN UNITS PER HOUR	
		CENTER 1	CENTER 2
1	1	0.40	
	2		0.50
2	1	0.50	1.00
Production hours available		500	400
Cost per hour		$600	$800

For the period under consideration, it is required that 200 units of product 1 and 200 units of product 2 be produced.

(a) Formulate a linear programming model to determine how best to meet these production goals. Treat the problem as a two-stage system.

(b) Repeat part (a), treating the problem a single-stage system.

3-46 In Exercise 3-45, suppose no fixed production requirements were given for the two finished products and the manufacturer wanted to determine his maximum profit production program. Product 1 sells for $3000 and product 2 for $3500. The maximum sales potential for product 1 is 250 units and for product 2 is 220 units.

(a) Formulate a linear programming model, treating the problem as a two-stage system.

(b) Repeat part (a), treating the problem as a single-stage system.

3-47 Consider a two-stage inventory system: raw material inventory and finished product inventory. The product is sold in a short selling season and there is no opportunity to resupply the raw material inventory once the season begins. The problem is to determine the amount of raw material and the amount of finished product to stock at the start of the season, given the following information:

Cost of a unit of raw material—$20

Cost of converting a unit of raw material into a finished product—$10

Scrap value of a finished unit—$5

Scrap value of a unit of raw material—$15

Selling price per unit—$50

Fraction of customers who will wait for production if out of finished stock = 0.20

Probability distribution of demand—$f(D) = 0.005$, for $200 \leq X \leq 400$

3-48 Solve the problem of Exercise 3-47, assuming demand is normally distributed with mean 300 and standard deviation 60.

3-49 Show that Equations 3-42 and 3-43 define the optimal solution to the model of Section 3-8.2.

3-50 Formulate and solve a model for the two-stage problem of Section 3-8.2 when demand is a discrete random variable having probability mass function $p(D)$.

3-51 Formulate a general M-stage model for the problem of Section 3-8.2. Assume that α_j is the fraction of customers who will wait for material to be processed from stage j into finished product, where $\alpha_j \leq \alpha_{j+1}$, $j = 1, 2, \ldots, M - 2$. (Stage M is to be the finished product inventory.) How would you solve for the optimal stock level at each stage?

3-52 Analyze the multistage base stock system of Section 3-8.3 for the case of demand in any time period of length t being a Poisson variable with mean λt.

3-53 A production-distribution system for a product has four stages in series. A raw material inventory precedes the first stage and is assumed to never run short. Inventories at other stages are controlled by base stock systems. Using the terminology and notation of Section 3-8.3, the production lead times in days are $\tau_1 = 6, \tau_2 = 10, \tau_3 = 20$, and $\tau_4 = 5$; the maximum service time at the finished goods inventory is to be $S_4 = 0$; the probabilities of exceeding the maximum service times at the stages are specified as $\alpha_1 = 0.10$, $\alpha_2 = 0.05$, $\alpha_3 = 0.05$, and $\alpha_4 = 0.01$; and the inventory holding costs per unit per year at the stages are $h_1 = \$4$, $h_2 = \$6$, $h_3 = \$10$, and $h_4 = \$15$. Daily demand for the product is assumed to be normally distributed with a mean of 100 and a standard deviation of 20. Find the optimal base stock levels for each stage.

3-54 Show that $E(I^+)$ and $E(I^-)$, defined by Equations 3-31 and 3-32, respectively, can be computed from

$$E(I^+) = \hat{\sigma}L'\left(\frac{-\hat{I}}{\hat{\sigma}}\right) = \hat{\sigma}L\left(\frac{\hat{I}}{\hat{\sigma}}\right)$$

$$E(I^-) = \hat{\sigma}L\left(\frac{-\hat{I}}{\hat{\sigma}}\right) = \hat{\sigma}L'\left(\frac{\hat{I}}{\hat{\sigma}}\right)$$

where $L'(u)$ and $L(u)$ are right- and left-hand unit-normal linear loss integrals, whose values are given in Table A-3 of the Appendix. (See also Exercise 2-61.) Also note that $E(I^+) - E(I^-) = \hat{I}$.

3-55 For the two-stage system of Section 3-8.4, suppose $\mu = 800$, $\sigma = 100$, $v(S_2) = e^{-S_2}$, $\tau_1 = 3$, and $\tau_2 = 5$. Use the results given in Exercise 3-54 in completing the following:

(a) If $S_1 = 1$ and $S_2 = 2$, find $\hat{I}$ and $\hat{J}$. What are the expected on-hand inventory positions? Repeat for $S_1 = 3$, $S_2 = 2$; $S_1 = 3$, $S_2 = 8$; and $S_1 = 0$, $S_2 = 2$.

(b) If $\hat{I} = 2500$ and $\hat{J} = 4000$, what are S_1 and S_2?

3-56 Suppose in the situation of Section 3-8.4, management has arbitrarily decided that $S_1 = 1$ and $S_2 = 1$ are good values for the service times at the semifinished and finished product inventories. The production lead times are $\tau_1 = 8$ and $\tau_2 = 4$. Time is measured in multiples of the review period, which is one week. Demand is normally distributed with $\mu = 1000$, $\sigma = 400$, and $v(S_2) = e^{-S_2/10}$.

(a) What are the target net inventories $\hat{I}$ and $\hat{J}$?

(b) At the start of a week, the finished goods inventory level is 1200. Production lots in progress at stage 2 and due to be completed within the next four weeks are $Y_1 = 700$, $Y_2 = 900$, $Y_3 = 700$, and $Y_4 = 800$. At the start of the same week, the semifinished net inventory is -100 (a backlog condition). Lots in progress at stage 1 have sizes $X_1 = 1200$, $X_2 = 800$, $X_3 = 1400$, $X_4 = 1000$, $X_5 = 600$, $X_6 = 1100$, $X_7 = 700$, and $X_8 = 1500$. What should be the size of the production order to be placed for finished goods at this time? What should be the size of the lots put into production at each stage?

(c) Rework part (b) assuming the current semifinished net inventory is 100.

(d) What are the average on-hand inventory levels?

3-57 *Purchasing and Production.* Consider a two-stage system that produces a single finished product from a single raw material and consists of a raw material inventory, a production facility, and a finished goods inventory. The demand rate for the product is known and constant at D units per unit time. Because the production rate, P, of the facility exceeds D, production is intermittant. Let A_2 be the production setup cost, C_2 be the processing cost per unit (excluding raw material cost), and X_2 be the production lot size. The raw material is purchased in lots of size X_1, and has a unit variable cost of C_1 and a fixed procurement cost per lot of A_1. It takes k units of raw material to produce one unit of product. No shortages are permitted at any inventory point.

(a) If raw material can be stocked *only during the time production takes place*, develop expressions for the optimal procurement and production lot sizes.

(b) Develop expressions for optimal X_1 and X_2, without the constraint of part (a).

(c) Under what conditions, if any, would the policy of part (a) be optimal?

3-58 A single product is produced by a two-stage production system, where each stage consists of a single production facility followed by an inventory. Production at each stage is in lots, with the lot size, X_1, at stage 1 twice the lot size, X_2, at stage 2. The demand rate on the inventory at stage 2 is constant at D units per unit time. The production rate at the first stage is $P_1 > D$. Production is unit by unit, with a processing time of τ_1. Because of inspection and transportation, there is a delay of length $\alpha_1 + \beta_1 X_1$ before a completed first-stage lot is available for use by the second stage. Until a unit is actually put into production at the second stage, it is considered to be in the first-stage inventory. The production process at stage 2 is such that X_2 units are withdrawn instantaneously from the first-stage inventory and simultaneously started into production at the second stage. After a processing time at stage 2 of $\gamma_2 + \delta_2 X_2$, the lot is available to satisfy demand. No shortages are allowed at either inventory. Derive expressions for the average inventory level at each stage. Do your results agree with those given by the formulas in Section 3-8.5?

3-59 For the serial system of Section 3-8.5, when there are two stages and production and usage of lots can occur simultaneously, write an appropriate cost model for finding the optimal lot sizes. Develop a solution method.

3-60 Repeat Exercise 3-59 for a three-stage system.

chapter 4
Production Planning—
Dynamic Models

4-1 Introduction

In this chapter, we are concerned with planning production over a future interval of time, called the *planning horizon*, during which the rate of demand for the product varies. We assume this time interval is divided into periods and that the planning problem is to establish a production rate for each period in the planning horizon. The demand rate in each period is assumed to be known, but is not necessarily constant from period to period. When the demand rate varies over time, the associated planning problem is said to be *dynamic*.

The following are some of the alternatives available to management in planning to meet a fluctuating demand:

1. Build inventories during periods of slack demand in anticipation of higher demand rates later in the planning interval.

2. Carry backorders or tolerate lost sales during periods of peak demand.

3. Use overtime in peak periods or undertime in slack periods to vary output while holding work force and facilities constant.

4. Use subcontracting in peak periods.

5. Vary capacity by changing the size of the work force through hiring and firing.

6. Vary capacity through changes in plant and equipment. Since we typically are concerned with planning horizons less than a year, we usually shall assume that facilities are fixed and thus that this alternative is not available to the planner.

The optimal combination of these methods involves proper tradeoffs between the following types of costs:

1. Procurement costs for product purchased from outside sources.

2. Production costs, which include any out-of-pocket costs that are associated with production under normal conditions and that vary with the production rate.

3. Inventory holding costs.

4. Shortage losses associated with backorders and lost sales.

5. Costs of increasing and decreasing work force levels. These include hiring and training costs and separation pay and other losses associated with firing or laying off workers.

6. Costs of deviating from normal capacity through use of overtime or undertime. Wage rate premiums for overtime work and opportunity losses because of underutilization of the work force are examples.

7. Cost of *changing* production rates. Examples are machine setup and takedown costs, opportunity losses because of lost production during change-over, and losses because of quality problems and inefficiencies resulting from schedule changes.

As we shall see, only certain of these management alternatives and costs are considered in any particular model found in the operations research literature.

☐**EXAMPLE 4-1** Table 4-1 contains a forecast of expected sales of a product over a one-year planning horizon, broken into 13 four-week periods. The seasonality of the demand pattern is apparent from observing the changes in the slope of the cumulative demand curve shown in Figure 4-1. The two dashed curves represent alternative production programs for the year. The first plan

TABLE 4-1 Demand Forecast for Example 4-1

PERIOD	EXPECTED DEMAND	CUMULATIVE DEMAND
1	100	100
2	180	280
3	220	500
4	150	650
5	100	750
6	200	950
7	250	1200
8	300	1500
9	260	1760
10	250	2010
11	240	2250
12	210	2460
13	140	2600

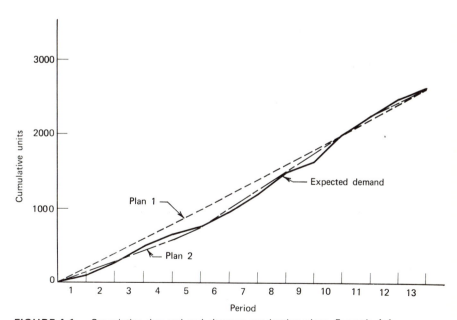

FIGURE 4-1. Cumulative demand and alternate production plans, Example 4-1.

TABLE 4-2 Analysis of Plan 1, Example 4-1

PERIOD	PRODUC-TION	INVENTORY	BACK-ORDERS	CAPACITY CHANGE	OVERTIME	SUB-CONTRACT
1	200	100	0	+20	0	0
2	200	120	0	0	0	0
3	200	100	0	0	0	0
4	200	150	0	0	0	0
5	200	250	0	0	0	0
6	200	250	0	0	0	0
7	200	200	0	0	0	0
8	200	100	0	0	0	0
9	200	40	0	0	0	0
10	200	0	10	0	0	0
11	200	0	50	0	0	0
12	200	0	60	0	0	0
13	200	0	0	0	0	0

is to produce at a constant rate of 200 units per period for the entire year. The second plan has a production rate of 150 units for each of the first five periods, 250 units for each of the next six periods, and 175 units for the last two periods. From Tables 4-2 and 4-3, one can compare the two plans with regard to inventories, backorders, overtime, subcontracting, and production rate changes. In developing these tables, it was assumed that all shortages are backordered,

TABLE 4-3 Analysis of Plan 2, Example 4-1

PERIOD	PRODUC-TION	INVENTORY	BACK-ORDERS	CAPACITY CHANGE	OVERTIME	SUB-CONTRACT
1	150	50	0	−30	0	0
2	150	20	0	0	0	0
3	150	0	50	0	0	0
4	150	0	50	0	0	0
5	150	0	0	0	0	0
6	250	50	0	+50	40	10
7	250	50	0	0	40	10
8	250	0	0	0	40	10
9	250	0	10	0	40	10
10	250	0	10	0	40	10
11	250	0	0	0	40	10
12	175	0	35	−25	0	0
13	175	0	0	0	0	0

that the regular time capacity can be varied up to 200 units per period, that the maximum overtime is 20 percent of regular time capacity, and that production on overtime is preferable to subcontracting. Assumed initial inventory was zero and assumed initial regular time production capacity was 180 units per period. We observe that Plan 1 has higher inventory costs than Plan 2, but has better performance with regard to the other measures. The preferred plan will depend on the costs of carrying inventory, incurring backorders, changing production rates, overtime, and subcontracting. □

The alternative production programs in Example 4-1 were selected somewhat arbitrarily by considering the cumulative demand pattern over the season. Many other plans could have been generated. The problem is to develop the best production program. The models presented in this chapter treat problems of this type.

4-2 Models with Linear Costs

If the relevant costs can be assumed to be linear functions of the variables defining the production program, the planning problem can be formulated as a linear programming model, provided any constraints are also linear. The availability of powerful algorithms for solving the general linear programming problem means that large-scale production planning problems then can be analyzed mathematically. Additionally, certain models have special structures that permit use of other highly efficient algorithms to obtain solutions.

In this section, three examples of linear programming formulations of dynamic planning problems are given. The first is a transportation model, which can be solved quickly by a special algorithm. The last two are in the general linear programming format. All involve a single product and a single production stage. Problems with nonlinear costs or involving multiple products or multiple stages are treated in later sections of this chapter.

4-2.1 A Model with Only Production and Inventory Costs

This model is appropriate for the situation where there are several production or procurement sources for a single product in each of T time periods, where for any source the product has a constant unit variable cost. The product may be stored from one period to the next at a known cost per unit. No shortages are to be planned. There is no fixed cost of production and no cost of changing production rates of the various sources. Each source has a given capacity in each time period, measured in the same units as the production requirements.

To formulate the problem symbolically, let

D_t = units required in period t, $(t = 1, 2, \ldots, T)$

m = number of sources of product in any period

P_{it} = capacity, in units of product, of source i in period t, $(i = 1, 2, \ldots, m)$

X_{it} = planned quantity to be obtained from source i in period t

c_{it} = variable cost per unit from source i in period t

h_t = cost to store a unit from period t to period $t + 1$

I_t = inventory level at the end of period t, after satisfying the requirements in period t

We assume that units procured during a period can be used to satisfy demand in that period.

The problem is to choose the $\{X_{it}\}$ to minimize the total relevant cost during the planning horizon,

$$Z = \sum_{t=1}^{T} \left[\sum_{i=1}^{m} c_{it}X_{it} + h_tI_t \right] \tag{4-1a}$$

subject to

$$X_{it} \le P_{it}, \qquad (i = 1, 2, \ldots, m; t = 1, 2, \ldots, T) \tag{4-1b}$$

$$I_t = I_{t-1} + \sum_{i=1}^{m} X_{it} - D_t, \qquad (t = 1, 2, \ldots, T) \tag{4-1c}$$

$$X_{it} \ge 0, \qquad (i = 1, 2, \ldots, m; t = 1, 2, \ldots, T) \tag{4-1d}$$

$$I_t \ge 0, \qquad (t = 1, 2, \ldots, T) \tag{4-1e}$$

The objective function (4-1a), is the sum over all time periods of the procurement costs and the inventory holding cost. The latter is based on the ending inventory for a period. Constraints (4-1b) result from the capacity limitations on the production sources. Constraints (4-1c) are material balance equations that relate the inventory variables to the production variables. These equations link successive time periods and are characteristic of multiperiod production planning models. Nonnegative production levels are insured by constraints (4-1d), while constraints (4-1e) enforce the requirement that no shortages be planned. Note that in addition to the costs, requirements, and capacities, the initial inventory, I_0, must be given.

By redefining our decision variables, we can observe that this problem has the structure of the transportation model of linear programming. Let

y_{ijk} = number of units produced by source i in period j to meet the requirements of period k

γ_{ijk} = unit variable cost of production of a unit by source i in period j and storage to period k, when it is used

The cost coefficient is

$$\gamma_{ijk} = c_{ij} + h_j + h_{j+1} + \cdots + h_{k-1}, \qquad (k \geq j)$$

Since we are not allowing shortages, $y_{ijk} = 0$ for $k < j$. This could be forced in a computer solution by assigning γ_{ijk} a very large value for $k < j$. The model is

$$\text{minimize } Z = \sum_{i=1}^{m} \sum_{j=1}^{T} \sum_{k=j}^{T} \gamma_{ijk} y_{ijk}$$

subject to

$$\sum_{k=j}^{T} y_{ijk} \leq P_{ij}, \qquad (i = 1, 2, \ldots, m; j = 1, 2, \ldots, T)$$

$$\sum_{i=1}^{m} \sum_{j=1}^{k} y_{ijk} = D_k, \qquad (k = 1, 2, \ldots, T)$$

$$y_{ijk} \geq 0$$

This formulation assumes either no initial inventory or that any initial inventory has already been allocated against requirements, starting with the first period, so that the D_k values are *net* requirements.[1] To explicitly include the allocation of initial inventory in the model, we let y_{0k} be the number of units of initial inventory used to satisfy demand in period k and let γ_{0k} be the associated unit inventory carrying cost. Then $\gamma_{0k} = h_1 + h_2 + \cdots + h_{k-1}$. (The already-existing initial inventory is assigned a "production" cost of zero.) The modified model is

$$\text{minimize } Z = \sum_{i=1}^{m} \sum_{j=1}^{T} \sum_{k=j}^{T} \gamma_{ijk} y_{ijk} + \sum_{k=1}^{T} \gamma_{0k} y_{0k} \qquad (4\text{-}2a)$$

subject to

$$\sum_{k=j}^{T} y_{ijk} \leq P_{ij}, \qquad (i = 1, 2, \ldots, m; j = 1, 2, \ldots, T) \qquad (4\text{-}2b)$$

$$\sum_{k=1}^{T} y_{0k} \leq I_0 \qquad (4\text{-}2c)$$

$$y_{0k} + \sum_{i=1}^{m} \sum_{j=1}^{k} y_{ijk} = D_k, \qquad (k = 1, 2, \ldots, T) \qquad (4\text{-}2d)$$

$$y_{0k} \geq 0, \qquad (k = 1, 2, \ldots, T) \qquad (4\text{-}2e)$$

$$y_{ijk} \geq 0 \qquad (4\text{-}2f)$$

The constraints (4-2b) reflect production capacity by source and time period, and the constraints (4-2d) insure that each period's demand is satisfied exactly. It is apparent that Equations 4-2a to 4-2f form a linear programming transportation model. Figure 4-2 is the usual tableau format for this model.

The algorithm for solving the transportation model can be applied to obtain

[1] Provide an argument that this is the optimal use of any initial inventory.

Destination / Source		Demand Period 1	Demand Period 2	. . .	Demand Period T	Unused Capacity	Capacity Available
Initial inventory		0	γ_{02}	. . .	γ_{0T}	$\gamma_{0,T+1}$	I_0
Period 1	1	γ_{111}	γ_{112}		γ_{11T}	0	P_{11}
	2	γ_{211}	γ_{212}		γ_{21T}	0	P_{21}
	. . .	. . .	. . .	. . .	. . .	. . .	. . .
	m	γ_{m11}	γ_{m12}		γ_{m1T}	0	P_{m1}
Period 2	1		γ_{122}		γ_{12T}	0	P_{12}
	2		γ_{222}		γ_{22T}	0	P_{22}
	. . .		. . .	. . .	. . .	. . .	. . .
	m		γ_{m22}		γ_{m2T}	0	P_{m2}
. . .					. . .	. . .	. . .
Period T	1				γ_{1TT}	0	P_{1T}
	2				γ_{2TT}	0	P_{2T}
	. . .			. . .	. . .	. . .	. . .
	m				γ_{mTT}	0	P_{mT}
Required quantity		D_1	D_2	. . .	D_T	S^*	

$$ {}^* S = I_0 + \sum_{i=1}^{m} \sum_{k=1}^{T} P_{ik} - \sum_{k=1}^{T} D_k. $$

FIGURE 4-2. Transportation tableau for the production planning model of Section 4-2.1. (Entries in the cells are unit costs.)

the optimal production program; however, a minimum-cost solution for this problem can be obtained immediately by the following procedure:

1. Satisfy demand in the first period by the least-cost sources.
2. Adjust capacities to indicate amounts remaining after step 1.
3. Satisfy demand in the second period by the least-cost sources.
4. Adjust available capacities.
5. Repeat steps 3 and 4, for periods 3, 4, . . . , T.

A further discussion of this algorithm is given in Section 4-3.3. At this point, however, we do caution the reader that this procedure must be modified for similar problems where backorders are allowed.

□**EXAMPLE 4-2**   Consider the demand schedule given in Table 4-1. Suppose that there is no initial inventory and that the sources of production in each period are regular time at a cost of $100 per unit, overtime at a cost of $107 per unit, and subcontracting at a cost of $113 per unit. The inventory holding costs are $2 per unit per period. No shortages are to be planned. Regular time capacity is 180 units in each period and overtime capacity is 36 units. Subcontracting up to 50 units is available in each period. Figure 4-3 is the transportation tableau and shows the optimal solution. Table 4-4 gives the optimal production program and the resulting inventory levels.

TABLE 4-4   Solution to Example 4-2

	PRODUCTION				
PERIOD	REGULAR TIME	OVERTIME	SUB-CONTRACTED	REQUIRE-MENTS	END-OF-PERIOD INVENTORY
1	140			100	40
2	180			180	40
3	180			220	0
4	180			150	30
5	180			100	110
6	180	36		200	126
7	180	36		250	92
8	180	36		300	8
9	180	36	36	260	0
10	180	36	34	250	0
11	180	36	24	240	0
12	180	30		210	0
13	140			140	0
Total	2260	246	94	2600	

Transportation tableau (Figure 4-3). Each cell shows the unit cost (boxed) with any allocation in bold below it.

Period	Source	Period 1	Period 2	Period 3	Period 4	Period 5	Period 6	Period 7	Period 8	Period 9	Period 10	Period 11	Period 12	Period 13	Slack	Capacity Available
1	Regular time	100 **100**	102	104 **40**	106	108	110	112	114	116	118	120	122	124	0 **40**	180
	Over-time	107	109	111	113	115	117	119	121	123	125	127	129	131	0 **36**	36
	Sub-contract	113	115	117	119	121	123	125	127	129	131	133	135	137	0 **50**	50
2	Regular time		100 **180**	102	104	106	108	110	112	114	116	118	120	122	0 **0**	180
	Over-time		107	109	111	113	115	117	119	121	123	125	127	129	0 **36**	36
	Sub-contract		113	115	117	119	121	123	125	127	129	131	133	135	0 **50**	50
3	Regular time			100 **180**	102	104	106	108	110	112	114	116	118	120	0 **0**	180
	Over-time			107	109	111	113	115	117	119	121	123	125	127	0 **36**	36
	Sub-contract			113	115	117	119	121	123	125	127	129	131	133	0 **50**	50
4	Regular time				100 **150**	102	104	106 **10**	108 **20**	110	112	114	116	118	0 **0**	180
	Over-time				107	109	111	113	115	117	119	121	123	125	0 **36**	36
	Sub-contract				113	115	117	119	121	123	125	127	129	131	0 **50**	50
5	Regular time					100 **100**	102 **20**	104 **60**	106	108	110	112	114	116	0 **0**	180
	Over-time					107	109	111	113	115	117	119	121	123	0 **36**	36
	Sub-contract					113	115	117	119	121	123	125	127	129	0 **50**	50
6	Regular time						100 **180**	102	104	106	108	110	112	114	0 **0**	180
	Over-time						107	109	111 **28**	113 **8**	115	117	119	121	0 **0**	36
	Sub-contract						113	115	117	119	121	123	125	127	0 **50**	50
7	Regular time							100 **180**	102	104	106	108	110	112	0 **0**	180
	Over-time							107	109 **36**	111	113	115	117	119	0 **0**	36
	Sub-contract							113	115	117	119	121	123	125	0 **50**	50
8	Regular time								100 **180**	102	104	106	108	110	0 **0**	180
	Over-time								107 **36**	109	111	113	115	117	0 **0**	36
	Sub-contract								113	115	117	119	121	123	0 **50**	50
9	Regular time									100 **180**	102	104	106	108	0 **0**	180
	Over-time									107 **36**	109	111	113	115	0 **0**	36
	Sub-contract									113 **36**	115	117	119	121	0 **14**	50
10	Regular time										100 **180**	102	104	106	0 **0**	180
	Over-time										107 **36**	109	111	113	0 **0**	36
	Sub-contract										113 **34**	115	117	119	0 **16**	50
11	Regular time											100 **180**	102	104	0 **0**	180
	Over-time											107 **36**	109	111	0 **0**	36
	Sub-contract											113 **24**	115	117	0 **26**	50
12	Regular time												100 **180**	102	0 **0**	180
	Over-time												107 **30**	109	0 **6**	36
	Sub-contract												113	115	0 **50**	50
13	Regular time													100 **140**	0 **40**	180
	Over-time													107	0 **36**	36
	Sub-contract													113	0 **50**	50
Requirements		100	180	220	150	100	200	250	300	260	250	240	210	140	858	3458

FIGURE 4-3. Transportation tableau for Example 4-2.

This model can be extended to include minimum inventory levels (Exercise 4-3), minimum production levels (Exercise 4-4), backlogging (Exercise 4-5), and multiple products (Exercise 4-6). However, in many situations a transportation model is not adequate to describe the decision problem. One such case of particular interest occurs when there is a cost of changing the production rate from one period to the next. The modeling of this problem is described in the next section. □

4-2.2 A Model with Production Rate Change Costs and Backlogging

This section contains a more general linear programming formulation of the production smoothing problem. The model includes penalties for increasing or decreasing production rates from one period to the next and it considers the cost of backorders. The following formulation is for a single product and a single production source in each period and assumes all shortages are backlogged. Let

X_t = quantity produced in period t, $(t = 1, 2, \ldots, T)$

I_t = net inventory at the end of period t

I_t^+ = on-hand inventory at the end of period t

I_t^- = backorder position at the end of period t

Δ_t^+ = increase in production rate from period $t - 1$ to t

Δ_t^- = decrease in production rate from period $t - 1$ to t

c_t = unit variable production cost in period t

h_t = inventory carrying cost per unit held from period t to $t + 1$

π_t = backorder cost per unit carried from period t to $t + 1$

λ_t = cost to increase the production rate by one unit from period $t - 1$ to period t

ω_t = cost to decrease the production rate by one unit from period $t - 1$ to period t

P_t = maximum production rate in period t

D_t = demand in period t

The problem is to choose $X_1, X_2, \ldots, X_T$ to minimize the sum of production costs, inventory-related costs, and production rate change costs over the planning horizon. That is, minimize

$$Z = \sum_{t=1}^{T} [c_t X_t + h_t I_t^+ + \pi_t I_t^- + \lambda_t \Delta_t^+ + \omega_t \Delta_t^-] \qquad (4\text{-}3a)$$

subject to, for $t = 1, 2, \ldots, T$,

$$I_t = I_{t-1} + X_t - D_t \tag{4-3b}$$

$$I_t = I_t^+ - I_t^- \tag{4-3c}$$

$$X_t = X_{t-1} + \Delta_t^+ - \Delta_t^- \tag{4-3d}$$

$$X_t \leq P_t \tag{4-3e}$$

$$X_t \geq 0 \tag{4-3f}$$

$$I_t^+ \geq 0 \tag{4-3g}$$

$$I_t^- \geq 0 \tag{4-3h}$$

$$\Delta_t^+ \geq 0 \tag{4-3i}$$

$$\Delta_t^- \geq 0 \tag{4-3j}$$

Note that the net inventory, I, is not constrained in sign and is defined in (4-3c) as the difference of two nonnegative variables. The initial inventory position, I_0, must be given in order to formulate (4-3b) for $t = 1$. Similarly, the initial production rate, X_0, must be provided to set up (4-3d) for $t = 1$.

Also observe that the vector of constraint coefficients for I_t^+ is linearly dependent with that of I_t^-. This means that I_t^+ and I_t^- cannot both be in a basic solution when h_t and π_t are positive, and hence that the constraint $I_t^+ \cdot I_t^- = 0$, implied by the definition of on-hand inventory and backorders, is automatically satisfied and does not have to be represented explicitly in the model. For the same reason, Δ_t^+ and Δ_t^- cannot both be in a basic solution. It is not difficult to show that (4-3b) and (4-3d) can be written as

$$I_t = I_0 + \sum_{k=1}^{t} (X_k - D_k) \tag{4-3k}$$

$$X_t = X_0 + \sum_{k=1}^{t} (\Delta_k^+ - \Delta_k^-) \tag{4-3l}$$

If one wishes to do so, the number of variables in the model may be reduced by using (4-3k) and (4-3l) to eliminate the $\{X_t\}$ and the $\{I_t\}$, thereby leaving the problem in terms of the $\{\Delta_t^+, \Delta_t^-, I_t^+, I_t^-\}$. In doing this, one must not forget to substitute into (4-3f); otherwise, negative production rates may result.

Finally, we point out that Δ_t^+ and Δ_t^- are often denoted in the literature by $(X_t - X_{t-1})^+$ and $(X_t - X_{t-1})^-$, respectively. The general convention is that, if F denotes any function,

$$(F)^+ = \max(0, F)$$

$$(F)^- = \max(0, -F)$$

Then

$$\Delta_t^+ \equiv (X_t - X_{t-1})^+ = \begin{cases} X_t - X_{t-1}, & \text{if } X_t > X_{t-1} \\ 0, & \text{if } X_t \leq X_{t-1} \end{cases}$$

$$\Delta_t^- \equiv (X_t - X_{t-1})^- = \begin{cases} 0, & \text{if } X_t \geq X_{t-1} \\ X_{t-1} - X_t, & \text{if } X_t < X_{t-1} \end{cases}$$

4-2.3 A Model with Employment Level and Overtime Decisions

In a situation similar to that of Section 4-2.2, suppose that the capacity in a period is a function of the work force level during the period and that there is a cost of changing the work force level from period to period. There is no cost to change the production rate; however, overtime is required when scheduled production is in excess of the regular time capacity of the work force. Production costs are higher on overtime than on regular time. Assume backorders are allowed.

The following notation is needed:

W_t = work force level in period t, measured in regular time man-hours

w_t^+ = increase in work force level from period $t - 1$ to t (in man-hours)

w_t^- = decrease in work force level from period $t - 1$ to t (in man-hours)

O_t = overtime scheduled in period t (in man-hours)

U_t = undertime scheduled in period t (in man-hours)

X_t = production scheduled for period t (in units of product)

m = number of man-hours required to produce one unit of product

c_t = unit variable cost, excluding labor, of product produced in period t

l_t = cost of a man-hour of labor on regular time in period t

l_t' = cost of a man-hour of labor on overtime in period t

e_t = cost to increase the work force level by one man-hour in period t

e_t' = cost to decrease the work force level by one man-hour in period t

The symbols I_t, I_t^+, I_t^-, h_t, π_t, and D_t have the same meaning as in Section 4-2.2.

Our problem is to choose the work force, production, and inventory levels to minimize the sum of labor costs, other production costs, inventory-related costs, and work force change costs. The model is

$$\text{minimize} \quad Z = \sum_{t=1}^T [c_t X_t + l_t W_t + l_t' O_t + h_t I_t^+ + \pi_t I_t^- + e_t w_t^+ + e_t' w_t^-]$$

(4-4a)

subject to, for $t = 1, 2, \ldots, T$,

$$I_t = I_{t-1} + X_t - D_t \tag{4-4b}$$

$$I_t = I_t^+ - I_t^- \tag{4-4c}$$

$$W_t = W_{t-1} + w_t^+ - w_t^- \tag{4-4d}$$

$$O_t - U_t = mX_t - W_t \tag{4-4e}$$

$$X_t \geq 0 \tag{4-4f}$$

$$I_t^+ \geq 0 \tag{4-4g}$$

$$I_t^- \geq 0 \tag{4-4h}$$

$$W_t \geq 0 \tag{4-4i}$$

$$w_t^+ \geq 0 \tag{4-4j}$$

$$w_t^- \geq 0 \tag{4-4k}$$

$$O_t \geq 0 \tag{4-4l}$$

$$U_t \geq 0 \tag{4-4m}$$

We make the following observations about this model:

1. Since from (4-4b),

$$I_t = I_0 + \sum_{k=1}^{t} (X_k - D_k)$$

we can substitute for I_t in (4-4c) and reduce the number of constraints.

2. From (4-4d),

$$W_t = W_0 + \sum_{k=1}^{t} (w_k^+ - w_k^-)$$

which we can use to eliminate W_t and reduce the number of variables.

3. To define the relationship between the overtime variable, O_t, the work force variable, W_t, and the production variable, X_t, it is necessary to introduce a variable for "undertime," U_t, in (4-4e). Because the regular time labor costs are included in the objective function, it is assumed that there is no cost associated with undertime.

4. The initial work force level, W_0, and the initial inventory position I_0, must be provided.

5. It would be natural to limit overtime to some fraction, θ, of regular time capacity. We then would add the constraints $O_t - U_t \leq \theta W_t$, for $t = 1, 2, \ldots, T$. (Why not use the form: $O_t \leq \theta W_t$?)

4-3 Dynamic Programming and Network Models

The multiperiod production planning problem often can be decomposed and formulated as a dynamic programming model. The utility of such a model may be limited, if extensive computations are required to obtain a solution. However, under certain conditions, knowledge of properties of the optimal solution will allow us to develop a solution procedure significantly more efficient than the usual method of solving dynamic programming problems.

In this section, we shall formulate a general dynamic programming model of the multiperiod problem and then shall examine several efficient solution algorithms for the cases of linear, convex, concave, and piecewise concave costs. We shall consider only a single product, and we may or may not be able to incorporate easily constraints on production rates and inventory levels. We shall assume that production scheduled for a period is available for use in that period.

4-3.1 A General Dynamic Programming Model

Let

X_t = production scheduled for period t $(t = 1, 2, \ldots, T)$

D_t = expected demand in period t

I_t = net inventory at the end of period t

$K_t(X_t, I_t)$ = cost, in period t, of producing X_t units and having an ending net inventory of I_t

$f_t(I)$ = the minimum cost attainable over periods $t, t + 1, \ldots, T$, when the net inventory at the start of period t is I

Consider the decision to be made in period t. If the inventory at the start of period t is $I_{t-1} = I$ and the production decision is X_t, the resulting cost in period t is $K_t(X_t, I_t)$. Furthermore, the ending inventory, I_t, which is strictly determined by I, X_t, and D_t, affects the minimum costs that can be obtained in the periods following t. Assuming that an optimal policy is followed after period t, the decision X_t results in a cost over the last $T - t + 1$ periods of $K_t(X_t, I_t) + f_{t+1}(I_t)$. The minimum value of this cost is $f_t(I)$, defined by the following recursive equation:

$$f_t(I) = \min_{X_t \geq 0} \left[K_t(X_t, I + X_t - D_t) + f_{t+1}(I + X_t - D_t) \right] \quad (4\text{-}5a)$$

for $t = 1, 2, \ldots, T$, where $f_{T+1}(I) \equiv 0$. Note that the inventory balance equation,

$$I_{t-1} + X_t - D_t = I_t \qquad (4\text{-}5b)$$

allows us to express $K_t(X_t, I_t)$ as a function of the *starting* inventory $I(= I_{t-1})$, as well as the production rate X_t.

We now can use standard dynamic programming means to solve for the optimal production schedule $\{X_t\}$. Addition of constraints, such as $X_t \leq P_t$ or $I_t \leq L_t$, would serve only to reduce the range of values to be considered for the decision variable or the state variable, thereby making our solution easier.

However, we shall seek algorithms more efficient than the usual dynamic programming solution procedures. For certain types of cost functions, we can learn something of the structure of the optimal solution and can then exploit this information to develop a good method of obtaining that solution.

In most cases, we shall assume that the inventory-related costs depend only on the net inventory and that production costs depend only on the production rate. Thus we can write

$$K_t(X_t, I_t) = C_t(X_t) + H_t(I_t) \qquad (4\text{-}6)$$

The following special forms will be considered:

(1) $C_t(X_t)$ and $H_t(I_t)$ *linear* (Figure 4-4):

$$C_t(X_t) = c_t X_t, \qquad \text{for } X_t \geq 0 \qquad (c_t \geq 0) \qquad (4\text{-}7a)$$

$$H_t(I_t) = \begin{cases} h_t I_t, & \text{for } I_t \geq 0 \qquad (h_t \geq 0) \\ -\pi_t I_t, & \text{for } I_t \leq 0 \qquad (\pi_t \geq 0) \end{cases} \qquad (4\text{-}7b)$$

(2) $C_t(X_t)$ and $H_t(I_t)$ *convex* (Figure 4-5):

$$C_t(X_t) \geq 0 \quad \text{convex for } X_t \geq 0 \qquad (4\text{-}8a)$$

$$H_t(I_t) \geq 0 \begin{cases} \text{convex for } I_t \geq 0 \\ \text{convex for } I_t \leq 0 \end{cases} \qquad (4\text{-}8b)$$

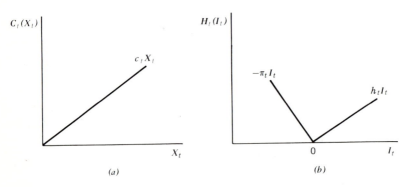

FIGURE 4-4.   Linear cost functions. (a) Production cost. (b) Inventory cost.

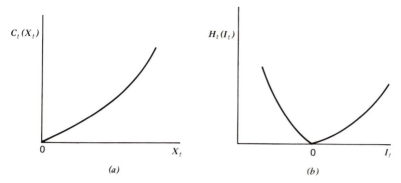

FIGURE 4-5. Convex cost functions. (a) Production cost. (b) Inventory cost.

(3) $C_t(X_t)$ and $H_t(I_t)$ *piecewise concave* (Figure 4-6):

$$C_t(X_t) \geq 0 \quad \text{concave for } X_t \geq 0 \tag{4-9a}$$

$$H_t(I_t) \geq 0 \begin{cases} \text{concave for } I_t \geq 0 \\ \text{concave for } I_t \leq 0 \end{cases} \tag{4-9b}$$

The latter case includes the commonly assumed model for the cost of a production lot

$$C_t(X_t) = \begin{cases} 0, & \text{if } X_t = 0 \\ A_t + c_t X_t, & \text{if } X_t > 0 \end{cases} \tag{4-10}$$

If there is a cost of *changing* the production rate, the problem is more complicated. Then the cost in a period depends not only on X_t and I_t, but also on the production rate in the previous period, X_{t-1}. A dynamic programming formulation would require two state variables at each stage (period)—the beginning net inventory and the production rate at the prior stage. This means a significant increase in computational effort.

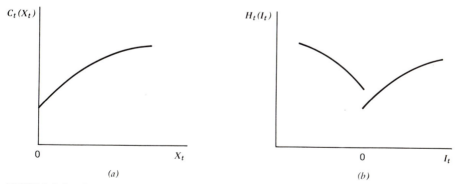

FIGURE 4-6. Concave and piecewise concave functions. (a) Production costs. (b) Inventory costs.

With production rate change costs, the model would be

$$f_t(I, X) = \min_{X_t \geq 0} \left[K_t(X_t, I_t, X) + f_{t+1}(I_t, X_t) \right] \tag{4-11}$$

where I is the ending net inventory and X is the production rate for period $t - 1$. The cost in period t might be of the form

$$K_t(X_t, I_t, X_{t-1}) = C_t(X_t) + H_t(I_t) + V_t(X_t, X_{t-1}) \tag{4-12}$$

where $V_t(X_t, X_{t-1})$ is the cost to change the production rate from X_{t-1} in period $t - 1$ to X_t in period t.

4-3.2 Network Representations

It is interesting and instructive to observe that dynamic planning problems can be conceptualized as network models. Several examples are now given to convey a better understanding of the structure of the decision problem and to provide a foundation for explaining some of the special algorithms to be presented later.

(1) Network Flow Model—No Shortages. Consider a single source network having T nodes in addition to the source. Arcs connect the source to each of the other nodes and connect node t to node $t + 1$, for $t = 1, 2, \ldots, T - 1$. Arcs lead from each of the T transhipment nodes to a sink (not shown in Figure 4-7). The flow in the arc leading from node t to the sink is required to be D_t (assuming that the initial inventory, I_0, has been allocated so that the $\{D_t\}$ are the net requirements that must be met by production). To assure a steady-state flow, assume that the flow imposed on the system at the source node is $F = \sum_{t=1}^{T} D_t$.

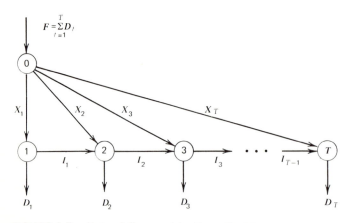

FIGURE 4-7. Network flow model with no shortages.

The resulting flow in arc $(0, t)$ is interpreted as X_t and the flow in arc $(t, t + 1)$ as I_t. No backlogging is assumed, so I_t is the on-hand inventory. Assume there is a cost associated with the flow in an arc, and let $C_t(X_t)$ and $H_t(I_t)$ give cost as a function of the flow level. The problem is to choose the minimum cost flow pattern. Stated mathematically, we want to select $X_1, X_2, \ldots, X_T$ to minimize

$$Z = \sum_{t=1}^{T} C_t(X_t) + \sum_{t=1}^{T-1} H_t(I_t) \tag{4-13a}$$

subject to

$$\sum_{t=1}^{T} D_t = \sum_{t=1}^{T} X_t \tag{4-13b}$$

$$X_1 = D_1 + I_1 \tag{4-13c}$$

$$X_t + I_{t-1} = D_t + I_t, \qquad (t = 2, 3, \ldots, T - 1) \tag{4-13d}$$

$$X_T + I_{T-1} = D_T \tag{4-13e}$$

$$I_t \geq 0, \qquad X_t \geq 0 \tag{4-13f}$$

The first constraint, representing conservation of flow at node 0, may be dropped, since it can be obtained by summing the other equality constraints.

This problem of minimum cost flow is exactly that of multiperiod production planning described in the previous section. [This network flow analogy and the one that follows for the backlogging case were noted by Zangwill (52).]

(2) Network Flow Model—Backorders Allowed. Define I_t^+ and I_t^- as the on-hand inventory and backorder position, respectively, at the end of period t. Then the net inventory position is $I_t = I_t^+ - I_t^-$. To represent the possibility of satisfying demand in a period through production in a later period, we add arcs from node $t + 1$ to node t, for $t = 1, 2, \ldots, T - 1$. Flow in arc $(t + 1, t)$ is the backorder position I_t^-. The resulting network is shown in Figure 4-8. In

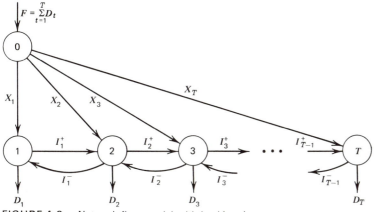

FIGURE 4-8. Network flow model with backlogging.

the algebraic formulation of this minimum cost flow model, we use the objective function

$$Z = \sum_{t=1}^{T} C_t(X_t) + \sum_{t=1}^{T-1} [H_t^+(I_t^+) + H_t^-(I_t^-)] \qquad (4\text{-}14\text{a})$$

where the inventory holding costs and backorder costs appear as separate functions. The constraints would be

$$\sum_{t=1}^{T} D_t = \sum_{t=1}^{T} X_t \qquad (4\text{-}14\text{b})$$

$$X_1 + I_1^- = D_1 + I_1^+ \qquad (4\text{-}14\text{c})$$

$$X_t + I_{t-1}^+ + I_t^- = D_t + I_{t-1}^- + I_t^+, \qquad (t = 2, 3, \ldots, T-1) \quad (4\text{-}14\text{d})$$

$$X_T + I_{T-1}^+ = D_T + I_{T-1}^- \qquad (4\text{-}14\text{e})$$

$$X_t \geq 0, \qquad I_t^+ \geq 0, \qquad I_t^- \geq 0 \qquad (4\text{-}14\text{f})$$

Again, constraint (4-14b) is redundant.

(3) Shortest Path Model—No Shortages. In a later section, we shall consider the case of concave production and inventory costs and no backlogging. It will be shown that an optimal program has the property that production in any period t must be one of these values: 0 or $\sum_{j=t}^{k} D_j$, for $k = t, t + 1, \ldots, T$. This results from the fact that if production takes place in a period, the entering inventory for that period must be zero; that is, $X_t I_{t-1} = 0$. Hence, it is sufficient to consider only programs having this property. Figure 4-9 is a network representing such programs for $T = 4$. Arc (j, k) represents a decision to supply the requirements for period $j + 1, j + 2, \ldots, k$ by production in period $j + 1$.

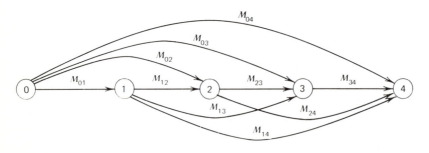

FIGURE 4-9. Shortest path model, no shortages.

This means

$$X_{j+1} = \sum_{t=j+1}^{k} D_t$$

$$X_t = 0, \quad \text{for } t = j + 2, j + 3, \ldots, k$$

$$I_j = I_k = 0$$

$$X_{k+1} > 0$$

If M_{jk} is the cost of satisfying requirements in periods $j + 1, j + 2, \ldots, k$ by production in period $j + 1$, arc (j, k) could be assumed to have *length* M_{jk}, and the production planning problem could be stated as a problem of finding the shortest path from node 0 to node T. There are several efficient algorithms for solving this type of problem.

4-3.3 Models with Convex Costs

We suppose that the cost of production and inventory in period t is given by

$$K_t(X_t, I_t) = C_t(X_t) + H_t(I_t) \tag{4-15}$$

where $C_t(X_t)$ is convex for $X_t \geq 0$, and $H_t(I_t)$ is convex for all values of the net inventory, I_t. Shortages are assumed to be backlogged, so I_t can take on negative values. The optimal production program can be determined with the following algorithm.

Convex Cost Algorithm. Each period's demand is to be filled in turn starting with period 1, then period 2, and so on, until all demands have been satisfied. When deciding how to meet demand in a period, use production sources in order of increasing marginal cost. Alternatives are production in the current period, production in a prior period with storage, and production in a later period with backlogging. More formally, suppose in using this approach, production has been planned to meet demand in periods $1, 2, \ldots, k - 1$, and now period k is being considered:

(1) There are T possible alternatives for satisfying the next unit of D_k, corresponding to increasing production by one unit in exactly one of the periods $1, 2, \ldots, T$. For each of these alternatives, compute the entire incremental cost from production, inventory, and backlogging. (In computing this incremental cost, it is assumed that both the original and the new partial production schedules are allocated against the demands in periods $1, 2, \ldots, k - 1$, and any part of the demand to be satisfied in period k, in a manner that minimizes total relevant costs.) Select the minimum cost alternative and adjust the production plan accordingly.

(2) If the demand for period k has not been completely filled, return to step 1 and determine how best to satisfy the next unit of period k's demand;

otherwise consider the requirements in period $k + 1$, and return to step 1 with $k = k + 1$. Continue through T periods.

The bulk of the work in using the algorithm is associated with determining the optimal allocation of a partial production schedule in step 1. An exception occurs when backorders are not allowed and inventory costs are linear, in which case the optimal program is obtained easily.

The convex model often results from situations where there are multiple production (or procurement) sources in a period and it is assumed that production costs are proportional to the quantity produced by a source. By assigning production first to the source with the lowest unit cost until its capacity is reached, then proceeding to use the next cheapest source to capacity, etc., one develops a total production cost that is convex in the total amount scheduled for the period. We already have seen an example of this in Section 4-2.1.

The transportation tableau (Figure 4-2) is a good way to organize a problem having convex piecewise-linear production costs and linear (proportional) inventory holding and backlogging costs. When backorders are permitted, the problem is more efficiently solved by the transportation algorithm of linear programming than by the convex cost algorithm described above. However, when backlogging is not allowed, the solution can be obtained immediately by the convex cost algorithm. The procedure was given in Section 4-2.1 and used in solving Example 4-2. We now give a second example.

☐**EXAMPLE 4-3** Production is to be planned over a four-period horizon, where the requirements by period are 20, 10, 40, and 30 units, respectively. Inventory holding costs are of the form $h_t I_t^+$, with $h_1 = 3$, $h_2 = 2$, and $h_3 = h_4 = 1$. No shortages are permitted. The production costs, which are convex, are given in Table 4-5. Entries in the table are the marginal production costs, which are assumed to be constant for the given range of X_t. Maximum production in a period is 35 units. The initial net inventory is zero and the final net inventory is to be zero.

TABLE 4-5 Marginal Production Costs for Example 4-3

RANGE OF PRODUCTION	PERIOD OF PRODUCTION, t			
	1	2	3	4
$1 \leq X_t \leq 8$	4	6	6	3
$9 \leq X_t \leq 17$	5	10	8	5
$18 \leq X_t \leq 25$	6	12	10	7
$26 \leq X_t \leq 35$	8	14	12	10

To solve the problem, we conceive of four sources of production in each period, with each source having a given capacity and proportional costs. Since inventory costs are also proportional, we can use the transportation tableau to organize our solution. Table 4-6 is the result. Numbers in the small square in the upper right-hand corner of each cell are incremental production cost plus any incremental inventory cost.

Assignments to the cells are made starting with period 1. When the demand in period 1 has been satisfied by allocation of production from the cheapest sources, the capacities in the right-hand column are adjusted to reflect the remaining capacity and we move to period 2. Period 2's demand is filled from the cheapest sources, and so on, until all requirements have been satisfied. The optimal production program is $X_1^* = 25$, $X_2^* = 10$, $X_3^* = 35$, and $X_4^* = 30$. For this program, $I_1^+ = 5$, $I_2^+ = 5$, $I_3^+ = 0$, and $I_4^+ = 0$. The minimum total cost is 713.

Now suppose that backorders are allowed and backorder costs in period t are $\pi_t I_t^-$, with $\pi_1 = 2$, $\pi_2 = 3$, $\pi_3 = 1$, and $\pi_4 = \infty$ (because we require $I_4^- = 0$). The associated transportation tableau and an optimal solution are shown in Table 4-7. The solution, $X_1^* = 25$, $X_2^* = 8$, $X_3^* = 32$, and $X_4^* = 35$, was obtained using the transportation algorithm. For this solution, the inventory levels are $I_1^+ = 5$, $I_2^+ = 3$, and $I_3^+ = I_4^+ = 0$, and backlogging occurs only in the third period when $I_3^- = 5$. The minimum cost is 708. Compare the solution for the backlog case with that of the no-backlog case.□

Bound Constraints on Production and Net Inventory. We may wish to impose constraints of the form $P_t' \leq X_t \leq P_t$, or $L_t' \leq I_t \leq L_t$.[2] These bound constraints create no problems when costs are convex. We can handle them by defining $C_t(X_t)$ and $H_t(I_t)$ to be infinite whenever $X_t < P_t'$ or $X_t > P_t$ and $I_t < L_t'$ or $I_t > L_t$, respectively.

Veinott (42) summarizes the effect of varying the bounds:

I. Optimal production in a period t is a *nondecreasing* function of:

    (1)   The requirements in any period $(D_1, D_2, \ldots, D_T)$.

    (2)   The upper and lower production capacity limits in the period (P_t', P_t).

    (3)   The upper and lower limits on net inventory in the given period and all succeeding periods $(L_j', L_j$, for $j = t, t + 1, \ldots, T)$.

II. Optimal production in a given period is a *nonincreasing* function of

    (1)   The upper and lower production capacity limits in every other period $(P_j', P_j$, for $j = 1, 2, \ldots, t - 1, t + 1, \ldots, T)$.

    (2)   The upper and lower limits on net inventory in any preceeding period $(L_j', L_j$, for $j = 1, 2, \ldots, t - 1)$.

---

[2] The latter constraint is equivalent to $I_t^+ \leq L_t$ and $I_t^- \leq -L_t'$, assuming $L_t' \leq 0$.

TABLE 4-6 Solution to Example 4-3, No Backlogging

PERIOD	SOURCE OF PRODUCTION	DEMAND PERIOD				UNUSED CAPACITY	CAPACITY
		1	2	3	4		
1	$1 \le X_1 \le 8$	4 [8]	7	9	10	0	8
	$9 \le X_1 \le 17$	5 [9]	8	10	11	0	9
	$18 \le X_1 \le 25$	6 [3]	9 [2]	11 [3]	12	0	8
	$26 \le X_1 \le 35$	8	11	13	14	0 [10]	10
2	$1 \le X_2 \le 8$		6 [8]	8	9	0	8
	$9 \le X_2 \le 17$		10	12 [2]	13	0 [7]	9
	$18 \le X_2 \le 25$		12	14	15	0 [8]	8
	$26 \le X_2 \le 35$		14	16	17	0 [10]	10
3	$1 \le X_3 \le 8$			6 [8]	7	0	8
	$9 \le X_3 \le 17$			8 [9]	9	0	9
	$18 \le X_3 \le 25$			10 [8]	11	0	8
	$26 \le X_3 \le 35$			12 [10]	13	0	10
4	$1 \le X_4 \le 8$				3 [8]	0	8
	$9 \le X_4 \le 17$				5 [9]	0	9
	$18 \le X_4 \le 25$				7 [8]	0	8
	$26 \le X_4 \le 35$				10 [5]	0 [5]	10
Requirements		20	10	40	30	40	140

TABLE 4-7   Solution to Example 4-3, Backlog Case

PERIOD	SOURCE OF PRODUCTION	DEMAND PERIOD 1	2	3	4	UNUSED CAPACITY	CAPACITY
1	$1 \le X_1 \le 8$	4 8	7	9	10	0	8
	$9 \le X_1 \le 17$	5 9	8	10	11	0	9
	$18 \le X_1 \le 25$	6 3	9 2	11 3	12	0	8
	$26 \le X_1 \le 35$	8	11	13	14	0 10	10
2	$1 \le X_2 \le 8$	8	6 8	8	9	0	8
	$9 \le X_2 \le 17$	12	10	12	13	0 9	9
	$18 \le X_2 \le 25$	14	12	14	15	0 8	8
	$26 \le X_2 \le 35$	16	14	16	17	0 10	10
3	$1 \le X_3 \le 8$	11	9	6 8	7	0	8
	$9 \le X_3 \le 17$	13	11	8 9	9	0	9
	$18 \le X_3 \le 25$	15	13	10 8	11	0	8
	$26 \le X_3 \le 35$	17	15	12 7	13	0 3	10
4	$1 \le X_4 \le 8$	9	7	4	3 8	0	8
	$9 \le X_4 \le 17$	11	9	6	5 9	0	9
	$18 \le X_4 \le 25$	13	11	8	7 8	0	8
	$26 \le X_4 \le 35$	16	14	11 5	10 5	0	10
Requirements		20	10	40	30	40	140

Additional results for the convex cost case are given in Exercises 4-26 and 4-27.

Treatment of Initial Inventory.   If the initial net inventory, I_0, is different from zero, the following should be done prior to applying the solution algorithm described above. If $I_0 > 0$, meaning that there is inventory on hand at time zero, subtract I_0 from the requirement D_1 for period 1 to obtain an adjusted demand for period 1. Should I_0 exceed D_1, set the adjusted demand for period 1 equal to zero and subtract $I_0 - D_1$ from D_2 to obtain the adjusted demand for period 2, and so on. Solve the problem using the adjusted demand values. Should there be backorders at time zero, that is, $I_0 < 0$, add the backorder quantity to D_1 to obtain an adjusted demand for period 1; then solve.

4-3.4 Models with Concave Costs

We now assume that $K_t(X_t, I_t)$ is concave and that no shortages are allowed. Later we shall consider the backorders case. We also assume $I_0 = I_T = 0$. Thus the model is to minimize the concave function

$$Z = \sum_{t=1}^{T} K_t(X_t, I_t)$$

subject to T linear constraints,

$$X_1 - D_1 = I_1$$
$$I_{t-1} + X_t - D_t = I_t, \qquad (t = 2, 3, \ldots, T - 1)$$
$$I_{T-1} + X_T - D_T = 0$$
$$I_t \geq 0, \qquad X_t \geq 0$$

It is well known that the minimum of a concave function subject to linear constraints occurs at an extreme point of the convex set formed by the constraints. An extreme-point solution will have at most T nonzero variables. If $D_t > 0$, then one or both of X_t and I_{t-1} must also be greater than zero. Since there are T constraints and only T variables in an extreme point solution, then *exactly* one of the variables I_{t-1} and X_t must be at a positive level. Thus all extreme point solutions, including the optimal one, would have the property $I_{t-1}X_t = 0$, for $t = 1, 2, \ldots, T$. Now if the demand is zero in some period k, it is feasible to have both $I_{k-1} = 0$ and $X_k = 0$, which means that an extreme point solution could have $I_{t-1} > 0$ and $X_t > 0$ for some $t \neq k$. However, such a solution cannot be the optimal one. To see this, note that if $I_{k-1} = X_k = 0$, we can find the minimum cost solution by decomposing the original problem into two independent problems: the planning of periods 1 through $k - 1$, and the planning of periods $k + 1$ through T. The first problem has $k - 1$ constraints, and hence $k - 1$ nonzero variables in its optimal solution, and the second has $T - k$ constraints and $T - k$ nonzero variables.

Therefore there would be only $T - 1$ nonzero variables in the optimal solution to the combined problem, and again this means that $I_{t-1}X_t = 0$.

Knowledge of this property of the optimal solution allows us to greatly reduce the decision and state spaces for solution of the dynamic programming model. It is necessary to consider only the following values for X_t: 0, D_t, $D_t + D_{t+1}, \ldots, D_t + D_{t+1} + \cdots + D_T$. Points in time where the inventory level is zero are called *regeneration points*. For every time period where production is scheduled, the start of the period (end of the prior period) is a regeneration point. We consider next some algorithms based on this property.

Forward Algorithm—No Backlogging. Let M_{jk} denote the cost of producing in period $j + 1$ to satisfy demands in periods $j + 1, j + 2, \ldots, k$ $(j = 0, 1, \ldots, T - 1; k = j + 1, j + 2, \ldots, T)$. M_{jk} includes inventory costs as well as production costs. Note that we are assuming that the end of period j and the end of period k are regeneration points; that is, $I_j = 0$ and $I_k = 0$. Then

$$X_{j+1} = D_{j+1} + D_{j+2} + \cdots + D_k \tag{4-16}$$

and

$$I_t = X_{j+1} - \sum_{r=j+1}^{t} D_r = \sum_{r=t+1}^{k} D_r, \qquad (t = j + 1, j + 2, \ldots, k - 1) \tag{4-17}$$

Therefore,

$$M_{jk} = C_{j+1}(X_{j+1}) + \sum_{t=j+1}^{k-1} H_t(I_t)$$

$$= C_{j+1}\left(\sum_{r=j+1}^{k} D_r \right) + \sum_{t=j+1}^{k-1} H_t\left(\sum_{r=t+1}^{k} D_r \right) \tag{4-18}$$

Let F_k denote the optimal policy costs for periods $1, 2, \ldots, k$, given $I_k = 0$. Then

$$F_k = \min_{0 \le j \le k-1} [F_j + M_{jk}], \qquad (k = 1, 2, \ldots, T) \tag{4-19}$$

and $F_0 \equiv 0$. This recurrence relation is equivalent to that of the problem of finding the shortest path through a network. (See Section 4-3.2, especially Figure 4-9.)

To organize computations, define α_{jk} to be the optimal cost for periods $1, 2, \ldots, k$ (a k-period horizon), when $I_k = 0$ and $j + 1$ is the period of last production; that is, when $X_{j+1} > 0$ and $X_{j+2} = X_{j+3} = \cdots = X_k = 0$. Then

$$\alpha_{jk} = F_j + M_{jk} \tag{4-20}$$

and

$$F_k = \min_{0 \le j \le k-1} [\alpha_{jk}] \tag{4-21}$$

Next construct the table shown in Figure 4-10. For a k-period horizon, the optimal last regeneration point is $j^*(k)$, defined by

$$\alpha_{j^*(k),k} = \min_{0 \le j \le k-1} \alpha_{jk} \tag{4-22}$$

Period of Last Production $(j+1)$	Last Regeneration Point (j)	Horizon (k)				
		1	2	3	...	T
1	0	α_{01}	α_{02}	α_{03}	...	α_{0T}
2	1		α_{12}	α_{13}	...	α_{1T}
3	2			α_{23}	...	α_{2T}
.	.					.
.	.					.
.	.					.
T	$T-1$					$\alpha_{T-1,T}$
$F_k = \min\limits_{j} \alpha_{jk}$		F_1	F_2	F_3		F_T
Optimal last regeneration point $[j^*(k)]$		$j^*(1)$	$j^*(2)$	$j^*(3)$		$j^*(T)$

FIGURE 4-10. Table for forward algorithm, no backlogging.

Given any regeneration point k, one can find the optimal last time point prior to k, $j^*(k)$, when the inventory is to be zero. This means that production last takes place in period $j^*(k) + 1$. By starting with $k = T$ and working backward, one can identify the regeneration points in the optimal solution.

An abbreviated discussion of this forward algorithm was given in Section 2-8.2 for the case of linear holding costs and production costs of the form (4-10).

☐**EXAMPLE 4-4** Production is to be planned for a four-period horizon. There is no initial inventory and the final inventory level is to be zero. No shortages are allowed. Production and inventory costs have the following forms:

$$C_t(X_t) = \begin{cases} 0, & \text{if } X_t = 0 \\ A_t + c_t X_t, & \text{if } X_t > 0 \end{cases}$$

$$H_t(I_t) = h_t I_t$$

Estimates of cost parameters and demand are given in Table 4-8. First consider the one-period problem $(k = 1)$:

$$M_{01} = A_1 + c_1 D_1 = 30 + (3)(20) = 90$$
$$F_1 = \alpha_{01} = F_0 + M_{01} = 0 + 90 = 90$$
$$\text{Solution: } j^*(1) = 0 \text{ and } X_1^* = 20$$

TABLE 4-8   Data for Example 4-4

PERIOD t	PREDICTED DEMAND D_t	SETUP COST A_t	UNIT VARIABLE COST c_t	UNIT HOLDING COST PER PERIOD h_t
1	20	$30	$3	$2
2	30	40	3	2
3	40	30	4	1
4	30	50	4	1

Next consider the two-period problem ($k = 2$):

$$M_{02} = A_1 + c_1(D_1 + D_2) + h_1 D_2 = 30 + (3)(20 + 30) + (2)(30) = 240$$

$$M_{12} = A_2 + c_2 D_2 = 40 + (3)(30) = 130$$

$$F_2 = \min \begin{cases} \alpha_{02} = F_0 + M_{02} = 0 + 240 = 240 \\ \alpha_{12} = F_1 + M_{12} = 90 + 130 = 220 \end{cases}$$

Solution: $F_2 = 220, j^*(2) = 1$, and $X_1^* = 20, X_2^* = 30$

For the three-period problem ($k = 3$):

$$M_{03} = A_1 + c_1(D_1 + D_2 + D_3) + h_1(D_2 + D_3) + h_2 D_3 = 520$$

$$M_{13} = A_2 + c_2(D_2 + D_3) + h_2 D_3 = 330$$

$$M_{23} = A_3 + c_3 D_3 = 190$$

$$F_3 = \min \begin{cases} \alpha_{03} = F_0 + M_{03} = 0 + 520 = 520 \\ \alpha_{13} = F_1 + M_{13} = 90 + 330 = 420 \\ \alpha_{23} = F_2 + M_{23} = 220 + 190 = 410 \end{cases}$$

Solution: $F_3 = 410, j^*(3) = 2$, and $X_1^* = 20, X_2^* = 30, X_3^* = 40$

Finally, for the four-period problem ($k = 4$):

$$M_{04} = A_1 + c_1(D_1 + D_2 + D_3 + D_4) + h_1(D_2 + D_3 + D_4)$$
$$+ h_2(D_3 + D_4) + h_3 D_4 = 760$$

$$M_{14} = A_2 + c_2(D_2 + D_3 + D_4) + h_2(D_3 + D_4) + h_3 D_4 = 510$$

$$M_{24} = A_3 + c_3(D_3 + D_4) + h_3 D_4 = 340$$

$$M_{34} = A_4 + c_4 D_4 = 170$$

$$F_4 = \min \begin{cases} \alpha_{04} = F_0 + M_{04} = 0 + 760 = 760 \\ \alpha_{14} = F_1 + M_{14} = 90 + 510 = 600 \\ \alpha_{24} = F_2 + M_{24} = 220 + 340 = 560 \\ \alpha_{34} = F_3 + M_{34} = 410 + 170 = 580 \end{cases}$$

Solution: $F_4 = 560, j^*(4) = 2$, and $X_1^* = 20, X_2^* = 30, X_3^* = 70$, and $X_4^* = 0$

These computations are summarized in Table 4-9.

TABLE 4-9 Determination of F_k and $j^*(k)$ from Values of α_{jk} for Example 4-4

j \ k	1	2	3	4
0	90*	240	520	760
1		220*	420	600
2			410*	560*
3				580
F_k	90	220	410	560
$j^*(k)$	0	1	2	2

Note that we successively solved problems having one-, two-, three-, and four-period horizons. To understand how the optimal production program is determined for the four-period problem, consider the information in Table 4-9. For $k = 4$, the optimal last regeneration point is 2. This means $I_2^* = 0$, $X_3^* = D_3 + D_4 = 70$, $I_3^* = D_4 = 30$, and $X_4^* = 0$. Since the inventory at the end of period 2 is zero, we let $k = 2$, and find that the optimal last regeneration point is 1. Thus $I_1^* = 0$ and $X_2^* = D_2 = 30$. For $k = 1$, $j^*(1) = 0$, so $X_1^* = D_1 = 20.\square$

Forward Algorithm—Backlogging Permitted. When shortages are allowed and backordered, the net inventory, I_t, may assume negative values. We now assume that

$$K_t(X_t, I_t) = C_t(X_t) + H_t^+(I_t^+) + H_t^-(I_t^-) \qquad (4\text{-}23)$$

where I_t^+ is the on-hand inventory and I_t^- is the backorder position at the end of period t, $I_t = I_t^+ - I_t^-$, and C_t, H_t^+, and H_t^- are concave. The optimal production policy has the property that at least two of the three quantities I_{t-1}^+, I_t^-, and X_t are zero. That is, demand in any period t is satisfied entirely from inventory (production in prior periods), or entirely by backlogging (production in future periods), or entirely from production in period t. This property may be proved through an argument somewhat more difficult than the one we gave in the no-backlogging case to show $I_{t-1}X_t = 0$. A proof is given by Zangwill (48).

This characteristic of the optimal solution means that if production takes place in period t and $j < t$ and $k \geq t$ are the nearest regeneration points (that is, $I_j = 0$ and $I_k = 0$) before and after t,

$$X_t = \sum_{r=j+1}^{k} D_r \qquad (4\text{-}24)$$

It is important to note that if j and k are two consecutive regeneration points, there will be exactly one period t, $j < t \leq k$, where production takes place.

We redefine M_{jk} to be the *minimum* cost of producing in exactly one of the periods $j + 1, j + 2, \ldots, k$ to satisfy the demand during these periods, when $I_j = I_k = 0$. Then

$$M_{jk} = \begin{cases} C_{j+1}(D_{j+1}), & \text{if } k = j + 1 \\ \min_{j+1 \leq t \leq k} \left[C_t(X_t) + \sum_{l=j+1}^{t-1} H_l^-(I_l^-) + \sum_{l=t}^{k-1} H_l^+(I_l^+) \right], & \text{for } k > j + 1 \end{cases} \quad (4\text{-}25)$$

where X_t is given by (4-24), and

$$I_l^- = \sum_{r=j+1}^{l} D_r, \quad \text{for } l = j + 1, j + 2, \ldots, t - 1 \quad (4\text{-}26)$$

$$I_l^+ = \sum_{r=l+1}^{k} D_r, \quad \text{for } l = t, t + 1, \ldots, k - 1 \quad (4\text{-}27)$$

The forward recursive relation is still

$$F_k = \min_{0 \leq j \leq k-1} [F_j + M_{jk}]$$

$$= \min_{0 \leq j \leq k-1} [\alpha_{jk}], \quad \text{for } k = 1, 2, \ldots, T \quad (4\text{-}28)$$

where $F_0 \equiv 0$. The preliminary optimization to find M_{jk} causes the backlog case to require more computational effort than the case where backlogging is not permitted.

□**EXAMPLE 4-5** Suppose in the situation of Example 4-4 that backlogging is permitted and that the backorder penalty function is

$$H_t^-(I_t^-) = \pi_t I_t^-$$

with $\pi_1 = 1$, $\pi_2 = 1$, $\pi_3 = 2$, and $\pi_4 = 2$. The first step is to compute M_{jk} for $k = 1, 2, 3,$ and 4 and all $j < k$. This involves finding the optimal period of production between the regeneration points j and k. We will denote this period by $t^*(j, k)$.

$$M_{01} = C_1(D_1) = 90; \quad t^*(0, 1) = 1$$

$$M_{02} = \min \begin{cases} C_1(D_1 + D_2) + H_1^+(D_2) = 240 \\ C_2(D_1 + D_2) + H_1^-(D_1) = 210 \end{cases}$$

$$= 210; \quad t^*(0, 2) = 2$$

$$M_{03} = \min \begin{cases} C_1(D_1 + D_2 + D_3) + H_1^+(D_2 + D_3) + H_2^+(D_3) = 520 \\ C_2(D_1 + D_2 + D_3) + H_1^-(D_1) + H_2^+(D_3) = 410 \\ C_3(D_1 + D_2 + D_3) + H_1^-(D_1) + H_2^-(D_1 + D_2) = 460 \end{cases}$$

$$= 410; \quad t^*(0, 3) = 2$$

Dynamic Programming and Network Models   217

$$M_{04} = \min \begin{cases} C_1\left(\sum_{r=1}^{4} D_r\right) + H_1^+(D_2 + D_3 + D_4) \\ \qquad\qquad + H_2^+(D_3 + D_4) + H_3^+(D_4) = 760 \\ C_2\left(\sum_{r=1}^{4} D_r\right) + H_1^-(D_1) + H_2^+(D_3 + D_4) + H_3^+(D_4) = 590 \\ C_3\left(\sum_{r=1}^{4} D_r\right) + H_1^-(D_1) + H_2^-(D_1 + D_2) + H_3^+(D_4) = 610 \\ C_4\left(\sum_{r=1}^{4} D_r\right) + H_1^-(D_1) + H_2^-(D_1 + D_2) \\ \qquad\qquad + H_3^-(D_1 + D_2 + D_3) = 780 \end{cases}$$

$$= 590; \ t^*(0, 4) = 2$$

$$M_{12} = C_2(D_2) = 130; \ t^*(1, 2) = 2$$

$$M_{13} = \min \begin{cases} C_2(D_2 + D_3) + H_2^+(D_3) = 330 \\ C_3(D_2 + D_3) + H_2^-(D_2) = 340 \end{cases}$$

$$= 330; \ t^*(1, 3) = 2$$

$$M_{14} = \min \begin{cases} C_2(D_2 + D_3 + D_4) + H_2^+(D_3 + D_4) + H_3^+(D_4) = 510 \\ C_3(D_2 + D_3 + D_4) + H_2^-(D_2) + H_3^+(D_4) = 490 \\ C_4(D_2 + D_3 + D_4) + H_2^-(D_2) + H_3^-(D_2 + D_3) = 620 \end{cases}$$

$$= 490; \ t^*(1, 4) = 3$$

$$M_{23} = C_3(D_3) = 190; \ t^*(2, 3) = 3$$

$$M_{24} = \min \begin{cases} C_3(D_3 + D_4) + H_3^+(D_4) = 340 \\ C_4(D_3 + D_4) + H_3^-(D_3) = 410 \end{cases}$$

$$= 340; \ t^*(2, 4) = 3$$

$$M_{34} = C_4(D_4) = 170; \ t^*(3, 4) = 4$$

Table 4-10 contains a summary of the computations. The next step is to solve for the F_k and the $j^*(k)$, using these values of M_{jk} in the recursive relation (4-28). The results are given in Table 4-11.

From Table 4-11 we see that the optimal regeneration points are 0, 2, and 4. For the regeneration points $j = 0$ and $k = 2$, Table 4-10 gives $t^*(0, 2) = 2$. Thus $X_1^* = 0$ and $X_2^* = 50$. Next we find $t^*(2, 4) = 3$, so $X_3^* = 70$ and $X_4^* = 0$. The cost of the program is 550. All inventory and backorder variables are zero, except $I_1^- = 20$ and $I_3^+ = 30$.□

Backward Algorithm—Backlogging Permitted. Zangwill (52) gives a backward algorithm for solving the backorder case. He also represents the problem as one of determining the minimal cost flow in a network (see Figure 4-8). The

TABLE 4-10 Determination of M_{jk} for Example 4-5

LAST REGENERATION POINT (j)	NEXT REGENERATION POINT (k)	PERIOD OF PRODUCTION (t)				$t^*(j, k)$	M_{jk}
		1	2	3	4		
0	1	90*				1	90
	2	240	210*			2	210
	3	520	410*	460		2	410
	4	760	590*	610	780	2	590
1	2		130*			2	130
	3		330*	340		2	330
	4		510	490*	620	3	490
2	3			190*		3	190
	4			340*	410	3	340
3	4				170*	4	170

property that in the optimal solution no more than one of the variables I_{t-1}^+, I_t^-, and X_t can be greater than zero is obtained by Zangwill through use of the following theorem about minimum cost flows in concave cost networks:[3]

> "*In a minimum cost network flow problem where the objective function is a concave function of the arc flows and the network has a single source, there is an optimal solution having the property that each node has an inward flow from at most one arc.*"

TABLE 4-11 Determination of F_k and $j^*(k)$ from Values of α_{jk} for Example 4-5

j \ k	1	2	3	4
0	90*	210*	410	590
1		220	420	580
2			400*	550*
3				570
F_k	90	210	400	550
$j^*(k)$	0	0	2	2

[3] The theorem assumes no capacity constraint on the flow in any arc.

The algorithm is as follows. Let β_j be the *optimal* cost from the beginning of period $j + 1$ to the end of period T, if j is a regeneration point, and let $\gamma_t(\varepsilon)$ be the *optimal* cost from the beginning of period t to the end of period T, if: (1) demand is backlogged ε periods at the end of period $t - 1$ and (2) production is carried out in period t. These definitions lead to the following recursive equations:

$$\beta_j = \min_{j < t \le T} \left[\sum_{l=j+1}^{t-1} H_l^- \left(\sum_{r=j+1}^{l} D_r \right) + \gamma_t(t - j - 1) \right] \qquad (4\text{-}29)$$

where $0 \le j \le T$ and $\beta_T \equiv 0$;

$$\gamma_t(\varepsilon) = \min_{t \le k \le T} \left[C_t \left(\sum_{r=t-\varepsilon}^{k} D_r \right) + \sum_{l=t}^{k-1} H_l^+ \left(\sum_{r=l+1}^{k} D_r \right) + \beta_k \right] \qquad (4\text{-}30)$$

where $0 \le \varepsilon \le t - 1$, $1 \le t \le T$, and $\gamma_{T+1} \equiv 0$.

Equation 4-29 assumes j is a regeneration point and finds the optimal time for the *next production*, which we will denote by $t^*(j)$. Equation 4-30 assumes production takes place in period t, at which time the backorder position is $I_{t-1}^- = D_{t-\varepsilon} + D_{t-\varepsilon+1} + \cdots + D_{t-1}$, and finds the optimal *next regeneration point*, $k^*(t, \varepsilon)$. The quantities β_j and $\gamma_t(\varepsilon)$ are calculated backward, starting with period T. For any period t, first find β_t and then compute $\gamma_t(\varepsilon)$ for $\varepsilon = 0, 1, 2, \ldots, t - 1$. The optimal program has cost β_0.

In case no backlogging is permitted, Zangwill's backward algorithm can be used by considering only $\varepsilon = 0$ and defining $\beta_j = \gamma_{j+1}(0)$, for all j.

□EXAMPLE 4-6   We shall use Zangwill's algorithm to solve the problem of Example 4-5. Important data are summarized in Table 4-12.

We start with $\beta_4 \equiv 0$ and proceed to compute $\gamma_4(\varepsilon)$, for $\varepsilon = 0, 1, 2, 3$; that is, we calculate the optimum cost for the last period, assuming production takes place in that period, for the possibilities of 0, 1, 2, or 3 periods of backlog at the start of the period. Since the ending net inventory is to be zero, the optimum last period policy is to produce a quantity equal to the demand in period 4, plus any backlog existing at the start of the period. Therefore, we have

TABLE 4-12   Data for Example 4-6

t	D_t	A_t	c_t	h_t	π_t
1	20	30	3	2	1
2	30	40	3	2	1
3	40	30	4	1	2
4	30	50	4	1	2

$k^*(4, \varepsilon) = 4$, and

$$\gamma_4(0) = C_4(D_4) + \beta_4 = 170 + 0 = 170$$
$$\gamma_4(1) = C_4(D_3 + D_4) + \beta_4 = 330 + 0 = 330$$
$$\gamma_4(2) = C_4(D_2 + D_3 + D_4) + \beta_4 = 450 + 0 = 450$$
$$\gamma_4(3) = C_4(D_1 + D_2 + D_3 + D_4) + \beta_4 = 530 + 0 = 530$$

Next we assume the end of period 3 is a regeneration point and compute the optimal cost in the last period, β_3. Obviously we must produce in period 4, which means $t^*(3) = 4$, and

$$\beta_3 = \gamma_4(0) = 170$$

Now we suppose we produce in period 3 and want to find the optimal cost over periods 3 and 4, for the possibilities of 0, 1, or 2 periods of backlog at the start of period 3.

$$\gamma_3(0) = \min \begin{cases} C_3(D_3) + \beta_3 = 190 + 170 = 360 \\ C_3(D_3 + D_4) + H_3^+(D_4) + \beta_4 = 310 + 30 + 0 = 340 \end{cases}$$
$$= 340; \text{ for which } k^*(3, 0) = 4$$

$$\gamma_3(1) = \min \begin{cases} C_3(D_2 + D_3) + \beta_3 = 310 + 170 = 480 \\ C_3(D_2 + D_3 + D_4) + H_3^+(D_4) + \beta_4 = 430 + 30 + 0 = 460 \end{cases}$$
$$= 460; \text{ for which } k^*(3, 1) = 4$$

$$\gamma_3(2) = \min \begin{cases} C_3(D_1 + D_2 + D_3) + \beta_3 = 390 + 170 = 560 \\ C_3(D_1 + D_2 + D_3 + D_4) + H_3^+(D_4) + \beta_4 = 510 + 30 + 0 = 540 \end{cases}$$
$$= 540; \text{ for which } k^*(3, 2) = 4$$

We next consider the end of period 2 to be a regeneration point and solve for β_2.

$$\beta_2 = \min \begin{cases} \gamma_3(0) = 340 \\ H_3^-(D_3) + \gamma_4(1) = 80 + 330 = 410 \end{cases}$$
$$= 340; \text{ for which } t^*(2) = 3$$

Assuming production takes place in period 2,

$$\gamma_2(0) = \min \begin{cases} C_2(D_2) + \beta_2 = 470 \\ C_2(D_2 + D_3) + H_2^+(D_3) + \beta_3 = 500 \\ C_2(D_2 + D_3 + D_4) + H_2^+(D_3 + D_4) + H_3^+(D_4) + \beta_4 = 510 \end{cases}$$
$$= 470; \text{ for which } k^*(2, 0) = 2$$

$$\gamma_2(1) = \min \begin{cases} C_2(D_1 + D_2) + \beta_2 = 530 \\ C_2(D_1 + D_2 + D_3) + H_2^+(D_3) + \beta_3 = 560 \\ C_2(D_1 + D_2 + D_3 + D_4) + H_2^+(D_3 + D_4) + H_3^+(D_4) + \beta_4 = 570 \end{cases}$$
$$= 530; \text{ for which } k^*(2, 1) = 2$$

If the end of period 1 is a regeneration point, we compute the optimal cost over the last three periods as follows:

$$\beta_1 = \min \begin{cases} \gamma_2(0) = 470 \\ H_2^-(D_2) + \gamma_3(1) = 490 \\ H_2^-(D_2) + H_3^-(D_2 + D_3) + \gamma_4(2) = 620 \end{cases}$$

$$= 470; \text{ for which } t^*(1) = 2$$

If production takes place in the first period, the optimal cost over all four periods is

$$\gamma_1(0) = \min \begin{cases} C_1(D_1) + \beta_1 = 560 \\ C_1(D_1 + D_2) + H_1^+(D_2) + \beta_2 = 580 \\ C_1(D_1 + D_2 + D_3) + H_1^+(D_2 + D_3) + H_2^+(D_3) + \beta_3 = 690 \\ C_1(D_1 + D_2 + D_3 + D_4) + H_1^+(D_2 + D_3 + D_4) \\ \qquad + H_2^+(D_3 + D_4) + H_3^+(D_4) + \beta_4 = 760 \end{cases}$$

$$= 560; \text{ for which } k^*(1, 0) = 1$$

Finally, considering the regeneration point at $t = 0$, we compute the minimum cost over the four-period horizon.

$$\beta_0 = \min \begin{cases} \gamma_1(0) = 560 \\ H_1^-(D_1) + \gamma_2(1) = 550 \\ H_1^-(D_1) + H_2^-(D_1 + D_2) + \gamma_3(2) = 610 \\ H_1^-(D_1) + H_2^-(D_1 + D_2) + H_3^-(D_1 + D_2 + D_3) + \gamma_4(3) = 780 \end{cases}$$

$$= 550; \text{ for which } t^*(0) = 2$$

These results are displayed in Tables 4-13 and 4-14.

To find the optimal production program, we must start with the regeneration point at time zero and work forward through time, alternating between Tables 4-13 and 4-14. For $j = 0$, we find $t^*(0) = 2$ from Table 4-13. This means that

TABLE 4-13 Determination of β_j and $t^*(j)$ in Example 4-6

REGENERATION POINT (j)	PERIOD OF NEXT PRODUCTION (t)				$t^*(j)$	β_j
	1	2	3	4		
0	560	550*	610	780	2	550
1		470*	490	620	2	470
2			340*	410	3	340
3				170*	4	170

Production Planning—Dynamic Models   222

TABLE 4-14 Determination of $\gamma_t(\varepsilon)$ and $k^*(t, \varepsilon)$ in Example 4-6

PERIOD OF PRODUCTION (t)	PERIODS OF BACKLOG SINCE LAST REGENERATION POINT (ε)	NEXT REGENERATION POINT (k) 1	2	3	4	$k^*(t, \varepsilon)$	$\gamma_t(\varepsilon)$
1	0	560*	580	690	760	1	560
2	0		470*	500	510	2	470
	1		530*	560	570	2	530
3	0			360	340*	4	340
	1			480	460*	4	460
	2			560	540*	4	540
4	0				170*	4	170
	1				330*	4	330
	2				450*	4	450
	3				530*	4	530

production first takes place in period 2. At this point we know that $X_1^* = 0$, $X_2^* > 0$, and that one period of backlog will be the net inventory status at the start of period 2. Going to Table 4-14 with $t = 2$ and $\varepsilon = 1$, we see that $k^*(2, 1) = 2$. This means $I_2^+ = I_2^- = 0$, implying $X_2^* = D_1 + D_2$. Since $j = 2$ is a regeneration point, we determine from Table 4-13 that the next period of production is $t^*(2) = 3$. Thus $X_3^* > 0$. Since $I_2 = 0$, we use $\varepsilon = 0$ to find the next regeneration point when $t = 3$. It is $k^*(3, 0) = 4$, so we know that $X_3^* = D_3 + D_4$ and $X_4^* = 0$. The optimal program is $X_1^* = 0$, $X_2^* = 50$, $X_3^* = 70$, and $X_4^* = 0$. It has a cost of $\beta_0 = 550$. Naturally, this agrees with the solution of Example 4-5, where the forward algorithm was applied to the same problem. $\square$

Treatment of Initial Inventory. When the initial net inventory is not zero, one first adjusts the demand schedule by subtracting any initial on-hand inventory from the original requirements, starting with period 1, or by adding any initial backlog to the requirements in period 1. This procedure is the same as that described for the convex cost case in Section 4-3.3.

Planning Horizon Theorems. When the production cost function is of the special form

$$C_t(X_t) = \begin{cases} A_t + c_t X_t, & \text{if } X_t > 0 \\ 0, & \text{if } X_t = 0 \end{cases}$$

and the inventory cost function is

$$H_t(I_t) = \begin{cases} h_t I_t, & \text{if } I_t \geq 0 \\ -\pi_t I_t, & \text{if } I_t \leq 0 \end{cases}$$

several authors have presented theorems that can reduce the computational effort required in applying the algorithms given in this section. Wagner and Whitin (45), Zabel (47), and Wagner (46) give results for the no-backlogging case, while Zangwill (52) analyzes the backlog case. Such findings often are called *planning horizon theorems* because they decompose the T-period problem into smaller problems that can be treated independently. This effectively reduces the decision space at each stage of optimization. An example is given in Exercise 4-40.

Some of the computations could have been eliminated in solving Examples 4-4, 4-5, and 4-6, had we made use of such theorems; however, we felt it better to explain the basic algorithms and illustrate them prior to mentioning possible refinements.

Bound Constraints on Production and Inventory.   When costs are concave and there are bound constraints of the form

$$P'_t \leq X_t \leq P_t$$

or

$$L'_t \leq I_t \leq L_t$$

the problem is much more difficult to solve, principally because it is difficult to characterize the structure of the optimal solution to the extent that an efficient algorithm can be developed.

Florian and Klein (11) have considered two cases: (1) the no-backlog case where $0 \leq X_t \leq P_t$ and $I_t \geq 0$ and (2) the backlog case where $0 \leq X_t \leq P_t$ and $I_t \geq - \sum_{k=t-\alpha+1}^{t} D_k$. The latter case limits backlogging to at most α periods, where α is an integer determined by management policy. They develop several properties of the optimal solution in each case and give solution algorithms for both problems when the production capacities are the same in each period.

Florian and Robillard (12) have constructed a branch-and-bound algorithm for solving the concave cost network flow problem with capacity constraints. Since the production planning problem can be modeled as a minimum-cost flow problem, the algorithm is applicable in our situation. However, no computational experience was reported.

Zangwill (48) shows that his backward algorithm is applicable for $0 \leq X_t \leq \infty$ and $- \sum_{k=t-\alpha+1}^{t} D_k \leq I_t \leq \infty$. This limitation of backlogging to at most α periods can be imposed by only considering $\varepsilon \leq \alpha$ in evaluating Equation 4-30.

If costs are linear, no difficulty is experienced because of bound constraints. We can solve the problem by a linear programming algorithm, or alternatively, we can recognize the problem as a capacitated transhipment problem and use the out-of-kilter algorithm of Ford and Fulkerson (13).

4-4 Production and Work Force Smoothing

4-4.1 Smoothing Problems and Aggregate Planning

In a sense, almost every model in this chapter could be called a production smoothing model, because it involves trade-offs between production costs and inventory-related costs and results in the determination of optimal production levels for each period, or equivalently, optimal changes in production levels from period to period. However, the term "production smoothing" typically is reserved for models that explicitly include costs of changing production levels from one period to the next. Such costs are called *smoothing costs*. Model (4-3) in Section 4-2.2 is an example of a linear programming formulation of a production smoothing problem, assuming that the cost of increasing or decreasing the production rate is a linear function of the change.

A related family of problems is concerned with capacity planning, as well as production level decisions, over the planning horizon. Capacity is a function of work force level and the amount of machinery and facilities available, and since only the former is usually variable in the short term, these problems often are called *work force smoothing problems*, or production and work force smoothing problems. Model (4-4) in Section 4-2.3 illustrates the inclusion of work force level change costs in a production planning problem. That model contains costs of hiring and firing in its objective function and expresses production capacity as a function of work force level in its constraints. The decision variables are work force size and production level for each period.

Another approach to modeling capacity change costs is discussed in Exercises 4-17 and 4-18, where it is assumed that the capacity in a period is controllable, with a given cost of changing capacity from one period to the next; however, capacity is not necessarily assumed to be dependent entirely on work force level and no work force level variables are included.

Aggregate Planning. So far in this chapter, we have discussed only single product models. These are appropriate in any of three situations: (1) only a single product is involved; (2) there are multiple products, but the production processes and resource availabilities are such that each product can be planned independently; and (3) there are multiple products, but for the decision problem at hand, it is sufficient to plan only their combined, or *aggregate*, level, without specifying production quantities for individual products. The latter situation is commonly the case when we are making decisions about capacity, typically work force level. For this reason, work force smoothing problems are often called *aggregate planning* problems in the literature.

In an aggregate planning problem, there is a single production variable, representing the total production of all products. This means that there must be some natural unit for measurement of aggregate output, such as tons for a steel mill, cases for a bottling plant, barrels for a refinery, machine-hours for a job shop, or man-hours for a maintenance department.

The solution to an aggregate model establishes the production capacity and the aggregate production level for each period. Naturally, it is necessary to follow this with a second-stage decision procedure to determine production quantities for individual products, using the output of the aggregate model as constraints. This two-stage approach to planning production and work force could result in an inferior solution to that obtained by combining decisions about individual item production quantities and the decision on work force level into one model. We illustrate the latter approach in Example 4-14 of Section 4-6, where we discuss multiple-item models. The principal disadvantage of multiple-item analysis over aggregate analysis has been the computational difficulty resulting from the size of the model. With advances in the size and speed of digital computers and improvements in mathematical programming software, this disadvantage is disappearing rapidly.

The economics of aggregate planning are similar to those of single-item planning, and the brief discussion of costs in Section 4-1 is relevant. More detailed descriptions of the setting and objectives of aggregate analysis can be found in Reference 4, Chapter 5, and Reference 15, Chapter 13. Since work force smoothing costs are characteristic of aggregate planning, most of the models of Section 4-4.3 are appropriate for such problems.

4-4.2 Models with Production Change Costs

To provide a general representation of the production smoothing problem, we recall the dynamic programming model (4-11), given in Section 4-3.1:

$$f_t(I, X) = \min_{X_t \geq 0} \left[K_t(X_t, I_t, X) + f_{t+1}(I_t, X_t) \right]$$

where

$$I_t = I + X_t - D_t$$

$f_t(I, X) =$ the minimum cost attainable over periods t, $t + 1$, ..., T, when the net inventory at the start of period t is I and the production level in period $t - 1$ was X

$K_t(X_t, I_t, X_{t-1}) =$ cost of production, inventory, shortages, and production change in period t, as a function of the production level and ending inventory in period t and the production level in period $t - 1$

The model has two state variables, I_{t-1} and X_{t-1}. This can greatly increase the amount of computation over that required for a model without smoothing costs and only one state variable.

Typically, we can write

$$K_t(X_t, I_t, X_{t-1}) = C_t(X_t) + H_t(I_t) + V_t(X_t, X_{t-1})$$

where we assume that the production, inventory-related, and smoothing costs are separable. The smoothing cost function, V_t, is defined to be zero when $X_t = X_{t-1}$, nonnegative otherwise. It is possible, but unlikely, that V_t will depend on production rates in periods prior to $t - 1$. If so, it must be structured to account for this dependence.

A variety of functional forms for smoothing costs appear in the literature:

$$V_t(X_t, X_{t-1}) = \lambda_t |X_t - X_{t-1}| \tag{4-31a}$$

$$V_t(X_t, X_{t-1}) = \lambda_t(X_t - X_{t-1})^+ + \lambda_t'(X_t - X_{t-1})^- \tag{4-31b}$$

$$V_t(X_t, X_{t-1}) = \lambda_t(X_t - X_{t-1})^2 \tag{4-31c}$$

$$V(X_t, X_{t-1}) = \begin{cases} v_t, & \text{if } X_t > 0 \text{ and } X_{t-1} = 0 \\ 0, & \text{otherwise} \end{cases} \tag{4-31d}$$

$$V_t(X_t, X_{t-1}) = \begin{cases} v_t, & \text{if } X_t > 0 \text{ and } X_{t-1} = 0 \\ v_t', & \text{if } X_t = 0 \text{ and } X_{t-1} > 0 \\ 0, & \text{otherwise} \end{cases} \tag{4-31e}$$

The forms (4-31a) and (4-31b) lend themselves to linear programming formulations. See model (4-3) in Section 4-2.2 and Exercise 4-12. Equation 4-31c is a simple convex function, assuming a quadratic model to represent a situation of increasing marginal change costs. The form (4-31d) is a start-up cost model. In this case, a cost v_t is incurred in period t if production takes place in period t but not in period $t - 1$, and is in addition to the production cost $C_t(X_t)$, which may include a setup cost, A_t, independent of X_{t-1}. A related model is (4-31e), which includes a shutdown cost as well as a start-up cost.

When the smoothing problem can be formulated as a linear programming model, we have an efficient solution procedure. However, when V_t is nonlinear, it is not so easy. Dynamic programming methods are not attractive, because there are two state variables. However, there are several more efficient algorithms for solving a few special cases. We next describe some of these results.

Zangwill (49) considers a situation where the cost functions C_t and H_t are concave and V_t is piecewise concave (see Figure 4-6b). No backlogging is allowed and the requirements are assumed *nondecreasing*, that is, $D_t \leq D_{t+1}$, for all t. He characterizes the optimal solution as having the following properties:

(1) If $\mathring{X}_t > 0$ and $X_{t-1} > 0$, then $X_t = X_{t-1}$

(2) If $X_t > 0$ and $X_{t-1} = 0$, then $I_{t-1} = 0$

Thus, production occurs in runs, where a run is a sequence of periods having the same positive production level in each period. Also no inventory is on hand at the start of the first period of the run. He then develops a solution algorithm for the special case

$$V_t(X_t, X_{t-1}) = \begin{cases} v_t, & \text{if } X_t > X_{t-1} \\ 0, & \text{if } X_t = X_{t-1} \\ v'_t, & \text{if } X_t < X_{t-1} \end{cases} \qquad (4\text{-}32)$$

The algorithm can be made more efficient for the simple production cost function

$$C_t(X_t) = \begin{cases} A_t + cX_t, & \text{if } X_t > 0 \\ 0, & \text{if } X_t = 0 \end{cases} \qquad (4\text{-}33)$$

We do not give the procedure, but refer the interested reader to Reference 49.

Sobel (39) analyses the problem of smoothing start-up and shutdown costs, using a smoothing cost structure similar to (4-31e) and assuming production and inventory costs are concave. He develops shortest-path network algorithms, of the type given in Section 4-3, for solution of two forms for V_t, and points out simplifications for special production cost functions.

☐**EXAMPLE 4-7**   [Suggested by a problem in Wagner (Reference 46, Chapter 9).] Consider a start-up cost smoothing problem where

$$C_t(X_t) = \begin{cases} A_t + c_t X_t, & \text{if } X_t > 0 \\ 0, & \text{if } X_t = 0 \end{cases}$$

$$c_1 \geq c_2 \geq \cdots \geq c_T, \qquad \text{(nonincreasing costs)}$$

$$H_t(I_t) \text{ concave for } I_t \geq 0$$

$$V_t(X_t, X_{t-1}) = \begin{cases} v_t, & \text{if } X_t > 0 \quad \text{and} \quad X_{t-1} = 0 \\ 0, & \text{otherwise} \end{cases}$$

No shortages are allowed, and $I_0 = I_T = 0$. For this cost structure, it is not difficult to show that an optimal solution has the property $I_{t-1}X_t = 0$. For suppose there was a period k having $I_k > 0$ and $X_k > 0$. Then, because $c_t \geq c_k$, for $t < k$, it is no more costly to reschedule the production of the amount I_{k-1} so that these units are now produced in period k. There will be no additional fixed costs or smoothing costs and at least the inventory cost $H_{t-1}(I_{t-1})$ will be averted.

Based on this property, the following backward algorithm can be used to obtain the optimal solution: Let

M_{jk} = cost of satisfying demand in periods $j + 1, j + 2, \ldots, k$, when j and k, $0 \leq j < k \leq T$, are two consecutive regeneration points and production *did* take place in period j

$\overline{M}_{jk}$ = same as M_{jk}, but assuming production *did not* take place in period j

β_j = optimal cost over periods $j + 1, j + 2, \ldots, T$, if j is a regeneration point and production *did* take place in period j

$\overline{\beta}_j$ = same as β_j, but assuming production *did not* take place in period j

An expression for M_{jk} was developed in Section 4-3.4 and given in Equation 4-18 for a general concave production cost function. For the production cost structure assumed in this example, we have

$$M_{jk} = \begin{cases} A_{j+1} + c_{j+1}D_{j+1}, & \text{if } k = j + 1 \\ A_{j+1} + c_{j+1} \sum_{r=j+1}^{k} D_r + \sum_{r=j+1}^{k-1} H_r \left(\sum_{l=r+1}^{k} D_l \right), & \text{if } k > j + 1 \end{cases} \quad (4\text{-}34)$$

Once M_{jk} is computed, we can quickly calculate $\overline{M}_{jk} = M_{jk} + v_{j+1}$.

The recursion for β_j involves finding the optimal next regeneration point, $k^*(j)$, following j. To do this, we must try all values $k = j + 1, j + 2, \ldots, T$ and choose the one giving the minimum cost. If $k = j + 1$, production will take place in periods $j + 1$ and $j + 2$, meaning that no start-up cost will be incurred in period $j + 2$; while if $k > j + 1$, production will take place in period $k + 1$, but not in k, resulting in a start-up cost in period $k + 1$. These considerations lead to

$$\beta_j = \min_{j < k \leq T} \left[M_{jk} + \begin{cases} \beta_{j+1}, & \text{if } k = j + 1 \\ \overline{\beta}_k, & \text{if } k > j + 1 \end{cases} \right] \quad (4\text{-}35)$$

If we replace M_{jk} with $\overline{M}_{jk}$ in (4-35), we have the recursion for $\overline{\beta}_j$; however, it is most easily computed from $\overline{\beta}_j = \beta_j + v_{j+1}$. Equation 4-35 holds for $j = 0$, $1, \ldots, T - 1$. We define $\overline{\beta}_T = \beta_T \equiv 0$, for completeness.

In using these relations, we compute $\beta_{T-1}, \overline{\beta}_{T-1}, \beta_{T-2}, \overline{\beta}_{T-2}, \ldots, \beta_0$, and $\overline{\beta}_0$, in that order. For each j, we note $k^*(j)$, the optimum next regeneration point. Once β_0 is computed, the optimal regeneration points (and hence the optimal production quantities) can be obtained for the entire T-period planning horizon.

This example illustrates again how knowledge of the properties of an optimal solution can help in the development of an efficient solution procedure. In this case, we obtained a backward shortest-path algorithm, with not much more computational effort than that required by the forward algorithm of Section 4-3.4, which did not involve production smoothing. □

4-4.3 Models with Work Force Change Costs

There have been a number of approaches to production planning when work force level decisions are involved. Most have included the formulation of a mathematical model, consisting of an economic objective function and relevant constraints, and solution of the model either by mathematical optimization methods or by computer-aided search procedures. A few analysts have intentionally avoided this approach and have developed decision rules based in part on subjective, logical considerations. In this section, we shall describe briefly some of the better-known mathematical approaches and defer discussion of heuristic methods until Section 4-4.4.

One of the earliest and best-known studies of the work force smoothing problem is the research of Holt, Modigliani, Muth, and Simon (20, 21). In the process of studying the aggregate planning policies of a large paint manufacturer, they formulated the following quadratic programming model: Let

W_t = work force level (workers) in period t, $t = 1, 2, \ldots, T$

X_t = aggregate production rate in period t

I_t = actual aggregate net inventory at the end of period t

I_t^* = desired (ideal) aggregate net inventory at the end of period t

Z = total cost during the planning horizon for work force, work force changes, overtime, inventory, shortages, and setups

The following costs are incurred in period t.

1. *Regular time payroll cost*. The model is

$$c_1 W_t + c_{13} \qquad (4\text{-}36)$$

The constants c_1 and c_{13} are nonnegative and represent, respectively, the variable cost of a worker on regular time in period t and the fixed labor cost in period t. While the constant c_{13} will not affect the solution once c_1 has been specified, it should be considered in the process of estimating c_1 from cost data.

2. *Work force change cost*. The model is

$$c_2(W_t - W_{t-1} - c_{11})^2 \qquad (4\text{-}37)$$

This is a quadratic function of the change in work force, where the constant c_{11} improves the fit when the costs of hiring and firing are different.

3. *Overtime cost*. The model is

$$c_3(X_t - c_4 W_t)^2 + c_5 X_t - c_6 W_t + c_{12} X_t W_t \qquad (4\text{-}38)$$

Typically, we assume that overtime costs are a linear function of the amount by which scheduled production X_t exceeds regular time capacity (here assumed to be proportional to the work force size and given by $c_4 W_t$). Holt et al., used a quadratic approximation to the typical piecewise linear model. The linear and multiplicative terms in (4-38) are to improve the fit, especially in case X_t is less than $c_4 W_t$, when the first term in the model erroneously generates "undertime" costs.

4. *Inventory-related costs.* The model is

$$c_7(I_t - I_t^*)^2 = c_7(I_t - c_8 - c_9 D_t)^2 \qquad (4\text{-}39)$$

Here the inventory-related costs of holding stock, carrying backorders, and making machine setups are assumed proportional to the square of the difference between the actual net inventory and the ideal net inventory. The assumption is that if $I_t > I_t^*$, excess inventory carrying costs will be incurred, while if $I_t < I_t^*$, excess backlogging costs will be experienced and setup costs will be increased because of reduced item lot sizes. Note that in the aggregate case, both the aggregate on-hand inventory and the aggregate backorder level can be nonzero at the same time (why?). Holt et al., assumed that the ideal inventory was a linear function of the expected aggregate demand in the period, that is, $I_t^* = c_8 + c_9 D_t$.

The complete optimization model is

$$\text{minimize} \quad Z = \sum_{t=1}^{T} [c_1 W_t + c_{13} + c_2(W_t - W_{t-1} - c_{11})^2 + c_3(X_t - c_4 W_t)^2$$

$$+ c_5 X_t - c_6 W_t + c_{12} X_t W_t + c_7(I_t - c_8 - c_9 W_t)^2] \quad (4\text{-}40a)$$

subject to

$$I_t = I_{t-1} + X_t - D_t, \qquad (t = 1, 2, \ldots, T) \qquad (4\text{-}40b)$$

Note that the model contains only inventory balance constraints and does not limit work force size or the amount of overtime.

By calculus methods, it can be shown (21) that the optimal solution for the first period in the planning horizon is of the following form:

$$W_1^* = \sum_{t=1}^{T} \lambda_t D_t + \rho_1 W_0 + \rho_2 I_0 + \rho_3 \qquad (4\text{-}41)$$

$$X_1^* = \sum_{t=1}^{T} \alpha_t D_t + \beta_1 W_0 + \beta_2 I_0 + \beta_3 \qquad (4\text{-}42)$$

In (4-41) and (4-42), I_0 and W_0 are the current net inventory and work force level, respectively, and the α's, β's, λ's and ρ's are constants depending on the c's in model (4-40). (What signs would you expect for $\rho_1, \rho_2, \beta_1,$ and β_2?)

If the $\{D_t\}$ are not known with certainty, a forecast must be used. In Reference 22, Chapter 6, it is shown that the proper forecast for period t is an unbiased estimate of the expected demand in that period. Under conditions of uncertainty, when it is desired to minimize the expected value of a quadratic objective function, such as (4-40a), it is possible to replace the random variable D_t with its expected value and proceed as in the deterministic case. Thus, we can use the decision rules (4-41) and (4-42) with estimates of expected demand, $E(D_t)$, in place of D_t. We do not need to estimate any other characteristics of the probability distribution of D_t.

Another factor that simplifies the forecasting problem is that the weights λ_t and α_t in the decision rules typically decrease rapidly as t increases. This means that only the first four or five periods must be forecasted with accuracy.

Although the decision rules are written only for the first period, they can be used to plan decisions in future periods. This involves repetitive application of the rules in a manner that simulates the decisions to be made over time, assuming demand materializes as expected. For example, if we have computed W_1^* and X_1^* from (4-41) and (4-42), we may assume $I_1 = I_0 + X_1^* - E(D_1)$, and compute

$$W_2^* = \sum_{t=1}^{T} \lambda_t E(D_{t+1}) + \rho_1 W_1^* + \rho_2 I_1 + \rho_3 \qquad (4\text{-}43a)$$

and

$$X_2^* = \sum_{t=1}^{T} \alpha_t E(D_{t+1}) + \beta_1 W_1^* + \beta_2 I_1 + \beta_3 \qquad (4\text{-}43b)$$

Note that we now must have a forecast for period $T + 1$. This process could be repeated for $t = 3, 4, \ldots, T$ to generate plans for the entire planning horizon. If the model is applied on a *moving horizon* basis, where at the end of each period, new forecasts are made for T future periods and the state variables I_0 and W_0 are updated, only the solution for P_1^* and W_1^* may be required. However, for related decisions requiring longer-range estimates of production and work force levels, it may be necessary to project tentative plans, and the approach described in this paragraph can be used.

Because the decision rules (4-41) and (4-42) are linear functions of the forecasts by period over the planning horizon and the current net inventory and work force levels, the model (4-40) is called the *linear decision rule* model. Further discussion of this approach, including an especially interesting discussion of costs and applications, can be found in Reference 22.

Hanssmann and Hess (17) give a linear programming formulation of the work force smoothing problem that parallels the linear decision rule model. It is very similar to model (4-4) of Section 4-2.3.

Taubert (41) develops and tests search procedures to optimize nonlinear mathematical programing models, such as (4-40). In a typical aggregate planning problem, the planning horizon will be 8 to 12 periods long, so that there will be about 20 decision variables. For a problem of this size, current computer-based search algorithms can explore the response surface defined by the objective function of the model and rapidly arrive at a (hopefully) good, although perhaps not optimal, solution. The advantage of the approach is its applicability to nonlinear models for which no efficient mathematical solution procedure can be found. A disadvantage is that the search procedure may terminate at a local optimum significantly inferior to the global optimum. Taubert reports good results with his methodology. He also describes his approach in Reference 4, Chapter 7.

Lippman, Rolfe, Wagner, and Yuan (29) have considered mathematical approaches to work force smoothing, when the cost of changing work force levels is a linear function of the change. In Reference 29 they characterize the optimal policy when production costs are convex, inventory costs are increasing, and demands are monotone increasing or decreasing. In Reference 30 they give solution algorithms and planning horizon results when all costs are linear and demands are monotone increasing or decreasing.

4-4.4 Other Approaches to Aggregate Planning

Parametric Production Planning. Jones (24) has developed an approach to production and work force planning that he calls *parametric production planning*. The procedure involves structuring a logical set of decision rules, which take current status information (such as inventory levels, work force levels, production rate) and a forecast of requirements over the lead time and compute changes to be made in work force size and production rate. These rules are a function of a few parameters, whose optimal values are determined through a search procedure involving simulation against historical demand and use of the actual cost structure of the organization (that is, retrospective simulation). The resulting rules are used each period on a moving horizon basis to plan production and work force for the next period.

For example, Jones proposed the following model for the same type of aggregate planning problem as in the linear decision rule model. Assuming the current time is $t = 0$, the work force level in period 1 is to be the current work force level, W_0, plus a fraction α of the difference between an ideal work force level, W_1^*, and W_0. W_1^* can be thought of as the level one would have if there were no work force change costs. Formally, this rule is

$$W_1 = W_0 + \alpha(W_1^* - W_0), \qquad 0 \le \alpha \le 1 \qquad (4\text{-}44)$$

which can also be written as

$$W_1 = \alpha W_1^* + (1 - \alpha)W_0, \qquad 0 \le \alpha \le 1$$

The latter form shows that the planned work force level in period 1 is to be a weighted average of the ideal level and the current level.

Jones proposes computing the ideal work force size by the following formula:

$$W_1^* = \sum_{t=1}^{T} b_t g(D_t^*) + b_1 g(I_1^* - I_0) \qquad (4\text{-}45)$$

where

$D_t^* =$ forecast of expected demand in period t

$g(\cdot) =$ a function that converts units of product into required man-hours of labor

$b_t =$ the weight given to the forecast for period t. These weights are assumed to be monotone-decreasing, nonnegative, and sum to unity

$I_1^* =$ a target inventory for the end of the first period. This is to be based on safety-stock considerations, not those of smoothing. It is determined externally in a manner not specifically defined by Jones

$I_0 =$ the current net inventory, so that $I_1^* - I_0$ is the inventory discrepancy to be corrected in the first period; hence, multiplication by the coefficient b_1

To reduce the number of parameters in the rule, Jones suggests computing the b_t values from

$$b_t = \frac{\beta^t}{\sum\limits_{t=1}^{T} \beta^t}, \qquad 0 \le \beta \le 1 \qquad (4\text{-}46)$$

Similarly, he proposes the following production level rule:

$$X_1 = g^{-1}(W_1) + \gamma[X_1^* - g^{-1}(W_1)], \qquad 0 \le \gamma \le 1 \qquad (4\text{-}47)$$

where

$g^{-1}(\cdot) =$ the inverse function converting man-hours into units of product, so that $g^{-1}(W_1)$ is the production capacity in period 1, if the work force level is W_1

$X_1^* =$ ideal production rate in period 1, given by

$$X_1^* = \sum\limits_{t=1}^{T} d_t D_t^* + d_1(I_1^* - I_0) \qquad (4\text{-}48)$$

The weights, $\{d_t\}$, are determined by choice of a single parameter δ, using the following equation:

$$d_t = \frac{\delta^t}{\sum\limits_{t=1}^{T} \delta^t}, \qquad 0 \le \delta \le 1 \qquad (4\text{-}49)$$

We note that Jones' decision rules are a function of four parameters, α, β, γ, and δ. Some criterion has to be established for selecting the best set of values for these parameters and an optimization procedure must be employed. Jones used a search procedure, where the response for any set of parameter values was determined by computing the costs of production, work force, work force change, inventories, and so forth, incurred in a simulation involving use of the rules against historical demand. Jones found that his procedure performed almost as well as the linear decision rule model. In Reference 24 he gives more details of the comparison of the two methods and provides other examples of his approach.

Management Coefficients Model. The usual approach in an operations research study of a production planning problem involves the construction of a model representing the expected economic payoff as a function of the decision variables, and the solution of the model by mathematical means to find the best decision values. This optimizing approach could be called *prescriptive*, in the sense that it results in prescribing a course of action for the decision maker, based on a rational analysis of how well his objectives are attained by the various alternatives available to him at the time. Bowman (3) has proposed a quite different methodology, which involves modeling the decision processes of the decision maker directly.

Bowman's procedure can be summarized briefly as follows. Consider the decision variable to be the dependent, or response, variable in the decision process and consider the various pieces of information available to the decision maker at the time he makes his decision to be the independent variables (which influence the decision). Based on interviews with the decision maker and other study of the problem situation, the analyst structures a model to represent the relationship between the dependent and independent variables. This model will contain several constants, or coefficients, which express the weights the decision maker attaches to the various pieces of information. These coefficients must be estimated in some manner, such as multiple regression analysis using historical data on past decisions and associated information. The numerical values for the coefficients can then be tested for statistical significance and independent variables that have little effect on the decision can be dropped. The revised model can then be used in the future, in effect, to predict the decision the decision maker would have made, given the same values of the independent variables (information).

For example, we might assume in an aggregate planning situation that the work force decision is influenced by the forecast of requirements, the current work force level, the current inventory, and the current production rate. This might lead to the linear model

$$\hat{W}_1 = \rho_0 + \rho_1 W_0 + \rho_2 I_0 + \rho_3 X_0 + \sum_{t=1}^{T} \lambda_t D_t \qquad (4\text{-}50)$$

Similar considerations might result in this model for production levels:

$$\hat{X}_1 = \beta_0 + \beta_1 W_0 + \beta_2 W_1 + \beta_3 X_0 + \beta_4 I_0 + \sum_{t=1}^{T} \alpha_t D_t \qquad (4\text{-}51)$$

The coefficients in each model would be estimated by least-squares methods. No costs would be involved.

For obvious reasons, the above approach has been called the *management coefficients* model. It is based on the idea that a manager makes good decisions on the average, but he suffers from inconsistency (or variability), in that the weights he attaches to the various information variables change from period to period depending on the most recent pressures. By using statistical methods, one can estimate the true weights. These then can be used in the model to help the decision maker, or we suppose, in some cases to replace him.

In tests by Bowman on aggregate planning problems, the management coefficients approach has not performed as well as other methods. However, it may have utility in other production management problems, particularly scheduling, where it is difficult to solve certain problems mathematically.

4-5 Adaptive Models For Production Control

4-5.1 Production Control Rules

Suppose that one of the previously described planning methods is used to establish a production plan over some interval of time, say six months or a year. This plan gives a production rate, X^*, and an ending inventory goal, I^*, for each period in the interval. Assume that the plan is considered a "preliminary" one, which at time zero establishes targets for production and inventory levels. However, as time passes, we may wish to adjust production rates from their originally planned levels, because actual demand differs from that forecasted at time zero. Some formal rules are needed to prescribe the changes to be made.

Let

X_t^* = the production rate originally established for period t under a preliminary plan made at time zero

X_t = the production rate finally decided on for period t

I_t^* = the planned inventory level at the end of period t

I_t = the actual inventory level at the end of period t

T = the number of periods in the planning horizon

τ = the production lead time

The production lead time is the number of periods between a decision to change the production rate and the time the change becomes effective. Thus, at the end of period t, we must specify $X_{t+\tau+1}$, the production rate in period $t + \tau + 1$ (which is assumed to be available for use in period $t + \tau + 1$). We already have decided on ("frozen") production becoming available in periods $t + 1$, $t + 2, \ldots, t + \tau$ at values of $X_{t+1}, X_{t+2}, \ldots, X_{t+\tau}$, which might differ from the originally planned quantities $X_{t+1}^*, X_{t+2}^*, \ldots, X_{t+\tau}^*$.

Define the correction or adjustment of production in period t as

$$\Delta_t = X_t - X_t^* \tag{4-52}$$

If D_t^* is the expected demand in period t and D_t is the actual demand,

$$I_t = I_{t-1} + X_t - D_t$$
$$I_t^* = I_{t-1}^* + X_t^* - D_t^*$$

A logical and simple production control rule is to schedule production rate $X_{t+\tau+1}$ equal to the originally planned rate, $X_{t+\tau+1}^*$, plus a correction equal to a fraction α of the inventory discrepancy projected at the end of period $t + \tau$. That is,

$$X_{t+\tau+1} = X_{t+\tau+1}^* + \alpha\left[I_t^* - I_t - \sum_{j=1}^{\tau}(X_{t+j} - X_{t+j}^*)\right]$$

$$= X_{t+\tau+1}^* + \alpha\left[I_t^* - I_t - \sum_{j=1}^{\tau}\Delta_{t+j}\right], \qquad 0 \le \alpha \le 1 \qquad (4\text{-}53)$$

In (4-53), $I_t^* - I_t$ is the current inventory discrepancy (shortage) and $-\sum_{j=1}^{\tau}\Delta_{t+j}$ is the additional discrepancy (shortage) that is projected to accrue over the lead time, because of production already scheduled differing from that planned originally.

☐**EXAMPLE 4-8** In Example 4-2, we used linear programming to develop a procurement program for a planning horizon of 13 four-week periods. The original forecasts and the resulting program for the first six periods are shown in the left-hand side of Table 4-15. Suppose the linear programming model is not to be run again and any modifications to the program will be computed using the rule (4-53) with $\alpha = 0.4$. Assume that the actual demands in the first

TABLE 4-15 Planned and Actual Production Programs for Example 4-8. (Status at End of Period 3)

	PLANNED			ACTUAL			
PERIOD (t)	FORE-CAST (D_t^*)	PRODUC-TION (X_t^*)	INVEN-TORY (I_t^*)	DEMAND (D_t)	PRODUC-TION (X_t)	ADJUST-MENT (Δ_t)	INVEN-TORY (I_t)
1	100	140	40	110	140	—	30
2	180	180	40	150	180	—	60
3	220	180	0	190	180	—	50
4	150	180	30		184	+4	
5	100	180	110		170	−10	
6	200	216	126		198	−18	

three periods are 110, 150, and 190. Also assume the production lead time is two periods ($\tau = 2$). Because of the lead time and because our original planning took place at time zero, actual production becoming available in the first three periods will equal the originally planned levels: $X_1 = 140, X_2 = 180, X_3 = 180$. At the end of period 1, the actual inventory will be

$$I_1 = X_1 - D_1 = 140 - 110 = 30$$

Now we compute the production level for period 4 using (4-53):

$$X_4 = X_4^* + \alpha\left[I_1^* - I_1 - \sum_{j=1}^{2}(X_{1+j} - X_{1+j}^*)\right]$$

$$= 180 + (0.4)[40 - 30 - (180 - 180) - (180 - 180)]$$

$$= 184$$

At the end of period 2, our actual inventory is $I_2 = 60$, and we calculate

$$X_5 = 180 + (0.4)[40 - 60 - (180 - 180) - (184 - 180)]$$

$$= 170.4 \cong 170$$

At the end of period 3, we find $I_3 = 50$ and compute

$$X_6 = 216 + (0.4)[0 - 50 - (184 - 180) - (170 - 180)]$$

$$= 198.4 \cong 198$$

This process is carried out each period as we progress through the planning horizon.□

To avoid continually making minor changes in the production plan, an alternative to (4-53) could be used:

$$X_{t+\tau+1} = \begin{cases} X_{t+\tau+1}^*, & \text{if } |\Delta_{t+\tau+1}| \le L \\ X_{t+\tau+1}^* + \Delta_{t+\tau+1}, & \text{if } |\Delta_{t+\tau+1}| > L \end{cases} \tag{4-54}$$

where L is some selected minimum change level and

$$\Delta_{t+\tau+1} = \alpha\left[I_t^* - I_t - \sum_{j=1}^{\tau} \Delta_{t+j}\right] \tag{4-55}$$

When a production control rule such as (4-53) or (4-54) is used to adjust a preliminary plan, it is desirable to have some idea of how the resulting fluctuations in inventory levels and production rates are related to the parameters of the rule, such as α and L. In the next section, the rule (4-53) is analyzed for the case of stochastic demand having a stationary probability distribution.

4-5.2 Effect on Production and Inventories

The control rule (4-53) gives the adjustment $\Delta_{t+\tau+1}$ shown in (4-55). For this rule, the difference between actual and planned inventory levels at the end of period $t + \tau$ can be represented as a linear combination of forecast errors for the periods $1, 2, \ldots, t + \tau$. The following derivation leads to Equation 4-60:

$$I_{t+\tau} - I^*_{t+\tau} = \left[I_t + \sum_{j=1}^{\tau} (X_{t+j} - D_{t+j}) \right] - \left[I^*_t + \sum_{j=1}^{\tau} (X^*_{t+j} - D^*_{t+j}) \right]$$

$$= I_t - I^*_t + \sum_{j=1}^{\tau} (X_{t+j} - X^*_{t+j}) - \sum_{j=1}^{\tau} (D_{t+j} - D^*_{t+j})$$

$$= I_t - I^*_t + \sum_{j=1}^{\tau} \Delta_{t+j} - \sum_{j=1}^{\tau} e_{t+j}$$

$$= E_{t+\tau} - \sum_{j=1}^{\tau} e_{t+j} \tag{4-56}$$

where $e_t \equiv D_t - D^*_t$ is the forecast error for period t and $E_{t+\tau}$ is the excess inventory at time $t + \tau$ *projected* at time t. Note that

$$E_{t+\tau} = I_t - I^*_t + \sum_{j=1}^{\tau} \Delta_{t+j} \tag{4-57}$$

and, from (4-55),

$$\Delta_{t+\tau+1} = -\alpha E_{t+\tau} \tag{4-58}$$

Next, one can show the recursive relation:

$$E_{t+\tau} = (1 - \alpha)E_{t+\tau-1} - e_t$$

Substituting successively for $E_{t+\tau-1}$, $E_{t+\tau-2}$, and so on, we obtain

$$E_{t+\tau} = (1 - \alpha)^{t+\tau}E_0 + \sum_{n=0}^{t+\tau} (1 - \alpha)^n e_{t-n}$$

We define $e_t = 0$, for $t \leq 0$, and note that the quantity E_0 might be interpreted as the excess inventory at $t = 0$; however, since the preliminary plan establishes inventory goals for periods $1, 2, \ldots, T$, based on a *given* initial inventory level, there is no initial inventory discrepancy and E_0 is zero. Thus,

$$E_{t+\tau} = \sum_{n=0}^{t-1} (1 - \alpha)^n e_{t-n} \tag{4-59}$$

Substituting in (4-56), we have

$$I_{t+\tau} - I^*_{t+\tau} = \sum_{n=0}^{t-1} (1 - \alpha)^n e_{t-n} - \sum_{n=1}^{\tau} e_{t+n} \tag{4-60}$$

Suppose that the demand process and the forecasting procedure result in forecast errors that are independent, identically distributed random variables with mean zero and variance σ_e^2. Then the inventory discrepancy, $\delta_{t+\tau} \equiv I_{t+\tau} - I_{t+\tau}^*$, will be a random variable having mean zero and variance

$$\sigma_\delta^2(t) = \sum_{n=0}^{t-1} (1 - \alpha)^{2n} \sigma_e^2 + \tau \sigma_e^2$$

$$= \left[\frac{1 - (1 - \alpha)^{2t}}{1 - (1 - \alpha)^2} + \tau \right] \sigma_e^2 \qquad (4\text{-}61)$$

If t is large, the standard deviation of the inventory discrepancy is approximately

$$\sigma_\delta \cong \left[\frac{1 + \tau(2\alpha - \alpha^2)}{2\alpha - \alpha^2} \right]^{1/2} \sigma_e \qquad (4\text{-}62)$$

Knowledge of σ_δ is useful in establishing safety-stock levels and in assessing the effect of a choice of α on variations in required working capital and warehouse space.

The deviation of planned production from actual production is given by

$$\Delta_{t+\tau+1} = -\alpha E_{t+\tau}$$

$$= -\alpha \sum_{n=0}^{t-1} (1 - \alpha)^n e_{t-n} \qquad (4\text{-}63)$$

The random variable $\Delta_{t+\tau+1}$ has mean zero and variance

$$\sigma_\Delta^2(t) = \alpha^2 \left[\frac{1 - (1 - \alpha)^{2t}}{1 - (1 - \alpha)^2} \right] \sigma_e^2 \qquad (4\text{-}64)$$

If t is large, the standard deviation of the difference between planned and actual production reduces to

$$\sigma_\Delta \cong \left[\frac{\alpha}{2 - \alpha} \right]^{1/2} \sigma_e \qquad (4\text{-}65)$$

The change in production rate from period to period is

$$X_t - X_{t-1} = (X_t^* - X_{t-1}^*) + (\Delta_t - \Delta_{t-1})$$

which can be thought of as the planned change (deterministic), plus an adjustment (stochastic) to the planned change. The quantity $\Delta_t - \Delta_{t-1}$ has mean zero and approximate standard deviation $\sigma_\Delta \sqrt{2}$. It follows that the change in production rate, $X_t - X_{t-1}$, has mean $X_t^* - X_{t-1}^*$ and standard deviation $\sigma_\Delta \sqrt{2}$, so that

$$\sigma_{X_t - X_{t-1}} \cong \left[\frac{2\alpha}{2 - \alpha} \right]^{1/2} \sigma_e \qquad (4\text{-}66)$$

The expected value of the *absolute value of the adjustment to the planned change* is about 0.8 times the standard deviation of $\Delta_t - \Delta_{t-1}$.

Since there are diseconomies associated with changing production rates from their preliminary levels as well as costs of changing production levels from period to period, it is important that one be able to evaluate the impact of a given α on production fluctuations.

To operate this type of production control rule, one must choose a value for α. As α *increases*, the standard deviation of inventory fluctuations about planned levels *decreases*, while the standard deviation of production fluctuations about planned levels *increases*. Large values for α make the system more responsive to forecast error, resulting in more substantial changes in production rates, but with lower inventory requirements. Small values for α have the opposite effect. Thus, we select a value of α by considering the tradeoff between inventory-related costs and production change costs. This might be done by simulation using historical or hypothetical demand and cost data.

This type of control rule is used to make adjustments to a plan established at time zero by some method, such as linear programming. The initial analysis was based on a forecast over the planning horizon, which is not modified as the actual demands during the interval are realized. The initial analysis procedure is not repeated; only the production control rule is applied periodically to correct for deviations from the plan. This is a *fixed-horizon* policy, as opposed to a *moving-horizon* policy, where instead of using a simple adaptive control rule each period, the entire original analysis would be repeated, using the same horizon length, but with the current starting inventory and new forecasts.

In closing this section, it should be mentioned that this presentation is similar to those found in Magee and Boodman (32) and Hanssmann (18). Also, the reader is cautioned that certain of the above results were based on the assumption of independence of forecast errors. In general, this is not true; forecast errors usually are correlated. So the expressions for the variances and standard deviations are only approximate.

□**EXAMPLE 4-9** For the situation of Example 4-8, assume that the forecasting procedure generates forecasts that are unbiased (zero expected error) and have an error standard deviation $\sigma_e = 20$. Then actual inventory levels will be distributed with mean equal to the planned inventory levels and standard deviation $\sigma_\delta = (1.89)\sigma_e = 37.8$, using (4-62) with $\tau = 2$ and $\alpha = 0.4$. To protect against running out of stock, we may want to adjust all planned inventory levels to be at least k standard deviations, where k is a constant whose choice depends on our desired risk of a stockout. For $k = 2$, we require all $I_t^* \geq 2\sigma_\delta = (2)(37.8) = 75.6$; while for $k = 1.5$, our minimum planned inventory is $(1.5)(37.8) = 56.7$, which means a lower inventory cost than when $k = 2$, but a higher risk of shortages. Also, in this situation, we can state that the standard deviation of period-to-period production rate changes will be approximately $\sigma_{X_t - X_{t-1}} = (0.71)\sigma_e = 14.2$, from (4-66).$\square$

4-6 Multiproduct Models

To this point we have considered single-item models, including those where the "product" is in fact the aggregate of a large number of individual items. In this section, we extend the analysis to situations where we have to develop separate production schedules for a number of products. Because these products use common facilities, labor, and materials, they must be considered jointly instead of planned independently by methods given in prior sections. Initially linear programming models will be discussed, followed by some examples of modeling and analysis when the cost structure is nonlinear.

4-6.1 Multiproduct Linear Programming Models

It is easy to extend the single product LP models given in Section 4-2 to include the multiproduct case. Essentially, we incorporate the characteristics of the product mix and process selection problems, described in Chapter 3 for a single time period, with the features of the dynamic planning problems described in prior sections of this chapter. Basic model components are the following: (1) inventory balance equations for each product to link successive time periods; and (2) capacity constraints for each period to represent resource limitations. We now give several examples that illustrate approaches to modeling some of the more important characteristics of multiproduct problems.

$\square$**EXAMPLE 4-10** *A Multiproduct, Multiperiod, Resource-Constrained Problem.* We suppose that a company produces n products and that the requirements by period over a T-period planning horizon are given for each product. Let D_{it} be the known demand for product i in period t. Our decision problem is to choose a production program $\{X_{it}\}$, where X_{it} is the production of product i scheduled for period t. This program will determine the net inventory, I_{it}, for each product i at the end of every period.

Assume there are K resources utilized in production and that b_{kt} is the amount of resource type k, $k = 1, 2, \ldots, K$, available for use in period t, $t = 1$, $2, \ldots, T$. In this model, we shall assume that any unused resource in period t cannot be carried forward to augment the available amount in period $t + 1$. Certainly this would be the case for resources such as labor man-hours, machine-hours, warehouse capacity, and working capital; however, if the resource is a raw material in limited supply or a given quantity of capital available for fixed investment, carry over to successive periods would be possible. (See Exercise 4-58 for consideration of the latter case.) Let a_{ik} be the quantity of resource k required to produce one unit of product i.

The production, inventory, and backlog costs are assumed to be proportional, leading to the following objective function:

$$Z = \sum_{i=1}^{n} \sum_{t=1}^{T} [c_{it} X_{it} + h_{it} I_{it}^{+} + \pi_{it} I_{it}^{-}] \qquad (4\text{-}67a)$$

This function is to be minimized by choice of the optimal $\{X_{it}\}$ conforming to the following constraints, for $i = 1, 2, \ldots, n$; $k = 1, 2, \ldots, K$; and $t = 1, 2, \ldots, T$:

$$\sum_{i=1}^{n} a_{ik} X_{it} \leq b_{kt} \qquad (4\text{-}67b)$$

$$I_{it} = I_{i,t-1} + X_{it} - D_{it} \qquad (4\text{-}67c)$$

$$I_{it} = I_{it}^{+} - I_{it}^{-} \qquad (4\text{-}67d)$$

$$X_{ij} \geq 0, \qquad I_{it}^{+} \geq 0, \qquad I_{it}^{-} \geq 0 \qquad (4\text{-}67e)$$

Note that constraints (4-67b) express the interdependence of the products, while (4-67c), (4-67d), and (4-67e) are for an individual product i. To make the problem somewhat more general, we add the following two bound constraints to this latter class:

$$L_{it}' \leq I_{it} \leq L_{it} \qquad (4\text{-}67f)$$

$$P_{it}' \leq X_{it} \leq P_{it} \qquad (4\text{-}67g)$$

where P_{it}' and P_{it} are nonnegative and typically $L_{it} \geq 0, L_{it}' \leq 0.\square$

□EXAMPLE 4-11 *Process Selection Decisions.*   Suppose that each product can be produced by several alternative processes (routings) in each period. Example 4-10 can be extended to consider this new feature by letting X_{ijt} be the number of units of product i produced by process j, ($j = 1, 2, \ldots, J_i$), in period t, and defining a_{ijk} to be the number of units of resource k required to produce one unit of product i by process j. If routing j does not utilize resource k, $a_{ijk} = 0$. The problem is to minimize

$$Z = \sum_{t=1}^{T} \sum_{i=1}^{n} \left[\sum_{j=1}^{J_i} c_{ijt} X_{ijt} + h_{it} I_{it}^{+} + \pi_{it} I_{it}^{-} \right]. \qquad (4\text{-}68a)$$

subject to

$$\sum_{i=1}^{n} \sum_{j=1}^{J_i} a_{ijk} X_{ijt} \leq b_{kt} \qquad (4\text{-}68b)$$

$$I_{it} = I_{i,t-1} + \sum_{j=1}^{J_i} X_{ijt} - D_{it} \qquad (4\text{-}68c)$$

$$I_{it} = I_{it}^+ - I_{it}^- \tag{4-68d}$$

$$L_{it}' \le I_{it} \le L_{it} \tag{4-68e}$$

$$P_{ijt}' \le X_{ijt} \le P_{ijt} \tag{4-68f}$$

$$I_{it}^+ \ge 0, \qquad I_{it}^- \ge 0 \tag{4-68g}$$

for all $i, j, k,$ and t.

Note that in problems such as those of Examples 4-10 and 4-11, we may want to constrain the solution to use a given *minimum* amount, b_{kt}', of resource k in period t. This would be the case, for example, if we felt it necessary to insure that a given department was scheduled for at least 80 percent of capacity each period, or that a particular subcontractor was assigned at least a given amount of work in a period. Equation 4-68b would be modified to[4]

$$b_{kt}' \le \sum_{i=1}^{n} \sum_{j=1}^{J_i} a_{ijk} X_{ijt} \le b_{kt} \tag{4-69}$$

□

□**EXAMPLE 4-12** *Product Mix Decisions.* In this example, we consider the problem of how best to use our resources when there are opportunities to sell up to given amounts of n products in each period of the planning horizon. The single-period version of this problem was described in Section 3-2. The only tricky point in going to the multiperiod case is the fact that production of an item may take place in a period different from its sale. In order to formulate constraints on both resource consumption and sales levels (from forecasts), it is necessary to identify both the period of production and the period of sale in defining decision variables. There are two principal approaches. One involves defining the decision variables to be X_{ijtv}, the amount of product i produced by process j in period t and sold in period v. The formulation of a model with this approach is left to Exercise 4-59. The second method requires definition of separate variables for the quantity produced in a period and the quantity sold in the period. To illustrate, let

X_{ijt} = the number of units of product i produced by process j in period t

S_{it} = the number of units of product i planned to be sold in period t

r_{it} = revenue, net of variable selling expense, from selling one unit of product i in period t

c_{ijt} = unit variable cost of producing a unit of product i by process j in period t

F_{it} = maximum projected sales potential for product i in period t

F_{it}' = minimum (required) level of planned sales for product i in period t

---

[4] This type of constraint is called a *range* constraint and is in effect a bound constraint on the slack variable for (4-68b).

As explained in Chapter 3, the quantities F'_{it} and F_{it} represent a range within which planned sales must fall. F_{it} is an upper limit specified by the forecasting system and management; F'_{it} is a lower limit determined by orders already booked for delivery in period t and management policy regarding minimum availability of the product.

The following is a typical model of the dynamic product mix problem: Find $\{X_{ijt}\}$ and $\{S_{it}\}$ to *maximize*

$$Z = \sum_{t=1}^{T} \sum_{i=1}^{n} \left[r_{it} S_{it} - \sum_{j=1}^{J_i} c_{ijt} X_{ijt} - h_{it} I_{it}^+ - \pi_{it} I_{it}^- \right] \tag{4-70a}$$

subject to

$$b'_{kt} \le \sum_{i=1}^{n} \sum_{j=1}^{J_i} a_{ijk} X_{ijt} \le b_{kt} \tag{4-70b}$$

$$I_{it} = I_{i,t-1} + \sum_{j=1}^{J_i} X_{ijt} - S_{it} \tag{4-70c}$$

$$I_{it} = I_{it}^+ - I_{it}^- \tag{4-70d}$$

$$L'_{it} \le I_{it} \le L_{it} \tag{4-70e}$$

$$F'_{it} \le S_{it} \le F_{it} \tag{4-70f}$$

$$X_{ijt} \ge 0, \qquad I_{it}^+ \ge 0, \qquad I_{it}^- \ge 0 \tag{4-70g}$$

In a product mix model, backorders usually are not considered; however, for completeness they are allowed in the formulation above. The interpretation is that sales are made for a given period at a price for that period and backorders constitute a late delivery. By setting $L'_{it} \ge 0$ and $I_{it}^- = 0$, the model can be modified to represent the no-backlog case.□

□**EXAMPLE 4-13** *Production Smoothing Problem.* In the prior three examples, we have considered only production costs, sales revenue, and inventory-related costs. Now we suppose that it is felt necessary to include a penalty cost for changing the production rate of a product from one period to the next. A single product model of this type was given in Section 4-2.2. Here we modify Example 4-11 by adding production rate change costs to illustrate the multiproduct case. This model also considers multiple routings for each product.

Suppose the cost of changing the production rate of product i by process j from $X_{ij,t-1}$ in period $t-1$ to X_{ijt} in period t is proportional to the absolute value of the change; that is, the cost in period t is given by

$$\lambda_{ijt} |X_{ijt} - X_{ij,t-1}|$$

where λ_{ijt} is a nonnegative constant. Let

$$\Delta_{ijt}^+ \equiv (X_{ijt} - X_{ij,t-1})^+$$

and

$$\Delta_{ijt}^- \equiv (X_{ijt} - X_{ij,t-1})^-$$

then

$$\Delta_{ijt}^+ + \Delta_{ijt}^- = |X_{ijt} - X_{ij,t-1}|$$

The problem is to choose the $\{X_{ijt}\}$ to minimize

$$Z = \sum_{t=1}^{T} \sum_{i=1}^{n} \left[\sum_{j=1}^{J_i} c_{ijt} X_{ijt} + h_{it} I_{it}^+ + \pi_{it} I_{it}^- + \sum_{j=1}^{J_i} \lambda_{ijt}(\Delta_{ijt}^+ + \Delta_{ijt}^-) \right] \quad (4\text{-}71\text{a})$$

subject to

$$b_{kt}' \leq \sum_{i=1}^{n} \sum_{j=1}^{J_i} a_{ijk} X_{ijt} \leq b_{kt} \quad (4\text{-}71\text{b})$$

$$I_{it} = I_{i,t-1} + \sum_{j=1}^{J_i} X_{ijt} - D_{it} \quad (4\text{-}71\text{c})$$

$$I_{it} = I_{it}^+ - I_{it}^- \quad (4\text{-}71\text{d})$$

$$L_{it}' \leq I_{it} \leq L_{it} \quad (4\text{-}71\text{e})$$

$$P_{ijt}' \leq X_{ijt} \leq P_{ijt} \quad (4\text{-}71\text{f})$$

$$X_{ijt} = X_{ij,t-1} + \Delta_{ijt}^+ - \Delta_{ijt}^- \quad (4\text{-}71\text{g})$$

$$I_{it}^+ \geq 0, \quad I_{it}^- \geq 0, \quad \Delta_{ijt}^+ \geq 0, \quad \Delta_{ijt}^- \geq 0 \quad (4\text{-}71\text{h})$$

for all i, j, k, and t. Note that the initial states $\{I_{i0}\}$ and $\{X_{ij0}\}$ must be supplied.

Comparing (4-71) with (4-68), we observe that to include production change costs we had to add $2n\bar{J}T$ variables and $n\bar{J}T$ constraints (4-71g), where $\bar{J}$ is the average number of routings for a product; that is,

$$\bar{J} = \frac{\left(\sum_{i=1}^{n} J_i \right)}{n} \quad (4\text{-}72)$$

$\square$

$\square$**EXAMPLE 4-14** *Production and Work Force Planning.* This final linear programming model will add work force level decisions to the situation of Example 4-10. It is an extension of the model of Section 4-2.3 to the multi-product case. For convenience, we repeat the notation. Let

W_t = work force level in period t, measured in regular time man-hours

w_t^+ = increase in work force level from period $t - 1$ to t

w_t^- = decrease in work force level from period $t - 1$ to t

O_t = overtime scheduled in period t, measured in man-hours

U_t = undertime scheduled in period t, measured in man-hours

X_{it} = production of product i in period t

m_i = number of man-hours required to produce a unit of product i

c_{it} = unit variable cost, exclusive of labor, of product i produced in period t

l_t = cost of a man-hour of labor on regular time in period t

l'_t = cost of a man-hour of labor on overtime in period t

e_t = cost to increase the work force level by one man-hour in period t

e'_t = cost to decrease the work force level by one man-hour in period t

θ = ratio of overtime capacity in man-hours to regular time work force level

We want to minimize

$$Z = \sum_{t=1}^{T} \left[l_t W_t + l'_t O_t + e_t w_t^+ + e'_t w_t^- + \sum_{i=1}^{n} (c_{it} X_{it} + h_{it} I_{it}^+ + \pi_{it} I_{it}^-) \right] \quad (4\text{-}73a)$$

subject to constraints

$$b'_{kt} \leq \sum_{i=1}^{n} a_{ik} X_{it} \leq b_{kt} \quad (4\text{-}73b)$$

$$I_{it} = I_{i,t-1} + X_{it} - D_{it} \quad (4\text{-}73c)$$

$$I_{it} = I_{it}^+ - I_{it}^- \quad (4\text{-}73d)$$

$$L'_{it} \leq I_{it} \leq L_{it} \quad (4\text{-}73e)$$

$$P'_{it} \leq X_{it} \leq P_{it} \quad (4\text{-}73f)$$

$$W_t = W_{t-1} + w_t^+ - w_t^- \quad (4\text{-}73g)$$

$$O_t - U_t = \sum_{i=1}^{n} m_i X_{it} - W_t \quad (4\text{-}73h)$$

$$O_t - U_t \leq \theta W_t \quad (4\text{-}73i)$$

$$W_t, w_t^+, w_t^-, O_t, U_t, X_{it}, I_{it}^+, I_{it}^- \geq 0 \quad (4\text{-}73j)$$

for all i, k, and t. $\square$

4-6.2 Multiproduct Models with Nonlinear Costs

When costs or resource utilizations are nonlinear functions of the production variables, solution of the problem becomes more difficult. In earlier sections of this chapter, we have given several algorithms for solution of the single-item problem, when costs are convex, concave, or piecewise concave. However, in the multiple-item case, capacity constraints resulting from resource limitations are not easily incorporated into such algorithms. Also, use of dynamic programming methods or nonlinear programming procedures is often realistic only for small problems, and multiproduct problems usually have many variables and constraints.

One approach is to ignore the resource constraints and independently determine an optimal production schedule for each product. The combination of the solutions obtained can then be checked to see if any resource constraint is violated. If not, the schedules are optimal for the capacity-constrained problem; otherwise, some other method must be employed to find the optimal solution.

If the costs are convex, it may be possible to use piecewise linear approximations to formulate and solve the problem as a linear programming model. If all cost are linear (proportional), except for the production cost function, which is of the simple form,

$$A_{it} \, \delta(X_{it}) + c_{it} X_{it}$$

where $\delta(X_{it})$ is 0 if $X_{it} = 0$, and 1 if $X_{it} > 0$, one of the approximate algorithms for solving the fixed charge problem may yield good results for small problems. Such an approach is described by Denzler (7). For more general cost functions, the following approach, attributed to Manne (33), may be applicable.

Assume there are n different products and let $\mathbf{D}_i = (D_{i1}, D_{i2}, \ldots, D_{iT})$ be the demand vector for product i. Denote the production schedule for product i by $\mathbf{X}_i = (X_{i1}, X_{i2}, \ldots, X_{iT})$ and the availability vector for resource type k by $\mathbf{B}_k = (b_{k1}, b_{k2}, \ldots, b_{kT})$. Let $r_{ikt}(X_i)$ be the quantity of resource k required in period t by the schedule $\mathbf{X}_i$ and define $\mathbf{R}_{ik} = [r_{ik1}(\mathbf{X}_i), r_{ik2}(\mathbf{X}_i), \ldots, r_{ikT}(\mathbf{X}_i)]$ to be the resource utilization vector for product i and resource k. Finally, let $\gamma_{it}(\mathbf{X}_i)$ be the total cost in period t resulting from the production program $\mathbf{X}_i$, and let $\Gamma_i(\mathbf{X}_i) = [\gamma_{i1}(\mathbf{X}_i), \gamma_{i2}(\mathbf{X}_i), \ldots, \gamma_{iT}(\mathbf{X}_i)]$ be the cost vector for product i. The decision problem is to find $\mathbf{X}_1, \mathbf{X}_2, \ldots, \mathbf{X}_n$ to minimize

$$\sum_{i=1}^{n} \sum_{t=1}^{T} \gamma_{it}(\mathbf{X}_i) \tag{4-74a}$$

subject to

$$\sum_{i=1}^{n} \mathbf{R}_{ik}(\mathbf{X}_i) \le \mathbf{B}_k, \qquad (k = 1, 2, \ldots, K) \tag{4-74b}$$

$$\mathbf{X}_i \in \mathbf{S}_i, \qquad (i = 1, 2, \ldots, n) \tag{4-74c}$$

The kT constraints (4-74b) are the resource availability constraints and express the interdependence between the production schedules of the different products. Additionally, there may be other constraints that apply only to a particular product. For example, $0 \le X_{it} \le P_{it}$, or $L'_{it} \le I_{it} \le L_{it}$. These constraints limit the feasible production programs for product i to a set $\mathbf{S}_i$. Following Lasdon and Terjung (28), we denote such constraints by (4-74c).

Suppose, through analysis of the structure of the model, we can classify the optimal solution $\mathbf{X}_i^*$ as one of a set $\mathbf{V}_i$. Let $\mathbf{V}_i = \{\mathbf{X}_{ij}\}$, where $\mathbf{X}_{ij}$ belongs to $\mathbf{S}_i$ and is a possibility for the optimal program. We assume the membership of $\mathbf{V}_i$ is finite and use j as a subscript to identify a particular member, $j = 1$, $2, \ldots, J_i$. Some examples will be provided presently to illustrate situations where a useful set $\mathbf{V}_i$ can be identified. At this point, we can remember the single-product, concave-cost case with no backlogging (Section 4-3.4), where a set $\mathbf{V}$ was found to consist of all schedules for which $I_{t-1}X_t = 0$. The set $\mathbf{V}_i$ is referred to as the set of *dominant* schedules for product i (33).

Next we formulate a 0–1 integer programming model to select the optimal programs from the dominant sets. Let

$$\theta_{ij} = \begin{cases} 1, & \text{if we choose } \mathbf{X}_i = \mathbf{X}_{ij} \\ 0, & \text{otherwise} \end{cases} \tag{4-76}$$

and to emphasize that the solution is now independent of the forms of $\mathbf{\Gamma}$ and $\mathbf{R}$, define

$$\mathbf{\Gamma}_{ij} \equiv \mathbf{\Gamma}_i(\mathbf{X}_{ij})$$

and

$$\mathbf{R}_{ijk} \equiv \mathbf{R}_{ik}(\mathbf{X}_{ij})$$

Then our problem is to choose $\{\theta_{ij}\}$ to minimize

$$\sum_{i=1}^{n} \sum_{j=1}^{J_i} \left(\sum_{t=1}^{T} \gamma_{ijt} \right) \theta_{ij} \tag{4-77a}$$

subject to

$$\sum_{j=1}^{J_i} \theta_{ij} = 1, \qquad (i = 1, 2, \ldots, n) \tag{4-77b}$$

$$\sum_{i=1}^{n} \sum_{j=1}^{J_i} \mathbf{R}_{ijk} \theta_{ij} \leq \mathbf{B}_k, \qquad (k = 1, 2, \ldots, K) \tag{4-77c}$$

$$\theta_{ij} = 0 \text{ or } 1 \tag{4-77d}$$

We observe that θ_{ij} is, in effect, an indicator variable to tell us which production program from the set $\mathbf{V}_i$ is to be used. Since there typically will be a very large number of these variables, 0–1 integer programming algorithms often are not suitable. In such a situation, Manne suggests replacing the constraint (4-77d) by

$$\theta_{ij} \geq 0 \tag{4-78}$$

and solving the model as a linear programming problem. If this is done, we may obtain fractional values for some of the $\{\theta_{ij}\}$. This has no meaning in the context of the model (4-77), since a program

$$\mathbf{X}_i' = \sum_{j=1}^{J_i} \theta_{ij} \mathbf{X}_{ij}$$

may not be in the set $\mathbf{V}_i$. However, if most values of the $\{\theta_{ij}\}$ are 0 or 1, we often can consider such a solution as an acceptable approximation to an optimal one. It can be shown that at most, KT products can have fractional θ_{ij}, so if n is large compared to KT, the number of fractional variables will be a small percentage of the total.[5]

$\square$ **EXAMPLE 4-15** *Loading Machines.* Lasdon and Terjung (28) report an application of a model of this type in planning production for four plants of a major corporation. There are n different products to be scheduled over a T-period horizon. Requirements by item and period are assumed given, and the relevant costs are inventory-related costs for holding stock or incurring shortages and production costs. Because the unit variable production costs seemed to be independent of the schedule, only machine changeover (setup) costs were included in the model. The products are produced on identical machines, but each product requires its own unique machine attachment, which the authors called "dies." Apparently the machines are presses or molding machines, which must be set up for a new product by replacing the die, or mold. It was assumed that any machine can produce any item and that setup cost is independent of the products involved in the changeover.

The following notation further defines the problem:

b_t = number of machines available in period t

D_{it} = requirements for item i in period t

ρ_i = production rate for a machine producing item i, in units per time period

N_i = number of molds available for item i

A = cost of a changeover,

m_{it} = number of machines assigned to produce product i in period t

$\mathbf{M}_i = (m_{i1}, m_{i2}, \ldots, m_{iT})$, the program for product i

I_{it} = net inventory of product i at the end of period t

$H_{it}(I_{it})$ = inventory-related costs for product i in period t, as a function of the ending net inventory

Z = total of setup costs and inventory costs over the planning horizon

The problem is to choose $\mathbf{M}_1, \mathbf{M}_2, \ldots, \mathbf{M}_n$ to minimize

$$Z = \sum_{i=1}^{n} \sum_{t=1}^{T} \left[A(m_{it} - m_{i,t-1})^+ + H_{it}(I_{it}) \right] \tag{4-79a}$$

[5] The proof is easy. There are $KT + n$ constraints, so at most $KT + n$ variables can be nonzero in the optimal solution. Let y be the number of products having fractional θ_{ij} values. Then $n - y$ products have exactly one $\theta_{ij} > 0$. This means $n - y + 2y \le KT + n$, or $y \le KT$.

subject to

$$I_{it} = I_{i,t-1} + \rho_i m_{it} - D_{it} \qquad \text{(4-79b)}$$

$$L'_{it} \le I_{it} \le L_{it} \qquad \text{(4-79c)}$$

$$m_{it} \le N_i \qquad \text{(4-79d)}$$

$$m_{it} = 0, 1, 2, \ldots, N_i \qquad \text{(4-79e)}$$

$$\sum_{i=1}^{n} m_{it} \le b_t \qquad \text{(4-79f)}$$

The term $(m_{it} - m_{i,t-1})^+$ is the increase in the number of machines producing product i from period $t-1$ to t. The initial conditions $\{m_{io}\}$, must be given.

The authors next define $\mathbf{V}_i = \{\mathbf{M}_i \mid \mathbf{M}_i$ satisfies constraints (4-79b) through (4-79e)$\}$, and denote the jth member of the set as $\mathbf{M}_{ij}$. Note that $\mathbf{M}_{ij}$ is a feasible production plan for product i. There are a finite number of such programs, since all m_{it} are integer valued and bounded. Note that the objective function (4-79a) can be written as

$$Z = \sum_{i=1}^{n} Z_i(\mathbf{M}_i),$$

where $Z_i(\mathbf{M}_i)$ is defined implicitly. Let $z_{ij} = Z_i(\mathbf{M}_{ij})$ and define

$$\theta_{ij} = \begin{cases} 1, & \text{if } \mathbf{M}_i = \mathbf{M}_{ij} \\ 0, & \text{otherwise} \end{cases}$$

The problem is now stated as one of choosing $\{\theta_{ij}\}$ to minimize

$$Z = \sum_{i=1}^{n} \sum_{j=1}^{J_i} z_{ij}\theta_{ij} \qquad \text{(4-80a)}$$

subject to

$$\sum_{j=1}^{J_i} \theta_{ij} = 1, \qquad (i = 1, 2, \ldots, n) \qquad \text{(4-80b)}$$

$$\sum_{i=1}^{n} \sum_{j=1}^{J_i} m_{ijt}\theta_{ij} \le b_t, \qquad (t = 1, 2, \ldots, T) \qquad \text{(4-80c)}$$

$$\theta_{ij} \ge 0 \qquad \text{(4-80d)}$$

Solving (4-80) as a linear programming model may yield up to T items having fractional values for θ_{ij}. In the application, the number of items was around 400, while the number of time periods was six, each being one week long. With n so much larger than T, no difficulties with fractional θ's would be expected. However, a major problem arises from the large number of variables in the model, resulting from the size of the sets $\mathbf{V}_i$. This leads to a search for an effective computational scheme. In their paper, Lasdon and Terjung report development of a procedure, which, for their problem, significantly reduces computation time over that required by standard decomposition methods [such as that used by Dzielinski and Gomory (9)].

In actual application of the model, some additional constraints were added. The first limits the total number of machine changes in a period to reflect the limited availability of manpower and equipment to make these changes:

$$\sum_{i=1}^{n} |m_{it} - m_{i,t-1}| \le e_t, \qquad (t = 1, 2, \ldots, T) \qquad (4\text{-}81)$$

The second limits the total number of items in production in any period to avoid production problems in prior manufacturing stages, which supply components for the final products:

$$\sum_{i=1}^{n} \delta(m_{it}) \le f_t, \qquad (t = 1, 2, \ldots, T) \qquad (4\text{-}82)$$

where

$$\delta(u) = \begin{cases} 0, & \text{if } u = 0 \\ 1, & \text{if } u > 0 \end{cases} \qquad (4\text{-}83)$$

The final set of constraints controls the number of items produced in period $t - 1$ and not produced in period t. Shutting down production of a product can involve scrapping or reworking component materials in process at prior manufacturing stages. These constraints hold down related costs:

$$\sum_{i=1}^{n} \delta(m_{i,t-1})[1 - \delta(m_{it})] \le g_t, \qquad (t = 1, 2, \ldots, T) \qquad (4\text{-}84)$$

Addition of constraints (4-81), (4-82), and (4-84) impose additional dependencies between the $\mathbf{M}_{ij}$, so they must be added to the model (4-80).□

□EXAMPLE 4-16 *Minimizing Overtime.* The original paper on this approach to multiproduct lot-size programming was by Manne (33). He modeled the problem of planning production of n items over a horizon of T periods for a machine shop, where there was a single limited resource, labor. For each product and each period, the product demand, D_{it}, is given and no shortages are allowed. The only costs included are production labor costs. Inventory holding costs were thought to be negligible and all production costs, other than labor, were assumed to be independent of the production program. If X_{it} is the production of product i in period t, the labor required by product i in period t is assumed to be the following concave function (measured in man-hours):

$$l_{it} = a_i \, \delta(X_{it}) + v_i X_{it} \qquad (4\text{-}85)$$

where $a_i > 0$, $v_i > 0$, and $\delta(X)$ is defined by (4-83).

The regular time capacity in period t is W_t man-hours. This work force will be maintained whether or not it is fully utilized. Overtime is allowed up to

W'_t man-hours in period t. The only labor cost affected by the program is the overtime labor cost, which is assumed to be proportional to the overtime hours. Let O_t be the amount of overtime scheduled in period t. The problem is to minimize

$$Z = \sum_{t=1}^{T} O_t \qquad (4\text{-}86\text{a})$$

subject to

$$\sum_{i=1}^{n} \sum_{t=1}^{T} \left[a_i\, \delta(X_{it}) + v_i X_{it} \right] - O_t \leq W_t \qquad (4\text{-}86\text{b})$$

$$O_t \leq W'_t \qquad (4\text{-}86\text{c})$$

$$\sum_{k=1}^{t} (X_{ik} - D_{ik}) \geq 0 \qquad (4\text{-}86\text{d})$$

$$X_{it} \geq 0, \qquad O_t \geq 0 \qquad (4\text{-}86\text{e})$$

$$\delta(X_{it}) = \begin{cases} 0, & \text{if } X_{it} = 0 \\ 1, & \text{if } X_{it} > 0 \end{cases} \qquad (4\text{-}86\text{f})$$

for all i and t. Note that constraint (4-86d) is the constraint that the ending inventory, I_{it}, for product i at the end of period t be nonnegative.

Manne shows that the only production programs that need be considered for product i are those conforming to constraints (4-86d) and (4-86e) and having the property that $I_{i,t-1} X_{it} = 0$. That is, the program should meet the demand requirements and be such that no inventory is carried into any period where production takes place. More formally, if $\mathbf{X}_i = (X_{i1}, X_{i2}, \ldots, X_{iT})$ is the time-phased production schedule for product i and $\mathbf{V}_i$ is the set of dominant schedules for product i, then

$$\mathbf{V}_i = \{\mathbf{X}_i \mid \mathbf{X}_i \text{ conforms to (4-86d), (4-86e), and}$$

$$I_{i,t-1} X_{it} = 0, t = 1, 2, \ldots, T\} \quad (4\text{-}87)$$

Denote the jth member of $\mathbf{V}_i$ by $\mathbf{X}_{ij}$, $j = 1, 2, \ldots, J_i$, and let X_{ijt} and l_{ijt} be the production quantity and required labor, respectively, in period t for this schedule. Finally, let $\theta_{ij} = 1$, if we choose $\mathbf{X}_i = \mathbf{X}_{ij}$, and 0 otherwise. Manne gives the following linear programming model for determining the optimal $\{\theta_{ij}\}$; minimize

$$Z = \sum_{t=1}^{T} O_t \qquad (4\text{-}88\text{a})$$

subject to, for all i and t,

$$\sum_{j=1}^{J_i} \theta_{ij} = 1 \qquad (4\text{-}88\text{b})$$

$$\sum_{i=1}^{n} \sum_{j=1}^{J_i} l_{ijt} \theta_{ij} - O_t \leq W_t \qquad (4\text{-}88\text{c})$$

$$O_t \leq W'_t \qquad \text{(4-88d)}$$

$$\theta_{ij} \geq 0, \qquad O_t \geq 0 \qquad \text{(4-88e)}$$

The solution to the model will have at most T items with fractional θ. This should be satisfactory if n is much larger than T. An upper bound to the number, J_i, of schedules for product i in the dominant set is 2^{T-1}, since (assuming $D_{i1} > 0$) production must take place in period 1 and may or may not be carried out in each of the other $T - 1$ periods. Of course, schedules can be arbitrarily deleted from $\mathbf{V}_i$ if they are considered undesirable for reasons external to the model. This means (4-88) will be a linear programming model with $2T + n$ rows and at most $n2^{T-1} + T$ variables.

We should emphasize that the characterization of the set of dominant schedules by (4-87) allowed the nonlinear model (4-86) to be stated as an equivalent linear model. It required analysis of the structure of (4-86) to state and prove (4-87), which has come to be known as Manne's "Dominance Theorem."□

□**EXAMPLE 4-17** *Planning Production and Work Force.* Following the work of Manne (33), Dzielinski, Baker, and Manne (8) developed an expanded model, which considers work force level decisions, as well as production lot-size decisions in each period. Because of a structure similar to that of the Manne model, the optimal solution consists of production schedules for each of the n products that have the property $I_{t-1}X_t = 0$ and that satisfy the constraint of no shortages. As in the previous example, the set of dominant schedules for product i will be denoted by $\mathbf{V}_i = \{\mathbf{X}_{ij}\}, j = 1, 2, \ldots, J_i$. The following notation describes the problem:

X_{ijt} = production of product i in period t, if schedule $\mathbf{X}_{ij}$ is used

θ_{ij} = (0, 1), depending on whether or not schedule $\mathbf{X}_{ij}$ is used for product i

W^r_{kt} = number of workers at facility k having work schedule r in period t ($k = 1, 2, \ldots, K; r = 1, 2, \ldots, R$). It is assumed that there are K facilities (departments) to be staffed and that at each facility the work force can be divided into mutually exclusive groups according to the shift and the number of hours per week worked. For example, "first shift, straight time" would be a different work schedule from "first shift, overtime" or "second shift, straight time"

w^+_{kt} = increase in the number of workers at facility k from period $t - 1$ to period t

w^-_{kt} = decrease in the number of workers at facility k from period $t - 1$ to period t

e_{kt}^r = number of hours a worker having work schedule r will work in period t

λ_{kt} = cost of hiring a worker at facility k in period t

λ'_{kt} = cost of laying off a worker at facility k in period t

ϕ_{kt}^r = cost per worker on work schedule r at facility k in period t

$M_{kt}(p)$ = maximum number of workers that can be employed on shift p ($p = 1, 2, 3$), at facility k in period t

a_{ikt} = setup labor, if product i is produced at facility k in period t

v_{ikt} = unit variable labor for product i at facility k in period t

l_{ijkt} = the number of man-hours required at facility k to produce X_{ijt} units of product i in period t

c_{it} = unit material cost for product i in period t

γ_{ij} = total material cost for product i over the planning horizon, when schedule $\mathbf{X}_{ij}$ is used

From the above definitions, we have

$$\gamma_{ij} = \sum_{t=1}^{T} c_{it} X_{ijt} \tag{4-89}$$

and

$$l_{ijkt} = \begin{cases} 0, & \text{if } X_{ijt} = 0 \\ a_{ikt} + v_{ikt} X_{ijt}, & \text{if } X_{ijt} > 0 \end{cases} \tag{4-90}$$

The problem is to choose $\{\theta_{ij}\}$ and $\{W_{kt}^r\}$ to minimize

$$\sum_{i=1}^{n} \sum_{j=1}^{J_i} \gamma_{ij} \theta_{ij} + \sum_{t=1}^{T} \sum_{k=1}^{K} \left[\sum_{r=1}^{R} \phi_{kt}^r W_{kt}^r + \lambda_{kt} w_{kt}^+ + \lambda'_{kt} w_{kt}^- \right] \tag{4-91a}$$

subject to, for all i, k, and t,

$$\sum_{i=1}^{n} \sum_{j=1}^{J_i} l_{ijkt} \theta_{ij} \leq \sum_{r=1}^{R} e_{kt}^r W_{kt}^r \tag{4-91b}$$

$$\sum_{j=1}^{J_i} \theta_{ij} = 1 \tag{4-91c}$$

$$\sum_{r=1}^{R} W_{kt}^r = \sum_{r=1}^{R} W_{k,t-1}^r + w_{kt}^+ - w_{kt}^- \tag{4-91d}$$

$$\sum_{r=1}^{R(1)} W_{kt}^r \leq M_{kt}(1) \tag{4-91e}$$

$$\sum_{r=R(1)+1}^{R(2)} W_{kt}^r \leq M_{kt}(2) \tag{4-91f}$$

$$\sum_{r=R(2)+1}^{R(3)} W_{kt}^r \leq M_{kt}(3) \tag{4-91g}$$

$$\theta_{ij},\, W_{kt}^r,\, w_{kt}^+,\, w_{kt}^- \geq 0 \tag{4-91h}$$

The first constraint insures that the total labor hours required at facility k in period t is no more than the total number of man-hours available, considering all workers at that facility. Equation 4-91d relates the number of workers at facility k in period t to the number in period $t - 1$. Constraints (4-91e), (4-91f), and (4-91g) limit the number of workers that can be assigned to each of the three shifts at facility k in period t. The integers $R(1)$, $R(2)$, and $R(3)$ identify the work schedules, r, corresponding to each shift.

For this model, it can be shown that at most, KT items can have fractional θ_{ij} values. This is the number of constraints in the set (4-91b).

We should note that the objective function contains no inventory carrying cost term. Dzielinski et al., define all cost components as being *discounted* back to the start of the planning horizon at an appropriate interest rate, reflecting the opportunity cost of capital. Since both material and labor costs are included in the model and because the inventory carrying rate is largely the cost of capital, the objective function implicitly charges for carrying inventory.□

The paper by Dzielinski, Baker, and Manne (8) is interesting because they test the lot-size programming (*LP*) model against a typical finished goods inventory control (*EOQ*) system by simulating their performance when used to schedule a hypothetical shop. The *LP* model was solved each period, using a moving *T*-period horizon. Tests were made for $T = 3$ and $T = 6$. Second-order exponential smoothing was used to generate necessary demand forecasts for both systems. The finished goods inventory control system was based on a periodic review (R, r) policy. Items were controlled independently, and when called for by the inventory control rules, orders were issued to the shop to restock the inventories. As the shop load varied over time, the work force levels were adjusted. It was found that the *LP* system performed significantly better than the *EOQ* system in all cost categories. (We recommend this paper as an example of how to test a model to determine its value in comparison with existing decision procedures.)

Dzielinski and Gomory (9) develop decomposition methods, based on the Dantzig-Wolfe principle, for facilitating solution of large problems of this type. Gorenstein (14) describes a modification of this model for planning tire production, and his work is interesting for several reasons. He uses two models. The first is a long-range model that sets production and work force levels for a planning horizon of six eight-week periods. The second is a shorter-range model, covering eight one-week periods, and establishes production plans by week, subject to labor and machine allocations imposed by the long-range plan. Gorenstein also considers production of semifinished tires and components and extends both models to account for precedence relationships in the production of the various products and components. In effect, he treats a system with several manufacturing stages, where it is necessary that production of components at prior stages be coordinated with production at later stages. Multistage systems are the subject of Section 4-7.

□**EXAMPLE 4-18** *Planning Production and Work Force, Profit Maximization and Convex Costs.* Bergstrom and Smith (1) developed and applied the following quadratic programming model, which in effect is an extension of the single (aggregate) product model of Holt et al., described in Section 4-4.3, to the multiproduct case and to a situation where the sales level in each period is a controllable variable. Let

X_{it} = production of product i in period t, $(i = 1, 2, \ldots, n; t = 1, 2, \ldots, T)$
W_t = work force level in period t
S_{it} = number of units of product i to be sold in period t
I_{it} = net inventory of product i at the end of period t

They assume that the revenue from the sale of S_{it} units of product i is a quadratic function:

$$R_{it} = r_{1it} + r_{2it}S_{it} + r_{3it}S_{it}^2 \qquad (4\text{-}92)$$

Inventory-related costs for product i in period t are given by

$$H_{it} = c_{i7}(I_{it} - c_{i8} - c_{i9}S_{it})^2 \qquad (4\text{-}93)$$

where $c_{i8} + c_{i9}S_{it}$ is the ideal net inventory.

The amount of labor needed to support the production program in period t is assumed to be

$$L_t = \sum_{i=1}^{n} k_i X_{it} \qquad (4\text{-}94)$$

where k_i is the standard man-hours per unit of product i. The variable production costs in period t are modeled as

$$(VC)_t = c_3(L_t - c_4 W_t)^2 + c_5 L_t - c_6 W_t + c_{12} L_t W_t \qquad (4\text{-}95)$$

Finally the work force change costs are

$$(WFC)_t = c_2(W_t - W_{t-1} - c_{11})^2 \qquad (4\text{-}96)$$

The problem is to choose the $\{X_{it}\}$, $\{S_{it}\}$, and $\{W_t\}$ to *maximize*

$$Z = \sum_{t=1}^{T} \left[\sum_{i=1}^{n} (R_{it} - H_{it}) - (VC)_t - (WFC)_t \right] \qquad (4\text{-}97a)$$

subject to

$$I_{it} = I_{i,t-1} + X_{it} - S_{it} \tag{4-97b}$$

for all i and t.

This quadratic model was solved by differentiating (4-97a) with respect to X_{it}, I_{it}, and W_t and equating the derivatives to zero. Equation 4-97b was used to express the sales variable in terms of the production and inventory variables. The resulting set of equations were then solved simultaneously using a digital computer. Bergstrom and Smith also describe an application of the model to production planning for a firm producing electric motors.□

4-7 Multistage Models

4-7.1 Structure of Multistage Models

To illustrate some of the characteristics of multistage models, when demand and other factors change with time, we consider the situation of Figure 4-11. A single finished product is manufactured in two stages. The first consists of a plant (department), which produces a semifinished product, and an inventory of that commodity. The second stage contains a plant (department), which converts the semifinished product into finished product, and the finished goods inventory, which is subjected to a known time-varying demand schedule. Each plant can use overtime in any period to produce in excess of its regular time capacity; however, production costs are higher on overtime than on regular time. The problem is to specify the regular time and overtime production quantities at each stage in each period, so that all external demand is satisfied on time.

We can better appreciate the structure of a problem if we formulate it

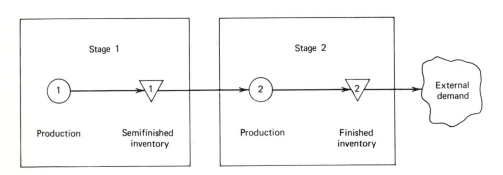

FIGURE 4-11. A two-stage serial production-inventory system.

symbolically, and for that purpose, we introduce the following notation:

X_{it} = regular time production at stage i in period t, ($i = 1, 2; t = 1, 2, \ldots, T$)

Y_{it} = overtime production at stage i in period t

I_{it} = inventory at stage i at the end of period t

P_{it} = regular time production capacity at stage i in period t

P'_{it} = overtime production capacity at stage i in period t

c_{it} = unit variable cost of regular time production at stage i in period t

c'_{it} = unit variable cost of overtime production at stage i in period t

h_{it} = cost of carrying a unit in inventory from period t to $t + 1$ at stage i

Z = total cost of production and inventory during the planning horizon

D_t = demand for finished product in period t

The problem is to choose $\{X_{it}\}$ and $\{Y_{it}\}$ to minimize

$$Z = \sum_{t=1}^{T} \sum_{i=1}^{2} [c_{it}X_{it} + c'_{it}Y_{it} + h_{it}I_{it}] \tag{4-98a}$$

subject to

$$I_{1t} = I_{1,t-1} + X_{1t} + Y_{1t} - X_{2t} - Y_{2t} \tag{4-98b}$$

$$I_{2t} = I_{2,t-1} + X_{2t} + Y_{2t} - D_t \tag{4-98c}$$

$$X_{it} \leq P_{it} \tag{4-98d}$$

$$Y_{it} \leq P'_{it} \tag{4-98e}$$

$$X_{it} \geq 0, \qquad Y_{it} \geq 0, \qquad I_{it} \geq 0 \tag{4-98f}$$

for all i and t. For convenience in this initial discussion of multistage systems, we have formulated the problem as a linear programming model.

Equations 4-98b are the material balance equations for the semifinished inventory between the two operations. For any period t, the ending inventory at stage 1 is equal to the inventory at the end of period $t - 1$, plus the production at stage 1 on regular time and overtime in period t, less the quantity withdrawn for regular time and overtime production at stage 2 in period t. These equations provide the linkage between stages and are characteristic of multistage models. Together with the nonnegativity requirement $I_{1t} \geq 0$, they insure that no shortages will be planned for the inventory between stages.

As written, (4-98b) assumes that one unit of the semifinished item is needed to produce one unit of the finished item. We could generalize slightly to explicitly include the situation where k units of semifinished material are required for each unit of finished product. Then

$$I_{1t} = I_{1,t-1} + X_{1t} + Y_{1t} - k(X_{2t} + Y_{2t}) \tag{4-99}$$

Multistage Models   259

An alternative to (4-99) is to define a unit of the first-stage commodity to be the amount necessary to produce one unit of finished product, and use the form (4-98b).

We may need to modify the inventory equations, (4-98b) and (4-98c), to account for production time. Production time (sometimes called "throughput" time) at a stage is the time interval between starting an item into production and having it available for use at the next stage. Let τ_i denote the production time, in periods, at stage i. The production variables, X_{it} and Y_{it}, are defined as the quantities *started* into production in period t, which means that these amounts would be *added to inventory* (and be available for withdrawal by the next stage) in period $t + \tau_i$. The inventory balance equations would be

$$I_{1t} = I_{1,t-1} + X_{1,t-\tau_1} + Y_{1,t-\tau_1} - X_{2t} - Y_{2t} \qquad (4\text{-}100)$$

$$I_{2t} = I_{2,t-1} + X_{2,t-\tau_2} + Y_{2,t-\tau_2} - D_t \qquad (4\text{-}101)$$

In these equations, the first-stage variables, $X_{1,t-\tau_1}$, $Y_{1,t-\tau_1}$, $t = 1, 2, \ldots, \tau_1$, and the second-stage variables, $X_{2,t-\tau_2}$, $Y_{2,t-\tau_2}$, $t = 1, 2, \ldots, \tau_2$, are work in process at time zero (resulting from prior decisions), which will be added to inventory during the planning horizon. Thus, they are known constants that must be specified as input to the model.

In formulating models of multistage processes when there are several sources of product at each stage, the analyst has two fundamental approaches. The first is to define separate production variables for each production source and each stage. We used this method in the model (4-98), when the sources were regular time and overtime at each stage in each time period. We could have used a second method that involves defining a finished goods production variable for every possible combination of source and stage. To illustrate, let X_{jklm} be the number of units of finished product produced by source l at stage 2 in period m, using semifinished product produced by source j at stage 1 in period k, $k \leq m$, where j or $l = 1$ indicates regular time production and j or $l = 2$ means overtime production. If we use the same notation for inventories, costs, and demands as in (4-98), we have the following new model:

$$\text{minimize} \quad Z = \sum_{k=1}^{T} \sum_{l=1}^{2} \sum_{m=k}^{T} [c_{1k}X_{1klm} + c'_{1k}X_{2klm}]$$

$$+ \sum_{j=1}^{2} \sum_{k=1}^{T} \sum_{m=k}^{T} [c_{2m}X_{jk1m} + c'_{2m}X_{jk2m}]$$

$$+ \sum_{t=1}^{T} [h_{1t}I_{1t} + h_{2t}I_{2t}] \qquad (4\text{-}102a)$$

subject to

$$I_{1t} = I_{10} + \sum_{j=1}^{2} \sum_{k=1}^{t} \sum_{l=1}^{2} \sum_{m=t+1}^{T} X_{jklm} \qquad (4\text{-}102b)$$

$$I_{2t} = I_{20} + \sum_{j=1}^{2} \sum_{k=1}^{t} \sum_{l=1}^{2} \sum_{m=1}^{t} X_{jklm} - \sum_{m=1}^{t} D_m \qquad (4\text{-}102\text{c})$$

$$\sum_{l=1}^{2} \sum_{m=t}^{T} X_{1tlm} \leq P_{1t} \qquad (4\text{-}102\text{d})$$

$$\sum_{l=1}^{2} \sum_{m=t}^{T} X_{2tlm} \leq P'_{1t} \qquad (4\text{-}102\text{e})$$

$$\sum_{j=1}^{2} \sum_{k=1}^{t} X_{jk1t} \leq P_{2t} \qquad (4\text{-}102\text{f})$$

$$\sum_{j=1}^{2} \sum_{k=1}^{t} X_{jk2t} \leq P'_{2t} \qquad (4\text{-}102\text{g})$$

$$X_{jklm} \geq 0, \qquad I_{1t} \geq 0, \qquad I_{2t} \geq 0 \qquad (4\text{-}102\text{h})$$

for all j, k, l, m, and t. Some of the elements of the model are difficult to recognize. The left-hand sides of inequalities (4-102d) and (4-102e) are the regular time and overtime production, respectively, at stage 1 in period t. Inequalities (4-102f) and (4-102g) are similar capacity constraints for stage 2. The stage 1 inventory equation, (4-102b), says that the inventory at the end of period t equals the initial inventory, plus any production on regular time and overtime at stage 1 during the first t periods that is to be used at stage 2 during the periods $t + 1$ to T. The stage 2 inventory equation, (4-102c), states that the inventory at the end of period t equals the initial inventory, plus the production on regular time and overtime at stage 2 during the first t periods, less the cumulative demand during the first t periods. The first set of terms in the objective function are production costs at stage 1; the second set, production costs at stage 2; and the third set, inventory holding costs at both stages.

The model (4-102) is less desirable than (4-98), because while both have $6T$ constraints, (4-102) has $2T(T + 1)$ production variables to $4T$ for model (4-98). Also, the definition of variables in (4-98) results in the solution to the model naturally being a production schedule for each stage. Therefore, we shall use the approach of defining separate production variables for each stage when modeling dynamic multistage systems.

The simple one-product, two-stage model described above can be generalized in many ways, including the following:

1. More than two production stages in series.

2. Multiple finished products and multiple semifinished products.

3. Multiple stages, not necessarily in series. Some stages may produce components used in the production of one or more finished products.

4. Multiple resource constraints at each stage.

5. Alternative production routings for products within a stage. This is the case of multiple production sources (processes) at each stage. Costs differ between processes, as do the resources used.

6. Allowance of backlogging. In most multistage systems, a shortage at any in-process inventory means an adjustment to production schedules at future operations, which may ultimately result in a delay in meeting demand for the finished product. Therefore the backlogging decisions are relevant to the final stage, where the finished product is produced.

7. Inclusion of distribution, or shipping, operations in the system. These operations can be treated in the same manner as a production operation.

8. Product mix decisions in the multiproduct case.

9. Inclusion of production smoothing costs in the objective function.

10. Nonlinear cost structures in the objective function.

In the following sections, we shall illustrate how some of these features can be modeled. Others will be left to the exercises at the end of the chapter. However, we make one final comment here. In practice, it is sometimes the case that a multistage system can be scheduled effectively by modeling the most important stage as a single-stage system, developing a production program for that stage, and based on this solution, sequentially scheduling operations at the other stages, often using more elementary planning models. Whether a large multistage model, which simultaneously considers decisions at every stage, or a set of smaller single-stage models, which plan stages in sequence, should be used is a matter to be decided through consideration of the relevant economics. Further discussion of this type of question can be found in Chapter 7.

4-7.2 Linear Programming Models

In this section, we give several examples of linear programming models of multistage systems. The obvious reason for concentrating on linear programming models is the availability of methods for solving very large linear programming problems. Dynamic multistage models tend to be large scale, since generally the number of constraints and variables is proportional to the number of stages, as well as to the number of time periods.

☐ **EXAMPLE 4-19** *An M-Stage Serial System, with Multiple Sources at Each Stage.* We generalize the problem of Section 4-7.1 to the case of M stages *in series*, each stage consisting of a production operation and an inventory. A single finished product is manufactured, and we assume that the units of production at each stage are defined to be the quantity needed for a unit of finished product. At any stage i, there may be several sources of production, such as regular time, overtime, subcontracting, different departments, different machines, different plants, etc. Let

X_{ijt} = the number of units of product at stage i produced by source j in period t, $(i = 1, 2, \ldots, M; j = 1, 2, \ldots, J_i; t = 1, 2, \ldots, T)$

c_{ijt} = unit production cost at stage i, source j, in period t

I_{it} = ending inventory at stage i, period t

h_{it} = inventory holding cost per unit, stage i, period t

P_{ijt} = capacity of source j, stage i, period t

D_t = finished goods demand, period t

We assume that the objective is to minimize the total production and inventory cost over the planning horizon, subject to a policy of no shortages. More formally, we want to choose the $\{X_{ijt}\}$ to minimize

$$Z = \sum_{t=1}^{T} \sum_{i=1}^{M} \left[\sum_{j=1}^{J_i} c_{ijt} X_{ijt} + h_{it} I_{it} \right] \tag{4-103a}$$

subject to, for $t = 1, 2, \ldots, T$,

$$I_{it} = I_{i,t-1} + \sum_{j=1}^{J_i} X_{ijt} - \sum_{j=1}^{J_{i+1}} X_{i+1,jt}, \quad (i = 1, 2, \ldots, M-1) \tag{4-103b}$$

$$I_{Mt} = I_{M,t-1} + \sum_{j=1}^{J_M} X_{Mjt} - D_t \tag{4-103c}$$

$$X_{ijt} \le P_{ijt}, \quad (i = 1, 2, \ldots, M; j = 1, 2, \ldots, J_i) \tag{4-103d}$$

$$X_{ijt} \ge 0, \quad I_{it} \ge 0, \quad (i = 1, 2, \ldots, M; j = 1, 2, \ldots, J_i) \tag{4-103e}$$

□

□**EXAMPLE 4-20** *Backlogging Allowed.* Suppose in the situation of Example 4-19 that backlogging is allowed for the finished goods inventory at a unit cost of π_t in period t. The revised model would be

$$\text{minimize} \quad Z = \sum_{t=1}^{T} \left[\sum_{i=1}^{M} \sum_{j=1}^{J_i} c_{ijt} X_{ijt} + \sum_{i=1}^{M-1} h_{it} I_{it} + h_{Mt} I_{Mt}^+ + \pi_t I_{Mt}^- \right] \tag{4-104a}$$

subject to

$$I_{it} = I_{i,t-1} + \sum_{j=1}^{J_i} X_{ijt} - \sum_{j=1}^{J_{i+1}} X_{i+1,jt}, \quad (i = 1, 2, \ldots, M-1) \tag{4-104b}$$

$$I_{Mt} = I_{M,t-1} + \sum_{j=1}^{J_M} X_{Mjt} - D_t \tag{4-104c}$$

$$I_{Mt} = I_{Mt}^+ - I_{Mt}^- \tag{4-104d}$$

$$0 \leq X_{ijt} \leq P_{ijt}, \qquad (i = 1, 2, \ldots, M; j = 1, 2, \ldots, J_i) \qquad \text{(4-104e)}$$

$$I_{it} \geq 0, \qquad (i = 1, 2, \ldots, M - 1) \qquad\qquad \text{(4-104f)}$$

$$I_{Mt}^+ \geq 0, \qquad I_{Mt}^- \geq 0 \qquad\qquad\qquad\qquad \text{(4-104g)}$$

for $t = 1, 2, \ldots, T$. The finished goods net inventory, I_{Mt}, is unconstrained in sign.$\square$

$\square$**EXAMPLE 4-21** *Multiple Products and Multiple Routings.* To illustrate modeling of a multistage system when each stage produces several products, each of which may have several alternative routings, we shall consider a two-stage system. The first stage produces n_1 different products that are used in the production of n_2 different finished products at the second stage. The requirements for each finished product are given by time period and must be satisfied with no shortages. Each stage has available certain resources (machine time at various production centers, man-hours of different labor types, raw materials, subcontracting capabilities, and so on), whose availability in each period is known. The problem is to meet the finished product requirements at minimum cost of production and inventory, subject to resource constraints at each stage.

Problems of this type are typical in industry. An example is a textile system, where the first stage consists of spinning plants manufacturing a number of different types of yarn and the second stage contains weaving plants that use the yarns in producing several styles of woven cloth. The time-phased requirements for each cloth style are given. There are several processes (routings) by which each yarn type can be produced. These routings differ in the combination of machine groups used in production of the yarn. Here a machine group can be defined as a set of identical machines at the same location (plant). Similarly, alternate routings exist for manufacture of a cloth style. The planner must determine a spinning and weaving schedule that allows the demand for cloth to be filled on time.

To formulate the model, let

X_{ijt} = number of units of (semifinished) product i produced by routing j at stage 1 in period t, $(i = 1, 2, \ldots, n_1; j = 1, 2, \ldots, J_i)$

Y_{pqt} = number of units of (finished) product p produced by routing q at stage 2 in period t, $(p = 1, 2, \ldots, n_2; q = 1, 2, \ldots, Q_p)$

D_{pt} = demand for finished product p in period t

I_{1it} = inventory of product i at stage 1 at the end of period t

I_{2pt} = inventory of product p at stage 2 at the end of period t

b_{1kt} = quantity of resource type k available at stage 1 in period t, $(k = 1, 2, \ldots, K)$

b_{2rt} = quantity of resource type r available at stage 2 in period t, $(r = 1, 2, \ldots, R)$

a_{ipq} = number of units of semifinished product i used to make one unit of finished product p by process q at stage 2

e_{ijk} = number of units of stage 1 resource k required to produce one unit of semifinished product i by process j

f_{pqr} = number of units of stage 2 resource r required to produce one unit of finished product p by process q

c_{1ijt} = cost to produce a unit of semifinished product i by process j at stage 1 in period t

c_{2pqt} = cost to produce a unit of product p by process q at stage 2 in period t

h_{1it} = cost to carry a unit of semifinished product i in inventory at stage 1 from period t to $t + 1$

h_{2pt} = cost to carry a unit of finished product p in inventory at stage 2 from period t to $t + 1$

We want to minimize

$$Z = \sum_{t=1}^{T} \left\{ \sum_{i=1}^{n_1} \left[\sum_{j=1}^{J_i} c_{1ijt} X_{ijt} + h_{1it} I_{1it} \right] + \sum_{p=1}^{n_2} \left[\sum_{q=1}^{Q_p} c_{2pqt} Y_{pqt} + h_{2pt} I_{2pt} \right] \right\} \quad (4\text{-}105a)$$

subject to the constraints:

$$I_{1it} = I_{1i,t-1} + \sum_{j=1}^{J_i} X_{ijt} - \sum_{p=1}^{n_2} \sum_{q=1}^{Q_p} a_{ipq} Y_{pqt} \quad (4\text{-}105b)$$

$$I_{2pt} = I_{2p,t-1} + \sum_{q=1}^{Q_p} Y_{pqt} - D_{pt} \quad (4\text{-}105c)$$

$$\sum_{i=1}^{n_1} \sum_{j=1}^{J_i} e_{ijk} X_{ijt} \leq b_{1kt} \quad (4\text{-}105d)$$

$$\sum_{p=1}^{n_2} \sum_{q=1}^{Q_p} f_{pqr} Y_{pqt} \leq b_{2rt} \quad (4\text{-}105e)$$

$$I_{1it} \geq 0, \qquad I_{2pt} \geq 0 \quad (4\text{-}105f)$$

$$X_{ijt} \geq 0, \qquad Y_{pqt} \geq 0 \quad (4\text{-}105g)$$

for all i, k, p, r, and t. The constraints (4-105b) are material balance equations for the semifinished inventories, while (4-105c) are for the finished goods inventories. Resource limitations are represented by (4-105d), for stage 1, and (4-105e), for stage 2. The constraints (4-105f) insure that all finished goods demand will be met and that the production programs at the two stages are coordinated to the extent that no shortages occur at between-stage inventories.□

□**EXAMPLE 4-22** *Product Mix Decisions.* In this example, we show how the multiproduct model of Example 4-21 can be extended to include decisions on product mix. Now, instead of being given a fixed set of production requirements for each product, we suppose that we are to find the most profitable production program over the planning horizon. The sales potential of a product p in period t is described by an upper limit, F_{pt}, which represents the maximum possible sales in period t, and a lower limit, F'_{pt}, which insures the availability of at least this much product in period t. (This method of establishing an authorized range for planned sales in period t is the same as that used in Example 4-12 of Section 4-6.1 for the single-stage case.)

Let S_{pt} be the planned sales of product p in period t and ϕ_{pt} be the unit variable revenue from the sale of product p in period t. Note that the $\{S_{pt}\}$ are decision variables, along with the $\{X_{ijt}\}$ and $\{Y_{pqt}\}$. The problem is to *maximize*

$$\sum_{t=1}^{T} \left\{ \sum_{p=1}^{n_2} \phi_{pt} S_{pt} - \sum_{i=1}^{n_1} \left[\sum_{j=1}^{J_i} c_{1ijt} X_{ijt} + h_{1it} I_{1it} \right] - \sum_{p=1}^{n_2} \left[\sum_{q=1}^{Q_p} c_{2pqt} Y_{pqt} + h_{2pt} I_{2pt} \right] \right\}$$

(4-106a)

subject to

$$I_{1it} = I_{1i,t-1} + \sum_{j=1}^{J_i} X_{ijt} - \sum_{p=1}^{n_2} \sum_{q=1}^{Q_p} a_{ipq} Y_{pqt}$$

(4-106b)

$$I_{2pt} = I_{2p,t-1} + \sum_{q=1}^{Q_p} Y_{pqt} - S_{pt}$$

(4-106c)

$$\sum_{i=1}^{n_1} \sum_{j=1}^{J_i} e_{ijk} X_{ijt} \le b_{1kt}$$

(4-106d)

$$\sum_{p=1}^{n_2} \sum_{q=1}^{Q_p} f_{pqr} Y_{pqt} \le b_{2rt}$$

(4-106e)

$$F'_{pt} \le S_{pt} \le F_{pt}$$

(4-106f)

$$I_{1it} \ge 0, \qquad I_{2pt} \ge 0$$

(4-106g)

$$X_{ijt} \ge 0, \qquad Y_{pqt} \ge 0$$

(4-106h)

for all i, k, p, r, and t.

The solution to this model will specify, for each production stage, how much of each product should be manufactured by each routing in each period, as well as how much of each finished product should be sold in each period. Also, the planned end-of-period inventories at each stage will be a direct output of the model's solution. Production and marketing management will be interested in several additional pieces of information provided by standard computer programs for solution of *LP* problems: for each stage, the resources that are completely utilized and the amount of unused capacity for those that are not; shadow prices for limiting resources; cost ranging on the objective function to determine the implications of price changes; and products having optimal solution values $S_{pt}^* = F_{pt}'$, when the lower limit is greater than zero.

The reader should compare the nature of the model of the multistage product mix problem of this example with that of the multistage process selection model of Example 4-21, and verify that in adding the product mix feature, we effectively added a third stage to the original two-stage model. This third stage, which we could call the "marketing stage," draws on the finished goods inventory and delivers to the customer, all in the same period. Its activities generate no costs, only revenues. This concept is illustrated in Figure 4-12.

A useful exercise for the reader would be consideration of how one would determine the various cost and revenue factors in the model. We will make only a few observations here. The ϕ_{pt} should be the variable revenue per unit, net of any variable selling and distribution costs. The first-stage production costs, c_{1ijt}, should include only variable costs of material, labor, power, and so on, at stage 1. The second-stage costs, c_{2pqt} should be only the *additional* variable costs incurred at stage 2. Any variable transportation costs must be allocated to the appropriate stage. Inventory carrying costs, h_{1it} and h_{2pt}, should be based

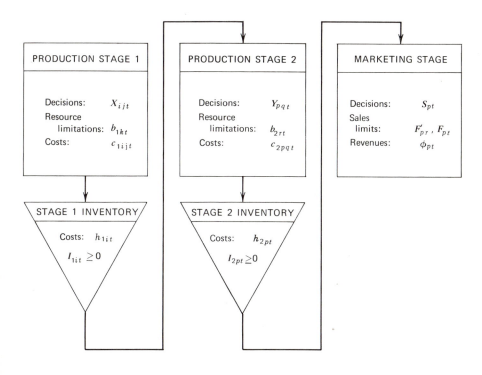

FIGURE 4-12. Multistage structure of Example 4-22.

on the length of the period and the value of the item. The latter could be the total variable cost expended on the item to that point in the production process. Since a product may have several production routings, an estimated average cost must be used. For example, suppose that an item in the second-stage inventory has an average total variable cost for the first two stages of $10, the annual carrying cost rate is 24 percent, and each period is a month long. Then $h_{2it} = (0.24/12)(10) = 0.20$, for all t. Finally, we remark that different inventory carrying-cost *rates* may be used for the various stages, especially when the risk of obsolescence depends on the production stage.☐

☐**EXAMPLE 4-23** *A Multilocation Production-Distribution Problem.* As a final example of linear programming models of multistage systems, consider the situation of Figure 4-13. A single finished product is produced by two plants, β_1 and β_2, and immediately distributed to three regional warehouses, γ_1, γ_2, and γ_3, where it is stored. All customer demand is shipped from these latter locations. The system also contains three other plants, α_1, α_2, and α_3, which each produce the same product, a major component part of the finished product produced at β_1 and β_2. Each of these component-producing plants maintains its own inventory of completed parts, which are shipped on demand to the assembly plants. The five plants and the three finished product warehouses are each at a different geographical location. Production costs vary among plants and shipping costs are, of course, a function of the source and the destination. Each plant has a known capacity in each period. The problem is to specify the least-cost production and distribution program for the system that satisfies given demand schedules for each finished goods warehouse.

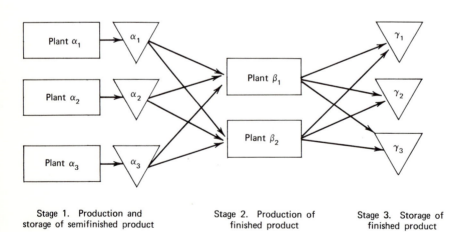

Stage 1. Production and storage of semifinished product

Stage 2. Production of finished product

Stage 3. Storage of finished product

FIGURE 4-13.   Production-distribution system for Example 4-23.

In modeling this system, we shall be more specific about the between-stage shipping pattern than we were in the model of Example 4-21. We identify the following decision variables:

X_{it} = number of units of semifinished product produced at plant i of stage 1 in period t

Y_{jkt} = number of units of finished product produced at plant j of stage 2 and shipped to finished goods warehouse k in period t

V_{ijt} = number of units of semifinished product shipped from plant i at stage 1 to plant j at stage 2 in period t

Note carefully that we have treated the transportation between the two production stages differently from the transportation between the final production stage and the regional warehouses. Since the production of a unit of semifinished product can take place in a period *prior* to its shipment to a stage 2 plant, we chose to define separate variables for the stage 1 production and the shipments between stages 1 and 2. However, second-stage production is not stored at the plant, but is shipped *immediately* to γ_1, γ_2, or γ_3. In such a situation, it is convenient to let the decision variable identify both the production source and the warehouse destination; hence, the definition of Y_{jkt}.

The following additional notation will be needed:

D_{kt} = given demand at warehouse k in period t

c_{1it} = cost to produce a unit of semifinished product at plant i of stage 1 in period t

c_{2jt} = cost to produce a unit of finished product at plant j of stage 2 in period t

g_{ijt} = cost to ship a unit of semifinished product from plant i at stage 1 to plant j at stage 2 in period t

g'_{jkt} = cost to ship a unit of finished product from plant j at stage 2 to regional warehouse k

I_{1it} = semifinished inventory at plant i, stage 1, at the end of period t

I_{3kt} = finished goods inventory at warehouse k at the end of period t

h_{1it}, h_{3kt} = unit inventory carrying costs at stages 1 and 3, respectively, in period t

P_{1it}, P_{2jt} = production capacities at stages 1 and 2, respectively, in period t

Z = total production and shipping cost during the planning horizon

We want to choose the $\{X_{it}\}$, $\{V_{ijt}\}$, and $\{Y_{jkt}\}$ to minimize

$$Z = \sum_{t=1}^{T}\left\{\sum_{i=1}^{3}[c_{1it}X_{it} + h_{1it}I_{1it}] + \sum_{i=1}^{3}\sum_{j=1}^{2}g_{ijt}V_{ijt}\right.$$

$$\left. + \sum_{j=1}^{2}\sum_{k=1}^{3}(c_{2jt} + g'_{jkt})Y_{jkt} + \sum_{k=1}^{3}h_{3kt}I_{3kt}\right\} \quad \text{(4-107a)}$$

subject to

$$I_{1it} = I_{1i,t-1} + X_{it} - \sum_{j=1}^{2}V_{ijt} \quad \text{(4-107b)}$$

$$\sum_{i=1}^{3}V_{ijt} = \sum_{k=1}^{3}Y_{jkt} \quad \text{(4-107c)}$$

$$I_{3kt} = I_{3k,t-1} + \sum_{j=1}^{2}Y_{jkt} - D_{kt} \quad \text{(4-107d)}$$

$$X_{it} \leq P_{1it} \quad \text{(4-107e)}$$

$$\sum_{k=1}^{3}Y_{jkt} \leq P_{2jt} \quad \text{(4-107f)}$$

$$I_{1it} \geq 0, \qquad I_{3kt} \geq 0 \quad \text{(4-107g)}$$

$$X_{it} \geq 0, \qquad V_{ijt} \geq 0, \qquad Y_{jkt} \geq 0 \quad \text{(4-107h)}$$

for all i, j, k, and t. Constraints (4-107b) and (4-107d) are inventory balance equations for the stage 1 and stage 3 inventories, respectively. The constraint (4-107c) insures that the quantity of parts shipped from all stage 1 locations in period t to plant j of stage 2 is equal to the quantity required by the production schedule for that plant in period t.

This model can be modified to include the following additional considerations: sale or purchase of semifinished product, overtime decisions, work force level decisions, inventory maximums and minimums, production lead times, limitations on size of shipments between plants, backlogging of finished goods demand, production rate change costs, multiple routings within plants, and multiple products. Also, there are other ways we might have defined the decision variables in this problem. Some of these extensions and variations are considered in Exercises 4-71 to 4-74.□

Naturally, all of the models given in this section could be formulated with nonlinear cost components if appropriate; however, such models often are difficult to solve, especially if the problem is large.

In the next section, we shall examine the network structure of multistage models and some algorithms based on the properties of solutions to network problems.

4-7.3 Network Models

It is not difficult to extend the network concepts of Section 4-3 to the multistage case. We do that in this section by considering first a network-based algorithm for solving a single product planning problem for a serial system with concave costs, and then more general network structures with linear costs.

A Single-Product, Multifacility Model with Concave Costs. Zangwill (52) considers the problem of planning production for each of M facilities over a planning horizon of T periods, where the facilities are arranged in series and numbered so that the output of facility j becomes the input to facility $j + 1$. An inventory is maintained between stages and the jth inventory follows production at facility j. The series structure of the problem is illustrated in Figure 4-14. The finished goods inventory following stage M is subjected to a known demand schedule and backorders are not allowed. It is assumed that production at facility j in period t can be used by facility $j + 1$ in the same period. This assumption is not binding, because time lags can be handled by redefining the decision variables to account for production lead times.

Let X_{jt} be the production at facility j in period t and I_{jt} be the inventory following facility j at the end of period t. The production cost in period t at stage j is $C_{jt}(X_{jt})$ and the inventory cost is $H_{jt}(I_{jt})$. Both functions are assumed concave for nonnegative arguments. Let D_t be the external demand in period t. The problem is to choose the $\{X_{jt}\}$ to minimize the total production and inventory costs over the planning horizon,

$$\sum_{t=1}^{T} \sum_{j=1}^{M} [C_{jt}(X_{jt}) + H_{jt}(I_{jt})] \tag{4-108a}$$

subject to the following constraints:

$$I_{jt} = I_{j,t-1} + X_{jt} - X_{j+1,t}, \quad (j = 1, 2, \ldots, M-1; t = 1, 2, \ldots, T) \tag{4-108b}$$

$$I_{Mt} = I_{M,t-1} + X_{Mt} - D_t, \quad (t = 1, 2, \ldots, T) \tag{4-108c}$$

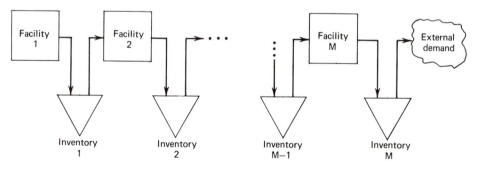

FIGURE 4-14. Serial multifacility system.

$$X_{jt} \geq 0, \qquad I_{jt} \geq 0 \tag{4-108d}$$

$$I_{j0} = I_{jT} = 0, \qquad (j = 1, 2, \ldots, M) \tag{4-108e}$$

The constraints (4-108b) are inventory balance equations for the in-process inventories, while (4-108c) are similar constraints for the finished goods inventory. We assume that all inventories are zero initially and that all inventories are to be zero at time T.

Zangwill develops properties of an optimal solution by noting the network flow analogy represented by Figure 4-15. Each node (j, t) represents a production stage and a time period. The flow through an arc is either production or

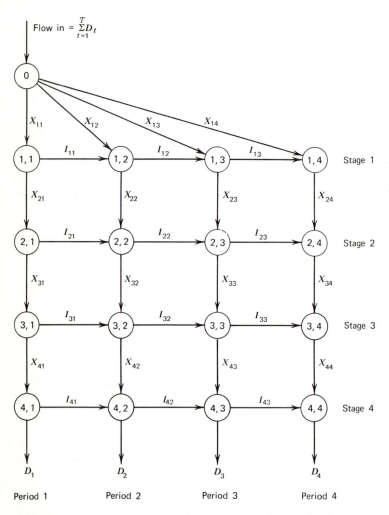

FIGURE 4-15. Multistage network flow model with $M = 4$, $T = 4$.

inventory. Flow into node (j, t) is from inventory carried forward from the prior period, $I_{j,t-1}$, and from production at facility j in the current period, X_{jt}. Flow out of node (j, t) is inventory carried forward to the next time period, I_{jt}, and production by facility $j + 1$ in the current period, $X_{j+1,t}$. The conservation of flow equation for node (j, t) is (4-108b). Exceptions to the above occur at the boundaries: the flows out of node (M, t) are the given external demand, D_t, and the inventory carried forward, I_{Mt}; there is no inventory flow out of nodes (j, T), since the final inventories are to be zero; and there is no inventory flow into nodes $(j, 1)$, since we assume initial inventories are zero. The single source node has an inward flow equal to $\sum_{t=1}^{T} D_t$, the total flow out of the system.

Observe that this network model is an extension of Figure 4-7 to the multistage case.

Since the cost functions defined on the arc flows are concave and the network has a single source, we know that any minimum cost flow is an extreme flow, which has the property that at most one arc entering a node will have a positive flow. (See Section 4-3.4 and Reference 51.) The nature of an extreme flow for a single-source, concave-cost network is illustrated in Figure 4-16, where only the arcs having positive flow are shown. Note the treelike structure, which has resulted in the name *arborescence* flow (51).

Using the above property of an extreme flow, Zangwill (52) develops the following results.

1. If the total flow into node (j, t), other than the source, is $f, f > 0$, then there are integers α and β, $t \leq \alpha \leq \beta \leq T$, such that

$$f = \sum_{r=\alpha}^{\beta} D_r \qquad (4\text{-}109)$$

Equation 4-109 says that the sum of the entering inventory plus the production at stage j in period t must be the exact sum of demands for periods $\alpha, \alpha + 1, \ldots,$ β, for some $t \leq \alpha \leq \beta \leq T$. For $t = 1$, we must have $\alpha = 1$, and if $j = M$, then $\alpha = t$.

2. If $j = M$, then the ending inventory for period t is

$$I_{Mt} = \begin{cases} \sum\limits_{r=t+1}^{\beta} D_r, & \text{for some } t < \beta \leq T \\ 0, & \text{for } \beta = t \end{cases} \qquad (4\text{-}110)$$

This states that when the flow into a last-stage node (M, t) is $\sum_{r=t}^{\beta} D_r, t \leq \beta \leq T$, the ending inventory will be zero if $t = \beta$ and will be the sum of the demands in periods $t + 1, t + 2, \ldots, \beta$, when $t < \beta \leq T$.

3. Now suppose $j = M - 1$, the next-to-last stage. If the flow into stage

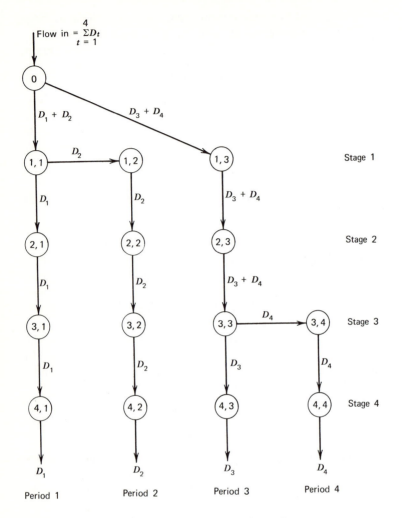

FIGURE 4-16. Arborescence structure of an extreme flow.

$(M - 1, t)$ is $\displaystyle\sum_{r=\alpha}^{\beta} D_r$, for $t \le \alpha \le \beta \le T$, then we have the following:

    (a) If $\alpha = t$, there is an integer γ, $t \le \gamma \le \beta$, such that

$$X_{Mt} = \sum_{r=\alpha}^{\gamma} D_r \tag{4-111}$$

and

$$I_{M-1,t} = \sum_{r=\gamma+1}^{\beta} D_r \tag{4-112}$$

    (b) If $\alpha > t$, $X_{Mt} = 0 \tag{4-113}$

and

$$I_{M-1,t} = \sum_{r=\alpha}^{\beta} D_r \qquad (4\text{-}114)$$

Equations 4-111 and 4-112 follow from the fact that if the requirements for period t, D_t, are transhipped through node $(M - 1, t)$, there must be production at stage M in period t; while (4-113) and (4-114) are verified by observing that if the requirements for period t were not shipped into node $(M - 1, t)$, they must reach node (M, t) by another path and since only one positive flow into (M, t) is permitted, $X_{Mt} = 0$.

4. If the flow into node (j, t), $j \leq M - 2$, is $\sum_{r=\alpha}^{\beta} D_r$, for some $t \leq \alpha \leq \beta \leq T$, there exists an integer γ, max $[t, \alpha - 1] \leq \gamma \leq \beta$, such that

$$X_{j+1,t} = \sum_{r=\alpha}^{\gamma} D_r \qquad (4\text{-}115)$$

and

$$I_{j,t} = \sum_{r=\gamma+1}^{\beta} D_r \qquad (4\text{-}116)$$

Definition of the range of γ insures that $X_{j+1,t} > 0$, if $\alpha = t$, and provides for the possibility that $X_{j+1,t} = 0$, when $\alpha > t$. The latter is implied by $\gamma = \alpha - 1$.

These properties are used in the following algorithm to determine the minimum cost program. Let the number of units shipped into any node (j, t) be denoted by

$$f(\alpha, \beta) = \sum_{r=\alpha}^{\beta} D_r, \quad \text{for } t \leq \alpha \leq \beta \leq T \qquad (4\text{-}117)$$

and let $K_{jt}(\alpha, \beta)$ be the optimal cost of shipping these $f(\alpha, \beta)$ units from node (j, t) to their destination nodes $(M, \alpha), (M, \alpha + 1), \ldots, (M, \beta)$. For a node (j, t) in the middle of the network, the flow leaving the node will be either production at stage $j + 1$ in period t or inventory at stage j carried into period $t + 1$; that is,

$$f(\alpha, \beta) = X_{j+1,t} + I_{jt} \qquad (4\text{-}118)$$

The immediate decision at node (j, t) is to choose an integer γ, $\alpha \leq \gamma \leq \beta$, such that

$$X_{j+1,t} = \sum_{r=\alpha}^{\gamma} D_r \qquad (4\text{-}119)$$

and

$$I_{jt} = \sum_{r=\gamma+1}^{\beta} D_r \qquad (4\text{-}120)$$

The immediate cost of this decision is the sum of production and inventory costs,

$$C_{j+1,t}\left(\sum_{r=\alpha}^{\gamma} D_r\right) + H_{jt}\left(\sum_{r=\gamma+1}^{\beta} D_r\right)$$

which to simplify notation can be written as $C_{j+1,t}[\alpha, \gamma] + H_{jt}[\gamma + 1, \beta]$. The remaining portion of the cost $K_{jt}(\alpha, \beta)$ is obtained by noting that the decision at node (j, t) results in a flow $f(\alpha, \gamma)$ into node $(j + 1, t)$ and a flow $f(\gamma + 1, \beta)$ into node $(j, t + 1)$. This leads to the following recursive relation:

$$K_{jt}(\alpha, \beta) = \min_{\alpha \le \gamma \le \beta} \{C_{j+1,t}[\alpha, \gamma]$$
$$+ H_{jt}[\gamma + 1, \beta] + K_{j+1,t}(\alpha, \gamma) + K_{j,t+1}(\gamma + 1, \beta)\} \quad (4\text{-}121)$$

The optimization at node (j, t) is illustrated in Figure 4-17.

Equation 4-121 is the general form of the recursive relation, but must be more carefully defined to handle all the special cases:

1. If $j = M$:

$$K_{Mt}(t, \beta) = H_{Mt}[t + 1, \beta] + K_{M,t+1}(t + 1, \beta) \quad (4\text{-}122)$$

which holds for $1 \le t \le T - 1$ and $t \le \beta \le T$. Note that if $t = T$,

$$K_{MT}(T, T) = 0 \quad (4\text{-}123)$$

2. If $j = M - 1$ and $\alpha = t$,

$$K_{M-1,t}(t, \beta) = \min_{t \le \gamma \le \beta} \{C_{Mt}[t, \gamma] + H_{M-1,t}[\gamma + 1, \beta]$$
$$+ K_{Mt}(t, \gamma) + K_{M-1,t+1}(\gamma + 1, \beta)\} \quad (4\text{-}124)$$

for $1 \le t \le T - 1$ and $t \le \beta \le T$. When $t = T$,

$$K_{M-1,T}(T, T) = c_{M,T}[T, T] \quad (4\text{-}125)$$

3. If $j = M - 1$ and $\alpha > t$:

$$K_{M-1,t}(\alpha, \beta) = H_{M-1,t}[\alpha, \beta] + K_{M-1,t+1}(\alpha, \beta) \quad (4\text{-}126)$$

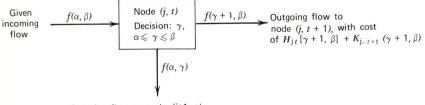

FIGURE 4-17. Decision process at node (j, t), assuming a given incoming flow $f(\alpha, \beta)$ and optimal decisions at nodes $(j + 1, t)$ and $(j, t + 1)$.

which holds for $2 \leq t \leq T - 1$ and $t < \alpha \leq \beta \leq T$. For $t = 1, \alpha = 1$ must be the case (otherwise the demand D_1 would not be met) and (4-124) is used.

4. If $1 \leq j \leq M - 2$:

$$K_{jt}(\alpha, \beta) = \underset{\max(t, \alpha - 1) \leq \gamma \leq \beta}{\text{minimum}} \{C_{j+1,t}[\alpha, \gamma] + H_{jt}[\gamma + 1, \beta]$$
$$+ K_{j+1,t}(\alpha, \gamma) + K_{j,t+1}(\gamma + 1, \beta)\} \quad (4\text{-}127)$$

for $2 \leq t \leq T - 1$ and $t \leq \alpha \leq \beta \leq T$. Note that if $\alpha = t$, then $X_{j+1,t}$ must be at least D_t. This leads to the definition of the lower bound on γ, as explained in the discussion following (4-116). When $t = T$,

$$K_{jT}(T, T) = C_{j+1,T}(T, T) + K_{j+1,T}(T, T) \quad (4\text{-}128)$$

If $t = 1$, then $\alpha = 1$ must hold and (4-127) can be used to compute $K_{j1}(1, \beta)$.

Equations 4-122 to 4-128 allow determination of the optimal disposition of a flow of $f(\alpha, \beta)$ into any node (j, t). To complete the algorithm, we have to include decisions at the source node, which actually are decisions about when to produce at the first stage. Consider the decision on X_{1t}. Let $K_{0t}(\alpha, T)$ be the minimum cost of shipping $\sum_{r=\alpha}^{T} D_r$ units from the source to satisfy the requirements at nodes $(M, \alpha), (M, \alpha + 1), \ldots, (M, T)$. This is the optimal cost of satisfying the demands $D_\alpha, D_{\alpha+1}, \ldots, D_T$, through production in periods t, $t + 1, \ldots, T$. Note that demand in the first $\alpha - 1$ periods is assumed to be satisfied through production in periods prior to t. Also observe that if $\alpha = t$, we must produce in period t at the first stage; otherwise we will not satisfy the requirement D_t in period t. If $\alpha > t$, X_{1t} may or may not be positive, depending on the economics. If we do produce in period t at the first stage, the production quantity can be indexed by an integer $\gamma, \alpha \leq \gamma \leq T$, since

$$X_{1t} = \sum_{r=\alpha}^{\gamma} D_r$$

For convenience in writing the following recursive relationship, the alternative of $X_{1t} = 0$ will be identified by letting $\gamma = \alpha - 1$. We then have

$$K_{0t}(\alpha, T) = \underset{\max(t, \alpha - 1) \leq \gamma \leq T}{\text{minimum}} \{C_{1t}[\alpha, \gamma] + K_{1t}(\alpha, \gamma) + K_{0,t+1}(\gamma + 1, T)\} \quad (4\text{-}129)$$

which holds for $2 \leq t \leq T - 1$ and $t \leq \alpha \leq T$. If $t = 1$, use (4-129) only with $\alpha = 1$. If $t = T$,

$$K_{0T}(T, T) = C_{1T}[T, T] + K_{1T}(T, T) \quad (4\text{-}130)$$

Finally, for completeness, define

$$K_{jt}(r + 1, r) = H_{jt}[r + 1, r] = C_{jt}[r + 1, r] = 0,$$

whenever these terms appear in applying any of the recursive equations.

We start the algorithm with $K_{MT}(T, T) = 0$ and work backward in j and t

until we find $K_{01}(1, T)$, which is the minimum cost attainable for the network. The procedure is best learned through study of an example.

☐**EXAMPLE 4-24** We consider a planning horizon of four periods for a production system consisting of three stages in series. The production and inventory costs at each stage have the following form:

$$C_{jt}(X_{jt}) = \begin{cases} 0, & \text{if } X_{jt} = 0 \\ A_j + c_j X_{jt}, & \text{if } X_{jt} > 0 \end{cases}$$

$$H_{jt}(I_{jt}) = h_j I_{jt}$$

Suppose $A_1 = 400$, $A_2 = 300$, $A_3 = 600$, $c_1 = 20$, $c_2 = 10$, $c_3 = 30$, $h_1 = 2$, $h_2 = 1$, and $h_3 = 3$. Demands for the single commodity are $D_1 = 100$, $D_2 = 300$, $D_3 = 200$, and $D_4 = 400$. No shortages are permitted.

Initially we observe that the unit variable production cost at each stage is constant and independent of the period of production. Since each stage must produce 1000 units and the total variable cost does not depend on when we produce, we drop the variable cost term from $C_{jt}(X_{jt})$ and retain only the setup cost. This simplifies the arithmetic somewhat.

Before going further, the reader is advised to draw the network for this problem and to trace out the alternatives as we consider them. We start with stage 3 and use (4-122) and (4-123):

$K_{34}(4, 4) = 0$

$K_{33}(3, 3) = H_{33}[4, 3] + K_{34}(4, 3) = 0 + 0 = 0$

$K_{33}(3, 4) = H_{33}[4, 4] + K_{34}(4, 4) = 1200 + 0 = 1200$

$K_{32}(2, 2) = H_{32}[3, 2] + K_{33}(3, 2) = 0 + 0 = 0$

$K_{32}(2, 3) = H_{32}[3, 3] + K_{33}(3, 3) = 600 + 0 = 600$

$K_{32}(2, 4) = H_{32}[3, 4] + K_{33}(3, 4) = 1800 + 1200 = 3000$

$K_{31}(1, 1) = H_{31}[2, 1] + K_{32}(2, 1) = 0 + 0 = 0$

$K_{31}(1, 2) = H_{31}[2, 2] + K_{32}(2, 2) = 900 + 0 = 900$

$K_{31}(1, 3) = H_{31}[2, 3] + K_{32}(2, 3) = 1500 + 600 = 2100$

$K_{31}(1, 4) = H_{31}[2, 4] + K_{32}(2, 4) = 2700 + 3000 = 5700$

Next we consider stage 2, using (4-124), (4-125), and (4-126):

$K_{24}(4, 4) = C_{34}[4, 4] = 600$

$\begin{aligned} K_{23}(3, 3) &= C_{33}[3, 3] + H_{23}[4, 3] + K_{33}(3, 3) + K_{24}(4, 3) \\ &= 600 + 0 + 0 + 0 = 600 \end{aligned}$

$\begin{aligned} K_{23}(3, 4) &= \min_{3 \le \gamma \le 4} \{C_{33}[3, \gamma] + H_{23}[\gamma + 1, 4] + K_{33}(3, \gamma) + K_{24}(\gamma + 1, 4)\} \\ &= \min [600 + 400 + 0 + 600; 600 + 0 + 1200 + 0] \\ &= 1600, \quad \text{for } \gamma^* = 3 \end{aligned}$

$$K_{23}(4, 4) = H_{23}[4, 4] + K_{24}(4, 4) = 400 + 600 = 1000$$

$$K_{22}(2, 2) = C_{32}[2, 2] + H_{22}[3, 2] + K_{32}(2, 2) + K_{23}(3, 2)$$
$$= 600 + 0 + 0 + 0 = 600$$

$$K_{22}(2, 3) = \min_{2 \le \gamma \le 3} \{C_{32}[2, \gamma] + H_{22}[\gamma + 1, 3] + K_{32}(2, \gamma) + K_{23}(\gamma + 1, 3)\}$$
$$= \min [600 + 200 + 0 + 600, 600 + 0 + 600 + 0]$$
$$= 1200, \quad \text{for } \gamma^* = 3$$

$$K_{22}(2, 4) = \min_{2 \le \gamma \le 4} \{C_{32}[2, \gamma] + H_{22}[\gamma + 1, 4] + K_{32}(2, \gamma) + K_{23}(\gamma + 1, 4)\}$$
$$= \min [600 + 600 + 0 + 1600, 600 + 400 + 600 + 1000,$$
$$600 + 0 + 3000 + 0]$$
$$= 2600, \quad \text{for } \gamma^* = 3$$

$$K_{22}(3, 3) = H_{22}[3, 3] + K_{23}(3, 3) = 200 + 600 = 800$$

$$K_{22}(3, 4) = H_{22}[3, 4] + K_{23}(3, 4) = 600 + 1600 = 2200$$

$$K_{22}(4, 4) = H_{22}[4, 4] + K_{23}(4, 4) = 400 + 1000 = 1400$$

$$K_{21}(1, 1) = C_{31}[1, 1] + H_{21}[2, 1] + K_{31}(1, 1) + K_{22}(2, 1)$$
$$= 600 + 0 + 0 + 0 = 600$$

$$K_{21}(1, 2) = \min_{1 \le \gamma \le 2} \{C_{31}[1, \gamma] + H_{21}[\gamma + 1, 2] + K_{31}(1, \gamma) + K_{22}(\gamma + 1, 2)\}$$
$$= \min [600 + 300 + 0 + 600, 600 + 0 + 900 + 0]$$
$$= 1500, \quad \text{for } \gamma^* = 1 \text{ or } 2$$

$$K_{21}(1, 3) = \min_{1 \le \gamma \le 3} \{C_{31}[1, \gamma] + H_{21}[\gamma + 1, 3] + K_{31}(1, \gamma) + K_{22}(\gamma + 1, 3)\}$$
$$= \min [600 + 500 + 0 + 1200, 600 + 200 + 900 + 800,$$
$$600 + 0 + 2100 + 0]$$
$$= 2300, \quad \text{for } \gamma^* = 1$$

$$K_{21}(1, 4) = \min_{1 \le \gamma \le 4} \{C_{31}[1, \gamma] + H_{21}[\gamma + 1, 4] + K_{31}(1, \gamma) + K_{22}(\gamma + 1, 4)\}$$
$$= \min [600 + 900 + 0 + 2600, 600 + 600 + 900 + 2200,$$
$$600 + 400 + 2100 + 1400, 600 + 0 + 5700 + 0]$$
$$= 4100, \quad \text{for } \gamma^* = 1$$

Next we make calculations for stage 1, using (4-127) and (4-128):

$$K_{14}(4, 4) = C_{24}[4, 4] + K_{24}(4, 4) = 300 + 600 = 900$$

$$K_{13}(3, 3) = C_{23}[3, 3] + H_{13}[4, 3] + K_{23}(3, 3) + K_{14}(4, 3)$$
$$= 300 + 0 + 600 + 0 = 900$$

$$K_{13}(3, 4) = \min_{3 \leq \gamma \leq 4} \{C_{23}[3, \gamma] + H_{13}[\gamma + 1, 4] + K_{23}(3, \gamma) + K_{14}(\gamma + 1, 4)\}$$
$$= \min [300 + 800 + 600 + 900, 300 + 0 + 1600 + 0]$$
$$= 1900, \quad \text{for } \gamma^* = 4$$

$$K_{13}(4, 4) = H_{13}(4, 4) + K_{14}(4, 4) = 800 + 900 = 1700$$

$$K_{12}(2, 2) = C_{22}[2, 2] + H_{12}[3, 2] + K_{22}(2, 2) + K_{13}(3, 2)$$
$$= 300 + 0 + 600 + 0 = 900$$

$$K_{12}(2, 3) = \min_{2 \leq \gamma \leq 3} \{C_{22}[2, \gamma] + H_{12}[\gamma + 1, 3] + K_{22}(2, \gamma) + K_{13}(\gamma + 1, 3)\}$$
$$= \min \{300 + 400 + 600 + 900, 300 + 0 + 1200 + 0\}$$
$$= 1500, \quad \text{for } \gamma^* = 3$$

$$K_{12}(2, 4) = \min_{2 \leq \gamma \leq 4} \{C_{22}[2, \gamma] + H_{12}[\gamma + 1, 4] + K_{22}(2, \gamma) + K_{13}(\gamma + 1, 4)\}$$
$$= \min [300 + 1200 + 600 + 1900, 300 + 800 + 1200 + 900,$$
$$300 + 0 + 2600 + 0]$$
$$= 2900, \quad \text{for } \gamma^* = 4$$

$$K_{12}(3, 3) = H_{12}[3, 3] + K_{13}(3, 3) = 400 + 900 = 1300$$

$$K_{12}(3, 4) = H_{12}[3, 4] + K_{13}(3, 4) = 1200 + 1900 = 3100$$

$$K_{12}(4, 4) = H_{12}[4, 4] + K_{13}(4, 4) = 800 + 1700 = 2500$$

$$K_{11}(1, 1) = C_{21}[1, 1] + H_{11}[2, 1] + K_{21}(1, 1) + K_{12}(2, 1)$$
$$= 300 + 0 + 600 + 0 = 900$$

$$K_{11}(1, 2) = \min_{1 \leq \gamma \leq 2} \{C_{21}[1, \gamma] + H_{11}[\gamma + 1, 2] + K_{21}(1, \gamma) + K_{12}(\gamma + 1, 2)\}$$
$$= \min [300 + 600 + 600 + 900, 300 + 0 + 1500 + 0]$$
$$= 1800, \quad \text{for } \gamma^* = 2$$

$$K_{11}(1, 3) = \min_{1 \leq \gamma \leq 3} \{C_{21}[1, \gamma] + H_{11}[\gamma + 1, 3] + K_{21}(1, \gamma) + K_{12}(\gamma + 1, 3)\}$$
$$= \min [300 + 1000 + 600 + 1500, 300 + 400 + 1500 + 1300,$$
$$300 + 0 + 2300 + 0]$$
$$= 2600, \quad \text{for } \gamma^* = 3$$

$$K_{11}(1, 4) = \min_{1 \leq \gamma \leq 4} \{C_{21}[1, \gamma] + H_{11}[\gamma + 1, 4] + K_{21}(1, \gamma) + K_{12}(\gamma + 1, 4)\}$$
$$= \min [300 + 1800 + 600 + 2900, 300 + 1200 + 1500 + 3100,$$
$$300 + 800 + 2300 + 2500, 300 + 0 + 4100 + 0]$$
$$= 4400, \quad \text{for } \gamma^* = 4$$

Finally, we consider the source node and use (4-129) and (4-130):

$$K_{04}(4, 4) = C_{14}[4, 4] + K_{14}(4, 4) = 400 + 900 = 1300$$

$$K_{03}(3, 4) = \min_{3 \le \gamma \le 4} \{C_{13}[3, \gamma] + K_{13}(3, \gamma) + K_{04}(\gamma + 1, 4)\}$$

$$= \min [400 + 900 + 1300, 400 + 1900 + 0]$$

$$= 2300, \quad \text{for } \gamma^* = 4$$

$$K_{03}(4, 4) = \min_{3 \le \gamma \le 4} \{C_{13}[4, \gamma] + K_{13}(4, \gamma) + K_{04}(\gamma + 1, 4)\}$$

$$= [0 + 0 + 1300, 400 + 1700 + 0]$$

$$= 1300, \quad \text{for } \gamma^* = 3 \quad \text{(this means } X_{13} = 0)$$

$$K_{02}(2, 4) = \min_{2 \le \gamma \le 4} \{C_{12}[2, \gamma] + K_{12}(2, \gamma) + K_{03}(\gamma + 1, 4)\}$$

$$= [400 + 900 + 2300, 400 + 1500 + 1300, 400 + 2900 + 0]$$

$$= 3200, \quad \text{for } \gamma^* = 3$$

$$K_{02}(3, 4) = \min_{2 \le \gamma \le 4} \{C_{12}[3, \gamma] + K_{12}(3, \gamma) + K_{03}(\gamma + 1, 4)\}$$

$$= \min [0 + 0 + 2300, 400 + 1300 + 1300, 400 + 3100 + 0]$$

$$= 2300, \quad \text{for } \gamma^* = 2 \quad \text{(this means } X_{12} = 0)$$

$$K_{02}(4, 4) = \min_{3 \le \gamma \le 4} \{C_{12}[4, \gamma] + K_{12}(4, \gamma) + K_{03}(\gamma + 1, 4)\}$$

$$= \min [0 + 0 + 1300, 400 + 2500 + 0]$$

$$= 1300, \quad \text{for } \gamma^* = 3 \quad \text{(this means } X_{12} = 0)$$

$$K_{01}(1, 4) = \min_{1 \le \gamma \le 4} \{C_{11}[1, \gamma] + K_{11}(1, \gamma) + K_{02}(\gamma + 1, 4)\}$$

$$= \min [400 + 900 + 3200, 400 + 1800 + 2300,$$

$$400 + 2600 + 1300, 400 + 4400 + 0]$$

$$= 4300, \quad \text{for } \gamma^* = 3$$

Having completed the computations, we must now work forward to extract the optimal production program, which has a cost of $K_{01}(1, 4) = 4300$. In computing $K_{01}(1, 4)$, we found $\gamma^* = 3$. This means $X_{11}^* = D_1 + D_2 + D_3 = 600$. Furthermore, it tells us that the flow into node (1, 1) is $f(1, 3) = 600$. Now we examine $K_{11}(1, 3)$ and see $\gamma^* = 3$, which implies $X_{21}^* = D_1 + D_2 + D_3 = 600$. This flows into node (2, 1), so we look up $K_{21}(1, 3)$ and find $\gamma^* = 1$. This says that $X_{31}^* = D_1 = 100$ and $I_{21}^* = D_2 + D_3 = 500$. The quantity I_{21}^* flows into node (2, 2), causing us to check the computation of $K_{22}(2, 3)$ and determine $\gamma^* = 3$. This tells us that $X_{32}^* = D_2 + D_3 = 500$. This is shipped into node (3, 2), where $D_2 = 300$ units leave the system and $D_3 = 200$ units move on to node (3, 3) to satisfy the demand in period 3. At this point, we have learned how production in period 1 at stage 1 is used in subsequent stages to meet the demands in periods 1, 2, and 3. Now we need to determine how the demand in period 4 is met by production at stage 1 in periods 2, 3, and 4. Considering $K_{02}(4, 4)$, we find $X_{12}^* = 0$. From $K_{03}(4, 4)$, it is seen that $X_{13}^* = 0$. Thus, $X_{14}^* = D_4 = 400$. Then obviously $X_{24}^* = X_{34}^* = 400$. The optimal solution is summarized in Table 4-16 and illustrated in Figure 4-18.□

TABLE 4-16 Optimal Production Schedule for Example 4-24

PRODUCTION STAGE	PERIOD			
	1	2	3	4
1	600	0	0	400
2	600	0	0	400
3	100	500	0	400

Extension to Permit Backlogging. We now suppose that demand can be backlogged. To accommodate this feature in the network structure, only the nodes for stage M need be altered, because all backlogging is reflected in delivery delays at the final stage. We add a directed arc from node $(M, t + 1)$ to node (M, t) for each $t = 1, 2, \ldots, T - 1$, and define a flow I_{Mt}^- on the arc.

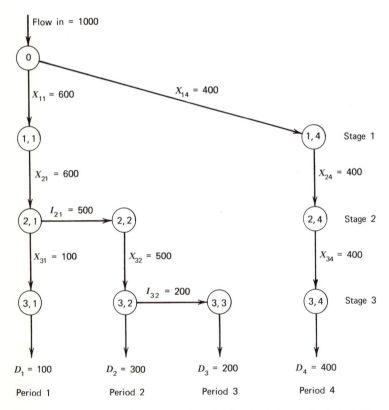

FIGURE 4-18. Network representation of optimal solution to Example 4-24.

This flow is the backlog position at stage M at the end of period t. We also interpret the flow in the directed arc from node (M, t) to $(M, t + 1)$ as $I_{M,t}^+$, the on-hand inventory at stage M at the end of period t. Finally, we define the arc flow cost functions $H_{Mt}^+(I_{Mt}^+)$ and $H_{Mt}^-(I_{Mt}^-)$, to represent the inventory costs and backlogging penalties, respectively, at stage M in period t. These functions are assumed concave for nonnegative arguments. The revised structure for stage M is shown in Figure 4-19, and the revised algebraic model is as follows: Minimize

$$Z = \sum_{t=1}^{T} \left\{ \sum_{j=1}^{M} C_{jt}(X_{jt}) + \sum_{j=1}^{M-1} H_{jt}(I_{jt}) + H_{Mt}^+(I_{Mt}^+) + H_{Mt}^-(I_{Mt}^-) \right\} \quad \text{(4-131a)}$$

subject to the constraints

$$I_{jt} = I_{j,t-1} + X_{jt} - X_{j+1,t}, \qquad (j = 1, 2, \ldots, M - 1) \quad \text{(4-131b)}$$

$$I_{Mt} = I_{M,t-1} + X_{Mt} - D_t \quad \text{(4-131c)}$$

$$I_{Mt} = I_{Mt}^+ - I_{Mt}^- \quad \text{(4-131d)}$$

$$X_{jt} \geq 0, \, I_{jt} \geq 0, \qquad (j = 1, 2, \ldots, M - 1) \quad \text{(4-131e)}$$

$$X_{Mt} \geq 0, \qquad I_{Mt}^+ \geq 0, \qquad I_{Mt}^- \geq 0 \quad \text{(4-131f)}$$

$$I_{j0} = I_{jT} = 0, \qquad (j = 1, 2, \ldots, M) \quad \text{(4-131g)}$$

for all t.

Because the revised network has only a single source and all arc flow costs are concave, we again know that at most one arc leading into a node will have positive flow. This fact leads to the following observations about the possible flows into a node:

1. For the last stage node (M, t), the inward flow $f(\alpha, \beta) = \sum_{r=\alpha}^{\beta} D_r$, for all

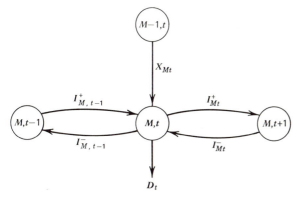

FIGURE 4-19. Flows in and out of node (M, t) with back-logging.

$1 \leq \alpha \leq t \leq \beta \leq T$. For node (M, T), β must equal T and $0 \leq \alpha \leq T$. For node $(M, 1)$, $\alpha = 1$ and $1 \leq \beta \leq T$.

2. At any other node (j, t), $j = 1, 2, \ldots, M - 1$, possible inward flow values are $f(\alpha, \beta)$, $1 \leq \alpha \leq \beta$, $t \leq \beta \leq T$. Except for $t = 1$, when α must be 1, and $t = T$, when $\beta = T$, α can exceed t for node (j, t), $j < M$.

The recursive relation for the last stage is

$$K_{Mt}(\alpha, \beta) = H^-_{M,t-1}[\alpha, t - 1] + H^+_{Mt}[t + 1, \beta] + K_{M,t-1}(\alpha, t - 1)$$
$$+ K_{M,t+1}(t + 1, \beta), \qquad 1 \leq \alpha \leq t \leq \beta \leq T \quad (4\text{-}132)$$

If $t = 1$, $\alpha = 1$:

$$K_{M1}(1, \beta) = H^+_{M1}[2, \beta] + K_{M2}(2, \beta), \qquad 1 \leq \beta \leq T \quad (4\text{-}133)$$

If $t = T$, $\beta = T$:

$$K_{MT}(\alpha, T) = H^-_{Mt}[\alpha, T - 1] + K_{M,T-1}(\alpha, T - 1), \qquad 1 \leq \alpha \leq T \quad (4\text{-}134)$$

The recursions for nodes (j, t), $j < M$, are

$$K_{jt}(\alpha, \beta) = \underset{\max(t,\alpha-1) \leq \gamma \leq \beta}{\text{minimum}} \{C_{j+1,t}[\alpha, \gamma] + H_{jt}[\gamma + 1, \beta]$$
$$+ K_{j+1,t}(\alpha, \gamma) + K_{j,t+1}(\gamma + 1, \beta) \quad (4\text{-}135)$$

which holds for $1 \leq \alpha \leq \beta$, $t \leq \beta \leq T$. If $t = 1$, α must equal 1 in (4-135). For $t = T$, $\beta = T$ and

$$K_{jT}(\alpha, T) = C_{j+1,T}[\alpha, T] + K_{j+1,T}(\alpha, T), \qquad 1 \leq \alpha \leq T \quad (4\text{-}136)$$

Decisions about first-stage production are analyzed using a recursion for $K_{0t}(\alpha, T)$, the minimum cost of satisfying the demands D_α, $D_{\alpha+1}, \ldots, D_T$, through production in periods t, $t + 1, \ldots, T$. Note that except for $t = 1$, when α must be 1, α can be less than t. The equations are

$$K_{0t}(\alpha, t) = \underset{\max(t,\alpha-1) \leq \gamma \leq T}{\text{minimum}} \{C_{1t}[\alpha, \gamma] + K_{1t}(\alpha, \gamma) + K_{0,t+1}(\gamma + 1, T)\} \quad (4\text{-}137)$$

which holds for $2 \leq t \leq T - 1$ and $1 \leq \alpha \leq T$. If $t = 1$, use (4-137) only with $\alpha = 1$. If $t = T$,

$$K_{0T}(\alpha, T) = C_{1T}[\alpha, T] + K_{1T}(\alpha, T), \qquad 1 \leq \alpha \leq T \quad (4\text{-}138)$$

Using Equations 4-132 to 4-138, one can solve for the optimal solution in the same manner as was done for the no-backlog case. However, there will be considerably more computation required because of the additional in-flow quantities possible at each node in the backlog situation.

Transhipment Models When Costs are Linear. Many multistage systems can be formulated as transhipment models and solved by the transportation algorithm (of linear programming). The arc flow costs must be linear (proportional), however. The following example illustrates the approach.

□**EXAMPLE 4-25** A single product is produced by a three-stage serial production system. Demands for the four periods comprising the planning horizon are 100, 300, 200, and 400 units, respectively. The production cost functions are of the form $C_{jt}(X_{jt}) = c_{jt}X_{jt}$, and the inventory holding cost functions are $H_{jt}(I_{jt}) = h_j I_{jt}$. The cost parameters are given in Table 4-17.

The problem as stated is almost identical with that of Example 4-24. We have dropped the fixed component of production cost and have made some changes in the variable production costs. Now we make one more change by allowing backorders at stage 3 in each period (except the last), at a cost of two per unit per period.

The network structure of this problem is that of Figure 4-15, for $M = 3$, with the last stage modified as shown in Figure 4-19 to permit backlogging. There is one source, node (0), and four sinks, nodes (3, 1), (3, 2), (3, 3), and (3, 4). All nodes, except (0), are also transhipment nodes. We form the problem in a transportation tableau (Figure 4-20) by providing a row for each pure source and each transhipment node and a column for each transhipment node and each pure sink (none in the backlog case). The available capacity of each source is the flow into the system at that source. For node (0), this is $\sum_{r=1}^{4} D_r = 1000$. The required quantity for each sink is the flow out of the system at that node. For each transhipment node, including those that are also sources or sinks, we add a quantity Q to both the requirements and the available quantity for that node. This is a device to account for transhipments through the node. Since the maximum amount that could possibly be transhipped through any node in our problem is the total demand over the planning horizon, we use $Q = 1000$. The cost coefficients are production, inventory, or backlog costs, depending on the nature of the arc connecting the row node to the column node.

Once put in the standard transportation tableau, the problem was solved by the transportation algorithm to obtain the minimum cost solution shown in Figure 4-20, and summarized in Tables 4-18 and 4-19 (page 287). The reader should verify that this solution is an arborescence flow by constructing a diagram

TABLE 4-17 Cost Factors for Example 4-25

STAGE	PRODUCTION COST, c_{jt}, IN PERIOD				INVENTORY COST, h_j
	1	2	3	4	
1	20	23	23	25	2
2	15	15	12	12	1
3	30	28	31	27	3

Node	(1,1)	(1,2)	(1,3)	(1,4)	(2,1)	(2,2)	(2,3)	(2,4)	(3,1)	(3,2)	(3,3)	(3,4)	Available quantity
Source	20 / 400	23	23 / 600	25									1000
(1,1)	0 / 600	2			15 / 400								1000
(1,2)		0 / 1000	2			15							1000
(1,3)			0 / 400	2			12 / 600						1000
(1,4)				0 / 1000				12					1000
(2,1)					0 / 600	1 / 300			30 / 100				1000
(2,2)						0 / 700	1			28 / 300			1000
(2,3)							0 / 400	1 / 600			31		1000
(2,4)								0 / 400				27 / 600	1000
(3,1)									0 / 1000	3			1000
(3,2)									2	0 / 1000	3		1000
(3,3)										2	0 / 1000	3	1000
(3,4)											2 / 200	0 / 800	1000
Required quantity	1000	1000	1000	1000	1000	1000	1000	1000	1100	1300	1200	1400	13,000

FIGURE 4-20. Transhipment problem of Example 4-25 in a transportation tableau.

similar to Figure 4-18. This problem, with linear costs, also could have been solved using the algorithm of Zangwill, previously described for the concave cost case. However, the availability of computer codes for solving transportation problems makes the transhipment formulation potentially useful.□

Network Models with Constraints. Considering the network flow model of the single-product multistage problem, we comment briefly on the effect of

TABLE 4-18 Optimal Production Program for Example 4-25

PRODUCTION STAGE	PERIOD			
	1	2	3	4
1	400		600	
2	400		600	
3	100	300		600

adding constraints on the arc flows. These constraints would either limit production, as indicated in (4-139), or inventory, as shown in (4-140):

$$P'_{jt} \leq X_{jt} \leq P_{jt} \qquad (4\text{-}139)$$

$$0 \leq I^+_{jt} \leq L_{jt} \qquad (4\text{-}140\text{a})$$

$$0 \leq I^-_{jt} \leq L'_{jt} \qquad (4\text{-}140\text{b})$$

When such constraints are present in the concave cost case, it no longer is true that the optimal solution has the property that at most one arc leading into a node will have positive flow. Thus, the algorithm of Zangwill, which was based on this property, does not solve the constrained problem.

If costs are linear (proportional), the constrained problem can be solved as a linear programming problem by a simplex-type algorithm or as a constrained network flow problem, using the out-of-kilter algorithm of Ford and Fulkerson (13).

4-8 Stochastic Models

To this point in Chapter 4 we have considered only deterministic models, which do not explicitly account for any uncertainties in the decision problem.

TABLE 4-19 Optimal Ending Net Inventory for Example 4-25

PRODUCTION STAGE	PERIOD			
	1	2	3	4
1	0	0	0	0
2	300	0	600	0
3	0	0	−200	0

In production planning, uncertainty may exist regarding a variety of factors, including product demand, production lead times, production rates, quality losses, selling prices, production costs, and resource availabilities. In Chapters 2 and 3, we presented several stochastic models of simple inventory and production problems, where typically the source of uncertainty was in the demand process. We either assumed a single time period was to be planned, or if there were a sequence of decision points, we assumed a stationary demand distribution and treated the problem as one in steady state. Now we consider the situation where we must plan for a horizon of T periods and all we know about demand is its probability distribution in any period, and that may differ from period to period.

A major difficulty in analyzing dynamic stochastic problems is that a solution for $X_1, X_2, \ldots, X_T$, made at time zero, must recognize that X_2 can be determined after D_1 is known, that X_3 can be based on the realized values of D_1 and D_2, and so on. The analysis at time zero will fix only X_1; the remaining production rates will be random variables whose value depends on the demand actually experienced in prior periods. It is difficult to construct practical models that account for this dependence of the production levels on the sequence of demand values. The common approaches involve either a moving horizon or a fixed horizon structure.

When a moving horizon structure is used, the analysis is repeated at the start of each period, always using a T-period horizon. The linear decision rule model, described in Section 4-4.3, is an example. For that model, it can be shown that use of expected demand in the decision rules developed through deterministic analysis will minimize expected costs. For other models, such as linear programming, we are not so fortunate. In these situations, we usually do not attempt to construct a stochastic model; instead, we assume that the adverse effects of uncertainty will be reduced because we are repeating the analysis each period, using current inventory data and updated forecasts of future demand. Thus, the production level for a period will be planned and replanned several times before we actually become committed to it. Also, we may establish inventory minimums (safety stock) and otherwise use conservative estimates to reflect the uncertainties we have.

In the fixed horizon structure, a given set of T periods is planned at time zero and the production rates are revised according to certain rules as time passes. However, no consideration is ever given to periods beyond the original set of T. In Section 4-5, we described a situation where a deterministic model was used initially to establish production and inventory goals for each period in the planning horizon and then a heuristic production control rule was used to adjust production rates as demand materialized. In the remainder of this section, we shall describe two fixed horizon approaches to constructing stochastic models that, at time zero, will develop a production plan that includes specific rules for determining any period's production rate after the demands in all prior periods are known. The first approach is dynamic programming and the second is separable convex programming.

4-8.1 Dynamic Programming Models for a Single Product

We now give a general dynamic programming model of a single-stage production planning problem under dynamic stochastic demand. Only a single product is produced, and we assume all shortages are backlogged. This is an extension of the model of Section 4-3.1 to the stochastic case. As in that section, we let X_t be the production rate in period t, I_t be the net inventory at the end of period t, $K_t(X_t, I_t)$ be the production, inventory, and backorder costs in period t, and D_t be the demand in period t, a random variable having known probability distribution $g_t(D_t)$. Assume the $\{D_t\}$ are mutually independent.

Let $f_t(I)$ be the *minimum expected cost* over the periods $t, t + 1, \ldots, T$, when I is the net inventory position at the start of period t. Then,

$$f_t(I) = \min_{X_t \geq 0} \left\{ \int_{-\infty}^{\infty} [K_t(X_t, I + X_t - D_t) + f_{t+1}(I + X_t - D_t)]g_t(D_t)\,dD_t \right\}$$

$$= \min_{X_t \geq 0} \left[\overline{K}_t(X_t) + \int_{-\infty}^{\infty} f_{t+1}(I + X_t - D_t)g_t(D_t)\,dD_t \right] \qquad (4\text{-}141)$$

where $\overline{K}_t(X_t)$ is the expected cost in period t. If we assume

$$K_t(X_t, I_t) = C_t(X_t) + H_t^+(I_t^+) + H_t^-(I_t^-)$$

where I_t^+ and I_t^- are the on-hand inventory and backorder level, respectively, at the end of period t, we have, for a given starting inventory I,

$$\overline{K}_t(X_t) = \int_{-\infty}^{\infty} C_t(X_t)g_t(D_t)\,dD_t + \int_{-\infty}^{I+X_t} H_t^+(I + X_t - D_t)g_t(D_t)\,dD_t$$

$$+ \int_{I+X_t}^{\infty} H_t^-(D_t - I - X_t)g_t(D_t)\,dD_t \qquad (4\text{-}142)$$

For completeness, we define $f_{T+1}(I) \equiv 0$.

The backward recursion (4-141) is solved first for $t = T$, then for $t = T - 1$, and so on, until $f_1(I)$ is obtained. This is the minimum cost for the T-period planning horizon. Given the initial inventory, one then can immediately find the optimal production level for period 1, X_1^*; however, it is not possible to state precisely the production rates that will be used in later periods. These will depend on the actual demand and production that are realized up to the start of the period in question, because they will determine the initial inventory for the period. As we proceed through time, we easily can determine the best

Stochastic Models   289

production rate for a period t, once I_{t-1} is known. No additional computations are required, since we had to obtain $f_t(I_{t-1})$ for every possible value of I_{t-1} in solving for $f_1(I_0)$.

If, at time zero, it is important to have estimates of the production rate for each period in the planning horizon, one can compute the expected inventory level at the start of a period and thereby obtain the expected production rate for that period. This is done in sequence, starting with the first period.

Exercises 4-78 and 4-79 require development of dynamic programming models for situations where some or all of the shortages are lost.

4-8.2 Chance-Constrained Programming Models

As an alternative to a dynamic programming formulation, we now shall consider a mathematical programming model. Let X_t be the production rate for period t, which will be determined after the demands $D_1, D_2, \ldots, D_{t-1}$ are known. Assume that the production lead time is negligible and that backlogging is permitted. Our policy will be stated as a sequence $R_1, R_2, \ldots, R_T$, from which we determine the production level in any period t by the rule $X_t = R_t - I_{t-1}$. (For the moment, assume that the random variable I_{t-1} will not be greater than R_t.) If I_0 is the initial inventory,

$$X_1 = R_1 - I_0$$
$$X_2 = R_2 - I_1$$
$$= R_2 - (I_0 + X_1 - D_1)$$
$$= R_2 - R_1 + D_1$$

and in general,

$$X_t = R_t - I_{t-1}$$
$$= R_t - (I_{t-2} + X_{t-1} - D_{t-1})$$
$$= R_t - R_{t-1} + D_{t-1} \qquad (4\text{-}143)$$

Now, define

$$\gamma_1 = R_1 - I_0 \qquad (4\text{-}144a)$$
$$\gamma_t = R_t - R_{t-1}, \qquad (t = 2, 3, \ldots, T) \qquad (4\text{-}144b)$$

Then our policy can be put in terms of the $\{\gamma_t\}$:

$$X_1 = \gamma_1 \qquad (4\text{-}145a)$$
$$X_t = \gamma_t + D_{t-1}, \qquad (t = 2, 3, \ldots) \qquad (4\text{-}145b)$$

The net inventory level at the end of period t is

$$I_t = I_0 + \sum_{j=1}^{t}(X_j - D_j)$$

$$= I_0 + \sum_{j=1}^{t}\gamma_j - D_t, \qquad (t = 1, 2, \ldots, T) \qquad (4\text{-}146)$$

To illustrate the determination of the optimal $\{\gamma_t\}$ by mathematical programming, we give a chance-constrained model of the type used by Charnes and Cooper in Reference 1 of Chapter 3. Suppose that the production cost in period t is a *convex* function, $C_t(X_t)$, of the quantity produced and that the inventory holding cost in period t is proportional to the ending on-hand inventory. No backlogging costs are to be included in the objective function; instead, we shall require the probability of a shortage to be small for each period. Because backlogging will not be extensive, we will approximate the on-hand ending inventory for a period by the ending net inventory, and write the inventory cost in period t as $h_t I_t$.

Letting $g_t(D_t)$ be the density function of D_t and using (4-145) and (4-146), we obtain the following expression for the expected costs over the planning horizon:

$$E(Z) = \sum_{t=1}^{T}\left\{\int_{-\infty}^{\infty} C_t(\gamma_t + D_{t-1})g_{t-1}(D_{t-1})\, dD_{t-1}\right.$$

$$\left. + h_t\left[I_0 + \sum_{j=1}^{t}\gamma_j - E(D_t)\right]\right\} \qquad (4\text{-}147)$$

This function is to be minimized, subject to the chance constraints

$$P\{I_t \geq L_t\} \geq \alpha_t, \qquad (\alpha_t \text{ large}) \qquad (4\text{-}148)$$

and

$$P\{X_t \geq 0\} = 1 \qquad (4\text{-}149)$$

for $t = 1, 2, \ldots, T$.

In Equation 4-148, L_t is the desired lower bound on net inventory and α_t is the desired minimum probability that the net inventory will actually exceed L_t. Both α_t and L_t are determined subjectively for each period. To show that this condition implies a linear constraint on the $\{\gamma_t\}$, we use (4-146) to write (4-148) as

$$P\left\{I_0 + \sum_{j=1}^{t}\gamma_j - L_t \geq D_t\right\} \geq \alpha_t$$

This implies that

$$I_0 + \sum_{j=1}^{t}\gamma_j - L_t \geq G_t^{-1}(\alpha_t) \qquad (4\text{-}150)$$

where $G_t(D_t)$ is the cumulative probability distribution of D_t and $G_t^{-1}(\alpha)$ is

100αth percentile of G_t. The right-hand side of (4-150) can be calculated or possibly read from a table, once the form of $g_t(D_t)$ is selected.

The constraint (4-149) is to insure that our decision rules do not specify a negative production level. If the smallest value (realistically) possible for D_t is $(D_t)_{\min}$, we can write this constraint as a linear function of γ_t:

$$\gamma_t + (D_{t-1})_{\min} \geq 0 \qquad (4\text{-}151)$$

Since the production cost functions are assumed to be convex, the objective function is of the form

$$E(Z) = \sum_{t=1}^{T} K_t(\gamma_t) \qquad (4\text{-}152)$$

where $K_t(\gamma_t)$ is convex in γ_t. Thus $E(Z)$ is a separable convex function of the $\{\gamma_t\}$, which is to be minimized subject to a set of linear constraints. This can be done relatively easily using the separable convex programming features available with some of the more recent linear programming software packages.

Once the $\{\gamma_t^*\}$ are found, the rule (4-145) is used to plan production as time passes; or, if it is desired, the $\{R_t^*\}$ may be computed from (4-144) and production planned by the rule $X_t^* = R_t^* - I_{t-1}$. There is no need to do any additional analysis unless the forecast of the demand distributions changes significantly. If this happens, the mathematical programming model must be solved again, using the new forecasts, either to the end of the original planning horizon or to a new horizon.

If we wish to incorporate backlogging costs in the objective function, we must include the expected on-hand inventory and the expected backorder position at the end of period t in our model. Then,

$$E(Z) = \sum_{t=1}^{T} \left\{ \int_{-\infty}^{\infty} C_t(\gamma_t + D_{t-1})g_{t-1}(D_{t-1})\, dD_{t-1} \right.$$
$$\left. + h_t \int_{-\infty}^{a} (a - D_t)g_t(D_t)\, dD_t + \pi_t \int_{a}^{\infty} (D_t - a)g_t(D_t)\, dD_t \right\} \qquad (4\text{-}153a)$$

where a is a function of t,

$$a = I_0 + \sum_{j=1}^{t} \gamma_j \qquad (4\text{-}153b)$$

and π_t is the backorder cost per unit in period t. The function (4-153) must be minimized subject to (4-151). This is not a simple matter, since (4-153a) is no longer a separable convex function of the $\{\gamma_t\}$. The difficulty of solving this more exact formulation in part explains the use of the chance-constrained model. (For an application of the latter, see Reference 1 of Chapter 3.)

We should point out that a randomized decision rule (see Section 3-7.1) may be superior to the deterministic rule (4-145) when the problem contains chance constraints such as (4-148). Since we only considered nonrandomized strategies, the methods described here may lead to a suboptimal policy.

Production Planning—Dynamic Models   292

4-9 References

1. **Bergstrom, G. L., and B. E. Smith,** "Multi-Item Production Planning—An Extension of the HMMS Rules," *Management Science*, **16** (10), 1970, B614–B629.

2. **Bowman, E. H.,** "Production Scheduling by the Transportation Method of Linear Programming," *Operations Research*, **3** (1), 1956, 100–103.

3. **Bowman, E. H.,** "Consistency and Optimality in Managerial Decision Making," *Management Science*, **9** (2), 1963, 310–321.

4. **Buffa, E. S., and W. H. Taubert,** *Production-Inventory Systems: Planning and Control*, Revised Edition, Richard D. Irwin, Homewood, Ill., 1972.

5. **Chang, R. H., and C. M. Jones,** "Production-Workforce Scheduling Extensions," *AIIE Transactions*, **2** (4), 1970, 326–333.

6. **Damon, W. W., and R. Schramm,** "A Simultaneous Decision Model for Production, Marketing and Finance," *Management Science*, **19** (2), 1972, 161–172.

7. **Denzler, D. R.,** "A Heuristic Production Lot Scheduling Model," *AIIE Transactions*, **2** (1), 1970, 59–63.

8. **Dzielinski, B. P., C. T. Baker, and A. S. Manne,** "Simulation Tests of Lot-Size Programming," *Management Science*, **9** (2), 1963, 229–258.

9. **Dzielinski, B. P., and R. E. Gomory,** "Optimal Programming of Lot Sizes, Inventory and Labor Allocations," *Management Science*, **11** (9), 1965, 875–890.

10. **Elmaghraby, S. E., and V. Y. Bawle,** "Optimization of Batch Ordering Under a Deterministic Variable Demand," *Management Science*, **18** (9), 1972, 508–517.

11. **Florian, M., and M. Klein,** "Deterministic Production Planning with Concave Costs and Capacity Constraints," *Management Science*, **18** (1), 1971, 12–20.

12. **Florian, M., and P. Robillard,** "An Implicit Enumeration Algorithm for the Concave Cost Network Flow Problem," *Management Science*, **18** (3), 1971, 184–193.

13. **Ford, L. R., and D. R. Fulkerson,** *Flows in Networks*, Princeton University Press, Princeton, N.J., 1962.

14. **Gorenstein, S.,** "Planning Tire Production," *Management Science*, **17** (2), 1970, 372–382.

15. **Groff, G. K., and J. F. Muth,** *Operations Management: Analysis for Decisions*, Richard D. Irwin, Homewood, Ill., 1972.

16. **Hadley, G.,** *Nonlinear and Dynamic Programming*, Addison-Wesley, Reading, Mass., 1964.

17. **Hanssmann, F., and S. W. Hess,** "A Linear Programming Approach to Production and Employment Scheduling," *Management Technology*, **1** (1), 1960, 46–51.

18. **Hanssmann, F.,** *Operations Research in Production and Inventory Control*, John Wiley & Sons, New York, 1962.

19. **Hausman, W. H., and J. O. McClain,** "A Note on the Bergstrom-Smith Multi-Item Production Planning Model," *Management Science,* **17** (11), 1971, 783–785.

20. **Holt, C. C., F. Modigliani, and H. A. Simon,** "A Linear Decision Rule for Production and Employment Scheduling," *Management Science,* **2** (1), 1955, 1–30.

21. **Holt, C. C., F. Modigliani, and J. F. Muth,** "Derivation of a Linear Decision Rule for Production and Employment," *Management Science,* **2** (2), 1956, 159–177.

22. **Holt, C. C., F. Modigliani, J. F. Muth, and H. A. Simon,** *Planning Production, Inventories and Work Force,* Prentice-Hall, Englewood Cliffs, N.J., 1960.

23. **Johnson, S. M.,** "Sequential Production Planning over Time at Minimum Cost," *Management Science,* **3** (4), 1957, 435–437.

24. **Jones, C. H.,** "Parametric Production Planning," *Management Science,* **13** (11), 1967, 843–866.

25. **Kalymon, B. A.,** "A Decomposition Algorithm for Arborescence Inventory Systems," *Operations Research,* **20** (4), 1972, 860–873.

26. **Kortanek, K., and A. L. Soyster,** "On the Status of Some Multi-Product Multi-Period Production Scheduling Models," *Management Science,* **17** (8), 1971, B560–B561.

27. **Kortanek, K. O., D. Sodaro, and A. L. Soyster,** "Multi-Product Production Scheduling via Extreme Point Properties of Linear Programming," *Naval Research Logistics Quarterly,* **15** 1968, 287–300.

28. **Lasdon, L. S., and R. C. Terjung,** "An Efficient Algorithm for Multi-Item Scheduling," *Operations Research,* **19** (4), 1971, 946–969.

29. **Lippman, S. A., A. J. Rolfe, H. M. Wagner, and J. S. C. Yaun,** "Optimal Production Scheduling and Employment Smoothing with Deterministic Demands," *Management Science,* **14** (3), 1967, 127–158.

30. **Lippman, S. A., A. J. Rolfe, H. M. Wagner, and J. S. C. Yaun,** "Algorithm for Optimal Production Scheduling and Employment Smoothing," *Operations Research,* **15** (6), 1967, 1011–1029.

31. **Love, S. F.,** "A Facilities in Series Inventory Model with Nested Schedules," *Management Science,* **18** (5), 1972, 327–338.

32. **Magee, J. R.,** *Production Planning and Inventory Control,* McGraw-Hill, New York, 1958.

33. **Manne, Alan S.,** "Programming of Economic Lot Sizes," *Management Science,* **4** (2), 1958, 115–135.

34. **Peterson, R.,** "Optimal Smoothing of Shipments in Response to Orders," *Management Science,* **17** (9), 1971, 597–607.

35. **Silver, E. A.,** "A Tutorial on Production Smoothing and Work Force Balancing," *Operations Research,* **15** (6), 1967, 985–1010.

36. **Sobel, M. J.,** "Production Smoothing with Stochastic Demand I: Finite Horizon Case," *Management Science*, **16** (3), 1969, 195–207.

37. **Sobel, M. J.,** "Smoothing Start-up and Shut-down Costs in Sequential Production," *Operations Research*, **17** (1), 1969, 133–144.

38. **Sobel, M. J.,** "Making Short-Run Changes in Production when the Employment Level is Fixed," *Operations Research*, **18** (1), 1970, 35–51.

39. **Sobel, M. J.,** "Smoothing Start-up and Shut-down Costs: Concave Case," *Management Science*, **17** (1), 1970, 78–91.

40. **Sobel, M. J.,** "Production Smoothing with Stochastic Demand II: Infinite Horizon Case," *Management Science*, **17** (11), 1971, 724–735.

41. **Taubert, W. H.,** "A Search Decision Rule for the Aggregate Scheduling Problem," *Management Science*, **14** (6), 1967, B343–B359.

42. **Veinott, A. F.,** "The Status of Mathematical Inventory Theory," *Management Science*, **12** (11), 1966, 745–777.

43. **Veinott, A. F.,** "Minimum Concave-Cost Solution of Leontief Substitution Models of Multi-Facility Inventory Systems," *Operations Research*, **17** (2), 1969, 262–291.

44. **Vergin, R. C.,** "Production Scheduling under Seasonal Demand," *Journal of Industrial Engineering*, **17** (5), 1966, 260–266.

45. **Wagner, H. M., and T. M. Whitin,** "Dynamic Version of the Economic Lot Size Model," *Management Science*, **5** (1), 1959, 89–96.

46. **Wagner, H. M.,** *Principles of Operations Research*, Prentice-Hall, Englewood Cliffs, N.J., 1969.

47. **Zabel, E.,** "Some Generalizations of an Inventory Planning Horizon Theorem," *Management Science*, **10** (3), 1964, 465–471.

48. **Zangwill, W. I.,** "A Deterministic Multi-Period Production Scheduling Model with Backlogging," *Management Science*, **13** (1), 1966, 105–119.

49. **Zangwill, W. I.,** "Production Smoothing of Economic Lot Sizes with Non-Decreasing Requirements," *Management Science*, **13** (3), 1966, 191–209.

50. **Zangwill, W. I.,** "A Deterministic Multiproduct, Multifacility Production and Inventory Model," *Operations Research*, **14** (3), 1966, 486–507.

51. **Zangwill, W. I.,** "Minimum Concave Cost Flows in Certain Networks," *Management Science*, **14** (7), 1968, 429–450.

52. **Zangwill, W. I.,** "A Backlogging Model and a Multi-Echelon Model of a Dynamic Economic Lot Size Production System—A Network Approach," *Management Science*, **15** (9), 1969, 506–527.

53. **Zoller, K.,** "Optimal Disaggregation of Aggregate Production Plans," *Management Science*, **17** (8), 1971, B533–B549.

4-10 Exercises

4-1 Compare the total costs of the two plans presented in Example 4-1, using the following cost factors:

Regular time unit variable production cost $100
Overtime unit variable production cost $110
Subcontracted unit cost $130
Inventory holding cost per unit per period $2
Backorder cost per unit per period $6
Production rate change cost per unit/period increase or decrease $10

Next, develop a third plan that involves no shortages and compute its cost.

4-2 Consider the model (4-1) presented in Section 4-2.1. First show that (4-1c) can be written as

$$I_t = I_0 + \sum_{k=1}^{t} \sum_{i=1}^{m} X_{ik} - \sum_{k=1}^{t} D_k, \qquad (t = 1, 2, \ldots, T)$$

Next, use this result to eliminate the inventory variables from the model and obtain the following formulation in terms of only the production variables:

$$\text{minimize} \quad Z = \sum_{t=1}^{T} \sum_{i=1}^{m} \left(c_{it} + \sum_{k=t}^{T} h_t \right) X_{it} + \text{(constant)}$$

subject to

$$X_{it} \le P_{it}, \qquad (i = 1, 2, \ldots, m; t = 1, 2, \ldots, T)$$

$$I_0 + \sum_{k=1}^{t} \sum_{i=1}^{m} X_{ik} \ge \sum_{k=1}^{t} D_k, \qquad (t = 1, 2, \ldots, T)$$

$$X_{it} \ge 0, \qquad (i = 1, 2, \ldots, m; t = 1, 2, \ldots, T)$$

Furthermore, show that if the inventory carrying cost is the same for every period, the objective function can be simplified somewhat to

$$Z = \sum_{t=1}^{T} \sum_{i=1}^{m} [c_{it} + (T - t + 1)h] X_{it} + \text{(constant)}$$

Is there any advantage to this formulation over that of model (4-1)?

4-3 Show how you would treat each of the following in the tableau format for the transportation model (Figure 4-2):

(a) Requirement that the inventory at the end of period T be a given value, I_T^*.

(b)   Requirement that the inventory at the end of each period be at least I^*.

(c)   Requirement that the inventory at the end of period t be I_t^*, for $t = 1, 2, \ldots, T$.

4-4   In the tableau format for the transportation model (Figure 4-2), how would you incorporate the requirement that the planned production by process i in period j be at least P_{ij}^*, where $P_{ij}^* < P_{ij}$?

4-5   In the tableau format for the transportation model (Figure 4-2), how would you allow backlogging at a backorder cost of π per unit backordered per period of time? Also show how models (4-1) and (4-2) would be modified for the backorder case.

4-6   Show how the algebraic models (4-1) and (4-2) would be modified to account for multiple products. Assume that the product requirements and the production capacities have a common unit of measurement, such as machine-hours or man-hours. How would Figure 4-2 be changed?

4-7   Only inventory and procurement costs are relevant to the following four-period production planning problem:

	PERIOD 1	PERIOD 2	PERIOD 3	PERIOD 4
Regular time production capacity	100	100	60	100
Overtime production capacity	20	20	10	10
Subcontracting source capacity	40	40	40	40
Regular time unit cost	$15	$16	$18	$20
Overtime unit cost	17	19	21	24
Subcontracting unit cost	20	21	22	23
Demand requirements	90	110	100	115

The initial inventory is five units. No shortages are to be planned. The inventory carrying cost is $1 per unit per period. Solve for the optimal procurement schedule.

4-8   For the situation of Exercise 4-7, what is the optimal production program if shortages can be backlogged at a cost of $2.20 per unit per period? Assume that no backorders are allowed at the end of the final period.

4-9   The following five-period production planning problem involves only production and inventory costs:

CAPACITIES AND UNIT COSTS

PERIOD	REQUIRE-MENTS	REGULAR TIME	OVERTIME	SUB-CONTRACTING
1	200	300 ($10)	100 ($13)	100 ($12)
2	400	300 ($10)	50 ($13)	100 ($15)
3	600	300 ($14)	100 ($13)	100 ($17)
4	500	400 ($13)	150 ($18)	100 ($19)
5	300	500 ($10)	100 ($18)	—

No shortages are allowed. The cost of storing a unit from one period to the next is $1.75. The initial inventory is 20 units.

(a) Develop the transportation tableau and solve for the optimal program.

(b) What is the solution if you must have a final inventory of 100 units?

(c) What is the solution if you must have an inventory of at least 100 units at the end of each period?

4-10 Suppose in the situation of Exercise 4-9, that backorders are allowed and that the cost to backlog one unit for one period is estimated to be $2.10. What is the optimal production program, if the only inventory constraint is that the final net inventory be zero?

4-11 For the situation of Exercise 4-9, suppose the company desires to stabilize production by requiring that, for every period, scheduled production must be at least 80 percent of regular time capacity.

(a) Formulate an algebraic model.

(b) Develop a transportation tableau for this problem and solve.

4-12 Production of a single product is to be planned over a horizon of T periods. The requirements, $D_1, D_2, \ldots, D_T$, are given. The cost in period t is assumed to be of the form

$$K_t(X_t, X_{t-1}, I_t) = c_t X_t + h_t I_t^+ + \pi_t I_t^- + \lambda_t |X_t - X_{t-1}|$$

where c_t, h_t, π_t, and λ_t are nonnegative constants and X_t, I_t^+, and I_t^- are nonnegative decision variables, having their usual meaning. Suppose it is required that $X_t \leq P_t$ and $I_t^+ \leq L_t$ in period t, $t = 1, 2, \ldots, T$. How would you solve this problem? Write the model.

4-13 Formulate the following single product, multiperiod production planning problem as a linear programming model:

PERIOD	DEMAND IN UNITS	UNIT PRODUCTION COST	UNIT CARRYING COST	COST OF UNIT CHANGE IN PRODUCTION RATE	
				DECREASE	INCREASE
1	100	$200	$10	$3	$4
2	150	195	10	4	6
3	120	210	10	3	6
4	180	200	10	3	6

The initial inventory is 10 units and the minimum inventory at the end of any period is to be 5 units. The plant is currently set up to produce at the rate of 110 units per period. Can this problem be solved by the transportation method?

4-14 *Production Lead Time.* In the model (4-3) of Section 4-2.2, suppose there is a time lag between production and the earliest use of a product. In particular, suppose that a unit produced in period t can be used to satisfy customer demand in period $t + \tau$, at the earliest. What modifications should be made to the model?

4-15 *Periods of Different Length.* In model (4-3) of Section 4-2.2, the production change costs were formulated assuming that all periods in the planning horizon were of the same length, so that the production quantities $\{X_t\}$ could also be interpreted as production rates (production per unit time), with the unit of time equal to the length of a period. How would you reformulate the model if periods were of different lengths? Let ζ_t be the length of period t. Also consider the effect on the determination of the inventory and backlog costs, h_t and π_t.

4-16 *Limitation on Backlogging.* In model (4-3) of Section 4-2.2, there was no limitation on the backorder level. Management may wish to impose one or both of the following types of constraints, as a matter of policy: (1) the maximum backorder position at the end of period t should be L'_t; (2) all demand should be satisfied within α periods. Reformulate the model adding these two constraints.

4-17 *Single Product Planning with Capacity Change Costs.* Formulate the following single product dynamic production planning problem as a linear programming model. Requirements $D_1, D_2, \ldots, D_T$ are given for the T-period planning horizon. Backorders are allowed in every period except the last. Unit inventory and backlog costs are h_t and π_t, respectively. Within each period, there are two sources of production, regular time at a unit cost of c_t and overtime at a unit cost of c_t'. Overtime capacity is a fraction θ of regular time capacity, P_t. Regular time capacity can be varied from period to period at a cost (by hiring workers, adding machines, and so on). Let P_0 be the regular time capacity at time zero, u_t and v_t be the capacity increase and decrease, respectively, planned for period t, and a_t and a_t' be the unit costs of capacity increases and decreases, respectively, in period t.

4-18 *Continuation of 4-17 to Include the Cost of Maintaining Capacity.* From the model of the problem of Exercise 4-17, note that it will never be desirable to reduce capacity. Why? Since this can be considered a deficiency of the model in a situation where money may be saved by lowering the capacity level, we may want to add to the objective function the term $\sum_{t=1}^{T} \alpha_t P_t$, where α_t is the cost of operating the production system per unit of capacity in period t. Does this simple extension appear reasonable? Discuss, considering the situation where capacity is a function of work force level and the case where it is a function of machinery and facilities primarily. How would you determine α_t? Can you think of other approaches to modeling the cost of capacity in a linear programming framework?

4-19 Formulate a linear programming model for the following production planning problem:

Number of time periods   3
Demand schedule $D_1 = 45, D_2 = 52, D_3 = 60$
Current regular time capacity   45 units per period
Overtime capacity   25 percent of regular time capacity
Unit variable cost $800 on regular time, $1000 on overtime
Inventory carrying cost $12 per unit per period
Cost to add one unit of capacity $240
Cost to reduce capacity by one unit $180
No shortages are to be planned

Note that the decision variables are the production level and capacity change in each period.

4-20 A manufacturer, producing a single product having a seasonal demand, is faced with decisions about production levels, work force size, and overtime during a planning horizon of six weeks. His capacity is determined by his work force level, which presently is 100 people, each working a 40-hour work week. Overtime, up to eight hours a week per man, is possible. Labor costs average $5 per hour, resulting in an overtime rate of $7.50 per hour. It takes 6.0 man-hours to produce a unit of product. Product costs other than labor are $50 per unit. The cost to carry a unit of inventory for one week is 40 cents. Shortages are back-ordered at an estimated cost of $1 per unit per week; however, company policy is to fill all orders within a two-week period. Costs to change work force are based on an estimated $240 to hire and train a worker and $180 to lay off a worker. Estimated requirements by week are 650, 700, 800, 900, 800, and 700 units. The current inventory level is 50 units. Formulate this problem as a linear programming model, assuming that new workers are able to produce at 100 percent effectiveness in the period they are hired.

4-21 *Continuation of 4-20 to Allow for Training and Production Lead Times.* Reformulate the model of Exercise 4-20 to account for each of the following variations:

(a) A worker hired in week t is not productive until week $t + 2$, when he completes training and starts work at 100 percent effectiveness.

(b) A worker hired in week t is not productive in week t, is 50 percent effective in week $t + 1$, and is 100 percent effective in week $t + 2$. (*Note:* By 50 percent effectiveness, we mean one unit per 12 man-hours.)

(c) Production scheduled for week t cannot be used to satisfy customer demand until period $t + 1$.

4-22 Solve the following three-period production planning problem using the dynamic programming model (4-5):

Demand: $D_1 = 2, D_2 = 4, D_3 = 1$
Demand and production are integer valued
No shortages are allowed
Initial and final inventories are zero

$$K_t(X_t, I_t) = \begin{cases} A_t + c_t X_t + h_t I_t, & \text{if } X_t > 0 \\ h_t I_t, & \text{if } X_t = 0 \end{cases}$$

Costs: $A_1 = 10, A_2 = 10, A_3 = 15, c_1 = 4, c_2 = 6, c_3 = 6,$
$h_1 = h_2 = h_3 = 1$

4-23 Solve the problem of Exercise 4-22 under each of the following additional conditions:

(a) The maximum production rate in any period is three units.

(b) The maximum inventory level at the end of any period is two units.

(c) Inventory is not to be carried into a period where production takes place; that is, $I_{t-1} X_t = 0$, for each period t.

Comment on how each of the above conditions reduces the computational effort required in solving 4-22.

4-24 Draw the network flow model for the six-period production program, $X_1 = 25, X_2 = 0, X_3 = 0, X_4 = 40, X_5 = 0,$ and $X_6 = 15,$ developed to satisfy demands $D_1 = 10, D_2 = 15, D_3 = 20, D_4 = 10, D_5 = 10,$ and $D_6 = 15.$ (See Figure 4-8.) Omit all arcs having zero flow. Note the treelike structure of the network, in the sense that at most one arc carries flow into a node. This type of flow is called an *arborescence* flow.

4-25 Solve the following three-period production planning problem using dynamic programming methods:

> Demand: $D_1 = 2, D_2 = 4, D_3 = 1$
> Demand and production are integer valued
> Shortages are backlogged
> Initial and final inventories are zero

$$K_t(X_t, I_t^+, I_t^-) = \begin{cases} A_t + c_t X_t + h_t I_t^+ + \pi_t I_t^-, & \text{if } X_t > 0 \\ h_t I_t^+ + \pi_t I_t^-, & \text{if } X_t = 0 \end{cases}$$

> Costs: $A_1 = 20, A_2 = 10, A_3 = 15, c_1 = 4, c_2 = 6, c_3 = 6,$
> $h_1 = h_2 = h_3 = 1, \pi_1 = \pi_2 = \pi_3 = 2$

Also solve the problem for the case where all shortages are lost sales at a cost of 10 per unit short in any period.

4-26 *Planning Horizon Result, Convex Cost Case.* Suppose that the production cost function is convex in the amount produced and is the same from period to period. Assume that no shortages are permitted and that inventory holding costs are negligible. There is no upper limit on production or inventory in a period. Define the cumulative demand through period t to be

$$R_t = \sum_{j=1}^{t} D_j, \qquad t = 1, 2, \ldots, T$$

and assume $R_0 = 0.$ The optimal solution can be obtained by first finding a set of integers

$$0 \equiv n_0 < n_1 < n_2 < \cdots < n_p \equiv T$$

by repeated use of the formula

$$\bar{D}(n_i, n_{i+1}) = \max \{\bar{D}(n_i, t); n_i < t \leq T\}$$

where $\bar{D}(n, t)$ is the average demand over periods $n + 1, n + 2, \ldots, t,$ and is computed by

$$\bar{D}(n, t) = \frac{R_t - R_n}{t - n}$$

An optimal solution is then

$$X_t^* = \bar{D}(n_i, n_{i+1}), \quad \text{for } n_i < t \leq n_{i+1}, \qquad i = 0, 1, \ldots, p - 1$$

Production Planning—Dynamic Models   302

In using the above, one first finds n_1, then n_2, then n_3, and so on. The $\{n_i\}$ are regeneration points and the production rate in periods between successive regeneration points is constant. Once n_1 has been determined, the finding of n_2 may proceed without consideration of the first n_1 periods. Thus n_1 could be called a planning horizon. (See Reference 42, p. 747 and Reference 46, p. 302.)

(a) Prove this algorithm yields an optimal solution.

(b) Show that if $D_{t+1} \geq D_t$ for all t, then $n_1 = T$ and $X_t^* = \bar{D}(0, T)$, for $t = 1, 2, \ldots, T$.

(c) Show that if $D_{t+1} \leq D_t$ for all t, then $n_i = i$, $p = T$, and $X_t^* = D_t$, for $t = 1, 2, \ldots T$.

(d) Use the algorithm to solve the following problem:

$$
\begin{array}{ccc}
D_1 = 4 & D_4 = 10 & D_7 = 15 \\
D_2 = 6 & D_5 = 6 & D_8 = 9 \\
D_3 = 10 & D_6 = 4 & D_9 = 12 \\
& C(X_t) = X_t^2 &
\end{array}
$$

4-27   Wagner (46, p. 300) gives the following result for the convex cost model of Section 4-3.3. Define R_t to be the cumulative demand and P_t to be the cumulative production through period t of a T-period planning horizon. That is,

$$
R_t = \sum_{j=1}^{t} D_j \quad \text{and} \quad P_t = \sum_{j=1}^{t} X_j
$$

Assume that there is some uncertainty about the $\{D_t\}$ and that the only firm statements that can be made about demand are of the form $\alpha_t \leq R_t \leq \beta_t$, for $t = 1, 2, \ldots, T$. If $P_t(\alpha)$ is an optimal production schedule assuming $R_t = \alpha_t$ and if $P_t(\beta)$ is an optimal production schedule assuming $R_t = \beta_t$, for $t = 1, 2, \ldots, T$, then the schedule that would be optimal for the demand actually realized has the property

$$
P_t(\alpha) \leq P_t^* \leq P_t(\beta)
$$

(a) Prove this result.

(b) Explain how this could be of value in production planning.

4-28   Example 4-3 in Section 4-3.3 was formulated as a transportation problem (Table 4-6), but the optimal solution was obtained by applying the special algorithm for the convex cost case. Solve the problem using the transportation method of linear programming and compare results.

4-29   *Convex Inventory Costs.* Consider the single product planning problem described by (4-3). Now suppose that the inventory holding costs in period t are charged at h_t per unit of on-hand inventory up to L_t units and h'_t, $h'_t > h_t$, per unit of on-hand inventory in excess of L_t. Also suppose that backorder costs are computed based on π_t per unit up to B_t units and π'_t, $\pi'_t > \pi_t$, for shortages over B_t. Rewrite the model to form a new linear programming problem incorporating these features. Would your model be appropriate if $h'_t < h_t$ or $\pi'_t < \pi_t$?

4-30 Consider a three-period production planning problem in which there can be both regular time and overtime production in each period. In every period, the regular time capacity is two units and the overtime capacity is two units. Demands in periods 1, 2, and 3 are two, seven, and three units, respectively. Regular time production cost is $4 per unit and overtime production cost is $7 per unit. Inventory holding costs are $1 per unit per period and backlogging costs are $2 per unit per period. There is no initial inventory and the final net inventory is to be zero. All shortages are backlogged.

(a) Construct the transportation tableau for this problem.

(b) Solve, using the transportation algorithm.

(c) Solve, using the *convex cost algorithm* of Section 4-3.3.

4-31 Determine the optimal production program for the following four-period problem: Production cost functions (convex), showing marginal costs:

PERIOD 1		PERIOD 2		PERIOD 3		PERIOD 4	
RANGE	COST	RANGE	COST	RANGE	COST	RANGE	COST
$0 < X_1 \leq 10$	$ 6	$0 < X_2 < 10$	$ 6	$0 < X_3 \leq 7$	$ 5	$0 < X_4 \leq 5$	$ 4
$10 < X_1 \leq 20$	9	$10 < X_2 \leq 20$	9	$7 < X_3 \leq 15$	10	$5 < X_4 \leq 10$	7
$20 < X_1 \leq 30$	14	$20 < X_2 \leq 30$	13	$15 < X_3 \leq 25$	15	$10 < X_4 \leq 30$	10
		$30 < X_2 \leq 40$	17			$30 < X_4 \leq 40$	15

Demand, inventory holding costs (proportional), backlogging costs (proportional):

PERIOD (t)	DEMAND (D_t)	INVENTORY (h_t)	BACKORDER (π_t)
1	18	1	2
2	25	1	2
3	28	2	3
4	25	2	3

4-32 Solve Exercise 4-25 assuming an initial backlog position of five units at time zero and using the following inventory carrying cost function for each period:

$$h_t(I_t^+) = \begin{cases} I_t^+, & 0 \le I_t^+ \le 3 \\ 3 + 3I_t^+, & I_t^+ > 3 \end{cases}$$

4-33 Solve the following production planning problem, assuming production costs in period t are $A_t + c_t X_t$, if $X_t > 0$ and inventory costs are $h_t I_t$.

t	D_t	A_t	c_t	h_t
1	10	50	7	1
2	6	60	8	1
3	14	40	8	2
4	18	60	4	2
5	12	60	6	1
6	10	90	6	1

No shortages are allowed. Give the production quantity and ending inventory for each period.

4-34 Rework 4-33 assuming that backorders are allowed and the backorder cost function is $\pi_t I_t^-$, with $\pi_1 = \pi_2 = \pi_3 = 3$ and $\pi_4 = \pi_5 = \pi_6 = 2$. Also assume the initial inventory is 12 units.

4-35 Solve the following five-period production planning problem:

PERIOD	REQUIRE- MENTS	PRODUCTION COST	INVENTORY COST	BACK- LOGGING COST
1	20	$50 + 7X_1$	$2I_1^+$	$3I_1^-$
2	10	$60 + 8X_2$	I_2^+	$20 + 3I_2^-$
3	40	$40 + 10X_3$	$10 + 2I_3^+$	$3I_3^-$
4	20	$100 + \sqrt{X_4}$	$2I_4^+$	$2\sqrt{I_4^-}$
5	30	$70 + 9X_5$	$2I_5^+$	$2I_5^-$

All shortages are backlogged. The final net inventory is to be zero.

4-36 Work Exercise 4-35 assuming that the on-hand inventory at the end of period 5 is to be 10 units.

4-37 Work Exercise 4-35 assuming that demand can be backlogged at most one period.

4-38 Solve the following six-period planning problem using Zangwill's backward algorithm for the concave cost case:

t	D_t	A_t	c_t	h_t	π_t
1	10	100	20	2	5
2	20	100	20	2	5
3	40	150	15	2	5
4	20	150	15	2	5
5	30	150	15	2	5
6	10	200	15	2	5

All shortages are backlogged. At the start of the planning horizon there is a backlog of 10 units. The inventory at the end of the sixth period is to be 10 units. Assume that company policy is to schedule so that demand is backlogged at most two periods.

4-39 Consider the forward algorithm given in Section 4-3.4 for solving the dynamic planning model with concave costs, when no shortages are allowed. Suppose

$$C_t(X_t) = \begin{cases} 0, & \text{if } X_t = 0 \\ A_t + c_t X_t, & \text{if } X_t > 0 \end{cases}$$

$$H_t(I_t) = h_t I_t$$

To assist in computations, find the following recursive relationships:

(a) Express M_{jk} in terms of $M_{j,k-1}$
(b) Express M_{jk} in terms of $M_{j-1,k}$

4-40 *Planning Horizon Theorem, Concave Cost Case.* Wagner (46, p. 309) gives the following results for the forward algorithm with no backlogging: If

$$(1) \quad C_t(X_t) = \begin{cases} 0, & \text{if } X_t = 0 \\ A_t + c_t X_t, & \text{if } X_t > 0 \end{cases}$$

$$(2) \quad c_t \geq c_{t+1}, \quad \text{for } t = 1, 2, \ldots, T - 1$$

and

$$(3) \quad H_t(I_t) = h_t I_t, \quad \text{for } I_t \geq 0$$

where $A_t \geq 0$, $c_t \geq 0$, and $h_t \geq 0$, then:

(A)   If $j*(k) = k - 1$, for $k \geq 2$, it is always optimal to schedule periods $1, 2, \ldots, k - 1$ as an independent time interval.

(B)   If $l \geq k$, then $j*(l) \geq j*(k)$.

Give a proof of (A) and (B). Explain the utility of these results.

4-41   *Warehousing Problem.* Consider an inventory system where a product (commodity) is purchased for resale. In period t, the unit purchase price is c_t and the unit selling price is r_t. Product purchased in period t cannot be sold until period $t + 1$. Inventory is stored in a warehouse whose capacity is L units. Assume inventory holding costs are negligible. The decision variables in each period are how much to purchase (X_t) and how much to sell (S_t). The planning horizon is T periods long.

(a)   Formulate the problem as a linear programming model.

(b)   Formulate the problem as a dynamic programming model. Show that the optimization at any stage is a linear programming problem having the following four extreme point solutions: $S_t = 0$, $X_t = 0$; $S_t = I$, $X_t = 0$; $S_t = 0$, $X_t = L - I$; $S_t = I$, $X_t = L$; where I is the inventory on hand at the start of period t. The optimal solution is one of these values. Explain the logic of this result. How would you determine which of these extreme points is optimal?

4-42   *Warehousing Problem* (*Extension*). In the situation of Exercise 4-41, suppose that the warehouse capacity, L, is also a decision variable. This might be the case if warehouse space had to be contracted for prior to the start of the planning horizon. What modifications should be made to the model? How might the solution proceed?

4-43   *Warehousing Problem* (*Extension*). One apparent shortcoming of the model for the warehousing problem of Exercise 4-41 is the failure to include inventory carrying costs. Modify the model to include an inventory carrying cost proportional to the dollar investment. Also add a second component of inventory cost related to the handling of inventory. That is, include an "in-out" charge for warehouse handling.

4-44   *The Caterer Problem.* A caterer must provide napkins for dinners on each of T consecutive days. The number of napkins required on day t is D_t. These requirements may be met by purchasing new napkins at a cost of c_1 cents per napkin or by laundering napkins soiled at an earlier dinner. Assume that two types of laundry service are available: regular service, which requires τ days and costs c_2 cents per napkin, and special service, which requires $v < \tau$ days and costs $c_3 > c_2$ cents per napkin. A laundering lead time of τ days means that a napkin soiled on day t could be cleaned in time for use again on day $t + \tau$. These napkins are custom designed for this set of dinners. They can be purchased in unlimited quantities, but will be of no value to the caterer after the last dinner. The problem is to determine the best program of purchasing and laundering to meet the demand for clean napkins each night. Naturally, for the problem to be interesting, we assume $c_3 < c_1$ and $\tau < T$.

(a)   Formulate an algebraic model of this optimization problem.

(b)   Show that the problem can be represented as a transportation model by giving the transportation tableau.

(c)   Solve the following problem: $T = 10$, $c_1 = 20$, $c_2 = 9$, $c_3 = 14$, $\tau = 4$, $v = 2$, $\{D_t\} = (200, 230, 250, 220, 290, 310, 240, 200, 250, 300)$.

(d)   Suppose that a napkin can be cleaned at most twice before it must be discarded. Repeat parts (a), (b), and (c).

(e)   Can you think of more practical applications of models of this type? (For example, maintenance of aircraft parts and procurement of reprocessible hospital supplies.)

4-45   Demand by period over a five-period horizon is expected to be 100, 150, 250, 400, and 450 units. The production cost in any period has the form of Equation 4-33, with $c = 100$. The fixed costs are $A_1 = 1000$, $A_2 = 1200$, $A_3 = 800$, $A_4 = 2000$, and $A_5 = 1500$. Inventory holding costs are proportional to ending inventory, with $h_1 = 10$, $h_2 = 15$, $h_3 = 12$, $h_4 = 20$, and $h_5 = 10$. Production rate change costs are given by Equation 4-32, with $v_1 = 2000$, $v'_1 = 1000$, $v_2 = 2000$, $v'_2 = 1800$, $v_3 = 3000$, $v'_3 = 2500$, $v_4 = 2500$, $v'_4 = 2000$, $v_5 = 2000$, and $v'_5 = 2000$. No shortages are allowed. Find the best production plan.

4-46   Consider the start-up cost problem described in Example 4-7. Use the algorithm defined by Equations 4-34 and 4-35 to solve the following problem:

t	D_t	A_t	c_t	v_t	h_t
1	100	200	10	100	2
2	200	200	10	100	2
3	150	250	9	100	1
4	100	250	8	50	2
5	180	200	8	50	1

4-47   Consider the situation described in Exercise 4-12. Show how you would formulate the problem as a linear programming model when there are upper bounds on the magnitude of production changes from one period to the next. Explain why this might be the case in practice.

4-48   Consider the situation described in Exercise 4-12; however, now suppose that the production change costs are of the form

$$V_t(X_t, X_{t-1}) = \begin{cases} \lambda_t |X_t - X_{t-1}|, & \text{if } |X_t - X_{t-1}| \le M_t \\ \omega_t |X_t - X_{t-1}|, & \text{if } |X_t - X_{t-1}| > M_t \end{cases}$$

where $\omega_t > \lambda_t$. Sketch the function V. Try to formulate a linear programming model of the problem. Repeat for the case where $\omega_t < \lambda_t$. What are your conclusions? Which situation is more likely to occur in practice?

4-49   The following aggregate planning model is an abbreviated version of Equation 4-40:

$$\text{minimize} \quad Z = \sum_{t=1}^{T} [c_1 W_t + c_2(W_t - W_{t-1})^2 \\ + c_3(X_t - c_4 W_t)^2 + c_5(I_t - c_6)^2]$$

subject to

$$I_t = I_{t-1} + X_t - D_t, \qquad (t = 1, 2, \ldots, T)$$

Derive expressions for W_1^* and X_1^*, assuming that W_0, I_0, and the $\{D_t\}$ are given. Verify that they are of the form given by (4-41) and (4-42).

4-50   For the aggregate planning model of Exercise 4-49, suppose that demand in each period is a random variable having density function $g_t(D_t)$.

(a)   Write an expression for the expected value of Z.

(b)   Show that $E(Z)$ will be minimized if the demand in period t is estimated by its expected value.

(c)   Show that the resulting solutions for W_1^* and X_1^* are the same as those obtained in Exercise 4-49, except that D_t is replaced by $E(D_t)$.

(d)   What assumptions, if any, had to be made about the independence of the $\{D_t\}$ in solving parts (a), (b), and (c)?

4-51   For the parametric production planning model of Jones, described by Equations 4-44 to 4-49, consider the extreme cases where the parameters α, β, γ, and δ are either 0 or 1. Explain the significance of each of these policies.

4-52   The parametric production planning rules, (4-44) and (4-47), are to be used with $T = 6$ and all parameters equal to 0.5. The present inventory level is 200 units and the current work force level is 30 workers, each of whom normally works 200 hours during a period. Ten man-hours are required to produce a unit of product. The desired inventory ending inventory levels for the next six periods are 250, 300, 300, 250, 200, and 250.

(a) What work force level and production rate would be planned for period 1?

(b) If the actual demands in the next six periods are 240, 320, 340, 300, 260, and 220, what work force and production decisions will be made?

4-53 *Management Coefficients Model.* As a result of studying an aggregate production planning process, it is hypothesized that the planner makes his decisions about work force level and production rate in the next period through consideration of current work force level, current net inventory, current production rate, and a forecast of demand by period for the next T periods. Linear models of the forms given by Equations 4-50 and 4-51 are assumed. Given that adequate historical data are available, show how one would estimate the coefficients in the models using multiple regression methods. Give the normal equations to be solved. Discuss how one would decide which variables should be dropped from the models. Discuss how one would use the models after the parameters have been estimated.

4-54 Prior to the start of a year, linear programming methods are used to establish planned production rates for each of 13 four-week periods during the year. The company will not repeat the *LP* analysis, but instead will use a rule of the form given in Equation 4-53 to adjust production rates as the year progresses. The original plan is the following:

PERIOD	DEMAND FORECAST	PLANNED PRODUCTION	PLANNED INVENTORIES
1	100	140	40
2	180	180	40
3	220	180	0
4	150	180	30
5	100	180	110
6	200	216	126
7	250	216	92
8	300	216	8
9	260	252	0
10	250	250	0
11	240	240	0
12	210	210	0
13	140	140	0

Suppose that the actual demand during the year turns out to be 120, 180, 250, 180, 120, 210, 200, 250, 200, 200, 200, 180, 150.

(a) What production rates would actually be scheduled during the year if the control constant is $\alpha = 0.4$ and the production lead time is $\tau = 2$? Also give the inventory levels that would result.

(b) Repeat part (a) for $\alpha = 0.4$ and $\tau = 1$. Compare results with those of part (a).

(c) Repeat part (a) for $\alpha = 0.8$ and $\tau = 2$. Compare results with those of parts (a) and (b).

4-55   Verify the following result, given in the proof of Equation 4-60 in Section 4-5.2:

$$E_{t+\tau} = (1 - \alpha)E_{t+\tau-1} - e_t$$

4-56   To determine the effect of the control constant α, do the following:

(a) Equation 4-62 gives the standard deviation of inventory discrepancy, δ, as a function of α, τ, and σ_e. Assume $\sigma_e = 1$ and plot curves of σ_δ versus α for $\tau = 1, 2$, and 4. What conclusions do you draw about the choice of α in using a production control rule such as Equation 4-53?

(b) Repeat part (a) for the standard deviation of the difference between planned and actual production, given by Equation 4-65.

(c) Repeat part (a) for the standard deviation of the change in production rate, given by Equation 4-66.

4-57   Suppose that the forecasting procedure used to predict demand in Exercise 4-54 is known to generate forecasts that are unbiased with an error standard deviation of $\sigma_e = 30$. If the production control rule has $\alpha = 0.4$ and $\tau = 2$, what minimum inventory levels should be planned so that the probability of no stockout in a period is approximately 0.95? What changes would have to be made in the production plan? Repeat for $\alpha = 0.4$ and $\tau = 1$. Repeat for $\alpha = 0.8$ and $\tau = 2$.

4-58   *Multiproduct Models with Carry-Over of Resources.* In model (4-67) of Example 4-10, it is assumed that the quantity of resource k available in period t is b_{kt}, regardless of the utilization of resource k in prior periods. This, in effect, is assuming that any unused amount of the resource in a period cannot be carried forward for use in future periods. This is proper for resources such as labor man-hours, machine-hours, and ton-miles of transportation capacity. However, if the resource is a raw material or investment capital, the amount available in period t is the sum of the unused amount in period $t - 1$ and the amount becoming available for the first time in period t. Reformulate (4-67) assuming that the first K_1 of the K resources are of the type that can be carried forward.

4-59   *Alternative Formulation of the Multiperiod Product Mix Problem.* In Example 4-12, we developed a product mix model using one set of variables to represent the production program and another set to represent the sales program. We did this because production and sale of a given unit of product may occur in different periods. Reformulate the problem using only one set of decision variables. Let X_{ijtv} be the amount of product i produced by process j in period t and sold in period v. Compare the two formulations. Do you see any advantages to one over the other?

4-60 Two products, A and B, are produced in the same department. Production is to be planned for the next three periods. The following information is given:

PRODUCT	REQUIREMENTS IN UNITS			PRODUCTION RATE IN UNITS PER HOUR	INITIAL INVENTORY
	PERIOD 1	PERIOD 2	PERIOD 3		
A	1000	2000	3000	10	300
B	5000	6000	4000	5	800

Overtime is available in each period and, in addition, Product B may be subcontracted up to 1000 units each period at a cost of $10 per unit. Capacities, in hours of production time, for each period and production costs are

SOURCE	CAPACITY IN HOURS			UNIT COSTS	
	PERIOD 1	PERIOD 2	PERIOD 3	A	B
Regular time	1000	1100	700	$15	$6
Overtime	200	200	100	20	9

Inventory carrying costs are $1.50 per unit per period for product A and $0.85 per unit per period for product B. No shortages are allowed.

(a) Formulate this planning problem as a linear programming model.

(b) Show that the problem can be solved as a transportation problem by giving the appropriate transportation tableau. (*Hint:* The requirements for each product must be measured in some standard units, which must be the same as that used to measure capacity.)

(c) Solve for the optimal production and subcontracting decisions.

4-61 A single facility produces two products, A and B. Production is to be planned over a four-period horizon. The following data are available:

	DEMAND IN UNITS		AVAILABLE CAPACITY IN MACHINE-HOURS	
PERIOD	A	B	REGULAR TIME	OVERTIME
1	50	100	450	200
2	70	100	480	200
3	200	50	500	100
4	100	100	400	170

	UNIT PRODUCT COST		UNIT INVENTORY COST PER PERIOD	PRODUCTION RATE IN HOURS PER UNIT	INVENTORY	
PRODUCT	REGULAR TIME	OVERTIME			INITIAL	FINAL
A	$30	$40	$10	2	40	50
B	60	72	16	4	20	50

(a) Give the algebraic formulation of this problem as a linear programming model.

(b) This problem can be formulated as a transportation-type linear programming model. Give the appropriate transportation tableau and solve for the optimal production program.

4-62 Consider a multiproduct production planning problem having the following characteristics:

(1) There are n products.

(2) The planning horizon is T periods.

(3) Product i requires k_i man-hours of labor per unit.

(4) The work force level in period t is W_t *man-hours*. This can be changed from period to period at a cost of α dollars per man-hour of change (either increase or decrease).

(5) The inventory holding cost per unit of product i in period t is h_{it}.

(6) Shortages are backordered at a cost of π_{it} per unit of product i in period t.

(7) The production cost in period t is c_{it} dollars per unit of product i.

(8) There is a cost of changing the production rate (independent of any work force change costs). This cost is λ_i dollars per unit of change in the production rate of product i from one period to the next (either increase or decrease).

(9) The cost per man-hour of work force in period t is ρ_t.

Formulate the problem of determining production and work force decisions over the planning horizon as a linear programming model. Assume the ending net inventory for each product is to be zero.

4-63 For the Lasdon-Terjung model, described in Example 4-15 of Section 4-6.2, show how you would include the constraints (4-81), (4-82), and (4-84) in the model (4-79).

4-64 For the type of planning problem studied by Manne, Dzielinski, Baker, Gorenstein et al., described by Examples 4-16 and 4-17, suppose that the requirements for a product over a four-period planning horizon are 1000, 1200, 800, and 900 units. The initial inventory is 600 units. List the set of dominant production schedules for this product. How would your solution be affected if the maximum production of the product is limited to 3000 units in any period?

4-65 A company has four plants, each of which manufactures the same product. Raw material costs differ from one plant to another, as do the production costs. There are five regional warehouses that supply customers. The selling price depends on the warehouse. Production and distribution is to be planned over a four-period horizon, based on the following information.

Plant costs and capacities:

	CAPACITY IN UNITS PER PERIOD		RAW MATERIAL COST PER UNIT	PRODUCTION COST PER UNIT	
PLANT	REGULAR TIME	OVERTIME		REGULAR TIME	OVERTIME
1	150	30	10	$15	20
2	200	30	9	18	24
3	175	35	12	14	18
4	100	20	8	13	18

Transportation costs (per unit):

	WAREHOUSE				
PLANT	1	2	3	4	5
1	$3	$1	$5	$7	$4
2	9	7	8	3	5
3	5	4	3	8	6
4	4	5	6	2	7

Sales potential, selling prices, and inventory costs:

	WAREHOUSE				
	1	2	3	4	5
Period 1: max. sales	80	110	150	100	150
min. sales	20	20	30	10	40
Period 2: max. sales	100	100	160	200	100
min. sales	30	30	30	30	30
Period 3: max. sales	70	130	120	110	130
min. sales	30	30	30	40	40
Period 4: max. sales	100	120	130	140	150
min. sales	20	60	20	20	20
Selling price	$34	$32	$31	$31	$31
Inventory cost per unit per period	$ 1	$ 2	$ 1	$ 1	$ 3

No inventories are maintained at the plants; all production is immediately shipped to the warehouses. There are no initial inventories. The problem is to maximize profits over the planning horizon, subject to sales and capacity constraints. Formulate a linear programming model.

4-66 Formulate a general algebraic model for the two-stage problem of Exercise 4-65. Assume there are n plants, m warehouses, and T time periods. Introduce notation for decision variables, costs, revenues, capacities, and sales limits.

4-67 Formulate the problem of Exercise 4-65 as a capacity-constrained network flow problem. Draw the network, indicating arc capacities and costs. Solve using the out-of-kilter algorithm of Ford and Fulkerson (13).

4-68 A plant produces two products, A and B. During the next three periods, the demand for A is expected to be 100, 200, and 150 units, and for B, 180, 220, and 100 units. Two operations are required to produce each product. For both products, the first operation is done in Department 1 and the second operation in Department 2. The following additional data are available:

PRODUCT	INITIAL INVENTORY	UNIT COST REGULAR TIME	UNIT COST OVERTIME	UNIT INVENTORY COST PER PERIOD
A	10	$30	$31	$2
B	20	28	32	3

	PRODUCTION RATE IN UNITS PER HOUR	
PRODUCT	OPERATION 1	OPERATION 2
A	2	4
B	1	5

CAPACITY IN MACHINE HOURS

	DEPARTMENT 1		DEPARTMENT 2	
PERIOD	REGULAR TIME	OVERTIME	REGULAR TIME	OVERTIME
1	250	50	100	20
2	250	50	50	20
3	200	50	50	20

(a) Assuming that both departments follow the same schedule in each period, that both operations are completed in the same period, and that no shortages are to be permitted, write a linear programming model of the planning problem.

(b) Now assume that the departments can follow different schedules and that in-process inventories of both products can be maintained between operations (departments). Let the in-process inventory holding cost per period be $1 for A and $1.50 for B. Formulate the appropriate model.

(c) Discuss the reason why the model of part (b) could have a lower-cost solution than that of part (a), even though part (b) involves additional inventory costs.

4-69 Repeat Exercise 4-68 assuming shortages of finished product can be backlogged at a cost per unit per period of $3 for A and $2 for B.

4-70 A production system consists of three facilities. Facility 1 produces Type A parts, Facility 2 makes Type B parts, and Facility 3 assembles the finished product. Each facility maintains an inventory of its product. It takes three type-A parts to make one Type B part, and two Type B parts and one Type A part are required for each unit of finished product. Regular time and overtime are available at each facility in each period. P_{jt} is the regular time production capacity at facility j in period t, $(t = 1, 2, \ldots, T)$, and overtime capacity is 20 percent of regular time capacity. The demand, D_t, for finished goods in period t is given for each period in the planning horizon. No shortages are to be allowed at any inventory point, and minimum inventory levels of 200 Type A and 100 Type B parts are required. Assume that unit regular time and overtime production costs and inventory carrying costs at each facility are known for each period. Formulate this problem as a linear programming model, defining any additional notation required.

4-71 Reformulate the model of Example 4-23 assuming that up to M_t units of semifinished product can be sold at a unit price of r_t in period t and that up to N_t units of semifinished product can be purchased at a unit cost of k_t in period t.

4-72 Show how each of the following features can be added to the model of Example 4-23:

(a) Backlogging of finished goods demand.

(b) Inventory maximums and minimums.

(c) A production lead time of τ_1 periods at stage 1 plants and τ_2 weeks at stage 2 plants.

(d) Limitations of the size of shipments between plants.

4-73 Modify the formulation of Example 4-23 to include each of the following at each plant:

(a) Production rate change costs.

(b) Work force level decisions at each plant.

(c) Overtime decisions.

(d) Multiple routings within plants.

4-74 Modify the formulation of Example 4-23 for the situation of multiple finished products, each of which uses one or more of multiple semifinished products produced by the plants at stage 1.

4-75   Three facilities are involved in the manufacture of an item. Facility 1 makes type A parts and facility 2 produces type B parts. At facility 3, two type A and three type B parts are assembled to make one unit of finished product C. Given the following information, formulate a linear programming model to aid in planning production at these facilities during the next three months. No shortages are to be planned. Assume that production at facilities 1 and 2 will be available in time for use by facility 3 in the same month.

FACILITY	INITIAL INVENTORY	UNIT PRODUCTION COST REGULAR TIME	UNIT PRODUCTION COST OVERTIME	UNIT INVENTORY COST PER MONTH
1	200	$20	$25	$1
2	150	30	31	2
3	100	15	18	4

		AVAILABLE CAPACITY (IN UNITS) ON REGULAR TIME AND OVERTIME					
	FINISHED	FACILITY 1		FACILITY 2		FACILITY 3	
	PRODUCT	REGULAR	OVER-	REGULAR	OVER-	REGULAR	OVER-
MONTH	DEMAND	TIME	TIME	TIME	TIME	TIME	TIME
1	180	250	50	400	100	150	50
2	320	300	50	400	100	200	80
3	120	200	100	300	100	100	40

4-76   Use Zangwill's algorithm, described in Section 4-7.3, to solve the following four-period multistage problem:

$$(1) \quad C_{jt}(X_{jt}) = \begin{cases} 0, & \text{if } X_{jt} = 0 \\ A_j + c_j X_{jt}, & \text{if } X_{jt} > 0 \end{cases}$$

with $A_1 = 600$, $A_2 = 400$, $A_3 = 800$

$$c_1 = 20, c_2 = 30, c_3 = 15$$

(2) $H_{jt}(I_{jt}) = h_j I_{jt}$

with $h_1 = 5$, $h_2 = 8$, $h_3 = 10$

(3) $D_1 = 400$, $D_2 = 200$, $D_3 = 600$, $D_4 = 800$

4-77 Production and inventory costs at each stage of a serial three-stage system are linear. Four periods are to be planned. Demand and unit costs are the following:

PERIOD	PRODUCTION COST AT STAGE			FINISHED PRODUCT DEMAND
	1	2	3	
1	20	30	15	400
2	23	28	17	200
3	26	27	21	600
4	23	24	26	800

Unit inventory holding costs per period at the three stages are 5, 6, and 8. Backlogging of finished product is permitted at a cost of 10 per unit backlogged per period. Assuming there is sufficient production capacity at each stage in each period, formulate the problem as a transhipment model and solve by the transportation method of linear programming.

4-78 Develop a dynamic programming model, similar to that of Section 4-8.1, for the case where shortages are not backlogged. Explain the nature of any shortage cost function you may include in your model.

4-79 Develop a dynamic programming model, similar to that of Section 4-8.1, for the case where a fraction α of shortages are backlogged and a fraction $(1 - \alpha)$ are lost.

4-80 A single product is to be produced and sold over a three-period planning horizon. Demand in any period t is a discrete random variable having probability distribution $p_t(D_t)$:

DEMAND	$p_1(D_1)$	$p_2(D_2)$	$p_3(D_3)$
0	0.1	0.2	0.4
1	0.2	0.4	0.3
2	0.4	0.3	0.3
3	0.2	0.1	0
4	0.1	0	0

Production costs are of the form

$$C_t(X_t) = \begin{cases} 0, & \text{if } X_t = 0 \\ A_t + c_t X_t, & \text{if } X_t > 0 \end{cases}$$

with $A_1 = 100$, $A_2 = 200$, $A_3 = 50$, $c_1 = 30$, $c_2 = 50$, and $c_3 = 40$. Inventory holding costs are $h_t I_t^+$, where $h_1 = 10$, $h_2 = 10$, and $h_3 = 20$. Shortages are backlogged at a cost $\pi_t I_t^-$, where $\pi_1 = \pi_2 = \pi_3 = 40$. Find the optimal production policy for each period. If $I_0 = 0$, how many units should be produced in the first period? What are the *expected* production levels in the second and third periods? If the demand in the first period is actually three units, how many units should be produced in the second period? At that point, what is the expected production in the third period?

4-81 Formulate the chance-constrained model given in Section 4-8.2 for a three-period planning horizon. Demand in each period is normally distributed with mean μ_t and standard deviation σ_t. Production costs are $C_t(X_t) = X_t^2$ and inventory costs are $h_t I_t$. Use the following data:

$$\mu_1 = 100 \qquad \sigma_1 = 10 \qquad h_t = 10,\ t = 1, 2, 3 \qquad I_0 = 0$$
$$\mu_2 = 200 \qquad \sigma_2 = 20 \qquad L_t = 10,\ t = 1, 2, 3$$
$$\mu_3 = 150 \qquad \sigma_3 = 10 \qquad \alpha_t = 0.05,\ t = 1, 2, 3$$

How would you convert the model into a linear programming formulation?

4-82 Discuss the formulation and solution of the chance-constrained model of Section 4-8.2 for each of the following cases:

(a) Linear production and inventory costs.

(b) Concave production and inventory costs.

(c) Convex production and inventory costs with no backlogging allowed. Shortages are lost.

(d) A constant production lead time of τ periods.

(e) Multiple products with resource constraints.

chapter 5
Operations Scheduling

5-1   Introduction

An important function of management is the coordination and control of complex activities, including optimum resource allocation in the performance of those activities. In Chapters 3 and 4, we were concerned with intermediate-range planning decisions, without giving attention to the sequence with which production activities were performed. There are other problems, which we call *scheduling* problems, where both resource allocation and sequence are important. In recent years, a number of quantitative approaches to several important types of scheduling problems have been proposed. The job shop scheduling problem, in which we must determine the order or sequence for processing a set of jobs through several machines in an optimum manner, has received considerable attention, and a variety of scheduling rules and procedures for certain types of job shops have evolved from these efforts. Network planning and control techniques have found wide application to the scheduling problems associated with project activities. Numerous procedures also have been proposed for determining optimal or near-optimal work station assignments for assembly lines.

This chapter will concentrate on three main types of scheduling problems: job shop scheduling, project scheduling, and assembly line balancing. Not all scheduling problems for these diverse systems can be efficiently solved, and in several instances heuristic techniques that yield nonoptimal, but relatively good solutions will be employed. In many cases, it may seem that a scheduling algorithm has been developed from an overly simplified model of the real system. However, such techniques have considerable value because through their study and use, the analyst is better able to understand the complex interrelationships among activities in the scheduling process.

5-2 Job Shop Scheduling

A job shop consists of a set of general purpose machines that perform operations on production orders or jobs. The jobs are often unique in that they result from a specific customer order. While we traditionally think of the job shop as a machine shop, the job shop process is the underlying model for a considerable number of operational systems such as maintenance activities, construction operations, and so on.

The job shop scheduling problem consists of determining the order or sequence in which the machines will process the jobs so as to optimize some measure of performance. Four factors serve to describe and classify a specific job shop scheduling problem. First, the job arrival pattern. If n jobs arrive simultaneously in a shop that is idle and immediately available for work, then the scheduling problem is said to be *static*. If jobs arrive intermittently, possibly according to a stochastic process, the scheduling problem is *dynamic*. Second, it is necessary to specify the number of machines, m, that compose the job shop. Third, the flow process of jobs through the machines must be specified. If all jobs follow the same routing, then the shop is a *flow shop*. The opposite extreme is the *randomly routed job shop*, in which jobs do not follow a common sequence of operations. Fourth, the criterion for evaluating the performance of the shop plays a critical role in the scheduling process.

A performance measure that we shall frequently employ is the makespan, or the total amount of time required to completely process all the jobs. Our objective then would be to develop a scheduling procedure that would minimize the makespan. Many other performance measures are often used to evaluate schedules, although we shall make only limited use of them. For example if d_i

TABLE 5-1   Processing Times for Example 5-1

JOB	MACHINE 1	MACHINE 2
1	13	3
2	2	5
3	1	3
4	4	6
5	5	7

is the due date of the ith job and C_i is the completion time of the ith job, then $L_i = C_i - d_i$ is a measure of the lateness of the ith job. Our goal could be to schedule jobs to minimize the average lateness per job. Alternatively, we may be more interested in the average tardiness per job, where the tardiness for job i is defined as $T_i = \max(0, L_i)$. Other typical performance measures are the average time a job is in the shop (average *flow time*), the average number of jobs in the shop, the variance of the distribution of flow time lateness, or tardiness, and the utilization of machines and labor.

An early graphical approach to scheduling problems was proposed by Henry L. Gantt. The Gantt chart simply displays job operations as a function of time on each machine. The chart usually consists of a horizontal bar for each machine, with idle and busy periods for a particular schedule designated. Inspection of the Gantt chart allows the schedule to be evaluated for makespan, machine idle time, and job waiting time. While the Gantt chart is an excellent display device, it has serious weakness as a scheduling technique because it does not provide any structured approach to schedule improvement. The analyst must use intuition to find an improved schedule.

□**EXAMPLE 5-1**   To illustrate the construction of a Gantt chart, consider a five-job, two-machine scheduling problem. Each job must be processed first on machine 1, then on machine 2. The processing times are shown in Table 5-1. Suppose we elect to process the jobs in the sequence {3, 2, 4, 5, 1}. The Gantt chart for this sequence is shown in Figure 5-1, page 324. From examining the Gantt chart, we see that the makespan for this sequence is 28 time units. Furthermore, there is no idle time on machine 1 until all jobs have been processed. There are four units of idle time on machine 2. Finally, jobs 2, 4, and 5 incur a total of six units of waiting time at machine 2.□

5-2.1 *n* Jobs, One Machine

The simplest job shop scheduling problem involves determining an optimal sequence for a set of n jobs to be processed by a single machine. Let $p_1, p_2, \ldots, p_n$

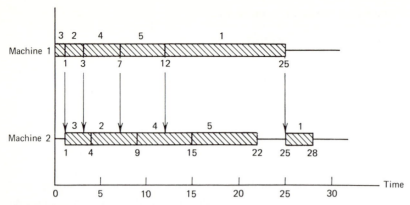

FIGURE 5-1. Gantt chart for the sequence {2, 3, 4, 5, 1}.

be the processing times (including any necessary setup time for the machine) of the jobs. We assume the processing times are known with certainty. A schedule will be just some permutation of the integers $1, 2, \ldots, n$ (clearly there are $n!$ such schedules). Furthermore, it is obvious that all schedules result in the same makespan, so that some alternative measure of performance must be chosen. Suppose we wish to determine a schedule such that the mean flow time is minimized.

Square brackets will be used to denote position in sequence in a schedule. Thus, [1] denotes the job that is in first position in the sequence, and $p_{[1]}$ would denote the processing time of that job. A schedule to minimize the mean flow time of n jobs on a single machine may be found by sequencing the jobs in order of nondecreasing processing time, that is, such that

$$p_{[1]} \le p_{[2]} \le \cdots \le p_{[n]}$$

This procedure is called *shortest processing time* sequencing (abbreviated SPT).

We may easily prove that sequencing the jobs according to the SPT rule results in a minimum mean flow time schedule. The flow time of a job in the kth position of an arbitrary sequence is

$$F_{[k]} = \sum_{i=1}^{k} p_{[i]}$$

The mean flow time of the entire n job sequence is just

$$\bar{F} = \frac{\sum_{k=1}^{n} F_{[k]}}{n} = \frac{\sum_{k=1}^{n} \sum_{i=1}^{k} p_{[i]}}{n}$$

$$= \frac{\sum_{i=1}^{n} (n - i + 1)p_{[i]}}{n}$$

Operations Scheduling   **324**

Now a sum of pairwise products of two sequences of numbers can be minimized by arranging one sequence in nonincreasing order and the other sequence in nondecreasing order. Since the coefficients $(n - i + 1)$ are already in nonincreasing order, $\bar{F}$ would be minimized by sequencing the jobs so that the processing times are in nondecreasing order. Thus, the SPT sequence results in a minimum mean flow time. One may also show that SPT minimizes the mean waiting time and the mean lateness.

In many situations, all jobs are not equally important. Suppose each job has an importance weight or value w_i (the larger w_i, the more important the job). We wish to schedule a set of n jobs so as to minimize the mean weighted flow time

$$\bar{F}_w = \frac{\sum\limits_{i=1}^{n} w_i F_i}{n}$$

This may be accomplished by sequencing the jobs so that

$$\frac{p_{[1]}}{w_{[1]}} \le \frac{p_{[2]}}{w_{[2]}} \le \cdots \le \frac{p_{[n]}}{w_{[n]}}$$

which is obviously a generalization of SPT.

□**EXAMPLE 5-2** Suppose we wish to schedule 6 jobs on a single machine. The processing time, weights, and ratios of processing time to weight are shown in the Table 5-2. To minimize $\bar{F}_w$, the jobs should be processed in the sequence {2, 5, 3, 6, 1, 4}.□

5-2.2 *n* Jobs, Two Machines

Consider the problem of scheduling a set of n jobs which must pass through two machines in the same technological order, that is, a two-machine flow shop problem. We wish to determine a schedule that minimizes the makespan for

TABLE 5-2 Data for Example 5-2

JOB	p_i	w_i	p_i/w_i
1	10	5	2.0
2	6	10	0.6
3	5	5	1.0
4	4	1	4.0
5	2	3	0.67
6	8	5	1.6

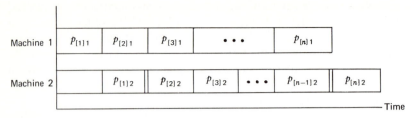

FIGURE 5-2.   Gantt chart of a two-machine schedule.

the n jobs. The procedure used to construct the schedule was developed by Johnson (14).

Let p_{ij} be the processing time of job i on machine j. Assume that all jobs are processed first on machine 1 and then on machine 2, and that no passing is allowed (that is, the sequence at machine 1 is preserved at machine 2). Johnson's procedure is as follows. Find the job with the minimum p_{ij}. If this minimum value occurs on machine 1 ($j = 1$), assign this job to the first available place in the sequence. If the minimum value occurs on machine 2 ($j = 2$), assign the job to the last available place in the sequence. Then remove this job from the list of jobs to be sequenced and repeat the process. Ties are resolved by randomly choosing either position in the sequence for the assignment. This process continues until all jobs have been sequenced.

We shall not prove the optimality of Johnson's algorithm, but by examining obvious lower bounds on makespan, one may develop an intuitive notion as to why it works. Let $p_{[i]1}$ be the processing time on machine 1 of the job in the ith position in the sequence. Define $p_{[i]2}$ similarly for machine 2. A schedule could be as shown in Figure 5-2. It is clear that the last job cannot be completed earlier than the time required to process all n jobs on machine 1 plus the time required to process the last job on machine 2. Thus

$$F \geq \sum_{i=1}^{n} p_{[i]1} + p_{[n]2} \tag{5-1}$$

Similarly, the last job cannot be completed in less time than required to process all n jobs on machine 2, plus the delay time before machine 2 can begin, or

$$F \geq \sum_{i=1}^{n} p_{[i]2} + p_{[1]1} \tag{5-2}$$

Now the summations in Equations 5-1 and 5-2 are unaffected by sequence, and so we may only influence these bounds by the choice of $p_{[n]2}$ and $p_{[1]1}$. Therefore, we would choose the job with the smallest p_{ij}. If $j = 1$, we would put that job first in sequence so as to minimize $p_{[1]1}$. If $j = 2$, we would put that job last in the sequence so as to minimize $p_{[n]2}$. Now with the first job sequenced, one

TABLE 5-3   Processing Times for Example 5-3

JOB	MACHINE 1	MACHINE 2
1	4	3
2	1	2
3	5	4
4	2	3
5	5	6

could repeat the same argument for the set of $n - 1$ remaining jobs. While not a proof, this does illustrate the logic upon which the procedure is based.

☐**EXAMPLE 5-3**   The processing times for five jobs on each of two machines is shown in Table 5-3. We wish to determine a minimum makespan schedule. Applying Johnson's algorithm, we see that min $\{p_{ij}\} = 1$ occurs for job 2 on machine 1. Therefore, job 2 is placed first in the sequence. Eliminating job 2, we find that $\min_{i \neq 2} \{p_{ij}\} = 2$ occurs for job 4 on machine 1, so job 4 is placed second in the sequence. Now $\min_{i \neq 2,4} \{p_{ij}\} = 3$ occurs for job 1 on machine 2, so job 1 is placed last in the sequence. We now find that $\min_{i \neq 1,2,4} \{p_{ij}\} = 4$ occurs for job 3 on machine 2, so job 3 is placed fourth (the last available place) in the sequence. Only job 5 remains, and it must be placed in the only available position in the sequence, third. Thus, the minimum makespan sequence is $\{2, 4, 5, 3, 1\}$. The Gantt chart for this sequence shown in Figure 5-3 reveals a makespan of 21 time units.☐

Jackson (12) has shown that Johnson's algorithm may be modified to produce a minimum makespan sequence of n jobs in a two-machine job shop (jobs may have different technological orderings). Partition the n jobs into four sets

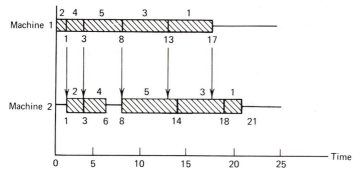

FIGURE 5-3.   Gantt chart for the sequence $\{2, 4, 5, 3, 1\}$.

defined as follows:

$\{A\}$ = the set of jobs that are processed *only* on machine 1

$\{B\}$ = the set of jobs that are processed *only* on machine 2

$\{AB\}$ = the set of jobs to be processed on machine 1 followed by machine 2

$\{BA\}$ = the set of jobs to be processed on machine 2 followed by machine 1

Sequence the jobs in $\{AB\}$ by Johnson's algorithm. Then sequence the jobs in $\{BA\}$ by Johnson's algorithm. Now select *any arbitrary* sequence for the jobs in $\{A\}$ and $\{B\}$. Finally, combine the sets of jobs in the following way, without changing the order within each set:

Machine 1: jobs in $\{AB\}$ before jobs in $\{A\}$ before jobs in $\{BA\}$

Machine 2: jobs in $\{BA\}$ before jobs in $\{B\}$ before jobs in $\{AB\}$

5-2.3 *n* Jobs, Three Machines

Considerable attention has been given to scheduling problems in the *n*-job, three-machine flow shop. Johnson's algorithm for the two-machine case may be extended to the three-machine case under certain circumstances. If either of the following two conditions are true, then Johnson's method is applicable:

$$\text{either} \quad \min \{p_{i1}\} \geq \max \{p_{i2}\}$$

$$\text{or} \quad \min \{p_{i3}\} \geq \max \{p_{i2}\}$$

That is, Johnson's method is applicable if machine 2 is completely dominated by either the first or third machine. The working procedure involves defining two dummy machines, say 1' and 2', with processing times

$$p_{i1'} = p_{i1} + p_{i2}$$

$$p_{i2'} = p_{i2} + p_{i3}$$

and applying Johnson's algorithm to this new two-machine problem.

□**EXAMPLE 5-4** Consider the four-job, three-machine scheduling problem in Table 5-4. All jobs are to be processed first on machine 1, then on machine 2, and last on machine 3. Since $\min \{p_{i1}\} = 5 > \max \{p_{i2}\} = 4$, Johnson's

TABLE 5-4 Processing Times for Example 5-4

JOB	MACHINE 1	MACHINE 2	MACHINE 3
1	8	2	4
2	5	4	5
3	6	1	3
4	7	3	2

TABLE 5-5 Processing Times

JOB	MACHINE 1′	MACHINE 2′
1	10	6
2	9	9
3	7	4
4	10	5

method is applicable. The processing times for the dummy machines 1′ and 2′ are shown in Table 5-5. Applying Johnson's method, we find that the optimal sequence for the jobs is $\{2, 1, 4, 3\}$.□

Giglio and Wagner (6) applied Johnson's method to 20 general six-job, three-machine flow shop problems that did not satisfy *either* of the required conditions. In 9 out of the 20 cases, an optimal solution was actually generated, and in 8 of the remaining cases, the solution obtained could be made optimal by interchanging two adjacent jobs. Apparently Johnson's method is a useful approximate procedure even if the optimality conditions are not satisfied. At least it would often provide a good starting point for further analysis.

Ignall and Schrage (11) have proposed a branch-and-bound algorithm for the general three-machine flow shop problem. This procedure requires us to describe the problem as a tree, in which each node represents a partial solution. At each node, a lower bound on makespan is computed for all nodes that emanate from it. It is easy to see that the flow shop scheduling problem can be expressed as a tree. The first node in the tree structure corresponds to the initial state, with no jobs scheduled. From this node, there are n branches corresponding to the n possible jobs that can be placed first in the sequence. From each of these nodes, there are $n - 1$ branches corresponding to the jobs available to be placed second in the sequence. Since there are $n!$ possible sequences, there are $1 + n + n(n - 1) + \cdots + n!$ nodes in the tree.

Each node represents a partial sequence containing from 1 to n jobs. Consider an arbitrary node, say P, with sequence J_r. That is, J_r is a particular subset of size r $(1 \leq r \leq n)$ of the n jobs. Let TIME1(J_r), TIME2(J_r), and TIME3(J_r) be the times at which machine 1, 2, and 3, respectively, complete processing on the jobs in J_r. Then a lower bound on the makespan of all schedules that begin with sequence J_r is

$$
\text{LB}(P) = \text{LB}(J_r) = \max \left\{
\begin{array}{l}
\text{TIME1}(J_r) + \sum\limits_{i \in \bar{J}_r} p_{i1} + \min\limits_{i \in \bar{J}_r} (p_{i2} + p_{i3}) \\[2ex]
\text{TIME2}(J_r) + \sum\limits_{i \in \bar{J}_r} p_{i2} + \min\limits_{i \in \bar{J}_r} (p_{i3}) \\[2ex]
\text{TIME3}(J_r) + \sum\limits_{i \in \bar{J}_r} p_{i3}
\end{array}
\right\} \quad (5\text{-}3)
$$

where $\bar{J}_r$ is the set of $n-r$ jobs that have not been scheduled.

TABLE 5-6 Processing Times for Example 5-5

JOB	MACHINE 1	MACHINE 2	MACHINE 3
1	12	5	13
2	6	10	3
3	9	11	18
4	17	16	4

The actual procedure consists of generating the nodes in the tree and computing the lower bounds associated with them. We always branch from the node with the smallest lower bound. To branch from a node, create a new node for every job not yet scheduled by attaching the unscheduled job to the end of the partial sequence of scheduled jobs. The lower bounds can then be computed from Equation 5-3.

As soon as a node has been found with all n jobs scheduled and a smallest lower bound, the problem is solved and the sequence at that node is optimal. In performing the above steps, dominance can be used to some extent. That is, if J_r and I_r are sequences containing the same r jobs, then if $\text{TIME2}(J_r) \leq \text{TIME2}(I_r)$ and $\text{TIME3}(J_r) \leq \text{TIME3}(I_r)$, the node associated with sequence I_r can be discarded as soon as node J_r is created.

☐**EXAMPLE 5-5**   Consider the four-job, three-machine flow shop scheduling problem shown in Table 5-6. To branch from node 0, we construct nodes 1, 2, 3, and 4 as shown in Figure 5-4. In computing the lower bounds, we need $\text{TIME1}(1) = 12$, $\text{TIME2}(1) = 17$, $\text{TIME3}(1) = 30$, $\text{TIME1}(2) = 6$, $\text{TIME2}(2) = 16$, $\text{TIME3}(2) = 19$, $\text{TIME1}(3) = 9$, $\text{TIME2}(3) = 20$, $\text{TIME3}(3) = 38$, $\text{TIME1}(4) = 17$, $\text{TIME2}(4) = 33$, and $\text{TIME3}(4) = 37$. The lower bounds are

$$LB(1) = \max \begin{Bmatrix} 12 + 32 + 13 = 57 \\ 17 + 37 + 3 = 57 \\ 30 + 25 = 55 \end{Bmatrix} = 57$$

$$LB(2) = \max \begin{Bmatrix} 6 + 38 + 18 = 62 \\ 16 + 32 + 4 = 52 \\ 19 + 35 = 54 \end{Bmatrix} = 62$$

$$LB(3) = \max \begin{Bmatrix} 9 + 35 + 13 = 57 \\ 20 + 31 + 3 = 54 \\ 38 + 20 = 58 \end{Bmatrix} = 58$$

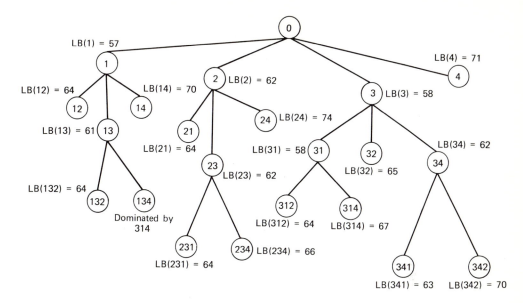

FIGURE 5-4. Tree for the four-job, three-machine problem in Example 5-5.

$$
LB(4) = \max \begin{cases} 17 + 27 + 13 = 57 \\ 33 + 26 + 3 = 62 \\ 37 + 34 = 71 \end{cases} = 71
$$

As LB(1) is the smallest lower bound, we branch from node 1. To compute the lower bounds, we need TIME1(12), TIME2(12), . . . , TIME3(14). These quantities may be computed as follows:

$$TIME1(12) = TIME1(1) + p_{21} = 12 + 6 = 18$$

$$TIME2(12) = \max \{TIME1(12) + p_{22}, TIME2(1) + p_{22}\}$$
$$= \max \{18 + 10 = 28, 17 + 10 = 27\} = 28$$

$$TIME3(12) = \max \{TIME2(12) + p_{23}, TIME3(1) + p_{23}\}$$
$$= \max \{28 + 3 = 31, 30 + 3 = 33\} = 33$$

$$TIME1(13) = TIME1(1) + p_{31} = 12 + 9 = 21$$

$$TIME2(13) = \max \{TIME1(13) + p_{32}, TIME2(1) + p_{32}\}$$
$$= \max \{21 + 11 = 32, 17 + 11 = 28\} = 32$$

$$TIME3(13) = \max \{TIME2(13) + p_{33}, TIME3(1) + p_{33}\}$$
$$= \max \{32 + 18 = 50, 30 + 18 = 48\} = 50$$

$$TIME1(14) = TIME1(1) + p_{41} = 12 + 17 = 29$$

$$\text{TIME2(14)} = \max \{\text{TIME1(14)} + p_{42}, \text{TIME2(1)} + p_{42}\}$$
$$= \max \{29 + 16 = 45, 17 + 16 = 33\} = 45$$
$$\text{TIME3(14)} = \max \{\text{TIME2(14)} + p_{43}, \text{TIME3(1)} + p_{43}\}$$
$$= \max \{45 + 4 = 49, 30 + 4 = 34\} = 49$$

The lower bounds are

$$\text{LB(12)} = \max \begin{cases} 18 + 26 + 20 = 64 \\ 28 + 27 + 4 = 59 \\ 33 + 22 = 55 \end{cases} = 64$$

$$\text{LB(13)} = \max \begin{cases} 21 + 23 + 13 = 57 \\ 32 + 26 + 3 = 61 \\ 50 + 7 = 57 \end{cases} = 61$$

and

$$\text{LB(14)} = \max \begin{cases} 29 + 15 + 13 = 57 \\ 45 + 21 + 3 = 69 \\ 49 + 21 = 70 \end{cases} = 70$$

Since LB(3) = 58 is now the smallest lower bound, we next branch from node 3. We need the quantities

$$\text{TIME1(31)} = \text{TIME1(3)} + p_{11} = 9 + 12 = 21$$
$$\text{TIME2(31)} = \max \{\text{TIME1(31)} + p_{12}, \text{TIME2(3)} + p_{12}\}$$
$$= \max \{21 + 5 = 26, 20 + 5 = 25\} = 26$$
$$\text{TIME3(31)} = \max \{\text{TIME2(31)} + p_{13}, \text{TIME3(3)} + p_{13}\}$$
$$= \max \{26 + 13 = 39, 38 + 13 = 51\} = 51$$
$$\text{TIME1(32)} = \text{TIME1(3)} + p_{21} = 9 + 6 = 15$$
$$\text{TIME2(32)} = \max \{\text{TIME1(32)} + p_{22}, \text{TIME2(3)} + p_{22}\}$$
$$= \max \{15 + 10 = 25, 20 + 10 = 30\} = 30$$
$$\text{TIME3(32)} = \max \{\text{TIME2(32)} + p_{23}, \text{TIME3(3)} + p_{23}\}$$
$$= \max \{30 + 3 = 33, 38 + 3 = 41\} = 41$$
$$\text{TIME1(34)} = \text{TIME1(3)} + p_{41} = 9 + 17 = 26$$
$$\text{TIME2(34)} = \max \{\text{TIME1(34)} + p_{42}, \text{TIME2(3)} + p_{42}\}$$
$$= \max \{26 + 16 = 42, 20 + 16 = 36\} = 42$$
$$\text{TIME3(34)} = \max \{\text{TIME2(34)} + p_{43}, \text{TIME3(3)} + p_{43}\}$$
$$= \max \{42 + 4 = 46, 38 + 4 = 42\} = 46$$

The lower bounds are

$$
LB(31) = \max \begin{cases} 21 + 23 + 13 = 57 \\ 26 + 26 + 3 = 55 \\ 51 + 7 = 58 \end{cases} = 58
$$

$$
LB(32) = \max \begin{cases} 15 + 29 + 21 = 65 \\ 30 + 21 + 4 = 55 \\ 41 + 17 = 58 \end{cases} = 65
$$

and

$$
LB(34) = \max \begin{cases} 26 + 18 + 13 = 57 \\ 42 + 15 + 3 = 60 \\ 46 + 16 = 62 \end{cases} = 62
$$

Since LB(31) is the smallest lower bound, we shall branch from node 31. Note that

TIME1(312) = TIME1(31) + p_{21} = 21 + 6 = 27

TIME2(312) = max {TIME1(312) + p_{22}, TIME2(31) + p_{22}}

$\qquad$ = max {27 + 10 = 37, 26 + 10 = 36} = 37

TIME3(312) = max {TIME2(312) + p_{23}, TIME3(31) + p_{23}}

$\qquad$ = max {37 + 3 = 40, 51 + 3 = 54} = 54

TIME1(314) = TIME1(31) + p_{41} = 21 + 17 = 38

TIME2(314) = max {TIME1(314) + p_{42}, TIME2(31) + p_{42}}

$\qquad$ = max {38 + 16 = 54, 26 + 16 = 42} = 54

TIME3(314) = max {TIME2(314) + p_{43}, TIME3(31) + p_{43}}

$\qquad$ = max {54 + 4 = 58, 51 + 4 = 55} = 58

The lower bounds are

$$
LB(312) = \max \begin{cases} 27 + 17 + 20 = 64 \\ 37 + 16 + 4 = 57 \\ 54 + 4 = 58 \end{cases} = 64
$$

and

$$
LB(314) = \max \begin{cases} 38 + 6 + 13 = 57 \\ 54 + 10 + 3 = 67 \\ 58 + 3 = 61 \end{cases} = 67
$$

Since the least lower bound is LB(13) = 61, we must backtrack to node 13.

We note that

$$\text{TIME1}(132) = \text{TIME1}(13) + p_{21} = 21 + 6 = 27$$

$$\text{TIME2}(132) = \max\{\text{TIME1}(132) + p_{22}, \text{TIME2}(13) + p_{22}\}$$
$$= \max\{27 + 10 = 37, 32 + 10 = 42\} = 42$$

$$\text{TIME3}(132) = \max\{\text{TIME2}(132) + p_{23}, \text{TIME3}(13) + p_{23}\}$$
$$= \max\{42 + 3 = 45, 50 + 3 = 53\} = 53$$

$$\text{TIME1}(134) = \text{TIME1}(13) + p_{41} = 21 + 17 = 38$$

$$\text{TIME2}(134) = \max\{\text{TIME1}(134) + p_{42}, \text{TIME2}(13) + p_{42}\}$$
$$= \max\{38 + 16 = 54, 32 + 16 = 48\} = 54$$

$$\text{TIME3}(134) = \max\{\text{TIME2}(134) + p_{43}, \text{TIME3}(13) + p_{43}\}$$
$$= \max\{54 + 4 = 58, 50 + 4 = 54\} = 58$$

Since TIME2(134) = TIME2(314) and TIME3(134) = TIME3(314), node 134 is dominated by node 314. The only lower bound which must be calculated is

$$\text{LB}(132) = \max\begin{cases} 27 + 17 + 20 = 64 \\ 42 + 16 + \quad 4 = 62 \\ 53 + \quad 4 \qquad\quad = 57 \end{cases} = 64$$

At this point, we must investigate either node 2 or node 34. Arbitrarily choose node 34. We find that

$$\text{TIME1}(341) = \text{TIME1}(34) + p_{11} = 26 + 12 = 38$$

$$\text{TIME2}(341) = \max\{\text{TIME1}(341) + p_{12}, \text{TIME2}(34) + p_{12}\}$$
$$= \max\{38 + 5 = 43, 42 + 5 = 47\} = 47$$

$$\text{TIME3}(341) = \max\{\text{TIME2}(341) + p_{13}, \text{TIME3}(34) + p_{13}\}$$
$$= \max\{47 + 13 = 60, 46 + 13 = 59\} = 60$$

$$\text{TIME1}(342) = \text{TIME1}(34) + p_{21} = 26 + 6 = 32$$

$$\text{TIME2}(342) = \max\{\text{TIME1}(342) + p_{22}, \text{TIME2}(34) + p_{22}\}$$
$$= \{32 + 10 = 42, 42 + 10 = 52\} = 52$$

$$\text{TIME3}(342) = \max\{\text{TIME2}(342) + p_{23}, \text{TIME3}(34) + p_{23}\}$$
$$= \max\{52 + 3 = 55, 46 + 3 = 49\} = 55$$

and the lower bounds are

$$\text{LB}(341) = \max\begin{cases} 38 + \quad 6 + 13 = 57 \\ 47 + 10 + \quad 3 = 60 \\ 60 + \quad 3 \qquad\quad = 63 \end{cases} = 63$$

and

$$\text{LB}(342) = \max \begin{cases} 32 + 12 + 18 = 62 \\ 52 + \ \ 5 + 13 = 70 \\ 55 + 13 \qquad = 68 \end{cases} = 70$$

As LB(2) = 62, we must still investigate node 2. Notice that

$$\text{TIME1}(21) = \text{TIME1}(2) + p_{11} = 6 + 12 = 18$$
$$\text{TIME2}(21) = \max \{\text{TIME1}(21) + p_{12}, \text{TIME2}(2) + p_{12}\}$$
$$= \max \{18 + 5 = 23, 16 + 5 = 21\} = 23$$
$$\text{TIME3}(21) = \max \{\text{TIME2}(21) + p_{13}, \text{TIME3}(2) + p_{13}\}$$
$$= \max \{23 + 13 = 36, 19 + 13 = 32\} = 36$$
$$\text{TIME1}(23) = \text{TIME1}(2) + p_{31} = 6 + 9 = 15$$
$$\text{TIME2}(23) = \max \{\text{TIME1}(23) + p_{32}, \text{TIME2}(2) + p_{32}\}$$
$$= \max \{15 + 11 = 26, 16 + 11 = 27\} = 27$$
$$\text{TIME3}(23) = \max \{\text{TIME2}(23) + p_{33}, \text{TIME3}(2) + p_{33}\}$$
$$= \max \{27 + 18 = 45, 19 + 18 = 37\} = 45$$
$$\text{TIME1}(24) = \text{TIME1}(2) + p_{41} = 6 + 17 = 23$$
$$\text{TIME2}(24) = \max \{\text{TIME1}(24) + p_{42}, \text{TIME2}(2) + p_{42}\}$$
$$= \max \{23 + 16 = 39, 16 + 16 = 32\} = 39$$
$$\text{TIME3}(24) = \max \{\text{TIME2}(24) + p_{43}, \text{TIME3}(2) + p_{43}\}$$
$$= \max \{39 + 4 = 43, 19 + 4 = 23\} = 43$$

and the lower bounds are

$$\text{LB}(21) = \max \begin{cases} 18 + 26 + 20 = 64 \\ 23 + 27 + \ \ 4 = 54 \\ 36 + 22 \qquad = 58 \end{cases} = 64$$

$$\text{LB}(23) = \max \begin{cases} 15 + 29 + 18 = 62 \\ 27 + 21 + \ \ 4 = 52 \\ 45 + 17 \qquad = 62 \end{cases} = 62$$

and

$$\text{LB}(24) = \max \begin{cases} 23 + 21 + 18 = 62 \\ 39 + 16 + 13 = 68 \\ 43 + 31 \qquad = 74 \end{cases} = 74$$

We must branch from node 23.

$$\text{TIME1}(231) = \text{TIME1}(23) + p_{11} = 15 + 12 = 27$$

$$\text{TIME2}(231) = \max \{\text{TIME1}(231) + p_{12}, \text{TIME2}(23) + p_{12}\}$$
$$= \max \{27 + 5 = 32, 27 + 5 = 32\} = 32$$
$$\text{TIME3}(231) = \max \{\text{TIME2}(231) + p_{13}, \text{TIME3}(23) + p_{13}\}$$
$$= \max \{32 + 13 = 45, 45 + 13 = 58\} = 58$$
$$\text{TIME1}(234) = \text{TIME1}(23) + p_{41} = 15 + 17 = 32$$
$$\text{TIME2}(234) = \max \{\text{TIME1}(234) + p_{42}, \text{TIME2}(23) + p_{42}\}$$
$$= \max \{32 + 16 = 48, 27 + 16 = 43\} = 48$$
$$\text{TIME3}(234) = \max \{\text{TIME2}(234) + p_{43}, \text{TIME3}(23) + p_{43}\}$$
$$= \max \{48 + 4 = 52, 45 + 4 = 49\} = 52$$

The lower bounds are

$$\text{LB}(231) = \max \begin{cases} 27 + 17 + 20 = 64 \\ 32 + 16 + 4 = 52 \\ 58 + 4 = 62 \end{cases} = 64$$

and

$$\text{LB}(234) = \max \begin{cases} 32 + 12 + 18 = 62 \\ 48 + 5 + 13 = 66 \\ 52 + 13 = 65 \end{cases} = 66$$

At this point, we see that the least lower bound on the tree is $\text{LB}(341) = 63$. Therefore, the optimal sequence is $\{3, 4, 1, 2\}$. $\square$

There are several other approaches to the three machine scheduling problem. Giglio and Wagner (6) and Story and Wagner (18) have used integer programming to formulate and solve the three-machine flow shop scheduling problem (see Exercise 5-25). Their computational results are not very encouraging, and branch-and-bound methods seem to have a clear advantage over the integer programming approach.

There are no simple general results known for the three-machine job shop scheduling problem (jobs may have different technological orderings). It is possible to formulate the three-machine job shop scheduling problem as an integer programming problem, but once again, this is not an efficient approach.

5-2.4 Two Jobs, m Machines

There is a simple graphical solution to the two-job, m-machine job shop scheduling problem. The procedure was first suggested by Akers and Friedman (1), and has been stated more completely by Hardgrave and Nemhauser (7).

TABLE 5-7 Processing Times

| | MACHINE | | | |
JOB	*a*	*b*	*c*	*d*
1	2	5	3	2
2	3	5	2	6

The procedure is best illustrated by an example. Suppose two jobs are to be processed on four machines. Let the machines be designated *a*, *b*, *c*, and *d*. Job 1 must be processed with the technological ordering *a*, *b*, *c*, *d*. The technological ordering of job 2 is *d*, *b*, *a*, *c*. The processing times are shown in Table 5-7. A graphical representation of the problem is shown in Figure 5-5. The axes represent the amount of work completed on the jobs, with the machine

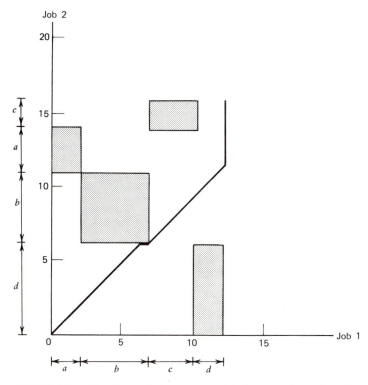

FIGURE 5-5. Graphical solution to a two-job, four-machine scheduling problem.

times laid out in the proper technological order (hence, the restriction to two jobs). The coordinates represent a possible state of completion of the two jobs. The Cartesian product of the job 1–job 2 processing times for each machine is shown as a shaded region. Clearly, these shaded regions are infeasible, as they represent simultaneous processing of both jobs on the same machine.

A solution to this problem is any line from the point $(0, 0)$ to the point $\left(\sum_{i=1}^{m} p_{i1}, \sum_{i=1}^{m} p_{i2} \right)$, which does not pass through a shaded region. The line may be composed of horizontal (work on job 1 only), vertical (work on job 2 only), and 45° (simultaneous work on both jobs) segments.

A minimum makespan schedule is a line that minimizes the length of vertical (or horizontal) segment, that is, a schedule that maximizes the amount of simultaneous processing. This schedule must be determined by trial and error. Usually, only a few lines must be drawn before the optimal solution is found. An optimal solution to the example problem is shown in Figure 5-5.

5-2.5 n Jobs, m Machines

The general n-job, m-machine job shop scheduling problem is quite formidable. The difficulties are entirely computational, as there are $(n!)^m$ possible schedules, and at least one of them must produce a minimum makespan (or optimize whatever measure of effectiveness has been chosen). There are no efficient exact solution procedures known. Various authors have formulated integer programming models of the job shop scheduling problem [see Conway, et al. (5), pp. 107–109], but computational results are not encouraging.

The branch-and-bound technique has been used by Brooks and White (3) and many other authors. The Brooks and White procedure is computationally prohibitive for large problems, but does appear to be more efficient than integer programming, especially for small problems.

A number of heuristic methods are used in the general job shop scheduling problem. Among the most widely used are a class of procedures known as *dispatching rules*. These are simply logical decision rules that enable a decision maker to select the next job for processing at a machine when that machine becomes available. Thus, the scheduling decisions are made sequentially over time instead of all at once. Dispatching procedures always include the concept of job *priority*. A priority is just a numerical attribute of a job defined in such a way that a job with the highest priority is scheduled next. We shall discuss priority assignment procedures in greater detail in Section 5-2.7.

5-2.6 Scheduling to Minimize Total Setup Costs

There are many practical situations in which it is unreasonable to assume that the time required to set up the facility for the next job is independent of the task that was just performed. That is, the setup time for the jobs to be processed are *sequence dependent*. For example, consider the bottling of different flavors of soft drinks on the same machine. Clearly the thoroughness of the cleaning of the machine required between any two flavors is dependent on both the flavor just bottled and the flavor for which the machine is being prepared.

In situations where setup time is sequence independent, it is customary to include setup time as part of the job processing time. However, if the setup times are sequence dependent, we must take explicit account of them. Let s_{ij} be the time required to change the facility over from job i to job j. The makespan is

$$F = \sum_{i=1}^{n} s_{[i-1][i]} + \sum_{i=1}^{n} p_{[i]}$$

where $s_{[0][1]}$ is the time required to bring the facility from the idle state to the conditions necessary to process the first job in the sequence. Since the sum of the processing times is constant, regardless of sequence, makespan is minimized by minimizing the sum of the setup times.

The task of minimizing the sum of the setup times is analogous to a classic combinatorial problem known as the *traveling salesman problem*. This is a problem in which a salesman, starting in one city, wishes to visit each of the remaining $n - 1$ cities once and only once and return to the start in such a way that minimizes the total distance traveled (or total time, or cost, etc.). Clearly each job in the scheduling problem corresponds to a city;[1] the setup time from one job to another corresponds to the distance between cities, and a schedule of the n jobs corresponds to a "tour" for the salesman.

The traveling salesman problem is closely related to the well-known assignment problem of linear programming. If we let

$$X_{ij} = \begin{cases} 1, & \text{if the tour involves a direct link from city } i \text{ to city } j \\ 0, & \text{otherwise} \end{cases}$$

then the assignment problem is

$$\min \sum_{i=1}^{n} \sum_{j=1}^{n} X_{ij} s_{ij} \tag{5-4}$$

subject to

$$\sum_{i=1}^{n} X_{ij} = 1, \qquad j = 1, 2, \ldots, n \tag{5-5}$$

---

[1] Actually, the scheduling problem corresponds to an $(n + 1)$-city problem, since the initial idle state of the machine must be considered.

$$\sum_{j=1}^{n} X_{ij} = 1, \qquad i = 1, 2, \ldots, n \tag{5-6}$$

$$X_{ij} = 0, 1 \tag{5-7}$$

The objective function, Equation 5-4, is the cost associated with any tour, and the constraints (5-5) and (5-6) insure that each city is visited once and only once. However, we have not constrained the problem so that a tour cannot return to its starting point until all n cities have been visited. Incorporation of this constraint converts a very simple mathematical programming problem into a complex combinatorial problem.

We shall describe a branch-and-bound solution offered by Little et al. (16) for the traveling salesman problem. Let $\mathbf{S} = \{s_{ij}\}$ be an $(n \times n)$ matrix of the distances (or times, costs, etc.) between city pairs. If $s_{ij} = s_{ji}$, the problem is said to be symmetric. The classical traveling salesman problem is symmetric, as s_{ij} represent distance. If the s_{ij} represent time, cost, and so forth, then the problem need not be symmetric. The procedure to be described is slightly more efficient for asymmetric problems.

A tour is just a permutation of the integers $1, 2, \ldots, n$, say

$$[1], [2], \ldots, [n]$$

and the length of the tour is

$$z = \sum_{i=2}^{n} s_{[i-1][i]} + s_{[n][1]}$$

In the construction of lower bounds on the optimum tour, the process of *reduction* is useful. Subtracting the smallest element in a row from every element in that row is called *row reduction*. A distance matrix with at least one zero in each row and column will be called a *reduced matrix* and could be obtained by reducing both rows *and* columns. Suppose h is the sum of the reducing constants. Now if z is the length of a tour under a matrix before reduction and z_1 the length of the tour under the reduced matrix, then

$$z = z_1 + h \tag{5-8}$$

Since a reduced matrix contains only nonnegative elements, h constitutes a lower bound on the length of a tour under the old matrix.

The branching process consists of, at some stage of a partial solution, deciding whether or not to incorporate the city pair (i, j) in the partial tour. This is illustrated by the tree in Figure 5-6. The "all tours" node is self-explanatory. The node labeled (i, j) represents all tours containing the city pair (i, j), while the node labeled $(\overline{i, j})$ represents all tours that do not. Similarly, for the nodes labeled (l, m) and $(\overline{l, m})$. If the branching process is carried far enough, some node will eventually represent a single tour.

Let LB(X) represent the lower bound on all tours contained in node X.

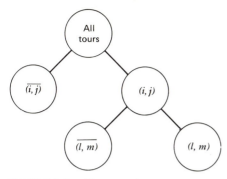

FIGURE 5-6. The start of a tree.

Clearly LB("all tours") is the sum of the constants required to reduce the original matrix. Consider branching from that node to a new node, say Y. Possible city pairs for inclusion in Y are those for which $s_{ij} = 0$. Now consider tours that do not contain (i, j). Since some city other than j will immediately follow city i and city j must be reached from some city other than i, those tours must include a distance at least equal to the sum of the smallest elements in row i and column j, excluding s_{ij}; that is,

$$\theta_{ij} = \min_{\substack{k \\ k \neq j}} s_{ik} + \min_{\substack{l \\ l \neq i}} s_{lj} \tag{5-9}$$

We elect to choose for inclusion in the current tour, that is, node Y, the city pair with the largest θ_{ij}. Call this city pair (u, v). In effect, this chooses to include the city pair that has the largest penalty associated with *not* including it. The lower bound on the node $\bar{Y}$, which excludes (u, v), is

$$\text{LB}(\bar{Y}) = \text{LB}(\text{"all tours"}) + \theta_{uv} \tag{5-10}$$

Now, since (u, v) are included in the tour, row u and column v may be deleted from the original matrix. Furthermore, (u, v) will be part of a partial tour starting at p and ending at m, and we must forbid connecting m to p as this would create a subtour. To accomplish this, set $s_{mp} = \infty$. Finally, the new **S** matrix may be reduced to form the lower bound for node Y as

$$\text{LB}(Y) = \text{LB}(\text{"all tours"}) + h \tag{5-11}$$

where h is the sum of the reducing constants. Then the process starts over again, branching from node Y just as we branched from the node "all tours."

If we continue this procedure, we eventually arrive at a node representing a single tour. If the lower bound on this node is less than or equal to the lower bounds on all other nodes, then the optimal solution has been found. If not, then those nodes with smaller lower bounds must be explored. The procedure is best learned through study of an example.

TABLE 5-8 Cost Matrix for Example 5-6

		1	2	3	4	5	6
				To			
	1	∞	13	11	2	7	9
	2	5	∞	10	6	8	4
	3	3	4	∞	7	4	6
From	4	8	11	3	∞	6	4
	5	9	2	6	8	∞	10
	6	6	5	4	7	8	∞

☐**EXAMPLE 5-6** Consider the six city traveling salesman problem where the cost of travel between city pairs is shown in Table 5-8. Note that $s_{ii} = \infty$ to prohibit linking a city with itself. The tree for this problem is shown in Figure 5-7. We shall now trace the construction of this tree. Consider the node "all tours." The lower bound is found by reducing the original **S** matrix first by rows and then by columns. The reduced matrix is given in Table 5-9, with the

TABLE 5-9 Reduced Cost Matrix for Example 5-6

		1	2	3	4	5	6	
					To			
	1	∞	11	9	0 ⑥	4	7	2
	2	1	∞	6	2	3	0 ②	4
	3	0 ①	1	∞	4	0 ②	3	3
From	4	5	8	0 ①	∞	2	1	3
	5	7	0 ⑤	4	6	∞	8	2
	6	2	1	0 ①	3	3	∞	4
						1		

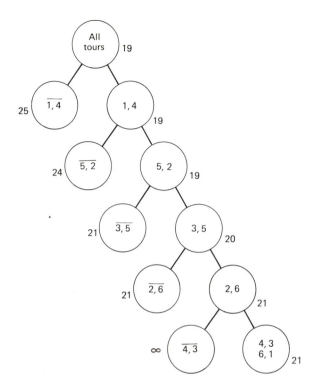

FIGURE 5-7. Tree for Example 5-6.

reducing constants shown in the right-hand and bottom margins. It is easily seen that the sum of these constants is 19, so LB("all tours") = 19. The θ_{ij} are computed from Equation 5-9, and are the circled numbers in Table 5-9. Since max $\{\theta_{ij}\} = \theta_{1,4} = 6$, we branch from "all tours" to the nodes $(1, 4)$ and $(\overline{1, 4})$. The lower bound on $(\overline{1, 4})$ is found by Equation 5-10 to be LB$(\overline{1, 4}) = 19 + 6 = 25$. Row 1 and column 4 are deleted, and $s_{4,1} = \infty$ to prevent subtours. The new cost matrix is shown in Table 5-10.

We note that the new cost matrix cannot be reduced further. Therefore, from Equation 5-11, LB$(1, 4) = 19 + 0 = 19$. We continue to explore the $(1, 4)$ branch. The θ_{ij} are shown as circled numbers in Table 5-10. Since max $\{\theta_{ij}\} = \theta_{5,2} = 5$, we branch from $(1, 4)$ to $(5, 2)$ and $(\overline{5, 2})$. We may compute LB$(\overline{5, 2}) = 19 + 5 = 24$. Deleting row 5 and column 2, and setting $s_{2,5} = \infty$, we obtain the new cost matrix shown in Table 5-11.

This new cost matrix cannot be reduced further, therefore, LB$(5, 2) = 19 + 0 = 19$, and we continue to explore the $(5, 2)$ branch. There are three possibilities for max $\{\theta_{ij}\} = \theta_{6,3} = \theta_{3,5} = \theta_{2,6} = 2$. Arbitrarily choose $(3, 5)$ as the next city pair to examine. We obtain LB$(\overline{3, 5}) = 19 + 2 = 21$. Deleting row 3 and

TABLE 5-10 New Cost Matrix

		To			
	1	2	3	5	6
From 2	1	∞	6	3	0 ②
3	0 ①	1	∞	0 ②	3
4	∞	8	0 ①	2	1
5	7	0 ⑤	4	∞	8
6	2	1	0 ①	3	∞

column 5 and setting $s_{2,3} = \infty$ yields a new cost matrix in which column 1 must be reduced by 1. This new reduced cost matrix is shown in Table 5-12. Also, LB(3, 5) = 19 + 1 = 20, and we continue to explore the (3, 5) branch. Since $\theta_{2,1} = \theta_{2,6} = \theta_{4,3} = \theta_{6,3} = 1$, several choices exist for the next branch. Arbitrarily choose (2, 6). This results in LB$(\overline{2, 6})$ = 20 + 1 = 21. Deleting row 2 and column 6 and setting $s_{6,3} = \infty$ yields the (2 × 2) cost matrix shown in Table 5-13, which has been reduced by 1. Since LB(2, 6) = 20 + 1 = 21, we continue to explore the (2, 6) path. By examining this last cost matrix, we see that either (6, 1) or (4, 3) may be chosen, and that the lower bound on either choice is still 21. Furthermore, choosing either city pair automatically forces us to include the other to form a complete tour. Since this final node has a lower bound of 21, and no other node on the tree has a smaller lower bound, the problem is solved. The optimum tour is {1, 4, 3, 5, 2, 6}.□

TABLE 5-11 New Cost Matrix

		To		
	1	3	5	6
From 2	1	6	∞	0 ②
3	0 ①	∞	0 ②	3
4	∞	0 ①	2	1
6	2	0 ②	3	∞

TABLE 5-12   New Reduced Cost Matrix

		To		
		1	3	6
From	2	0 ①	∞	0 ①
	4	∞	0 ①	1
	6	1	0 ①	∞

TABLE 5-13   Final Reduced Cost Matrix

		To	
		1	3
From	4	∞	0 ⊘
	6	0 ⊘	∞

This solution procedure is relatively efficient. Little et al., report solving problems up to 40 cities in less than nine minutes on an IBM 7090 computer. Problems involving up to approximately 20 cities may be solved in a few seconds. In general, adding 10 cities to the problem seems to multiply the solution time by a factor of 10. It appears to be computationally advantageous to branch to the right (the inclusive branch) unless the lower bounds dictate otherwise. This seems to assist in reaching an optimum solution quickly.

5-2.7 Priority Dispatching in Dynamic Job Shops

The scheduling procedures that we have presented in previous sections depend heavily on the static nature of the problem. That is, all jobs to be scheduled are already available or may be thought of as arriving at the facility simultaneously. The static problem leads to decision rules whose structure and development is algebraic. The dynamic job shop scheduling problem, in which jobs arrive at random during some time interval, leads to solution techniques of an entirely different nature. These solution techniques consist essentially of priority dispatching procedures in which all jobs are assigned a priority such that a job with the smallest priority number is scheduled first.

A number of results from priority queueing would seem useful in resolving the dynamic job shop scheduling problem. However, only limited success has been achieved through this approach. Principally, the results available deal with the single-channel, single-server queue that corresponds to a single-facility job shop, and multiple-channel queues that correspond to several facilities in parallel. There are some limited approaches to queues in tandem (series), and Jackson (13) has established sufficient conditions under which a general network of queues, which corresponds to a general job shop, may be decomposed and treated as a set of independent queues. These results are discussed at length in Conway et al. (5, Chapters 8, 9, and 10).

An alternative to the probabilistic or queueing methods discussed above would be actual experimentation with various scheduling procedures, such as priority dispatching rules, in a real job shop. This is usually not practical, however, and even if it was, there would be a considerable loss of generality. One could not always be certain whether a particular result was due to the scheduling procedure being tested or to some undetected condition in the shop.

This problem may be overcome to a large extent by performing experiments with a hypothetical job shop on a digital computer through Monte Carlo simulation. The general procedure consists of developing a computer program that simulates the arrival of jobs and controls the flow of these jobs through the various processing facilities. In addition, the program may assign due dates or other attributes to the jobs, and it usually contains lists and files to record the state of the job shop and compute various measures of effectiveness. Through the use of such a computer program, various scheduling procedures and their impact on shop performance may be investigated under relatively homogenous conditions. Many authors have reported such studies. The report by Conway (4) contains a very complete investigation of 92 priority dispatching rules and their effect on several measures of performance. Conway et al. (5, Chapter 11) also discuss the findings of several more investigations.

The results of these studies seem to indicate that in many situations the SPT priority rule is of dominating importance. We saw in Section 5-2.1 that SPT optimized mean flow time in a static single-machine problem. It is somewhat surprising that it emerges as a superior rule for many complex dynamic problems as well. Regardless of the measure of performance, the SPT rule is among the best of the many procedures that have been investigated. For a given measure of performance, it is usually possible to produce a rule that performs better than SPT. However, for reasonable measures of performance, the rules that appear to be better are much more complex and often would require elaborate information systems for implementation. The SPT rule is extremely simple, both in statement and implementation, and is very close to the rules used by real-world job shops.

A practical objection to the use of SPT is the general belief that jobs with long processing times would experience unusually long waiting times. This general belief is incorrect. Conway et al. (5) report the mean and variance of flow time for 8700 jobs processed through a nine-machine random-routed job shop using the SPT, FCFS (first-come, first-served) and RANDOM (next job chosen at random from among those available) priority rules. Their results are reproduced in Table 5-14. We see that SPT actually has a *smaller* variance of flow time than either FCFS or RANDOM. Thus, it would seem that the often-heard objection to SPT is erroneous.

There are, of course, many other priority dispatching rules that could be employed in a job shop. For example, several rules that are related to the shortest processing time concept are:

LWKR	*Least Work Remaining*	Job priority equals the sum of the processing times for all operations not yet performed.
TWK	*Total Work*	Job priority equals the sum of the processing times of all operations of the job.
FOPR	*Fewest Operations Remaining*	Job priority equals the number of operations yet to be performed on the job.

In general, SPT tends to result in fewer jobs in queue when compared to the above priority rules. It is also much easier to implement in practice.

In any job shop, there are various types of information available about the status of the work centers, and it would seem reasonable to incorporate this information into a decision rule in an attempt to improve shop performance. For example, it does not seem particularly useful to select a job on the basis of SPT if, after processing, that job goes to a machine that already has a large

TABLE 5-14 Mean and Variance of Flow Time for 8700 Jobs in a Nine-Machine Random Routed Job Shop

PRIORITY RULE	MEAN	VARIANCE
SPT	34.02	2,318
FCFS	74.43	5,739
RANDOM	74.70	10,822

backlog of work. One priority rule that attempts to deal with this problem is

WINQ   *Work in Next Queue*   The job that would subsequently move to the machine with the least work is assigned the highest priority. Jobs waiting for the last operation have priority zero.

Clearly, WINQ is independent of job processing time. It can reduce the number of jobs in queue, when compared to such rules as FCFS and RANDOM, but usually does not perform as well in this respect as SPT. The type of input data required for WINQ would be reasonably difficult to provide in an actual job shop, and the actual computation of priorities is considerably more complex than under SPT.

An important measure of performance in actual job shops is the satisfaction of preassigned due dates. Many priority dispatching rules have been devised to deal explicitly with due date related criteria. Some of these rules are:

DDATE   *Due Date*   The job priority equals its due date.

SLACK   *Slack Time*   The job priority equals the time remaining before its due date minus any remaining processing time.

S/ROP   *Slack/Remaining Operation*   The job priority equals the slack time divided by the number of remaining operations.

All of these rules generally yield a substantial improvement over such rules as FCFS with respect to the number of jobs that are late. The S/ROP rule is probably the best in terms of mean lateness and standard deviation of lateness. However, SPT does nearly as well, as it does not require as much information. As a general rule, S/ROP operates best when the machine utilization is only moderately high (say up to approximately 85 percent) and SPT operates best at high machine utilizations (say in excess of 90 percent). An alternating priority rule that uses SPT during relatively high congestion periods and S/ROP during less congested periods would likely perform very well. A further discussion of these results is given by Conway (4).

When jobs arrive at random, one must consider the possibility of preemption. The two possible extremes are preempt-resume and preempt-repeat. Preempt-resume implies that a job that has been preempted has the same total processing time despite interruption. Preempt-repeat implies that if a job is interrupted, all processing time up to the point of preemption is lost and the job must begin anew when it is reprocessed. Most real systems probably operate somewhere between these two extremes. For example, an interrupted job may lose the setup time portion of its total processing time.

Under preempt-resume, the dynamic scheduling problem essentially reduces to the static case. Upon arrival of a job, the scheduling decision is reviewed using only the remaining processing time for the job currently on the facility, and the static sequencing rule optimal for the particular situation could be employed. The preempt-repeat situation is not so simple, and no general results are known. If advance information is available about arriving jobs, it may be optimal to insert idle time in the schedule. For example, if we are scheduling a single facility and it is known that a job that will cause preemption will arrive before any of the jobs currently available can be processed, then no processing should be performed.

5-3 Project Scheduling

Project scheduling is distinguished from job shop and other related types of scheduling by the nonrepetitive nature of the work. A project is usually thought of as a one-time effort, although this may not always be the case. Similar efforts may have been undertaken previously, but not on a production basis. For example, the construction of a building, a highway, or a ship might be thought of as typical projects. In addition, periodic maintenance operations, administration of research and development programs, installation of a new computer facility, and the development and implementation of a new management information system are also activities that can be treated by project scheduling methods. The essential components of a project are usually the degree of nonrepetitiveness, the time frame, and the magnitude of costs involved.

A number of techniques have been developed to assist in planning, scheduling, and control of projects. The most popular methods are the Critial Path Method (CPM) and the Program Evaluation and Review Technique (PERT). These techniques decompose the project into a number of activities, represent the precedence relationships among activities through a network, and then determine a critical or bottleneck path through the network. CPM and PERT differ primarily in their treatment of uncertainty in activity time estimates.

5-3.1 The Critical Path Method (CPM)

CPM was developed for E. I. duPont de Nemours in 1957 and was first applied to construction and maintenance of chemical plants. Since then, the use of CPM has grown at a rapid rate. There are numerous articles in trade and professional journals reporting both applications and methodological developments, and many computer programs to perform the calculation have been developed.

The critial path method starts with the construction of a network or arrow diagram that represents the precedence relationships among activities in the project. Network construction is a planning function, and is the most difficult

Activity	Duration	Immediate Predecessor
(1, 2)	4	—
(2, 4)	7	(1, 2)
(2, 3)	8	(1, 2)
(2, 5)	6	(1, 2)
(4, 6)	15	(2, 4), (2, 3)
(3, 5)	9	(2, 3)
(5, 6)	12	(2, 5), (3, 5)
(6, 7)	8	(4, 6), (5, 6)

(a)

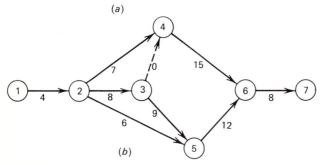

(b)

FIGURE 5-8. A typical project and network. (a) Activities in the project. (b) Project network.

aspect of CPM. It involves detailed analysis and thought, especially for large projects. The benefits of this effort may be considerable, as it will produce a clear understanding of what must be accomplished. In fact, the logical statement of the project obtained from the network model may be the greatest benefit of CPM.

Suppose a project consisted of the activities, time durations, and precedence relationships shown in Figure 5-8a. The network representation of this project is shown in Figure 5-8b. The arcs in this network represent activities and the nodes represent events. An event is simply a point marking the end of one activity and the start of a new group of activities. The number along the arc represents the duration of that activity. This is the activities-on-arcs, or AOA system of network representation. There is another possible approach in which the activities are graphically represented by the nodes and the arrows represent only the precedence relationships. This activities-on-nodes (AON) system is not widely used, although it often simplifies network construction. The primary disadvantage of the AON system is that few CPM computer programs accept it and hand calculations under AON are slightly more difficult.

The dashed line in Figure 5-8b is called a dummy activity, and it has a zero duration. It has been necessary to introduce the dummy to indicate the dependency of activity (4, 6) on activity (2, 3). Other situations may require the use of dummy activities. For example, consider the parallel activities originating at

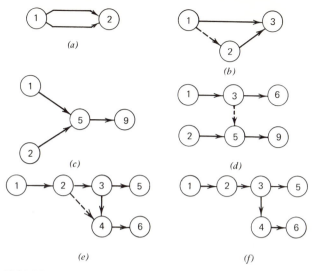

FIGURE 5-9. Network modeling situations.

node 1 and terminating at node 2 in Figure 5-9a. We cannot distinguish between the two activities, as they both are labeled (1, 2). By adding a dummy activity, as shown in Figure 5-9b, the two activities are uniquely identified. Alternatively, we could combine the two activities into one, but this may destroy the detail needed in the network. Another use of dummy activities occurs when one activity is only partially dependent on another. For example, consider the three activities shown in Figure 5-9c. If activity (5, 9) is only partially dependent on (1, 5), we must split (1, 5) into two parts, say (1, 3) and (3, 6), such that (5, 9) depends on (1, 3), and represent this dependency with a dummy. This is shown in Figure 5-9d. Dummy activities must be used efficiently, however, to avoid cluttering the network. Consider the dummy activity (2, 4) in Figure 5-9e. Evidently, (4, 6) depends on (1, 2), (2, 3), and (3, 4), but the dependency on (1, 2) is clear without the dummy. Therefore, we would eliminate the unnecessary dummy and represent the network as in Figure 5-9f.

As a general guide to network construction, Moder and Phillips (17) have given the following rules:

1. No activity can begin until all activities preceding it are complete.

2. Neither the length nor the direction of an arc has any significance. It implies precedence only.

3. Two events can be directly connected by at most one activity.

4. Each event number must be unique.

5. A network may have only one initial and one terminal event.

We shall assume that the events in the AOA network are indexed by i

$(i = 1, 2, \ldots, n)$. Thus, an activity could be represented by (i, j) where $i < j$. The following additional notation will be used:

t_{ij} = duration for activity (i, j)

E_i = earliest occurrence time for event i

L_i = latest occurrence time for event i

ES_{ij} = earliest start time for activity (i, j)

EF_{ij} = earliest finish time for activity (i, j)

LS_{ij} = latest allowable start time for activity (i, j)

LF_{ij} = latest allowable finish time for activity (i, j)

S_{ij} = total slack or float for activity (i, j)

FS_{ij} = free slack or float for activity (i, j)

The procedure for computing the critical path has four stages. It does not explicitly require the ES_{ij}, EF_{ij}, LS_{ij}, and LF_{ij} values, but we shall present formulas for their calculation for completeness.

The first stage consists of a forward pass through the network to compute the earliest event times (and the earliest start and earliest finish times if desired for each activity). This is accomplished by the following procedure:

1. Set the start time of the initial event to zero.

2. Start each activity as soon as its predecessor event occurs.

3. Calculate early event time as the maximum of the earliest finish time of activities terminating at the event.

These steps are applied sequentially, passing through the network from initial to terminal event. Expressed mathematically, we have

$$E_1 = 0 \tag{5-12}$$

and

$$E_j = \max \{E_{i_1} + t_{i_1, j}, E_{i_2} + t_{i_2, j}, \ldots, E_{i_u} + t_{i_u, j}\}, \qquad j > 1 \tag{5-13}$$

where $i_1, i_2, \ldots, i_u$ indicate the preceding events of the u activities that terminate at event j. The formulas for the earliest start and earliest finish values are

$$ES_{ij} = E_i \tag{5-14}$$

and

$$EF_{ij} = E_i + t_{ij} \tag{5-15}$$

respectively.

The second stage of the CPM calculations is to conduct a backward pass through the network to determine the latest occurrence time for each event (and the latest start and latest finish time for each activity, if you wish). Usually, we set the latest event time for the terminal event equal to the earliest event time for that event. However, any arbitrary upper limit on project completion time could be used. The steps in this backward pass are:

1.   Set the latest time for the terminal event equal to the earliest time for that event.

2.   Start each activity at the latest time of its successor event less the duration of the activity.

3.   Determine event time as the minimum of the latest start times of all activities emanating from the event.

Apply these steps sequentially, passing through the network from terminal to initial event. Expressed mathematically,

$$L_n = E_n \qquad (5\text{-}16)$$

and

$$L_i = \min \{L_{j_1} - t_{i,j_1}, L_{j_2} - t_{i,j_2}, \ldots, L_{j_v} - t_{i,j_v}\}, \qquad i < n \quad (5\text{-}17)$$

where $j_1, j_2, \ldots, j_v$ indicate the successor events of the v activities that emanate from event i. The formulas for the latest finish and latest start values are

$$LF_{ij} = L_j \qquad (5\text{-}18)$$

and

$$LS_{ij} = L_j - t_{ij} = LF_{ij} - t_{ij} \qquad (5\text{-}19)$$

respectively.

The third stage of the CPM calculations is to determine the slack times for the events and activities in the project. Slack time for an *event* is just the difference between its latest and earliest occurrence times,

$$S_i = L_i - E_i \qquad (5\text{-}20)$$

The *total slack* for *activity* (i, j) is the time by which that activity could be extended without changing the total project duration. It is computed as the difference between the latest occurrence time for event j and the earliest finish time for activity (i, j),

$$S_{ij} = L_j - E_i - t_{ij} \qquad (5\text{-}21)$$

The *free slack* for any activity is the amount of time that activity completion can be delayed without affecting the earliest start time for any other activity in the network. Mathematically,

$$FS_{ij} = E_j - E_i - t_{ij} \qquad (5\text{-}22)$$

The final stage is to determine the *critical path*, which consists of all activities with zero slack ($S_{ij} = 0$). Essentially, this says that an activity belongs on the critical path if any delay of that activity will delay the completion time of the project. Activities with nonzero slack can be used to smooth work loads by moving their start times within the limits of available slack without affecting project completion time.

□**EXAMPLE 5-7** To illustrate the CPM calculations, consider the project described in Figure 5-8. The forward pass computations begin with $E_1 = 0$, and then we obtain

$$E_2 = E_1 + t_{1,2} = 0 + 4 = 4$$

$$E_3 = E_2 + t_{2,3} = 4 + 8 = 12$$

$$E_4 = \max \{E_2 + t_{2,4}, E_3 + t_{3,4}\} = \max \{4 + 7, 12 + 0\} = 12, \text{etc.}$$

The values of E_i for the remaining portion of the network are shown in the square boxes to the left of each node in the network in Figure 5-10. As a result of these calculations, we find that the earliest occurrence time for event 7 is 41 time periods. Thus, 41 time periods is the earliest possible completion time for the project. The backward pass calculations for the latest event times begin by setting $L_7 = 41$, and then computing

$$L_6 = L_7 - t_{6,7} = 41 - 8 = 33$$

$$L_5 = L_6 - t_{5,6} = 33 - 12 = 21$$

$$L_4 = L_6 - t_{4,6} = 33 - 15 = 18$$

$$L_3 = \min \{L_4 - t_{3,4}, L_5 - t_{3,5}\} = \{18 - 0, 21 - 9\} = 12, \text{etc.}$$

The remaining values of L_i are shown in circles to the right of each node in the network of Figure 5-10. The slack times may be computed according to Equation 5-21. For example, the slack time for activity (4, 6) is seen to be

$$S_{4,6} = L_6 - E_4 - t_{4,6} = 33 - 12 - 15 = 6$$

and the slack time for activity (5, 6) is

$$S_{5,6} = L_6 - E_5 - t_{5,6} = 33 - 21 - 12 = 0$$

The slack for each activity is shown enclosed in parentheses immediately

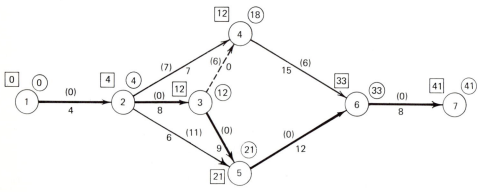

FIGURE 5-10.   CPM calculations for Example 5-7.

adjacent to the activity. Finally, the critical path is determined as those activities with zero slack, or $\{(1, 2), (2, 3), (3, 5), (5, 6), (6, 7)\}$. $\square$

An analysis such as that illustrated above would be performed at the outset of a project. However, periodic updating and revision of the network is necessary to achieve project control. In some instances, noncritical activities may be delayed and as a result, slacks for all activities may be changed. Thus, activities that were formerly not critical may become critical and necessitate managerial decisions to keep the project on schedule. The length of the revision cycle will depend on the expected duration of the project, the variability in activity duration estimates, and the nature of the economic consequences of late completion.

The computational procedure for periodic updating of the network consists of the following steps:

    1.   Introduce a dummy activity before the initial event having a duration equal to the time interval between the time of updating and the start of the project.

    2.   Set the activity durations of all completed activities to zero.

    3.   Revise the durations of all activities that are only partially complete to show the remaining duration from the time of updating.

    4.   Modify the durations of any future activities, if necessary.

    5.   If desirable, schedule a final project completion date equal to a target date.

    6.   Calculate the event times, slack, and critical path for this updated network in the usual fashion.

There are a number of modifications to the basic CPM procedure. We may often have resource constraints that must be satisfied. These types of problems generally deal with either smoothing resource demands with a constraint on total project completion time, or minimizing project completion time with constraints on resource availability. Frequently, situations arise in which the total project completion time exceeds some allowable upper limit. Then we would be interested in reducing the project completion time in a least-cost manner. An introduction to these procedures is given in Section 5-3.3.

A Linear Programming Approach to CPM.   It is not difficult to see that finding the critical path is equivalent to finding the *longest path* through a network. To demonstrate that this problem can be formulated as a linear program, let node 1 be designated as the *source*, let the terminal node n be designated as the *sink*, and assume that a unit of flow must travel through the network from source to sink. The activity durations, t_{ij}, may be thought of as the *length* of arc (i, j). Therefore, the longest path through the network is the solution to

$$\text{maximize} \sum_{\substack{(i,\,j) \text{ in} \\ \text{network}}} \sum t_{ij} X_{ij} \tag{5-23a}$$

subject to

$$\sum_{\substack{(1,\,j) \text{ in} \\ \text{network}}} X_{1j} = 1 \tag{5-23b}$$

$$\sum_{\substack{(k,\,j) \text{ in} \\ \text{network}}} X_{kj} - \sum_{\substack{(i,\,k) \text{ in} \\ \text{network}}} X_{ik} = 0, \qquad \text{for all } k \neq 1 \text{ or } n \tag{5-23c}$$

$$\sum_{\substack{(i,\,n) \text{ in} \\ \text{network}}} X_{in} = 1 \tag{5-23d}$$

$$X_{ij} \geq 0, \qquad \text{for all } (i, j) \text{ in network} \tag{5-23e}$$

There are several special algorithms, other than the usual simplex method, that can be employed to solve the longest path problem (5-23).

5-3.2 Program Evaluation and Review Technique (PERT)

PERT was originally developed in 1958 to 1959 as part of the Polaris Fleet Ballistic Missile Program of the United States Navy. The primary difference between PERT and CPM is that PERT takes explicit account of the uncertainty in the activity duration estimates. The PERT approach consists of specifying a probability distribution for each activity duration. The probability distribution is specified by three estimates of the activity duration: a most likely duration, denoted by m_{ij} for activity (i, j); an optimistic duration, denoted a_{ij}; and a pessimistic duration, denoted b_{ij}.

The beta distribution, shown in Figure 5-11, is usually assumed to be the probability model for activity duration. However, if historical information about activity durations is available, then some other more appropriate standard probability distribution or even an empirical distribution may be employed. In most projects, there will be little or no historical activity duration data available, due to the nonrepetitive nature of the tasks. Under these conditions, the beta distribution is not an unreasonable choice. The beta is a unimodal distribution defined for nonnegative arguments between arbitrary lower (a_{ij}) and upper (b_{ij}) limits with mode m_{ij}. The skewness of the distribution depends upon the location of m_{ij} relative to a_{ij} and b_{ij}. Assuming the beta distribution for activity duration, the mean and variance of activity duration are approximately

$$\bar{t}_{ij} = \frac{a_{ij} + 4m_{ij} + b_{ij}}{6} \tag{5-24}$$

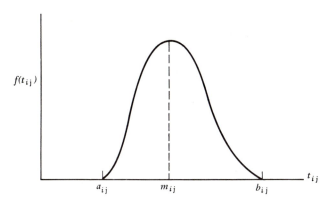

FIGURE 5-11. Beta distribution for duration of activity (i, j).

and

$$\sigma_{ij}^2 = \frac{(b_{ij} - a_{ij})^2}{36} \tag{5-25}$$

respectively.

The network construction phase of PERT is identical to that of CPM. Furthermore, once $\bar{t}_{ij}$ and σ_{ij}^2 are computed for each activity, the critical path determination is identical to CPM. The earliest and latest event times for the network are random variables. Therefore, the computations yield *mean* event times, which we shall denote by $\bar{L}_i$ and $\bar{E}_i$. The variance of activity duration, σ_{ij}^2, is not used during the critical path computations. Once the critical path is determined, probability statements may be made about the total project duration and about the slack at any event.

These probability statements will, in general, not be exact. A typical project network consists of series, parallel, converging, and diverging branches. Determining the exact probability distribution of project duration for such a general project network would be very difficult. PERT makes the simplifying assumption that the mean and variance of project duration, say $\bar{t}_p$ and $\sigma_p{}^2$, respectively, are just the sums of the means and variances of durations of activities on the critical path. Expressed mathematically,

$$\bar{t}_p = \sum_{(i,\,j)\,\in\,U} \bar{t}_{ij} \tag{5-26}$$

and

$$\sigma_p{}^2 = \sum_{(i,\,j)\,\in\,U} \sigma_{ij}^2 \tag{5-27}$$

where U denotes the set of activities on the critical path. In addition, Equation 5-27 requires the assumption that activity durations for activities on the critical path are independent random variables. Finally, PERT appeals to the

Project Scheduling 357

central limit theorem to assume the normal distribution as the probability model for project duration time. These assumptions cause the mean, and often the variance, of project duration time to be underestimated, and there is a probability that some other path will actually be the critical path.

As a result of these simplifying assumptions, *approximate* probability statements may be made about total project duration. We should be very careful about using these probability statements, as it is quite possible that the required assumptions do not hold.

☐**EXAMPLE 5-8** Suppose the project shown in Figure 5-10 had the most likely, optimistic, and pessimistic activity durations shown in columns (1), (2), and (3) respectively, of Table 5-15. The activity duration means and variances may be computed by Equations 5-24 and 5-25 and are shown in columns (4) and (5) of Table 5-15. The critical path calculations shown in Figure 5-10 are still valid. Applying the central limit theorem, the probability distribution of total project duration is approximately normal with mean $\bar{t}_p = 41$ and variance $\sigma_p^2 = 8.778$ computed from Equations 5-26 and 5-27, respectively. Therefore, the probability that the project requires less than (say) 45 time periods is, approximately

$$Pr\{E_7 < 45\} = Pr\left\{Z < \frac{45 - 41}{\sqrt{8.778}}\right\} = Pr\{Z < 1.350\} \simeq 0.91$$

where E_7 is assumed to be normally distributed with mean 41 and variance 8.778, and Z is the standard normal random variable. From this calculation, we see that if 45 time periods is the target completion data for the project, then there is approximately a 91 percent chance of completing the project on time.☐

TABLE 5-15 Activity Duration Means and Variances for Project Network in Figure 5-10

ACTIVITY	(1) m_{ij}	(2) a_{ij}	(3) b_{ij}	(4) $\bar{t}_{ij}$ (DURATION MEAN)	(5) σ_{ij}^2 (DURATION VARIANCE)
(1, 2)	4	2	6	4	0.444
(2, 4)	7	4	10	7	1.000
(2, 3)	7	6	14	8	1.778
(2, 5)	6	3	9	6	1.000
(4, 6)	14	12	22	15	2.778
(3, 5)	10	2	12	9	2.778
(5, 6)	9	6	12	12	1.000
(6, 7)	7	5	15	8	2.778

It is also possible to compute an approximate $100(1 - \alpha)$ percent confidence interval for project completion time. If t is the true project completion time, then

$$Pr\{\bar{t}_p - z_{\alpha/2}\sigma_p \leq t \leq \bar{t}_p + z_{\alpha/2}\sigma_p\} = 1 - \alpha$$

approximately, where $z_{\alpha/2}$ denotes a percentage point of the standard normal distribution such that $Pr\{Z > z_{\alpha/2}\} = \alpha/2$. Thus, the approximate $100(1 - \alpha)$ percent confidence interval is

$$\bar{t}_p - z_{\alpha/2}\sigma_p \leq t \leq \bar{t}_p + z_{\alpha/2}\sigma_p$$

For example, a 95 percent confidence interval estimate of project completion time for the project shown in Figure 5-10 and whose activity durations are given in Table 5-15 is

$$41 - (1.96)(3.682) \leq t \leq 41 + (1.96)(3.682)$$

or

$$33.783 \leq t \leq 48.216$$

We may also find the probability of positive slack at any event in the network, that is, $Pr\{S_i > 0\} = Pr\{L_i - E_i > 0\}$. Events with a small probability of positive slack are likely to become critical events and management attention may be focused on them as the project progresses. The mean early and late occurrence times for event i, $\bar{E}_i$ and $\bar{L}_i$, respectively, are computed during the forward and backward pass. Furthermore, let the variance of the random variable L_i, say $\sigma_{L_i}^2$, be the sum of the variances of activities along the backward path leading to event i, and the variance of E_i, say $\sigma_{E_i}^2$, be the sum of the variances of activities along the forward path leading to event i. Thus, the random variable $L_i - E_i$ has estimated mean $\bar{L}_i - \bar{E}_i$ and estimated variance $\sigma_{L_i}^2 + \sigma_{E_i}^2$. We also assume that $L_i - E_i$ follows the normal distribution. Therefore,

$$Pr\{S_i > 0\} = Pr\{L_i - E_i > 0\}$$

$$= Pr\left\{Z > \frac{-(\bar{L}_i - \bar{E}_i)}{\sqrt{\sigma_{L_i}^2 + \sigma_{E_i}^2}}\right\}$$

which can be evaluated using tables of the standard normal cumulative distribution function. For example, consider event 4 in Figure 5-10. We see that $\bar{L}_4 = 18$ and $\bar{E}_4 = 12$. The variances $\sigma_{L_4}^2$ and $\sigma_{E_4}^2$ are found using the activity duration variances in column (5) of Table 5-15 as

$$\sigma_{L_4}^2 = \sigma_{6,7}^2 + \sigma_{4,6}^2 = 2.778 + 2.778 = 5.556$$

and

$$\sigma_{E_4}^2 = \sigma_{1,2}^2 + \sigma_{2,4}^2 = 0.444 + 1.000 = 1.444$$

Thus,

$$\bar{L}_4 - \bar{E}_4 = 6, \qquad \sigma_{L_4}^2 + \sigma_{E_4}^2 = 7$$

and
$$L_4 - E_4 \sim N(6, 7)$$

The probability of positive slack at event 4 is

$$Pr\{S_4 > 0\} = Pr\left\{Z > \frac{-6}{\sqrt{7}}\right\} \simeq 0.87$$

Since the probability of positive slack at event 4 is large, it is unlikely that event 4 will become critical.

5-3.3 Resource Allocation in Project Network Models

Our discussion of project network models so far has emphasized the time element. Usually, however, both time and resources are of interest to the project manager. Often, only limited resources are available, and they should be utilized in an optimum manner. There are three general kinds of resource allocation problems:

1. *Time-Cost Trade-off.* We are interested in reducing the project completion time by allocating more resources to certain activities.

2. *Resource Leveling.* The problem is to commit the resources to the project activities at as constant a rate as possible, subject to the time constraints of the activities. A typical resource considered is the work force. Resource leveling techniques would result in a work force of nearly constant size throughout the project.

3. *Scheduling to Satisfy Resource Constraints.* We wish to determine the minimum project duration that can be achieved when the available resources are subject to constraints.

For reasons of space, we shall discuss only the time-cost trade-off problem. Most techniques for solving the resource leveling problem and the scheduling with resource constraint problem are heuristic in nature. An excellent discussion of resource allocation procedures is given by Moder and Phillips (17, Chapters 6 and 7).

In most projects, the activity durations of some or all activities can be reduced by the allocation of more resources. Of course, this causes an increase in the direct cost for these activities. The usual purpose of compressing activity durations is to reduce the project completion time. It is frequently useful to be able to determine the minimum project cost associated with each completion time.

A linear programming formulation of the time-cost trade-off problem can

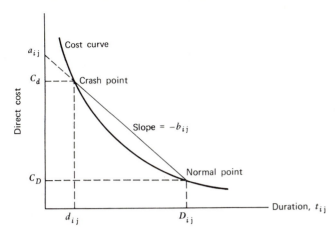

FIGURE 5-12. Linear approximation of a convex time-cost curve.

be given for the case where the function relating *direct* cost to time for each activity is continuous and convex, and where activities are assumed independent. A typical convex time-cost curve is shown in Figure 5-12. We assume that a linear approximation to the convex time-cost curve is a sufficiently good approximation (see Figure 5-12). Only two points are required to define the linear approximation: a "normal" activity duration and cost (D_{ij}, C_D), and a "crash" or fully expedited duration and cost (d_{ij}, C_d). In some instances, a piecewise-linear approximation may be necessary. See Figure 5-13.

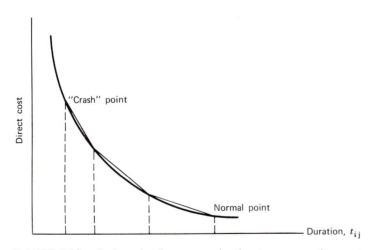

FIGURE 5-13. A piecewise-linear approximation to a convex time-cost curve for activity (i, j).

The direct cost of any feasible schedule is

$$TC = \sum_{\substack{(i, j) \text{ in} \\ \text{network}}} (a_{ij} - b_{ij}t_{ij}) \tag{5-28}$$

where each activity duration must satisfy $d_{ij} \leq t_{ij} \leq D_{ij}$. But we see minimizing TC is equivalent to maximizing

$$\sum_{\substack{(i, j) \text{ in} \\ \text{network}}} b_{ij}t_{ij} \tag{5-29}$$

since the a_{ij}'s are constants. If θ is the upper limit on project completion time, then the minimum cost solution satisfies

$$\max \sum_{\substack{(i, j) \text{ in} \\ \text{network}}} b_{ij}t_{ij} \tag{5-30a)}$$

subject to

$$d_{ij} \leq t_{ij} \leq D_{ij}, \qquad \text{for } (i, j) \text{ in network} \tag{5-30b}$$

$$E_i + t_{ij} - E_j \leq 0, \qquad \text{for } (i, j) \text{ in network} \tag{5-30c}$$

$$-E_1 + E_n \leq \theta \tag{5-30d}$$

where E_i is the occurrence time of event i, and E_1 can be set arbitrarily equal to zero.

We may solve (5-30) for all θ between θ_d, the "all-crash" project duration (all activities at their crash durations) and θ_D, the "all normal" project duration (all activities at their normal durations) by parametric linear programming. The result is a piecewise-linear project cost curve, shown in Figure 5-14, which plots the minimum project direct cost against the project duration. It is also possible to incorporate the *indirect* project costs (which usually increase with time) into

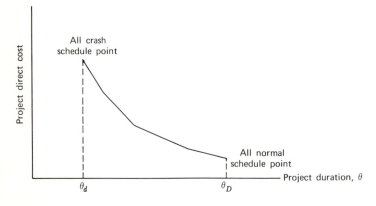

FIGURE 5-14. A typical piecewise-linear project direct cost curve.

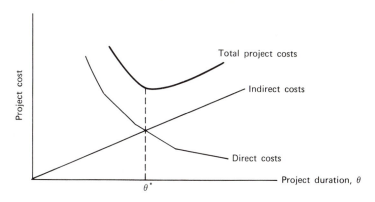

Project cost

Total project costs

Indirect costs

Direct costs

Project duration, θ

θ^*

Least—cost project duration

FIGURE 5-15. A typical total project cost curve.

the analysis, to produce a *total* project cost curve, such as shown in Figure 5-15. From this function, the optimum (least-cost) project duration can be found.

While the time-cost trade-off problem (5-30) could be solved by parametric linear programming, it is usually not efficient computationally to do so. It is more efficient to formulate the dual of (5-30) and use the Ford-Fulkerson maximum flow network algorithm to solve it. We shall not give a complete discussion of the procedure, but in general the process is as follows. An all-normal schedule and cost for the project is first computed. Then a reduction in project completion time is forced by expediting the critical activities with the smallest time-cost slopes. As the project completion time is reduced, new activities become critical. The analysis is then repeated, until all activities are at their crash durations. The result is the same cost curve shown in Figure 5-14.

5-4 Assembly Line Balancing

Assembly lines are characterized by the movement of the workpiece from one work station to the next. The individual tasks required to complete the product are divided and assigned to the work stations so that each station performs the same operation on every unit of product. The workpiece remains at each station for a duration of time called the *cycle time*. An *assembly line balancing problem* consists of assigning the individual tasks to the work stations in such a way that some appropriate measure of line performance is optimized. If a line is balanced perfectly, then all stations have an equal amount of work to perform, and smooth product flow with no delay should be achieved. We note that the overall design of a production line includes planning the proper sequence of operations, setting the production rate for the line, and balancing the load on the individual work stations.

To define the assembly line balancing problem more specifically, suppose that a set of n *tasks* are to be performed on each workpiece, with the ith task having processing or *performance time* p_i. These tasks must be assigned to k ($k \leq n$) work stations. The *total work content* of the product is the sum of the performance times, that is,

$$\sum_{i=1}^{n} p_i$$

The order in which the tasks are to be performed is not unrestricted; that is, there are *precedence relations* among the tasks. In addition, there may be other more elaborate restrictions, such as zoning constraints, which prevent grouping certain tasks at the same work station, or the must-do task, which must be performed at a particular work station. We shall not discuss assembly line balancing methods for dealing with constraints more elaborate than general precedence relations.

The criteria for choosing a balance are usually related to idle time. If c is the cycle time, then the idle time, say I, is

$$I = kc - \sum_{i=1}^{n} p_i \tag{5-31}$$

Frequently, it is convenient to work with the *balance delay*

$$d = \frac{kc - \sum_{i=1}^{n} p_i}{kc} \tag{5-32}$$

We see that assigning tasks to work stations so that idle time (or d) is minimized will minimize the number of assembly hours per unit of product.

Assume that the performance times p_i are expressed as integers, and that they are known with certainty. Then, given a cycle time, a necessary condition for zero balance delay is that $\sum_{i=1}^{n} p_i/c$ be integer. This condition is necessary, because if balance delay is zero, the ratio $\sum_{i=1}^{n} p_i/c$ will always be integer. However, the condition is not sufficient as it is possible to have $\sum_{i=1}^{n} p_i/c$ integer, yet, because of precedence constraints, not be able to assign the tasks to the work stations so as to make the balance delay zero.

There would seem to be several equivalent criteria related to idle time. For example, minimizing total idle time is equivalent to minimizing the number of work stations k, or the cycle time, or kc. Thus, several possible approaches to developing a line balancing algorithm exist. The usual approach is to find the minimum number of stations to balance the line for a given cycle time. This is repeated for various cycle times, and the balance that yields the minimum idle time is selected. The range of possible cycle times is

$$p_{\max} \le c \le \sum_{i=1}^{n} p_i$$

where $p_{\max}$ denotes the longest performance time of the set of tasks. Clearly, these upper and lower bounds on c are based on practical considerations and are of little real assistance in selecting a cycle time. Usually, the expected demand for the product implies a cycle time, since the production rate (in units of product/unit time) is just $1/c$. If this implied cycle time is smaller than the cycle time that minimizes idle time, then overtime, a second shift, duplicating bottleneck work stations, or a second production line may be required to meet demand. If the implied cycle time is larger than the cycle time that minimizes idle time, then the production line need not be operated continuously or its resources can be shared with other products.

The assembly line balancing problem has received considerable attention in the past several years, and, as a result, there are a great many solution procedures. The procedures may be classified generally as either exact methods that guarantee an optimal solution, or heuristic methods that may yield only approximately optimal solutions. The exact methods are usually mathematical programming formulations. Many types of heuristic methods have been proposed, ranging from simple procedures easily performed by hand to complex algorithms that require a computer for problem solutions.

Virtually all line balancing techniques assume the task performance times to be constants whose values are known with certainty. In reality, the performance times are usually random variables. To overcome this difficulty, production line designers often load work stations to less than 100 percent of full capacity. This provides a safety factor to absorb random variation in performance time, as well as an allowance for worker rest and change of pace. The percentage of full capacity to which a station should be loaded depends on the variability of performance times and whether the tasks are performed by machines or human operators.

5-4.1 Mathematical Programming Formulations

Held et al. (8) have offered a dynamic programming formulation of the assembly line balancing problem that minimizes the number of work stations for a given cycle time. Let $\{J_1, J_2, \ldots, J_n\}$ be the set of tasks to be performed. A *feasible subset* is a subset of the n tasks that can be executed in some order without any other tasks being done and a *feasible subsequence* is a subsequence of the n tasks that can be performed in the indicated order without any other tasks being done. The "cost" of a feasible subsequence is the number of fully loaded work stations it requires plus the time in the last station. The cost of a feasible subset is the minimum of the costs of its associated feasible subsequences. The basis of the dynamic programming formulation is the relationship

cost of sequence $\{J_a, J_b, \ldots, J_i, J_j\}$

$$= \text{cost of sequence } \{J_a, J_b, \ldots, J_i\} + \Delta(J_j)$$

where

$$\Delta(J_j) = \begin{cases} p_j, \text{ if } J_j \text{ fits in the last station of } \{J_a, J_b, \ldots, J_i\} \\ p_j \text{ in the next station plus idle time in the last station of} \\ \{J_a, J_b, \ldots, J_i\}, \text{ if } J_j \text{ does not fit} \end{cases}$$

Then for a subset V,

cost of $V = \min_{J_i \notin V} [\text{cost of } \{V - J_i\} + \Delta(J_i)]$, such that $\{V - J_i\}$ is feasible

$$(5\text{-}32)$$

Equation 5-32 is used in a recursive manner to obtain the costs of subsets with two tasks from those with one, then the costs of subsets with three tasks from those with two, etc. Eventually, the cost of the entire n-task line is obtained. For small- and medium-size problems, this procedure is relatively efficient. For large assembly lines, however, computer storage capacity is exceeded. The authors have developed approximation methods for dealing with large problems.

Several authors have proposed integer programming formulations of the assembly line balancing problem. These formulations are discussed by Ignall (10). For the most part, integer programming models are not practical computationally and the dynamic programming model of Held, et al., is more efficient. However, Thangavelu and Shetty (19) have recently offered an integer programming formulation and an algorithm that takes advantage of the special structure of the problem and appears to be quite efficient.

The Thangavelu and Shetty model may be described as follows. There are n tasks $\{J_1, J_2, \ldots, J_n\}$ with performance times $p_1, p_2, \ldots, p_n$, and a set of precedence relations. If J_u should precede J_v, then the subscripts are ordered so that $u < v$. Let

$$X_{ij} = \begin{cases} 1 \text{ if task } J_j \text{ is assigned to station } i, \quad (i = 1, 2, \ldots, k) \\ 0 \text{ otherwise} \end{cases}$$

where k is an upper limit on the number of stations required. The total time of all tasks assigned to a station must not exceed the cycle time, or

$$\sum_{j=1}^{n} X_{ij} p_j \leq c, \quad i = 1, 2, \ldots, k \quad (5\text{-}33)$$

It is required that all tasks be performed. This is expressed by

$$\sum_{i=1}^{k} X_{ij} = 1, \qquad j = 1, 2, \ldots, n \tag{5-34}$$

The precedence relations are expressed by

$$X_{hv} \leq \sum_{i=1}^{h} X_{iu}, \qquad h = 1, 2, \ldots, k; \quad (u, v) \in \mathcal{R} \tag{5-35}$$

where the set $\mathcal{R} = \{(u, v) \mid \text{task } J_u \text{ should immediately precede task } J_v\}$. If there are R immediate precedence relations, we shall need kR inequalities of the form in Equation 5-35 to account for precedence constraints.

The objective is to minimize the number of stations required. The number of stations cannot be less than the smallest integer greater than

$$\sum_{j=1}^{n} p_j / c$$

Let k_0 denote the smallest number of stations theoretically possible. Thus, the objective function is

$$\min Z = \sum_{i=1}^{k} \sum_{j=1}^{n} C_{ij} X_{ij} \tag{5-36}$$

where

$$C_{ij} = \begin{cases} p_j \left[\sum_{h \in F} p_h + 1 \right]^{(i - k_0 - 1)}, & i = k_0 + 1, \ldots, k; \quad j \in F \\ 0 \text{ otherwise} \end{cases}$$

and $F = \{j \mid \text{task } J_j \text{ need not precede any other task}\}$. This objective function makes the use of more than k_0 stations very costly and forces tasks to be assigned to the earliest possible station on the line. In fact, one unit of a later assignment is more costly than the sum of all preceding assignments. Since at least the first k_0 stations *must* be used, they need not be assigned a cost. Also, only tasks that have no followers need positive costs, as they may be placed last on the line.

Thangavelu and Shetty note that Equation 5-35 can be replaced by

$$\sum_{i=1}^{k} (k - i + 1)(X_{iu} - X_{iv}) \geq 0, \qquad (u, v) \in \mathcal{R} \tag{5-37}$$

because any solution satisfying (5-35) has

$$X_{iu} = \begin{cases} 1 \text{ for some } i = r \\ 0 \text{ otherwise} \end{cases}$$

$$X_{iv} = \begin{cases} 1 \text{ for some } i = h \\ 0 \text{ otherwise} \end{cases}$$

Thus, (5-35) and (5-37) are satisfied if and only if $r \leq h$, which implies that J_r precedes J_h. The algorithm employed requires that constraints be in inequality form. Thus, (5-34) is replaced by the $n + 1$ inequalities

$$1 - \sum_{i=1}^{k} X_{ij} \geq 0, \qquad j = 1, 2, \ldots, n$$

$$-n + \sum_{i=1}^{k} \sum_{j=1}^{n} X_{ij} \geq 0 \tag{5-38}$$

and the final problem statement is

$$\min Z = \sum_{i=1}^{k} \sum_{j=1}^{n} C_{ij} X_{ij} \tag{5-39a}$$

subject to

$$\sum_{j=1}^{n} X_{ij} p_j \leq c, \qquad i = 1, 2, \ldots, k \tag{5-39b}$$

$$1 - \sum_{i=1}^{k} X_{ij} \geq 0, \qquad j = 1, 2, \ldots, n \tag{5-39c}$$

$$-n + \sum_{i=1}^{k} \sum_{j=1}^{n} X_{ij} \geq 0 \tag{5-39d}$$

$$\sum_{i=1}^{k} (k - i + 1)(X_{iu} - X_{iv}) \leq 0, \qquad (u, v) \in \mathscr{R} \tag{5-39e}$$

$$X_{ij} = 0, 1 \tag{5-39f}$$

In general, $(k + n + R + 1)$ inequality constraints are required.

A modification of Balas' additive algorithm for zero-one integer programs is developed for the problem given by Equation 5-39. The modification consists of eliminating or simplifying certain steps of the Balas algorithm to account for the special structure of the problem. Numerical results indicate that this algorithm is approximately 50 percent faster than the dynamic programming procedure of Held et al. This is very encouraging, as previous integer programming models of the assembly line balancing problem have performed quite poorly. It seems that the Thangavelu and Shetty procedure is the most efficient exact solution method available, and is capable of solving moderately sized problems with up to 50 tasks in a few seconds of computer time.

5-4.2 Heuristic Assembly Line Balancing Procedures

The exact methods currently available for solving assembly line balancing problems, while capable of solving problems of moderate size, are not as yet computationally practical for large problems involving 75 to 100 or more tasks and 10 to 15 or more stations. Approximate solutions to large-scale assembly line balancing problems are usually found by heuristic procedures.

Ignall (10) reviews several line balancing techniques and points out two factors in favor of heuristic approaches. First, line balancing problems grow in size very rapidly. He estimates that a line with 70 tasks and 105 precedence relations has $70!/2^{105} = 10^{85}$ feasible sequences. No implicit enumeration technique, no matter how efficient, could hope to solve such a problem in a short amount of computer time. As virtually all line balancing methods attempt to minimize the number of work stations for a given cycle time, several different cycle times will have to be investigated to compare minimum cycle time balances over a range of the number of stations. This means a given method may have to be used several times to produce a final solution to the problem. Second, a practical problem will involve zone constraints or other complex restrictions not easily dealt with analytically. Therefore, an experienced engineer will have to modify the final balance to incorporate these practical considerations. It seems reasonable not to spend valuable time pursuing an optimal balance, but instead to produce a good approximate balance fairly quickly and determine the final balance through engineering personnel.

Kilbridge and Wester (15) have proposed a heuristic technique for balancing assembly lines that attempts to obtain a balance by assigning those tasks with the fewest predecessors to the first available station on the line. The details of the procedure are illustrated in the following example.

☐**EXAMPLE 5-9** Consider the nine-task problem whose precedence relations are shown in Figure 5-16, and whose performance times are shown in Table 5-16. The directed graph in Figure 5-16 is called a precedence diagram. The Kilbridge and Wester method requires the addition of column labels to the precedence diagram. These labels are the Roman numbers in Figure 5-16.

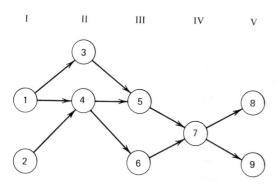

FIGURE 5-16.   Precedence diagram for Example 5-9.

TABLE 5-16 Performance Times for Example 5-9

TASK	PERFORMANCE TIME
1	5
2	3
3	6
4	8
5	$10 = p_{max}$
6	7
7	1
8	5
9	3
	$\sum_{i=1}^{n} p_i = 48$

Tasks that have no predecessors are placed in column I, tasks that are preceded directly by those in column I are placed in column II, tasks that are immediately preceded by those in column II are placed in column III, etc. We see that this results in a precedence diagram that places each task as far to the left as possible. Intracolumn movement of tasks is unrestricted, as there are no precedence constraints *within* a column. Furthermore, many tasks can be moved from their current columns to a column further right without violating precedence constraints.

To determine the possible cycle times for which $\sum_{i=1}^{n} p_i/c$ is an integer, and thus, the possible cycle times yielding a perfect balance, we write $\sum_{i=1}^{n} p_i$ as a product of prime numbers. In our example, since $\sum_{i=1}^{n} p_i = 48$, we have

$$2 \times 2 \times 3 \times 2 \times 2 = 48$$

Since we must require $10 \leq c \leq 48$, it is easily seen that the ratio $\sum_{i=1}^{n} p_i/c$ is an integer for

$$c_1 = 2 \times 2 \times 3 \times 2 \times 2 = 48$$
$$c_2 = 2 \times 2 \times 2 \times 3 \quad = 24$$
$$c_3 = 2 \times 2 \times 2 \times 2 \quad = 16$$
$$c_4 = 2 \times 2 \times 3 \quad = 12$$

Thus, perfect balance can possibly be achieved with

$$k_1 = \frac{\sum\limits_{i=1}^{n} p_i}{c_1} = \frac{48}{48} = 1 \text{ station (trivial)}$$

$$k_2 = \frac{\sum\limits_{i=1}^{n} p_i}{c_2} = \frac{48}{24} = 2 \text{ stations}$$

$$k_3 = \frac{\sum\limits_{i=1}^{n} p_i}{c_3} = \frac{48}{16} = 3 \text{ stations}$$

$$k_4 = \frac{\sum\limits_{i=1}^{n} p_i}{c_4} = \frac{48}{12} = 4 \text{ stations}$$

To illustrate the procedure, we shall balance the $c = 16$ case. It is useful to construct a table containing detailed information about the tasks taken from each column of the precedence diagram. This is shown as Table 5-17. We shall attempt to assign tasks to station 1. Scan the "cumulative sum" column of Table 5-17 until we find the smallest cumulative sum that is greater than or equal to the cycle time, 16. The value found is the cumulative sum of the tasks in columns I and II, that is, 22. Since the tasks in column I require eight units of time and have the fewest predecessors of the available tasks, they will be

TABLE 5-17 Tabular Representation of Precedence Diagram

COLUMN NUMBER	TASK	p_i	SUM OF p_i	CUMULATIVE SUM OF p_i
I	1	5		
	2	3	8	8
II	3	6		
	4	8	14	22
III	5	10		
	6	7	17	39
IV	7	1	1	40
V	8	5		
	9	3	8	48

TABLE 5-18 Modified Table 5-17 After Assignment of Tasks to Station 1

COLUMN NUMBER	TASK	p_i	SUM OF p_i	CUMULATIVE SUM OF p_i
I	1	5		
	2	3		
II	4	8	16	16
	3	6	6	22
III	5	10		
	6	7	17	39
IV	7	1	1	40
V	8	5		
	9	3	8	48

assigned to station 1. Now $c - 8 = 16 - 8 = 8$ time units are left. Scan column II and see if any combination of tasks total eight time units. We find that task 4 is acceptable. Therefore, move task 4 to the top of the column II list and assign it to station 1, along with tasks 1 and 2. In general, if a choice between two or more tasks exists, always use the task with the longest performance time first. The status of the solution is now shown by Table 5-18.

Scan the "cumulative sum" column of Table 5-18 to find the smallest cumulative sum greater than or equal to $2 \times 16 = 32$. The cumulative sum for column III is 39. Assigning task 3 to station 2 yields $c - 6 = 16 - 6 = 10$ units of time available in this station. Search column III for any combination of tasks whose times total 10. We find that task 5 qualifies. Therefore, we also assign task 5 to station 2. The status of the solution is shown in Table 5-19. Repeating these steps for station 3, it is easily seen that the smallest cumulative sum greater than or equal to $3 \times 16 = 48$ is the cumulative sum for column V, that is, 48. Since there are exactly 16 time units of unassigned work remaining, tasks 6, 7, 8, and 9 may be assigned to station 3.

The final station assignments are shown in Figure 5-17. We see that the Kilbridge and Wester method has resulted in a perfect balance, as there is no idle time in any station. We may easily verify that for $c = 12$ and $c = 24$, there are no perfect balances using the minimum number of stations. Therefore, the best solution to the problem seems to be the perfect balance attained with $c = 16$ and $k = 3$ stations. □

TABLE 5-19 Modified Table 5-18 After Assignment of Tasks to Station 2

COLUMN NUMBER	TASK	p_i	SUM OF p_i	CUMULATIVE SUM OF p_i	
I	1	5			Station 1
	2	3			
II	4	8	16	16	
	3	6			Station 2
III	5	10	16	32	
	6	7			
IV	7	1	8	40	Unassigned Tasks
V	8	5			
	9	3	8	48	

The Kilbridge and Wester method is, in general, very good for large cycle times when one station crosses several columns. However, for low cycle times, where one column may require two or more stations, much manipulation of the tasks is necessary and there is no guarantee of good results.

Arcus (2) has developed the computer-based line balancing heuristic COMSOAL (Computer Method of Sequencing Operations for Assembly Lines). The essential idea behind COMSOAL is the random generation of a

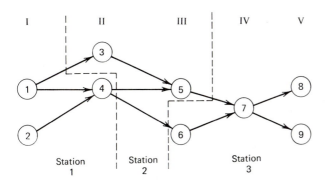

FIGURE 5-17. Final station assignments for Example 5-9 using Kilbridge and Wester's method.

feasible sequence. Such a sequence may be constructed by assigning a positive probability of selection to each task that will fit in the current station, and then selecting one of the tasks at random. This procedure is repeated until all tasks have been assigned.

□**EXAMPLE 5-10** Consider the assembly line balancing problem described in Example 5-9. Assume that a cycle time of 16 is desired. If tasks 1 and 2 are assigned to the first work station, then either task 3 or 4 could also be assigned. Suppose probability 1/2 is assigned to both task 3 and 4, and one selected at random, say task 3. Then the first work station is full, and task 4 *must* be assigned to station 2. As tasks 5 or 6 could also be assigned to station 2, probability 1/2 would be assigned to each, and so on, until a feasible solution to the problem is obtained.□

Arcus' computer program generates 1000 feasible sequences, and chooses the solutions that use the smallest number of stations as optimum. The program also accumulates the idle time of the current partial solution, and abandons that solution when its accumulated idle time exceeds the total idle time of the previous best solution. This feature may save considerable computer time.

COMSOAL in its most elementary form assigns equal probability to all the tasks that could fit into the current work station. However, Arcus explored other methods for weighting the assigned probabilities. His best procedure weights the probability assignment in inverse proportion to the number of places the task can go in the sequence. To illustrate this idea, return to Example 5-10 and consider the probabilities assigned to tasks 3 and 4. Task 3 is followed by tasks 5, 7, 8, and 9, so task 3 cannot be later than fifth in the sequence. That is, task 3 can be second, or third, or fourth, or fifth, a total of four positions. Similarly, task 4 can be in any one of two positions. So task 4 would be assigned a higher probability of selection than task 3 in the ratio 4:2. This results in probability 4/6 for task 4 and probability 2/6 for task 3.

COMSOAL is an efficient assembly line balancing technique, especially for large problems involving many tasks and work stations. It generally produces solutions with fewer work stations than other heuristic techniques. In terms of computing time, COMSOAL appears to be 3 to 10 times faster than the dynamic programming procedure of Held, et al., and 1.5 to 5 times faster than Thangavelu and Shetty's integer programming method. However, it does not necessarily produce the optimum solution to every problem. For large assembly line balancing problems, COMSOAL is the best technique currently available.

Helgeson and Birnie (9) have proposed the Ranked Positional Weight Method for assembly line balancing. The *positional weight* of task i is defined as its performance time p_i plus the sum of the performance times for all tasks that follow task i. Tasks are ranked in descending order of the positional weights, and then assigned to stations in order of the ranking. If a task takes longer than

TABLE 5-20 Ranked Positional Weights

TASK	1	2	4	3	5	6	7	8	9
Positional weight	48	37	34	25	19	16	9	5	3
Immediate predecessors			1, 2	1	3, 4	4	5, 6	7	7

the time remaining in the station or would violate precedence constraints, it is passed over and the next task is tried. As soon as no further tasks can be assigned to the current station, the next station is started, beginning with the first of the tasks that have been passed over.

☐**EXAMPLE 5-11**   The ranked positional weights for the assembly line balancing problem described in Example 5-9 are shown in Table 5-20. To balance this line for a cycle time of 16, we would assign task 1, which has the largest positional weight, to the first station. Tasks 2 and 4 have the next largest positional weights and are also assigned to station 1. As station 1 is now full, task 3 must be assigned to station 2, followed by task 5. Now station 2 is full, and tasks 6, 7, 8, and 9 are successively assigned to station 3. We see that the Ranked Positional Weight Method produces a perfect three-station balance.☐

As a general rule, the Ranked Positional Weight Method produces a preliminary balance in a very short period of time, although the balance may be far from optimum. Thus, examination and improvement of this preliminary balance by an experienced engineer is an important step in the method. To provide a second preliminary balance for the engineer to work with, Helgeson and Birnie proposed an inverse positional weight, which is just the ranked positional weight of the backward balancing problem obtained by turning the arrows of the original problem around.

5-5   References

1.   **Akers, S. B., Jr., and J. Friedman,** "A Non-numerical Approach to Production Scheduling Problems," *Operations Research*, **3** (4), 1955.

2.   **Arcus, A. L.,** "COMSOAL: A Computer Method of Sequencing Operations for Assembly Lines," *International Journal of Production Research*, **4** (4), 1966.

3.   **Brooks, G. H., and C. R. White,** "An Algorithm for Finding Optimal or Near-Optimal Solutions to the Production Scheduling Problem," *Journal of Industrial Engineering*, **16** (1), 1965.

4.   **Conway, R. W.,** *An Experimental Investigation of Priority Assignment In a Job Shop*, RM-3789-PR, The Rand Corporation, Santa Monica, California, 1964.

5. **Conway, R. W., W. L. Maxwell, and L. W. Miller,** *Theory of Scheduling*, Addison-Wesley, Reading, Mass., 1967.

6. **Giglio, R. H., and H. M. Wagner,** "Approximate Solutions to the Three-Machine Scheduling Problem," *Operations Research*, **12** (2), 1964.

7. **Hardgrave, W. W., and G. L. Nemhauser,** "A Geometric Model and Graphical Algorithm for a Sequencing Problem," *Operations Research*, **11** (6), 1963.

8. **Held, M., R. M. Karp, and R. Shareshian,** "Assembly Line Balancing—Dynamic Programming with Precedence Constraints," *Operations Research*, **11** (3), 1963.

9. **Helgeson, W. P., and D. P. Birnie,** "Assembly Line Balancing Using the Ranked Positional Weight Technique," *Journal of Industrial Engineering*, **6** (6), 1961.

10. **Ignall, E. J.,** "A Review of Assembly Line Balancing," *Journal of Industrial Engineering*, **16** (4), 1965.

11. **Ignall, E. J., and L. E. Schrage,** "Application of the Branch and Bound Technique to Some Flow-Shop Scheduling Problems," *Operations Research*, **13** (3), 1965.

12. **Jackson, J. R.,** "An Extension of Johnson's Results on Job-Lot Scheduling," *Naval Research Logistics Quarterly*, **3** (3), 1956.

13. **Jackson, J. R.,** "Networks of Waiting Lines," *Operations Research*, **5** (4), 1957.

14. **Johnson, S. M.,** "Optimal Two- and Three-Stage Production Schedules with Setup Times Included," *Naval Research Logistics Quarterly*, **1** (1), 1954.

15. **Kilbridge, M. D., and L. Wester,** "A Heuristic Method of Assembly Line Balancing," *Journal of Industrial Engineering*, **12** (4), 1961.

16. **Little, John D. C., K. G. Murty, D. W. Sweeney, and C. Karel,** "An Algorithm for the Traveling Salesman Problem," *Operations Research*, **11** (6), 1963.

17. **Moder, J. J., and C. R. Phillips,** *Project Management with CPM and PERT*, Reinhold Publishing Company, New York, 1964.

18. **Story, A. E., and H. M. Wagner,** "Computational Experience with Integer Programming for Job-Shop Scheduling," Chapter 14 in *Industrial Scheduling*, (J. F. Muth and G. L. Thompson, eds.), Prentice-Hall, Englewood Cliffs, N.J., 1963.

19. **Thangavelu, S. R., and C. M. Shetty,** "Assembly Line Balancing by Zero- One Integer Programming," *AIIE Transactions*, **III** (1), 1971.

5-6   Exercises

5-1   A small factory produces five different products, each of which pass through a drill press, milling machine, and grinder, in that order. The processing time in hours of each product is shown below. Construct a Gantt chart of the sequence {5, 4, 3, 1, 2}, and determine the makespan.

From examining the chart, can you easily find an improved schedule?

	PRODUCT				
MACHINE	1	2	3	4	5
Drill press	2	3	6	5	4
Milling machine	1	4	3	5	8
Grinder	6	2	7	3	9

5-2 Six jobs are to be processed on a punch press. The processing times are shown below. Determine a sequence that minimizes the average flow time.

JOB	1	2	3	4	5	6
p_i	5	2	1	4	7	3

5-3 Five jobs are to be scheduled through a paint shop according to SPT. The processing times and the due dates (d_i) for the jobs are shown below. Determine the lateness of each job under the SPT schedule. What is the mean lateness? Can you find another schedule with a smaller mean lateness?

JOB	1	2	3	4	5
p_i	8	7	6	4	10
d_i	10	15	24	28	23

5-4 An automobile repair shop must schedule six jobs for its single air conditioning specialist. Each job is for a different customer, and the shop manager has ranked the jobs assigning a priority to each so that a priority of 1 is the most important, a priority of 2 is the next most important, etc. Determine, from the data shown below, the best sequence in terms of mean weighted flow time.

JOB	1	2	3	4	5	6
Priority	4	1	2	3	6	5
p_i	40	30	25	45	50	36

5-5 Show that SPT sequencing for n jobs on a single machine minimizes the mean lateness.

5-6 Show that sequencing n jobs on one machine, so that jobs with the longest processing times are performed first, maximizes the mean flow time. This rule is *antithetical* to SPT; that is, it produces a sequence *opposite* to that produced by SPT.

5-7 Five jobs are to be processed on a single machine. The processing times and importance weights are shown below. Find a schedule that minimizes the mean weighted flow time.

JOB	1	2	3	4	5
w_i	10	6	5	4	7
p_i	20	16	25	31	17

5-8 *Single Machine Sequencing with Due Dates.* Suppose n jobs are to be processed on a single machine, and each job has a due date, d_i, ($i = 1, 2, \ldots, n$). Show that if the jobs are sequenced according to nondecreasing due dates, the maximum lateness is minimized.

5-9 Small electric motors used in the production department of a heavy machinery plant break down at random during the two shifts of production operations. The maintenance department repairs these motors on the third shift and tries to have all motors available for use the next day. The maintenance mechanic must schedule the repairs, that is, determine the sequence in which the motors are to be repaired. Assuming only one mechanic is available, in what sequence should the following motors be repaired?

Motor number	14	20	362	7	251	109	46	299
Estimated repair time (minutes)	45	30	60	25	15	45	90	75

5-10 *Preempt-Repeat in a One-Machine Job Shop.* Consider scheduling the following four jobs on a single machine, subject to a preempt-repeat scheme; that is, an arriving job can preempt a job in progress, but the preempted job must be completely repeated when returned to the machine. Find a schedule for the four jobs that minimizes the mean flow time.

JOB	1	2	3	4
Arrival time	0	1	3	5
Processing time	4	1	3	2

5-11 *SPT Sequencing With Incomplete Information.* Suppose a schedule for n jobs on a single machine must be found, where the processing times for the jobs are not known exactly until after processing takes place. That is, the processing times of the n jobs, say $p_1, p_2, \ldots, p_n$ are unobserved random variables. Let $A_1, A_2, \ldots, A_n$ be a set of *estimates* of the processing times of the n jobs, and assume that these estimates will be used to construct the sequence. Thus, the resulting SPT sequence is

$$A_{[1]} \le A_{[2]} \le \cdots \le A_{[n]}$$

The necessary condition to obtain the optimal mean flow time schedule is only that the estimates be sufficiently close to the true processing time to obtain the correct relative ordering. It is *not* necessary that $A_i = p_i$. For example, find the optimal schedule for the jobs with the estimates of processing time in column 1 below and compare it with the schedule that would be obtained if the true values of processing time shown in column 2 were known.

JOB	(1) A_i	(2) p_i
1	6	5
2	10	8
3	1	2
4	4	5
5	11	9

5-12 *Parallel Machines.* Six jobs arrive simultaneously at a job shop with two identical parallel machines. That is, each job has only one operation, but there are two machines available to perform the processing. The processing times of the jobs are shown below. Renumber the jobs so that $p_1 \leq p_2 \leq \cdots \leq p_6$, and assign job 1 to machine 1 and job 2 to machine 2. Then each time a machine finishes a job, assign from among those jobs waiting the job with the shortest processing time. Find the mean flow time for this scheduling rule. Can you find a schedule that produces a smaller mean flow time? How do you think this scheduling rule will work for the general case of n jobs and two parallel identical machines? How would you apply this rule to n jobs and m parallel identical machines?

JOB	1	2	3	4	5	6
Processing time, p_i	4	7	6	5	4	2

5-13   Eight jobs must pass through a lathe and a surface grinder, in that order. The processing times are shown below. Determine a minimum makespan sequence. Draw the Gantt chart for the schedule and determine the makespan, job waiting time, and machine idle time.

JOB	1	2	3	4	5	6	7	8
Lathe	4	9	8	7	9	10	15	4
Surface grinder	6	5	10	3	1	12	6	7

5-14   Five jobs must be processed through a two-machine flow shop. The processing times and a set of due dates for these jobs are shown below. Determine a minimum makespan schedule. Find the maximum lateness and the mean lateness. Can you find another schedule with a smaller maximum lateness?

JOB	PROCESSING TIME		DUE DATE
	MACHINE 1	MACHINE 2	
1	1	3	5
2	2	5	12
3	4	1	16
4	3	2	20
5	6	4	25

5-15 Six jobs must be processed through a two-machine flow shop. The processing times are shown below. Find a minimum makespan schedule. Construct a Gantt chart of this schedule and find the makespan, average flow time, and machine idle time. Does the minimum makespan schedule minimize the average flow time?

JOB	1	2	3	4	5	6
Machine 1	4	8	1	7	6	5
Machine 2	6	2	3	9	2	10

5-16 A set of 10 jobs must be processed through a two-machine job shop. The technological orderings and processing times of the jobs are shown below. Use Jackson's extention of Johnson's two-machine flow shop algorithm to find a minimum makespan schedule. Construct a Gantt chart of the schedule and determine the makespan and machine idle time.

JOB	MACHINE NUMBER FOR:		PROCESSING TIMES	
	OPERATION 1	OPERATION 2	OPERATION 1	OPERATION 2
1	1	2	4	6
2	1		3	
3	1		4	
4	1	2	5	2
5	2	1	1	2
6	2		1	
7	2	1	7	8
8	2		3	
9	2	1	6	7
10	1	2	2	4

5-17 The following five jobs are to be processed through a three-machine flow shop. Find a minimum makespan schedule for this flow shop.

JOB	PROCESSING TIMES		
	MACHINE 1	MACHINE 2	MACHINE 3
1	8	3	2
2	6	4	5
3	4	2	6
4	9	1	4
5	5	3	9

Construct a Gantt chart for the schedule and find the idle time for each machine. Find the makespan.

5-18 Seven jobs must be processed through an assembly operation, an inspection station, and a packing and shipping station. The processing times of these jobs in each operation is shown below. Find a minimum makespan for performing the seven jobs.

JOB	1	2	3	4	5	6	7
Assembly	10	16	14	21	12	15	19
Inspection	12	8	5	4	7	1	9
Packing and shipping	16	5	8	7	3	1	4

5-19 Consider the three-machine flow shop scheduling problem shown in the following table:

	PROCESSING TIMES		
JOB	MACHINE 1	MACHINE 2	MACHINE 3
1	5	6	9
2	4	7	6
3	9	5	8
4	6	8	5

(a) Why is Johnson's algorithm not applicable?

(b) Find a minimum makespan schedule using the branch-and-bound technique described in Section 5-2.3.

5-20 Use the branch-and-bound method to find a minimum makespan schedule for the following three machine flow shop problem.

	PROCESSING TIMES		
JOB	MACHINE 1	MACHINE 2	MACHINE 3
1	1	4	2
2	3	3	4
3	2	5	1
4	4	2	3

5-21 Consider the three-machine flow shop problem described in Exercise 5-20. Apply Johnson's method to obtain an approximate solution and compare it with the solution obtained by the branch-and-bound method.

5-22 Find a minimum makespan schedule for the three machine flow shop problem shown below.

	PROCESSING TIMES		
JOB	MACHINE 1	MACHINE 2	MACHINE 3
1	7	5	3
2	6	9	8
3	13	6	5
4	2	4	7

5-23 Find a minimum makespan schedule for the three-machine flow shop problem shown below.

	PROCESSING TIMES		
JOB	MACHINE 1	MACHINE 2	MACHINE 3
1	6	5	5
2	9	4	10
3	5	3	7
4	8	4	10
5	7	4	8

5-24 *A Three-Machine Job Shop Problem*. Four jobs are to be processed through three machines. The technological orderings and processing times are given in the table below.

	MACHINE NUMBER FOR:			PROCESSING TIMES		
JOB	OPERA-TION 1	OPERA-TION 2	OPERA-TION 3	OPERA-TION 1	OPERA-TION 2	OPERA-TION 3
1	2	1	3	4	6	2
2	1	2	3	5	4	2
3	1	3	2	2	3	7
4	2	3	1	4	3	5

(a)   Find a feasible schedule for processing the jobs.

(b)   Construct a Gantt chart for the schedule in part (a). What is the makespan and the machine idle time? Do you see any obvious improvements in the schedule found in part (a)?

5-25   *An Integer Programming Model of the Three-Machine Flow Shop* (see References 6 and 18). Consider an n-job, three-machine flow shop scheduling problem where the objective is to minimize makespan. Let

$$X_{ij} = \begin{cases} 1, & \text{if job } i \text{ is assigned to position } j \text{ in the sequence} \\ 0, & \text{otherwise} \end{cases}$$

$Z_j^{\,k}$ = idle time on machine k before the start of the job in position j

$Y_j^{\,k}$ = idle time for the job in position j between the end of processing on machine k and the beginning on machine $k + 1$

p_{ik} = processing time of job i on machine k

The constraints are

$$\sum_{i=1}^{n} X_{ij} = 1, \qquad (j = 1, 2, \dots, n)$$

$$\sum_{j=1}^{n} X_{ij} = 1, \qquad (j = 1, 2, \dots, n)$$

$$Z_{j+1}^2 + \sum_{i=1}^{n} X_{i,j+1} p_{i2} + Y_{j+1}^2 - Y_j^{\,2}$$

$$- \sum_{i=1}^{n} X_{ij} p_{i3} - Z_{j+1}^3 = 0, \qquad (j = 1, 2, \dots, n-1)$$

$$\sum_{i=1}^{n} X_{i,j+1} p_{i1} + Y_{j+1}^1 - Y_j^{\,1}$$

$$- \sum_{i=1}^{n} X_{ij} p_{i2} - Z_{j+1}^2 = 0, \qquad (j = 1, 2, \dots, n-1)$$

Since minimizing the makespan is equivalent to minimizing idle time on the third machine, the objective function is

$$\min \sum_{j=1}^{n} Z_j^{\,3}$$

(a)   What is the physical significance of each constraint equation?

(b)   Write out the constraints and objective function completely for the integer programming model, using the data in Exercise 5-20.

(c)   In general, how large will the integer program be; that is, how many variables and how many constraints are necessary? Comment on computational requirements.

(d) Suppose the jobs may have different technological orderings. What modifications in the above model would be required?

5-26 Two jobs must be processed through five machines, say a, b, c, d, and e. Job 1 must be processed in the order a, b, d, c, e and job 2 must be processed in the order d, a, b, e, c. The processing times are shown below. Find a minimum makespan schedule for the two jobs, given these processing times:

	MACHINE				
JOB	a	b	c	d	e
1	2	3	4	6	2
2	4	1	2	2	5

5-27 Two jobs are to be processed on four machines, say a, b, c, and d. Job 1 has the technological ordering a, c, d, b and job 2 has the technological ordering c, d, a, b. The processing times are shown below. Find a minimum makespan schedule for the two jobs.

	MACHINE			
JOB	a	b	c	d
1	10	6	15	12
2	15	10	9	20

5-28 A small job shop consists of a lathe, a drill press, a milling machine, and a grinder. Two jobs are available for processing. Job 1 requires lathe, drill press, grinder, and milling machine operations, and job 2 requires drill press, lathe, grinder, and milling machine operations, in that order. The processing times are shown below. Find a minimum makespan schedule.

	MACHINE			
JOB	LATHE	DRILL PRESS	MILLING MACHINE	GRINDER
1	10	20	35	15
2	20	25	18	30

5-29 Find a minimum makespan schedule for the two-job, six-machine job shop, whose processing times are shown below. Job 1 must be processed with the technological ordering a, b, e, c, f, d and job 2 requires b, c, f, a, d, e.

JOB	MACHINE					
	a	b	c	d	e	f
1	4	2	6	8	3	1
2	2	5	7	8	4	3

5-30 The cost matrix for a five-city traveling salesman problem is shown below. Find a minimum cost tour using the branch-and-bound algorithm described in Section 5-2.6.

From \ To	1	2	3	4	5
1	∞	8	7	4	1
2	5	∞	2	3	2
3	3	7	∞	6	9
4	10	7	2	∞	4
5	1	5	6	3	∞

5-31 A paint company mixes and cans six different colors of latex paint on the same machine. The setup times for each color depend on the color that was processed previously. A table of the setup times is shown below. Find

From \ To	Red	White	Blue	Green	Yellow	Grey
Red	∞	18	10	10	10	15
White	2	∞	4	3	2	3
Blue	5	18	∞	8	10	11
Green	6	17	7	∞	8	9
Yellow	4	12	5	4	∞	5
Grey	5	13	4	3	5	∞

a sequence for producing and canning the six colors that minimizes the total setup costs.

5-32 A soft drink company bottles seven flavors of product on a single machine. The setup time for a flavor depends on the flavor that was bottled previously. Pungent flavors may require that the machine be cleaned and flushed with a caustic solution, while other flavors require less elaborate preparation. The standard costs of changing the machine from one flavor to another are shown in the table below. In what order should the seven flavors be bottled?

	To						
	Cola	Grape	Orange	Root beer	Lemon-lime	Ginger ale	Diet cola
Cola	∞	16	17	4	24	30	12
Grape	20	∞	22	3	24	29	15
Orange	17	20	∞	3	22	27	13
From Root beer	34	26	30	∞	32	34	33
Lemon-lime	21	17	20	3	∞	22	20
Ginger ale	12	15	12	1	18	∞	17
Diet cola	15	16	13	2	20	21	∞

5-33 *The "Closest-Unvisited-City" Algorithm for the Traveling Salesman Problem.* A heuristic algorithm for the traveling salesman problem is to always travel to the closest city that has not yet been visited. That is, from any row k in the S matrix travel to the city denoted by the column that contains the minimum cost element s_{kj}, excluding cities already visited. While this heuristic does not always generate an optimal tour, it is a commonsense procedure, and one might be interested in its performance characteristics. There are two possible versions of the closest unvisited city algorithm. The arbitrary origin version assumes that one city (row in S) be designated as the start (and end) of the tour. The all-origin version requires that all cities be successively chosen as the starting point and the best of the resulting tours be chosen. In general, the performance of the closest unvisited city algorithm worsens as the number of cities increase, and the all-origins procedure is roughly twice as good as the arbitrary origin approach. Consider the distance matrix shown below:

To

		1	2	3	4	5	6
	1	∞	3	10	5	17	4
	2	5	∞	8	11	2	25
From	3	8	16	∞	5	9	5
	4	4	5	7	∞	11	14
	5	18	9	13	4	∞	7
	6	21	7	15	6	20	∞

(a) Find the tour generated by arbitrarly choosing city 2 as the origin.

(b) Find the best tour generated using the all-origins approach. How much improvement is obtained with respect to the solution in part (a)?

(c) Find the optimal tour using the branch-and-bound approach. How does it compare to the solutions in parts (a) and (b)?

5-34 Consider a three-machine flow shop in which jobs arrive at random. The arrival times and processing times for 10 jobs are shown in the table below.

		PROCESSING TIMES		
JOB	ARRIVAL TIME	MACHINE 1	MACHINE 2	MACHINE 3
1	0	4	1	5
2	0	3	2	4
3	2	1	3	2
4	3	2	1	4
5	5	3	2	1
6	5	5	3	2
7	6	1	1	3
8	8	2	2	4
9	10	1	4	5
10	11	3	2	1

Study the behavior of this shop, assuming that SPT is used to sequence jobs on the various machines. What is the makespan of the 10 jobs? What is the machine idle time?

5-35 Consider a two-machine flow shop in which jobs arrive at random. The arrival times and processing times for 15 jobs are shown below. Study

JOB	1	2	3	4	5	6	7	8	9	10	11	12	13	14	15
Arrival time	0	0	1	2	4	6	8	8	10	10	11	13	15	16	18
Machine 1	2	1	4	5	3	1	4	2	1	2	5	7	9	6	5
Machine 2	2	3	1	4	1	3	2	1	5	2	4	3	7	1	2

the behavior of this shop, using both SPT and first-come, first-served rules to schedule the jobs. Which method seems to give the best results for this example?

5-36 Show that for scheduling n jobs through an m-machine flow shop to minimize makespan, one need only consider schedules that require the same job sequence on machines 1 and 2, and the same job sequence on machines $m - 1$ and m.

5-37 A small research project is defined by the network shown below. Find the critical path.

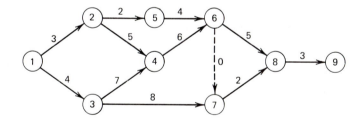

5-38 An engineering firm has agreed to undertake the design, fabrication, and testing of a prototype transmission for a major automobile firm. They have identified the following activities and their associated times and precedence relationships. Construct the network diagram that represents this project. Find the critical path.

ACTIVITY	TIME (WEEKS)	IMMEDIATE PREDECESSORS
1. Establish design specifications	1	—
2. Mechanical design	5	1
3. Electrical design	2	1
4. Final design review	1	2, 3
5. Prepare test vehicle	0.5	1, 2
6. Fabricate prototype	2	4
7. Conduct test	3	5, 6
8. Prepare blueprints	0.5	7
9. Prepare final report	1	8

5-39 Find at least four errors or unnecessary symbols in the project network shown below.

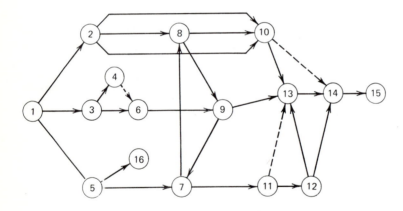

5-40 Consider the servicing of an automobile at a gasoline station to be a project. Construct an appropriate project network assuming that two attendants are available.

5-41 *Activities on Nodes.* Make a list of the activities that constitute the project shown in Exercise 5-37 and write down the precedence relationships. Then from this list, construct a project network using the activities on nodes (AON) method. Compare the resulting network with the one in Exercise 5-37. Notice that no dummy activity is required (this is a feature of the AON method).

5-42 The annual shutdown maintenance on a 50,000 horsepower steam turbine can be represented by the following list of activities:

ACTIVITY	DURATION	IMMEDIATE PREDECESSOR
1. Shut down turbine	2	—
2. Close steam lines	5	—
3. Remove case	3	1
4. Cool steam lines	8	2
5. Disconnect steam lines	10	2
6. Remove old bearings	4	1, 4
7. Remove valves	9	3, 6
8. Remove tubing	6	3, 6
9. Repair steam lines	7	4
10. Replace steam lines	2	4, 5
11. Replace valves	14	7
12. Replace tubing	8	8
13. Replace bearings	6	9, 10
14. Lubricate	11	7, 8
15. Replace case	15	12, 13

(a) Construct the project network.

(b) Prepare a table giving earliest and latest start and finish, total slack, and free slack for each activity.

(c) Identify the critical path.

5-43 The installation of a new digital computer can be described by the following activities:

ACTIVITY	DURATION (WEEKS)	IMMEDIATE PREDECESSOR
1. Write specifications	10	—
2. Request for bids	0.5	1
3. Construct facility exterior	20	1
4. Preparation of bids	5	2
5. Evaluate bids	3	4
6. Construct facility interior	10	3
7. Choose computer	1	4
8. Choose support equipment	1	7
9. Wire facility interior	2	3, 7
10. Install computer	3	9
11. Install support equipment	1	8
12. Evaluate system	2	10, 11

Construct a network diagram of this project. Find the critical path. Find the early and late start, and early and late finish times of each activity and display them in a table.

5-44 A list of activities and the precedence relationships that describe a project are given below. However, the AOA network does not express the proper precedence relationship. Construct a correct AOA network.

ACTIVITY	IMMEDIATE PREDECESSORS
a	—
b	—
c	a, b
d	c, b
e	b
f	e, d
g	d
h	g, f

5-45 Suppose the activity durations for the computer installation project described in Exercise 5-43 were uncertain, but estimates of the optimistic, pessimistic, and most likely times were available, as shown below. Draw

	ACTIVITY DURATION		
ACTIVITY	OPTIMISTIC	MOST LIKELY	PESSIMISTIC
1	8	10	14
2	0.5	1	2
3	16	20	25
4	3	5	8
5	2	3	4
6	7	10	12
7	1	2	3
8	0.5	2	4
9	0.75	2	2.75
10	1.5	3	4
11	0.75	1	1.5
12	1	2	3

the network and find the critical path for the project. Construct an approximate 95 percent confidence interval on the project duration.

5-46 Assume that the activity durations for the steam turbine maintenance described in Exercise 5-42 cannot be determined exactly. For the optimistic, most likely, and pessimistic times, estimates are shown below.

(a) Construct the network and find the critical path for the project.

(b) Compute a 99 percent confidence interval on project completion time.

(c) Find the probability of positive slack for each event in the network. Do these calculations indicate that any events not now on the critical path are likely to become critical?

(d) Find a time, say x, such that the probability of project completion time exceeding x is less than 0.1, approximately.

	ACTIVITY DURATION		
ACTIVITY	OPTIMISTIC	MOST LIKELY	PESSIMISTIC
1	1	2	3
2	4	5	7
3	1	3	5
4	6	8	10
5	8	10	12
6	3	4	6
7	7	9	10
8	4	6	7
9	6	7	8
10	1	2	3
11	10	14	16
12	7	8	10
13	4	6	7
14	9	11	12
15	13	15	18

5.47 The PERT network for a small project is shown on page 394 along with the estimated activity durations. Find the critical path, and compute an approximate 95 percent confidence interval on project completion time.

What is the probability that the project will take more than 25 time periods?

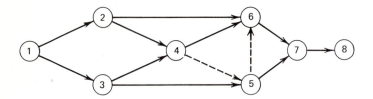

TIME ESTIMATES

ACTIVITY	a_{ij}	m_{ij}	b_{ij}
(1, 2)	2	3	4
(1, 3)	2	4	6
(2, 4)	5	6	7
(2, 6)	4	5	6
(3, 4)	7	8	10
(3, 5)	6	7	9
(4, 6)	3	5	6
(5, 7)	3	4	5
(6, 7)	1	2	3
(7, 8)	1	2	3

5-48   For the PERT network shown below, find the critical path and compute an approximate 95 percent confidence interval on project completion time.

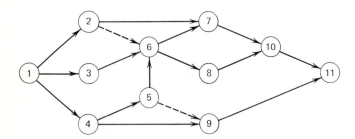

ACTIVITY	TIME ESTIMATES		
	a_{ij}	m_{ij}	b_{ij}
(1, 2)	3	4	5
(1, 3)	5	6	8
(1, 4)	2	3	4
(2, 7)	7	9	10
(3, 6)	10	12	15
(4, 5)	2	4	5
(4, 9)	5	7	8
(5, 6)	6	8	9
(6, 7)	12	13	15
(6, 8)	8	10	11
(7, 10)	7	9	12
(8, 10)	1	2	4
(9, 11)	1	3	4
(10, 11)	5	6	7

5-49 Consider the nine-task assembly line balancing problem whose precedence diagram is shown below. The performance time of each task is shown immediately above the node representing the task.

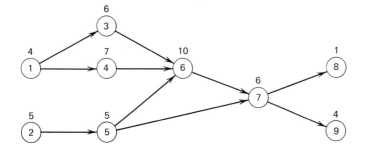

(a) Using the Kilbridge and Wester method, find a balance for $c = 16$, if possible.

(b) Investigate the other feasible cycle times using Kilbridge and Wester's method. Do any perfect balances exist?

(c) Using the Ranked Positional Weight Method find a balance for $c = 16$, if possible.

5-50 An assembly line for a television set subassembly is shown in the precedence diagram below. The task performance times in minutes are shown directly above the nodes representing the tasks.

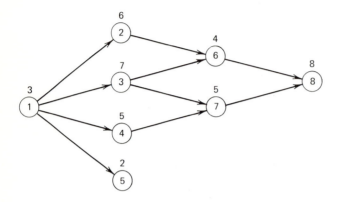

(a) What values of cycle times would potentially yield perfect balances? Find the number of units produced per hour at each cycle time.

(b) Try to obtain a perfect balance for a cycle time of 10 minutes using Kilbridge and Wester's technique.

(c) Apply COMSOAL to this problem for a cycle time of 10 assuming that the probabilities of selecting available tasks are equal. Generate three solutions. Is any solution optimal?

5-51 Consider the assembly line balancing problem shown below. The performance times for the tasks are shown above the nodes. Does a zero idle time balance exist? Use Kilbridge and Wester's method.

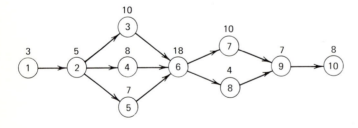

5-52 Consider the assembly line balancing problem shown on page 397. The performance times for the tasks are shown above the nodes. Try to balance the line using COMSOAL for a cycle time of 15. Assume that equal probabilities are assigned to available tasks. Generate five solutions.

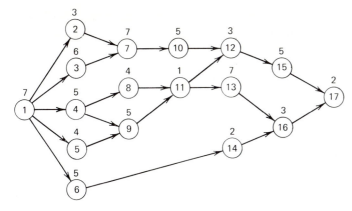

5-53 Try to find a four-station balance for the assembly line shown below using the Kilbridge and Wester method. The performance times for the tasks are shown above the nodes. Do three-station or five-station balances exist?

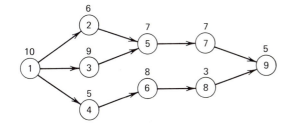

5-54 Try to find a five-station balance for the assembly line shown below using the Ranked Positional Weight method. The performance times for the tasks are shown above the nodes.

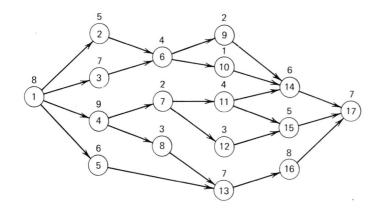

5-55 Formulate the nine-task assembly line balancing problem described in Exercise 5-49 as an integer programming problem. Assume a cycle time of 12 is desired.

5-56 Formulate the eight-task assembly line balancing problem described in Exercise 5-50 as an integer programming problem. Assume a cycle time of 10 is desired.

5-57 *The Least-Cost Testing Sequence Problem.* Suppose that units of product must be subjected to n sequential independent tests. Each unit is tested in a specific sequence until it either fails to pass a test and is rejected with no further tests conducted, or until it passes the nth test and is accepted. A schematic representation of the process is shown below. Let C_i be

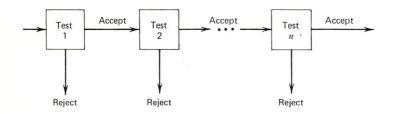

the cost per unit of conducting the ith test and p_i be the probability of acceptance at the ith test. The expected cost per item for any testing sequence is

$$C = C_1 + p_1 C_2 + p_1 p_2 C_3 + \cdots + (p_1 p_2 \cdots p_{n-1})C_n$$

Show that the least-cost testing sequence is given by ordering the tests such that

$$\frac{C_{[1]}}{1 - p_{[1]}} \leq \frac{C_{[2]}}{1 - p_{[2]}} \leq \cdots \leq \frac{C_{[n]}}{1 - p_{[n]}}$$

chapter 6
Forecasting Systems

6-1 Introduction

6-1.1 Nature and Uses of Forecasts

Management often is concerned with predicting future values of a time-oriented variable. The sequence of values of the variable usually is called a *time series*. Estimates of future values of a time series are used frequently as a basis for managerial decision making. For example, forecasts of demand for a product may be needed to schedule production or regulate inventories for that product. While many applications of forecasting are concerned with product demand, there are many other industrial time series for which forecasts would be extremely useful, such as quality characteristics for a product, costs, facility or equipment utilization, work load, and cash flow. Forecasts of various time series find wide application as inputs to inventory control systems, item or aggregate production planning and scheduling models, cost control models, and many other management information systems. We have studied several models in earlier chapters for which forecasts of demand are an essential component.

There are two general ways that we may estimate future values of a time series. We may subjectively estimate, or *predict*, these values. Prediction usually involves anticipating qualitative factors, such as the effect of introducing a new product, competitive action, or a major change in the national economy. Because predictions require skill, experience, and judgment, not all time series can be successfully predicted. Alternatively, we may *forecast* future values of a time series. Specifically, forecasting involves analyzing past data and projecting it into the future, usually by employing some appropriate mathematical model. Forecasting is the process of drawing inferences about the future from historical data. (This distinction between prediction and forecasting is not universal, but it is used in this text.)

It is important to note that the forecast is an estimate of a future observation assuming that the underlying time series continues as it has in the recent past. Because forecasting is an objective process, we know which factors have been considered in the forecast and which have not. When some factor causes changes in the basic nature of the underlying time series, and the decision maker has knowledge of that change, this information often can be incorporated into the forecast. To some extent, then, a forecast may serve as an input for a prediction. In reality, many forecasting systems operate this way, with management having the opportunity to modify the forecast in some fashion as part of the decision-making process.

There are many potential uses of forecasts. For example, if reliable forecasts of product demand for the next six months were available, a production control manager could accurately plan production schedules, work-force assignments, distribution of product, and certain capacity needs. If longer-range forecasts, say one year or more, were available, financial and facilities planning could utilize this information. In general, the uses of a forecast are limited to a large extent by the lead time over which that forecast is made. Short-range forecasts are for only a few time periods ahead, and at most for a year into the future. Their utility is primarily in production scheduling, inventory planning, and other activities which can be accomplished or affected in the short run. Long-range forecasts may project as much as five or ten years into the future. Decisions requiring a long lead time to implement, such as when and where to build new plants, will be partially based on long-range forecasts. Inherently, short-range forecasts are more accurate than long-range forecasts, since there is greater likelihood that the underlying time series will be affected by external environ-

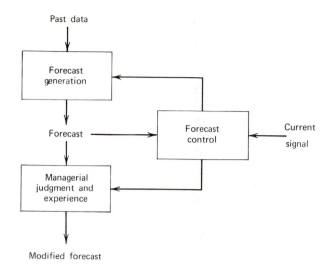

Past data

Forecast
generation

Forecast

Forecast
control

Current
signal

Managerial
judgment and
experience

Modified forecast

FIGURE 6-1. The forecasting system.

mental factors over a long period of time than over a short one. Usually, quite different techniques are used to produce these two kinds of forecasts.

The process of generating forecasts is not isolated. To be effective and efficient, forecasting must be imbedded in a management control system such as the one shown in Figure 6-1. In this figure, the forecast is a result of inference from data. However, the forecast is only a basis for decision making, and managerial judgment and experience must be brought to bear on the forecast as part of the decision-making process. Finally, a comparison between the forecast and the actual signal may cause modifications in either the forecast generation procedure or the way in which management interprets the forecast, or perhaps both.

This chapter concentrates on mathematical and statistical methods for generating short-term forecasts. The methods we shall present are applicable to a variety of situations and relatively simple, so that they may be routinely applied to a large number of time series. We shall also discuss several aspects of forecast control.

6-1.2 Sources of Data

Assume that the time series data available is of a discrete nature, that is, information becomes available only at certain points in time. The process generating this data may be either discrete or continuous. If it is continuous, then we are dealing with a sampled-data system. Let the data be x_t, ($t = 1, 2, \ldots$), where the subscript t represents time. The unit of time represented by $\Delta t = (t + 1) - t$ is called the sampling interval. It may be a second, a day, a week, or several weeks, depending on the nature of the application. Obviously, the choice of sampling interval (when such a choice can be made) will have considerable influence on the data, and also on the forecasting system itself.

Data that is truly representative of the process under study is an essential part of a successful forecasting system. For example, the control of inventories and production should be based on a forecast of demand, that is, the actual requirements of the customer. Frequently, the only data readily available are sales, or shipments to customers, or invoices, or some other similar statistic. All of these measures may be quite different from demand. Sales does not include unfulfilled or lost demand due to inventory shortages, and shipments very often give a highly distorted picture of demand. It is usually worthwhile to obtain the correct type of data, even if an information system must be developed for this purpose.

The data in a forecasting system are subject to recording and transmission errors, and therefore should be screened in an effort to eliminate errors. Small errors will be very difficult to detect, but they usually will have little effect on the performance of the forecasting system. Larger errors can be detected more easily, and corrected. Also, the forecasting system should not react to extraordinary signals. If we are forecasting demand, any transaction data identified as unusual or extreme should, of course, affect the inventory records, but should not be included in the data used by the forecasting system. For example, suppose a plant routinely supplies several other companies with a certain product. When a new company begins to use this product, it will probably require a large shipment as initial stock. This excess demand should be considered extraordinary, and should not be allowed to influence excessively the forecast of future demand.

In developing forecasting models, the analyst should become thoroughly familiar with the data used by the forecasting system. It is useful to plot the data against time, and attempt to ascertain the existence of long-term trends, periodic or cyclic variation, or other reasonably stable patterns of behavior.

6-1.3 Models and Criteria

Forecasting problems involve describing the process or phenomena that generates a sequence of data, or a set of observations. We shall be interested in either forecasting the expected value of future observations or the form of the probability distribution from which these observations will be generated. In either event, it is usually necessary to represent the behavior of the observations by a mathematical model that can be projected into the future. It is necessary that the model be a good representation of the observations in any local segment of time close to the present. We usually do not require the model to represent very old observations as they probably have little influence on the present, or observations far into the future, beyond the lead time over which the forecast is made. Once a valid model for the time series process has been established, an appropriate forecasting technique can be developed.

Several typical characteristics of time series are shown in Figure 6-2a–c. Occasionally time series exhibit abnormal patterns of behavior, such as step functions, impulses, unusual increases in sales following introduction of a new product, or marked decreases in sales as a product is phased out. Several of these unusual situations are illustrated in Figure 6-2d–g. We shall discuss forecasting techniques for models that account for three basic types of time series

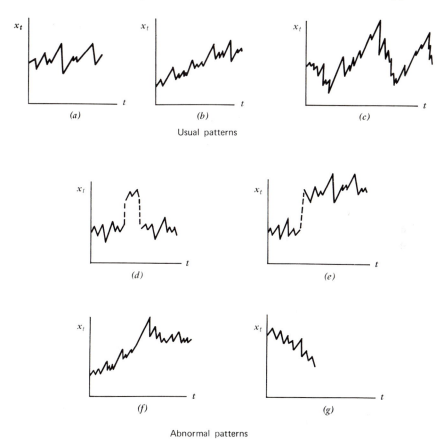

FIGURE 6-2. Time series characteristics. (a) Constant process. (b) Linear trend. (c) Cyclic variation. (d) Impulse. (e) Step function. (f) New product growth. (g) Product phased out.

characteristics: constant processes, linear and quadratic trends, and cyclic or periodic variation. Various combinations of these patterns will also be considered.

Many of the models that we shall use to represent time series will be algebraic or transcendental functions of time, or some composite model that combines both algebraic and transcendental components. For example, if the observations are random samples from some probability distribution, and if the mean of that distribution does not change with time, then the constant model

$$x_t = a + \varepsilon_t \qquad (6\text{-}1)$$

may be employed, where a is the unknown mean and ε_t is a random error component. Usually we shall find it convenient to make some assumptions about the random error component, such as, for example, $E(\varepsilon_t) = 0$, and $V(\varepsilon_t) = \sigma_\varepsilon^2$. If the mean of the distribution changes linearly with time, then the linear trend model

$$x_t = a + bt + \varepsilon_t \qquad (6\text{-}2)$$

may be appropriate. Cyclic variation may be accounted for by introducing transcendental components into the model, say

$$x_t = a_0 + a_1 \sin \frac{2\pi t}{12} + a_2 \cos \frac{2\pi t}{12} + \varepsilon_t \qquad (6\text{-}3)$$

which would account for a 12-period cycle. We shall also discuss other approaches to cyclic variation.

The forecasting problem consists of estimating the unknown parameters in the appropriate time series model, and once these unknown parameters have been estimated, projecting the model into the future to obtain a forecast. For example, let $\hat{a}$ and $\hat{b}$ be estimates of the unknown parameters a and b in Equation 6-2. If we are currently at the end of period t, then the forecast of the signal in some future period $t + \tau$ would be

$$\hat{x}_{t+\tau} = \hat{a} + \hat{b}[t + \tau]$$

Thus, the forecast simply projects the estimate of the trend component, $\hat{b}$, τ periods into the future. We shall consider a variety of techniques for estimating the unknown parameters of time series models.

In developing a forecasting system, there are various criteria useful in judging the success of a given technique, or in discriminating among alternatives. Most measures of effectiveness concerned with forecast accuracy utilize some function of the forecast error in a period, which for period t we denote by $e_t = x_t - \hat{x}_t$. In developing estimators for model parameters, we shall use a least-squares criteria of accuracy. That is, the unknown parameters will be estimated so as to minimize the sum of squares of the forecast error. These errors may be discounted in time away from the most recent observation, to attach less importance to older data. In addition to forecast accuracy, we should also like the computations involved in the forecasting procedure to be reasonably simple. In many applications, it may be necessary periodically to compute forecasts for hundreds or thousands of different time series. Even with the use of high-speed computers, the amount of time required to perform the necessary calculations will be an important consideration.

6-2 Regression Methods

In this section, the notation and methodology of regression methods applied in estimating parameters of time series models is developed. Initially, least-squares analysis of a model with trend is presented and then the general procedure is described more formally.

Many time series can be adequately described by a simple linear function of time. We may write this function, including noise as

$$x_t = a + bt + \varepsilon_t \tag{6-4}$$

We shall consider estimating the unknown parameters a and b by least-squares regression. The only assumptions required regarding the random error component are $E(\varepsilon_t) = 0$, $V(\varepsilon_t) = \sigma_\varepsilon^2$, and $Cov(\varepsilon_i, \varepsilon_j) = 0$ for $i \neq j$. That is, the average error is zero, the error variance is σ_ε^2, and the errors are uncorrelated random variables.

Assume that there are T periods of data available, say $x_1, x_2, \ldots, x_T$. We wish to estimate a and b, say by $\hat{a}$ and $\hat{b}$, such that the sum of squares of residuals

$$SS_E = \sum_{t=1}^{T} [x_t - \hat{a} - \hat{b}t]^2 \tag{6-5}$$

is minimized. Therefore, it is necessary that $\hat{a}$ and $\hat{b}$ satisfy

$$\frac{\partial SS_E}{\partial \hat{a}} = -2 \sum_{t=1}^{T} [x_t - \hat{a} - \hat{b}t] = 0 \tag{6-6}$$

and

$$\frac{\partial SS_E}{\partial \hat{b}} = -2 \sum_{t=1}^{T} [x_t - \hat{a} - \hat{b}t](t) = 0 \tag{6-7}$$

Equations 6-6 and 6-7 may be written as

$$\hat{a} \sum_{t=1}^{T} (1) + \hat{b} \sum_{t=1}^{T} t = \sum_{t=1}^{T} x_t \tag{6-8}$$

$$\hat{a} \sum_{t=1}^{T} t + \hat{b} \sum_{t=1}^{T} t^2 = \sum_{t=1}^{T} t x_t \tag{6-9}$$

Equations 6-8 and 6-9 are called the *least-squares normal equations*. Using $\sum_{t=1}^{T} t = T(T + 1)/2$ and $\sum_{t=1}^{T} t^2 = T(T + 1)(2T + 1)/6$, the solution to the normal equations is easily found to be

$$\hat{a} = \frac{2(2T + 1)}{T(T - 1)} \sum_{t=1}^{T} x_t - \frac{6}{T(T - 1)} \sum_{t=1}^{T} t x_t \equiv \hat{a}(T) \tag{6-10}$$

$$\hat{b} = \frac{12}{T(T^2 - 1)} \sum_{t=1}^{T} t x_t - \frac{6}{T(T - 1)} \sum_{t=1}^{T} x_t \equiv \hat{b}(T) \tag{6-11}$$

It is convenient to denote our estimators of the unknown parameters as a function of time, that is, $\hat{a}(T)$ and $\hat{b}(T)$, where T is the time at which the estimates are computed. The forecast for some future period, say $T + \tau$, would be

$$\hat{x}_{T+\tau} = \hat{a}(T) + \hat{b}(T)[T + \tau] \tag{6-12}$$

As a new observation becomes available, new estimates of the parameters a and b may be computed.

☐**EXAMPLE 6-1** The weekly demand record following the introduction of a new product is available to us and is shown in Table 6-1 below. We shall use this data to estimate the parameters in the linear trend model. Since $\sum_{t=1}^{5} x_t = 75$, and $\sum_{t=1}^{5} t x_t = 251$, we may compute

$$\hat{a}(5) = \frac{2(11)}{5(4)} (75) - \frac{6}{5(4)} (251) = 7.2$$

and

$$\hat{b}(5) = \frac{12}{5(24)} (251) - \frac{6}{5(4)} (75) = 2.6$$

using Equations 6-10 and 6-11. The forecasting equation is

$$\hat{x}_{5+\tau} = 7.2 + 2.6(5 + \tau)$$

TABLE 6-1 Weekly Demand Data

WEEK (t)	DEMAND (x_t)
1	10
2	12
3	15
4	18
5	20

The forecast of demand for the next week, that is, $\tau = 1$, is

$$\hat{x}_6 = 7.2 + 2.6(6) = 22.8 \cong 23 \qquad \qquad \square$$

Frequently, we may have reason to suspect that some equation other than a simple linear relationship will provide a better model for a time series. So long as the desired relationship is *linear in the unknown parameters*, we may use multiple linear regression to find the least-squares estimators. For example, suppose the required relationship is

$$x_t = a_0 + a_1 t + a_2 t^2 + \varepsilon_t$$

Since this relationship is linear in the unknown parameters (the a_i's), we may use multiple regression to estimate the parameters. As another example the model

$$x_t = a_0 + a_1 t + a_2 \sin 2\pi t + a_3 e^{-t} + \varepsilon_t$$

is also linear in the unknown parameters. Generally, models such as these are called *linear models*.

We assume that the general model is

$$x_t = \sum_{i=1}^{n} a_i f_i(t) + \varepsilon_t, \qquad t = 1, 2, \ldots, T \qquad (6\text{-}13)$$

where a_i is the coefficient of the ith term in the model and the independent variables $f_i(t)$, $i = 1, 2, \ldots, n$, are appropriate functions of time[1]. Once again, we assume that $E(\varepsilon_t) = 0$, $V(\varepsilon_t) = \sigma_\varepsilon^2$, and $Cov(\varepsilon_i, \varepsilon_j) = 0$ for $i \neq j$.

It is convenient to express Equation 6-13 in matrix notation. Let $\mathbf{a}$ denote the $(n \times 1)$ column vector whose ith element is a_i and $\mathbf{f}(t)$ denote the $(n \times 1)$ column vector whose ith element is the ith independent variable $f_i(t)$. Then we may write Equation 6-13 as

$$x_t = \mathbf{a}'\mathbf{f}(t) + \varepsilon_t, \qquad t = 1, 2, \ldots, T \qquad (6\text{-}14)$$

where the prime (') denotes the transpose operation. If $\hat{\mathbf{a}}' = [\hat{a}_1, \hat{a}_2, \ldots, \hat{a}_n]$ denotes the vector of estimates of $\mathbf{a}$, the tth residual is

$$e_t = x_t - \hat{x}_t = x_t - \hat{\mathbf{a}}'\mathbf{f}(t)$$

We seek the estimator of $\mathbf{a}$ that minimizes the weighted[2] sum of squares of the residuals,

$$SS_E = \sum_{t=1}^{T} W_{tt}^2 e_t^2 \qquad (6\text{-}15)$$

We see that W_{tt} is the square root of the weight given to the tth residual.

Let $\mathbf{x} = [x_1, x_2, \ldots, x_T]$ be a $(1 \times T)$ row vector of the observations,

---

[1] Much of the notation in this chapter follows that of Brown (2).

[2] The reason for weighting the residuals will soon become apparent.

$\mathbf{e} = [e_1, e_2, \ldots, e_T]$ be a $(1 \times T)$ row vector of residuals, $\mathbf{F}$ be a $(n \times T)$ matrix of the independent variables such that

$$\mathbf{F} = \begin{bmatrix} f_1(1) & f_1(2) & \cdots & f_1(T) \\ f_2(1) & f_2(2) & \cdots & f_2(T) \\ . & . & & . \\ . & . & & . \\ . & . & & . \\ f_n(1) & f_n(2) & \cdots & f_n(T) \end{bmatrix}$$

and $\boldsymbol{\varepsilon} = [\varepsilon_1, \varepsilon_2, \ldots, \varepsilon_T]$ be a $(1 \times T)$ row vector of the model error components. Now in matrix notation the model is

$$\mathbf{x} = \mathbf{a}'\mathbf{F} + \boldsymbol{\varepsilon} \tag{6-16}$$

and, for a vector of estimates $\hat{\mathbf{a}}$, the residuals are

$$\mathbf{e} = \mathbf{x} - \hat{\mathbf{a}}'\mathbf{F} \tag{6-17}$$

The weighted sum of squared residuals is

$$\begin{aligned} SS_E &= (\mathbf{eW})(\mathbf{eW})' \\ &= \mathbf{eWW}'\mathbf{e}' \\ &= \mathbf{eW}^2\mathbf{e}' \\ &= (\mathbf{x} - \hat{\mathbf{a}}'\mathbf{F})\mathbf{W}^2(\mathbf{x} - \hat{\mathbf{a}}'\mathbf{F})' \\ &= \mathbf{xW}^2\mathbf{x}' - \hat{\mathbf{a}}'\mathbf{FW}^2\mathbf{x}' - \mathbf{xW}^2\mathbf{F}'\hat{\mathbf{a}} + \hat{\mathbf{a}}'\mathbf{FW}^2\mathbf{F}'\hat{\mathbf{a}} \end{aligned}$$

where $\mathbf{W}$ is the $(T \times T)$ diagonal matrix

$$\mathbf{W} = \begin{bmatrix} W_{11} & 0 & \cdots & 0 \\ 0 & W_{22} & \cdots & 0 \\ . & . & . & . \\ . & . & . & . \\ . & . & . & . \\ 0 & 0 & \cdots & W_{TT} \end{bmatrix}$$

It is necessary that the least-squares estimators satisfy

$$\frac{\partial SS_E}{\partial \hat{\mathbf{a}}} = -2\mathbf{FW}^2\mathbf{x}' + 2\mathbf{FW}^2\mathbf{F}'\hat{\mathbf{a}} = 0$$

and thus the least-squares normal equations are

$$\mathbf{FW}^2\mathbf{F}'\hat{\mathbf{a}} = \mathbf{FW}^2\mathbf{x}'$$

or

$$\mathbf{G\hat{a}} = \mathbf{g}$$

where $\mathbf{G} = (\mathbf{FW})(\mathbf{FW})'$ is a matrix of weighted sums of squares and cross-products of the independent variables, and $\mathbf{g} = \mathbf{FW}^2\mathbf{x}'$ is a vector of weighted sums of cross-products of the independent and dependent variables. In scalar notation we may write $G_{ij} = \sum_{t=1}^{T} W_{tt}^2 f_i(t) f_j(t)$ for $i, j = 1, 2, \ldots, n$, and $g_i = \sum_{t=1}^{T} W_{tt}^2 x_t f_i(t)$ for $i = 1, 2, \ldots, n$.

The solution to the normal equations is

$$\mathbf{\hat{a}} = \mathbf{G}^{-1}\mathbf{g} \equiv \mathbf{\hat{a}}(T) \qquad (6\text{-}19)$$

if $\mathbf{G}^{-1}$ exists. Occasionally, it will be convenient to denote the least-squares estimators as $\mathbf{\hat{a}}(T)$ to indicate that they depend on the point in time that they are computed. The least-squares estimators $\mathbf{\hat{a}}$ are unbiased for the true unknown parameters $\mathbf{a}$ since

$$E(\mathbf{\hat{a}}) = E(\mathbf{G}^{-1}\mathbf{g}) = (\mathbf{FW}^2\mathbf{F}')^{-1}\mathbf{FW}^2 E(\mathbf{x}') = \mathbf{F}'^{-1}\mathbf{F}^{-1}\mathbf{FF}'\mathbf{a} = \mathbf{a}$$

The variance-covariance matrix of the least-squares estimators is

$$\mathbf{V} = E(\mathbf{\hat{a}} - \mathbf{a})(\mathbf{\hat{a}} - \mathbf{a})' = \sigma_\varepsilon^2 \mathbf{G}^{-1}\mathbf{FW}^2(\mathbf{FW}^2)'\mathbf{G}^{-1} \qquad (6\text{-}20)$$

since $E(\boldsymbol{\varepsilon}'\boldsymbol{\varepsilon}) = \sigma_\varepsilon^2 \mathbf{I}$. If $\mathbf{W}$ is the unit matrix (all data receives the same weight), then $\mathbf{V} = \sigma_\varepsilon^2 \mathbf{G}^{-1} = \sigma_\varepsilon^2 (\mathbf{FF}')^{-1}$.

For a particular linear model and the least-squares estimates at time T, say $\mathbf{\hat{a}}(T)$, the forecast for some future period $T + \tau$ would be

$$\hat{x}_{T+\tau} = \mathbf{\hat{a}}'(T)\mathbf{f}(T + \tau) \qquad (6\text{-}21)$$

where $\mathbf{f}'(T + \tau) = [f_1(T + \tau), f_2(T + \tau), \ldots, f_n(T + \tau)]$ is the vector of independent variables evaluated at $T + \tau$. The variance of the forecast is

$$V(\hat{x}_t) = V\{\mathbf{\hat{a}}'(T)\mathbf{f}(t)\} = \mathbf{f}'(t)V\{\mathbf{\hat{a}}'(T)\}\mathbf{f}(t) = \mathbf{f}'(t)\mathbf{V}\mathbf{f}(t)$$

In many practical situations the variance σ_ε^2 is unknown. If the model is an adequate description of the true process we may estimate σ_ε^2 by the mean square error

$$\hat{\sigma}_\varepsilon^2 = \frac{\mathbf{ee}'}{T - n} = \frac{\sum_{t=1}^{T}(x_t - \hat{x}_t)^2}{T - n} \qquad (6\text{-}22)$$

Regression procedures form the basis for many forecasting techniques. While multiple linear regression would appear to require considerable computational effort, for certain types of models, independent variables, and choice of weights, very efficient procedures can be derived. Many of the results developed in this section will be employed again in this chapter as we study specific forecasting methods. More complete treatments of regression are available by Draper and Smith (7) and Graybill (9).

6-3 Moving Average Methods

This section presents two elementary forecasting techniques based on the moving average. The moving average technique results from applying the least-squares criterion to a data record of fixed length, where each data point is weighted equally. Techniques for both constant and linear trend processes are presented.

6-3.1 A Constant Process

In this section we shall consider a time series generated by a constant process plus random error, or noise. The time series model is

$$x_t = a + \varepsilon_t \qquad (6\text{-}23)$$

where ε_t is a random variable such that $E(\varepsilon_t) = 0$ and $V(\varepsilon_t) = \sigma_\varepsilon^2$, and a is an unknown parameter. It is possible that in different widely separated parts of the sequence of observations the value of a will be different, but in any local segment of time a is a constant.

To forecast future values of the time series we must estimate the unknown parameter in Equation 6-23, that is, a. Suppose all observations through period T, say $x_1, x_2, \ldots, x_T$, are available. If we weight these observations equally, the least-squares criterion is to choose $\hat{a}$ so as to minimize

$$SS_E \sum_{t=1}^{T} (x_t - \hat{a})^2$$

From $dSS_E/d\hat{a} = 0$ we obtain

$$\hat{a} = \frac{1}{T} \sum_{t=1}^{T} x_t \qquad (6\text{-}24)$$

which is just the arithmetic mean, or sample mean, of the T observations.

The arithmetic mean includes all past observations of x_t. Since the value of a can change gradually with time, it is reasonable to place more weight on current observations than on those obtained a long time ago. Suppose we decide to use only the most recent N periods of data. The least squares criterion becomes

$$SS_E = \sum_{t=T-N+1}^{T} (x_t - \hat{a})^2$$

and from $dSS_E/d\hat{a} = 0$ we obtain

$$\hat{a} = \frac{1}{N} \sum_{t=T-N+1}^{T} x_t \equiv M_T \qquad (6\text{-}25)$$

Thus M_T is the average of the most recent N observations. At each period the oldest observation is discarded and the newest one added to the set. For this reason, M_T is called an N-period *moving average*. It easily can be verified that an alternative form for Equation 6-25 is

$$M_T = M_{T-1} + \frac{x_T - x_{T-N}}{N} \qquad (6\text{-}26)$$

Equation 6-26 allows us to obtain M_T directly from the previous value, M_{T-1}. The forecast for any future period is just

$$\hat{x}_{T+\tau} = \hat{a} = M_T$$

☐**EXAMPLE 6-2** The last six days demand for a hydraulic jack are $x_1 = 19$, $x_2 = 24$, $x_3 = 22$, $x_4 = 19$, $x_5 = 20$, and $x_6 = 16$. We see, from (6-25), that

$$M_6 = \tfrac{1}{6}[16 + 20 + 19 + 22 + 24 + 19] = 20$$

Therefore $\hat{a} = M_6 = 20$. The forecast for the next day is $\hat{x}_7 = \hat{a} = 20$. Moving ahead one day, suppose $x_7 = 22$. Then to compute M_7 we drop x_1 and add x_7 to obtain

$$M_7 = \tfrac{1}{6}[22 + 16 + 20 + 19 + 22 + 24] = 20.5$$

Alternatively, we may use Equation 6-26 to obtain

$$M_7 = 20 + \frac{22 - 19}{6} = 20.5$$

☐

The behavior of this simple moving average method is a function of the choice of the number of observations to be averaged. If N is large, the moving average will react slowly to changes in the parameter a, and when N is smaller, the moving average will react more quickly. That is, if the time series process operates with some constant $a = a_1$, say, and then suddenly shifts to $a = a_2$, it will take N observations for the moving average to yield forecasts consistent with the new value of a. However, if the random errors are independent random variables, the variance of successive estimates $\hat{a}$ is σ_ε^2/N, so for small N, the variance of $\hat{a}$ will be relatively large. When the process is really constant we would like to use a large value of N, and when the process is changing we would like to use a small value of N.

In many applications, it would be difficult to frequently change the number of observations averaged, as this may involve redesigning computer files or programs. Often, this inflexibility with regard to N is a major reason for using other forecasting methods. Furthermore, an N-period moving average requires that all N observations must be saved. For even a moderate number of different time series, it is clear that the total number of observations carried would soon become prohibitively large.

6-3.2 A Linear Trend Process

Many time series can be adequately described by the simple linear trend model

$$x_t = a + bt + \varepsilon_t \tag{6-27}$$

where a and b are unknown parameters and ε_t is a random error component such that $E(\varepsilon_t) = 0$ and $V(\varepsilon_t) = \sigma_\varepsilon^2$. Once again we assume that in any local segment of time, a and b are constants.

To estimate the unknown parameters a and b, we employ least-squares regression using only the most recent N observations. The criterion to be minimized is

$$SS_E = \sum_{t=T-N+1}^{T} (x_t - \hat{a} - \hat{b}t)^2$$

From $\partial SS_E/\partial \hat{a} = \partial SS_E/\partial \hat{b} = 0$ we obtain the normal equations

$$N\hat{a} + \frac{N}{2}(2T + 1 - N)\hat{b} = \sum_{t=T-N+1}^{T} x_t \tag{6-28a}$$

$$\frac{N}{2}(2T + 1 - N)\hat{a} + \frac{N}{6}[(N - 1)(2N - 1) + 6T(T + 1 - N)]\hat{b}$$

$$= \sum_{t=T-N+1}^{T} tx_t \tag{6-28b}$$

To simplify the computations, shift the origin to the center of the data, that is, from $t = 0$ to $t = \bar{t}$, where $\bar{t} = \dfrac{1}{N}\displaystyle\sum_{t=T-N+1}^{T} t = T - (N - 1)/2$. Therefore, we make the transformation

$$t' = t - \left[T - \frac{N - 1}{2}\right]$$

Now $(N - 1)/2$ is the new coded index for the latest period (T). Substituting for T in Equations 6-28a and 6-28b, we obtain the transformed normal equations

$$N\hat{a}' + (0)\hat{b} = \sum_{t'=-(N-1)/2}^{(N-1)/2} x_{t'} \tag{6-29a}$$

$$(0)\hat{a}' + \frac{N(N^2 - 1)}{12}\hat{b} = \sum_{t'=-(N-1)/2}^{(N-1)/2} t'x_{t'} \tag{6-29b}$$

Note that the transformation $t' = t - \bar{t}$ will not affect the slope $\hat{b}$, but will transform the intercept into

$$\hat{a}' = \hat{a} + \hat{b}\bar{t}$$

and also that

$$\sum_{t'=-(N-1)/2}^{(N-1)/2} x_{t'} = \sum_{t=T-N+1}^{T} x_t$$

The solution to the normal equations 6-29a and 6-29b is

$$\hat{a}'(T) \equiv \hat{a}' = \frac{1}{N} \sum_{t=T-N+1}^{T} x_t = M_T \tag{6-30}$$

$$\hat{b}(T) \equiv \hat{b} = \frac{12}{N(N^2-1)} \sum_{t'=-(N-1)/2}^{(N-1)/2} t' x_{t'}$$

$$= \frac{12}{N(N^2-1)} \left[\frac{N-1}{2} x_T + \frac{N-3}{2} x_{T-1} \right.$$

$$\left. + \cdots - \frac{N-3}{2} x_{T-N+2} - \frac{N-1}{2} x_{T-N+1} \right]$$

$$\equiv W_T \tag{6-31}$$

It is possible to obtain the estimates recursively as

$$\hat{a}'(T) = M_T = M_{T-1} + \frac{1}{N}(x_T - x_{T-N}) \tag{6-32}$$

and

$$\hat{b}(T) = W_T = W_{T-1} + \frac{12}{N(N^2-1)} \left[\frac{N-1}{2} x_T + \frac{N+1}{2} x_{T-N} - N M_{T-1} \right] \tag{6-33}$$

If we wish to express the results in terms of the original intercept, then $\hat{b}(T)$ is unchanged and

$$\hat{a}(T) = M_T - W_T \left(T - \frac{N-1}{2} \right) \tag{6-34}$$

To forecast τ periods into the future we merely extrapolate the trend. The forecasting equation is

$$\hat{x}_{T+\tau} = \hat{a}(T) + \hat{b}(T)[T + \tau]$$

$$= \hat{a}'(T) + \hat{b}(T) \left[\frac{N-1}{2} + \tau \right]$$

$$= M_T + W_T \left[\frac{N-1}{2} + \tau \right] \tag{6-35}$$

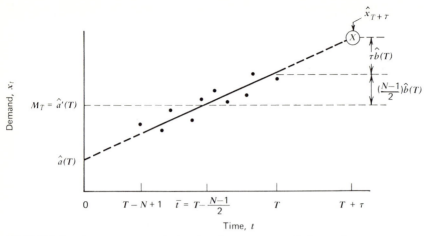

FIGURE 6-3. Least-squares analysis using the most recent N observations.

This process is illustrated in Figure 6-3. Note that the moving average, M_T, lags behind the expected demand in the current period, T, by an amount $[(N-1)/2]b$. Thus, to forecast for period $T + \tau$, we first must "correct" the moving average for the lag by adding $[(N-1)/2]\hat{b}(T)$ and then extrapolate by adding $\tau\hat{b}(T)$.

These results may be put into a slightly different and often more useful form. Suppose that our linear process had no noise component, say

$$x_t = a + bt$$

At time t the moving average is

$$M_t = \frac{1}{N}\left[x_{t-N+1} + x_{t-N+2} + \cdots + x_t\right]$$

$$= x_t - \frac{N-1}{2}b$$

$$= a + bt - \left(\frac{N-1}{2}\right)b \qquad (6\text{-}36)$$

Consider a moving average *of* the moving averages, called the *double moving average*

$$M_t^{[2]} = \frac{1}{N}\left[M_{t-N+1} + M_{t-N+2} + \cdots + M_t\right] \qquad (6\text{-}37\text{a})$$

$$= M_{t-1}^{[2]} + \frac{1}{N}\left[M_t - M_{t-N}\right] \qquad (6\text{-}37\text{b})$$

The quantity $M_t^{[2]}$ denotes a second-order statistic, not a squared quantity.

Forecasting Systems 414

Note that

$$M_t^{[2]} = x_t - (N - 1)b$$
$$= a + bt - (N - 1)b \qquad (6\text{-}37c)$$

Therefore, solving Equations 6-36 and 6-37c for a and b, we obtain

$$a = 2M_t - M_t^{[2]} - bt \qquad (6\text{-}38)$$

$$b = \frac{2}{N - 1}[M_t - M_t^{[2]}] \qquad (6\text{-}39)$$

so that

$$x_t = a + bt = 2M_t - M_t^{[2]} \qquad (6\text{-}40)$$

When the process has noise, it seems logical to use the statistics M_t and $M_t^{[2]}$ to estimate a, b, and x_t according to Equations 6-38, 6-39, and 6-40, respectively. Thus, a forecast for period $T + \tau$, made at the end of period T, would be

$$\hat{x}_{T+\tau} = \hat{x}_T + \hat{b}(T)\tau$$

$$= 2M_T - M_T^{[2]} + \tau\left(\frac{2}{N - 1}\right)[M_T - M_T^{[2]}] \qquad (6\text{-}41)$$

The results obtained by this method will not agree exactly with those obtained from Equation 6-35.

□**EXAMPLE 6-3** The weekly sales of a 5000 BTU air conditioner are shown in the second column of Table 6-2 below. The process generating this data is

TABLE 6-2 Weekly Sales and Forecasts for an Air Conditioner

WEEK	DEMAND	M_t	$M_t^{[2]}$	$\hat{x}_t$
1	10			
2	12			
3	15			
4	14			
5	16	13.4		
6	19	15.2		
7	18	16.4		
8	21	17.6		
9	23	19.4	16.40	
10	20	20.2	17.76	23.90
11	22	20.8	18.85	23.86
12	24	22.0	20.00	23.00
13	23	22.4	20.96	24.56
14	21	22.0	21.48	22.78
15	25	23.0	22.04	24.44

thought to be well-approximated by a linear trend model, and a five-week double moving average is to be used to forecast sales one week ahead. The single moving averages, M_t, can be computed for each week from $5, 6, \ldots, 15$ and are shown in the third column of Table 6-2. The double moving averages, $M_t^{[2]}$, are computed using Equations 6-37a or 6-37b for each week $9, 10, \ldots, 15$. The one-week ahead forecast made at the end of week t are computed according to Equation 6-41 for $\tau = 1$ and are shown in the last column of Table 6-2 for period $t + 1$. For example,

$$\hat{x}_{10} = 2M_9 - M_9^{[2]} + (1)(\tfrac{2}{4})[M_9 - M_9^{[2]}]$$
$$= 2(19.4) - (16.40) + \tfrac{1}{2}[19.4 - 16.40] = 23.90 \qquad \square$$

6-4 Exponential Smoothing Methods

In this section, a development and discussion of exponential smoothing and several related forecasting methods is presented. Exponential smoothing and its variants represent the most widely used class of forecasting methods because they are reasonably accurate and computationally efficient. The procedure will be developed from the weighted least-squares criterion.

6-4.1 Single Exponential Smoothing for a Constant Process

Consider the constant time series model

$$x_t = a + \varepsilon_t$$

where ε_t is a random error component. We shall assume that $E(\varepsilon_t) = 0$, $V(\varepsilon_t) = \sigma_\varepsilon^2$, and that the errors are independently distributed random variables. We could use the N-period simple moving average, developed in Section 6-3.1, to estimate a, and hence to forecast for some future period. In this section, we shall present an alternative method, called *simple exponential smoothing*.[3]

Suppose we wish to estimate a such that the following sum of weighted squared residuals is minimized:

$$SS_E = \sum_{t=1}^{T} \beta^{T-t}(x_t - \hat{a})^2, \qquad 0 < \beta < 1$$

---

[3] Other names for this method of forecasting a constant process are *first-order exponential smoothing* and *single smoothing*.

where β^{T-t} is the weight given to the tth residual. Note that the weights decrease with the age of the data. Proceeding as before, $\hat{a}$ must satisfy

$$\frac{dSS_E}{d\hat{a}} = -2\sum_{t=1}^{T} \beta^{T-t}(x_t - \hat{a}) = 0$$

or

$$\hat{a}\sum_{t=1}^{T} \beta^{T-t} = \sum_{t=1}^{T} \beta^{T-t}x_t$$

Solving for $\hat{a}$ we obtain

$$\hat{a} = \left(\frac{1-\beta}{1-\beta^T}\right)\sum_{t=1}^{T} \beta^{T-t}x_t \equiv S_T$$

Subtracting S_{T-1} from S_T,

$$S_T = \frac{1}{(1-\beta^T)}[(1-\beta)x_T + \beta(1-\beta^{T-1})S_{T-1}] \qquad (6\text{-}42)$$

Let $\alpha = 1 - \beta$ and assume that T is large so that $\beta^T \cong 0$ in Equation 6-42. Then

$$S_T = \alpha x_T + (1-\alpha)S_{T-1} \qquad (6\text{-}43)$$

The operation defined by (6-43) is called *simple exponential smoothing*, and S_T is called the smoothed value or smoothed statistic. The constant α is called the *smoothing constant*.

A heuristic development of exponential smoothing that has great intuitive appeal is often given. Suppose that the new value of the smoothed statistic in period T is defined to be the old value of the smoothed statistic computed in period $T - 1$ plus a fraction, say α, of the difference between the current observation and the old smoothed statistic. This difference is the error from using S_{T-1} to forecast the current period's result. Expressed mathematically, the procedure for revising the smoothed statistic considering current forecast error is

$$S_T = S_{T-1} + \alpha(x_T - S_{T-1})$$

or

$$S_T = \alpha x_T + (1-\alpha)S_{T-1}$$

which is identical to Equation 6-43. Thus, exponential smoothing is a procedure that updates the smoothed statistic proportionally to the difference between the smoothed statistic and the data.

The statistic S_T is a linear combination of all past observations. This is easily seen by first substituting for S_{T-1} in Equation 6-43 to obtain

$$S_T = \alpha x_T + (1-\alpha)[\alpha x_{T-1} + (1-\alpha)S_{T-2}]$$

Exponential Smoothing Methods   417

and then continuing to substitute recursively for S_{T-i} for $i = 2, 3, \ldots$, until finally

$$S_T = \alpha \sum_{k=0}^{T-1} \beta^k x_{T-k} + \beta^T S_0 \tag{6-44}$$

The weights given to past observations decrease geometrically with age. The weights sum to unity, since for large T,

$$\alpha \sum_{k=0}^{\infty} \beta^k = \frac{\alpha}{1 - \beta} = 1$$

so that exponential smoothing is an averaging process in which unequal weights are assigned to the observations. If the smoothing constant is 0.2, then the previous observations have weight 0.16, 0.128, 0.1024, and so on. A comparison of these weights with those of a five-period moving average are shown in Figure 6-4. Because the weights appear to decline exponentially when connected by a smooth curve, the name "exponential smoothing" has been applied to this technique.

The exponential smoothing process yields an unbiased estimator of a, since

$$E(S_T) = E\left[\alpha \sum_{k=0}^{\infty} \beta^k x_{T-k} \right] = \alpha \sum_{k=0}^{\infty} \beta^k E[x_{T-k}] = \alpha \sum_{k=0}^{\infty} \beta^k a = a$$

Therefore, we would be justified in using S_T as an estimator of the unknown parameter a, that is,

$$\hat{a} = S_T \tag{6-45}$$

Forecasts of future observations, say at period $T + \tau$, would be obtained from

$$\hat{x}_{T+\tau} = S_T \tag{6-46}$$

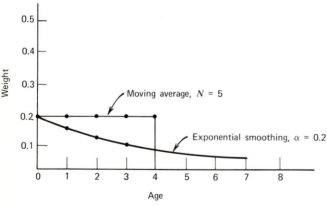

FIGURE 6-4. Weights of past observations.

The choice of α is important in exponential smoothing. Essentially, the response of the forecast to changes in the parameter a is a function of the relative size of α. The lower α, the slower the response. Higher values of α will cause the smoothed value to react quickly—not only to real changes but also to random fluctuations. In general, the value of α should be somewhere between 0.01 and 0.30. The value of α is related to the value of N in a moving average. The average age of the data in an N-period moving average is

$$\bar{A} = \frac{1}{N} \sum_{i=0}^{N-1} i = \frac{N-1}{2}$$

In exponential smoothing, the weight given to data k periods ago is $\alpha\beta^k$. Therefore, the average age is

$$\bar{A} = \alpha \sum_{i=0}^{\infty} i\beta^i = \frac{\beta}{\alpha}$$

Thus if we wish to define an exponential smoothing system that is equivalent to an N-period moving average, then set $\beta/\alpha = (N-1)/2$, which implies

$$\alpha = \frac{2}{N+1}$$

We shall discuss the choice of α more thoroughly in Section 6-4.6.

Exponential smoothing requires a starting value, S_0. If historical data are available, then one could use a simple average of the most recent N observations as S_0. If there is no reliable past data available, then some subjective prediction must be made. If this prediction is likely to be inaccurate, a larger value of α may be used in the first few periods to allow early demand history to rapidly modify the initial estimate.

☐**EXAMPLE 6-4**   A large heating contractor wishes to forecast the number of installations of water heaters per week. He has the following available data:

WEEK	1	2	3	4	5	6	7	8	9	10
Number of installations	15	18	10	12	20	17	22	16	14	20

An examination of the data persuades him to assume a constant model, and use simple exponential smoothing. Assuming $\alpha = 0.1$, arbitrarily, then

$$S_{11} = (0.1)x_{11} + (0.9)S_{10}$$

Exponential Smoothing Methods   **419**

But there is no starting value, S_{10} (note that we could redefine the origin of time to be $t = 10$, and thus the starting value could be denoted S_0). Since the average of the first 10 weeks' demand is 16.6, it is not unreasonable to use $S_{10} = 16.6$. Thus the forecast for any future period, say $10 + \tau$ would be

$$\hat{x}_{10+\tau} = 17$$

after rounding. Suppose the actual number of installations in week 11 is 15. Then

$$S_{11} = (0.1)(15) + (0.9)(16.60) = 16.44$$

and the forecast is

$$\hat{x}_{11+\tau} = 16$$

The one-period ($\tau = 1$) forecast versus the actual number of installations for the weeks 11 through 25 is shown in Table 6-3.□

TABLE 6-3 Demand and Forecasts of Water Heater Installations

WEEK (t)	x_t	S_t	$\hat{x}_t$
1	15		
2	18		
3	10		
4	12		
5	20		
6	17		
7	22		
8	16		
9	14		
10	20	16.60	
11	15	16.44	17
12	12	16.00	16
13	16	16.00	16
14	20	16.40	16
15	22	16.96	16
16	17	16.96	17
17	15	16.76	17
18	10	16.08	17
19	16	16.07	16
20	20	16.46	16
21	19	16.71	16
22	24	17.44	17
23	18	17.50	17
24	15	17.25	17
25	20	17.53	17

6-4.2 Double Exponential Smoothing for a Linear Trend Process

The concept of exponential smoothing can be easily extended to estimating the parameters in the linear model

$$x_t = a + bt + \varepsilon_t \tag{6-47}$$

where we assume that $E(\varepsilon_t) = 0$ and $V(\varepsilon_t) = \sigma_\varepsilon^2$. If simple exponential smoothing were applied to the signal x_t in Equation 6-47, we would obtain, in period T

$$S_T = \alpha x_T + (1 - \alpha)S_{T-1} \tag{6-48}$$

Now

$$E(S_T) = E\left[\alpha \sum_{k=0}^{T-1} \beta^k x_{T-k} + \beta^T S_0\right]$$

$$= \alpha \sum_{k=0}^{T-1} \beta^k E[x_{T-k}] + \beta^T S_0$$

$$= \alpha \sum_{k=0}^{T-1} \beta^k [a + b(T - k)] + \beta^T S_0$$

As $T \to \infty$, $\beta^T \to 0$, and we may write

$$E(S_T) = (a + bT)\alpha \sum_{k=0}^{\infty} \beta^k - b\alpha \sum_{k=0}^{\infty} k\beta^k$$

so that

$$E(S_T) = a + bT - \frac{\beta}{\alpha}b = E(x_T) - \frac{\beta}{\alpha}b \tag{6-49}$$

That is, the simple exponential smoothing statistic S_T will tend to lag behind the true signal by an amount equal to $(\beta/\alpha)b$.

Now suppose we apply the exponential smoothing operator to the output of Equation 6-48. This would result in

$$S_T^{[2]} = \alpha S_T + (1 - \alpha)S_{T-1}^{[2]} \tag{6-50}$$

where the notation $S_T^{[2]}$ implies "double exponential smoothing," not the square of exponential smoothing. By proceeding as above, we may show that

$$E(S_T^{[2]}) = E(S_T) - \frac{\beta}{\alpha}b$$

therefore

$$b = \frac{\alpha}{\beta}\left[E(S_T) - E(S_T^{[2]})\right] \tag{6-51}$$

Thus, it seems logical to estimate b at the end of period T by

$$\hat{b}(T) = \frac{\alpha}{\beta}[S_T - S_T^{[2]}] \tag{6-52}$$

The signal at the end of period T may be obtained from Equations 6-49 and 6-51 as

$$E(x_T) = E(S_T) + \frac{\beta}{\alpha} \cdot \frac{\alpha}{\beta}[E(S_T) - E(S_T^{[2]})]$$

$$= 2E(S_T) - E(S_T^{[2]})$$

The estimate of this signal would be

$$\hat{x}_T = 2S_T - S_T^{[2]} \tag{6-53}$$

To forecast τ periods into the future using double exponential smoothing, the appropriate forecasting equation is

$$\hat{x}_{T+\tau} = \hat{x}_T + \tau\hat{b}(T)$$

$$= 2S_T - S_T^{[2]} + \tau\frac{\alpha}{\beta}[S_T - S_T^{[2]}]$$

$$= (2 + \gamma)S_T - (1 + \gamma)S_T^{[2]} \tag{6-54}$$

where $\gamma = \tau(\alpha/\beta)$.

We have not estimated the intercept directly. However, if necessary, this can be done easily. The estimate of the intercept at time T with the original time origin is just

$$\hat{a}(T) = \hat{x}_T - T\hat{b}(T)$$

$$= 2S_T - S_T^{[2]} - T\frac{\alpha}{\beta}[S_T - S_T^{[2]}]$$

If we think of the origin of time as shifted to T, then $\hat{a}(T) = \hat{x}_T$.

In initiating double smoothing, values must be given to S_0 and $S_0^{[2]}$. These initial conditions may be obtained from estimates of the two coefficients $\hat{a}(0)$ and $\hat{b}(0)$, which in turn may be estimated from historical data using simple linear regression. If no historical data is available, it is necessary to estimate $\hat{a}(0)$ and $\hat{b}(0)$ subjectively. Given initial estimates $\hat{a}(0)$ and $\hat{b}(0)$, the equations for estimating the coefficients in terms of the smoothed statistics, that is, Equations 6-52 and 6-53, may be solved to yield the initial smoothed values

$$S_0 = \hat{a}(0) - \frac{\beta}{\alpha}\hat{b}(0) \tag{6-55}$$

and

$$S_0^{[2]} = \hat{a}(0) - 2\frac{\beta}{\alpha}\hat{b}(0) \tag{6-56}$$

□**EXAMPLE 6-5** An operations research analyst for a time-sharing computer utility wishes to forecast billings by his firm for computer service. The company has been in business two years; however, he considers the billings for these two years not indicative of current business operations, as the company was not well established. He believes the billings to be increasing linearly with time, and furthermore, his best subjective estimates of the parameters of this linear relationship are (in thousands of dollars), $\hat{a}(0) = 95$ and $\hat{b}(0) = 1.0$. The analyst decides to use double exponential smoothing with $\alpha = 0.1$. Using these estimates, the required initial values for double smoothing are

$$S_0 = 95 - \frac{(0.9)}{(0.1)}(1) = 86$$

and

$$S_0^{[2]} = 95 - 2\frac{(0.9)}{(0.1)}(1) = 77$$

Therefore, the forecast (in thousands of dollars) for month 1 is

$$\hat{x}_1 = \left[2 + (1)\frac{(0.1)}{(0.9)}\right]S_0 - \left[1 + (1)\frac{(0.1)}{(0.9)}\right]S_0^{[2]}$$

$$= (2.111)(86) - (1.111)77$$

$$= 95.999$$

$$\cong 96$$

Suppose the actual billing in month 1 was 98. Then the smoothed statistics would be revised as follows:

$$S_1 = \alpha x_1 + (1 - \alpha)S_0 = (0.1)(98) + (0.9)(86) = 87.20$$

$$S_1^{[2]} = \alpha S_1 + (1 - \alpha)S_0^{[2]} = (0.1)(87.20) + (0.9)(77) = 78.02$$

and the forecast for month 2 would be

$$\hat{x}_2 = (2.111)S_1 - (1.111)S_1^{[2]}$$

$$= (2.111)(87.20) - (1.111)(78.02)$$

$$= 97.399$$

$$\cong 97$$

The monthly billings for the next year and their forecasts using this procedure are shown in Table 6-4 (page 424). The graph in Figure 6-5 (page 424) plots the actual versus predicted billings.□

TABLE 6-4 Forecasts of Monthly Billings Using Double Exponential Smoothing

MONTH (t)	x_t	S_t	$S_t^{[2]}$	$\hat{x}_t$
0		86.00	77.00	
1	98	87.20	78.02	96
2	94	87.88	79.01	97
3	99	88.99	80.00	98
4	104	90.49	81.05	99
5	108	92.24	82.17	101
6	100	93.02	83.26	103
7	106	94.32	84.36	104
8	104	95.29	85.45	105
9	118	97.56	86.66	106
10	109	98.70	87.87	110
11	102	99.03	88.98	111
12	116	100.73	90.16	110

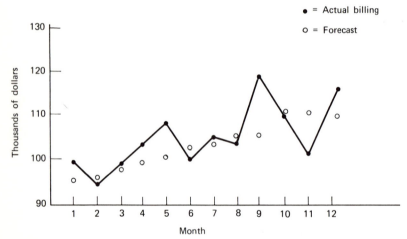

• = Actual billing

o = Forecast

FIGURE 6-5. Actual billing versus forecast.

6-4.3 Higher-Order Polynomial Models

Exponential smoothing can be used to estimate the coefficients in general polynomial models. Suppose, for example, the time series model is the quadratic

$$x_t = a + bt + \tfrac{1}{2}ct^2 + \varepsilon_t \tag{6-57}$$

where we assume that $E(\varepsilon_t) = 0$ and $V(\varepsilon_t) = \sigma_\varepsilon^2$. We may use the first three exponentially smoothed statistics, computed at the end of period T

$$S_T = \alpha x_T + (1 - \alpha)S_{T-1}$$
$$S_T^{[2]} = \alpha S_T + (1 - \alpha)S_{T-1}^{[2]} \qquad (6\text{-}58)$$
$$S_T^{[3]} = \alpha S_T^{[2]} + (1 - \alpha)S_{T-1}^{[3]}$$

to estimate the coefficients in the model (6-57) as

$$\hat{a}(T) = 3S_T - 3S_T^{[2]} + S_T^{[3]}$$

$$\hat{b}(T) = \frac{\alpha}{2\beta^2}\left[(6 - 5\alpha)S_T - 2(5 - 4\alpha)S_T^{[2]} + (4 - 3\alpha)S_T^{[3]}\right] \qquad (6\text{-}59)$$

$$\hat{c}(T) = \left(\frac{\alpha}{\beta}\right)^2\left[S_T - 2S_T^{[2]} + S_T^{[3]}\right]$$

The forecast of any future observation, say at time $T + \tau$, would be

$$\hat{x}_{T+\tau} = \hat{a}(T) + \hat{b}(T)\tau + \tfrac{1}{2}\hat{c}(T)\tau^2 \qquad (6\text{-}60)$$

This procedure is usually called *triple exponential smoothing*.

Starting values must be provided for three smoothed statistics. Note that Equation 6-58 may be solved for the smoothed statistics as follows.

$$S_T = \hat{a}(T) - \frac{\beta}{\alpha}\hat{b}(T) + \frac{\beta(2 - \alpha)}{2\alpha^2}\hat{c}(T)$$

$$S_T^{[2]} = \hat{a}(T) - \frac{2\beta}{\alpha}\hat{b}(T) + \frac{2\beta(3 - 2\alpha)}{2\alpha^2}\hat{c}(T) \qquad (6\text{-}61)$$

$$S_T^{[3]} = \hat{a}(T) - \frac{3\beta}{\alpha}\hat{b}(T) + \frac{3\beta(4 - 3\alpha)}{2\alpha^2}\hat{c}(T)$$

Equation 6-61 can be used to estimate the required initial values for the smoothed statistics, S_0, $S_0^{[2]}$, and $S_0^{[3]}$, in terms of predictions (or least squares estimates) of the model coefficients, $\hat{a}(0)$, $\hat{b}(0)$, and $\hat{c}(0)$.

These results may be generalized to the case of an nth degree polynomial model, say

$$x_t = \xi_t + \varepsilon_t = a_0 + a_1 t + \frac{a_2}{2}t^2 + \cdots + \frac{a_n}{n!}t^n + \varepsilon_t \qquad (6\text{-}62)$$

where, as usual, ε_t is a random variable with zero expectation and variance σ_ε^2. We shall use the first $n + 1$ exponentially smoothed statistics to estimate the coefficients in the model (6-62). Exponential smoothing of *order k* is defined as

$$S_T^{[k]} = \alpha S_T^{[k-1]} + (1 - \alpha)S_{T-1}^{[k]}$$

where, for convenience, we let $S_T^{[1]} = S_T = \alpha x_T + (1 - \alpha)S_{T-1}$ (simple

Exponential Smoothing Methods   425

exponential smoothing). Notice that the partial derivatives of the noise-free process ξ_t with respect to t are

$$\xi_t^{(k)} = \frac{\partial^k \xi_t}{\partial t^k} = \sum_{j=k}^{n} \frac{a_j}{(j-k)!} t^{j-k}, \qquad k = 1, 2, \ldots, n;$$

$$= 0, \qquad\qquad k = n+1, n+2, \ldots$$

To obtain the coefficient a_k, evaluate $\xi_t^{(k)}$ at $t = 0$:

$$a_k = \left. \frac{\partial^k \xi_t}{\partial t^k} \right|_{t=0}$$

Therefore, taking the current observation t as the origin of time

$$E(x_{t+\tau}) = \sum_{k=0}^{n} \frac{a_k}{k!} \tau^k = \sum_{k=0}^{n} \frac{\tau^k}{k!} [\xi_t^{(k)}]_{t=0}$$

Brown (2) has shown that

$$S_t^{[p]} = \sum_{k=0}^{n} (-1)^k \frac{\xi_t^{(k)}}{k!} \frac{\alpha^p}{(p-1)!} \sum_{j=0}^{\infty} j^k \beta^j \frac{(p-1+j)!}{j!}, \qquad p = 1, 2, \ldots, n+1$$

(6-63)

Equation 6-63 expresses a relationship between the exponentially smoothed statistics for a noise-free process and the derivatives $\xi_t^{(k)}$. Now Equation 6-63 can be written in the form

$$\mathbf{S}_t = \mathbf{M}\mathbf{a} \qquad (6\text{-}64)$$

where $\mathbf{S}_t' = [S_t^{[1]}, S_t^{[2]}, \ldots, S_t^{[p]}]$, $\mathbf{a}' = [a_0(t), a_1(t), \ldots, a_n(t)]$, and $\mathbf{M}$ is an $[(n+1) \times p]$ matrix involving infinite sums of the smoothing constant,

$$M_{ik} = \frac{(-1)^k \alpha^i}{k!(i-1)!} \sum_{j=0}^{\infty} j^k \beta^j \frac{(i-1+j)!}{j!}$$

which can all be written in closed form.

To solve Equation 6-64 for $\mathbf{a}$, we must require that $p = n+1$, that is, we must have the first $n+1$ exponentially smoothed statistics. If $p = n+1$, then the solution to (6-64) is

$$\hat{\mathbf{a}} = \mathbf{M}^{-1}\mathbf{S}_t \qquad (6\text{-}65)$$

which expresses the model coefficients as functions of the first $n+1$ exponentially smoothed statistics. When the process includes random error with zero expectation, it seems reasonable to estimate the model coefficients by $\hat{\mathbf{a}}$. The forecast for period τ made at the end of period T would be

$$\hat{x}_{T+\tau} = \hat{a}_0(T) + \hat{a}_1(T)\tau + \hat{a}_2(T)\frac{\tau^2}{2!} + \cdots + \hat{a}_n(T)\frac{\tau^n}{n!} \qquad (6\text{-}66)$$

□**EXAMPLE 6-6**   We shall derive the results for triple smoothing presented at the start of this section to demonstrate the general procedure. The model is given by Equation 6-57, and since $p = n + 1 = 2 + 1 = 3$,

$$\mathbf{S}_t = \begin{bmatrix} S_t \\ S_t^{[2]} \\ S_t^{[3]} \end{bmatrix} \qquad \mathbf{a} = \begin{bmatrix} a(t) \\ b(t) \\ c(t) \end{bmatrix}$$

The elements of the **M** matrix are

$$\mathbf{M} = \begin{bmatrix} 1 & -\dfrac{\beta}{\alpha} & \dfrac{\beta(2 - \alpha)}{2\alpha^2} \\[2mm] 1 & -\dfrac{2\beta}{\alpha} & \dfrac{2\beta(3 - 2\alpha)}{2\alpha^2} \\[2mm] 1 & -\dfrac{3\beta}{\alpha} & \dfrac{3\beta(4 - 3\alpha)}{2\alpha^2} \end{bmatrix}$$

It is clear that $\mathbf{S}_t = \mathbf{Ma}$ is identical to Equation 6-61. We can show that the inverse of **M** is

$$\mathbf{M}^{-1} = \begin{bmatrix} 3 & -3 & 1 \\[2mm] \dfrac{\alpha(6 - 5\alpha)}{2\beta^2} & \dfrac{-2\alpha(5 - 4\alpha)}{2\beta^2} & \dfrac{\alpha(4 - 3\alpha)}{2\beta^2} \\[2mm] \left(\dfrac{\alpha}{\beta}\right)^2 & -2\left(\dfrac{\alpha}{\beta}\right)^2 & \left(\dfrac{\alpha}{\beta}\right)^2 \end{bmatrix}$$

and $\hat{\mathbf{a}} = \mathbf{M}^{-1}\mathbf{S}_t$ is clearly Equation 6-59.□

6-4.4   Winters' Method for Seasonal Variation

Exponential smoothing is an efficient technique for estimating the coefficients in a polynomial model. However, there are many time series processes that cannot be adequately described by a polynomial model. For example, many industrial time series have cyclical or *seasonal* variation, and this variation could not be easily followed by a polynomial model. This seasonal variation may be accounted for by several methods. We shall present an approach to forecasting a time series with seasonal variation that is due to Winters (15).

Winters' method assumes that the time series model is

$$x_t = (a + bt)c_t + \varepsilon_t \tag{6-67}$$

where a is the base signal, sometimes called the "permanent component," b is a linear trend component, c_t is the seasonal factor for period t, and ε_t is a random error component. This model incorporates both a linear trend and a seasonal effect. If no trend computation is required, then we may delete b from the model. We have assumed the seasonal factor to be multiplicative. Procedures for other types of seasonal factors (that is, additive) may be developed (see Exercise 6-19). We shall assume that the season contains L periods, and define the seasonal factors such that

$$\sum_{t=1}^{L} c_t = L \tag{6-68}$$

The procedure for periodically revising estimates of the model parameters and for forecasting is the following. At the end of any period T, after observing x_T,

1. Revise the estimate of the permanent component:

$$\hat{a}(T) = \alpha \left[\frac{x_T}{\hat{c}_T(T - L)} \right] + (1 - \alpha)[\hat{a}(T - 1) + \hat{b}(T - 1)] \tag{6-69}$$

where $0 < \alpha < 1$ is a smoothing constant.

2. Revise the estimate of the trend component:

$$\hat{b}(T) = \beta[\hat{a}(T) - \hat{a}(T - 1)] + (1 - \beta)\hat{b}(T - 1) \tag{6-70}$$

where $0 < \beta < 1$ is a second smoothing constant.

3. Revise the estimate of the seasonal factor for period T:

$$\hat{c}_T(T) = \gamma \left[\frac{x_T}{\hat{a}(T)} \right] + (1 - \gamma)\hat{c}_T(T - L) \tag{6-71}$$

where $0 < \gamma < 1$ is a third smoothing constant.

4. Forecast for any future period $T + \tau$ using

$$\hat{x}_{T+\tau} = [\hat{a}(T) + \tau\hat{b}(T)]\hat{c}_{T+\tau}(T + \tau - L) \tag{6-72}$$

Remember that the quantity in the parenthesis for $\hat{a}(\cdot)$, $\hat{b}(\cdot)$, and $\hat{c}_t(\cdot)$ indicates the time of computation of the estimate. Thus, $\hat{c}_T(T - L)$ represents an estimate of the seasonal factor for period T, computed one season (L periods) ago, when the last opportunity to observe this part of the seasonal pattern occurred.

Each of the three equations [(6-69), (6-70), (6-71)] represent smoothing of an estimate based on current information with an estimate based on information prior to the current period. They were developed heuristically, rather than objectively through use of a criterion such as least squares. There are three smoothing constants and a value must be specified for each.

From Equation 6-69, we note that the origin of time for the forecasting model (6-72) is shifted in computing $\hat{a}(T)$, such that it always is at the end of the current period T. Thus, $\hat{x}_T = \hat{a}(T)\hat{c}_T(T)$.

In initiating this forecasting model, values must be specified for $\hat{a}(0)$, $\hat{b}(0)$, and $\hat{c}_t(0)$ for $t = 1, 2, \ldots, L$. Historical information, if available, may be used to provide some or all of the initial estimates. For example, if data from the past two seasons are available, we may estimate the trend over the two seasons as $(\bar{x}_2 - \bar{x}_1)/L$, where $\bar{x}_1$ is the average demand during the first season and $\bar{x}_2$ is the average demand during the most recent season. Then a reasonable initial estimate of trend would be $\hat{b}(0) = (\bar{x}_2 - \bar{x}_1)/L$. Now the expected values of the observations are

$$E(x_1) = [a - (2L - 1)b]c_1$$

$$\cdot$$
$$\cdot$$
$$\cdot$$

$$E(x_L) = [a - Lb]c_L$$
$$E(x_{L+1}) = [a - (L - 1)b]c_1$$

$$\cdot$$
$$\cdot$$
$$\cdot$$

$$E(x_{2L-1}) = [a - b]c_{L-1}$$
$$E(x_{2L}) = ac_L$$

where we have chosen the last period $(2L)$ as the origin of time. Taking any two of these equations that are L periods apart, it is possible to isolate the seasonal factor as

$$c_t = \frac{E(x_{t+L}) - E(x_t)}{Lb}, \qquad t = 1, 2, \ldots, L$$

When actual observations obscured by noise are available, it seems reasonable to estimate the starting seasonal factors by

$$\hat{c}_t(0) = \frac{x_{t+L} - x_t}{L\hat{b}(0)}, \qquad t = 1, 2, \ldots, L$$

However, this procedure usually will yield poor results because of randomness in the demand pattern, especially when $\hat{b}(0)$ is small. We suggest that the estimates computed in this manner be treated as tentative and that they be revised once the permanent component is estimated. To obtain an estimate of a, note that

$$\sum_{t=1}^{2L} E(x_t) = 2La - 3L^2b + 2b \sum_{t=1}^{L} tc_t$$

Using $\sum_{t=1}^{2L} x_t$ to estimate the left-hand side, $\hat{b}(0)$ to estimate b, and the tentative

$\{\hat{c}_t(0)\}$ to estimate the $\{c_t\}$, we can solve for an estimate $\hat{a}(0)$. Now the tentative estimates of the seasonal factors can be replaced by improved estimates, based on $\hat{a}(0)$ and $\hat{b}(0)$. Since

$$E(x_t) = [a - (2L - t)b]c_t$$
$$E(x_{t+L}) = [a - (L - t)b]c_t$$

for $t = 1, 2, \ldots, L$, we now might estimate c_t using each equation and averaging the results:

$$\hat{c}_t(0) = \frac{1}{2}\left[\frac{x_t}{\hat{a}(0) - (2L - t)\hat{b}(0)} + \frac{x_{t+L}}{\hat{a}(0) - (L - t)\hat{b}(0)}\right]$$

for $t = 1, 2, \ldots, L$.

A widely used scheme to estimate the initial seasonal factors is simply to divide the demand in each period by the average demand per period over the season. This procedure works quite well if there is *no trend* present. However, a significant trend component will adversely affect estimates of seasonal factors obtained by this method.

□EXAMPLE 6-7   The demand for a 5000 BTU 110 V window air conditioner is seasonal, with a larger portion of the demand occurring during the spring and summer months. Historical data for 1970 is available and shown in Table 6-5. We assume that the trend component is zero, so seasonal factors are computed by dividing the monthly demand by the monthly average for the year. These seasonal factors are shown in the last column of Table 6-5. The

TABLE 6-5   Historical Data (1970)

MONTH	DEMAND	ESTIMATED SEASONAL FACTOR
January	4	0.48
February	2	0.24
March	5	0.60
April	8	0.96
May	11	1.32
June	13	1.56
July	18	2.16
August	15	1.80
September	9	1.08
October	6	0.72
November	5	0.60
December	4	0.48
Total	100	12.00

TABLE 6-6   Computed Results for Current Year (1971)

MONTH	ACTUAL DEMAND	$\hat{a}(t)$	$\hat{b}(t)$	$\hat{c}_t(t)$	FORECAST MADE ONE PERIOD PRIOR
January	5	8.72	0.043	0.53	4.0
February	4	10.34	0.200	0.31	2.1
March	7	10.77	0.223	0.63	6.3
April	7	10.25	0.149	0.82	10.6
May	15	10.59	0.158	1.37	13.7
June	17	10.78	0.161	1.56	16.8
July	24	10.97	0.164	2.17	23.6
August	18	10.91	0.142	1.73	20.0
September	12	11.06	0.143	1.08	11.9
October	7	10.91	0.114	0.68	8.1
November	8	11.49	0.161	0.65	6.6
December	6	11.82	0.178	0.49	5.6
Total	130				129.3

initial parameters are

$$\hat{b}(0) = 0$$

$$\hat{a}(0) = 100/12 = 8.3$$

and the smoothing constants to be used are $\alpha = 0.2$, $\beta = 0.1$, and $\gamma = 0.5$. The values for $\hat{a}(t)$, $\hat{b}(t)$, $\hat{c}_t(t)$, and the forecast are computed from Equations 6-69, 6-70, 6-71, and 6-72, respectively, and are shown in Table 6-6. For example, in January, we would obtain

$$\hat{x}_{\text{Jan.}} = [\hat{a}(0) + \hat{b}(0)]\hat{c}_{\text{Jan.}}(\text{Jan. 1970}) = (8.3 + 0)(0.48) = 3.98 \simeq 4.0.$$

Since the actual January 1971 demand was 5, we obtain from Equation 6-69

$$\hat{a}(\text{Jan.}) = \alpha\left[\frac{x_{\text{Jan.}}}{\hat{c}_{\text{Jan.}}(\text{Jan. 1970})}\right] + (1 - \alpha)[\hat{a}(0) + \hat{b}(0)]$$

$$= (0.2)\left[\frac{5}{0.48}\right] + (0.8)(8.3) = 8.72$$

from (6-70)

$$\hat{b}(\text{Jan.}) = \beta[\hat{a}(\text{Jan.}) - \hat{a}(0)] + (1 - \beta)\hat{b}(0)$$

$$= (0.1)(8.72 - 8.3) + (0.9)(0) = 0.043$$

and from (6-71)

$$\hat{c}_{\text{Jan.}}(\text{Jan. 1971}) = \gamma\left[\frac{x_{\text{Jan.}}}{\hat{a}(\text{Jan.})}\right] + (1 - \gamma)\hat{c}_{\text{Jan.}}(\text{Jan. 1970})$$

$$= 0.5\left[\frac{5}{8.72}\right] + (0.5)(0.48) = 0.53$$

The forecast for February would be

$$\hat{x}_{\text{Feb.}} = [\hat{a}(\text{Jan.}) + \hat{b}(\text{Jan.})]\hat{c}_{\text{Feb.}}(\text{Feb. 1970})$$
$$= (8.72 + 0.043)(0.24) = 2.1$$

The remaining entries in Table 6-6 are computed in a similar fashion.□

Note that as we revise the estimates of the seasonal factors, they may not add to the length of the season. A possible modification of Winters' method would be to "normalize" the seasonal factors at the end of every season.

6-4.5 Adaptive Smoothing

A procedure that is equivalent to exponential smoothing has been developed by Brown (2, 4). Called *adaptive smoothing*, the technique involves using polynomial, transcendental, or exponential functions as the independent variables in a discounted multiple regression model. If polynomial functions are employed, the adaptive smoothing approach produces forecasts identical to multiple smoothing, except that the calculations are organized so that estimates of the model parameters are obtained directly instead of through the smoothed statistics. Exercise 6-18 asks the reader to take this approach with the linear trend model.

The most important use of adaptive smoothing is with trigonometric functions, such as sine and cosine, to model a seasonal demand process. For example, a simple sinusoidal model is

$$x_t = a_1 + a_2 \sin \frac{2\pi t}{12} + \varepsilon_t$$

The behavior of this model (without the error component) is depicted in Figure 6-6.

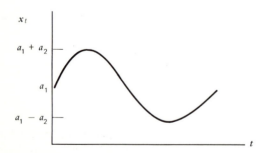

FIGURE 6-6.   A sinusoidal model.

The introduction of transcendental terms into the process allows considerable flexibility so far as the selection of a time series model is concerned. By appropriate choice of terms, a wide variety of time series patterns may be modeled. For example, sine waves have three characteristics that may be easily modified; the amplitude (height), phase angle (origin), and cycle length. Thus

$$x = a \sin \omega t$$

defines a sine wave with amplitude a and origin at $t = 0$. If ωt is expressed in radians, a 12-period season is obtained by setting $\omega = 2\pi/12$. The origin of the sine wave may be shifted λ periods by defining

$$x = a \sin \omega(t + \lambda)$$

However, it is usually more convenient to use an equivalent sine-cosine pair. Since

$$\sin (u + v) = \cos u \sin v + \sin u \cos v$$

we may rewrite the sine wave with arbitrary origin as

$$x = a \sin \omega(t + \lambda)$$
$$= a \cos \omega\lambda \sin \omega t + a \sin \omega\lambda \cos \omega t$$
$$= a_1 \sin \omega t + a_2 \cos \omega t$$

It is also possible to construct composite models that contain polynomial terms. For example, the four-parameter model

$$x_t = a_1 + a_2 t + a_3 \sin \frac{2\pi t}{12} + a_4 \cos \frac{2\pi t}{12} + \varepsilon_t$$

would impose a sinusoidal variation with arbitrary origin on a steady growth (or decline). The behavior of this model is depicted in Figure 6-7. A very useful model is a 12-point sine wave with one harmonic of the basic wave form and

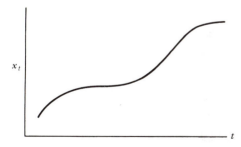

FIGURE 6-7. A sinusoidal model with a linear trend.

trend, say

$$x_t = a_1 + a_2 t + a_3 \sin \frac{2\pi t}{12} + a_4 \cos \frac{2\pi t}{12} + a_5 \sin \frac{4\pi t}{12} + a_6 \cos \frac{4\pi t}{12} + \varepsilon_t$$

The inclusion of the harmonic allows a great variety of seasonal patterns to be modeled. The choice of a model is important and will have a significant effect on the success of the application. There are several time series analysis techniques useful in determining the frequencies and amplitudes present, and thus aid in the selection of model components.

In general, let us suppose that the model is

$$x_t = \sum_{i=1}^{n} a_i f_i(t) + \varepsilon_t, \qquad t = 1, 2, \ldots, T \tag{6-73}$$

where the $f_i(t)$ are the independent variables (the polynomial or transcendental terms), and there are T observations available. From the results of Section 6-2, Equation 6-73 may be written in matrix notation as

$$x_t = \mathbf{a}'\mathbf{f}(t) + \varepsilon_t, \qquad t = 1, 2, \ldots, T$$

We shall estimate the coefficients $\mathbf{a}$ by discounted least squares, where the $(T \times T)$ matrix of weights is the diagonal matrix

$$\mathbf{W}^2 = \text{diag}\,(\beta^{T-1}, \beta^{T-2}, \ldots, \beta, 1)$$

Using Equation 6-19, the coefficients $\mathbf{a}$ that minimize

$$SS_E = \sum_{t=1}^{T} \beta^{T-t}[x_t - \hat{\mathbf{a}}'\mathbf{f}(t)]^2$$

are

$$\hat{\mathbf{a}}(T) = \mathbf{G}(T)^{-1}\mathbf{g}(T) \tag{6-74}$$

where

$$G_{ij}(T) = \sum_{t=1}^{T} \beta^{T-t} f_i(t) f_j(t), \qquad i, j = 1, 2, \ldots, n$$

and

$$g_i(T) = \sum_{i=1}^{T} \beta^{T-t} x_t f_i(t), \qquad i = 1, 2, \ldots, n$$

We must require that $T \geq n$ for $\mathbf{G}(T)^{-1}$ to exist.

If Equation 6-74 were used for periodic forecasting, the parameters $\hat{\mathbf{a}}$ would need to be revised at the end of each time period to take into account the data realized since the last revision of the model. This involves computing $\mathbf{G}(T)^{-1}$ at the end of each time period. The computations associated with solving Equation 6-74 each time the forecast is to be revised would be prohibitive if a large number of series were being analyzed.

Adaptive smoothing is a very efficient direct method of updating the coefficients that does not involve Equation 6-74. In effect, this method smoothes the old coefficients with the forecast error for the current period to obtain new coefficients.

It will be convenient to always have the origin of time of the model to be the end of the current period, say T. This requires that the origin of time be shifted each period; therefore, at the end of any period, the regression equations to be solved will be based on

$$SS_E = \sum_{j=0}^{T-1} \beta^j [x_{T-j} - \mathbf{f}'(-j)\hat{\mathbf{a}}(T)]^2$$

Notice that the subscript on x indicates the calendar time period associated with the observation and T in $\hat{\mathbf{a}}(T)$ indicates the calendar time at which these coefficients are estimated; however, $\mathbf{f}(-j)$ indicates that the mathematical functions $\mathbf{f}$ are to be evaluated at $-j$.

Now suppose that all the functions $f_i(t)$ are such that their values at time $t + 1$ are linear combinations of the values of the same functions at the previous time t. Thus

$$f_i(t + 1) = L_{i1}f_1(t) + L_{i2}f_2(t) + \cdots + L_{in}f_n(t), \qquad i = 1, 2, \ldots, n$$

Letting $\mathbf{L}$ be the $(n \times n)$ matrix of the L_{ij}, we may write

$$\mathbf{f}(t + 1) = \mathbf{L}\mathbf{f}(t) \tag{6-75}$$

For example, consider a variation of the quadratic trend model, say

$$x_t = a_1 + a_2 t + \tfrac{1}{2}a_3 t(t - 1) + \varepsilon_t$$

Then $f_1(t) = 1$, $f_2(t) = t$, $f_3(t) = \tfrac{1}{2}t(t - 1)$, and it is easily verified that

$$\mathbf{L} = \begin{bmatrix} 1 & 0 & 0 \\ 1 & 1 & 0 \\ 0 & 1 & 1 \end{bmatrix}$$

The only functions for which such a transition property exists are polynomials, exponentials, and sinusoidals. The appropriate $\mathbf{L}$ matrix may be written down by inspection from the type of functions used in the model (see Exercise 6-20). Also notice that given $\mathbf{L}$ and $\mathbf{f}(0)$, we may find $\mathbf{f}(t) = \mathbf{L}^t\mathbf{f}(0)$.

Let

$$\mathbf{G}(T) = \sum_{j=0}^{T-1} \beta^j \mathbf{f}(-j)\mathbf{f}'(-j) = \mathbf{G}(T - 1) + \beta^{T-1}\mathbf{f}(-T + 1)\mathbf{f}'(-T + 1)$$

It can be shown that if the functions $f_i(t)$ do not decay too rapidly,[4] the matrix

---

[4] A steady-state $\mathbf{G}$ always exists if $\mathbf{f}(t)$ are trigonometric or polynomial functions. If $f_i(t) = e^{-at}$, then we must require that $\beta < e^{-2a}$.

$\mathbf{G}(T)$ approaches a limit $\mathbf{G}$, where

$$\mathbf{G} \equiv \lim_{T \to \infty} \mathbf{G}(T) = \sum_{j=0}^{\infty} \beta^j \mathbf{f}(-j)\mathbf{f}'(-j) \qquad (6\text{-}76)$$

Thus, $\mathbf{G}^{-1}$ need be computed only once. Furthermore, at time T, we may write

$$\mathbf{g}(T) = \sum_{j=0}^{T-1} \beta^j x_{T-j} \mathbf{f}(-j)$$

$$= x_T \mathbf{f}(0) + \sum_{j=1}^{T-1} \beta^{j-1} x_{T-j} \mathbf{f}(-j)$$

$$= x_T \mathbf{f}(0) + \beta \sum_{j=1}^{T-1} \beta^{j-1} x_{T-j} \mathbf{L}^{-1} \mathbf{f}(-j+1)$$

$$= x_T \mathbf{f}(0) + \beta \mathbf{L}^{-1} \sum_{k=0}^{T-2} \beta^k x_{T-1-k} \mathbf{f}(-k)$$

or

$$\mathbf{g}(T) = x_T \mathbf{f}(0) + \beta \mathbf{L}^{-1} \mathbf{g}(T-1)$$

Thus, $\mathbf{g}(T)$ may be obtained recursively from $\mathbf{g}(T-1)$.

Using the steady-state value for $\mathbf{G}(T)$ in Equation 6-74, we may write

$$\hat{\mathbf{a}}(T) = \mathbf{G}^{-1}\mathbf{g}(T) = \mathbf{G}^{-1}[x_T \mathbf{f}(0) + \beta \mathbf{L}^{-1}\mathbf{g}(T-1)] \qquad (6\text{-}78)$$

Since $\mathbf{g}(T-1) = \mathbf{G}\hat{\mathbf{a}}(T-1)$, Equation 6-78 becomes

$$\hat{\mathbf{a}}(T) = x_T \mathbf{G}^{-1}\mathbf{f}(0) + \beta \mathbf{G}^{-1}\mathbf{L}^{-1}\mathbf{G}\hat{\mathbf{a}}(T-1)$$

This is of the form

$$\hat{\mathbf{a}}(T) = \mathbf{h}x_T + \mathbf{H}\hat{\mathbf{a}}(T-1) \qquad (6\text{-}79)$$

where

$$\mathbf{h} = \mathbf{G}^{-1}\mathbf{f}(0)$$

and

$$\mathbf{H} = \beta \mathbf{G}^{-1}\mathbf{L}^{-1}\mathbf{G}$$

Equation 6-79 may be simplified further. Notice that

$$\mathbf{L}^{-1}\mathbf{G} = \mathbf{L}^{-1}\mathbf{G}(\mathbf{L}')^{-1}\mathbf{L}'$$

$$= \sum_{j=0}^{\infty} \beta^j \mathbf{L}^{-1}\mathbf{f}(-j)\mathbf{f}'(-j)(\mathbf{L}')^{-1}\mathbf{L}'$$

$$= \sum_{j=0}^{\infty} \beta^j [\mathbf{L}^{-1}\mathbf{f}(-j)][\mathbf{L}^{-1}\mathbf{f}(-j)]'\mathbf{L}'$$

$$= \sum_{j=0}^{\infty} \beta^j \mathbf{f}(-j+1)\mathbf{f}'(-j+1)\mathbf{L}'$$

Letting $k = j + 1$, we obtain

$$\mathbf{L}^{-1}\mathbf{G} = \beta^{-1}\left[\sum_{k=1}^{\infty}\beta^k\mathbf{f}(-k)\mathbf{f}'(-k)\right]\mathbf{L}'$$

$$= \beta^{-1}[\mathbf{G} - \mathbf{f}(0)\mathbf{f}'(0)]\mathbf{L}'$$

Thus,

$$\mathbf{H} = \beta\mathbf{G}^{-1}\mathbf{L}^{-1}\mathbf{G}$$

$$= \mathbf{G}^{-1}[\mathbf{G} - \mathbf{f}(0)\mathbf{f}'(0)]\mathbf{L}'$$

$$= [\mathbf{I} - \mathbf{G}^{-1}\mathbf{f}(0)\mathbf{f}'(0)]\mathbf{L}'$$

Since $\mathbf{h} = \mathbf{G}^{-1}\mathbf{f}(0)$, we see that

$$\mathbf{H} = \mathbf{L}' - \mathbf{h}\mathbf{f}'(0)\mathbf{L}'$$

$$= \mathbf{L}' - \mathbf{h}[\mathbf{L}\mathbf{f}(0)]'$$

$$= \mathbf{L}' - \mathbf{h}\mathbf{f}'(1)$$

Now Equation 6-79 may be written as

$$\hat{\mathbf{a}}(T) = \mathbf{h}x_T + [\mathbf{L}' - \mathbf{h}\mathbf{f}'(1)]\hat{\mathbf{a}}(T - 1)$$

$$= \mathbf{L}'\hat{\mathbf{a}}(T - 1) + \mathbf{h}[x_T - \mathbf{f}'(1)\hat{\mathbf{a}}(T - 1)] \qquad (6\text{-}80)$$

Let $\hat{x}_T$ be the forecast for period T, made at the end of period $T - 1$. Thus, since $\hat{x}_T = \mathbf{f}'(1)\hat{\mathbf{a}}(T - 1)$, Equation 6-80 becomes

$$\hat{\mathbf{a}}(T) = \mathbf{L}'\hat{\mathbf{a}}(T - 1) + \mathbf{h}[x_T - \hat{x}_T] \qquad (6\text{-}81)$$

The quantity in brackets in Equation 6-81 is just the single-period forecast error, or

$$e_1(T) = x_T - \hat{x}_T$$

Finally, we see that the estimates of the coefficients in period T are just linear combinations of the estimates made in the previous period and the single-period forecast error, that is

$$\hat{\mathbf{a}}(T) = \mathbf{L}'\hat{\mathbf{a}}(T - 1) + \mathbf{h}e_1(T) \qquad (6\text{-}82)$$

The coefficients in the model are modified each period for two reasons. The first is to shift the origin of time, and the second is to adapt or modify the coefficients according to the forecast error for the period just ended. These two purposes are accomplished by the first and second terms, respectively, in Equation 6-82. The $(n \times 1)$ vector $\mathbf{h}$ is sometimes called the "smoothing vector."

The forecast for period $T + \tau$, made at the end of period T, would be computed from

$$\hat{x}_{T+\tau} = \hat{\mathbf{a}}'(T)\mathbf{f}(\tau) = \sum_{i=1}^{n}\hat{a}_i(T)f_i(\tau), \qquad \tau = 1, 2, \ldots \qquad (6\text{-}83)$$

This procedure requires an initial estimate of the coefficients, $\hat{\mathbf{a}}(0)$. This may be obtained subjectively, or through analysis of historical data.

☐**EXAMPLE 6-8**   We shall illustrate the foregoing ideas by applying them to the six-parameter harmonic model

$$x_t = a_1 + a_2 t + a_3 \sin \frac{2\pi t}{12} + a_4 \cos \frac{2\pi t}{12} + a_5 \sin \frac{4\pi t}{12} + a_6 \cos \frac{4\pi t}{12} + \varepsilon_t$$

The independent variables, coefficients in period T, and smoothing vector are

$$
\mathbf{f}(t) = \begin{bmatrix} 1 \\ t \\ \sin \dfrac{2\pi t}{12} \\ \cos \dfrac{2\pi t}{12} \\ \sin \dfrac{4\pi t}{12} \\ \cos \dfrac{4\pi t}{12} \end{bmatrix}
\qquad
\mathbf{a}(T) = \begin{bmatrix} a_1(T) \\ a_2(T) \\ a_3(T) \\ a_4(T) \\ a_5(T) \\ a_6(T) \end{bmatrix}
\qquad
\mathbf{h} = \begin{bmatrix} h_1 \\ h_2 \\ h_3 \\ h_4 \\ h_5 \\ h_6 \end{bmatrix}
$$

It can be shown (see Exercise 6-20) that the transition matrix is

$$
\mathbf{L} = \begin{bmatrix}
1 & 0 & 0 & 0 & 0 & 0 \\
1 & 1 & 0 & 0 & 0 & 0 \\
0 & 0 & 0.866 & 0.5 & 0 & 0 \\
0 & 0 & -0.5 & 0.866 & 0 & 0 \\
0 & 0 & 0 & 0 & 0.5 & 0.866 \\
0 & 0 & 0 & 0 & -0.866 & 0.5
\end{bmatrix}
$$

The smoothing equations are found, by substituting $\mathbf{L}$ into Equation 6-82, to be

$$\hat{a}_1(T) = \hat{a}_1(T - 1) + \hat{a}_2(T - 1) + h_1 e_1(T)$$
$$\hat{a}_2(T) = \hat{a}_2(T - 1) + h_2 e_1(T)$$
$$\hat{a}_3(T) = 0.866\hat{a}_3(T - 1) - 0.5\hat{a}_4(T - 1) + h_3 e_1(T)$$
$$\hat{a}_4(T) = 0.5\hat{a}_3(T - 1) + 0.866\hat{a}_4(T - 1) + h_4 e_1(T)$$
$$\hat{a}_5(T) = 0.5\hat{a}_5(T - 1) - 0.866\hat{a}_6(T - 1) + h_5 e_1(T)$$
$$\hat{a}_6(T) = 0.866\hat{a}_5(T - 1) + 0.5\hat{a}_6(T - 1) + h_6 e_1(T)$$

where, of course,

$$e_1(T) = x_T - \hat{x}_T = x_T - \mathbf{f}'(1)\hat{\mathbf{a}}(T - 1)$$

and the forecast for any period $T + \tau$, made at the end of period T, is

$$\hat{x}_{T+\tau} = \mathbf{f}'(\tau)\hat{\mathbf{a}}(T)$$

Numerical values must be assigned to the elements of the smoothing vector, $\mathbf{h}$. Example 6-9 describes their computation.☐

☐**EXAMPLE 6-9** It would be of interest to demonstrate the computations required to obtain the elements of the smoothing vector for a specific model. Brown (4, pp. 144–149) gives details for the six-parameter harmonic model discussed in Example 6-8. Since for any model, the smoothing vector is found from

$$\mathbf{h} = \mathbf{G}^{-1}\mathbf{f}(0)$$

our problem essentially consists of finding the matrix $\mathbf{G}$. From Equation 6-76, we see that

$$\mathbf{G} = \sum_{j=0}^{\infty} \beta^j \mathbf{f}(-j)\mathbf{f}'(-j)$$

a symmetric matrix whose diagonal elements are the weighted sums of squares of the independent variables and whose off-diagonal elements are the weighted sums of cross-products of the independent variables. Thus, for the six-parameter harmonic model

$$\mathbf{G} = \begin{bmatrix} \mathbf{A} & \mathbf{B}(1) & \mathbf{B}(2) \\ \mathbf{B}(1) & \mathbf{C}(1,1) & \mathbf{C}(1,2) \\ \mathbf{B}(2) & \mathbf{C}(1,2) & \mathbf{C}(2,2) \end{bmatrix}$$

where the submatrices $\mathbf{A}$, $\mathbf{B}(v)$ and $\mathbf{C}(u, v)$ of order 2×2 are

$$\mathbf{A} = \begin{bmatrix} \sum\limits_{j=0}^{\infty} \beta^j & -\sum\limits_{j=0}^{\infty} j\beta^j \\ -\sum\limits_{j=0}^{\infty} j\beta^j & \sum\limits_{j=0}^{\infty} j^2\beta^j \end{bmatrix}$$

$$\mathbf{B}(v) = \begin{bmatrix} -\sum\limits_{j=0}^{\infty} \beta^j \sin v\omega j & \sum\limits_{j=0}^{\infty} \beta^j \cos v\omega j \\ \sum\limits_{j=0}^{\infty} j\beta^j \sin v\omega j & -\sum\limits_{j=0}^{\infty} j\beta^j \cos v\omega j \end{bmatrix}$$

for $v = 1, 2$, and

$$\mathbf{C}(u, v) = \begin{bmatrix} \displaystyle\sum_{j=0}^{\infty} \beta^j \sin u\omega j \sin v\omega j & -\displaystyle\sum_{j=0}^{\infty} \beta^j \sin u\omega j \cos v\omega j \\[2em] -\displaystyle\sum_{j=0}^{\infty} \beta^j \cos u\omega j \sin v\omega j & \displaystyle\sum_{j=0}^{\infty} \beta^j \cos u\omega j \cos v\omega j \end{bmatrix}$$

for $u = 1, 2$ and $v = u + 1$ where $\omega = 2\pi/12$. Closed form expressions for the elements of the submatrices $\mathbf{A}$ and $\mathbf{B}(v)$ may be found by using z-transforms as

$$\mathbf{A} = \begin{bmatrix} \dfrac{1}{1 - \beta} & \dfrac{-\beta}{(1 - \beta)^2} \\[1.5em] \dfrac{-\beta}{(1 - \beta)^2} & \dfrac{\beta(1 + \beta)}{(1 - \beta)^3} \end{bmatrix}$$

$$\mathbf{B}(v) = \begin{bmatrix} \dfrac{-\beta \sin v\omega}{1 - 2\beta \cos v\omega + \beta^2} & \dfrac{1 - \beta \cos v\omega}{1 - 2\beta \cos v\omega + \beta^2} \\[1.5em] \dfrac{\beta(1 - \beta^2) \sin v\omega}{[1 - 2\beta \cos v\omega + \beta^2]^2} & \dfrac{-2\beta^2 + \beta(1 + \beta^2) \cos v\omega}{[1 - 2\beta \cos v\omega + \beta^2]^2} \end{bmatrix}$$

The trigonometric identities

$$\sin a \sin b = -\tfrac{1}{2}[\cos (a + b) - \cos (a - b)]$$
$$\cos a \cos b = \tfrac{1}{2}[\cos (a + b) + \cos (a - b)]$$
$$\cos a \sin b = \tfrac{1}{2}[\sin (a + b) - \sin (a - b)]$$
$$\sin a \cos b = \tfrac{1}{2}[\sin (a + b) + \sin (a - b)]$$

allow the elements of $\mathbf{C}(u, v)$ to be expressed as

$$\mathbf{C}(u, v) = \tfrac{1}{2} \begin{bmatrix} -\left(\dfrac{c_1}{d_1} - \dfrac{c_2}{d_2}\right) & -\left(\dfrac{c_3}{d_1} + \dfrac{c_4}{d_2}\right) \\[1.5em] -\left(\dfrac{c_3}{d_1} - \dfrac{c_4}{d_2}\right) & \left(\dfrac{c_1}{d_1} + \dfrac{c_2}{d_2}\right) \end{bmatrix}$$

where

$$c_1 = 1 - \beta \cos (u + v)\omega$$
$$c_2 = 1 - \beta \cos (u - v)\omega$$
$$c_3 = \beta \sin (u + v)\omega$$
$$c_4 = \beta \sin (u - v)\omega$$
$$d_1 = 1 - 2\beta \cos (u + v)\omega + \beta^2$$
$$d_2 = 1 - 2\beta \cos (u - v)\omega + \beta^2$$

We see that the elements of **G** are completely determined by choosing β. Note that

$$\mathbf{f}(0) = \begin{bmatrix} 1 \\ 0 \\ 0 \\ 1 \\ 0 \\ 1 \end{bmatrix}$$

For $\beta = 0.90$, say, and $\omega = 2\pi/12$, it is relatively easy to show that

$$\mathbf{h} = \begin{bmatrix} 0.17030 \\ 0.00853 \\ 0.05453 \\ 0.15542 \\ 0.07055 \\ 0.14285 \end{bmatrix}$$

The smoothing vectors for several other models are given by Brown (2, pp. 178–195).□

6-4.6 Choice of Smoothing Constant

In any application of exponential smoothing, it is necessary to specify a value for the smoothing constant (or constants) in the model. This section will discuss some approaches to a rational basis for selecting the smoothing constant.

The smoothing constant controls the number of past realizations of the time series that influence the forecast. Small values of the smoothing constant include many past observations, and the forecasting system will respond slowly to changes in the parameters of the time series model. Larger values of the smoothing constant include less historical data and the forecasting system responds more rapidly. However, a large smoothing constant may cause the system to respond to random variations in the signal and be oversensitive. Brown (2) discusses the response characteristics of exponential smoothing to various standard signals, such as the impulse, ramp, and step functions.

As a general rule, the smoothing constant α for a constant model should be somewhere between 0.01 and 0.3. A widely used technique is to carry out a sequence of trials on a set of actual historical data using several different values for the smoothing constant, and select that value of α that optimizes some measure of effectiveness such as minimum sum of squares error. Of course, this approach also may be used for more complicated models. Various modifications of this concept are often employed. For example, if three years of historical data are available, one might use the first two years to optimize the smoothing constant and then simulate a forecast for each month of the remaining year to see how the "optimum" smoothing constant will react to fresh data.

If the results of a set of trials indicate an optimum value of α for a constant model that is greater than 0.3, then the validity of the model should be questioned. The data may be significantly autocorrelated, in which case the methods of Section 6-10 should be considered. Plotting the data may reveal trends or cyclic patterns that will lead to a large smoothing constant, but that should be dealt with by employing a more appropriate model.

For polynomial and transcendental models, it is possible to define an *equivalent value of the smoothing constant* such that estimates of the constant term in the model are the same. That is, suppose α_1 is used in single smoothing. Then the equivalent value of the smoothing constant for a model with n terms would be

$$(1 - \alpha_n)^n = 1 - \alpha_1$$

Many practitioners prefer to have available several values of the smoothing constant, and use an appropriate value at different times. For example, a normal value for α when the process seems stable may be 0.1; however, in addition, the value 0.25 may be used when the coefficients in the underlying process seem to be changing more rapidly. A number of procedures have been developed for maintaining control of the smoothing constant and automatically shifting from one value to another. These *adaptive control procedures*, as they are often called, are discussed in Section 6-8.

If we can make certain assumptions about the basic characteristics of the time series, it is often possible to develop rigorously an optimum value of the smoothing constant. For example, it is possible to determine the optimum smoothing constant for simple smoothing where the time series has exponential autocorrelation.

6-5 Forecasting Over Lead Times

In most of the examples presented thus far, we have assumed that management is interested in producing a forecast for the next time period, or for a single arbitrary point τ periods into the future. Many times we are interested in forecasting for each of several future periods. That is, we must forecast over some *lead time* or planning horizon. Typically, for production and inventory planning problems, we are interested in forecasting demand up to 12 future time periods.

To illustrate how this may be done, suppose the current period is T and we are interested in forecasting demand over the next w periods, say $T + 1$, $T + 2, \ldots, T + w$. We may obtain this forecast by indexing time in our forecasting model to $T + 1, T + 2, \ldots, T + w$ and computing $\hat{x}_{T+1}, \hat{x}_{T+2}, \ldots, \hat{x}_{T+w}$. Then the forecast of cumulative demand for the lead time of w periods is

$$\hat{X}_w(T) = \sum_{t=T+1}^{T+w} \hat{x}_t$$

In this manner, it is quite simple to produce a forecast of demand for any w-period lead time.

We may also compute the variance of the forecasts at any future point in time as

$$V(\hat{x}_t) = \mathbf{f}'(t)\mathbf{V}\mathbf{f}(t)$$

where the variance-covariance matrix $\mathbf{V}$ is defined by Equation 6-20. If the independent variables include an unbounded polynomial term, then $V(\hat{x}_t)$ depends on the future point in time for which the forecast is being made. Brown (2) shows that, in general, the variance of the forecast with a linear model increases as a linear function of time, and with a quadratic model, it increases as a quadratic function of time. A model that does not contain any unbounded polynomial function has nearly the same variance of the forecast for any future point in time. This is quite important, as a manager usually does not think of a forecast merely as a point estimate, but often wants a range of values. Thus, it may be necessary to present a probability statement about the values that future observations may take on. The variance of the forecast will be required to do this.

The forecast error is

$$e_t = x_t - \hat{x}_t$$

and the variance of the forecast error is

$$V(e_t) = \sigma_\varepsilon^2 + \mathbf{f}'(t)\mathbf{V}\mathbf{f}(t)$$

if the random variables ε_t are serially independent. Thus, the variance of forecast error also increases as a function of time. Intuitively, this seems quite reasonable, as we should be less confident about our model the further into the future we attempt to forecast.

Now consider the variance of the cumulative forecast, say $V\{\hat{X}_w(T)\}$. Since

$$\hat{X}_w(T) = \sum_{t=T+1}^{T+w} \hat{x}_t$$

$$= \sum_{t=T+1}^{T+w} \hat{\mathbf{a}}'(T)\mathbf{f}(t)$$

Forecasting Over Lead Times   443

we see that

$$V\{\hat{X}_w(T)\} = \left[\sum_{t=T+1}^{T+w} \mathbf{f}(t)\right]' \mathbf{V}\left[\sum_{t=T+1}^{T+w} \mathbf{f}(t)\right]$$

It is easily shown that the variance of the cumulative forecast error for the w-period lead time is

$$w\sigma_\varepsilon^2 + \left[\sum_{t=T+1}^{T+w} \mathbf{f}(t)\right]' \mathbf{V}\left[\sum_{t=T+1}^{T+w} \mathbf{f}(t)\right]$$

It is not surprising to see that the variance of the forecast error increases as the number of periods in the lead time increases.

·The reader is reminded that when using the adaptive smoothing formulations of Section 6-4.5 the origin of time is assumed to be at the end of the current period T. Then, $T = 0$ would be used in the preceding equations.

6-6 The Tracking Signal and Analysis of Forecast Errors

No forecasting system will produce perfect forecasts of future observations. There will always be some discrepancy between the forecast for period t, say $\hat{x}_t$, and the actual observation for that period, x_t. Mathematically, we define the forecast error as

$$e_t = x_t - \hat{x}_t \qquad (6\text{-}84)$$

Analysis of the forecast errors can frequently reveal many useful characteristics of both the forecasting system and the time series. We shall discuss several methods for this analysis.

An examination of the errors may indicate that they arise from a stable system, that is, a true time series model for which the assumed time series model is an adequate approximation. If this is the case, we would expect the average value of the forecast errors to be nearly zero. In itself, however, this information may not be very useful without knowledge of the *variability* of forecast errors, as large positive and negative errors would tend to cancel each other. We see that the variance of the forecast errors is

$$V(e_t) = V(x_t) + V(\hat{x}_t)$$

or

$$\sigma_e^2 = \sigma_\varepsilon^2 + \sigma_{\hat{x}}^2 \qquad (6\text{-}85)$$

assuming that x_t and $\hat{x}_t$ are independent. For a constant model, we may show that

$$\sigma_{\hat{x}_t}^2 = \frac{\alpha}{2 - \alpha} \sigma_\varepsilon^2$$

and thus

$$\sigma_e^2 = \frac{2}{2 - \alpha} \sigma_\varepsilon^2$$

In addition to the mean and variance of forecast error, it may be useful to have some knowledge of the form of the probability distribution. There is a great deal of theoretical and empirical justification for assuming that the forecast errors are normally distributed (approximately). In any practical problem, this assumption could be easily checked by simulating the forecast of historical data and examining the resulting errors.

The *tracking signal* is a useful device for monitoring and controlling forecast errors. We shall discuss two forms of the tracking signal, one based on the sum of the forecast errors and the other based on a smoothed error.

Consider the sum of the forecast errors in the current period, say period T,

$$Y(T) = \sum_{t=1}^{T} e_t$$

or equivalently

$$Y(T) = Y(T - 1) + e_T \tag{6-86}$$

If there is a consistent bias in the forecasts, the errors will have the same sign for several periods, and the sum $Y(T)$ will tend to become nonzero. Brown (2) has shown that for a constant model

$$\sigma_Y^2 = \frac{1}{1 - \beta^2} \sigma_\varepsilon^2$$

and, in general, for a model with n parameters

$$\sigma_Y^2 \simeq \frac{1}{1 - \beta^{2n}} \sigma_\varepsilon^2$$

If $|Y(T)|$ is greater than some relatively large multiple of σ_Y, we could not expect this to occur by chance, and would conclude that the forecasting system is no longer adequately tracking the process. That is, if

$$\left| \frac{Y(T)}{\sigma_Y} \right| < K \tag{6-87}$$

the forecasting system is performing adequately. We almost always do not know σ_Y exactly, and must estimate it. Actually, since $\sigma_Y^2 = [1/(1 - \beta^{2n})]\sigma_\varepsilon^2$, it suffices to estimate σ_ε^2.

Suppose that forecast error is normally distributed with mean zero and variance σ_e^2. Then the *mean absolute deviation*, Δ, is

$$\Delta = E\{|e - E(e)|\} = 2 \int_0^\infty (e - 0)n(e; 0, \sigma_e^2)\, de = \sqrt{\frac{2}{\pi}}\, \sigma_e \simeq 0.8\sigma_e \quad (6\text{-}88)$$

This approximation holds quite well, even for nonnormal data. At the end of period T, we may estimate the mean absolute deviation by either

$$\hat{\Delta}(T) = \alpha\, |e(T)| + (1 - \alpha)\, \hat{\Delta}(T - 1) \quad (6\text{-}89a)$$

or

$$\hat{\Delta}(T) = \frac{1}{N} \sum_{t = T - N + 1}^{T} |e_t| \quad (6\text{-}89b)$$

Equation 6-89a is more efficient. Thus, we see that $\hat{\sigma}_e^2 = \left[\dfrac{\hat{\Delta}(T)}{0.8}\right]^2$. For single smoothing, $\sigma_\varepsilon^2 = \dfrac{2 - \alpha}{2}\, \sigma_e^2$, so $\hat{\sigma}_\varepsilon^2 = \left(\dfrac{2 - \alpha}{2}\right)\left[\dfrac{\hat{\Delta}(T)}{0.8}\right]^2$ and thus,

$$\hat{\sigma}_Y^2 = \left(\frac{1}{1 - \beta^2}\right)\left(\frac{2 - \alpha}{2}\right)\left[\frac{\hat{\Delta}(T)}{0.8}\right]^2 = \frac{1}{2\alpha}\left[\frac{\hat{\Delta}(T)}{0.8}\right]^2$$

For the relationship between σ_ε^2 and σ_e^2 for other models, refer to Brown (2, Chapter 12).

For simple exponential smoothing, the tracking signal based on the sum of the forecast errors is

$$\left|\frac{Y(T)}{\hat{\Delta}(T)}\right| < \frac{K}{0.8}\sqrt{\frac{1}{2\alpha}} = C_1 \quad (6\text{-}90)$$

where K may be chosen from tables of the standard normal cumulative distribution function to provide an approximate level of significance. Quite often, especially when dealing with other than a constant model, instead of choosing K, one may directly choose C_1. Typical values of C_1 for most models are between 4 and 6.

It is also possible to base the tracking signal on the smoothed error in period T, say

$$Z(T) = \alpha e_T + (1 - \alpha)Z(T - 1)$$

The appropriate tracking signal would be

$$\left|\frac{Z(T)}{\hat{\Delta}(T)}\right| < C_2 \quad (6\text{-}91)$$

It is clear that the ratio $\left|\dfrac{Z(T)}{\hat{\Delta}(T)}\right|$ can never exceed 1.0. The proper value for C_2 is usually between 0.2 and 0.4.

If Equation 6-89a is used to compute the mean absolute deviation, a starting value, $\hat{\Delta}(0)$, must be supplied. Simulation using historical data is one approach, or frequently a relationship can be found between average demand and the standard deviation of forecast errors, and this estimated standard deviation used to provide a starting value $\hat{\Delta}(0)$.

If the tracking signal exceeds the control limit on two or three successive observations, this is a clear indication that something is wrong with the forecasting system. When the tracking signal goes out of control, the quantity $Y(T)$ [or $Z(T)$] should be reset to zero to prevent a false out of control signal in future periods. Finding the reason for the out of control signal involves many of the same procedures that one would use when initially identifying an appropriate time series model. We must usually either add another term (or terms) to the current time series model or increase the smoothing constant because certain model parameters are changing rapidly.

□EXAMPLE 6-10   To illustrate the calculations required for the cumulative error tracking signal, consider the demand data shown in column (1) of Table 6-7. Suppose that at some point prior to January, it has been determined that a constant time series model is appropriate and a smoothing constant $\alpha = 0.1$ selected. We also know that $S_{Dec.} = 100.00$, $Y(Dec.) = 0.00$, and $\hat{\Delta}(Dec.) = 2.00$. The forecast for January is $\hat{x}_{Jan.} = S_{Dec.} = 100.00$. Forecasts for the remaining months are computed in the usual fashion (Equations 6-43 and 6-46) and are shown in column 2 of Table 6-7. The forecast error and cumulative error for each month are shown in columns 3 and 4. The mean absolute deviation for each month, shown in column 5, is computed from Equation 6-89a. For example

$$\hat{\Delta}(Jan.) = \alpha \, |e_{Jan.}| + (1 - \alpha)\hat{\Delta}(Dec.)$$
$$= 0.1 \, |1.00| + (0.9)(2.00) = 1.90$$

TABLE 6-7   Sample Calculations for the Cumulative Error Tracking Signal

t	(1) x_t	(2) $\hat{x}_t$	(3) e_t	(4) $Y(t)$	(5) $\hat{\Delta}(t)$	(6) $Y(t)/\hat{\Delta}(t)$
January	101	100.00	1.00	1.00	1.90	0.53
February	104	100.10	3.90	4.90	2.10	1.69
March	98	100.49	-2.49	2.41	2.14	1.03
April	110	100.24	9.76	12.17	2.90	4.20*
May	120	101.22	18.78	30.95	4.49	8.80*
June	118	103.10	14.90	45.85	5.53	8.29*

Finally, the tracking signal for each month is computed by dividing the current cumulative error by the current mean absolute deviation. If we choose ± 4 as the detection threshold for the tracking signal, then the first out-of-control response is generated in April, followed by out-of-control values for May and June.☐

While we have concentrated primarily on the cumulative error form of the tracking signal, this method does appear to have some disadvantages relative to the smoothed error version. Suppose there was a very large, but random, error in the forecast for a particular time period. This would increase the smoothed error and the cumulative error, but assume that the increase is not quite enough to generate an out-of-control signal. Now, suppose many periods go by with small errors averaging zero. The cumulative error remains at its large value, but the smoothed error decreases toward zero. At some point in time, a second large, random error with the same sign as the previous one occurs. The cumulative sum tracking signal will *incorrectly* generate an out-of-control signal, but the smoothed error version would not. As another example, suppose the cumulative sum tracking signal was just less than the detection threshold, and a perfect forecast occurs. Since the error is zero, the cumulative sum will not change and the mean absolute deviation will become smaller. The net effect will be to *increase* the value of the tracking signal, perhaps above the detection threshold. If a smoothed error tracking signal is employed, a perfect forecast will cause the smoothed error to decrease along with the mean absolute deviation, resulting in little change in the tracking signal.

6-7 Forecasting the Probability Distribution of Demand

In certain situations, the probability distribution of the signal may be more important than the individual observations. For example, an inventory manager might be much more interested in the probability of a demand between 140 and 150 units next period than he would be in a single-number forecast. Therefore, we would be interested in forecasting probabilities instead of individual future observations.

Suppose that x_t is a random variable having probability distribution function G, that is, $Pr\{x_t \leq \theta\} = G(\theta)$. Usually, the exact form of G is unknown and must be estimated. We require that G be stationary, or changing very slowly with time. The forecasting problem is, for a given p, $0 < p < 1$, to find $\hat{\theta}_p$, an estimate of θ_p, such that $G(\theta_p) = p$. That is, we wish to find an estimator of θ_p such that the probability is p of observing a future realization smaller than θ_p.

Assume that the observations are measured on a scale with $n + 1$ class limits, say

$$X_0 < X_1 < X_2 < \cdots < X_n$$

The class limits must be defined so that each observation x_t is assigned to one and only one class. That is, there is only one k such that

$$X_{k-1} < x_t \leq X_k$$

The class limits X_0 and X_n should be finite, and there should be between 10 and 20 classes. The classes do not have to be of the same width, but may be defined to obtain information in relation to interest.

Let p_k be the probability that the random variable x_t falls in the interval from X_{k-1} to X_k, that is,

$$p_k = Pr\{X_{k-1} < x_t \leq X_k\}; \qquad k = 1, 2, \ldots, n \qquad (6\text{-}92)$$

We see that $\sum_{k=1}^{n} p_k = 1$. Furthermore, since

$$\sum_{j=1}^{k} p_j = Pr\{x_t \leq X_k\} = G(X_k)$$

we may estimate the unknown distribution function G by estimating the n probabilities p_k. We shall write these probabilities as an $(n \times 1)$ column vector $\mathbf{p}$, where

$$\mathbf{p} = \begin{bmatrix} p_1 \\ p_2 \\ \cdot \\ \cdot \\ \cdot \\ p_n \end{bmatrix}$$

Denote the estimates of these probabilities at time t as

$$\hat{\mathbf{p}}(t) = \begin{bmatrix} \hat{p}_1(t) \\ \hat{p}_2(t) \\ \cdot \\ \cdot \\ \cdot \\ \hat{p}_n(t) \end{bmatrix}$$

Thus, the estimate of $G(X_k)$ is $\hat{G}(X_k) = \sum_{j=1}^{k} \hat{p}_j(t)$.

Suppose the tth observation x_t is associated with the kth class interval, that is, $X_{k-1} < x_t \leq X_k$. Define an $(n \times 1)$ column vector $\mathbf{u}_k$ that has $n - 1$ zero's and a one as the kth component. We may revise the previous period's estimates

$\hat{p}(t-1)$ in light of the current information according to

$$\hat{p}(t) = \alpha u_k + (1 - \alpha)\hat{p}(t-1) \tag{6-93}$$

It is not difficult to show that $\hat{p}(t)$ is unbiased $[E\{\hat{p}(t)\} = p]$ and the variance of the kth estimated probability is $\sigma^2_{\hat{p}_k} = \dfrac{\alpha}{2 - \alpha} p_k(1 - p_k)$. See Exercise 6-30.

An initial estimate of the probabilities $\hat{p}(0)$ is required. This may be a subjective estimate, or may be obtained through an analysis of historical data.

Consider the forecasting problem. Suppose we have available the n probabilities $\hat{p}(t)$ and are given a probability of interest, say p. We wish to estimate a value θ_p such that the probability of a future observation being smaller than θ_p is p, that is, $G(\theta_p) = p$. If p is such that one of the class limits exactly satisfies $p = \hat{G}(X_k)$, the problem is easily solved by estimating θ_p with $\hat{\theta}_p = X_k$. However, if

$$\hat{G}(X_{k-1}) < p < \hat{G}(X_k)$$

then we may estimate θ_p by linear interpolation as

$$\hat{\theta}_p = \frac{[\hat{G}(X_k) - p]X_{k-1} + [p - \hat{G}(X_{k-1})]X_k}{\hat{G}(X_k) - \hat{G}(X_{k-1})} \tag{6-94}$$

It may be desirable to use other interpolation schemes near the tails of the distribution or if the class limits in the region of interest are widely spaced.

□**EXAMPLE 6-11** Suppose that at time $t - 1$ the data in Table 6-8 concerning the daily demand of an electronic component are available. The observation in period t is $x_t = 34$. Thus, the vector $u_4' = [0, 0, 0, 1, 0]$, and using $\alpha = 0.1$,

TABLE 6-8   Demand Data

k	CLASS LIMIT, X_k	PROBABILITY, $\hat{p}_k(t-1)$	$\hat{G}(X_k)$
0	0		0.00
1	10	0.60	0.60
2	20	0.15	0.75
3	30	0.15	0.90
4	40	0.05	0.95
5	50	0.05	1.00

we may update the probabilities according to Equation 6-93 as

$$\hat{\mathbf{p}}(t) = 0.1 \begin{bmatrix} 0 \\ 0 \\ 0 \\ 1 \\ 0 \end{bmatrix} + 0.9 \begin{bmatrix} 0.60 \\ 0.15 \\ 0.15 \\ 0.05 \\ 0.05 \end{bmatrix} = \begin{bmatrix} 0.540 \\ 0.135 \\ 0.135 \\ 0.145 \\ 0.045 \end{bmatrix}$$

The new estimated distribution function is $\hat{G}(0) = 0.00$, $\hat{G}(10) = 0.540$, $\hat{G}(20) = 0.675$, $\hat{G}(30) = 0.810$, $\hat{G}(40) = 0.955$, and $\hat{G}(50) = 1.00$. Suppose we wish to find θ_p such that the probability of demand less than θ_p is 0.9. This value is, from Equation 6-94

$$\hat{\theta}_{0.9} = \frac{[0.955 - 0.9]30 + [0.9 - 0.810]40}{0.955 - 0.810} = 36.2 \qquad \square$$

6-8 Adaptive Control Models

In Section 6-5, we discussed the use of tracking signals to monitor forecasting systems and provide a basis for managerial control of these systems. Forecast control procedures based on the tracking signal usually require direct management action as part of the control procedure. That is, the control procedures are not automatic. If a large number of time series are routinely forecasted, it may be quite time consuming for management to examine all series for which the tracking signal indicates an out-of-control condition and either choose a new model or modify the smoothing constant. In many applications, it is desirable to monitor the system *automatically*.

A number of schemes have been developed to monitor and modify automatically the value of the smoothing constant in exponential smoothing. These techniques are usually called *adaptive control* smoothing models, because the smoothing constant adapts itself to changes in the time series. The decision rules employed in these adaptive control models are usually quite simple, and are easily executed by a computer without management intervention. We shall briefly discuss several adaptive control smoothing models.

Chow (5) has described a procedure for adaptive control of a single exponential smoothing constant. Thus, Chow's method would be applicable to any form of exponential smoothing that employs only one smoothing constant. His procedure requires that three equally spaced values for the smoothing constant be chosen; a nominal value (α_0), an upper value (α_h), and a lower value (α_l). Thus,

$$\alpha_h = \alpha_0 + \delta$$
$$\alpha_l = \alpha_0 - \delta \qquad (6\text{-}95)$$

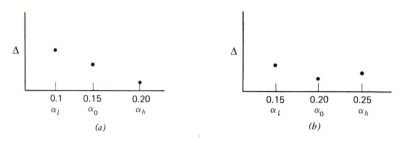

FIGURE 6-8. Chow's adaptive control exponential smoothing. (*a*) Time period *t*. (*b*) Time period $t + 1$.

where δ is an arbitrarly chosen constant. Chow used values of δ of approximately 0.05. Each period, three forecasts are computed, one using each value of the smoothing constant. The forecast associated with the nominal value α_0 is used as the actual forecast. The mean absolute deviation[5] is computed each period for each of the three forecasts. These mean absolute deviations are denoted $\Delta(\alpha_0)$, $\Delta(\alpha_h)$, and $\Delta(\alpha_l)$, to indicate the value of the smoothing constant employed. The decision rule for changing the value of the smoothing constant is based on the mean absolute deviation. If $\Delta(\alpha_0)$ is less than both $\Delta(\alpha_h)$ and $\Delta(\alpha_l)$, then no change is made. If $\Delta(\alpha_h) < \Delta(\alpha_0)$, then we set $\alpha_0 = \alpha_h$. The new upper and lower values of the smoothing constant are chosen according to Equation 6-95 using the new α_0. If $\Delta(\alpha_l) < \Delta(\alpha_0)$, we would set $\alpha_0 = \alpha_l$ and revise the upper and lower values similarly. Should both $\Delta(\alpha_l)$ and $\Delta(\alpha_h)$ be smaller than $\Delta(\alpha_0)$, we would adjust α_0 in the direction of the smallest mean absolute deviation. After each revision, the mean absolute deviations are reset to zero and the process begun anew. The procedure is illustrated in Figure 6-8 for the case $\Delta(\alpha_h) < \Delta(\alpha_0)$ at time *t*.

Chow reported several experimental trials of his procedure in an industrial setting with good results. The number of items indicated out of control by the tracking signal were significantly reduced. The major drawback to this procedure is that three forecasts must be computed each period and the amount of data that must be carried by the data processing system is greatly increased.

Roberts and Reed (13) have also proposed an adaptive control technique for monitoring the exponential smoothing constant. Their method is essentially an extension of Chow's to the case of a smoothing procedure with several smoothing constants (for example, Winters' method, described in Section 6-4.4). Their procedure uses a two-level factorial design in which each smoothing constant is held at a high and low level. All possible combinations of the high and low levels, as well as a center point, are run. The designs for a two-parameter

---

[5] Chow also experimented with the current absolute deviation, but could find no clear-cut advantage to either approach.

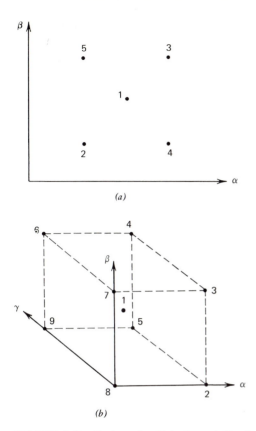

(a)

(b)

FIGURE 6-9. Designs for Roberts and Reed's method. (a) A two-parameter design. (b) A three-parameter design.

and a three-parameter model are shown in Figures 6-9a and 6-9b. A complete replication of each design point is called a *cycle*. Every time a new observation becomes available, a cycle is run. Thus, if k smoothing parameters are under control, then $2^k + 1$ forecasts must be computed each period. The actual forecast is always made using the combination of smoothing parameters at the center of the design.

The measure of forecast effectiveness employed is the squared forecast error. Let SS_{ij} be the squared forecast error at design point i in cycle j. Then after n cycles, the *average* squared forecast error at design point i is

$$\overline{SS}_i = \frac{1}{n} \sum_{j=1}^{n} SS_{ij}$$

The control procedure consists of computing the "effects" of each smoothing parameter in the same fashion that the main effects in an analysis of variance would be estimated and adjusting the parameters (and hence the design) if one or more of these parameters are significant.

For the two-parameter case, the effects of α and β, say E_α and E_β, are

$$E_\alpha = \tfrac{1}{2}(\overline{SS}_3 + \overline{SS}_4 - \overline{SS}_2 - \overline{SS}_5)$$

$$E_\beta = \tfrac{1}{2}(\overline{SS}_3 + \overline{SS}_5 - \overline{SS}_2 - \overline{SS}_4)$$

The smoothing parameters should be changed if either E_α, E_β, or both are outside the approximate 99 percent error limits [6]

$$\pm 3\sqrt{\frac{1}{n}}\, s$$

where s is an estimate of the standard deviation of the errors that may be easily computed using a range method (see Reference 13 for details and further references). To illustrate the technique, suppose E_α was below the lower error limit for a particular cycle, that is, $E_\alpha < -3\sqrt{(1/n)}s$. This indicates that $\overline{SS}_2 + \overline{SS}_5$ is considerably larger than $\overline{SS}_3 + \overline{SS}_4$, so we should shift the entire design to the right, adopting the high value of α as the new central value and leaving the values of β unchanged. Of course, then the old values of $\overline{SS}_i$ must be discarded and new ones computed over several cycles.

For the three-parameter case, the effects are

$$E_\alpha = \tfrac{1}{4}(\overline{SS}_2 + \overline{SS}_3 + \overline{SS}_4 + \overline{SS}_5 - \overline{SS}_6 - \overline{SS}_7 - \overline{SS}_8 - \overline{SS}_9)$$

$$E_\beta = \tfrac{1}{4}(\overline{SS}_3 + \overline{SS}_4 + \overline{SS}_6 + \overline{SS}_7 - \overline{SS}_2 - \overline{SS}_5 - \overline{SS}_8 - \overline{SS}_9)$$

$$E_\gamma = \tfrac{1}{4}(\overline{SS}_4 + \overline{SS}_5 + \overline{SS}_6 + \overline{SS}_9 - \overline{SS}_2 - \overline{SS}_3 - \overline{SS}_7 - \overline{SS}_8)$$

and the approximate 99 percent error limits are

$$\pm 3\sqrt{\frac{1}{2n}}\, s$$

The operation of the three-parameter control technique is similar to the two-parameter case.

Roberts and Reed tested this adaptive control procedure with several artificially generated time series. The test series contained impulse, ramp, trend, or seasonal variation so that the performance of the technique to changing

---

[6] These error limits are only approximate, as the squared errors at the design points within a cycle are not independent random variables. That is, the same data point is used $2^k + 1$ times to compute forecast errors. Comparing the estimated effects to the error limits is not a proper statistical test of significance.

time series models could be investigated. The results of these tests indicated that forecast accuracy and rate of response to dynamic signals were significantly better using the adaptive control procedure.

Another adaptive control scheme has been suggested by Montgomery (11). His technique is similar to the Roberts and Reed method but uses a different experimental design. The control scheme is based on the simplex, which, like the two-level factorial, is an orthogonal first-order experimental design. However, the simplex requires only one more observation than the number of factors under investigation. Thus, if k smoothing parameters are being controlled, $N = k + 1$. The N observations are taken at the vertices of a regular-sided simplex, which for a two-parameter smoothing method ($k = 2$) is an equilateral triangle and for the three-parameter smoothing technique ($k = 3$) is a tetrahedron. These designs are shown in Figure 6-10. The design

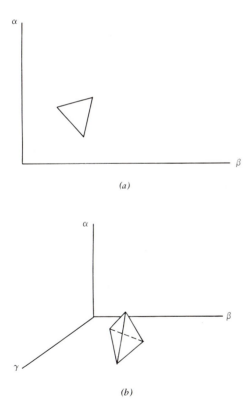

(a)

(b)

FIGURE 6-10. Simplex designs for Montgomery's method. (a) Simplex design in two dimensions. (b) Simplex design in three dimensions.

matrix $\mathbf{D}$ for a simplex of arbitrary orientation and edge length may be constructed from the last k columns of $N^{1/2}\mathbf{H}$, where $\mathbf{H}$ is any $(N \times N)$ orthogonal matrix having elements in the first column equal. The design points are the rows of the $\mathbf{D}$ matrix. The jth row of $\mathbf{D}$ will be denoted vectorially by $\mathbf{d}_j'$, and will contain a particular combination of smoothing parameters. The advantage of this design relative to a factorial is that each period only k forecasts need be computed.

To apply this technique to a two-parameter or a three-parameter exponential smoothing model, adjust the smoothing parameters according to the following rules:

1. Denote by e_i the current absolute forecast error at the ith design point; that is, $e_i = |\hat{x}_i - x_i|$, $i = 1, 2, \ldots, N$. Let the maximum value of e_i occur at design point $\mathbf{d}_j'$. Form a new simplex by deleting $\mathbf{d}_j'$ from $\mathbf{D}$ and substituting the new design point,

$$\mathbf{d}_j'^* = 2k^{-1}(\mathbf{d}_1' + \mathbf{d}_2' + \cdots + \mathbf{d}_{j-1}' + \mathbf{d}_{j+1}' + \cdots + \mathbf{d}_N') - \mathbf{d}_j'$$

Calculate the forecast for the next period using the smoothing parameters, which are the elements of $\mathbf{d}_j'^*$.

2. Apply rule 1 unless a design point has occurred in N successive simplexes without being eliminated. Should this situation arise for the ith design point, discard e_i and calculate the forecast for the next period using the smoothing parameters in $\mathbf{d}_i'$. Then apply rule 1.

3. Should e_i be the maximum absolute current error in the nth simplex and e_i^* be the maximum absolute current error in the $n + 1$st simplex, do not return to the nth design. Instead of oscillating, move from the $n + 1$st design by discarding the second largest absolute current error.

Montgomery tested this technique for several artificially generated time series and found it to be superior to nonadaptive exponential smoothing. Computationally, this scheme is more efficient than the Roberts and Reed method, as only k forecasts (as compared to $2^k + 1$ for Roberts and Reed) are required each period. The amount of information to be carried by the data processing system would seem to be correspondingly reduced, also. No extensive comparison of the accuracy or response characteristics of these two methods has been reported.

6-9 Bayesian Methods in Forecasting

In many forecasting problems, there is no useful historical information available at the time the initial forecast is required. Thus, the initial forecasts must be based on subjective considerations. As time series information becomes available, we must modify our subjective estimates in light of the actual data. Bayesian methods are often useful in statistical inference problems of this general type. This section deals with an application of Bayesian decision theory to forecasting problems.

Cohen (6) has presented a Bayesian forecasting procedure for the constant time series model

$$x_t = a + \varepsilon_t \tag{6-96}$$

where a is the unknown mean and ε_t is a random error such that $\varepsilon_t \sim N(0, \sigma_\varepsilon^2)$. As in exponential smoothing, forecasts of future observations x_t may be made by estimating a.

The estimation procedure makes use of Bayes theorem. Let x be a random variable with density function f characterized by the unknown parameter θ. We shall write this density as $f(x \mid \theta)$ to indicate that the density depends on the value taken on by θ. The parameter θ is assumed to be a random variable with probability density $f(\theta)$, which is called the *prior* density for θ. The prior density for θ measures our subjective or "degree-of-belief" information about θ. If we are relatively confident about the value of θ, we would choose a prior distribution with a small variance. If we are relatively uncertain about θ, we might choose a prior with a larger variance.

Assume there is available a random sample of n observations of x, and the joint density of these observations is $f(x_1, x_2, \ldots, x_n \mid \theta)$. From Bayes theorem, we see that the density function of θ given the sample results, called the *posterior* density for θ, is just

$$f(\theta \mid x_1, x_2, \ldots, x_n) = \frac{f(x_1, x_2, \ldots, x_n \mid \theta)f(\theta)}{\displaystyle\int_\theta f(x_1, x_2, \ldots, x_n \mid \theta)f(\theta) \, d\theta} \tag{6-97}$$

The *Bayes estimator* of θ, denoted θ^*, is defined as the expected value of the posterior density for θ, or

$$\theta^* = \int_\theta \theta f(\theta \mid x_1, x_2, \ldots, x_n) \, d\theta \tag{6-98}$$

This procedure may be employed to estimate a in Equation 6-96. Since $\varepsilon_t \sim N(0, \sigma_\varepsilon^2)$, we see that $x_t \sim N(a, \sigma_\varepsilon^2)$. Assume the prior density for a to be normal with mean a_0 and variance σ_0^2. That is, a is a random variable and our subjective knowledge about a is summarized by a normal density with mean a_0 and variance σ_0^2. We also assume that the parameter σ_ε^2 is known.

After n realizations of the time series have been observed, say $x_1, x_2, \ldots, x_n$, we would like to find the Bayes estimator of a. In the absence of prior data, we would estimate a by $\bar{x} = (1/n) \sum_{i=1}^{n} x_i$. Notice that the conditional density

$$f(\bar{x} \mid a) = [(\sigma_\varepsilon^2/n)2\pi]^{-1/2} \exp\left\{ -\frac{1}{2} \cdot \frac{(\bar{x} - a)^2}{(\sigma_\varepsilon^2/n)} \right\}$$

Thus, the posterior density is

$$f(a \mid \bar{x}) = \frac{(2\pi\sigma_0\sigma_\varepsilon/\sqrt{n})^{-1} \exp\left\{-\dfrac{1}{2}\left[\dfrac{(\bar{x}-a)^2}{(\sigma_\varepsilon^2/n)} + \dfrac{(a-a_0)^2}{\sigma_0^2}\right]\right\}}{\displaystyle\int_{-\infty}^{\infty} (2\pi\sigma_0\sigma_\varepsilon/\sqrt{n})^{-1} \exp\left\{-\dfrac{1}{2}\left[\dfrac{(\bar{x}-a)^2}{(\sigma_\varepsilon^2/n)} + \dfrac{(a-a_0)^2}{\sigma_0^2}\right]\right\} da}$$

$$= \frac{1}{\sqrt{2\pi}\left(\dfrac{1}{\sigma_0^2} + \dfrac{1}{(\sigma_\varepsilon^2/n)}\right)^{-1/2}} \exp\left\{-\dfrac{1}{2}\left[\dfrac{a - \dfrac{\bar{x}\sigma_0^2 + a_0(\sigma_\varepsilon^2/n)}{\sigma_0^2 + (\sigma_\varepsilon^2/n)}}{\left(\dfrac{1}{\sigma_0^2} + \dfrac{1}{(\sigma_\varepsilon^2/n)}\right)^{-1/2}}\right]^2\right\}$$

which we recognize as a normal density with mean

$$\frac{\bar{x}\sigma_0^2 + a_0(\sigma_\varepsilon^2/n)}{\sigma_0^2 + (\sigma_\varepsilon^2/n)}$$

and variance

$$\left(\frac{1}{\sigma_0^2} + \frac{1}{(\sigma_\varepsilon^2/n)}\right)^{-1}$$

From Equation 6-98, the Bayes estimator of a is the expected value of the posterior, so

$$a^*(n) = \frac{\bar{x}\sigma_0^2 + a_0(\sigma_\varepsilon^2/n)}{\sigma_0^2 + (\sigma_\varepsilon^2/n)}$$

or

$$a^*(n) = \frac{n}{u+n}\,\bar{x} + \frac{u}{u+n}\,a_0$$

where $u = \sigma_\varepsilon^2/\sigma_0^2$.

We see that the Bayes estimator of a is just a weighted average of the sample mean and the subjective estimate of a (the prior mean, a_0). Furthermore, $a^*(n)$ can be written as

$$a^*(n) = \alpha x_n + (1 - \alpha)a^*(n - 1) \tag{6-99}$$

where $\alpha = 1/(u + n)$, a form *not unlike* exponential smoothing.

Thus, Equation 6-99 could be used to blend subjectively new data each period with the previous estimate $a^*(n - 1)$ to produce an estimate $a^*(n)$. Forecasts for future periods, say $\hat{x}_{n+\tau}$, would be simply

$$\hat{x}_{n+\tau} = a^*(n)$$

We see that as the number of time periods increases, more weight is given to the actual data. Eventually, at some point in time when enough data is available, a permanent forecasting procedure perhaps involving exponential smoothing should be adopted.

□**EXAMPLE 6-12** Suppose we wish to forecast the demand for a new product. We suspect that demand is normally distributed and that a constant model is appropriate, but no historical information is available. A reasonable prior density for a is $N(50, 4)$, and $\sigma_\varepsilon^2 = 9$. For period 1, the forecast is

$$\hat{x}_1 = 50$$

Suppose the actual demand in period 1 is $x_1 = 56$. Now, the Bayes estimate of a is

$$a^*(1) = \frac{1}{(9/4) + 1}(56) + \frac{(9/4)}{(9/4) + 1}(50) \simeq 52$$

from Equation 6-99. Thus, the forecast for period 2 is

$$\hat{x}_2 = 52$$

Suppose the actual demand in period 2 is 58. Then

$$a^*(2) = \frac{1}{(9/4) + 2}(58) + \frac{(13/4)}{(9/4) + 2}(52) \simeq 53$$

and $\hat{x}_3 = 53$. This procedure would be continued until sufficient data had been accumulated to develop a permanent forecasting system.□

We may also treat a time series model with a linear trend component using the Bayesian approach. Suppose the time series is represented by

$$x_t = a + bt + \varepsilon_t$$

This model can be rewritten as

$$x_t = a' + b(t - \bar{t}) + \varepsilon_t \tag{6-100}$$

where $a' = a + b\bar{t}$ and $\bar{t} = (n + 1)/2$. This transformation admits orthogonal least squares estimators of a' and b, say $\hat{a}' = \sum_{t=1}^{n} x_t/n$ and $\hat{b} = \sum_{t=1}^{n} x_t(t - \bar{t})/SS_{tt}$, where $SS_{tt} = \sum_{t=1}^{n} (t - \bar{t})^2$. These estimators, $\hat{a}'$ and $\hat{b}$, are independent and are sufficient statistics for a' and b.

Let the prior densities for a' and b be $g(a')$ and $g(b)$. Consider the posterior density for b given the observations $x_1, x_2, \ldots, x_n$, say $f(b \mid x_1, x_2, \ldots, x_n)$. We use the fact that $\hat{b}$ is a sufficient statistic for b to find a useful form for $f(b \mid x_1, x_2, \ldots, x_n)$. Now

$$f(x_1, x_2, \ldots, x_n \mid a', b) = f(\hat{a}' \mid a')f(\hat{b} \mid b)c(x_1, x_2, \ldots, x_n)$$

and the joint density of the sample and b is

$$f(b, x_1, x_2, \ldots, x_n) = \int f(\hat{b} \mid b)g(b)f(\hat{a}' \mid a')g(a')c(x_1, x_2, \ldots, x_n) \, da'$$

$$= f(\hat{a}')f(\hat{b}, b)c(x_1, x_2, \ldots, x_n) \tag{6-101}$$

Bayesian Methods in Forecasting   459

where $c(x_1, x_2, \ldots, x_n)$ is a function of the sample data. Integrating out b in (6-101)

$$f(x_1, x_2, \ldots, x_n) = f(\hat{b})f(\hat{a}')c(x_1, x_2, \ldots, x_n)$$

and the posterior density is

$$f(b \mid x_1, x_2, \ldots, x_n) = \frac{f(b, x_1, x_2, \ldots, x_n)}{f(x_1, x_2, \ldots, x_n)} = \frac{f(\hat{b}, b)}{f(\hat{b})} = f(b \mid \hat{b})$$

Therefore, the Bayes estimator of b is

$$b^* = E(b \mid \hat{b}) \tag{6-102}$$

Similarly, since $\hat{a}'$ is a sufficient statistic for a', the Bayes estimator of a' can be shown to be

$$(a')^* = E(a' \mid \hat{a}') \tag{6-103}$$

Now, suppose the prior densities for b and a' are normal, say $b \sim N(b_0, \sigma_b^2)$ and $a' \sim N(a_0', \sigma_{a'}^2)$, and further assume that $\varepsilon_t \sim N(0, \sigma_\varepsilon^2)$. We assume that σ_ε^2 is known. The exact form of the Bayes estimators may be easily developed. Since $\hat{b}$ is independent of $\hat{a}'$ and

$$f(\hat{b} \mid b) = [SS_{tt}/(2\pi\sigma_\varepsilon^2)]^{1/2} \exp - \left\{ \frac{SS_{tt}}{2\sigma^2}(\hat{b} - b)^2 \right\}$$

we may show that the posterior density $f(b \mid \hat{b})$ is normal with mean

$$\frac{SS_{tt}\hat{b}\sigma_b^2 + b_0\sigma_\varepsilon^2}{SS_{tt}\sigma_b^2 + \sigma_\varepsilon^2}$$

The Bayes estimator of b is just the mean of the posterior, so

$$b^* = \frac{w}{w + \sigma_\varepsilon^2}\hat{b} + \frac{\sigma_\varepsilon^2}{w + \sigma_\varepsilon^2}b_0 \tag{6-104}$$

where $w = SS_{tt}\sigma_b^2$. Similarly, the Bayes estimator for a' is

$$(a')^* = \frac{z}{z + \sigma_\varepsilon^2}\hat{a}' + \frac{\sigma_\varepsilon^2}{z + \sigma_\varepsilon^2}a_0' \tag{6-105}$$

where $z = n\sigma_{a'}^2$.

We observe that both Bayes estimators are just simple weighted averages of the least-squares estimators and the prior means. Furthermore, the value placed on the sample information is inversely proportional to the variance of the time series data. As the length of the time series increases, the Bayes estimators approach the least-squares estimators. These results are directly comparable to those of Cohen for the constant model. Equations 6-104 and 6-105 can be used to successively blend the subjective estimates of a' and b with observational data until sufficient experience has been achieved to develop a permanent forecasting system.

6-10   The Box-Jenkins
Models

Most of the forecasting techniques discussed in previous sections of this chapter are based on exponential smoothing, which is derived from the discounted least-squares criterion (see Sections 6-4.1 and 6-4.3). This approach assumes that the mean of the time series is a deterministic function of time, and actual observations are generated by adding a random error component to the mean. For example, Equation 6-47 says that the mean is a *linear* deterministic function of time, to which a realization of the random variable $\{\varepsilon_t\}$ is added to produce the tth observation, x_t. If the $\{\varepsilon_t\}$ are assumed to be independent random variables, then the $\{x_t\}$ are also independent. This assumption is frequently made, even when it is unwarranted.

Successive observations in many time series are highly *dependent*. If this is the case, then the models presented previously are inappropriate, because they do not take advantage of this dependency in the most effective way. This is not to say that exponential smoothing methods do not work for time series in which observations are dependent; they may work reasonably well. However, forecasting methods are available that exploit this dependency and generally produce superior results. We now turn our attention to some of these alternative models.

Many of these alternative models assume that a time series in which successive observations are dependent can be modeled as a linear combination of independent random variables, say ε_t, ε_{t-1}, ε_{t-2}, ..., that are drawn from a stable distribution, usually assumed normal with mean zero and variance σ_ε^2. The sequence of random variables ε_t, ε_{t-1}, ε_{t-2}, ..., is often called a *white noise process*. The linear combination of the $\{\varepsilon_t\}$ could be written as

$$x_t = \mu + \psi_0 \varepsilon_t + \psi_1 \varepsilon_{t-1} + \psi_2 \varepsilon_{t-2} + \cdots \qquad (6\text{-}106)$$

where the $\psi_i (i = 0, 1, \ldots)$ are weights and μ determines the level of the process. Equation 6-106 is usually called a *linear filter*. Clearly successive observations of x_t are dependent, because they are generated from the same previous realizations of $\{\varepsilon_t\}$, and are normally distributed if the $\{\varepsilon_t\}$ are normally distributed. In light of (6-106), it is reasonable to define a time series model as a *function that transforms the time series into a white noise process.*[7]

Time series models derived from Equation 6-106 have been reported extensively in the statistics literature. Box and Jenkins (1) have unified this methodology and evolved a philosophy for its use. For this reason, time series models derived from (6-106) are often called *Box-Jenkins models*. We shall now briefly present their approach to forecasting.

---

[7] This definition, and much of the terminology and notation of this section, is derived from Box and Jenkins (1).

6-10.1 A Class of Time Series Models

The linear filter (6-106) would not be a very useful model in practice, as it contains an infinite number of unknown parameters (the ψ weights). Our approach will be to develop *parsimonious* models, that is, models that contain few parameters, yet are useful in modeling time series.

An alternate way of writing (6-106) is in terms of the backward shift operator, B, defined such that

$$B\varepsilon_t = \varepsilon_{t-1}$$

and

$$B^j\varepsilon_t = \varepsilon_{t-j};$$

Using this notation, the linear filter (6-106) becomes

$$x_t - \mu = (\psi_0 B^0 + \psi_1 B^1 + \psi_2 B^2 + \cdots)\varepsilon_t$$

or

$$x_t - \mu = \Psi(B)\varepsilon_t$$

where $\Psi(B) = \psi_0 B^0 + \psi_1 B^1 + \psi_2 B^2 + \cdots$.

Models derived from (6-106) are capable of representing both *stationary* and *nonstationary* time series. By stationary, we imply that the time series fluctuates randomly about a constant mean level, and by nonstationary we imply that the time series has no natural mean. Generally, if the sequence of weights ψ_0, $\psi_1, \ldots$ in (6-106) is finite or infinite and convergent the time series is stationary with mean μ. If $\psi_0, \psi_1, \ldots$ is infinite and diverges the time series is non-stationary and μ is only a reference point for the level of the series.

Autoregressive Models. It is convenient to work with the time series defined in terms of deviations from μ. Therefore, let $\tilde{x}_t = x_t - \mu$, for all t. An important special case of (6-106) is the model

$$\tilde{x}_t = \phi_1\tilde{x}_{t-1} + \phi_2\tilde{x}_{t-2} + \cdots + \phi_p\tilde{x}_{t-p} + \varepsilon_t \qquad (6\text{-}107)$$

Equation 6-107 is called an *autoregressive* process, because the current observation, $\tilde{x}_t$, is "regressed" on previous values $\tilde{x}_{t-1}, \tilde{x}_{t-2}, \ldots \tilde{x}_{t-p}$. The process contains p unknown parameters $\phi_1, \phi_2, \ldots, \phi_p$; therefore we would specifically refer to (6-107) as an autoregressive process of order p, abbreviated AR(p). Clearly the AR(p) process is a special case of the linear filter model (6-106), since we can substitute successively for $\tilde{x}_{t-j}$ on the right-hand side of (6-107) to obtain an infinite series in the ε's.

Two important autoregressive processes are the AR(1) process

$$\tilde{x}_t = \phi_1\tilde{x}_{t-1} + \varepsilon_t$$

and the AR(2) process

$$\tilde{x}_t = \phi_1\tilde{x}_{t-1} + \phi_2\tilde{x}_{t-2} + \varepsilon_t$$

Both of these processes are frequently useful in modeling time series.

Equation 6-107 can be written in terms of the backward shift operator as

$$\tilde{x}_t = (\phi_1 B + \phi_2 B^2 + \cdots + \phi_p B^p)\tilde{x}_t + \varepsilon_t$$

or

$$(1 - \phi_1 B - \phi_2 B^2 - \cdots - \phi_p B^p)\tilde{x}_t = \varepsilon_t \qquad (6\text{-}108)$$

Letting

$$\Phi_p(B) = 1 - \phi_1 B - \phi_2 B^2 - \cdots - \phi_p B^p$$

Equation 6-108 becomes

$$\Phi_p(B)\tilde{x}_t = \varepsilon_t \qquad (6\text{-}109)$$

The autoregressive model may be used to represent both stationary and nonstationary time series. Box and Jenkins show that if the roots of the polynomial $\Phi_p(B) = 0$ lie *outside* the unit circle, the process is stationary. This is equivalent to saying that, for example, in the AR(1) process we must have

$$|\phi_1| < 1$$

and in the AR(2) process

$$\phi_1 + \phi_2 < 1$$
$$\phi_2 - \phi_1 < 1$$
$$|\phi_2| < 1$$

for stationarity. While it is theoretically possible to model a nonstationary time series by an appropriately chosen autoregressive process, this is not usually done, because more effective methods are available.

Moving Average Models. Consider the special case of the linear filter (6–106) with only the first q weights nonzero. This yields

$$\tilde{x}_t = \varepsilon_t - \theta_1 \varepsilon_{t-1} - \theta_2 \varepsilon_{t-2} - \cdots - \theta_q \varepsilon_{t-q}$$
$$= (1 - \theta_1 B - \theta_2 B^2 - \cdots - \theta_q B^q)\varepsilon_t$$
$$= \Theta_q(B)\varepsilon_t \qquad (6\text{-}110)$$

say, where $-\theta_1, -\theta_2, \ldots, -\theta_q$ are the *finite* set of weights from (6-106). The model (6-110) is called a *moving average process* of order q, abbreviated MA(q). Two important and very useful special cases are the MA(1) process

$$\tilde{x}_t = \varepsilon_t - \theta_1 \varepsilon_{t-1}$$

and the MA(2) process

$$\tilde{x}_t = \varepsilon_t - \theta_1 \varepsilon_{t-1} - \theta_2 \varepsilon_{t-2}$$

The name "moving average" may be somewhat misleading, as the weights $\theta_i (i = 1, 2, \ldots, q)$ need not sum to unity or be positive.

There is an interesting duality between the moving average and autoregressive processes. For example, consider the MA(1) process

$$\tilde{x}_t = \varepsilon_t - \theta_1 \varepsilon_{t-1}$$
$$= (1 - \theta_1 B) \varepsilon_t$$

which solved for ε_t yields

$$\varepsilon_t = (1 - \theta_1 B)^{-1} \tilde{x}_t$$

Now if $|\theta_1| < 1$, this last equation becomes

$$\varepsilon_t = \left(\sum_{j=0}^{\infty} \theta_1{}^j B^j \right) \tilde{x}_t$$
$$= (1 + \theta_1 B + \theta_1{}^2 B^2 + \cdots) \tilde{x}_t$$

which is an infinite-order autoregressive process with weights $\phi_j = \theta_1{}^j$. That is, we have *inverted* the MA(1) process to obtain an AR(∞) process. The condition

$$|\theta_1| < 1$$

is called the *invertibility* condition for an MA(1) process. In general, for the MA(q) model to be invertible to an AR(∞) process we must require that the roots of $\Theta_q(B) = 0$ must lie outside the unit circle. However, moving average processes are *stationary* for any choice of the weights. This duality holds true for autoregressive processes as well; that is, the finite AR(p) process can be inverted to give an infinite-order moving average process.

Mixed Autoregressive-Moving Average Models. In building an empirical model of an actual time series, it may lead to a more parsimonious model to include *both* autoregressive and moving average parameters. This leads to the mixed autoregressive-moving average model of order (p, q)

$$\tilde{x}_t = \phi_1 \tilde{x}_{t-1} + \phi_2 \tilde{x}_{t-2} + \cdots + \phi_p \tilde{x}_{t-p}$$
$$- \theta_1 \varepsilon_{t-1} - \theta_2 \varepsilon_{t-2} - \cdots - \theta_q \varepsilon_{t-q} + \varepsilon_t$$

or

$$\Phi_p(B) \tilde{x}_t = \Theta_q(B) \varepsilon_t \tag{6-111}$$

which would be abbreviated ARMA(p, q). For example, a particularly useful model is the ARMA(1, 1) process

$$\tilde{x}_t - \phi_1 \tilde{x}_{t-1} = \varepsilon_t - \theta_1 \varepsilon_{t-1}$$

which can be written as

$$\tilde{x}_t = \phi_1 \tilde{x}_{t-1} + \varepsilon_t - \theta_1 \varepsilon_{t-1}$$

The stationarity and invertibility conditions for the AR(p) and MA(q) processes establish these properties for the ARMA (p, q) process. For example, the ARMA(1, 1) process is *stationary* if $|\phi_1| < 1$ and *invertible* if $|\theta_1| < 1$.

Nonstationary Processes. As previously discussed, many time series behave as if they have no constant mean; that is, in any local segment of time the observations look like those in any other segment, apart from their average. We call such a time series *nonstationary in the mean.* Similarly, it is possible for a time series to exhibit nonstationary behavior in *both mean and slope,* that is, apart from the mean and slope, observations in different segments of time look very much alike.

To understand how nonstationary behavior can be incorporated into a time series model, consider the discrete, deterministic signals shown in Figure 6-11.

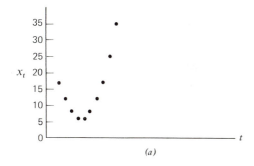

(a)

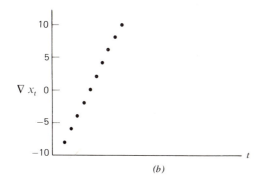

(b)

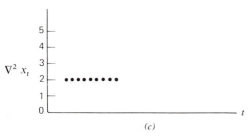

(c)

FIGURE 6-11. Reducing a discrete, nonstationary signal to a stationary signal.

The function in Figure 6-11*a* exhibits nonstationary behavior in both mean and slope. Its first difference, however, shown in Figure 6-11*b*, is nonstationary in the mean only. Finally the second difference, shown in Figure 6-11*c*, is stationary. Therefore, it seems reasonable to use differencing to reduce a nonstationary stochastic time series to a stationary one.

Define the (backward) difference operator, ∇, such that

$$\nabla x_t = x_t - x_{t-1} \qquad (6\text{-}112)$$

Clearly, ∇ can be expressed in terms of the backward shift operator B as $\nabla = (1 - B)$, allowing higher degrees of differencing to be expressed as $\nabla^2 = (1 - B)^2, \nabla^3 = (1 - B)^3, \ldots, \nabla^d = (1 - B)^d, \ldots$. For example, $\nabla^2 x_t = (1 - B)^2 x_t = x_t - 2x_{t-1} + x_{t-2}$. The difference operator always operates on the original observations. Differencing produces a new series $w_t = \nabla^d x_t = \nabla^d \tilde{x}_t$. In general, the new series $\{w_t\}$ may not have a zero mean.

The mathematical model for the *autoregressive integrated moving average* process of order (p, d, q), denoted ARIMA(p, d, q), is

$$\Phi_p(B)\, \nabla^d x_t = \Theta_q(B)\varepsilon_t \qquad (6\text{-}113)$$

An alternate way of writing (6-113) is

$$\Phi_p(B)w_t = \Theta_q(B)\varepsilon_t$$

If the differenced series w_t has a nonzero mean, say μ_w, then the ARIMA process would be

$$\Phi_p(B)(w_t - \mu_w) = \Theta_q(B)\varepsilon_t$$

The effect of allowing μ_w to be nonzero is to introduce a deterministic polynomial term into the eventual forecast function, and for this reason we usually assume that $\mu_w = 0$, unless the data indicates otherwise. For a more complete discussion of including deterministic functions of time in the model, see Box and Jenkins (1, pp. 91–94, 193–195).

In practice, most time series can be adequately modeled by an ARIMA process in which p, d, and q do not exceed 2. For example, an important process is the ARIMA$(1, 1, 1)$ process

$$(1 - \phi_1 B)\, \nabla x_t = (1 - \theta_1 B)\varepsilon_t$$

or

$$x_t = (1 + \phi_1)x_{t-1} - \phi_1 x_{t-2} + \varepsilon_t - \theta_1 \varepsilon_{t-1}$$

Notice that for appropriate choices of p and q with $d = 0$, the ARIMA process includes the autoregressive, moving average, and mixed models discussed previously as special cases. Thus, the ARIMA(p, d, q) process in Equation 6-113 represents a useful and flexible class of time series models.

Calculation of the ψ Weights. It is useful in forecasting to be able to express any ARIMA(p, d, q) model in terms of the ψ weights of the linear filter (6-106).

Forecasting Systems   466

To see how this may be done, recall that the linear filter can be written as

$$\tilde{x}_t = \Psi(B)\varepsilon_t$$

or

$$\varepsilon_t = \frac{\tilde{x}_t}{\Psi(B)}$$

Substituting into (6-113) with the x_t corrected for μ yields

$$\Phi_p(B)\, \nabla^d\tilde{x}_t = \Theta_q(B)\frac{\tilde{x}_t}{\Psi(B)}$$

or

$$\Psi(B)\Phi_p(B)(1 - B)^d\tilde{x}_t = \Theta_q(B)\tilde{x}_t$$

Therefore, the ψ weights may be obtained by equating coefficients of like powers of B in the expansion

$$(\psi_0 + \psi_1 B + \psi_2 B^2 + \cdots)(1 - \phi_1 B - \phi_2 B^2 - \cdots - \phi_p B^p)(1 - B)^d$$
$$= (1 - \theta_1 B - \theta_2 B^2 - \cdots - \theta_q B^q)$$

For example, consider the ARMA(1, 1) model

$$(1 - \phi_1 B)\tilde{x}_t = (1 - \theta_1 B)\varepsilon_t$$

To find the ψ weights we would equate coefficients of like powers of B in

$$(\psi_0 + \psi_1 B + \cdots)(1 - \phi_1 B) = (1 - \theta_1 B)$$

For B^0, this yields $\psi_0 = 1$. For B^1, we find $\psi_1 = \phi_1 - \theta_1$. For B^2 the coefficients are

$$\psi_2 - \phi_1\psi_1 = 0$$

which yields $\psi_2 = \phi_1(\phi_1 - \theta_1)$. It is not difficult to show that the jth ψ weight is $\psi_j = \phi_1^{j-1}(\phi_1 - \theta_1)$.

Seasonal Models. Differencing will not produce stationarity in seasonal time series. In general, the models presented in this section are not appropriate for seasonal data. The interested reader is referred to Chapter 9 of Box and Jenkins (1), where a useful class of models for seasonal time series is discussed.

6-10.2 Forecasting with the Box-Jenkins Models

In Reference 1, Box and Jenkins present a general philosophy for the development of an appropriate time series model and its use in forecasting. Their approach consists of a three-step iterative procedure. First, a tentative model is identified from actual data. Then the unknown parameters in the model are estimated. Finally, diagnostic checks are performed to determine the adequacy of the model, or to indicate possible improvements.

Identification. Tentative identification of a time series model is done by analysis of historical data. Usually, at least 50 observations are required to achieve satisfactory results. The primary tool used in this analysis is the auto-correlation function.

Consider the stationary time series $x_1, x_2, \ldots, x_N$. The theoretical auto-correlation function is

$$\rho_k = \frac{E[(x_t - \mu)(x_{t+k} - \mu)]}{\sigma_x^2}, \qquad k = 0, 1, \ldots \qquad (6\text{-}114)$$

where σ_x^2 is the variance of the series. The quantity ρ_k is called the auto-correlation at lag k. Obviously, $\rho_0 = 1$. The theoretical autocorrelation function is never known with certainty, and must be estimated. A satisfactory estimate of ρ_k is the sample autocorrelation function

$$\hat{\rho}_k = \frac{\dfrac{1}{N-k} \sum_{t=1}^{N-k} (x_t - \bar{x})(x_{t+k} - \bar{x})}{\dfrac{1}{N} \sum_{t=1}^{N} (x_t - \bar{x})^2}, \qquad k = 0, 1, \ldots, K \qquad (6\text{-}115)$$

For useful results, we would usually compute the first $K \le N/4$ autocorrelations.

As a supplemental aid the partial autocorrelation or conditional correlation function often proves useful. We shall define the partial autocorrelation coefficient ϕ_{kk} as the kth coefficient in an autoregressive process of order k. It can be shown (see Reference 1, Chapter 3), that the partial autocorrelation coefficients satisfy the following *Yule-Walker equations:*

$$\rho_j = \phi_{k1}\rho_{j-1} + \phi_{k2}\rho_{j-2} + \cdots + \phi_{kk}\rho_{j-k}, \qquad j = 1, 2, \ldots, k \quad (6\text{-}116)$$

We may estimate the partial autocorrelation coefficients by substituting $\hat{\rho}_j$ for ρ_j in (6-116), yielding

$$\hat{\rho}_j = \phi_{k1}\hat{\rho}_{j-1} + \phi_{k2}\hat{\rho}_{j-2} + \cdots + \phi_{kk}\hat{\rho}_{j-k}, \qquad j = 1, 2, \ldots, k \quad (6\text{-}117)$$

and solving the resulting equations for $k = 1, 2, \ldots, K$ to obtain $\hat{\phi}_{11}, \hat{\phi}_{22}, \ldots,$ $\hat{\phi}_{KK}$, the sample partial autocorrelation function.[8]

From the sample (estimated) autocorrelation and partial autocorrelation function, which can be conveniently exhibited by a graph, a tentative model is selected by comparison with the *theoretical* autocorrelation and partial

---

[8] Sample partial autocorrelations computed from (6-117) are sensitive to round-off errors. For a fuller discussion, see Box and Jenkins (1, Chapter 3).

autocorrelation function patterns. These theoretical patterns are shown in Table 6-9.

By "tailing off" in Table 6-9, we mean that the function has an approximately exponential, sinusoidal, or geometric decay, with a relatively large number of nonzero values. By "cutting off" we mean that the function truncates abruptly, with only a very few nonzero values. Notice that the duality referred to earlier between the autoregressive and moving average processes is also evident in Table 6-9. The autoregressive process has an autocorrelation function that tails off and a partial autocorrelation function that cuts off, while the moving average process has an autocorrelation function that cuts off and a partial autocorrelation function that tails off.

The standard errors of the autocorrelation and partial autocorrelation function are useful in identifying nonzero values. Box and Jenkins show that the estimated standard error of the kth autocorrelation coefficient is

$$S(\hat{\rho}_k) \simeq N^{-1/2}\left[1 + 2\sum_{j=1}^{k-1} r_j\right] \qquad (6\text{-}118)$$

where

$$r_j = \begin{cases} \hat{\rho}_j & \text{if } \rho_j \neq 0 \\ 0 & \text{if } \rho_j = 0 \end{cases}$$

The estimated standard error of the kth partial autocorrelation coefficient is

$$S(\hat{\phi}_{kk}) \simeq N^{-1/2} \qquad (6\text{-}119)$$

Generally, we will assume an autocorrelation or partial autocorrelation to be zero if the absolute value of its estimate is less than twice its standard error. It is useful to plot the limits $\pm 2S(\hat{\rho}_k)$ and $\pm 2S(\hat{\phi}_{kk})$ directly on the graphs of the functions.

The sample autocorrelation and partial autocorrelation functions of non-stationary time series die down extremely slowly from a value of one. If this type of behavior is exhibited, the usual approach is to compute the auto-correlation and partial autocorrelation functions for the first difference of the

TABLE 6-9 Behavior of Theoretical Autocorrelation and Partial Autocorrelation Functions for Stationary Models

MODEL	AUTOCORRELATION FUNCTION	PARTIAL AUTOCORRELATION FUNCTION
AR(p)	Tails off	Cuts off after lag p
MA(q)	Cuts off after lag q	Tails off
ARMA(p, q)	Tails off; exhibits damped sine wave after ($q - p$) lags	Tails off; exhibits damped sine wave after ($p - q$) lags

series. If these functions behave according to Table 6-9, then one degree of differencing is necessary to achieve stationarity. If not, then we must try successively higher-order differencing until stationary behavior is produced.

The actual identification of time series requires skill obtained by practice. Several excellent examples of identification are given in Box and Jenkins (1, Chapter 6).

Estimation. Once the time series has been tentatively identified, the usual procedure is to obtain the least-squares estimates of the model parameters. In Section 6-2 we defined a linear model as a relationship linear in the unknown parameters. It is easy to see that this implies that if a model is linear, then the partial derivative of the ε_t with respect to any parameter is not a function of the parameters. For example, consider the AR(p) process

$$\tilde{x}_t = \phi_1 \tilde{x}_{t-1} + \phi_2 \tilde{x}_{t-2} + \cdots + \phi_p \tilde{x}_{t-p} + \varepsilon_t$$

or

$$\varepsilon_t = \tilde{x}_t - \phi_1 \tilde{x}_{t-1} - \phi_2 \tilde{x}_{t-2} - \cdots - \phi_p \tilde{x}_p$$

Since

$$\frac{\partial \varepsilon_t}{\partial \phi_i} = \tilde{x}_{t-i}, \qquad i = 1, 2, \ldots, p$$

is not a function of the ϕ_i, we may estimate the parameters in an AR(p) process by *linear least squares*.

□**EXAMPLE 6-13**   We shall illustrate the above ideas by obtaining the linear least squares estimators for the AR(2) process

$$\tilde{x}_t = \phi_1 \tilde{x}_{t-1} + \phi_2 \tilde{x}_{t-2} + \varepsilon_t$$

Suppose N observations are available. Then we may write the data for the AR(2) model in matrix form as

$$\begin{bmatrix} \tilde{x}_3 \\ \tilde{x}_4 \\ \cdot \\ \cdot \\ \cdot \\ \tilde{x}_{N-1} \\ \tilde{x}_N \end{bmatrix} = \begin{bmatrix} \tilde{x}_2 & \tilde{x}_1 \\ \tilde{x}_3 & \tilde{x}_2 \\ \cdot & \cdot \\ \cdot & \cdot \\ \cdot & \cdot \\ \tilde{x}_{N-2} & \tilde{x}_{N-3} \\ \tilde{x}_{N-1} & \tilde{x}_{N-2} \end{bmatrix} \begin{bmatrix} \phi_1 \\ \phi_2 \end{bmatrix} + \begin{bmatrix} \varepsilon_3 \\ \varepsilon_4 \\ \cdot \\ \cdot \\ \cdot \\ \varepsilon_{N-1} \\ \varepsilon_N \end{bmatrix}$$

or

$$\mathbf{x} = \mathbf{Z}\boldsymbol{\phi} + \boldsymbol{\varepsilon}$$

Therefore, from the results of Section 6-2, the estimated autoregressive parameters are

$$\hat{\boldsymbol{\phi}} = (\mathbf{Z}'\mathbf{Z})^{-1}\mathbf{Z}'\mathbf{x}$$

Notice that we have used only the last $N - 2$ observations because the quantities x_0 and x_{-1}, required by the AR(2) process at time $t = 1$, do not exist. An alternate solution to this starting value problem is to set $x_0 = x_{-1} = 0$ and use the full set of N observations. If N is large, the least-squares estimators are insensitive to the latter approach.☐

Estimation of the moving average model parameters is not so simple. For example, consider the MA(1) process

$$\tilde{x}_t = \varepsilon_t - \theta_1 \varepsilon_{t-1}$$

or

$$\varepsilon_t = (1 - B\theta_1)^{-1} \tilde{x}_t$$

The first derivative is

$$\frac{d\varepsilon_t}{d\theta_1} = B(1 - B\theta_1)^{-2}$$

a function of the unknown parameter θ_1. Therefore, the parameters in models with moving average terms cannot be estimated by linear least squares. A treatment of *nonlinear* least squares is beyond the scope of this book, but rough estimates of the parameters may be obtained by applying direct search techniques to the sum of squares function

$$SS_E = \sum_{t=1}^{N} (x_t - \hat{x}_t)^2$$

Several efficient algorithms for nonlinear least squares are discussed at an elementary level by Draper and Smith (7), and a more advanced treatment is in Chapter 7 of Box and Jenkins (1).

Diagnostic Checking. If the fitted model is appropriate, it should transform the observations to a white noise process. Thus, a logical method of diagnostic checking is to compute the residuals, say $e_t = x_t - \hat{x}_t$, then construct and examine their autocorrelation function. If the model is appropriate, the residual autocorrelation function should have no structure to identify, that is, the auto-correlations should not differ significantly from zero for all lags greater than one. Box and Jenkins (1, Chapter 8) present additional methods of diagnostic checking, including a test for lack of fit. Careful residual analysis can often indicate potential improvements in the model.

Forecasting. Once the correct time series model has been identified, its parameters estimated, and diagnostic checks performed, the model may be used to generate forecasts that are optimal in a minimum mean square error sense. Denote the current period by T, and assume that we wish to forecast the signal in period $T + \tau$. Let $\hat{x}_{T+\tau}$ (or $\hat{\tilde{x}}_{T+\tau}$ if the series is corrected for the mean) represent the forecast for period $T + \tau$.

The forecasts may be obtained by taking expectation at origin T of the model written at time $T + \tau$. As a general rule, the forecast for period $T + \tau$ must be built up from the forecasts for periods $T + 1, T + 2, \ldots, T + \tau - 1$. In this procedure, the x_{T+j} that have not occurred at time T are replaced by their forecasts $\hat{x}_{T+j}$, the ε_{T-j} that have occurred are estimated from $e_{T-j} = x_{T-j} - \hat{x}_{T-j}$, and the ε_{T+j} that have not occurred are replaced by zeros. For example, consider the ARIMA(1, 1, 1) model, written at the end of time $T + \tau$:

$$x_{T+\tau} = (1 + \phi_1)x_{T+\tau-1} - \phi_1 x_{T+\tau-2} + \varepsilon_{T+\tau} - \theta_1 \varepsilon_{T+\tau-1}$$

On taking expectation at time T we find for $\tau = 1$

$$E[x_{T+1}] \equiv \hat{x}_{T+1} = (1 + \phi_1)x_T - \phi_1 x_{T-1} - \theta_1 e_T$$

since $E[\varepsilon_{T+1}] = 0$, and at the end of time T, ε_T may be estimated by the residual at time T, $e_T = x_T - \hat{x}_T$. For $\tau \geq 2$ we would obtain by similar reasoning

$$E[x_{T+\tau}] \equiv \hat{x}_{T+\tau} = (1 + \phi_1)\hat{x}_{T+\tau-1} - \phi_1 \hat{x}_{T+\tau-2}$$

It is also possible to generate the forecasts using the model expressed in terms of the ψ weights. In general, at origin T, we may write

$$x_{T+\tau} = \psi_1 \varepsilon_{T+\tau-1} + \cdots + \psi_{\tau-1}\varepsilon_{T+1}$$
$$+ \psi_\tau \varepsilon_T + \psi_{\tau+1}\varepsilon_{T-1} + \cdots + \varepsilon_{T+\tau} \quad (6\text{-}120)$$

However, at times $t > T$ we would replace the corresponding ε_t by zero and at times $t \leq T$ we would replace ε_t by e_t, so the forecast may be written as

$$\hat{x}_{T+\tau} = \hat{\psi}_\tau e_T + \hat{\psi}_{\tau+1} e_{T-1} + \cdots \quad (6\text{-}121)$$

The estimated weights $\hat{\psi}_\tau, \hat{\psi}_{\tau+1}, \ldots$ can be obtained from the $\{\hat{\phi}_i\}$ and $\{\hat{\theta}_j\}$ as previously described.

Probability limits on the forecast at any lead time may also be computed. The variance of the τ-step ahead forecast error is

$$V(\tau) = \left\{ 1 + \sum_{j=1}^{\tau-1} \psi_j^2 \right\} \sigma_\varepsilon^2$$

Thus, approximate $100(1 - \alpha)$ percent probability limits on the forecast for period $T + \tau$ would be computed from

$$\hat{x}_{T+\tau} \pm z_{\alpha/2} \left\{ 1 + \sum_{j=1}^{\tau-1} \hat{\psi}_j^2 \right\}^{1/2} s_\varepsilon \quad (6\text{-}122)$$

where s_ε is an estimate of σ_ε and $z_{\alpha/2}$ is a percentage point of the standard normal density such that $Pr\{Z \geq z_{\alpha/2}\} = \alpha/2$.

□**EXAMPLE 6-14** The weekly sales of a plastic container since its introduction nearly six years ago are shown in Table 6-10. The container is manufactured by an injection molding process, and has become widely used by

TABLE 6-10 Weekly Sales of A Plastic Container, x_t (300 Observations, Read Across)

592	1208	1864	2508	3160	3792	4419	5023	5626	6250
6903	7564	8223	8900	9569	10226	10823	11304	11785	12252
12724	13339	13940	14514	15102	15648	16212	16725	17217	17839
18463	19094	19718	20342	20966	21563	22167	22802	23431	24044
24562	25131	25676	26205	26718	27215	27767	28389	28974	29502
30022	30542	31044	31556	32092	32636	33196	33772	34347	34915
35502	36078	36643	37219	37804	38381	38974	39513	40044	40634
41237	41853	42430	42977	43529	44081	44657	45277	45917	46517
47100	47692	48241	48802	49399	49992	50601	51214	51855	52499
53127	53763	54387	54979	55591	56219	56843	57491	58127	58767
59264	59777	60298	60779	61348	61942	62521	63041	63576	64082
64550	65074	65594	66168	66664	67204	67711	68272	68837	69414
70012	70617	71211	71701	72214	72740	73283	73889	74509	75115
75743	76351	76971	77585	78169	78745	79309	79918	80563	81184
81761	82318	82855	83384	83921	84476	85028	85647	86275	86889
87493	88097	88737	89361	90017	90668	91313	91938	92575	93156
93669	94182	94695	95201	95679	96183	96783	97397	97989	98603
99223	99839	100478	101095	101724	102333	102902	103516	104157	104784
105411	106026	106626	107214	107806	108418	109048	109688	110321	110961
111586	112211	112828	113437	114038	114663	115288	115904	116519	117121
117688	118280	118916	119548	120130	120647	121210	121773	122350	122947
123540	124102	124705	125255	125769	126325	126893	127501	128133	128769
129402	129994	130491	130996	131565	132142	132719	133280	133863	134435
134997	135587	136187	136812	137424	138024	138648	139272	139909	140534
141171	141768	142329	142878	143423	144000	144585	145168	145738	146294
146832	147364	147920	148520	149128	149744	150342	150902	151407	151895
152396	152885	153390	153939	154520	155129	155742	156374	157006	157648
158295	158951	159655	160339	161039	161723	162410	163050	163698	164366
165031	165680	166321	166934	167559	168193	168882	169580	170277	170954
171602	172220	172852	173500	174136	174764	175364	175956	176560	177197

several pharmaceutical houses as a package for a prescription drug. From examining Table 6-10, we see that demand has increased steadily, causing an explosive behavior in the time series. The sample autocorrelation function for this series computed from Equation 6-115 is shown in Figure 6-12 (page 474). We see that the autocorrelation function does not die down rapidly, and conclude from this that the time series is nonstationary. Therefore, some degree of differencing will be necessary to produce stationarity.

The first difference of the time series, say $w_t = \nabla x_t$, $(t = 1, 2, \ldots, 300)$, shown in Table 6-11, is plotted in Figure 6-13 (page 475). From looking at these displays, it appears that the nonstationary behavior of the original series has been eliminated by differencing. This is confirmed by the sample autocorrelation function of w_t, shown in Figure 6-14a (page 475), which exhibits the sinusoidal decay of a stationary series.

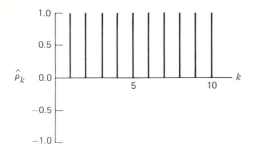

FIGURE 6-12. Sample auotocorrelation function for the data in Table 6-10.

TABLE 6-11 The First Difference of Weekly Plastic Container Sales, $w_t = \nabla x_t$

592	616	656	644	652	632	627	604	603	624
653	661	659	677	669	657	597	481	481	467
472	615	601	574	588	546	564	513	492	622
624	631	624	624	624	597	604	635	629	613
518	569	545	529	513	497	552	622	585	528
520	520	502	512	536	544	560	576	575	568
587	576	565	576	585	577	593	539	531	590
603	616	577	547	552	552	576	620	640	600
583	592	549	561	597	593	609	613	641	644
628	636	624	592	612	628	624	648	636	640
497	513	521	481	569	594	579	520	535	506
468	524	520	574	496	540	507	561	565	577
598	605	594	490	513	526	543	606	620	606
628	608	620	614	584	576	564	609	645	621
577	557	537	529	537	555	552	619	628	614
604	604	640	624	656	651	645	625	637	581
513	513	513	506	478	504	600	614	592	614
620	616	639	617	629	609	569	614	641	627
627	615	600	588	592	612	630	640	633	640
625	625	617	609	601	625	625	616	615	602
567	592	636	632	582	517	563	563	577	597
593	562	603	550	514	556	568	608	632	636
633	592	497	505	569	577	577	561	583	572
562	590	600	625	612	600	624	624	637	625
637	597	561	549	545	577	585	583	570	556
538	532	556	600	608	616	598	560	505	488
501	489	505	549	581	609	613	632	632	642
647	656	704	684	700	684	687	640	648	668
665	649	641	613	625	634	689	698	697	677
648	618	632	648	636	628	600	592	604	637

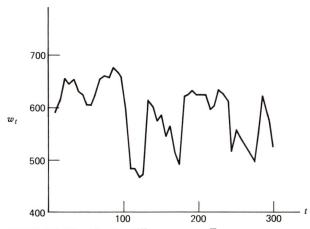

FIGURE 6-13. The first difference, $w_t = \nabla x_t$.

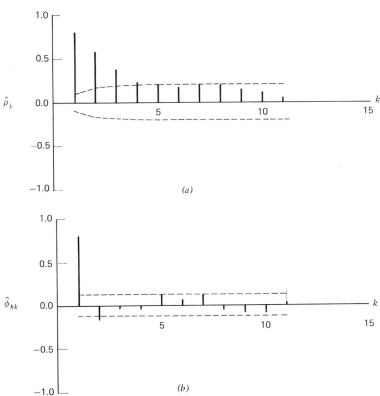

(a)

(b)

FIGURE 6-14. Sample autocorrelation and partial autocorrelation function for the series $w_t = \nabla x_t$. (a) Sample autocorrelation function. (b) Sample partial autocorrelation function.

Having determined that one degree of differencing is necessary, we must now select the proper model from the ARIMA(p, 1, q) class. The sample auto-correlation and partial autocorrelation functions for w_t are shown in Figure 6-14, along with two standard error limits (shown as dashed lines). The auto-correlation function tails off sinusoidally, while the partial autocorrelation function cuts off abruptly after two lags. This is indicative of the AR(2) process

$$\tilde{w}_t = \varepsilon_t + \phi_1 \tilde{w}_{t-1} + \phi_2 \tilde{w}_{t-2}$$

where the $\tilde{w}_t$ are the values of w_t corrected for the mean. Obtaining the least-squares estimators of ϕ_1 and ϕ_2 as indicated in Example 6-13, we find that $\hat{\phi}_1 = 0.93$ and $\hat{\phi}_2 = -0.17$. Therefore, the tentative ARIMA(2, 1, 0) process is

$$(1 - 0.93B + 0.17B^2) \nabla x_t = \varepsilon_t$$

or

$$x_t = x_{t-1} + 0.93(x_{t-1} - x_{t-2}) - 0.17(x_{t-2} - x_{t-3}) + \varepsilon_t$$

The autocorrelation function of the residuals generated from this model is shown in Figure 6-15. Since there are no significantly nonzero autocorrelations beyond lag zero, we would conclude that the residuals are a white noise process. Therefore, we conclude that the ARIMA(2, 1, 0) model is appropriate.

Forecasts of future observations may be obtained by taking expectation at origin T of the model written at time $T + \tau$, as described previously. This yields the forecasting equations

$$\hat{x}_{T+1} = x_T + 0.93(x_T - x_{T-1}) - 0.17(x_{T-1} - x_{T-2})$$
$$\hat{x}_{T+2} = \hat{x}_{T+1} + 0.93(\hat{x}_{T+1} - x_T) - 0.17(x_T - x_{T-1})$$
$$\hat{x}_{T+3} = \hat{x}_{T+2} + 0.93(\hat{x}_{T+2} - \hat{x}_{T+1}) - 0.17(\hat{x}_{T+1} - x_T)$$
$$\hat{x}_{T+\tau} = \hat{x}_{T+\tau-1} + 0.93(\hat{x}_{T+\tau-1} - \hat{x}_{T+\tau-2}) - 0.17(\hat{x}_{T+\tau-2} - \hat{x}_{T+\tau-3}), \quad \tau \geq 4$$

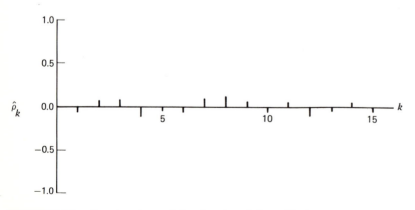

FIGURE 6-15. Sample autocorrelation function of the residuals.

To illustrate, we may forecast the observation at time 301 as

$$\hat{x}_{301} = x_{300} + 0.93(x_{300} - x_{299}) - 0.17(x_{299} - x_{298})$$
$$= 177{,}197 + 0.93(177{,}197 - 176{,}560) - 0.17(176{,}560 - 175{,}956)$$
$$= 177{,}695 \qquad \square$$

6-11 References

1. **Box, G. E. P., and G. M. Jenkins,** *Time Series Analysis, Forecasting and Control,* Holden-Day, San Francisco, 1970.

2. **Brown, R. G.,** *Smoothing, Forecasting and Prediction of Discrete Time Series,* Prentice-Hall, Englewood Cliffs, N.J., 1963.

3. **Brown, R. G.,** *Statistical Forecasting for Inventory Control,* McGraw-Hill Book Company, New York, 1959.

4. **Brown, R. G.,** *Decision Rules for Inventory Management,* Holt, Rinehart and Winston, New York, 1967.

5. **Chow, W. M.,** "Adaptive Control of the Exponential Smoothing Constant," *Journal of Industrial Engineering,* **XVI** (5), 314–317, 1965.

6. **Cohen, G. D.,** "Bayesian Adjustment of Sales Forecasts in Multi-Item Inventory Control Systems," *Journal of Industrial Engineering,* **XVII** (9), 474–479, 1966.

7. **Draper, N. R., and H. Smith,** *Applied Regression Analysis,* John Wiley and Sons, New York, 1968.

8. **Giffin, W. C.,** *Introduction to Operations Engineering,* Richard D. Irwin, Inc., Homewood, Ill., 1971.

9. **Graybill, F. A.,** *Introduction to Linear Statistical Models, Vol. I,* McGraw-Hill Book Company, New York, 1961.

10. **Montgomery, D. C.,** "An Introduction to Short-Term Forecasting," *Journal of Industrial Engineering,* **XIX** (10), 500–503, 1968.

11. **Montgomery, D. C.,** "Adaptive Control of Exponential Smoothing Parameters by Evolutionary Operation," *AIIE Transactions,* **2** (3), 268–269, 1970.

12. **Morrison, N.,** *Introduction to Sequential Smoothing and Prediction,* McGraw-Hill Book Company, New York, 1969.

13. **Roberts, S. D., and R. Reed,** "The Development of a Self-Adaptive Forecasting Technique," *AIIE Transactions,* **1** (4), 314–322, 1969.

14. **Trigg, D. W., and A. G. Leach,** "Exponential Smoothing with an Adaptive Response Rate," *Operational Research Quarterly,* **18** (1), 53–59, 1967.

15. **Winters, P. R.,** "Forecasting Sales by Exponentially Weighted Moving Averages," *Management Science,* **6** (3), 324–342, 1960.

6-12 Exercises

6-1 The number of lots of a particular fastener sold per week by a local company is shown below. Fit a straight line of the form $x_t = a + bt + \varepsilon_t$ to this data. Does it appear that this equation adequately represents the process? Estimate the error variance.

Week	1	2	3	4	5	6	7	8	9	10
Sales	78	74	80	79	80	83	82	85	78	89

6-2 The monthly maintenance expense in the manufacturing department of an electronics plant has been recorded for the past 18 months and is shown below. Fit a straight line of the form $x_t = a + bt + \varepsilon_t$ to this data. Estimate the error variance.

Month	1	2	3	4	5	6	7	8	9
Expense	880	812	830	1000	1160	1310	1360	1300	1250

Month	10	11	12	13	14	15	16	17	18
Expense	1315	1475	1590	1650	1920	2250	2180	2360	2400

6-3 The monthly sales of furniture in a city is thought to be linearly related to the number of new home starts. Data for the past year is available below. Fit a straight line to this data (can you use Equations 6-10 and 6-11 to estimate a and b? Why or why not?).

Monthly number of new home starts	100	110	96	114	120	160
Monthly furniture sales/$1000	46.1	47.3	45.0	47.2	48.1	53.8
Monthly number of new home starts	150	124	93	88	104	116
Monthly furniture sales/$1000	54.0	51.7	44.9	45.2	45.4	49.5

6-4   Suppose we wish to fit a regression model of the form

$$x_t = a + bt + ct^2 + \varepsilon_t$$

where ε is a random error such that $E(\varepsilon) = 0$ and $V(\varepsilon) = \sigma^2$. Find the least-squares estimators of the coefficients a, b, and c.

6-5   Using the results of Exercise 6-4, fit the model $x_t = a + bt + ct^2 + \varepsilon_t$ to the data below. Estimate the error variance. How many degrees of freedom are associated with experimental error?

t	1	2	3	4	5	6
x	9	13	15	22	35	50

6-6   *Weighted Simple Linear Regression.* Suppose the data for the simple linear regression model $x_t = a + bt + \varepsilon_t$ are such that we can no longer assume $V(\varepsilon_t)$ to be constant. Instead, $V(\varepsilon_t) = \sigma_t^2 = \sigma^2/w_t$, where the weights w_t are known constants. Show that the least-squares normal equations are

$$\hat{a} \sum_{t=1}^{T} w_t + \hat{b} \sum_{t=1}^{T} tw_t = \sum_{t=1}^{T} w_t x_t$$

$$\hat{a} \sum_{t=1}^{T} tw_t + \hat{b} \sum_{t=1}^{T} t^2 w_t = \sum_{t=1}^{T} tw_t x_t$$

6-7   Consider the data shown below, which represent the monthly delivery of a certain model automobile to a dealer.

Month	1	2	3	4	5	6	7	8	9	10	11	12	13
Deliveries	52	64	85	90	82	75	73	41	59	95	85	60	50

Fit the regression model

$$x_t = a_0 + a_1 \cos \frac{\pi t}{3} + a_2 \sin \frac{\pi t}{3} + \varepsilon_t$$

to these data using least squares.

6-8   Consider the data shown on page 480, which represents the past four years of demand for a double-knit polyester textile fabric.

MONTH	1968	1969	1970	1971
January	317	460	538	626
February	194	400	570	690
March	312	392	601	680
April	316	447	565	673
May	325	452	585	615
June	338	517	604	718
July	317	572	527	745
August	350	395	603	767
September	428	410	604	728
October	411	579	790	788
November	495	582	714	793
December	410	558	655	777

(a) Use a six-month moving average to forecast demand for a one-period lead time. Assume that a constant model is appropriate.

(b) Assume that a linear trend process is generating this data. Use a double moving average with $n = 6$ months to forecast demand for a one month lead time. Compare the results with those obtained in part (a).

6-9 For the data in Exercise 6-8, forecast demand for a one period lead time using simple exponential smoothing with $\alpha = 0.1$. Then repeat the forecasting procedure using double exponential smoothing ($\alpha = 0.1$). Which technique appears to give better results?

6-10 The monthly demand for a plastic container is shown below. Using

MONTH	1968	1969	1970	1971
January	143	189	359	332
February	138	326	264	244
March	195	289	315	320
April	225	293	361	437
May	175	279	414	534
June	389	552	647	830
July	454	674	836	1011
August	618	827	901	1081
September	770	1000	1104	1400
October	564	502	874	1123
November	327	512	683	713
December	235	300	352	487

the first two years of data, select an appropriate exponential smoothing forecasting technique. Then use this model to forecast the last two years of the data using a one period lead time. How well does this model seem to perform?

6-11 *Alternate Procedure for Linear Trend.* There are several approaches to forecasting linear trends through exponential smoothing. One alternate procedure often appearing in the literature involves the following:

$$\hat{x}_{T+\tau} = S_T + \frac{(1-\alpha)}{\alpha}\hat{b}_T + \tau\hat{b}_T$$

where $\hat{b}_T$, the estimator of the trend component, is

$$\hat{b}_T = \alpha(S_T - S_{T-1}) + (1-\alpha)\hat{b}_{T-1}$$

and $S_T = \alpha x_T + (1-\alpha)S_{T-1}$. Typically, this is called "exponential smoothing, corrected for trend." Give an explanation for the development of these equations. Show that they are equivalent to the double smoothing procedure of Section 6-4.2.

6-12 *Alternate Procedure for Linear Trend.* Consider an alternate forecasting procedure for linear trends, namely

$$\hat{x}_{T+\tau} = S_T + \frac{(1-\alpha)}{\alpha}\hat{b}_T + \tau\hat{b}_T$$

where $\hat{b}_T = \alpha(S_T - S_{T-1}) + (1-\alpha)\hat{b}_{T-1}$. Show that $\hat{x}_{T+\tau}$ is an unbiased estimator of $E(x_{T+\tau})$.

6-13 *Alternate Procedure for Linear Trend.* Consider the following procedure for forecasting a process with trend:

$$\hat{x}_{T+\tau} = \hat{a}(T) + \tau\hat{b}(T)$$

where $\hat{a}(T)$ is an estimate of the expected demand in period T and $\hat{b}(T)$ is an estimate of trend, computed at the end of period T by

$$\hat{a}(T) = \delta X_T + (1-\delta)[\hat{a}(T-1) + \hat{b}(T-1)]$$
$$\hat{b}(T) = \theta[\hat{a}(T) - \hat{a}(T-1)] + (1-\theta)\hat{b}(T-1)$$

where δ and θ are smoothing constants. Note that this is Winters' model without seasonality. Show that this procedure is equivalent to double exponential smoothing with a smoothing constant α if $\delta = \alpha(2-\alpha)$ and $h_2 = \alpha/(2-\alpha)$.

6-14 Consider the data sets shown below. For each set, use the first two years to select an appropriate exponential smoothing forecasting model. Then test the model by forecasting the last three years of data, using a one period lead time. Compute the tracking signal. Do any points fall out of control?

	A					B				
	1967	1968	1969	1970	1971	1967	1968	1969	1970	1971
January	205	190	245	216	156	84	49	50	69	55
February	212	212	220	205	210	49	45	57	45	45
March	178	238	220	140	205	46	28	62	72	42
April	218	244	190	216	178	41	58	48	42	99
May	255	215	148	195	216	43	47	42	62	34
June	236	198	205	180	212	75	48	26	53	52
July	208	168	198	210	238	94	48	87	34	48
August	195	186	201	220	228	26	69	95	68	51
September	180	208	198	218	195	31	84	46	57	68
October	172	205	224	238	219	84	75	93	48	65
November	246	210	245	295	164	74	80	66	92	55
December	200	205	235	218	215	94	41	67	74	62

6-15 Develop an exponential smoothing forecasting model for the data shown below, assuming we wish to use a one-period lead time. How does the performance of the model change if we wish to forecast two periods ahead? If we wish to forecast three periods ahead? Use the tracking signal to help detect differences in performance.

READ DOWN				
100	178	134	160	162
68	130	154	184	230
144	105	158	135	215
109	136	162	210	260
150	129	110	180	225
145	145	178	144	247
99	103	178	184	240
125	135	110	208	218
107	108	181	205	229
118	103	192	198	195
145	162	195	210	190
89	92	170	188	245

6-16 Consider the seasonal time series shown below. Use Winters' method with $\alpha = 0.2$, $\beta = 0.1$, and $\gamma = 0.2$ to forecast the last two years of data for a one-month lead time. Use the first two years of data to determine appropriate starting parameters for the model.

	1968	1969	1970	1971
January	391	388	398	380
February	350	375	343	370
March	385	355	325	332
April	295	340	343	334
May	324	288	345	281
June	290	230	301	240
July	290	320	315	318
August	315	300	320	390
September	309	335	360	371
October	350	401	348	328
November	328	400	412	329
December	390	390	402	402

6-17 Using the seasonal time series in Exercise 6-16, fit the model

$$x_t = a_1 + a_2 t + a_3 \sin \frac{2\pi t}{12} + a_4 \cos \frac{2\pi t}{12} + \varepsilon_t$$

Forecast the data with a one-month lead time using adaptive smoothing to update the coefficients in the model. Rework the problem assuming we wish to forecast two periods ahead.

6-18 Derive the estimates of the coefficients in the linear trend model

$$x_t = a_1 + a_2 t + \varepsilon_t$$

using the general adaptive smoothing approach. Show that the computations in this case are equivalent to double smoothing.

6-19 Suppose we wish to use an additive seasonal model, say

$$x_t = a + bt + c_t + \varepsilon_t$$

where $c_t = $ an additive seasonal effect. Develop a procedure similar to Winter's method for using this model.

6-20 The transition matrix $\mathbf{L}$ for adaptive smoothing can be written down by inspection of the terms in the model. Show that the following types of model terms yield the given transition matrices.

Linear model: $x_t = a_1 + a_2 t + \varepsilon_t,$ $\mathbf{L} = \begin{bmatrix} 1 & 0 \\ 1 & 1 \end{bmatrix}$

Trigonometric model: $x_t = \sin \omega t + \cos \omega t + \varepsilon_t,$

$$\mathbf{L} = \begin{bmatrix} \cos \omega & \sin \omega \\ -\sin \omega & \cos \omega \end{bmatrix}$$

Trigonometric model: $x_t = \sin \omega t + \cos \omega t + t \sin \omega t + t \cos \omega t + \varepsilon_t,$

$$\mathbf{L} = \begin{bmatrix} \cos \omega & \sin \omega & 0 & 0 \\ -\sin \omega & \cos \omega & 0 & 0 \\ \cos \omega & \sin \omega & \cos \omega & \sin \omega \\ -\sin \omega & \cos \omega & -\sin \omega & \cos \omega \end{bmatrix}$$

Exponential model: $x_t = e^{at} + te^{a(t-1)} + \varepsilon_t,$ $\mathbf{L} = \begin{bmatrix} e^a & 0 \\ 1 & e^a \end{bmatrix}$

Combinations: When the model is a combination of these forms, the transition matrix can be constructed by placing these simple matrices along the main diagonal.

6-21   The concentration of the output of a chemical process is an important quality characteristic. A series of concentration readings taken every two hours is shown below. Develop an appropriate model for forecasting future observations one period ahead.

READ DOWN						
17.1	16.9	16.7	17.3	17.5	17.8	18.1
17.0	16.8	17.4	17.2	17.4	17.5	17.5
16.6	17.4	17.2	17.4	17.6	18.1	17.4
16.3	17.1	17.4	16.8	17.3	17.5	17.4
16.1	17.0	17.0	17.1	17.0	17.4	17.6

6-22   Consider the irregular 12-point periodic function

$$x_t = a_0 + \sum_{j=1}^{4} \left[a_j \sin \frac{2\pi j t}{12} + b_j \cos \frac{2\pi j t}{12} \right] + \varepsilon_t$$

This model contains four harmonic frequencies and can describe almost any periodic process that is observed 12 times during the period of the lowest frequency. Write down the transition matrix and the equations for updating the coefficients. Describe how you would find the smoothing vector.

6-23 *A 13-Point Periodic Function.* Consider the model

$$x_t = a_0 + \sum_{j=1}^{4} \left[a_j \sin \frac{2\pi jt}{13} + b_j \cos \frac{2\pi jt}{13} \right] + \varepsilon_t$$

In this model, there are 13 observations during the period of the lowest frequency. Thus, this model would be applicable to situations in which the company observes sales in four-week accounting periods rather than calendar months. Write down the transition matrix and the equations for updating the coefficients. Describe how you would find the smoothing vector.

6-24 *A Growing Sine Wave Model.* The model

$$x_t = a_1 + a_2 t + (a_3 + a_4 t) \sin \frac{2\pi t}{12} + (a_5 + a_6 t) \cos \frac{2\pi t}{12} + \varepsilon_t$$

is called a growing sine wave model, as it can account for growing amplitude or shifting phase angles. Write down the transition matrix and the equations for updating the coefficients. How would you obtain the elements of the smoothing vector $\mathbf{h}$?

6-25 Suppose an appropriate time series model is thought to be

$$x_t = a_1 + a_2 c^t + \varepsilon_t$$

where c is an arbitrary constant. Derive equations for updating the estimates of a_1 and a_2 using adaptive smoothing with $\beta = 0.9$ and $c = 2$.

6-26 The viscosity of a chemical product is monitored from batch to batch. As it is an important quality characteristic, it seems desirable to forecast this value. Using the data below, develop an appropriate technique for

READ DOWN

8.6	8.3	9.7	9.2	9.7
8.4	8.1	9.5	8.8	9.9
8.3	8.1	9.5	8.7	10.0
8.3	8.1	9.5	8.8	10.1
8.1	8.4	9.5	9.3	10.2
8.2	8.5	9.9	9.6	9.4
8.3	8.7	9.7	10.0	9.2
8.5	9.0	9.5	9.4	9.6
8.1	9.3	9.1	9.8	9.5
8.1	9.3	8.9	8.9	8.6
7.9	9.5	9.3	9.3	9.0
8.0	9.6	9.0	9.4	9.6

forecasting the viscosity of the next batch. Test your model by applying a tracking signal.

6-27 Consider the forecasts made in Exercise 6-16 using Winters' model. Use a tracking signal based on the sum of the errors to monitor the last two years forecasts. Does this indicate that the model is performing adequately? Perform the same test using a tracking signal based on the smoothed error and compare the results.

6-28 The following information is available at time $t - 1$ about the probability distribution of demand for replacements for a valve in a large chemical plant. Suppose demand in the next three periods is 45, 58, and 69 units, respectively. For each period, find the updated probabilities and the new estimated cumulative distribution function using $\alpha = 0.1$. For each period, find θ_p such that the probability of demand less than θ_p is 0.85.

k	CLASS LIMIT X_k	PROBABILITY $\hat{p}_k(t - 1)$	$\hat{G}(X_k)$
0	0		0.00
1	20	0.20	0.20
2	40	0.20	0.40
3	50	0.20	0.60
4	60	0.30	0.90
5	65	0.10	1.00
6	70		

6-29 At the end of January, the probability distribution of demand for an aircraft spare part is as shown below.

k	CLASS LIMIT X_k	PROBABILITY $\hat{p}_k(t - 1)$	$\hat{G}(X_k)$
0	0		0.00
1	2	0.15	0.15
2	4	0.20	0.35
3	6	0.24	0.59
4	7	0.25	0.74
5	8	0.22	0.96
6	12	0.04	1.00

The demands for the next six months are as follows:

February	March	April	May	June	July
6	8	7	4	10	2

For each period, find the updated probabilities and the new estimated cumulative distribution function using $\alpha = 0.2$. For each period, find θ_p such that the probability of demand less than θ_p is 0.95.

6-30 Show that the smoothing procedure of Equation 6-93 yields unbiased estimates. Show that the variance of the kth estimated probability is

$$\sigma_{\hat{p}_k}^2 = \frac{\alpha}{2 - \alpha} p_k(1 - p_k)$$

6-31 Give an expression for an approximate $100(1 - \delta)$ percent confidence interval for the elements of the estimated probability vector $\hat{\mathbf{p}}(t)$ used in forecasting the probability distribution of demand, where δ is the level of significance.

6-32 We are interested in forecasting the probability distribution of a random variable using $\alpha = 0.10$. Before observing the next value of x, the results to date were the following:

k	CLASS LIMIT $X_{k-1} < x \le X_k$	PROBABILITY $\hat{p}_k$	$\hat{G}(X_k)$
1	$0 < x \le 100$	0.10	0.10
2	$100 < x \le 200$	0.20	0.30
3	$200 < x \le 300$	0.30	0.60
4	$300 < x \le 400$	0.20	0.80
5	$400 < x \le 600$	0.20	1.00

(a) If the next observation is $x = 190$, what would be the revised estimates of the probabilities?

(b) Compute an approximate 95 percent confidence interval estimate for p_4.

6-33 The capacity of a motel is 100 rooms. Assume that we have estimated the demand for these rooms to be a Poisson random variable with mean 80 rooms per day.

(a)   What is the probability that the motel has more than one vacancy?

(b)   What is the probability distribution of demand over a three-day lead time? What is the probability that at least one room is vacant over the three-day period?

(c)   Management is considering adding 10 rooms to the motel capacity. If they do, this will increase the basic cost of operation (including mortgage interest) from $500 per day to $600 per day. The average cost of a room is $12 per day. Does this capacity expansion seem wise in view of your forecast of demand?

6-34   A motel has records showing the number of rooms occupied each night over a long interval. These data are to be used to develop a probability distribution for the number of rooms demanded on a night. The problem is that many nights the motel has been full and no record of unfilled demand on those nights is available. How would you proceed to use the historical data? How would you proceed if it were desired to update the model periodically in the future? Does the use for the probability model affect your choice of a forecasting procedure?

6-35   Consider the data shown in Exercise 6-15. Using Winters' method with $\alpha = 0.2$, $\beta = 0.1$, and $\gamma = 0.2$, forecast the last two years of data, assuming that forecasts are to be made monthly for the total demand in the next three months. Use the first three years of data to establish starting parameters for the model.

6-36   For the data shown in Exercise 6-8, assume that a linear trend process is an appropriate model. Use double smoothing with $\alpha = 0.1$ to make monthly forecasts for a four-period lead time for the last three years of data. Use the first year of data to determine appropriate starting values for the model parameters.

6-37   For the seasonal data shown in Exercise 6-16, use the model

$$x_t = a_1 + a_2 t + a_3 \sin 30t + a_4 \cos 30t + a_5 \sin 60t + a_6 \cos 60t + \varepsilon_t$$

to forecast the last two years of data for a one-period lead time. Use the first two years to help determine values for the a_i. Use Equation 6-82 to revise the coefficients in the forecasting equation every period. The forecast is computed from Equation 6-83 with $\tau = 1$. Note that the arguments of the sine and cosine functions are expressed in degrees. How does this differ from the models discussed in the text?

6-38   A company is introducing a new product line, and has no historical information to assist them in developing a forecasting procedure. The operations research department, working together with the sales manager, has estimated that demand is probably normally distributed with variance $\sigma_\varepsilon^2 = 100$. A reasonable prior density for the unknown mean a is normal with mean 60 and variance 4. Set up a Bayes estimator for the unknown demand. Now suppose the first five demands are 48, 62, 74, 60, and 54. Revise the Bayes estimator successively in light of each new observation.

6-39   A manufacturer of style goods is introducing a new product. He suspects that demand will follow a linear trend process and that the variance of demand is $\sigma_\varepsilon^2 = 50$. Logical prior densities for the unknown parameters are $a \sim N(50, 4)$ and $b \sim N(10, 1)$. Set up a Bayesian procedure for forecasting demand. The first six observations are 68, 74, 77, 90, 98, and 110. Revise the Bayes estimator successively in light of each new observation.

6-40   Consider the Bayes estimators, Equations 6-104 and 6-105, for the parameters a' and b in the linear trend model. These estimators smooth the current least-squares estimators with the prior means. Develop alternate forms for $b*$ and $(a')*$ that smooth the most recent *observation* with the previous Bayes estimators, that is, find the constants $\theta_1, \theta_2, \phi_1$, and ϕ_2 in

$$b*(n) = \theta_1 x_n + \theta_2 b*(n - 1)$$
$$[a'(n)]* = \phi_1 x_n + \phi_2 [a'(n - 1)]*$$

6-41   *Blending Prior Information and Observational Data: The Constant Model.* Suppose that demand for an item can be described by the constant model $x_t = a + \varepsilon_t$, where $V(x_t) = \sigma_\varepsilon^2$ is known and $E(x_t) = a$ is unknown. A prior estimate of a is a_0 and the variance of a_0 is $V(a_0) = \sigma_{a_0}^2$. A simple approach to estimating a (and hence, forecasting $x_{t+\tau}$) is to blend the prior estimate a_0 with the current observed average demand, say $\bar{x}$, to obtain

$$\hat{a} = (1 - \theta)\bar{x} + \theta a_0$$

where θ is simply a weighting coefficient. One useful criterion for selecting θ is to minimize the variance of forecast error, that is, $V(x_t - \hat{a})$. Find the value of θ that minimizes $V(x_t - \hat{a})$, assuming that $Cov(\bar{x}, a_0) = 0$.

6-42   *Blending Prior Information and Observational Data: A Linear Trend Model.* Suppose the linear trend model $x_t = a' + b(t - \bar{t}) + \varepsilon_t$ describes the time series process. Assume that $V(x_t) = \sigma_\varepsilon^2$. Prior subjective estimates of the unknown parameters a' and b, say a_0' and b_0, are available where $V(a_0') = \sigma_{a_0}^2$ and $V(b_0) = \sigma_{b_0}^2$. The forecast for period $t + \tau = T$ is to be obtained by blending these prior estimates with the least-squares estimates of a' and b at time t, say $\hat{a}'$ and $\hat{b}$, as

$$\hat{x}_T = \theta \hat{a}' + (1 - \theta)a_0' + [\delta \hat{b} + (1 - \delta)b_0](T - \bar{T})$$

Assuming the forecast errors $\hat{x}_T - x_T$ to be independent random variables, find the weights (θ and δ) that minimize the variance of forecast error.

6-43 Weekly demand for a spare part is assumed to have the following Poisson distribution:

$$p(x \mid \lambda) = e^{-\lambda}\lambda^x/x!, \qquad x = 0, 1, 2, \ldots$$

The mean, λ, of the demand distribution is not known with certainty, but is assumed to have a gamma density

$$g(\lambda) = \frac{b^a}{(a-1)!} \lambda^{a-1} e^{-b\lambda}, \qquad \lambda > 0$$

where a and b are parameters having subjectively established values. In the week following the establishment of this prior distribution, d parts were demanded. What is the revised (posterior) distribution of λ? What value would you use for the mean of the Poisson distribution in order to make probability statements about weekly usage? How would you operate this Bayesian procedure on a weekly basis?

6-44 Verify the recursive form for W_T given by Equation 6-33.

6-45 How would you establish an initial value, $\hat{\Delta}(0)$, for the smoothed mean absolute deviation?

6-46 What role, if any, do goodness-of-fit procedures such as the Kolmogorov-Smirnov test and the Chi-square test play in developing forecasts?

6-47 What is the probability that a normally distributed random variable will differ from its mean by more than twice its mean absolute deviation?

6-48 Simple exponential smoothing with $\alpha = 0.10$ is used weekly on a constant process with a mean of 100. Suppose for one week *only* the demand comes from a constant process having a mean of 300. In future weeks the process mean reverts to its original level of 100. What is the expected *bias* in the smoothed statistic computed t weeks after the week of the impulse?

6-49 *A Hybrid Exponential Smoothing Model.* A soft drink bottler is interested in forecasting the number of cases of product to produce each day. He decides to smooth the daily demand x_t in the usual fashion, assuming a linear trend model. The bottler knows that the daily temperature has a pronounced effect on soft drink sales. Let $\hat{F}_{T+1}$ be the estimate of the maximum temperature for tomorrow, made at the end of the current day. He decides to use the decision rule, add

$$\beta \begin{cases} (\hat{F}_{T+1} - 85°), & \hat{F}_{T+1} > 85° \\ 0, & 65° \le \hat{F}_{T+1} \le 85° \\ (65° - \hat{F}_{T+1}), & \hat{F}_{T+1} < 65° \end{cases}$$

cases to the forecast of demand, where $\beta = 100$. Write a single fore-casting equation to incorporate *both* the smoothed statistics and the temperature effect. Show how the smoothed statistics would be updated.

6-50 Suppose simple exponential smoothing is used to forecast demand from a constant process, $x_t = a + \varepsilon_t$, where $V(x_t) = \sigma_\varepsilon^2$. Show that the variance of the forecast, $\hat{x}_{T+\tau} = S_T$, is $\sigma_{\hat{x}}^2 = \left(\dfrac{\alpha}{2 - \alpha}\right)\sigma_\varepsilon^2$ and that the variance of the forecast error, $e_t = x_t - \hat{x}_t$, is $\sigma_e^2 = \left(\dfrac{2}{2 - \alpha}\right)\sigma_\varepsilon^2$.

6-51 Suppose an N-period moving average is used to forecast demand from a constant process, $x_t = a + \varepsilon_t$, where $V(x_t) = \sigma_\varepsilon^2$. Find the variance of the following:

(a) The forecast for period $T + \tau$, $\hat{x}_{T+\tau} = M_T$.

(b) The cumulative forecast, $\hat{X}_w(T) = \displaystyle\sum_{t=T+1}^{T+w} \hat{x}_t$.

(c) The forecast error, $e_t = x_t - \hat{x}_t$.

(d) The cumulative forecast error, $E_w = X_w(T) - \hat{X}_w(T)$

$$= \sum_{t=T+1}^{T+w} e_t.$$

6-52 First-order exponential smoothing is used to forecast demand from a constant process, $x_t = a + \varepsilon_t$, where $V(x_t) = \sigma_\varepsilon^2$. The tracking signal usually has as its numerator one of the following two estimators of the expected forecast error:

$$Y(T) = Y(T - 1) + e_T, \quad \text{or} \quad Z(T) = \alpha e_T + (1 - \alpha)Z(T - 1)$$

where $e_T = x_T - \hat{x}_T$. Show that

$$\sigma_Y^2 = \left(\frac{1}{1 - \beta^2}\right)\sigma_\varepsilon^2 \quad \text{and} \quad \sigma_Z^2 = \left[\frac{\alpha}{(1 + \beta)^2}\right]\sigma_\varepsilon^2$$

where $\beta = 1 - \alpha$.

6-53 The president of a large corporation is interested in predicting the monthly sales of his firm. He believes sales to be growing linearly, and as he is a Bayesian, is willing to give you his opinion as to the expected sales level in the current month and the sales increase from month to month, both in the form of probability distributions. He wants to develop a forecasting system, based on Bayesian methods, to predict demand by month up to a year in the future. The forecasts are to be made at the end of each month, after using the latest sales figures to revise the model, always projecting ahead 12 months. Develop a procedure for doing this.

6-54 Modern inventory control systems often require an estimate of the standard deviation of demand over the replenishment lead time in order to compute safety stocks or reorder points. Let x_t be the demand in period t, $t = 1, 2, \ldots, T$. Consider the following methods of estimating the standard deviation of x computed at time T and denoted by $\hat{\sigma}_x(T)$:

(a) $\hat{\sigma}_x(T) = \sqrt{\sum_{t=1}^{T} (x_t - \bar{x})^2 / (T - 1)}$, where $\bar{x} = \dfrac{1}{T} \sum_{t=1}^{T} x_t$

(b) $\hat{\sigma}_x(T) = \dfrac{1.25}{T} \sum_{t=1}^{T} |x_t - \bar{x}|$

(c) $\hat{\sigma}_x(T) = \sqrt{\alpha(x_T - \hat{x}_T)^2 + (1 - \alpha)\hat{\sigma}_x^2(T - 1)}$, $\quad 0 < \alpha < 1$

What can you say about the relative accuracy or efficiency of these methods? Which method would you be likely to choose?

6-55 Suppose that demand for a product over the replenishment lead time is known to be Poisson distributed. Denote total lead time demand by X_τ, and *average* lead time demand by $\bar{X}_\tau$. Consider using as an estimator of the standard deviation of demand the statistic

$$\hat{\sigma}_x = \sqrt{\bar{X}_\tau}$$

Do you suspect that this is a reasonable estimator? Why or why not?

6-56 Consider the linear filter model (6-106). If the weights ψ_i, $(i = 1, 2, \ldots)$, form a convergent series the process x_t is stationary, and if they diverge the process is nonstationary. Give an argument as to why this is so.

6-57 The linear filter model (6-106) can be written in another form as a linear combination of the previous $\tilde{x}_{t-j}$ and the current ε_t, say

$$\tilde{x}_t = \sum_{j=1}^{\infty} \pi_j \tilde{x}_{t-j} + \varepsilon_t$$

Find a general relationship between the ψ weights in (6-106) and the π weights.

6-58 Show that the AR(p) process given in Equation 6-107 is just a special case of the linear filter model (6-106). Note that this is equivalent to showing that the AR(p) process is *invertible* to an infinite-order moving average process. Are any conditions necessary on the ϕ_i to insure invertibility? Compare this with the invertibility conditions for a moving average process.

6-59 *Autocorrelation Function of an* AR(p) *Process.* An important recurrence relation for the AR(p) process

$$\tilde{x}_t = \phi_1 \tilde{x}_{t-1} + \phi_2 \tilde{x}_{t-2} + \cdots + \phi_p \tilde{x}_{t-p} + \varepsilon_t$$

is obtained by multiplying both sides by $\tilde{x}_{t-k}$, taking expectation, and dividing by σ_x^2. Show that this recurrence relation is the difference equation

$$\rho_k = \phi_1 \rho_{k-1} + \phi_2 \rho_{k-2} + \cdots + \phi_p \rho_{k-p}, \qquad k \geq 1$$

6-60 *Continuation of Exercise* 6-59. For the stationary AR(1) process, the difference equation in Exercise 6-59 becomes

$$\rho_k = \phi_1 \rho_{k-1}, \qquad k \geq 1$$

Show that the solution to this difference equation is

$$\rho_k = \phi_1^k, \qquad k \geq 0$$

Graph the theoretical autocorrelation function for an AR(1) process with ϕ_1 positive. Repeat the graph for ϕ_1 negative.

6-61 *Continuation of Exercise* 6-59. Using the difference equation in Exercise 6-59, show that a reasonable estimate of ϕ_1 in an AR(1) process is

$$\hat{\phi}_1 = \hat{\rho}_1$$

and that reasonable estimates of ϕ_1 and ϕ_2 in an AR(2) process are

$$\hat{\phi}_1 = \frac{\hat{\rho}_1(1 - \hat{\rho}_1)}{1 - \hat{\rho}_1^2}$$

and

$$\hat{\phi}_2 = \frac{\hat{\rho}_2 - \hat{\rho}_1^2}{1 - \hat{\rho}_1^2}$$

Explain why these estimates are sometimes called *Yule-Walker estimates*.

6-62 Box and Jenkins (1, p. 69) show that the theoretical autocorrelation function for an MA(1) process is

$$\rho_1 = \frac{-\theta_1}{1 + \theta_1^2}$$

and $\rho_k = 0$ for $k = 2, 3, \ldots$. Using this relationship, find an estimator for the parameter θ_1 in terms of the estimated autocorrelation coefficient $\hat{\rho}_1$. For an invertible process, find a range of feasible values for ρ_1.

6-63   Write the forecast function at time $T + \tau$ for the following processes:

   (a)   AR(1)

   (b)   MA(2)

   (c)   ARMA(2, 1)

   (d)   ARMA(1, 2)

   (e)   ARIMA(2, 1, 1)

   (f)   ARIMA(2, 1, 0)

   (g)   ARIMA(1, 2, 1)

6-64   Consider the data in Exercise 6-8. Compute the autocorrelation and partial autocorrelation functions and determine the appropriate model. Estimate the model parameters.

6-65   Repeat Exercise 6-64 using the data in Exercise 6-26.

chapter 7
Systems Design and Implementation

This chapter discusses some practical considerations in using operations research methodology, especially prescriptive models such as those described in previous chapters, in management systems for production and inventory control. The discussion is brief and confined to specifics relevant to the development of production-inventory systems. It is not our intention to give a general treatment of operations research or systems design methodology; these subjects are well-covered in existing literature.

Initially, we shall discuss the development of production-inventory systems and then consider the operation of these systems.

7-1 The System Development Process

The development of an improved management system consists of the following sequence of activities:

1. Problem identification and definition.

2. Development of a design for the improved system (often called a *conceptual design*).

3. Economic justification of the improved system.

4. Detailed design and implementation.

At the conclusion of the system development phase, the management system should be operating routinely without need for assistance from those who developed the system.

7-1.1 Problem Identification

Typically, a project for the development of an improved production-inventory system has its origin with one or more managers who are unhappy about what they perceive to be signs of poor performance. A marketing manager may be concerned about noncompetitive delivery promises, late deliveries, or out-of-stock conditions. A production manager may be displeased with short production runs, the number of setups and changeovers, unrealistic production goals, and idle machines and labor. A controller may be alarmed by high inventory levels or the amount of overtime and subcontracting required to meet the schedule. Often the situation has degenerated to an open conflict between marketing and manufacturing, with each blaming the other for the apparent problems that exist. As a result of concern over these symptoms of poor production planning, a study of the problem area is authorized, directed either by internal staff or outside consultants.

The first step for the study team is to become familiar with the current state of affairs. This will involve interviews with people in marketing, production, production planning, controllership, and so on, visits to plants and customer service centers, and collection and analysis of a large amount of data. The following list illustrates some of the information to be gathered in each major sector of the system:

A. Marketing (merchandising, sales)
    1. Description of the product line. Major classifications; number of items within each class; complementary items; substitutable items.

2. Volatility of product line. Number of new items introduced each season and number of old items phased out; average life of an item.
3. Items produced to inventory and items produced to order, under current policies.
4. Nature of the market. Number and type of customers; distribution channels.
5. Characteristics of customer orders. Completeness; delivery time allowed; effect of late deliveries or partial shipments.
6. Characteristics of demand by product line. Seasonality; special promotions; trends over life cycle of an item; sales volume.
7. How marketing managers see their role in planning production and inventories. Interaction with production and production planning; relevant marketing policies; marketing responsibilities (for inventories, for example).
8. Extent to which marketing managers understand the general principles of production and inventory management and the effect of their decisions on production and inventories.
9. Forecasting procedures. How forecasts for financial planning and production planning are developed; frequency; accuracy; reasons for forecast errors.
10. Pricing policies. Discount schedules.
11. Sales histories for selected items.

B. Production

1. Facilities. Plants and warehouses in the system; processing centers and machine groups; capacities; current utilization.
2. Production processes. Processes by which each product can be produced; number and type of in-process items.
3. Inventory accumulations. Where in the system; capacity constraints; effect of shortages.
4. Lead times for production at the various stages.
5. Costs for selected items. Variable production costs; change-over and setup costs; overtime costs; economics of changing production rates.
6. Capacity changes. Feasibility; economics of changing work force levels.
7. How production managers see their role in planning production and inventories. Interaction with marketing and production planning; production responsibilities (for meeting a given schedule, for example).
8. Extent to which production managers understand marketing and customer service considerations.
9. Production histories for selected items.

C. Production planning and others (financial, customer service, data processing)
1. Present production planning system. Policies; role of central planning group; role of plant production planning and scheduling; information flow; frequencies.
2. Data processing system. Order processing; inventory accounting; production reporting; reports and frequency; inquiry capabilities.
3. Forecasting procedures. Past performance.
4. Inventory histories for selected items.
5. Inventory holding costs.
6. Explicit description of how production planning and scheduling decisions are made.
7. Procurement and subcontracting decisions.
8. Economics of shortages of finished goods or late deliveries.
9. Experience with mathematical programming or other quantitative decision procedures.
10. Personnel. Competency; analytical capability; understanding of principles and techniques; staffing.

The preceding list will seem long and tedious to many readers; however, those who have participated in such studies probably will find the list incomplete. Our point is that a great deal of information must be collected from all relevant functional units of the organization before one is in a position to define the problem and structure an improved system.

Evaluation of the collected information to determine if there are problems, and, if so, what the causes are, is largely an art, requiring experience, intelligence, and wisdom. The performance of the existing system must be analyzed to define areas for improvement and the feasibility of proceeding with the design of an improved system must be assessed.

If the decision is to proceed, the scope of the new system must be defined. This might involve a statement of the product lines, inventory points, and facilities to be included, as well as the extent to which the subsystems of forecasting, production planning, capacity planning, scheduling (loading and sequencing), and inventory control are to be reworked.

To further define the problem, objectives must be established for the system. Often these are in the form of constraints imposed by policies, such as delivery time or inventory investment; others are quantifiable factors, such as inventory costs and production change costs, which when summed, create the objective function for system operating decisions.

Finally, the sources of uncertainty in the system must be identified and evaluated. A major role of the production-inventory control system is to minimize the impact of uncertainty on the organization's performance. An understanding of where uncertainty arises, the significance of each type, and the possibility of probabilistic description is necessary to effectively design such a system.

7-1.2 Conceptual Design

In this phase of the development process, alternatives for system design are generated and analyzed. Usually this is done by developing subsystem designs and integrating them to form the whole system. For example, there may be subsystems for forecasting, work force planning, production planning, machine loading, materials purchasing, and finished goods inventory control. Naturally, these systems cannot be treated independently and some coordination is required between their designers. This is true also if data processing systems, such as order processing, production reporting, inventory accounting, and sales reporting, are being redesigned at the same time as the production control system.

The role of mathematical models usually is to analyze the existing state of the production-inventory system in light of forecasts of future requirements and stated management goals in order to determine actions to be taken, such as ordering material, changing the production rate, and assigning priorities to jobs. Once a model of a decision problem has been formulated, it should be tested for validity and feasibility. If the model recommends courses of action that line managers would never adopt, the reason is that some objectives or constraints have been overlooked, and the model is not a valid representation of the real problem. Initial formulations of linear programming models, for example, often lack validity in production planning applications.

Assuming a valid model can be formulated, the question of its feasibility arises. Are the data acquisition and reduction requirements reasonable? Is the required computer time prohibitive? Is there enough technical talent in the organization to operate and maintain the model? Are managers who are to use the output of the model able to understand its significance and can they be sold on the utility of the analytical approach? Are conditions likely to change and cause the model to become obsolete? All of these questions bear on the feasibility of incorporating the mathematical model into the system.

It is desirable that a model be viewed as an analytical tool that either *describes* expected results from a given decision or, through analysis, *recommends* (not *prescribes*) actions to be taken. Except for routine inventory control policies, the output of prescriptive models is only one input to a manager who must actually make the decision. For the model to be useful, the manager must understand its assumptions and limitations and should know how to use its analytical capabilities most effectively. This requires an educational program, usually on a continuing basis.

The conceptual design of the improved system should be described in a formal report that should include an economic justification. This serves as the basis for deciding on implementation.

7-1.3 Economic Justification

The cost of the improved system must be justified in the same manner as one would justify capital investment in new machinery. The new system will require an initial expenditure for detailed development and installation. This can be thought of as an investment that must be recovered with a return over the life of the system. Once the new system is in operation, there will be periodic costs for operation and maintenance. These costs can be more or less than those of the old system. If mathematical models are imbedded in the decision-making procedures of the new system, operating costs will probably be higher, because of the technical personnel required to maintain the system and continually educate others in the use of the models.

System development costs can be estimated with good accuracy by experienced analysts, once the activities necessary to implement the system have been defined and the time period for installation has been decided upon. The use of CPM methods (see Section 5-3) to aid in planning the implementation also facilitates cost estimation. Development costs are primarily for manpower, travel, and computer time.

Estimation of system operating costs should be relatively easy, assuming that the conceptual design is in sufficient detail. One needs to know the proposed organization and the volume of transactions and analyses in order to predict manpower and computer costs. By also estimating the operating costs of the present system, one can determine the change expected if the proposed system is installed.

Benefits from the new system can accrue from increased sales revenue or decreased costs of production, distribution, inventories, and shortages. Sales might increase because of better delivery capability stimulating demand, or because improved utilization of facilities effectively increases output that can be sold. Production cost savings can arise from larger lot sizes, fewer setups, better sequencing to reduce changeover costs, smoother production and work force levels, and reductions in the use of overtime or less efficient production processes. Distribution costs can be reduced by improved locations of inventories and by better assignment of production to plants or customer orders to warehouses. Inventory costs can be reduced through improved forecasts, which allow smaller safety stocks and reduce the risk of obsolescence, or by improved scheduling, which cuts the in-process inventory (and for most systems this would also reduce the production lead time, thereby lowering the safety stock requirements at the finished goods inventory). Shortage losses can be averted by improved inventory availability or by better scheduling to meet due dates. The nature and components of each of these types of cost have been discussed in prior chapters.

It can be a major problem to estimate the benefits from the improved system. Unless the current situation is extremely bad, for example, where a 10 percent decrease in the average inventory investment will justify the new system and experience strongly indicates that this reduction is attainable, some analysis must be done. A common approach is to simulate the operation of the proposed system assuming it had been used over, say, the past two years. The simulated performance of the proposed system is then compared with the actual performance of the old system during the same period of time. Use of actual historical data for simulation purposes is sometimes referred to as *retrospective simulation*. Naturally, if the future is expected to differ appreciably from the immediate past, simulation tests should use anticipated conditions. In this case, there is the additional problem of predicting how the existing system will perform in the future.

Once the development costs and year-by-year changes in operating costs and benefits have been estimated, several measures of effectiveness can be computed for the new system. If a life for recovery of the investment is specified, the rate of return on investment can be computed. However, because of uncertainty about the life of the system, one may place more emphasis on the payback period, computed either with or without a required return on investment. The payback period approach is a breakeven analysis, with system life as the breakeven variable. Together with a list of the intangible (nonquantifiable) factors bearing on the decision, these measures serve as the basis for evaluating the proposed system.

If the proposed system is approved, data on the performance of the existing system should be used to establish benchmarks by which the actual performance of the new system can be compared once it is installed. These benchmarks should be agreed to by all concerned prior to implementation.

7-1.4 Implementation

This phase of the system development process involves detailed design and installation. Analytical procedures (models) must be refined, programmed, tested, and documented. Data requirements must be defined and information systems developed to acquire and organize the input for models and management reports. Programs must be written to prepare reports summarizing the output of the models. All computer and data processing procedures must be tested and documented.

The noncomputerized portion of the system must be developed. Responsibilities for various aspects of system operation and maintenance must be defined and assigned to appropriate persons in marketing, production, production planning, data processing, systems, etc. These people must be educated in the overall operation of the system, the details of their responsibilities, the nature of the information to be provided them, and the relevant considerations in decisions they must make and information they must supply to others. When quantitative methods are a part of the system, care must be taken to tailor the educational approach to the individual. While a systems analyst may find an algebraic statement of a linear programming model interesting and informative, a marketing manager will not.

Implementation activities should be planned carefully and be closely controlled. As we mentioned earlier, critical path planning methods are useful for these purposes.

7-1.5 Personnel and Other Resources

From the foregoing discussion, it is obvious that a number of types of people must actively participate in the development of the system. They fall into four major categories:

1. Management systems analysts.
2. Data processing specialists.
3. Line managers.
4. Staff managers.

The first category includes individuals with the executive capability to plan and direct phases of the project, as well as technical specialists in the design of such systems and in mathematical methods of operations research. Also, there are data processing systems analysts and computer programmers required to convert the system design into a functioning information system.

The participation of operating personnel from the outset of the project is essential. Management representatives from marketing and production should be an integral part of the system development team. Naturally, managers from other areas, such as production planning, materials management, customer service, data processing (operations), purchasing, and traffic would be included as appropriate. Failure to include these people can result in implementation difficulties and ineffective system performance once installed. They must believe the system can help improve their performance or they will not use it properly. Throughout the system design effort, it should be remembered that *it is their system*.

Other resources required in addition to the system development team are computer time for testing programs and models, management time for interviews, and clerical time for gathering data and typing reports and manuals.

7-2   System Operation

In this section, we briefly comment on certain aspects of the system once it has been designed and installed. They involve obtaining the most effective use of the analytical procedures in the system, maintenance of the system, education of personnel, and the role of the system designers after the system is in operation.

7-2.1   Routine Decisions

The mathematical models and other analytical procedures of the system that provide recommended courses of action to management on a routine, periodic basis should be continually monitored to evaluate the quality of their output, the degree and method of use of the output by managers, problems being experienced, and the quality of decisions made by the model-manager combination. The objectives are to see that models are "fine-tuned" to current conditions, to insure that managers are making proper use of the analytical tools, and to identify areas for improvement in system operation.

To aid in this process, certain reports may be prepared periodically for review by higher management, as well as by the systems analysts. For example, the accuracy of a forecasting system could be monitored by comparing actual versus forecasted sales for certain products or product lines, say, by month for the past 12 months. This could be done for both the statistical forecast and the forecast finally decided on by management.

Periodically, performance measures, such as turnover rates, percentage of orders delivered on time, average inventory levels, and machine efficiencies should be reported, showing historical as well as current results to allow observation of trends.

After the new system has been in operation about a year, comparison of current performance with the performance benchmarks established for the old system should be made.

7-2.2   Nonroutine Decisions

Once the system is operating routinely, systems analysts can begin to develop new uses for the models. A linear programming model of a production system might be used along with price-demand curves to evaluate the effect of contemplated price changes, or it might be used to judge the impact of a new product on operations, or it could aid in determining the desirability of capital investment for capacity expansion. The possibility of using production planning models to answer "what if" questions is highly significant and should not be overlooked.

7-2.3 Maintenance

Mathematical models used on a periodic basis, such as linear programming, require continued maintenance. Products are added or dropped, capacities are changed, costs or standards are revised, and policies are modified. These necessitate changing certain of the variables and parameters in the model or modifying the structure of the model.

Hopefully, the system designers will carefully consider maintenance problems and develop procedures that permit operating personnel to routinely modify the models. This is important, because if changes are not made promptly, the model becomes obsolete and is not used.

Checks should be made periodically on the accuracy of information in the system. Source data, current status information, and parameters of the models can be monitored by sampling or by specially prepared error checking programs.

7-2.4 Education

Education of personnel involved in system operation is essential. Personnel transfers, reorganization, initial misunderstandings, and forgetfulness result in a deterioration of system performance unless there is a continuing program of training. People must be reminded of the importance of their role in the system and trained in the details of their work.

This is especially true when quantitative methods are involved. For instance, a new marketing manager probably will not comprehend the nature and limitations of the statistical forecasting system that generates reports that he must analyze; he will not appreciate the significance and importance of his role in the forecasting process; and he will not understand how the forecast is to be used. He may have to be sold on the system as well as trained in its use.

Without an organized program of education, many of the analytical procedures in the system will cease to be used and a lot of good operations research work will have been wasted.

7-2.5 Operating Responsibility

The system should be designed and installed so that it can be run by the operating people in marketing, production, production planning, etc. Systems analysts and operations research specialists should not be involved in the routine operation of the system. We have seen several situations where an operations research department develops a linear programming application, sells the utility of the model, and then ends up maintaining and periodically running the model. With successes like these, the operations research department soon will be involved more with operating old systems than with participating in the design of new or improved ones.

One solution to the problem of being able to turn a complex management system over to operating people is to make certain that the operating departments have the technical competence to understand the system. This may mean upgrading the quality of managers, changing the organizational structure, and hiring people with management science knowledge to work in production planning, marketing, production, and data processing. Operations research is more successful and mathematical models are more effectively used in organizations where not all of the operations research talent is in the operations research department.

7-3   References

1. **Ackoff, R. L.,** *Scientific Method: Optimizing Applied Research Decisions*, John Wiley & Sons, Inc., New York, 1962.

2. **Driebeek, N. J.,** *Applied Linear Programming*, Addison-Wesley, Reading, Massachusetts, 1969.

3. **Wagner, H. M.,** *Principles of Operations Research*, Prentice-Hall, Englewood Cliffs, N.J., 1969.

Appendix

TABLE A-1 Poisson Distribution Function

$$P(u) = \sum_{x=0}^{u} \frac{e^{-\lambda}\lambda^x}{x!}$$

				λ				
u	0.01	0.05	0.10	0.20	0.30	0.40	0.50	0.60
0.	0.9900	0.9512	0.9048	0.8187	0.7408	0.6703	0.6065	0.5488
1.	1.0000	0.9988	0.9953	0.9825	0.9631	0.9384	0.9098	0.8781
2.	1.0000	1.0000	0.9998	0.9989	0.9964	0.9921	0.9856	0.9769
3.	1.0000	1.0000	1.0000	0.9999	0.9997	0.9992	0.9982	0.9966
4.	1.0000	1.0000	1.0000	1.0000	1.0000	0.9999	0.9998	0.9996
5.	1.0000	1.0000	1.0000	1.0000	1.0000	1.0000	1.0000	1.0000

Table A-1 (*continued*)

u	0.70	0.80	0.90	λ 1.00	1.10	1.20	1.30	1.40
0.	0.4966	0.4493	0.4066	0.3679	0.3329	0.3012	0.2725	0.2466
1.	0.8442	0.8088	0.7725	0.7358	0.6990	0.6626	0.6268	0.5918
2.	0.9659	0.9526	0.9371	0.9197	0.9004	0.8795	0.8571	0.8335
3.	0.9942	0.9909	0.9865	0.9810	0.9743	0.9662	0.9569	0.9463
4.	0.9992	0.9986	0.9977	0.9963	0.9946	0.9923	0.9893	0.9857
5.	0.9999	0.9998	0.9997	0.9994	0.9990	0.9985	0.9978	0.9968
6.	1.0000	1.0000	1.0000	0.9999	0.9999	0.9997	0.9996	0.9994
7.	1.0000	1.0000	1.0000	1.0000	1.0000	1.0000	0.9999	0.9999
8.	1.0000	1.0000	1.0000	1.0000	1.0000	1.0000	1.0000	1.0000

u	1.50	1.60	1.70	λ 1.80	1.90	2.00	2.10	2.20
0.	0.2231	0.2019	0.1827	0.1653	0.1496	0.1353	0.1225	0.1108
1.	0.5578	0.5249	0.4932	0.4628	0.4337	0.4060	0.3796	0.3546
2.	0.8088	0.7834	0.7572	0.7306	0.7037	0.6767	0.6496	0.6227
3.	0.9344	0.9212	0.9068	0.8913	0.8747	0.8571	0.8386	0.8194
4.	0.9814	0.9763	0.9704	0.9636	0.9559	0.9473	0.9379	0.9275
5.	0.9955	0.9940	0.9920	0.9896	0.9868	0.9834	0.9796	0.9751
6.	0.9991	0.9987	0.9981	0.9974	0.9966	0.9955	0.9941	0.9925
7.	0.9998	0.9997	0.9996	0.9994	0.9992	0.9989	0.9985	0.9980
8.	1.0000	1.0000	0.9999	0.9999	0.9998	0.9998	0.9997	0.9995
9.	1.0000	1.0000	1.0000	1.0000	1.0000	1.0000	0.9999	0.9999
10.	1.0000	1.0000	1.0000	1.0000	1.0000	1.0000	1.0000	1.0000

Table A-1 (*continued*)

u	2.30	2.40	2.50	λ 2.60	2.70	2.80	2.90	3.00
0.	0.1003	0.0907	0.0821	0.0743	0.0672	0.0608	0.0550	0.0498
1.	0.3309	0.3084	0.2873	0.2674	0.2487	0.2311	0.2146	0.1991
2.	0.5960	0.5697	0.5438	0.5184	0.4936	0.4695	0.4460	0.4232
3.	0.7993	0.7787	0.7576	0.7360	0.7141	0.6919	0.6696	0.6472
4.	0.9162	0.9041	0.8912	0.8774	0.8629	0.8477	0.8318	0.8153
5.	0.9700	0.9643	0.9580	0.9510	0.9433	0.9349	0.9258	0.9161
6.	0.9906	0.9884	0.9858	0.9828	0.9794	0.9756	0.9713	0.9665
7.	0.9974	0.9967	0.9958	0.9947	0.9934	0.9919	0.9901	0.9881
8.	0.9994	0.9991	0.9989	0.9985	0.9981	0.9976	0.9969	0.9962
9.	0.9999	0.9998	0.9997	0.9996	0.9995	0.9993	0.9991	0.9989
10.	1.0000	1.0000	0.9999	0.9999	0.9999	0.9998	0.9998	0.9997
11.	1.0000	1.0000	1.0000	1.0000	1.0000	1.0000	0.9999	0.9999
12.	1.0000	1.0000	1.0000	1.0000	1.0000	1.0000	1.0000	1.0000

u	3.50	4.00	4.50	λ 5.00	5.50	6.00	6.50	7.00
0.	0.0302	0.0183	0.0111	0.0067	0.0041	0.0025	0.0015	0.0009
1.	0.1359	0.0916	0.0611	0.0404	0.0266	0.0174	0.0113	0.0073
2.	0.3208	0.2381	0.1736	0.1247	0.0884	0.0620	0.0430	0.0296
3.	0.5366	0.4335	0.3423	0.2650	0.2017	0.1512	0.1118	0.0818
4.	0.7254	0.6288	0.5321	0.4405	0.3575	0.2851	0.2237	0.1730
5.	0.8576	0.7851	0.7029	0.6160	0.5289	0.4457	0.3690	0.3007
6.	0.9347	0.8893	0.8311	0.7622	0.6860	0.6063	0.5265	0.4497
7.	0.9733	0.9489	0.9134	0.8666	0.8095	0.7440	0.6728	0.5987
8.	0.9901	0.9786	0.9597	0.9319	0.8944	0.8472	0.7916	0.7291
9.	0.9967	0.9919	0.9829	0.9682	0.9462	0.9161	0.8774	0.8305
10.	0.9990	0.9972	0.9933	0.9863	0.9747	0.9574	0.9332	0.9015
11.	0.9997	0.9991	0.9976	0.9945	0.9890	0.9799	0.9661	0.9467
12.	0.9999	0.9997	0.9992	0.9980	0.9955	0.9912	0.9840	0.9730
13.	1.0000	0.9999	0.9997	0.9993	0.9983	0.9964	0.9929	0.9872
14.	1.0000	1.0000	0.9999	0.9998	0.9994	0.9986	0.9970	0.9943
15.	1.0000	1.0000	1.0000	0.9999	0.9998	0.9995	0.9988	0.9976
16.	1.0000	1.0000	1.0000	1.0000	0.9999	0.9998	0.9996	0.9990
17.	1.0000	1.0000	1.0000	1.0000	1.0000	0.9999	0.9998	0.9996
18.	1.0000	1.0000	1.0000	1.0000	1.0000	1 0000	0.9999	0.9999
19.	1.0000	1.0000	1.0000	1.0000	1.0000	1.0000	1.0000	1.0000

Table A-1 (*continued*)

u	7.50	8.00	8.50	λ 9.00	9.50	10.0	15.0	20.0
0.	0.0006	0.0003	0.0002	0.0001	0.0001	0.0000	0.0000	0.0000
1.	0.0047	0.0030	0.0019	0.0012	0.0008	0.0005	0.0000	0.0000
2.	0.0203	0.0138	0.0093	0.0062	0.0042	0.0028	0.0000	0.0000
3.	0.0591	0.0424	0.0301	0.0212	0.0149	0.0103	0.0002	0.0000
4.	0.1321	0.0996	0.0744	0.0550	0.0403	0.0293	0.0009	0.0000
5.	0.2414	0.1912	0.1496	0.1157	0.0885	0.0671	0.0028	0.0001
6.	0.3782	0.3134	0.2562	0.2068	0.1649	0.1301	0.0076	0.0003
7.	0.5246	0.4530	0.3856	0.3239	0.2687	0.2202	0.0180	0.0008
8.	0.6620	0.5925	0.5231	0.4557	0.3918	0.3328	0.0374	0.0021
9.	0.7764	0.7166	0.6530	0.5874	0.5218	0.4579	0.0699	0.0050
10.	0.8622	0.8159	0.7634	0.7060	0.6453	0.5830	0.1185	0.0108
11.	0.9208	0.8881	0.8487	0.8030	0.7520	0.6968	0.1848	0.0214
12.	0.9573	0.9362	0.9091	0.8758	0.8364	0.7916	0.2676	0.0390
13.	0.9784	0.9658	0.9486	0.9261	0.8981	0.8645	0.3632	0.0661
14.	0.9897	0.9827	0.9726	0.9585	0.9400	0.9165	0.4657	0.1049
15.	0.9954	0.9918	0.9862	0.9780	0.9665	0.9513	0.5681	0.1565
16.	0.9980	0.9963	0.9934	0.9889	0.9823	0.9730	0.6641	0.2211
17.	0.9992	0.9984	0.9970	0.9947	0.9911	0.9857	0.7489	0.2970
18.	0.9997	0.9993	0.9987	0.9976	0.9957	0.9928	0.8195	0.3814
19.	0.9999	0.9997	0.9995	0.9989	0.9980	0.9965	0.8752	0.4703
20.	1.0000	0.9999	0.9998	0.9996	0.9991	0.9984	0.9170	0.5591
21.	1.0000	1.0000	0.9999	0.9998	0.9996	0.9993	0.9469	0.6437
22.	1.0000	1.0000	1.0000	0.9999	0.9999	0.9997	0.9673	0.7206
23.	1.0000	1.0000	1.0000	1.0000	0.9999	0.9999	0.9805	0.7875
24.	1.0000	1.0000	1.0000	1.0000	1.0000	1.0000	0.9888	0.8432
25.	1.0000	1.0000	1.0000	1.0000	1.0000	1.0000	0.9938	0.8878
26.	1.0000	1.0000	1.0000	1.0000	1.0000	1.0000	0.9967	0.9221
27.	1.0000	1.0000	1.0000	1.0000	1.0000	1.0000	0.9983	0.9475
28.	1.0000	1.0000	1.0000	1.0000	1.0000	1.0000	0.9991	0.9657
29.	1.0000	1.0000	1.0000	1.0000	1.0000	1.0000	0.9996	0.9782
30.	1.0000	1.0000	1.0000	1.0000	1.0000	1.0000	0.9998	0.9865
31.	1.0000	1.0000	1.0000	1.0000	1.0000	1.0000	0.9999	0.9919
32.	1.0000	1.0000	1.0000	1.0000	1.0000	1.0000	1.0000	0.9953
33.	1.0000	1.0000	1.0000	1.0000	1.0000	1.0000	1.0000	0.9973
34.	1.0000	1.0000	1.0000	1.0000	1.0000	1.0000	1.0000	0.9985
35.	1.0000	1.0000	1.0000	1.0000	1.0000	1.0000	1.0000	0.9992

TABLE A-2 Distribution Function and Ordinates of the Standard Normal Density

$$\phi(z) = \frac{1}{\sqrt{2\pi}} e^{-(1/2)z^2}$$

$$\Phi(z) = \int_{-\infty}^{z} \phi(t)\, dt$$

z	$\Phi(z)$	$\phi(z)$	z	$\Phi(z)$	$\phi(z)$
0.00	0.500000	0.398942	0.37	0.644309	0.372548
0.01	0.503989	0.398922	0.38	0.648027	0.371154
0.02	0.507978	0.398863	0.39	0.651732	0.369728
0.03	0.511966	0.398763	0.40	0.655422	0.368270
0.04	0.515953	0.398623	0.41	0.659097	0.366782
0.05	0.519939	0.398444	0.42	0.662757	0.365263
0.06	0.523922	0.398225	0.43	0.666402	0.363714
0.07	0.527903	0.397966	0.44	0.670032	0.362135
0.08	0.531881	0.397668	0.45	0.673645	0.360527
0.09	0.535856	0.397330	0.46	0.677242	0.358890
0.10	0.539828	0.396953	0.47	0.680823	0.357225
0.11	0.543795	0.396536	0.48	0.684386	0.355533
0.12	0.547758	0.396080	0.49	0.687933	0.353813
0.13	0.551717	0.395586	0.50	0.691463	0.352065
0.14	0.555670	0.395052	0.51	0.694974	0.350292
0.15	0.559618	0.394479	0.52	0.698468	0.348493
0.16	0.563559	0.393869	0.53	0.701944	0.346668
0.17	0.567495	0.393219	0.54	0.705401	0.344818
0.18	0.571424	0.392532	0.55	0.708840	0.342944
0.19	0.575345	0.391806	0.56	0.712260	0.341046
0.20	0.579260	0.391043	0.57	0.715661	0.339124
0.21	0.583166	0.390242	0.58	0.719043	0.337180
0.22	0.587064	0.389404	0.59	0.722405	0.335213
0.23	0.590954	0.388529	0.60	0.725747	0.333225
0.24	0.594835	0.387617	0.61	0.729069	0.331215
0.25	0.598706	0.386668	0.62	0.732371	0.329184
0.26	0.602568	0.385684	0.63	0.735653	0.327133
0.27	0.606420	0.384663	0.64	0.738914	0.325062
0.28	0.610261	0.383606	0.65	0.742154	0.322973
0.29	0.614092	0.382515	0.66	0.745373	0.320864
0.30	0.617912	0.381388	0.67	0.748571	0.318737
0.31	0.621720	0.380227	0.68	0.751748	0.316593
0.32	0.625516	0.379031	0.69	0.754903	0.314432
0.33	0.629300	0.377801	0.70	0.758036	0.312254
0.34	0.633072	0.376537	0.71	0.761148	0.310060
0.35	0.636831	0.375241	0.72	0.764237	0.307851
0.36	0.640577	0.373911	0.73	0.767305	0.305628

Table A-2 (*continued*)

z	$\Phi(z)$	$\phi(z)$	z	$\Phi(z)$	$\phi(z)$
0.74	0.770350	0.303389	1.17	0.879000	0.201214
0.75	0.773372	0.301138	1.18	0.881000	0.198863
0.76	0.776373	0.298873	1.19	0.882977	0.196521
0.77	0.779350	0.296595	1.20	0.884930	0.194186
0.78	0.782304	0.294305	1.21	0.886861	0.191860
0.79	0.785236	0.292004	1.22	0.888768	0.189543
0.80	0.788144	0.289692	1.23	0.890651	0.187236
0.81	0.791030	0.287369	1.24	0.892512	0.184937
0.82	0.793892	0.285037	1.25	0.894350	0.182649
0.83	0.796730	0.282695	1.26	0.896165	0.180371
0.84	0.799546	0.280344	1.27	0.897958	0.178104
0.85	0.802337	0.277985	1.28	0.899727	0.175848
0.86	0.805105	0.275618	1.29	0.901475	0.173602
0.87	0.807850	0.273245	1.30	0.903200	0.171369
0.88	0.810570	0.270864	1.31	0.904902	0.169147
0.89	0.813267	0.268478	1.32	0.906583	0.166937
0.90	0.815940	0.266085	1.33	0.908241	0.164740
0.91	0.818589	0.263688	1.34	0.909877	0.162555
0.92	0.821213	0.261286	1.35	0.911492	0.160384
0.93	0.823814	0.258881	1.36	0.913085	0.158225
0.94	0.826391	0.256471	1.37	0.914657	0.156080
0.95	0.828944	0.254059	1.38	0.916207	0.153948
0.96	0.831472	0.251644	1.39	0.917736	0.151831
0.97	0.833977	0.249228	1.40	0.919243	0.149728
0.98	0.836457	0.246810	1.41	0.920730	0.147639
0.99	0.838913	0.244390	1.42	0.922196	0.145564
1.00	0.841345	0.241971	1.43	0.923642	0.143505
1.01	0.843752	0.239551	1.44	0.925066	0.141460
1.02	0.846136	0.237132	1.45	0.926471	0.139431
1.03	0.848495	0.234714	1.46	0.927855	0.137417
1.04	0.850830	0.232297	1.47	0.929219	0.135418
1.05	0.853141	0.229882	1.48	0.930563	0.133435
1.06	0.855428	0.227470	1.49	0.931888	0.131469
1.07	0.857690	0.225060	1.50	0.933193	0.129518
1.08	0.859929	0.222654	1.51	0.934478	0.127583
1.09	0.862143	0.220251	1.52	0.935745	0.125665
1.10	0.864334	0.217852	1.53	0.936992	0.123763
1.11	0.866500	0.215458	1.54	0.938220	0.121878
1.12	0.868643	0.213069	1.55	0.939429	0.120009
1.13	0.870762	0.210686	1.56	0.940620	0.118157
1.14	0.872857	0.208308	1.57	0.941792	0.116323
1.15	0.874928	0.205936	1.58	0.942947	0.114505
1.16	0.876976	0.203572	1.59	0.944083	0.112704

Table A-2 (*continued*)

z	$\Phi(z)$	$\phi(z)$	z	$\Phi(z)$	$\phi(z)$
1.60	0.945201	0.110921	2.03	0.978822	0.050824
1.61	0.946301	0.109155	2.04	0.979325	0.049800
1.62	0.947384	0.107406	2.05	0.979818	0.048792
1.63	0.948449	0.105675	2.06	0.980301	0.047800
1.64	0.949497	0.103961	2.07	0.980774	0.046823
1.65	0.950528	0.102265	2.08	0.981237	0.045861
1.66	0.951543	0.100587	2.09	0.981691	0.044915
1.67	0.952540	0.098926	2.10	0.982135	0.043984
1.68	0.953521	0.097282	2.11	0.982571	0.043068
1.69	0.954486	0.095657	2.12	0.982997	0.042166
1.70	0.955434	0.094049	2.13	0.983414	0.041280
1.71	0.956367	0.092459	2.14	0.983822	0.040408
1.72	0.957284	0.090887	2.15	0.984222	0.039550
1.73	0.958185	0.089333	2.16	0.984614	0.038707
1.74	0.959070	0.087796	2.17	0.984996	0.037878
1.75	0.959941	0.086277	2.18	0.985371	0.037063
1.76	0.960796	0.084777	2.19	0.985738	0.036262
1.77	0.961636	0.083293	2.20	0.986096	0.035475
1.78	0.962462	0.081828	2.21	0.986447	0.034701
1.79	0.963273	0.080380	2.22	0.986791	0.033941
1.80	0.964070	0.078950	2.23	0.987126	0.033194
1.81	0.964852	0.077538	2.24	0.987454	0.032460
1.82	0.965620	0.076143	2.25	0.987775	0.031740
1.83	0.966375	0.074766	2.26	0.988089	0.031032
1.84	0.967116	0.073407	2.27	0.988396	0.030337
1.85	0.967843	0.072065	2.28	0.988696	0.029655
1.86	0.968557	0.070741	2.29	0.988989	0.028985
1.87	0.969258	0.069433	2.30	0.989276	0.028327
1.88	0.969946	0.068144	2.31	0.989556	0.027682
1.89	0.970621	0.066871	2.32	0.989830	0.027048
1.90	0.971283	0.065616	2.33	0.990097	0.026427
1.91	0.971933	0.064378	2.34	0.990358	0.025817
1.92	0.972571	0.063157	2.35	0.990613	0.025218
1.93	0.973196	0.061953	2.36	0.990863	0.024631
1.94	0.973810	0.060765	2.37	0.991106	0.024056
1.95	0.974412	0.059595	2.38	0.991344	0.023491
1.96	0.975002	0.058441	2.39	0.991576	0.022937
1.97	0.975581	0.057304	2.40	0.991802	0.022395
1.98	0.976148	0.056183	2.41	0.992024	0.021862
1.99	0.976704	0.055079	2.42	0.992240	0.021341
2.00	0.977250	0.053991	2.43	0.992451	0.020830
2.01	0.977784	0.052919	2.44	0.992656	0.020328
2.02	0.978308	0.051864	2.45	0.992857	0.019837

Table A-2 (*continued*)

z	$\Phi(z)$	$\phi(z)$	z	$\Phi(z)$	$\phi(z)$
2.46	0.993053	0.019356	2.79	0.997365	0.008140
2.47	0.993244	0.018885	2.80	0.997445	0.007915
2.48	0.993431	0.018423	2.81	0.997523	0.007697
2.49	0.993613	0.017971	2.82	0.997599	0.007483
2.50	0.993790	0.017528	2.83	0.997673	0.007274
2.51	0.993963	0.017095	2.84	0.997744	0.007071
2.52	0.994132	0.016670	2.85	0.997814	0.006873
2.53	0.994297	0.016255	2.86	0.997882	0.006679
2.54	0.994457	0.015848	2.87	0.997948	0.006491
2.55	0.994614	0.015449	2.88	0.998012	0.006307
2.56	0.994766	0.015060	2.89	0.998074	0.006127
2.57	0.994915	0.014678	2.90	0.998134	0.005953
2.58	0.995060	0.014305	2.91	0.998193	0.005782
2.59	0.995201	0.013940	2.92	0.998250	0.005616
2.60	0.995339	0.013583	2.93	0.998305	0.005454
2.61	0.995473	0.013234	2.94	0.998359	0.005296
2.62	0.995604	0.012892	2.95	0.998411	0.005143
2.63	0.995731	0.012558	2.96	0.998462	0.004993
2.64	0.995855	0.012232	2.97	0.998511	0.004847
2.65	0.995976	0.011912	2.98	0.998559	0.004705
2.66	0.996093	0.011600	2.99	0.998605	0.004567
2.67	0.996208	0.011295	3.00	0.998650	0.004432
2.68	0.996319	0.010997	3.10	0.999032	0.003267
2.69	0.996428	0.010706	3.20	0.999313	0.002384
2.70	0.996533	0.010421	3.30	0.999517	0.001723
2.71	0.996636	0.010143	3.40	0.999663	0.001232
2.72	0.996736	0.009871	3.50	0.999767	0.000873
2.73	0.996833	0.009606	3.60	0.999841	0.000612
2.74	0.996928	0.009347	3.70	0.999892	0.000425
2.75	0.997020	0.009094	3.80	0.999928	0.000292
2.76	0.997110	0.008847	3.90	0.999952	0.000199
2.77	0.997197	0.008605	4.00	0.999968	0.000134
2.78	0.997282	0.008370			

TABLE A-3 Unit Normal Linear-Loss Integrals

$$L(u) = \int_{-\infty}^{u} (u - z)\phi(z)\, dz$$

$$L'(u) = \int_{u}^{\infty} (z - u)\phi(z)\, dz$$

where $\phi(z) = (1/\sqrt{2\pi})e^{-(1/2)z^2}$. $L(u)$ and $L'(u)$ are the left-hand and right-hand unit normal linear-loss integrals, respectively. To evaluate unit normal linear-loss integrals, the following identities are useful:

1. $\Phi(u) = \int_{-\infty}^{u} \phi(z)\, dz$ (standard normal distribution function)
2. $L(u) = u\Phi(u) + \phi(u)$
3. $L'(u) = u\Phi(u) + \phi(u) - u$
4. $L(u) = L'(u) + u$
5. $L'(-u) = L'(u) + u = L(u)$
6. $L(-u) = L(u) - u = L'(u)$

u	$L'(u)$	$L(u)$	u	$L'(u)$	$L(u)$
0.00	0.398942	0.398942	0.25	0.286345	0.536345
0.01	0.393962	0.403962	0.26	0.282351	0.542351
0.02	0.389022	0.409022	0.27	0.278396	0.548396
0.03	0.384122	0.414122	0.28	0.274480	0.554480
0.04	0.379262	0.419262	0.29	0.270601	0.560601
0.05	0.374441	0.424441	0.30	0.266761	0.566761
0.06	0.369660	0.429660	0.31	0.262960	0.572960
0.07	0.364919	0.434919	0.32	0.259196	0.579196
0.08	0.360218	0.440218	0.33	0.255470	0.585470
0.09	0.355557	0.445557	0.34	0.251782	0.591782
0.10	0.350935	0.450935	0.35	0.248131	0.598131
0.11	0.346354	0.456354	0.36	0.244518	0.604518
0.12	0.341811	0.461811	0.37	0.240943	0.610943
0.13	0.337309	0.467309	0.38	0.237404	0.617404
0.14	0.332846	0.472846	0.39	0.233903	0.623903
0.15	0.328422	0.478422	0.40	0.230439	0.630439
0.16	0.324038	0.484038	0.41	0.227012	0.637012
0.17	0.319693	0.489693	0.42	0.223621	0.643621
0.18	0.315388	0.495388	0.43	0.220267	0.650267
0.19	0.311122	0.501122	0.44	0.216949	0.656949
0.20	0.306895	0.506895	0.45	0.213667	0.663667
0.21	0.302707	0.512707	0.46	0.210422	0.670422
0.22	0.298558	0.518558	0.47	0.207212	0.677212
0.23	0.294448	0.524448	0.48	0.204038	0.684038
0.24	0.290377	0.530377	0.49	0.200900	0.690900

Table A-3 (*continued*)

u	L'(u)	L(u)	u	L'(u)	L(u)
0.50	0.197797	0.697797	0.94	0.093279	1.033279
0.51	0.194729	0.704729	0.95	0.091556	1.041556
0.52	0.191696	0.711696	0.96	0.089858	1.049858
0.53	0.188698	0.718698	0.97	0.088185	1.058185
0.54	0.185735	0.725735	0.98	0.086537	1.066537
0.55	0.182806	0.732806	0.99	0.084914	1.074914
0.56	0.179912	0.739912	1.00	0.083316	1.083316
0.57	0.177051	0.747051	1.01	0.081741	1.091741
0.58	0.174225	0.754225	1.02	0.080191	1.100191
0.59	0.171432	0.761432	1.03	0.078664	1.108664
0.60	0.168673	0.768673	1.04	0.077160	1.117160
0.61	0.165947	0.775947	1.05	0.075680	1.125680
0.62	0.163254	0.783254	1.06	0.074223	1.134223
0.63	0.160594	0.790594	1.07	0.072789	1.142789
0.64	0.157967	0.797967	1.08	0.071377	1.151377
0.65	0.155373	0.805373	1.09	0.069987	1.159987
0.66	0.152810	0.812810	1.10	0.068620	1.168620
0.67	0.150280	0.820280	1.11	0.067274	1.177274
0.68	0.147781	0.827781	1.12	0.065950	1.185950
0.69	0.145315	0.835315	1.13	0.064647	1.194647
0.70	0.142879	0.842879	1.14	0.063365	1.203365
0.71	0.140475	0.850475	1.15	0.062104	1.212104
0.72	0.138102	0.858102	1.16	0.060863	1.220863
0.73	0.135760	0.865760	1.17	0.059643	1.229643
0.74	0.133448	0.873448	1.18	0.058443	1.238443
0.75	0.131167	0.881167	1.19	0.057263	1.247263
0.76	0.128916	0.888916	1.20	0.056103	1.256103
0.77	0.126694	0.896694	1.21	0.054962	1.264962
0.78	0.124503	0.904503	1.22	0.053840	1.273840
0.79	0.122340	0.912340	1.23	0.052737	1.282737
0.80	0.120207	0.920207	1.24	0.051653	1.291653
0.81	0.118103	0.928103	1.25	0.050587	1.300587
0.82	0.116028	0.936028	1.26	0.049540	1.309540
0.83	0.113981	0.943981	1.27	0.048510	1.318510
0.84	0.111962	0.951962	1.28	0.047499	1.327499
0.85	0.109972	0.959972	1.29	0.046505	1.336505
0.86	0.108009	0.968009	1.30	0.045528	1.345528
0.87	0.106074	0.976074	1.31	0.044569	1.354569
0.88	0.104166	0.984166	1.32	0.043626	1.363626
0.89	0.102285	0.992285	1.33	0.042700	1.372700
0.90	0.100431	1.000431	1.34	0.041791	1.381791
0.91	0.098604	1.008604	1.35	0.040898	1.390898
0.92	0.096803	1.016803	1.36	0.040021	1.400021
0.93	0.095028	1.025028	1.37	0.039159	1.409159

Table A-3 (*continued*)

u	L'(u)	L(u)	u	L'(u)	L(u)
1.38	0.038314	1.418314	1.82	0.013573	1.833573
1.39	0.037484	1.427484	1.83	0.013232	1.843232
1.40	0.036668	1.436668	1.84	0.012900	1.852900
1.41	0.035868	1.445868	1.85	0.012575	1.862575
1.42	0.035083	1.455083	1.86	0.012257	1.872257
1.43	0.034312	1.464312	1.87	0.011946	1.881946
1.44	0.033556	1.473556	1.88	0.011642	1.891642
1.45	0.032813	1.482813	1.89	0.011345	1.901345
1.46	0.032085	1.492085	1.90	0.011054	1.911054
1.47	0.031370	1.501370	1.91	0.010770	1.920770
1.48	0.030669	1.510669	1.92	0.010493	1.930493
1.49	0.029982	1.519982	1.93	0.010222	1.940222
1.50	0.029307	1.529307	1.94	0.009957	1.949957
1.51	0.028645	1.538645	1.95	0.009698	1.959698
1.52	0.027997	1.547997	1.96	0.009445	1.969445
1.53	0.027360	1.557360	1.97	0.009198	1.979198
1.54	0.026736	1.566736	1.98	0.008956	1.988956
1.55	0.026125	1.576125	1.99	0.008721	1.998721
1.56	0.025525	1.585525	2.00	0.008490	2.008490
1.57	0.024937	1.594937	2.01	0.008266	2.018266
1.58	0.024361	1.604361	2.02	0.008046	2.028046
1.59	0.023796	1.613796	2.03	0.007832	2.037832
1.60	0.023242	1.623242	2.04	0.007623	2.047623
1.61	0.022700	1.632700	2.05	0.007418	2.057418
1.62	0.022168	1.642168	2.06	0.007219	2.067219
1.63	0.021647	1.651647	2.07	0.007024	2.077024
1.64	0.021137	1.661137	2.08	0.006834	2.086834
1.65	0.020637	1.670637	2.09	0.006649	2.096649
1.66	0.020147	1.680147	2.10	0.006468	2.106468
1.67	0.019668	1.689668	2.11	0.006292	2.116292
1.68	0.019198	1.699198	2.12	0.006120	2.126120
1.69	0.018738	1.708738	2.13	0.005952	2.135952
1.70	0.018288	1.718288	2.14	0.005788	2.145788
1.71	0.017847	1.727847	2.15	0.005628	2.155628
1.72	0.017415	1.737415	2.16	0.005472	2.165472
1.73	0.016992	1.746992	2.17	0.005320	2.175320
1.74	0.016579	1.756579	2.18	0.005172	2.185172
1.75	0.016174	1.766174	2.19	0.005028	2.195028
1.76	0.015777	1.775777	2.20	0.004887	2.204887
1.77	0.015390	1.785390	2.21	0.004750	2.214750
1.78	0.015010	1.795010	2.22	0.004616	2.224616
1.79	0.014639	1.804639	2.23	0.004485	2.234485
1.80	0.014276	1.814276	2.24	0.004358	2.244358
1.81	0.013920	1.823920	2.25	0.004234	2.254234

Table A-3 (*continued*)

u	L'(u)	L(u)	u	L'(u)	L(u)
2.26	0.004114	2.264114	2.69	0.001096	2.691096
2.27	0.003996	2.273996	2.70	0.001060	2.701060
2.28	0.003882	2.283882	2.71	0.001026	2.711026
2.29	0.003770	2.293770	2.72	0.000993	2.720993
2.30	0.003662	2.303662	2.73	0.000961	2.730961
2.31	0.003556	2.313556	2.74	0.000930	2.740930
2.32	0.003453	2.323453	2.75	0.000900	2.750900
2.33	0.003352	2.333352	2.76	0.000870	2.760870
2.34	0.003255	2.343255	2.77	0.000842	2.770842
2.35	0.003159	2.353159	2.78	0.000814	2.780814
2.36	0.003067	2.363067	2.79	0.000787	2.790787
2.37	0.002977	2.372977	2.80	0.000761	2.800761
2.38	0.002889	2.382889	2.81	0.000736	2.810736
2.39	0.002804	2.392804	2.82	0.000712	2.820712
2.40	0.002721	2.402721	2.83	0.000688	2.830688
2.41	0.002640	2.412640	2.84	0.000665	2.840665
2.42	0.002561	2.422561	2.85	0.000643	2.850643
2.43	0.002484	2.432484	2.86	0.000622	2.860622
2.44	0.002410	2.442410	2.87	0.000601	2.870601
2.45	0.002338	2.452338	2.88	0.000581	2.880581
2.46	0.002267	2.462267	2.89	0.000561	2.890561
2.47	0.002199	2.472199	2.90	0.000542	2.900542
2.48	0.002132	2.482132	2.91	0.000524	2.910524
2.49	0.002067	2.492067	2.92	0.000506	2.920506
2.50	0.002004	2.502004	2.93	0.000489	2.930489
2.51	0.001943	2.511943	2.94	0.000472	2.940472
2.52	0.001884	2.521884	2.95	0.000456	2.950456
2.53	0.001826	2.531826	2.96	0.000440	2.960440
2.54	0.001770	2.541770	2.97	0.000425	2.970425
2.55	0.001715	2.551715	2.98	0.000410	2.980410
2.56	0.001662	2.561662	2.99	0.000396	2.990396
2.57	0.001610	2.571610	3.00	0.000382	3.000382
2.58	0.001560	2.581560	3.10	0.000267	3.100267
2.59	0.001511	2.591511	3.20	0.000185	3.200185
2.60	0.001464	2.601464	3.30	0.000127	3.300127
2.61	0.001418	2.611418	3.40	0.000086	3.400086
2.62	0.001374	2.621374	3.50	0.000058	3.500058
2.63	0.001330	2.631330	3.60	0.000039	3.600039
2.64	0.001288	2.641288	3.70	0.000025	3.700025
2.65	0.001247	2.651247	3.80	0.000017	3.800017
2.66	0.001208	2.661208	3.90	0.000011	3.900011
2.67	0.001169	2.671169	4.00	0.000007	4.000007
2.68	0.001132	2.681132			

Index